D1523673

The Peoples of Africa

THE PEOPLES OF AFRICA

An Ethnohistorical Dictionary

James S. Olson

GREENWOOD PRESS
Westport, Connecticut • London

Library of Congress Cataloging-in-Publication Data

Olson, James Stuart.
    The peoples of Africa : an ethnohistorical dictionary / James S.
Olson.
        p.   cm.
    Includes bibliographical references and index.
    ISBN 0–313–27918–7 (alk. paper)
        1. Ethnology—Africa—Dictionaries.   2. Ethnohistory—Africa—
Dictionaries.   3. Africa—Social life and customs—Dictionaries.
    I. Title.
    GN645.O47   1996
    305.8'0096—dc20   95–36433

British Library Cataloguing in Publication Data is available.

First published in 1996

Greenwood Press, 88 Post Road West, Westport, CT 06881
An imprint of Greenwood Publishing Group, Inc.

Printed in the United States of America

The paper used in this book complies with the
Permanent Paper Standard issued by the National
Information Standards Organization (Z39.48–1984).

10 9 8 7 6 5 4 3 2 1

Contents

Preface

Reports out of Africa frequently make the front pages of American and European newspapers and become sound bites on nightly television programs. Occasionally, the news is good. In 1994, apartheid died in South Africa, and black majority rule became a reality. Millions of people celebrated the triumph of democracy. Far more often, the news is not so good, ranging from the dismal to the apocalyptic. Drought, famine, war, civil war, genocide, ethnic discord, deadly diseases, and poverty appear to stalk the continent. But beneath the horrific headlines is another reality. Africa is home to more than 700 million people, all of whom are trying to make the most of their lives, worshiping their gods, raising their families, building their communities, and supporting themselves. In terms of cultural diversity, it is the richest of continents, a bewildering kaleidoscope of thousands of discrete ethnic entities whose group identities are focused and distinct.

In *The Peoples of Africa: An Ethnohistorical Dictionary,* I have tried to provide a brief introduction to most of these individual groups. It has been, of course, a daunting task. When years separate anthropological field research from the publication of results, the data often become quickly dated. Defining ethnicity is never easy, and, in Africa, an ethnic group can also be divided and subdivided by regional, dialect, and clan classifications. Ethnic groups are never static entities fixed in time, especially in Africa, where a population explosion, rapid urbanization, and political instability have worked to blur ethnic lines. In the cities, intermarriage between people from different ethnic groups is accelerating, so the emergence of new ethnic groups is occurring constantly. Many of the new groups, as well as a good number of the older ones, have not yet been studied by scholars. For these reasons, I cannot say that this book is truly comprehensive. No doubt, many groups have been overlooked, largely because they have escaped the attention of scholars. Nevertheless, I have tried to provide a brief description and, where possible, a population estimate of more than 1,800 ethnic communities in Africa. An asterisk (*) in the text indicates a separate essay on the group.

I would like to acknowledge the assistance of the reference librarians at Sam Houston State University in Huntsville, Texas, and at Texas A&M University in College Station, Texas, for their assistance.

The Peoples of Africa

A

AANZA. The Aanzas are a relatively small ethnic group living today in southeastern Zaire, northwestern Zambia, and southwestern Tanzania. Most of the Aanzas, however, are located between Lake Mweru and Lake Tanganyika in Zaire. They live in a highland region that permits them to farm as well as to raise cattle for meat and milk. The Aanzas speak a Bantu* language.
REFERENCE: Irving Kaplan et al. *Zaire: A Country Study.* 1978.

ABABA. *See* ABABDA.

ABABDA. The Ababda (Ababa) are one of the subgroups of the Beja* of Sudan. In fact, they are the northernmost of the Beja peoples, living in northeastern Sudan and southeastern Egypt, between the Nile and the Red Sea. They speak a Northern Cushitic language, as do other Beja groups, and they have traditionally been a pastoral people, wandering in groups of one to twelve families in search of pasture for their sheep, goat, or camel herds. Their traditional housing consists of rectangular, portable dwellings woven from goat hair. Although the Beja groups have been in the region for more than 4,000 years, the Ababda did not emerge as a self-conscious ethnic group until the sixteenth century. The Ababda live primarily on dairy products, particularly camel's milk, as well as on meat from slaughtered stock and small amounts of grain. They raise sorghum in wadi beds; they plant just after rain storms but do not tend the crop until harvest. The Ababda are Muslims, but their religious life still has elements of pre-Islamic custom. Within the last forty years, however, the Ababda have become increasingly acculturated into Egyptian Arabic society. The Ababda population exceeds 250,000 people. Closely associated with the Ababda are the Qireijab,* a highly Arabized group of Beja who fish in the Red Sea.
REFERENCES: Andrew Paul. *A History of the Beja Tribes of the Sudan.* 1954; John Spencer Trimingham. *Islam in Sudan.* 1949.

ABACHA. *See* BASSA-KWOMU.

ABADJA. The Abadjas are one of the many subgroups of the Igbos,* an ethnic group of nearly fifteen million people living today in southern and southeastern Nigeria.

ABAHANZA. The Abahanza are a prominent clan of the Hutus* in Burundi. They claim to be, along with the Abajiji and Abavuma, one of the three oldest Hutu families in Burundi.

ABAHUTU. *See* HUTU.

ABAJA. The Abajas are one of the many subgroups of the Igbo* people, an ethnic group with a population of nearly fifteen million people living today in southern and southeastern Nigeria.

ABAJIJI. The Abajiji are a prominent clan of the Hutus* in Burundi. They claim to be, along with the Abahanza and Abavuma, one of the three oldest Hutu families in Burundi.

ABAKAN. *See* KPAN.

ABAKWARIGA. The term "Abakwariga" is a collective reference for the Kutumbawa,* Maguzawa,* and Gwandari* peoples of northwestern Nigeria, all of whom speak a Hausa* language.
REFERENCE: A. Chukwudi Unomah. "The Gwandara Settlements of Lafia to 1900." In Elizabeth Isichei, ed. *Studies in the History of Plateau State, Nigeria.* 1982.

ABALUYIA. *See* LUHYA.

ABAM. The Abams are one of the many subgroups of the Igbo* people of southern and southeastern Nigeria.

ABANLIKU. *See* OBANLIKU.

ABANYOM. The Abanyoms, also known as Befuns, are an ethnic group living today in the Ikom Division of southern Cross River State in Nigeria. Most Abanyoms are farmers and workers. Their population today is approximately 20,000 people. They speak a Bantu* language and are closely related to the Ekoi people.
REFERENCE: *Language Survey of Nigeria.* 1976.

ABARAMBO. The Abarambo people live on the south side of the Uelé River in northeastern Zaire. They are a Sudanic people whose language is clas-

sified by ethnolinguists as part of the central Sudanic cluster. They migrated
from Sudan to the northern and northeastern Congo Basin in the late seventeenth
and early eighteenth centuries. Today, they live near Poko, Isiro, and Rungu in
Zaire, between the Ituri River and the Uelé River. The Abarambos have absorbed
a number of surrounding ethnic groups during the past century.
REFERENCES: F. Scott Bobb. *Historical Dictionary of Zaire.* 1988; Irving Kaplan et
al. *Zaire: A Country Study.* 1978.

ABARUE. The Abarues are a major subgroup of the Shona* peoples of Zimbabwe and Mozambique. Abarue society is subdivided into a number of strong
clan systems, including the Chokos, Tembos, Makates, Chiwares, Mucatus, Chilendjes, and Nyangurus.

ABASUBA. The Abasubas are a Bantu*-speaking people who originated in
Uganda and migrated to the Rusinga Island region of Kenya. In recent decades,
they have been all but assimilated by the Nilotic*-speaking Luo* people in the
area, although the Abasubas still maintain a distinct sense of identity.
REFERENCE: W. Thomas Connelly. ''Population Pressure, Labor Availability, and Agricultural Disintensification: The Decline of Farming on Rusinga Island, Kenya.'' *American Ethnology* 22 (June 1994): 145–70.

ABATSA. *See* BASSA-KWOMU.

ABAVUMA. The Abavuma are a prominent clan of the Hutus* in Burundi.
They claim to be, along with the Abajiji and Abahanza, one of the three oldest
Hutu families in Burundi.

ABBE. *See* ABÉ.

ABBEY. *See* ABÉ.

ABDALLAB. The Abdallabs are an Arab* group who are today scattered
throughout the Central Sudan and Blue Nile region. They are descendants of
the great sixteenth-century leader Abdallah Jamma. During the Hamaj wars in
the eighteenth century, they were driven from their homeland in Qerri and scattered out to their present locations.
REFERENCE: Carolyn Fluehr-Lobban, Richard A. Lobban, Jr., and John Obert Voll.
Historical Dictionary of Sudan. 1992.

ABÉ. The Abé people, also known as the Abbe or Abbey, are an ethnic group
living in the Agboville area of Ivory Coast. Although they speak a Lagoon
language, which is part of the extremely complex group of languages along the
southeastern coast of Ivory Coast, they maintain a social structure that places
them within an Akan* culture group. Traditionally, the Abé people have had

only the most rudimentary form of centralized political structure, with loyalties extending not far beyond the village level. The Abé resisted French colonial expansion until 1910, when the French decisively defeated them. Their population is approximately 180,000 people.
REFERENCES: G. T. Dumestre. *Atlas Linguistique de Côte d'Ivoire: Les Langues de la Région Lagunaire.* 1971; Robert E. Handloff et al. *Côte d'Ivoire: A Country Study.* 1990.

ABGAL. The Abgals are, with a population exceeding 400,000 people, the largest of the Issa* clans in the Horn of Africa.

ABIDJI. The Abidjis, also known as the Aris, are part of the Lagoon cluster of peoples of Ivory Coast. They are concentrated in the subprefecture of Sikensi. Like the other peoples of the southeast coast and lagoons of Ivory Coast, they practice cash-crop farming and engage in the production and trade of palm oil. Some Abidjis still fish as well to provide themselves with a protein source. They are part of a large Akan* culture group. The Abidji population today exceeds 50,000 people.
REFERENCES: Robert E. Handloff et al. *Côte d'Ivoire: A Country Study.* 1990; Robert J. Mundt. *Historical Dictionary of Côte d'Ivoire.* 1995.

ABINU. The Abinus are one of the main subgroups of the Yoruba* people of Nigeria. Most Abinus can be found today living in the eastern reaches of Kwara State in western Nigeria.

ABISI. *See* PITI.

ABISSA. The Abissas are a subgroup of the Maba* people of Chad.

ABJUKRU. *See* ADJUKRU.

ABON. The Abon (Abong) people are a small ethnic group living today in the Tigon District of the Mambilla Division of Gongola State in Nigeria. They are concentrated especially around the town of Abong. The Abons are primarily subsistence farmers who speak a non-Bantu language that is part of the Ti-Batu group.
REFERENCE: *Language Survey of Nigeria.* 1976.

ABONG. *See* ABON.

ABONWA. *See* ABURÉ.

ABORA. The Abora, also known as the Abura, are a subgroup of the Fante* people, an Akan* group, of Ghana. Most Aboras live in the central region

of Ghana, approximately fifteen miles north of Saltpond. Their 1990 population was estimated at approximately 4,500 people. Most of them are small farmers.
REFERENCE: Daniel M. McFarland. *Historical Dictionary of Ghana.* 1995.

ABORO. *See* BIROM.

ABOURÉ. *See* ABURÉ.

ABRON. The Abron (Abrong)—also known as the Boron, Bron, Brong, Bono, Doms, and Tchaman—are an Akan* people living in Bondoukou Department in Ivory Coast and across the border in Ghana and Burkina-Faso. The Abron in Ghana live primarily in the towns of Sunyani, Techiman, Kintampo, and Atebubu. Ethnologists estimate that the Abron settled in their present homeland sometime in the fifteenth century. Under the legendary King Adou Bini, the Abron claim to have founded the Bondoukou Empire back then. Although the Abrons have an Akan social structure and matrilineal systems of descent, they have not experienced real centralized authority in recent centuries. The Abron population today exceeds 100,000 people. They are divided into such subgroups as the Gyaman.
REFERENCES: Alexander Alland, Jr. "Native Therapists and Western Medical Practitioners among the Abron of Ivory Coast." *Transactions of the New York Academy of Sciences* 26 (1964): 714–25; Robert E. Handloff et al. *Côte d'Ivoire: A Country Study.* 1990.

ABU CHARIB. *See* ABU SHARIB.

ABU SHARIB. The Abu Sharibs are one of the seven Tama*-speaking peoples of Sudan and Chad. They live today in Chad and are surrounded by the Tama to the east, the Marari* to the southeast, the Maba* to the south and west, and the Mimi* to the north. Their occupations revolve around the production of cattle, goats, and camels. The Abu Sharib population today exceeds 50,000 people, and the administrative center of their region is the town of Am Zoer. They were converted to Islam centuries ago and are known for the intensity of their devotions.
REFERENCE: Paul Doornbos. "Tama-Speaking Peoples." In Richard V. Weekes, ed. *Muslim Peoples.* 1984.

ABUA. The Abua people are an ethnic group of approximately 60,000 people who today live in a 170-square-mile region of the Niger Delta—the Abua-Odual and Ahoada divisions of Rivers State. The nearest towns are Degema and Ahoada. The Abua farm and fish, trading farm products for fish brought to them by the Kalabari* Ijo.
REFERENCES: Ekpo Eyo. "Abua Masquerades." *African Arts* 7 (Spring 1974): 52–55; *Language Survey of Nigeria.* 1976.

ABUAKWA AKYEM. The Abuakwa Akyems, sometimes called the Abuaswa Akim or simply Akim, are the largest subgroup of the Akyem,* a major Akan* group of Ghana. The Abuakwa Akyem live in eastern Ghana, where they emerged from the Adansi* people. The chief Abuakwa Akyem settlement in Ghana today is the city of Kibi. Although most Abuakwa Akyems are small farmers, they enjoy occupational diversity ranging from blue-collar to professional jobs. Demographers estimate the Abuakwa Akyem population today at approximately 275,000 people.
REFERENCE: Daniel M. McFarland. *Historical Dictionary of Ghana.* 1995.

ABUAN. *See* ABUA.

ABUASWA AKIM. *See* ABUAKWA AKYEM.

ABURA. *See* ABORA.

ABURÉ. The Aburé—also known as the Abouré, Agoua, Abonwa, and Compa—are an ethnic group living primarily in the departments of Grand-Bassam, Bonoua, and Aboisso in extreme southeastern Ivory Coast. Their language is classified as part of the Lagoon cluster of Niger-Congo languages. Most of the Aburés are commercial farmers. The Aburé revolted against French incursions into their homeland in the 1890s, but they could not hold out militarily. The Aburé population today is approximately 35,000 people.
REFERENCE: Robert J. Mundt. *Historical Dictionary of Côte d'Ivoire.* 1995.

ABUSEMEN. The Abusemen are one of the subgroups of the Lisi* people of Chad. They are a Nilotic* people who today make their living as nomadic and semi-nomadic pastoralists, although many are also farming today.

ABYSSINIAN. *See* AMHARA.

ACANJJ. *See* AKAN.

ACHAWA. *See* YAO.

ACHEWA. *See* CHEWA.

ACHIM. *See* AKYEM.

ACHIPETA. *See* CHIPETA.

ACHODE. *See* ATWODE.

ACHOLI. *See* ACOLI.

ACILOWE. *See* LOMWE.

ACOLI. The Acoli (Acholi) are an East African, Nilotic* ethnic group living in north-central Uganda and southern Sudan. Their current population exceeds 500,000 people. They are also heavily concentrated in the cities of Gulu and Lira in Uganda. The Acoli speak a Western Nilotic language closely related to that of the Luo* of Kenya and the Shilluk* of Sudan. Their own oral traditions say that the Acoli arrived in their present location about three centuries ago after a migration from the north. The Acoli are divided into a number of subgroups, such as the Pacua Acoli, the Paimol Acoli, the Pacabol Acoli, the Pabala Acoli, the Parumo Acoli, and the Adilang Acoli. The economy of the rural Acoli revolves around transhumant pastoralism, with the men raising some cattle and the women trying to raise millet, cassava, sesame, sweet potatoes, and sometimes cotton and tobacco for cash. Of all of Uganda's ethnic groups, they are among the least developed and the least acculturated to Western technologies. Their entire cultural life revolves around cattle, which they raised in large numbers until late in the nineteenth century when disease and enemy raids destroyed their herds. Because of severe droughts in northeastern Africa during the 1980s and early 1990s, the Acoli have faced dire economic circumstances.
REFERENCES: *African Encyclopedia.* 1974; K. S. Gourlay. "The Practice of Cueing Among the Karimojon of North-East Uganda." *Journal of Ethnomusicology* 16 (May 1972): 240–46; Okot P'Bitek. "Horn of My Love." *African Arts* 7 (Winter 1973/1974): 56–61.

ACULO. The Aculos are a Grusi*-speaking people of Ghana and Burkina-Faso. They are scattered throughout the Upper Region of Ghana where most of them work as small farmers. They are closely related to the Sisalas and Kasenas,* who also live in the Upper Region. A few Aculos are scattered across the northern border of Ghana in Burkina-Faso as well. Most of them are concentrated near the border between Ghana and Burkina-Faso around the village of Prata.
REFERENCE: Daniel M. McFarland. *Historical Dictionary of Ghana.* 1995.

AD TEKLE. The Ad Tekles are one of the three subdivisions of the Bet Asgede people of Eritrea and Ethiopia. In the nineteenth century, they adopted the Muslim religion and the Tigre* language of the Tigre people, over whom they presided as feudal lords. Most Ad Tekles are nomadic pastoralists.

AD TEMARYAM. The Ad Temaryams are one of the three subgroups of the Bet Asgede people of Eritrea and Ethiopia. In the nineteenth century, they adopted the Muslim religion and the Tigre* language of the Tigre people, over whom they presided as feudal lords. Most Ad Temaryams live in Keren District.

ADA. The Adas are one of the subgroups of the Adangbe* peoples of the Accra Plain and coastal inselbergs of southeastern Ghana. Most of them make their livings as small farmers. The Ada population of Ghana today exceeds 150,000 people.

ADA. *See* KUTURMI.

ADAL. *See* AFAR.

ADAMPA. *See* ADANGBE.

ADANGBE. The Adangbes—also known as the Adangmes, Adampas, and Dangmes—comprise a major cluster of related ethnic groups in southeastern Ghana. They live in close association with the Ga* people of the region. The Adangbes are especially concentrated along the coast and on inselbergs in the Accra Plain. Most of them are small farmers. The Adangbes are divided into a number of subgroups, each of which possesses a very strong sense of ethnic identity. The Adangbe subgroups include the Adas,* Kpongs, Manya Krobos, Ningos, Shais, Pramprams, and Osudokus. They are related culturally and linguistically to the Ewe* people. The Adangbe population, including the Ga in Ghana today, is approximately 1.5 million people.
REFERENCES: Mary Kropp. *Adangme Vocabularies.* 1970; Daniel M. McFarland. *Historical Dictionary of Ghana.* 1995.

ADANGME. *See* ADANGBE.

ADANSI. The Adansis are an ethnic group of contemporary Ghana. Most of the Adansis live on both sides of the border between the Ashanti Region and the Central Region of southern Ghana. They are primarily small farmers.
REFERENCE: Daniel M. McFarland. *Historical Dictionary of Ghana.* 1995.

ADARA. *See* KADARA.

ADARAWA. The Adarawas are one of the Hausa* people of Niger.

ADELE. The Adeles are a small ethnic group of several thousand people living on both sides of the border in southwestern Togo and southeastern Ghana. They are especially concentrated to the northeast of Krakye. Most Adeles are small farmers. Ethnologists classify them as one of the Central Togo groups of people.
REFERENCE: Daniel M. McFarland. *Historical Dictionary of Ghana.* 1995.

ADIKUMMU. *See* SUKUR.

ADILANG. *See* ACOLI.

ADIOURKROU. *See* ADJUKRU.

ADJA. The Adja (Aja) people are part of the Ewe* cluster of southern Benin and Togo. They are a branch of the Yoruba* people who migrated out of Oyo, Nigeria, in the thirteenth century and settled in Nuatja and Tado. They claim to have originated in Adja-Tojo, today a small village in southern Togo. Early in the 1700s, the Adja split into two groups. One group migrated south and became known as the Western Adjas or the Ewes; the other group established the Allada kingdom in what is today Benin. In Togo, the Adja are concentrated in the Anécho and Atakpamé regions. Their language forms the foundation of all the languages between the Volta River and the Ouemé River—Ouatchi,* Evegbé,* Voudou, Kpessi, Fongbé, and Guin. The Adja population probably exceeds 500,000 people. They are primarily farmers, raising maize, millet, manioc, and plaintains.
REFERENCES: Samuel Decalo. *Historical Dictionary of Togo.* 1976; Samuel Decalo. *Historical Dictionary of Benin.* 1994.

ADJAO. *See* YAO.

ADJOUKROU. *See* ADJUKRU.

ADJUKRU. The Adjukru—also known as the Adjoukrou, Adiourkrou, Adyu-kru, Boubouri, and Odjukru—are a unique ethnic group in Ivory Coast. They are obviously of Kru* origins, but they also have many characteristics of the Lagoon peoples among whom they live in Dabou. Their own traditions have them migrating to their present area from the northwest. The other Lagoon peoples claim to have come from the east. Also, unlike the Lagoon groups, the Adjukru maintain elaborate age-group hierarchies in their social structure. The Adjukru are concentrated along the western portion of the Ebrie lagoon near the town of Dabou. Economically, the Adjukru are farmers and are deeply involved in palm oil production and the palm oil trade. Their population today is approximately 75,000 people.
REFERENCES: Robert E. Handloff et al. *Côte d'Ivoire: A Country Study.* 1990; H. Memel-Fote, *Le système politique de Lodjoukrou.* 1980; Robert J. Mundt. *Historical Dictionary of Côte d'Ivoire.* 1995; John M. Stewart. ''Downstep and Floating Low Tones in Adioukrou.'' *Journal of African Languages and Linguistics* 5 (1983): 57–78.

ADONG. *See* LUNGU.

ADOUMA. The Adouma are an ethnic group speaking a Mbédé* language. They are concentrated on the left bank of the upper Ogooué River near Lastourville in Gabon. They are expert canoemen and traditionally made their

living as fishermen before the arrival of Europeans. Their own historical traditions have them migrating to the Lastourville area from the east or south-east, moving down the Sébé River to the Ogooué River. During the years of the African slave trade, the Adouma sold slaves in return for salt, guns, gun-powder, fabrics, and copper utensils. Lastourville was an Adouma village before the arrival of the French. In recent years, large numbers of Adouma have been migrating down-river toward Port Gentil.
REFERENCE: David E. Gardinier. *Historical Dictionary of Gabon.* 1994.

ADYUKRU. *See* ADJUKRU.

ADYUMBA. The Adyumbas are an ethnic group who speak a Myènè* language in the Bantu* linguistic group; they live in the Lake Azingo region in Estuary Province and Moyen-Ogooué Province in Gabon. Historically, the Adyumbas were a clan of the Mpongwe* people, who were skilled canoemen and made their living off of the Ogooué River. Two centuries ago, they lived on the banks of Nazareth Bay at the mouth of the Ogooué River, but conflict with the Ombéké people drove them toward the west where they live today. Today, most Adyumbas are fishermen, small farmers, or local merchants.
REFERENCES: K. David Patterson. *The Northern Gabon Coast to 1875.* 1975; David E. Gardinier. *Historical Dictionary of Gabon.* 1994.

AFAKANI. *See* DEFAKA.

AFANGO. *See* BIROM.

AFAO. *See* ELOYI.

AFAR. The Afar, who are known as Danakil in Arabic and Adal in Amharic, are a Muslim people living in the eastern reaches of the Horn of Africa. The Afar Triangle consists of 55,000 square miles of territory spread out through Shoa, Wollo, and Tigre provinces and northern Harer Province, in Ethiopia, southern Eritrea, and Djibouti. Much of their territory is lowland deserts and salt pans; temperatures there are the hottest on the planet. Approximately 400,000 Afar live in Ethiopia, while another 135,000 are in Djibouti. Along the coast, some Afar make their living as fishermen, but most are pastoral nomads who work herds of sheep, cattle, goats, and camels. Although they are nomadic, Afar wandering is regionally confined to existing water supplies.

   The Afar are Sunni Muslims, although features of their original animistic faith still survive. Ever since the eighteenth century, there has been contact and con-flict between Christian Ethiopians and Afar Muslims, but the Afar have valued their ethnic identity highly and have maintained a distinctly separate culture. They remain faithful to their eastern Cushitic language and have resisted all attempts by Ethiopian and Djibouti politicians to transform them into settled farmers. Afar society has traditionally been divided into four sultanates—the Tajoura and Raheito sultanates in Djibouti and the Aussa and Biru sultanates in Ethiopia. Within each sultanate, there is a series of federations headed by chiefs. The primary function of the chiefs is to mediate controversies involving water and grazing rights. The Afar are also divided into patrilineal groups known as *mela,* or tribes, who define themselves in terms of lineage or territory.

Over the centuries, the Afar served as guides for Arab* slavers in the trans-Red Sea slave trade. At the turn of the twentieth century, when a railroad between Addis Ababa and Djibouti City was completed, the Afar were introduced to a commercial economy and valuable trade goods; over the course of the century, they began to supply more and more meat, butter, milk, and hides to buyers in the cities. In recent years, the Afar have had to deal with the problems of overgrazing, drought, and war in the Horn of Africa. Famine has devastated them, as did the ongoing battle between the central Ethiopian government and the Eritrean secessionists. In Djibouti, they find themselves under Issa* and Somali* domination and caught between the Ethiopian and Somali struggle in the Ogaden.

REFERENCES: Victor Englebert. ''The Danakil: Nomads of Ethiopia's Wasteland.'' *National Geographic* 147 (1970): 186–212; I. M. Lewis. *Peoples of the Horn: Somali, Afar, and Saho.* 1955; Enid Parker. ''Afar Stories, Riddles, and Proverbs.'' *Journal of Ethiopian Studies* 9 (1971); 219–87.

AFATIME. *See* AVATIME.

AFEMMAI. *See* YEKHEE.

AFFADE. The Affades are a small ethnic group living today primarily in the Rann Kalabalge District of Dikwa Division in Borno State, Nigeria. They speak a Chadic language, and many ethnologists consider them to be a subgroup of the Kotokos.* Most Affades make their living herding livestock and working small subsistence farms.

AFIZAREK. *See* AFUSARI.

AFKABIYE. *See* GUDUF.

AFO. *See* ELOYI.

AFRAN QALLA. The Afran Qalla are actually a cluster of four Oromo* subgroups: Obora, Nole, Babile, and Alla. They are primarily Muslims living around the city of Harer, Ethiopia, where they work as sedentary farmers.

AFRIKANER. The term ''Afrikaner'' is used today to refer to the more than 2.2 million people in South Africa who are descendants of the original

Boer, or Cape Dutch, settlers of the Cape Colony. Over the centuries, they assimilated some French* and German* settlers in South Africa as well. Their culture is distinct because of their Afrikaner language, their Calvinist faith expressed in the Dutch Reformed Church, and their powerful sense of racial identity as white people. Those Boers who engaged in the Great Trek to Transvaal and Natal in the nineteenth century even developed a sense of being God's chosen people. Afrikaners constitute 55 percent of the white population of South Africa and have been generally known for their creation of apartheid and their conservative, often fanatical, opposition to black majority rule.
REFERENCE: T. D. Moodie. *The Rise of Afrikanerdom: Power, Apartheid, and the Afrikaner Civil Religion.* 1975.

AFRO-PORTUGUESE. *See* MESTICO.

AFU. *See* ELOYI.

AFUNU. The Afunus are one of the Bantu*-speaking peoples of Nigeria. They are classified as part of the Plateau cluster of peoples who occupy central Nigeria. Most Afunus practice subsistence horticulture, raising ginger, millet, guinea corn, beans, and citrus products; they live in social systems characterized by patrilineal descent and patrifocal residence. In recent years, they have begun migrating to towns and cities looking for work.
REFERENCE: Donald G. Morrison et al. *Black Africa: A Comparative Handbook.* 1989.

AFUSARE. *See* AFUSARI.

AFUSARI. The Afusaris (Afusares, Jaris, Jarawas, Fizeres, Fesereks, Afizareks, Fezeres, Jarawan Dutses) are a people living today in the Plateau State of Nigeria, as well as in the Bauchi State. They are especially concentrated in the Karawa, Gwong, Forum, Gashish, and Jal districts of Jos Division and the Jema'a District of Jema'a Division of Kadima State. They are sometimes called the Hill Jarawa. They live in a series of villages where they have made the transition, in recent decades, to small farming. Hunting, however, has long been of religious and ritual significance to them. The consumption of meat and beer is considered among life's most important activities. Hunting tends to be a communal activity, complete with hunting dogs, horses, and brush fires to flush out game animals. Most Afusaris are subsistence farmers, however, raising millet, cassava, maize, yams, beans, peas, melons, pumpkins, goats, sheep, and chickens.
REFERENCES: *Language Survey of Nigeria.* 1976; Charles Meek. *The Northern Tribes of Nigeria.* 1969; Jean-Claude Muller. "Intertribal Hunting Among the Rukuba." *Ethnology* 21 (1982): 203–14.

AFUTU. *See* EFUTU.

AGARI. *See* GURE-KAHUGU.

AGAU. *See* AGAW.

AGAVE. The Agaves, who are also identified as the Crophy people, are an Ewe* ethnic group of Ghana. They are concentrated in the eastern reaches of the Accra Plain west of the Volta River and north of Songaw Lagoon and Ada. Most of them make their livings as small farmers.
REFERENCE: Daniel M. McFarland. *Historical Dictionary of Ghana.* 1985.

AGAW. The Agaw (Agew) people are an ethnic group living in central and northern Ethiopia and Eritrea. They are closely related, culturally and linguistically, with the neighboring Amhara* and Tigre* peoples. Ethnologists believe the Agaws have been living there for thousands of years, much longer than the Amharas and Tigres, and that they were the progenitors of what some anthropologists now call the Ethiopian ''type.'' They speak a Cushitic language. Most Agaws are farmers who raise millet, coffee, and castor oil plants. Today, intermarriage between Agaw, Amhara, and Tigre people is common. Several Agaw subgroups still maintain distinct identities, however, in spite of the cultural assimilation occurring. Those groups include the Bilen (Bogos) in Eritrea, and the Kemnant, Kwara, and Beta Israels.* The Agaw are divided religiously between several Christian denominations and the Sunni Muslim faith. The Agaw population today exceeds 240,000 people. The largest of the Agaw subgroups is the Awi.*
REFERENCES: *African Encyclopedia.* 1974; Harold D. Nelson et al. *Ethiopia: A Country Study.* 1980; Chris Prouty and Eugene Rosenfeld. *Historical Dictionary of Ethiopia and Eritrea.* 1994.

AGBARAGBA. *See* EFUTOP.

AGBARI. *See* GBARI.

AGBIRI. *See* GURE-KAHUGU.

AGBO. *See* LEGBO.

AGEW. *See* AGAW.

AGNAGAN. The Agnagans are a small ethnic group of several thousand people living on both sides of the border in southwestern Togo and southeastern Ghana, east of Lake Volta. Most Agnagans are small farmers. Ethnologists classify them as one of the Central Togo groups of people.
REFERENCE: Daniel M. McFarland. *Historical Dictionary of Ghana.* 1995.

AGNI. *See* ANYI.

AGOI. The Agois (Ro Bambanis, Ibamis), who call themselves the Wa Bambanis, are a small ethnic group living today in the Oubra Division of Cross River State in Nigeria. The Agoi population today is approximately 20,000 people. They speak a language that is included in the Cross River group of the Benue-Congo family.
REFERENCE: *Language Survey of Nigeria.* 1976.

AGOMA. *See* KAGOMA.

AGONA. The Agonas are one of the Fante* subgroups of people living today in southwestern Ghana. Their population there today is approximately 150,000 people. See AKAN.

AGONLINU. The Agonlinus are a subgroup of the Fon* people of Benin. They live in the southern third of the country and work as farmers, raising maize, millet, manioc, and plantains. They can also be found in Togo, primarily in the Atakpamé region. The Agonlinus speak a Ewe* dialect.

AGOUA. *See* ABURÉ.

AGRU. *See* ALLADIAN.

AGWAGWUNE. The Agwagwune people are a tiny ethnic group living today in Nigeria. Most of them are small farmers living in the Akamkpa Division of Cross River State. Ethnolinguists classify their language as part of the Cross River group of the Benue-Congo family.
REFERENCE: *Language Survey of Nigeria.* 1976.

AHAFO. The Ahafos are one of the major ethnic subdivisions of the Akan* people. They are concentrated in the Western Region and Brong-Ahafo Region in western Ghana and across the border in Ivory Coast. The number of Ahafos in Ghana today exceeds 50,000 people.

AHANTA. The Ahantas are an ethnic group in contemporary Ghana. Most of the Ahantas live along the coast of western Ghana, primarily in the Western Region. They make their livings as small farmers and fishermen. They are considered to be a subgroup of the Nzima* people. There are approximately 200,000 Ahantas in Ghana today.
REFERENCE: Daniel M. McFarland. *Historical Dictionary of Ghana.* 1995.

AHEL BERIKALLAH. The Ahel Berikallahs are a particularly devout ethnic group of Muslims who live on both sides of the border between Mauri-

tania and Western Sahara in what is today Morocco. Their population is approximately 2,000 people. They are known as a *zawiya* people—especially dedicated to the Koran.
REFERENCE: Tony Hodges. *Historical Dictionary of Western Sahara.* 1982.

AHEL BRAHIM OU DAOUD. The Ahel Brahim ou Daouds are a core ethnic group of the Reguibat* es-Sahel people of the Western Sahara in what is today Morocco. Their current population exceeds 10,000 people. Perhaps half of them live in such cities as El-Ayoun and Smara and in small towns in the Saguia el-Hamra area. The others live nomadic lives in a region reaching from Saguia el-Hamra in the north to Bir Moghrein in Mauritania in the south.
REFERENCE: Tony Hodges. *Historical Dictionary of Western Sahara.* 1982.

AHEL CHEIKH MA EL-AININ. The Ahel Cheikh Ma el-Ainin are the result of a recent process of ethnogenesis. They are descendants of Cheikh Ma el-Ainin, the individual who led a series of anticolonial political movements in the 1890s and early 1900s. He had thirty-three sons, and all of his descendants have coalesced ethnically into a group with a powerful sense of identity. They are widely known in southern Morocco, Mauritania, and Western Sahara for their political and intellectual abilities.
REFERENCE: Tony Hodges. *Historical Dictionary of Western Sahara.* 1982.

AHEL ES-SAHEL. The term Ahel es-Sahel is a collective reference to the Saharawis* of Western Sahara.

AHEL MOHAMMED BEN BRAHIM. The Ahel Mohammed Ben Brahim people are a subgroup of the Mejat* people of Western Sahara in what is today Morocco. They live along the coast and make their living as fishermen.

AHIZI. *See* AIZI.

AHLON. The Ahlons are classified as part of the Central Togo cluster of peoples in West Africa. The Ahlons live east of Lake Volta in southern Ghana and across the border in western Togo. Most of them are farmers and fishermen.
REFERENCE: Daniel M. McFarland. *Historical Dictionary of Ghana.* 1995.

AHO. *See* ELOYI.

AHOULAN. The Ahoulan are part of the cluster of Ewe*-speaking peoples of Togo. Their population today exceeds 27,000 people. They live primarily in the Lomé region and along the Togo-Ghana border. They make their living as fishermen. Tourist visits to the scattered Ahoulan villages on the beaches are quite common and provide an excellent source of foreign currency.
REFERENCE: Samuel Decalo. *Historical Dictionary of Togo.* 1976.

AIKE. *See* AKE.

AIT ATMAN. The Ait Atman are one of the major subgroups of the Tekna* peoples of Western Sahara in what is today Morocco. According to their own legends, they were originally a semi-nomadic people who have been engaged in constant warfare over the generations with the more sedentary Ait Jmel,* the other major Tekna group. Today, their division is more geographical, with the Ait Atman dominating the eastern Tekna regions and the Ait Jmel the western regions. The Ait Atman are themselves divided into the following subgroups: Azouafid, Id Ahmed, Ait Oussa,* and Id Brahim.

AIT JMEL. The Ait Jmel are one of the major subgroups of the Tekna* peoples of Western Sahara in what is today Morocco. According to their own legends, they were originally a sedentary people who have been engaged in constant war over the generations with the more nomadic Ait Atman,* the other major Tekna group. Today, the Ait Atman dominate the eastern Tekna regions and the Ait Jmel the western regions. The Ait Jmel are themselves divided into the following subgroups: the Ait Lahsen,* Izarguien,* and Yagout,* who are primarily nomadic people, and the more sedentary Ait Moussa Ou Ali of the Goulimine region and the Oulad Bou Laouilet.

AIT LAHSEN. The Ait Lahsens are a subgroup of the Ait Jmel,* who are part of the Tekna* group of peoples in Western Sahara in what is today Morocco. They are the dominant ethnic group of the Ait Jmel groupings. Their nomadic range traditionally reached from the Oued Noun region of southern Morocco to Saguia el-Hamra. They are divided into the following subgroups: Injouren, Ait Bou Meghout, Ait Yahya, Rouimiat, Ait Bou Guezzaten, Ait Hassein, Ait Saad, and Id Daoud Ou Abdallah. In the 1970s, most Ait Lahsens began to become more sedentary and settled permanently in small towns in southern Morocco. Tan-Tan has a large concentration of Ait Lahsens. They also settled in small towns in Western Sahara.

AIT OUSSA. The Ait Oussas are today one of the primary subgroups of the Tekna* peoples of Western Sahara in what is today Morocco. They have traditionally been a semi-nomadic people whose general regional homeland surrounded the oasis town of Assa. During the 1950s, the Ait Oussas were particularly active in the anticolonial resistance movements in Western Sahara and Morocco. In recent years, they aligned themselves with the Moroccan government against the Polisario Front movement.

AIT WARYAGHAR. The Ait Waryaghars are one of the major Berber* groups of Morocco, at least in terms of their political influence. They are concentrated in the Al-Hmam District of the Rif region of northwestern Morocco. During the Rif rebellion against the French in the 1920s, the Ait Waryaghars played a central role.

AIZI. The Aizi—also known as the Ahizi and Kpokpo—are a unique ethnic group of Ivory Coast. They are obviously of Kru* origins, but they also have many characteristics of the Lagoon peoples among whom they live in Jacqueville. Their own traditions have them migrating to their present area from the northwest. The other Lagoon peoples claim to have come from the east. Also, unlike the Lagoon groups, the Aizi maintain elaborate age group hierarchies in their social structure. The Aizi are concentrated along the western portion of the Ebrie lagoon near the town of Jacqueville. Economically, the Aizi are farmers and are deeply involved in palm oil production and the palm oil trade. Their population today is approximately 75,000 people.
REFERENCES: C. Bonnefoy. ''Tiagba—Notes sur un Village Aizi.'' *Études Eburnéenes* 3 (1954): 7–129; Robert J. Mundt. *Historical Dictionary of Côte d'Ivoire.* 1995.

AIZO. The Aizos are one of the Fon* peoples of contemporary Togo and Benin; some can also be found in Ghana. Most of them are subsistence farmers who raise maize, millet, manioc, and plantains. They are concentrated in the southern region of Togo and Benin, along the coast from Lomé to Ouidah. Ethnologists believe that they originated in Ghana and migrated to region in the seventeenth century. Their current population exceeds 225,000 people, and they constitute an important element in the political, commercial, and administrative elite of Togo and Benin.
REFERENCES: Samuel Decalo. *Historical Dictionary of Benin.* 1994; Donald G. Morrison et al. *Black Africa: A Comparative Handbook.* 1989.

AJA. *See* ADJA.

AJANJI. *See* JANJI.

AJAUA. *See* YAO.

AJAUA. The Ajaua people, whose population today exceeds 500,000 people, live in Niassa and Tete provinces in Mozambique and across the border in Malawi. During the past several centuries, they have made the transition from a hunting lifestyle to one based on farming. Most of them are Muslims.
REFERENCE: Mario Azevedo. *Historical Dictionary of Mozambique.* 1991.

AJURAN. The Ajuran people are part of the Eastern Hamatic cluster of peoples who live today in far northwestern Kenya, southern Ethiopia, and eastern Somalia. They speak a Somali* language and have a current population of approximately 60,000 people. The Ajurans are a pastoral people who also cultivate small plots of land.
REFERENCE: Donald G. Morrison et al. *Black Africa: A Comparative Handbook.* 1989.

AKA. The Aka are part of the Western cluster of Pygmies.* They live primarily in the Central African Republic and number approximately 5,000 people.

AKA. The Aka, not to be confused with the Aka subgroup of the Western cluster of Pygmies,* is a subgroup of the Mbutis, themselves a Pygmy subgroup. These Aka live in the northwestern reaches of the Ituri forest in Zaire.

AKAJUK. *See* EKAJUK.

AKAMBA. The Akambas are an ethnic group living today in the Kitui District of the Eastern Province of Kenya. Their economy revolves around the production of cattle, sheep, goats, millet, maize, and cow-peas. Large numbers of Akambas are also seasonal migrant workers earning cash for the commercial economy.
REFERENCE: Michael O'Leary. "The Growth and Decline of Household Herds in Eastern Kitui, Kenya." *Ethnos* 45 (1980): 211–29.

AKAN. The Akan (Akanny, Akani, Acanjj, Hecanny) people of West Africa live in the tropical rain forests and savannas in southern Ghana, the western Volta region, Togo, and the Ivory Coast. Those living in the tropical rain forest are farmers, while those in the savannas have traditionally been herdsmen. Large numbers of the Akan are migrating to the major cities of Ghana, Burkina-Faso, Togo, and Ivory Coast, where they work in a variety of industrial and service occupations. By the early 1990s, more than seven million people spoke the Akan language, which is divided into four basic subgroups, all part of the Kwa* group of the Niger-Congo linguistic family: Twi,* Fante,* Nzima,* and Anyi*-Baule.* Akan civilization first appeared around 1000 A.D., emerging from the northern Brong savanna, the Etsi coast, and the Adanse forest. Large Akan kingdoms, most notably the Asante* Empire, appeared between 1600 and 1850. Historically, the Akan peoples exchanged gold and kola nuts for salt and slaves. Until the Spanish conquest of the New World, the Akan "Gold Coast" was the main source of gold in Europe.
    Akan social organization is based on the matrilineal clan and a matrilineal descent system. Rapid urbanization in recent years, however, has placed severe pressures on the matrilineal clan system. Most Akan people still practice their indigenous religious traditions—including the worship of ancestors, fertility festivals, and harvest festivals—although most of the Akan have converted, at least nominally, to Christianity and Islam. Approximately two-thirds of the Akan identify themselves as Christians, while less than 10 percent are Muslim; the Muslims are divided between the Sunni and Shafi rites. The Akan generally see themselves as ethnically superior to surrounding groups. The major Akan sub-

divisions include the Akuapem,* Akyem,* Kwahu,* Ahafo,* Asante,* Abron,* Denkyira,* Assin,* Nzima, Fante, and Baule. The Baules and the Abrons are primarily in Ivory Coast.
REFERENCES: James Anquandah. ''State Formation Among the Akan of Ghana.'' *Sankofa, The Journal of Archaeological and Historical Studies* 1 (1975): 47–57; J. B. Christiansen. *Double Descent Among the Fante.* 1954; E. T. Meyerowitz. *Akan Traditions of Origins.* 1952.

AKANI. *See* AKAN.

AKANIGUI. *See* KANIGUI.

AKANNY. *See* AKAN.

AKASSA. The Akassa are a subgroup of the Ijaw* people of Nigeria. They are concentrated in the Brass Local Government Area of Rivers State.

AKAYON. *See* KIONG.

AKE. The Ake (Akye, Aike) people are a small ethnic group living today in the Lafia Division of Plateau State in Nigeria. They are especially concentrated in the Assaiko District, where most of them work as small farmers. Their language is classified as part of the Benue group of Benue-Congo languages.
REFERENCE: *Language Survey of Nigeria.* 1976.

AKEBOU. The Akebous are a small ethnic group of several thousand people living on both sides of the border in southwestern Togo and southeastern Ghana. Most Akebous are small farmers. Ethnologists classify them as one of the Central Togo groups of people.
REFERENCE: Donald G. Morrison et al. *Black Africa: A Comparative Handbook.* 1989.

AKÈLÈ. *See* BAKÈLÈ.

AKIÉ. *See* ATTIE.

AKIM. *See* ABUAKWA AKYEM.

AKOIYANG. *See* KIONG.

AKOKO. The Akokos are one of the main subgroups of the Yoruba* people of Nigeria. Most Akokos can be found today living in the northeastern reaches of Ondo State, especially in Akoko District. They can also be found in the Ijumu District of the Kabba Division in Kwara State.

AKONTO. *See* MBEMBE.

AKOT. The Akots are a major subdivision of the Atuot* peoples of the southern Sudan.

AKPAFU. The Akpafu homeland is in the Volta region of Ghana. The Akpafus live between Lake Volta on the west and the border with Togo on the east. A number of them also live across the border in Togo as well. Their contemporary population numbers approximately 20,000 people, and they live in the four villages of Akpafu-Mempeasem, Akpafu-Todzi, Akpafu-Odomi, and Akpafu-Adoko. Those villages are all located on a ridge resting between the central Togo and Nkonya hills. Some ethnologists have identified Akpafu origins in Ethiopia. Before their eighteenth-century arrival at their present location, the Akpafu fell under Akwamu* and then Asante* domination. They identify themselves as the Mawu and speak a Kwa* language. Their economy revolves around the production of rice and cocoa, and they also raise goats, sheep, rabbits, and poultry.
REFERENCE: V. Kofi Agawu. "Music in the Funeral Traditions of the Akpafu." *Journal of Ethnomusicology* 32 (Winter 1988): 75–105.

AKPANZHI. *See* KPAN.

AKPA-YACHE. The Akpa-Yaches are a relatively small ethnic group of Nigeria. They can be found particularly in the Akunga and Boju districts of the Oturkpo Division of Benue State, as well as in the Ogoja Division of Cross River State. They are closely related to the Idomas.*
REFERENCE: *Language Survey of Nigeria.* 1976.

AKPE. The Akpes are a little-known ethnic group living today in Nigeria. Most Akpes live in the Akoko Division of Ondo State and speak a Kwa* language. They are primarily subsistence farmers.
REFERENCE: *Language Survey of Nigeria.* 1976.

AKPET-EHOM. The Akpet-Ehoms, also known as the Ukpets, are a small ethnic group living today in Cross River State in Nigeria. They are concentrated especially in Akampka Division. Most Akpet-Ehoms labor as subsistence farmers. Their language is classified with the Cross River group of the Benue-Congo family.
REFERENCE: *Language Survey of Nigeria.* 1976.

AKPOSO. The Akposo (Akposso) constitute one of the prominent ethnic groups in central Togo, primarily in the mountains of the Akposo District of the Plateau region, west of Atakpamé and across the border in Ghana. Ethnographers believe the Akposo reached their present location after being driven there by the ex-

pansionist Ewe* and Asante* peoples. During the Ashanti-Akposo War of 1869–1873, more than one-third of all the Akposo were either slaughtered or sold into slavery. After the British* conquest of the region in 1874, as well as the subsequent German* pacification, Asante power declined, and the Akposo felt safe to move from the isolation of the mountains to the foothills. The Akposo are animist in their religious loyalties. Today, they maintain coffee and cocoa plantations located up to seventy miles from their mountain villages. The Akposo work the fields only twice a year, coming out of their villages only temporarily. The current Akposo population stands at approximately 90,000 people. They are known to their neighbors as being an ethnocentric people who are highly suspicious of outsiders.
REFERENCE: Samuel Decalo. *Historical Dictionary of Togo.* 1976.

AKPOSSO. *See* AKPOSO.

AKRAMAN. *See* GOMOA.

AKU. The term ''Aku'' is used to refer to a group of Yoruba* from Nigeria who exist today within the Krio* people of Freetown, Sierra Leone. They arrived in Freetown in the 1820s from eastern Nigeria and never lost their separate identity. Although most Krios are Christians, the Akus are devout Muslims who still speak Yoruba.
REFERENCE: Irving Kaplan et al. *Area Handbook of Sierra Leone.* 1976.

AKU. The term ''Aku'' is used in Gambia to refer to people of mixed African and European descent. They are a creole population of approximately 6,000 people in The Gambia. Although they constitute only 1 percent of the Gambian population, they are highly influential in business and the professions.
REFERENCE: David P. Gamble. *The Gambia.* 1988.

AKUAPEM. The Akuapem (Akwapim) are one of the major ethnic subdivisions of the Akan* people. Most of the Akuapems live in the southern reaches of the Eastern Region of Ghana. Their population in contemporary Ghana exceeds 450,000 people.

AKUNAKUNA. The Akunakunas are an ethnic group living today in southern Cross River State in Nigeria, as well as across the border in western Cameroon. They are closely related to the Efiks* and Ibibios.* The Akunakuna language is of Bantu* origins. Most of them are farmers, raising yams and palm oil. Large numbers of them also work in Nigerian cities. The Akunakuna population today exceeds 350,000 people.
REFERENCE: Donald G. Morrison et al. *Black Africa: A Comparative Handbook.* 1989.

AKURI. The Akuri, or Agru, are a subgroup of the Alladian* people of Ivory Coast.

AKURUMBA. *See* KURUMBA.

AKURUMI. *See* KURAMA.

AKWA. The Akwas are a prominent subgroup of the Duala* people of coastal Cameroon. Actually, they are a lineage group. Because of their skills as commercial traders, linguists, and political negotiators, they have emerged as an extremely influential Cameroonian people. King Akwa signed the Anglo-Duala Treaty of 1852 and the German protectorate treaty of 1884. The Akwas protested German land expropriation policies in the early 1900s and provided the genesis of Cameroonian nationalism. Betote Akwa was a leading Cameroonian politician in the 1950s and early 1960s.
REFERENCE: Mark DeLancey and H. M. Mokeba. *Historical Dictionary of the Republic of Cameroon.* 1990.

AKWAHU. *See* KWAHU.

AKWAMU. The Akwamus, also known historically as the Aquamboes and Oquies, are an ethnic group that today is concentrated along the border between the Eastern Region and the Volta Region of eastern Ghana. Akwamu traditions give them an origin to the north, but they expanded into southern Ghana in the seventeenth century, conquering the Akuapem by 1646, Accra by 1681, and Agona by 1689. The Akwamu Kingdom peaked in the early eighteenth century when it extended across southern Ghana into Benin. Akwamu fortunes then began to decline gradually, and, in 1886, they submitted to British sovereignty. Most Akwamus today work as small farmers, businessmen, laborers, and professionals. There are more than 50,000 Akwamu people in Ghana today.
REFERENCE: Daniel M. McFarland. *Historical Dictionary of Ghana.* 1995.

AKWAPIM. *See* AKUAPEM.

AKYÉ. *See* ATTIE.

AKYE. *See* AKE.

AKYEM. The Akyem (Akem) are one of the major ethnic subdivisions of the Akan* people. They are concentrated demographically in the western portions of the Eastern Region of Ghana. Their own oral traditions trace their origins to what is today the Adansi area of southwestern Ghana in the sixteenth century. They were forced to migrate eastward in the seventeenth century because of Denkyira* expansion, and they settled between the contemporary cities

of Kibi and Oda in the Atewa Hills. They were widely known as traders of gold, slave, and salt in the eighteenth and nineteenth centuries. The Akyem are divided into three major subdivisions: Abuakwa (Abuaswa) Akyem,* Bosume (Basome) Akyem,* and Kotoku Akyem.* In terms of population today, there are approximately 275,000 Abuakwa Akyem, 30,000 Bosume Akyem, and 100,000 Kotoku Akyems. Other Akyem subgroups total approximately 100,000 people.
REFERENCES: Irving Kaplan et al. *Area Handbook for Ghana.* 1971; Daniel M. McFarland. *Historical Dictionary of Ghana.* 1995.

ALABA. The Alaba are a Muslim subgroup of the Sadama* people of southwestern Ethiopia. Many also consider them to be a subgroup of the Kembatta.*

ALADA. *See* EGUN.

ALAGOA. The Alagoas (Alago, Arago) are an ethnic group living today in Plateau State, Nigeria, especially in the Doma, Keana, Obi, Awe, and Assaikio districts of the Lafia Division. They call themselves the Idoma-Nokwus. Like the Jukuns,* with whom they have had a long association, the Alagoas have a system of sacred kingships and hereditary political offices. They are also related to the Idomas and Gomeis.* Most Alagoas are subsistence farmers, raising guinea corn, maize, and millet. They are especially concentrated in the Lafia and Awe districts. Their contemporary population exceeds 120,000 people.
REFERENCES: Ade Adefuye. ''The Alago Kingdoms: A Political History.'' In Elizabeth Isichei, ed. *Studies in the History of Plateau State, Nigeria.* 1982; *Language Survey of Nigeria.* 1976.

ALEGE. The Aleges are a small ethnic group living in the Obudu Division of Cross River State in Nigeria. They speak a Bendi language, which is part of the Cross River group of the Benue-Congo family.
REFERENCE: *Language Survey of Nigeria.* 1976.

ALENSAW. The Alensaws are one of the many subgroups of the Igbo,* an ethnic group of nearly fifteen million people living today in southern and southeastern Nigeria.

ALETA. The Aleta are one of the major subgroups of the Sadama* people of southwestern Ethiopia.

ALFANEMA. The Alfanema are a Molé-Dagbane* people of the Yendi region of northern Ghana. Most of them are pastoralists.

REFERENCE: Phyllis Ferguson. "Islamization in Dagbon: A Study of the Alfanema of Yendi." Ph.D. dissertation. Cambridge University. 1972.

ALI. The Ali people are a small ethnic group living in and around Lobaye in the Central African Republic and across the border in Congo. The region is equatorial rain forest, and most Alis are small farmers, raising coffee, cacao, kola nuts, and pepper for cash and a variety of other crops for consumption. Ethnologists believe that the Alis are the result of a recent process of ethnogenesis, resulting from the mixing of various Bantu* peoples in the region and several Baya groups.
REFERENCE: Pierre Kalck. *Historical Dictionary of the Central African Republic.* 1992.

ALLA. The Alla are a subgroup of the Afran Qallo, themselves a subgroup of the Oromo* of Ethiopia. They are primarily Muslims living around the city of Harer who work as sedentary farmers.

ALLADIAN. The Alladians, also known as the Nladja-wron or Jack-Jacks, are one of the Lagoon ethnic groups of Ivory Coast. The Alladians are a matrilineal society with a tradition of having a strong chieftaincy. They are an Akan* people; as such, they depend on gold to play an important role in their ceremonial lives. The Alladian population today exceeds 20,000 people, most of whom live on the barrier island between the lagoon and the Gulf of Guinea. Traditionally the Alladian economy revolved around fishing, but, ever since the nineteenth century, they also have engaged in the palm oil trade, selling the palm oil produced by the ethnic groups living on the inland side of the lagoon. The Alladians are divided into three subgroups: the Aware, the Kovu, and the Akuri (Agru).
REFERENCES: Marc Augé. "Status, Power, and Wealth: Relations of Lineage, Dependence, and Production in an Alladian Society." In D. Seddon, ed. *Relations of Production: Marxist Approaches to Economic Anthropology.* 1978; Robert J. Mundt. *Historical Dictionary of Côte d'Ivoire.* 1995.

ALOMWE. *See* LOMWE.

ALUND. *See* LUNDA.

ALUR. The Alur are an East African people who live on the northern edge of Lake Albert in western Uganda and northeastern Zaire. The Alurs are of Nilotic* extraction. Over the course of the last several centuries, the Alur have acquired reputations as negotiators because of their ability to help settle disputes among more warlike groups, like the Azandés* and Mangbetus.* The Alur divide themselves into relatively small political groupings with chiefs as executives. The chiefs also have religious authority, since the Alur believe that they can intercede with dead ancestors to guarantee favorable conditions for the people. The Alur

population today exceeds 500,000 people. They speak an eastern Sudanic language. The Alur economy is relatively prosperous since they rotate crops in what is considered to be already excellent soil.
REFERENCES: F. Scott Bobb. *Historical Dictionary of Zaire.* 1988; Rita M. Byrnes et al. *Uganda: A Country Study.* 1992; Aidan Southall. *Alur Society.* 1956.

AMANA. *See* EMANE.

AMANYA. *See* NZIMA.

AMAP. *See* AMO.

AMARANI. The Amarani are a unique people living today primarily in the city of Brava, Somalia. They are not ethnic Somalis.* They can also be found in Baarawe, Merca, Mogadishu, and Afgoy. They speak a Swahili* language and work primarily as merchants or sailors. The Amarani claim to be the original inhabitants of the Brava region. Ethnologists believe they came to Somalia from southern Arabia, where they were fleeing Islamic expansion, and married with local peoples.
REFERENCE: Margaret Castagno. *Historical Dictionary of Somalia.* 1975.

AMARAR. The Amarar are one of the major subdivisions of the Beja* peoples of the Sudan. They speak a Northern Cushitic language. The Amarar population today exceeds 350,000 people, most of whom live in a 25,000-square-mile region along the Red Sea, extending from Port Sudan in the south to Mohammed Ghol in the north and reaching westward to an ethnic frontier with the Bisharin,* approximately half-way to the Nile. The Amarar are Muslims, although the pastoral Amarar are somewhat perfunctory in their religious devotions; their indigenous, animistic traditions still have a powerful hold on the people. Rural Amarar are characterized by their large crown of curly hair, complete with long ringlets hanging down from the head. The semi-nomadic pastoral herders live in portable, rectangular goat-skin houses, while sedentary Amarar live in permanent, mud-walled homes. Their herds consist largely of camels and sheep. In recent years, the Amarar have become increasingly integrated into a cash economy, primarily because of the need to pay government taxes. Severe droughts have also damaged their herds of goats, sheep, cattle, and camels, forcing increasingly large numbers of Amarar to settle down into permanent farming communities where government-financed irrigation systems allow them to raise cotton and other crops commercially. There are two subgroups of the Amarar: the Amarar proper and the Otman.*
REFERENCES: S. A. el-Arifi. "Pastoral Nomadism in the Sudan." *East African Geographical Review* 13 (1975): 89–103; Roushdi A. Henin. "Economic Development and Internal Migration in the Sudan." *Sudan Notes and Records* 44 (1963): 100–119; Andrew Paul. *A History of the Beja Tribes of the Sudan.* 1954.

AMASI. The Amasis are a relatively small ethnic group living today in the Manyu Prefecture of the Southwest Province of Cameroon. Their most immediate neighbors are the Denyas* and the Assumbos.* Most Amasis are subsistence farmers.
REFERENCE: Samson Negbo Abangma. *Modes in Denya Discourse.* 1987.

AMAVUNDLE. *See* VUNDLE.

AMBA. The Ambas are part of the Azandé*-Mangbetu* cluster of peoples in Zaire.

AMBAMBA. The Ambambas are a subgroup of the Mbete* people of southeastern Gabon and Congo. The Ambamba population today is approximately 20,000 people, most of whom are small farmers.

AMBO. The Ambo are a subgroup of the Chewa* people of Malawi, eastern Zambia, and central Mozambique. Their current population exceeds 300,000 people, most of whom are Roman Catholics. The Ambo economy revolves around the production of maize, beans, and rice. Regionally, the Ambo are known for their skills as wood carvers.
REFERENCE: John J. Grotpeter. *Historical Dictionary of Zambia.* 1979.

AMBO. The Ambos (Ovambos) and the closely related Kwanyamas* are ethnic groups living in southern Angola and northern Namibia, in what is often referred to as Ovamboland. Several thousand Ambos also live in Zambia. Because of their remote location off the main slave-trading thoroughfares and their pastoral lifestyle, the Ambos remained highly isolated until the early nineteenth century. No single political entity ever controlled the larger Ambo region, but several smaller states did emerge. The most powerful of these was the Kwanyama state, which appeared in the late nineteenth century. The Kwanyama economy revolved around the production of cattle, the export of slaves and ivory, and iron ore production. They hunted the elephants in the region to near-extinction by the 1880s. The Ambos and Kwanyamas resisted German authority in Namibia and Portuguese authority in Angola, and they were not conquered until 1917. Since that time, the Ambos have lived in an economically underdeveloped region, working as migrant laborers, small farmers, and herders. Political conflict in southern Africa in modern times has forced tens of thousands of Ambos into refugee status. The Ambos are subdivided into the following subgroups: the Kwanyamas, Ndongas, Kuamis, Ngandjeras, Mbalantus, Kualuthis, and Nkolonkati-Eundas.
REFERENCES: Susan H. Broadhead. *Historical Dictionary of Angola.* 1992; Reginald H. Green, Marja-Liisa Kiljunen, and Kimmo Kiljunen. *Namibia: The Last Colony.* 1981.

AMBUNDU. Ambundu is one of the major subdivisions of the language of the

Mbundu* people of north-central Angola. The other subdivision is Awka-luanda.*

AMERICO-LIBERIAN. During the middle decades of the nineteenth century, the American Colonization Society settled more than 16,000 African Americans in Liberia. Most of them were black people from Maryland, Virginia, North Carolina, and Georgia. These immigrants, who came to be known as Americo-Liberians, settled along the coast from Robertsport to Harper. They became the political, social, and economic elite of Liberia, although, in recent decades, intermarriage with indigenous Liberians has diluted some of that identity. Also, the coup d'état of April 12, 1980, which overthrew the regime of President William R. Tolbert, ended more than a century of Americo-Liberian control of the Liberian government. In recent years, intermarriage between Americo-Liberians and people from other groups has been so extensive that the term "Kwi" is now a more widely used description than Americo-Liberians.
REFERENCE: D. Elwood Dunn and Svend H. Holsoe. *Historical Dictionary of Liberia.* 1985.

AMHARA. The Amhara (Abyssinians) comprise one of the largest, if not the largest, ethnic groups in Ethiopia. They constitute the dominant culture, from whom all of Ethiopia's prominent rulers have come. Their population exceeds twelve million people today, in spite of the problems of war and famine that have plagued Ethiopia since the early 1970s. Amharic is the official language of Ethiopia. The Amhara live in central Ethiopia. They are closely related to the Tigrinya* people. The vast majority of the Amhara are subsistence farmers, raising cereal grains and oil plants. They also raise cattle. Coffee is their major cash crop. They live in compact villages with land communally owned. The Amhara speak a Semitic language and trace their origins back to King Solomon, but ethnologists believe that they arrived in Ethiopia in the fourth century after a long-term migration from southern Arabia. They then mixed with the various Agaw* peoples in the region. Most Amharas are members of the Coptic Ethiopian Orthodox Church.
REFERENCE: Allan Hoben. "Social Stratification in Traditional Amhara Society." In Arthur Tuden and L. Plotnikob, eds. *Social Stratification in Africa.* 1970.

AMIR. *See* BENI-AMER.

AMO. The Amos (Amon, Among, Timap, Ba) are a relatively small ethnic group, part of the Plateau cluster of peoples, living in the Amo District of the Jos Division in Plateau State, Nigeria, as well as in the Lere District of the Saminaka Division of Kaduna State. They call themselves Amaps. Their material culture for centuries closely resembled that of the neighboring Hausas.* Most Amos are small farmers who also engage in hunting. They live on the north-

ern edge of the Jos Plateau. The Amo population today is approximately 16,000
people.
REFERENCES: Harold D. Gunn. *The Peoples of the Plateau Area of Nigeria,* 1953;
Elizabeth Isichei, ed. *Studies in the History of Plateau State, Nigeria.* 1982; *Language
Survey of Nigeria.* 1976; Jean-Claude Muller. ''Intertribal Hunting Among the Rukuba.''
Ethnology 21 (1982): 203–14.

AMON. *See* AMO.

AMON. *See* UMON.

AMONG. *See* AMO.

AMPIKA. *See* BOLE.

AMTUL. *See* TAL.

AMU. The Amus are a Swahili*-speaking people who today live in Kenya.

ANA. The Ana are an ethnic group in central Togo. The Ana are concentrated
in Atakpamé, primarily in the Gnagna and Djama quarters, as well as between
Atakpamé and Sokodé on the Togo-Benin border. Ethnologists identify the Ana
as the most western of the Yoruba* peoples. In fact, the Ana trace their origins
to the Ife* in Nigeria, and their language is a dialect of Ife Yoruba. They are
animist in their religious loyalities and practice a traditional animist religion
whose roots are clearly attached to the pantheon of *orishas* in the Yoruba religion. Historically, until the era of European imperialism, the Ana were vassals
to the Dahomey kingdom.
REFERENCE: Samuel Decalo. *Historical Dictionary of Togo.* 1976.

ANAANG. *See* ANANG.

ANAFEJANZI. *See* JANJI.

ANAG. The Anags are a subgroup of the Nubian* people of the Sudan.

ANAGO. The Anagos are one of the many subgroups of the Yoruba* peoples
of West Africa. They can be found especially today in southern Benin.

ANAGUTA. *See* NARAGUTA.

ANAKAZA. The Anakaza (Annakaza) people are a subgroup of the Daza*
people of Chad. The Dazas are a major subgroup of the Tebu* people.

The Anakazas are headquartered in Borkou, but they also live in an arc from Faya-Largeau to Kirdimi. Anakaza nomads wander the area from Oum Chalouba to the Djourab and Mortcha rivers. Some Anakaza clans claim strong ties to the Bideyats. The Anakazas are a highly independent, politically divided people whom the French considered virtually ungovernable. In recent years, their most promiment representative in Chadian politics has been Hissene Habré.
REFERENCE: Samuel Decalo. *Historical Dictionary of Chad.* 1987.

ANANG. The Anang (Anaang, Annang) are an ethnic group living in the Abak, Ikot Ekpene, and Opobo divisions of Cross River State, Nigeria. They speak a language closely related to that of the neighboring Efik* and Ibibio* peoples. Most Anangs make their living as farmers, raising yams and palm oil. Their contemporary population exceeds 800,000 people.
REFERENCE: Donald G. Morrison et al. *Black Africa: A Comparative Handbook.* 1989.

ANCHEYA. *See* CHEWA.

ANDONI. *See* OBOLO.

ANÉ. The Ané are the ethnic group in Togo who founded Anécho between 1663 and 1690. They originated in the area of El Mina, Ghana, and came to Togo under the leadership of Quam-Bessou, a Fante* prince. Eventually they adopted the Ouatchi* dialect and, along with the neighboring Ga* peoples, they became known as the Mina,* themselves a part of the Ewe* cluster. Today, the Ané population exceeds 60,000 people, most of whom live in and around Ané-cho and the coastal areas of Togo.
REFERENCE: Samuel Decalo. *Historical Dictionary of Togo.* 1976.

ANEMORO. *See* LEMORO.

ANEP. *See* NDOE.

ANGA. The Anga people—also known as the Nngas and Kerangs—live in the Pankshin, Wokkos, Ampan, Kabwir, Garran, Talipai, Chip, and Amper districts of the Pankshin Division of Plateau State in Nigeria. They can also be found in the Kanam District of the Langtang Division. Their current population exceeds 100,000 people. The Angas speak a Chadic language that is part of the Sura-Gerka group.
REFERENCE: *Language Survey of Nigeria.* 1976.

ANGAN. *See* KAMANTAM.

ANGLO. *See* BRITISH.

ANGONI. *See* NGONI.

ANGUNI. *See* NGONI.

ANIGUTA. The Anigutas are a people living today in the Plateau State of Nigeria. They live in a series of villages where hunting has recently become less important than subsistence agriculture.
REFERENCE: Jean-Claude Muller. ''Intertribal Hunting Among the Rukuba.'' *Ethnology* 21 (1982): 203–14.

ANIRAGO. *See* GURE-KAHUGU.

ANKULU. *See* IKULU.

ANKWAI. *See* GOMEI.

ANKWE. *See* GOMEI.

ANLO. The Anlo, also known as the Awuna, are one of the most prominent subgroups (clans) of the Ewe* people of Togo and Ghana. They are concentrated on the coast of Togo, between the Volta River in Ghana and the border between Togo and Ghana. There are nearly 10,000 members of the Anlo-Ewe clan, and most of them live in Anloga. They are a well-educated, upwardly mobile people who have generated resentment and animosity among other Ewe groups because of their success and their alliance with the hated Asante* in the nineteenth century. Anlo traditions place their origins near Notsie in modern Togo, from which they migrated in the seventeenth century. They fought repeated wars with the Adas, who joined with the Danes and later the British.* The Anlo were finally forced into submission only after British troops crushed the Anlo rebellion in 1884 and burned the Anlo capital city of Anloga.
REFERENCE: Daniel M. McFarland. *Historical Dictionary of Ghana.* 1995.

ANNAKAZA. *See* ANAKAZA.

ANNANG. *See* ANANG.

ANNIYA. The Anniyas are a major subgroup of the Oromo* peoples of Ethiopia. Most of the Anniyas are Sunni Muslims who live near the city of Harer. They work as sedentary farmers.

ANNO. *See* CHOKOSSI.

ANNUAK. *See* ANUAK.

ANOUFOU. *See* CHOKOSSI.

ANOWURU. *See* LEMORO.

ANTAIFASY. The Antaifasy people are considered by some African ethnologists to be a subgroup of the Antaisaka* people of Madagascar. The contemporary Antaifasy population exceeds 140,000 people, and most of them live in and around the coastal city of Farafangana in Fianarantsoa Province. In recent years, large numbers of Antaifasies have migrated to the north and northeast in search of seasonal labor. They trace their own origins to the African mainland.
REFERENCES: Maureen Covell. *Madagascar: Politics, Economics and Society.* 1987; Harold D. Nelson et al. *Area Handbook for the Malagasy Republic.* 1973.

ANTAIMORO. The Antaimoros are a subgroup of the Antaisaka* peoples of Madagascar. Their contemporary population is approximately 500,000 people, most of whom live in the valleys and barren hills of Fianarantsoa Province on the east coast of the island. They claim to be the descendants of Arab* travelers who arrived in the region centuries ago and married local women. Antaimoro society is divided into a caste system, with the upper caste consisting of people who claim pure Arab descent. Antaimoro religion is a mixture of Islam and local animistic traditions.
REFERENCES: Maureen Covell. *Madagascar: Politics, Economics and Society.* 1987; Harold D. Nelson et al. *Area Handbook for the Malagasy Republic.* 1973.

ANTAISAKA. The Antaisakas (Taisakas, Tesakis) are the largest of the southeastern ethnic groups in Madagascar. Today, the Antaisaka population exceeds 650,000 people, and they are divided into a number of subgroups, including the Antaimoros,* Antambahaoka,* Antaifasy,* and Sahafatra. Most of them live in and around the city of Farafangana. In the Antaisaka social structure, the nobility is composed of several kinship groups who migrated in the seventeenth century from the Mangoky River Valley in the western coastal plain to the Mananara River Valley of the eastern coast. The commoners are of mixed Bara,* Sakalava,* and other origins. In Madagascar, the Antaisakas make up the majority of migrant workers. Those Antaisakas who are not migrant laborers are farmers who raise rice.
REFERENCES: Maureen Covell. *Madagascar: Politics, Economics and Society.* 1987; Harold D. Nelson et al. *Area Handbook for the Malagasy Republic.* 1973.

ANTAIVA. *See* MENABE.

ANTAMBAHAOKA. The Antambahaokas are a subgroup of the Antaisaka* peoples of Madagascar. Their population today is approximately 50,000 people, most of whom live in the lower Mananjary River Valley. They claim

to be descended from a single ancestor, King Ramina, who supposedly migrated to Madagascar from Mecca. Although they are not Muslims, their culture has many Islamic influences. Most Antambahaokas are farmers, raising rice and cassava, although substantial numbers have good educations and work for the government and private business.
REFERENCES: Maureen Covell. *Madagascar: Politics, Economics and Society.* 1987; Harold D. Nelson et al. *Area Handbook for the Malagasy Republic.* 1973.

ANTANALA. *See* TANALA.

ANTANDROY. The Antandroy (Tandruy), or "people of the thorn bush," live between the Mandrare and Menara rivers in far southern Madagascar. Their contemporary population exceeds 600,000 people. Many ethnologists classify the Antanosy* as a subgroup of the Antandroy. They claim to have Sakalava* ethnic origins. They are primarily a pastoral people, raising cattle, but they also produce cassava, millet, maize, and rice. Their harsh, arid homeland keeps them relatively isolated from other people in Madagascar. Large numbers of Antandroy men migrate seasonally to work for cash.
REFERENCES: Maureen Covell. *Madagascar: Politics, Economics and Society.* 1987; Harold D. Nelson et al. *Area Handbook for the Malagasy Republic.* 1973.

ANTANKARANA. The Antankaranas are considered a subgroup of the Sakalava* peoples of Madagascar, although their ethnic origins involve Arabs* and Betsimisarakas* as well. Most of them live on the far northern tip of the island, from Cap d'Ambre to the Sambirano River. They are primarily cattle herders, but many Antankaranas raise rice, maize, and cassava as well. Large numbers of them also work on the plantations of the eastern Madagascar coast and in factories and meat canneries in towns and cities.
REFERENCES: Maureen Covell. *Madagascar: Politics, Economics, and Society.* 1987; Harold D. Nelson et al. *Area Handbook for the Malagasy Republic.* 1973.

ANTANOSY. The Antanosy people are a subgroup of the Antandroy* peoples of the plains of Madagascar. Their population today exceeds 350,000 people, most of whom live in and around Faradofay. They can also be found in the Onilahy River Valley and northward in Manja, Miandrivazo, and on the island of Nosy Be. Their own traditions identify their ethnic origins as a mix of Antambahaokas,* French,* Arab,* and Indian.* Most Antanosy people are farmers raising rice and cattle. They are divided into a number of smaller chiefdoms.
REFERENCES: Maureen Covell. *Madagascar: Politics, Economics and Society.* 1987; Harold D. Nelson et al. *Area Handbook for the Malagasy Republic.* 1973.

ANTIBOINA. The Antiboinas are a subgroup of the Sakalava* peoples of the plains of Madagascar.

ANTIFASY. *See* ANTAIFASY.

ANTIFIHERENA. The Antifiherenas are a subgroup of the Sakalava* peoples of the plains of Madagascar.

ANTIMAILAKA. The Antimailakas are a subgroup of the Sakalava* peoples of the plains of Madagascar.

ANTIMARAKA. The Antimarakas are a subgroup of the Sakalava* peoples of the plains of Madagascar.

ANTIMENA. The Antimenas are a subgroup of the Sakalava* peoples of the plains of Madagascar.

ANTIMERINA. *See* MERINA.

ANTIMILANJA. The Antimilanjas are a subgroup of the Sakalava* peoples of the plains of Madagascar.

ANTISIHANAKA. *See* SIHANAKA.

ANUAK. The Anuak (Annuak, Anyuak) people of the Sudan and Ethiopia pre-date the arrival of Nilotic* peoples in the region, although their language today is distinctly Nilotic. They live along the Blue Nile River in eastern Sudan and western Ethiopia. Most Anuaks are sedentary herders of sheep and goats, and they maintain small gardens and farms as well. Unlike other Nilotic peoples of the region—the Gumuz,* Barya,* Kunama,* and Berti*—the Anuak economy does not revolve around the production of cattle. Most of them are sedentary farmers, raising millet as their staple. They are part of the Shilluk* cluster of peoples. In the history of the Anglo-Egyptian Sudan, the Anuaks kept up a guerrilla war against British authority until 1921. Their highly decentralized political system and remote location have left them with a strong sense of separate identity.
REFERENCES: *African Encyclopedia.* 1974; Carolyn Fluehr-Lobban, Richard A. Lobban, Jr., and John Obert Voll. *Historical Dictionary of Sudan.* 1992.

ANUM. The Anum, or Anum-Boso,* are one of the Guan* peoples of Ghana. The Anum population today is approximately 50,000 people.

ANUM-BOSO. The Anum-Boso people are a small ethnic group in contemporary Ghana. Most of them live and work as small farmers in the Eastern Region. They are part of the Guan* ethnic cluster.
REFERENCE: Daniel M. McFarland. *Historical Dictionary of Ghana.* 1995.

ANWAIN. *See* ESAN.

ANYANG. *See* DENYA.

ANYANJA. *See* NYANJA.

ANYARAN. *See* UKAAN.

ANYI. The term "Anyi" is used to refer to a cluster of peoples in Ivory Coast and Ghana who are part of the Kwa* branch of the Niger-Congo language family. They are subdivided into such groups as the Anyis proper, Nzimas,* Aburés,* Abrons,* and Ehotiles (Mekyibos*).
REFERENCES: Donald G. Morrison et al. *Black Africa: A Comparative Handbook.* 1989; Linda Stevenson. "Agni Proverbs." *African Art* 6 (Spring 1973): 53–55.

ANYI. The Anyi (Agni), also known as the Ton and Kotoko, are a Twi-speaking group whose Akan* language is part of the Kwa* branch of the Niger-Congo language family. Their population exceeds 100,000 people and is concentrated in southeastern Ivory Coast—especially east of the Comoé River in the Dimob-kro, Aboisso, Abengourou, and Dondoukou districts of Bongfouanou Depart-ment—and across the border in southwestern Ghana. The Anyi are closely related to the Baule* of Ivory Coast. They practice farming and animal hus-bandry. Their system of social organization is matrilineal. The Anyi are pri-marily Christians and animists. About 2 percent of them are Sunni Muslims of the Maliki and Shafi schools. Syncretic systems are common among all of their religions. Since the British* and French* conquests of Ghana, Togo, and Ivory Coast, the Anyi have become increasingly Westernized and view themselves as superior to the surrounding, non-Akan peoples. They were the first people of the Ivory Coast to come into contact with Europeans, and they are the most Christianized people in the region. The Anyi can be divided into a number of subgroups, including the Béttiés, Binis, Bonas, Jaublins, Moronous, Ndenyes, and Sanwis.
REFERENCES: James Anquandah. "State Formation Among the Akan of Ghana." *San-kofa, The Journal of Archaeological and Historical Studies* 1 (1975): 47–57; J. B. Chris-tiansen. *Double Descent Among the Fante.* 1954; E. T. Meyerowitz. *Akan Traditions of Origins.* 1952; Claude Perrot, "Le processus de formation d'une ethie: Les Anyi-Ndenye de Côte d'Ivorie." *Revue Français d'histoire d'Outre-Mer* 68 (1981): 427–29; Linda Stevenson. "Agni Proverbs." *African Art* 6 (Spring 1973): 53–55.

ANYI-BAULE. *See* ANYI, BAULE, or AKAN.

ANYIMA. *See* LENYIMA.

ANYUAK. *See* ANUAK.

ANYUNGWE. The Anyungwes are an ethnic group living on both sides of the lower Zambezi River in Mozambique. They can also be found in the Tete District of Mozambique. The Anyungwes trace their origins back to the Tongas* and Magangas* and represent an ethnic hybrid of the two groups. Most Anyungwes make their living fishing, farming, and raising livestock.
REFERENCE: Mario Azevedo. *Historical Dictionary of Mozambique.* 1991.

AOWIN. The Aowin, also known as the Awowin, are an ethnic group living along the southern border between Ivory Coast and Ghana. They are surrounded by Nzima* and Sefwi* peoples and speak an Akan* language. The Aowins are so closely related to the Anyi* people that they are considered a subgroup of them by many ethnologists. Most Aowins are small farmers. The Aowin population in Ghana today is approximately 50,000 people.

APAK. The Apaks are a major subdivision of the Atuot* people of the southern Sudan.

APEMANIM. The Apemanims are a subgroup of the Assin* people of Ghana.

APINDJI. The Apindjis are an ethnic group in Gabon. Their traditional homeland was on the east side of the middle N'Gounié River, north of Mouila, in N'Gounié Province. They supported themselves by fishing and by growing subsistence crops on the river banks. The Apindjis are well known regionally for their skills as canoemen and navigators. Two centuries ago, they were living on the upper Ogooué River and had a large population. A series of epidemics in 1877 and the great famine of 1922 brought about widespread death and population decline among the Apindjis. The Apindji religion, known as Bwiti, is today gaining converts among the Fang.* By the 1960s, relatively few Apindjis were still living on the middle N'Gounié River. Most of them have migrated to Lambaréné, Sindara, and Fougamou.
REFERENCES: Paul B. Du Chaillu. *My Apindji Kingdom.* 1871; David E. Gardinier. *Historical Dictionary of Gabon.* 1994; Stanislaus Swiderski. "Les agents éducatifs traditionnels chez les Apindji." *Revue de Psychologie des Peuples* 21 (1966): 194–220.

APOI. The Apois are a subgroup of the Izon* peoples of Rivers State in Nigeria.

APPA. *See* TAROK.

APPOLO. *See* NZIMA.

APPOLONIAN. *See* NZIMA.

AQUAMBOE. *See* AKWAMU.

ARAB. The Arabs are one of the world's largest and most rapidly growing ethnic groups. Arabic speakers range from the Atlantic coast of northwest Africa, across North Africa, onto the Arabian Peninsula, and from there into Asia Minor and India. Their population today totals more than 165,000,000 people, and they constitute the majority population in fifteen nations. More than 90 percent of them are Muslims, primarily since the Prophet Mohammed gave birth to Islam in the Arabian Peninsula in the seventh century. In Africa, large Arab populations can be found in Morocco, Libya, Egypt, Sudan, Tunisia, Algeria, Chad, Sudan, Mali, Niger, and Ethiopia. Substantial numbers of Arabs can also be found in Mauritania, Burkina-Faso, northern Nigeria, northern Benin, Tanzania, and the Central African Republic. Many African nations, such as Chad and Sudan, have ongoing struggles for power between Arabs, who dominate the northern reaches of those countries, and black Africans, who predominate in the south. Throughout Africa, the Arabs are subdivided and subdivided again into thousands of ethnic groups and subgroups based on the particular Muslim sect, Arabi dialect, and regional adaptation. There are no common physical features of Arabs, but they are united by the language, which is a Semitic language of the Afro-Asiatic linguistic family. Arab culture first emerged in the deserts among people known as Bedouins,* or desert nomads, although Arabs are also deeply engaged in the commercial activities of cities.
REFERENCES: Edward Atiyah. *The Arabs.* 1968; Philip Hitti. *History of the Arabs.* 1960; Maxine Rodinson. *The Arabs.* 1981.

ARAGO. *See* ALAGOA.

ARBORE. The Arbore are a tiny ethnic group of only 2,000 people who live today in Ethiopia. They speak a Cushitic language.
REFERENCE: M. L. Bender, J. D. Bowen, R. L. Cooper and C. A. Ferguson, eds. *Language in Ethiopia.* 1976.

AREGWE. *See* IRIGWE.

AREWA. The Arewas are a subgroup of the Maouri* people of Niger.

ARGOBBA. The Argobba are a Muslim people in Ethiopia. They speak a Semitic language. Their current population is under 9,000, and they are concentrated in two distinct communities. The Northern Argobba live in approximately twenty-five separate villages at the foot of the slopes of the East African Rift Valley, from just below Ankober to Dessie, a distance of about 190 miles. They are farmers, who raise sorghum and maize for their own needs and coffee, cotton, and tobacco as cash crops. There are approximately 6,000 Northern Argobba. There are approximately twenty Southern Argobba villages, and they are located about fifteen miles southeast of the city of Harer. The Argobba interact with neighboring Oromo* and Somali* peoples. Most of the Northern Argobba are bilingual in Argobba, Amharic, and Oromo, while the Southern Argobba have all but lost the use of their native language; most of them speak Oromo. The real exception among the Southern Argobba are the residents of Kurumi, who speak Harari.*

In recent years, the Argobba have suffered considerably, both culturally and economically. Significant intermarriage is occurring with neighboring ethnic groups, and droughts in Ethiopia have hurt their agriculture. The Southern Argobba have also suffered from the Ogaden War of 1978 and the continuing political instability in the region. Most ethnologists are now predicting the disappearance of the Argobba in the next generation.
REFERENCES: William Shack. *The Central Ethiopians: Amhara, Tigre and Related Peoples.* 1974; Volker Stitz. "The Western Argobba of Yifat, Central Ethiopia." *Proceedings of the United States Conference on Ethiopian Studies.* 1975; J. Spencer Trimingham. *Islam in Ethiopia.* 1965.

ARI. *See* ABIDJI.

ARI. The Ari people are an ethnic group living today in Ethiopia. The Aris are part of the Omotic* cluster of peoples in southern Ethiopia. The Aris plant ensete and other grains and practice animal husbandry for a living. Like most other Omotic peoples in the region, the Aris have remained loyal to their indigenous religious traditions. Their population today exceeds 40,000 people.
REFERENCE: Harold D. Nelson et al. *Ethiopia: A Country Study.* 1980.

ARIANGULU. *See* SANYE.

ARINDRANO. The Arindranos are a subgroup of the Betsileo* peoples of the central plateau of Madagascar.

ARISI. *See* ARSSI.

ARMA. The Armas of Mali are actually a unique subgroup of the Songhais.* They descend from the sixteenth-century invaders of Morocco—usually Irish, English, and Spanish soldiers—who were captured by the Sultan of Morocco and drafted into his trans-Saharan trading adventures. These Europeans met and married Songhai women, and their descendants evolved into the ruling class of Timbuktu in Mali. Today, the Armas number about 20,000 people, living in and around Timbuktu, as well as in the Niger Bend and inland Niger Delta. They are Muslims.
REFERENCE: Pascal Imperato. *Historical Dictionary of Mali.* 1986.

ARMENIAN. There are tens of thousands of people of Armenian descent

scattered throughout Africa. The most concentrated group of Armenians lives in Cairo (approximately 15,000 in 1990). The Egyptian Armenians have lived there for centuries, although there has been a steady out-migration since the revolution in 1952. Several thousand Armenians also live in Ethiopia.
REFERENCE: Helen C. Metz et al. *Egypt: A Country Study.* 1991.

ARNA. The Arna people are a highly independent, nomadic ethnic group wandering the frontier region between Chad and Niger. Neither country exercises any real police power in the region, and many non-Arnas consider them little more than ethnic bandits. They are a subgroup of the Tebus* and are under the leadership of Angata Yoskoimi.
REFERENCE: Samuel Decalo. *Historical Dictionary of Chad.* 1987.

ARO. The Aro people are a subgroup of the Igbo* peoples of Nigeria. They are widely known, and have been so known for centuries, for their skills as merchants and traders. The Aro population today exceeds 700,000 people. They are extremely well-educated and constitute a dominant economic and professional group in the region.
REFERENCE: Kenneth Onwuka Dike and Felicia Ekejiuba. *The Aro of Southeastern Nigeria, 1650–1980.* 1990.

AROKWA. *See* ERUWA.

AROSIEN. The Arosiens are one of the ethnic groups of Western Sahara in what is today Morocco. They recognize their ancestral founder to be Sidi Ahmed al-Arosi, a sixteenth-century leader whose family claimed to be direct descendants of the Prophet Mohammed. There are three subgroups of the Arosiens—the Oulad Khalifa, Oulad Sidi Bou Mehdi, and Ahel Sidi Brahim—all of them directly descended from Arosi's three sons. The Arosiens are a nomadic people whose migrating region is near Bir Enzaren. When they settle temporarily, it is usually in Bir Enzaren and Dakhla.
REFERENCE: Tony Hodges. *Historical Dictionary of Western Sahara.* 1982.

AROUNDE. *See* KAONDE.

ARRINGEU. *See* PONGU.

ARSI. *See* ARSSI.

ARSSI. The Arssi—also known as the Arsi, Arisi, and Arusi—are one of the major subgroups of the Oromo* people of Ethiopia. They are among the southern cluster of the Oromos in Ethiopia. Most of the Arssi live in Bale Province, beyond the Awash River southeast of Shewa. A substantial number of them are Muslims, but the Islamic conversion process did not begin until the late nineteenth century, so pre-Islamic beliefs and rituals are still common. Their economy revolves around a mixture of sedentary agriculture and cattle raising.

ARTAJ. *See* BERI.

ARTIQA. The Artiqa are a small, surviving subgroup of the larger group of Beja* peoples in Sudan. They were originally not part of the Beja group, but, in the nineteenth and twentieth centuries, they gradually fell within the Beja cultural orbit. They live on the Red Sea coastal plain south of Port Sudan.

ARUM. The Arums (Arum-Chessus) are a relatively small Nigerian ethnic group. They speak a Bantu* language and live on the southwestern edge of the Jos Plateau in Plateau State, especially in the Mama District of Akwanga Division. Their most immediate ethnic neighbors are the Rindres, Chessus,* Turkwans,* Kantanas,* and Ninzams.* Most Arums are subsistence farmers, who raise millet, guinea corn, maize, and a variety of other products.
REFERENCES: Elizabeth Isichei, ed. *Studies in the History of Plateau State, Nigeria.* 1982; *Language Survey of Nigeria.* 1976.

ARUSHA. The Arusha people are often described by ethnologists as ''agricultural Masais.'' Their language and culture closely resemble those of the Masai,* but, beginning in the 1930s, many Arushas settled near the upper Burka River region of Tanzania and abandoned nomadic pastoralism for agriculture. Today they own very few livestock. The Arushas raise coffee for cash and bananas, corn, and beans as staples. They have a population of about 130,000 people.
REFERENCE: Laura S. Kurtz. *Historical Dictionary of Tanzania.* 1978.

ARUSHI. *See* ARSSI.

ARUSI. *See* ARSSI.

ARUSSI. *See* ARSSI.

ASANGON. The Asangon people are part of the Bongue* cluster of the Ndowe* peoples of Equatorial Guinea.

ASANTE. The Asante, who total nearly two million people, are a Twi*-speaking group whose Akan* language is part of the Kwa* branch of the Niger-Congo language family. They practice farming and animal husbandry, and their system of social organization is matrilineal. They are subdivided into tribal groups, including the Kumasi (Kumase), Mampong, Bekwai, Kokofu, Nsuta, Dwaben (Juaben), Effiduase, Asokore, Ejiso (Edwiso), Bonwire, Assumigya, and Senfi. The Asante are Christians, Muslims, and animists, with syncretic systems common among them. Of the roughly 150,000 Asante who are Muslims, most follow the Sunni school of the Maliki tradition; a minority of Asante Muslims adhere to the Shafi rite. Since the British* conquest of Ghana, Togo, and Ivory Coast, the Asante have become increasingly Westernized and view themselves as superior to the surrounding, non-Akan peoples. Most Asante are subsistence farmers, whose major cash crop is cocoa. They also produce gold, palm-oil products, timber, rubber, citrus fruits, and kola nuts for cash. Their main food crops are yams, cocoyams, maize, and plantains. Family inheritance is determined by matrilineal descent. The Asante were founded as a nation around 1600 through the confederation of a number of small Akan states. Their territory expanded over the next 200 years to include most of present-day central and southern Ghana. Great Britain conquered the region in 1901, but the Asante have still maintained their separate ethnic identity.

REFERENCES: James Anquandah. ''State Formation Among the Akan of Ghana.'' *Sankofa, The Journal of Archaeological and Historical Studies* 1 (1975): 47–57; J. B. Christiansen. *Double Descent Among the Fante.* 1954; E. T. Meyerowitz. *Akan Traditions of Origins.* 1952.

ASAWERDA. The Asawerdas are a subgroup of the Saho* people of Ethiopia. Their current population exceeds 20,000 people.

ASBEN. The Asbens are one of the Tuareg* peoples of Niger.

ASEN. *See* ASSIN.

ASENNIZE. *See* SHANI.

ASHANTI. *See* ASANTE.

ASHILUANDA. The Ashiluandas are an ethnic group living on the island of Luanda off the coast of Angola. They are part of the larger Kongo* cluster of peoples. Like the Solongos,* the Ashiluandas make their living as fishermen in the coastal Atlantic Ocean.

REFERENCE: Thomas Collelo et al. *Angola: A Country Study.* 1991.

ASHRAF. The Ashraf are a small, surviving subgroup of the larger group of Beja* peoples in Sudan. They were originally not part of the Beja group, but, beginning in the nineteenth and twentieth centuries, they gradually came under Beja cultural influences. The Ashraf live on the Red Sea coastal plain and the hills of the Tokar delta south of Port Sudan.

REFERENCE: P. T. Demeny. *The Demography of the Sudan.* 1968.

ASI. *See* SANYE.

ASI MOUSSA OU ALI. The Asi Moussa Ou Alis are a subgroup of the Ait Jmel* people of Western Sahara, who are part of the larger Tekna* group of peoples.

ASIGA. *See* LEYIGHA.

ASIN. *See* ASSIN.

ASOKORE. The Asokores are one of the primary subdivisions of the Asante* people of Ghana.

ASONGORI. The Asongori are a settled ethnic group who today live west and north of the Masalit* people in Ouadai Prefecture and Biltine Prefecture in Chad. They are closely related culturally to the Mabas,* from whom they split in the seventeenth century.
REFERENCE: Samuel Decalo. *Historical Dictionary of Chad.* 1987.

ASSALE. The Assales are a subgroup of the Hassaunas,* a large group of ethnic Arabs* living today in Chad.

ASSIN. The Assin (Asen) are one of the major ethnic subdivisions of the Akan* people. They are concentrated in Central Region of Ghana, where they are surrounded by the Denkyira* and Twifu* to the west, the Adansi* to the north, the Akyem* to the east, and the Fante* to the south. The Assin are divided into two subgroups. The Assin Apemanim (Apimenem) live east of the Cape Coast-Kumasi highway, with their capital city at Manso. The Assin Attendansu (Atandanso) live on the west side of the highway. Their capital is at Nyankumasi. The number of Assin people in Ghana today is approximately 135,000.
REFERENCE: Daniel M. McFarland. *Historical Dictionary of Ghana.* 1995.

ASSIN APEMANIM. *See* ASSIN.

ASSIN APIMENEM. *See* ASSIM.

ASSIN ATANDANSO. *See* ASSIN.

ASSIN ATTENDANSU. *See* ASSIN.

ASSOKO. *See* NZIMA.

ASSUMBO. The Assumbos are a relatively small ethnic group living today in the Manyu Prefecture of the Southwest Province of Cameroon. Their most immediate neighbors are the Denyas* and the Amasis.* Assumbos can also

be found across the border in eastern Nigeria. Most Assumbos are subsistence farmers.
REFERENCE: Samson Negbo Abangma. *Modes in Denya Discourse.* 1987.

ASSUMIGYA. The Assumigyas are one of the primary subdivisions of the Asante* people of Ghana.

ASU. *See* PARE.

ASUNGOR. The Asungor are one of the Tama*-speaking peoples of Sudan and Chad. They live on the Chad side of the border and are closely, even intimately, related to the Erenga* who live across the border in Sudan. The Asungor population today is approximately 60,000 people, most of whom are settled pastoralists, raising cattle, camels, and goats, and performing small-scale subsistence agriculture. The main Asungor commercial and marketing centers are the towns of Molou and Toumtouma. The Asungor are overwhelmingly Muslims.
REFERENCE: Paul Doornbos. "Tama-Speaking Peoples." In Richard V. Weekes, ed. *Muslim Peoples.* 1984.

ATAK. *See* JIRU-KIR.

ATALA. *See* DEGEMA.

ATANDE. The Atande are a small ethnic group of several thousand people living in Mozambique. Most of them are small subsistence farmers who reside along the banks of the lower Zambezi River in Capoche and Mucanha. During the late eighteenth and nineteenth centuries, they actively participated in the slave trade, capturing and selling other Africans to Portuguese traders.
REFERENCE: Mario Azevedo. *Historical Dictionary of Mozambique.* 1991.

ATEN. *See* GANAWURI.

ATEWE. The Atewes are a major subgroup of the Shona* peoples of Zimbabwe and Mozambique. They are descended from the Rodzi people, who defeated the original inhabitants of the region, the Wazamoi. The Atewes are closely related to the Manhicas* (Manyica). They are subdivided into the Nyantaza, Nyampisi, Chiwawa, Mwanya, Chirumba, Banda, Marunga, Chilendje, Tembo, and Makat clans, which are matrilineal.

ATI. *See* ETSU.

ATIÉ. *See* ATTIE.

ATSAM. *See* CHAWAI.

ATTENDANSU. The Attendansus are a subgroup of the Assin* people of Ghana.

ATTI. *See* ETSU.

ATTIE. The Attie, who have also been called the Akié, Akyé, and Atié, are an ethnic group living west of the Comoé River and north of the city of Abidjan in Ivory Coast. Although ethnolinguists often classify them as one of the Lagoon peoples of Ivory Coast, because they speak a language related to others in the area, they are very similar socially to the Anyi* and Baule* peoples. They probably were part of the great migration to that area from the east. The Atties have never been organized into a central state. Age groups are very prominent in Attie society. Today, the vast majority of Attie are Christians who make their living producing coffee and cocoa. They also support themselves through fishing. The Attie population today is approximately 275,000 people.
REFERENCES: Robert J. Mundt. *Historical Dictionary of Côte d'Ivoire.* 1995; Denise Paulme. "Mission en Pays Atié, Côte d'Ivoire." *Homme* 5 (1965): 105–9; Denise Paulme. "Première approche des Atié (Côte d'Ivoire)." *Cahiers d'Études Africaines* 6 (1966): 86–120.

ATUOT. The Atuots (Attuots, Atwats) live in the Upper Nile River valley of Sudan, particularly in the Lakes Province fifty miles west of the Nile. Their population exceeds 50,000 people. The Atuots are divided into six subgroups, based on their regional locations and different dialects of the same Nilotic* language. The major Atuot subdivisions are the Apaks, Luacs, Jileks, Akots, Rorkecs, and Kueks. Like the neighboring Dinkas,* their economy and culture revolve around cattle production. They are closely associated with the Nuers.* They speak a Nilotic language. Until the outbreak of the Sudanese civil war in 1983, the Atuots (Leek Nuer) of southern Sudan were being incorporated into the national political economy of Sudan more effectively, and less traumatically, than many Nuer communities east of the White Nile. They are cattle raisers, and many Atuot cattle camps are named after the color of the ox, bull, or cow that was sacrificed by a group of settlers to mark, and therefore establish, a particular territory as their own. They are a polytheistic people. The creation of government courts, the collection of tribute, and the establishment of roads, markets, schools, missions, and medical facilities are gradually affecting Atuot nomadism.
REFERENCES: John W. Burton. *A Nilotic World: The Atuot-Speaking Peoples of the Southern Sudan.* 1987; Carolyn Fluehr-Lobban, Richard A. Lobban, Jr., and John Obert Voll. *Historical Dictionary of Sudan.* 1992.

ATWAT. *See* ATUOT.

ATWODE. The Atwode people, sometimes called the Atyoti or Achode, are an ethnic group living today in the northern portion of the Volta Region and the southeastern Northern Region of Ghana, as well as across the border in Togo. They are closely related culturally to the Ewe* peoples, and they make their livings as small farmers. The number of Atwode people in Ghana today exceeds 10,000. They are considered to be part of the Guan* cluster of peoples.
REFERENCE: Daniel M. McFarland. *Historical Dictionary of Ghana.* 1995.

ATYOTI. *See* ATWODE.

AUGA. *See* UKAAN.

AULLIMINDEN. The Aullimindens are one of the Tuareg* peoples of Niger.

AUSHI. The Aushis (Ushi) are a Bantu*-speaking people who today can be found living in the far southeastern tip of Zaire and across the border in Zambia, north and east of the upper Luapula River and west of Lake Bangweulu. They are descended from the Lubas.* Most Aushis are small subsistence farmers today. Some of them also raise cattle. Their population exceeds 200,000 people. Included in the Aushi cluster of peoples are the Ushis, Ngumbos, Mukulus, Ungas, and Kabendes.
REFERENCES: John J. Grotpeter. *Historical Dictionary of Zambia.* 1979; Irving Kaplan et al. *Zaire: A Country Study.* 1978.

AUYOKAWA. The Auyokawas are a subgroup of the Hausa* peoples of Nigeria.

AVANDE. *See* EVANT.

AVATIME. The Avatime peoples, also known as the Afatime, are part of the Central Togo cluster of peoples who live in Ghana. They essentially form an enclave in the Volta Region, surrounded by the Ewes,* but are also scattered in southwestern Togo. Ethnologists believe that the Avatime were once a much larger people who became overwhelmed by the in-migration of the Ewes. The chief of the Avatime lives in Vane, although the most important Avatime settlement is at Amedzofe, Ghana. The contemporary Avatime population is approximately 20,000 people.
REFERENCE: Daniel M. McFarland. *Historical Dictionary of Ghana.* 1995.

AVICO. The Avicos are a subgroup of the larger Ngangela* cluster of peoples living today in Angola.

AVIKAM. The Avikam—also known as the Brignan, Gbanda, and Lahou—are part of the Lagoon cluster of peoples of Ivory Coast. They are concentrated in the subprefecture of Grand-Lahou. Like the other peoples of the southeast coast and lagoons of Ivory Coast, they practice cash-crop farming and engage in the production and trade of palm oil. Some Avikam still fish as well to provide themselves with a protein source. They are part of the large Akan* culture group.
REFERENCES: Robert E. Handloff et al. *Côte d'Ivoire: A Country Study.* 1990; Robert J. Mundt. *Historical Dictionary of Côte d'Ivoire.* 1995.

AVUKAYA. The Avukayas are a relatively small ethnic group living west of the White Nile River in the central Al Istiwai region of southern Sudan. They are closely related to the Moru* and speak a language that is part of the central branch of the Nilo-Saharan family of languages. The Avukayas are small farmers.
REFERENCE: Helen C. Metz et al. *Sudan: A Country Study.* 1992.

AWAK. The Awaks (Awoks) live in the Kaltungo District of the Gombe Division in Gongola State. They call themselves the Adamawa and are part of the larger Waja* group. Most Awaks are subsistence farmers.
REFERENCE: *Language Survey of Nigeria.* 1976.

AWANDJI. The Awandji people of Gabon speak a Mbédé* language and live south of Lastourville on the upper Ogooué River. They are closely related, ethnically and linguistically, to the Adouma,* who live downriver from them on the Ogooué. In their traditional economy, the Awandjis brought meat that they had hunted to the Adoumas and exchanged it for fish. In 1923, France imposed a head tax on the Awandjis and followed that up with forced labor contracts for the construction of the Congo-Ocean Railroad in 1926. In 1927, when the French began demanding regular food shipments from the Awandjis to French military outposts, the Awandjis rebelled. A guerrilla war against the French, led by Chief Wongo, continued until 1929.
REFERENCE: David E. Gardinier. *Historical Dictionary of Gabon.* 1994.

AWARE. The Aware are a subgroup of the Alladian* peoples of Ivory Coast.

AWEMBA. *See* BEMBA.

AWHAWFIA. The Awhawfias are one of the many subgroups of the Igbo* people, an ethnic group of nearly fifteen million people living today in southern and southeastern Nigeria.

AWHAWZARA. The Awhawzaras are one of the many subgroups of the Igbo* people of southern and southeastern Nigeria.

AWI. The Awis are an ethnic group living today in Ethiopia. They speak a Central Cushitic language and are closely related to the Agaw* peoples. The Awis are concentrated southwest of Lake Tana in western Ethiopia. The Awis are surrounded by Amhara*-speaking people. The Awi population today exceeds 90,000 people, most of whom are small farmers and cattle raisers who remain loyal to their traditional religious beliefs. They call their language Awngi.
REFERENCE: Harold D. Nelson et al. *Ethiopia: A Country Study.* 1980.

AWKALUANDA. Awkaluanda is one of the major subdivisions of the Mbundu* language of Angola. The other subdivision is Ambundu.*

AWLAD JEMA. The Awlad Jemas are a subgroup of the Maba* people of Sudan.

AWLAD SULAYMAN. The Awlad Sulaymans are a primarily Arab* subgroup in Libya, Sudan, and Chad. Most of them are nomadic pastoralists or farmers. The Awlad Sulaymans in Chad migrated there from Libya in the nineteenth century.

AWOK. *See* AWAK.

AWORI. The Aworis are one of the main subgroups of the Yoruba* people of Nigeria. Most Aworis can be found today living in the southern reaches of Ogun State and in western Lagos State in western Nigeria.

AWOWIN. *See* AOWIN.

AWTANZU. The Awtanzus are one of the many subgroups of the Igbo* people of southern and southeastern Nigeria.

AWUNA. *See* ANLO.

AWUNA. The Awunas are a subgroup of the Grusis.* They live on the border of Ghana and Burkina-Faso.

AWUTU. The Awutu, also known as the Obutu, are a subgroup of the Guan* people of Ghana and live in the vicinity of Gomoa, Ghana. Their language is closely related to the Akan* languages. Most Awutu make their living as small

farmers and laborers. The contemporary Awutu population exceeds 55,000 people.
REFERENCE: Daniel M. McFarland. *Historical Dictionary of Ghana.* 1995.

AYA. *See* AYU.

AYADEGHE. The Ayadeghes are a subgroup of the Ibibio* peoples of Nigeria.

AYAMAT. *See* JAMAT.

AYEMBA. *See* BEMBA.

AYIGA. *See* LEYIGHA.

AYIGBÉ. The term "Ayigbé" is a pejorative reference to the Ewe,* Ga,* and Mina* people in Togo, Benin, and Ghana.

AYIKIBEN. *See* YUKUBEN.

AYU. The Ayus (Ayas) are a relatively small Nigerian ethnic group. They speak a Bantu* language and live in the Jema'a Division of Plateau State. Their most immediate ethnic neighbors are the Rons,* Madas,* and Ninzams.* Most Ayus are subsistence farmers who raise millet, guinea corn, maize, and a variety of other products.
REFERENCE: Elizabeth Isichei, ed. *Studies in the History of Plateau State, Nigeria.* 1982.

AZA. The Aza are a subgroup of the Dazaga,* themselves a subgroup of the Tebu* peoples of the Sahel and Sahara of Sudan, Chad, and Niger. In Chad, the Aza are a vassal group to the Teda* and Daza* peoples, living among them and working as blacksmiths, metalworkers, leatherworkers, potters, and hairdressers. In Niger, the Aza maintain their own herds of camels and cattle. All Aza are Muslims and speak the Dazaga language as their primary tongue. The children of Aza who have been freed from slavery constitute a separate caste known as the Kamaya. The Aza population numbers several thousand people.

AZAGHWANA. *See* DGHWEDE.

AZANDÉ. The Azandé (Zande) people today live in southwestern Sudan, northern Zaire, and southeastern Central African Republic. They are divided into two subgroups: the Bandias and the Vungaras. The Vungaras are the larger of the two. The Azandé did not exist as a distinct ethnic group until the beginning of the nineteenth century, when Ngoura, leader of the Kogobili clan, migrated with his people to the region. Along the way, they conquered and absorbed many ethnic groups, creating a new group, the Azandé, in the process. They are known in central Africa for their warrior qualities. That process of assimilation is still going on in central Africa. They are a farming people who live by shifting bush cultivation, relocating locally to new land as soon as existing lands experience soil exhaustion. Most of the Azandé remain loyal to their indigenous religion. They arrived in their present location in the Bahr al-Ghazal River Valley after displacing the existing peoples in the nineteenth century. Their total population today exceeds one million people. Because of their location, the Azandé have suffered over the years because of sleeping sickness, a disease endemic to their ethnic homeland. They have also been hurt over the years because of ongoing conflicts with the Dinkas.*

REFERENCES: E. E. Evans-Pritchard. *The Azande, History and Political Institutions.* 1971; Carolyn Fluehr-Lobban, Richard A. Lobban, Jr., and John Obert Voll. *Historical Dictionary of Sudan.* 1992; Pierre Kalck. *Historical Dictionary of the Central African Republic.* 1992; Andre Singer and Brian V. Street. *Zande Themes.* 1972.

AZARZIR. The Azarzirs are one of the Moor* subgroups living today in Mauritania.

AZEBO. *See* RAYA.

AZNA. Although the Fulbe* people of Niger use the term "Azna" to refer to all non-Muslim Hausas,* the term refers more specifically to a group of people living between Madaoua and Birni-N'Konni in Niger. The Aznas are considered a subgroup of the Hausas, probably a mix of the Tyenga people and the Songhai* people, who were driven there in the eleventh century by aggressive Tuaregs.* The Aznas are especially concentrated today in Darey, Lugu, and Birni N'Konni.

REFERENCE: Samuel Decalo. *Historical Dictionary of Niger.* 1989.

AZORA. *See* CHOKOBO.

AZOUAFID. The Azouafids are a subgroup of the Ait Atman* people of Western Sahara. The Ait Atman are themselves a subgroup of the Tekna* peoples.

AZURA. The Azuras are a small ethnic group living today in the grassy savannas and volcanic hills of the southern region of the state of Kaduna in Nigeria and in the Karta region of Mali. They are surrounded by the Konos* and Kiballos* to the west, the Katabs* and Chawais* to the south, and the Amos* and Rukubas* to the east. They are closely related to the Kuramas* and migrated to their present location in the Jere District early in the twentieth century, coming from the Zaria area. They make their living in a mixed economy of subsistence agriculture and livestock raising. Their lifestyle closely resembles that of the neighboring Hausas.* Until recently, the Azuras married endogamously or to Kuramas.

REFERENCES: Elizabeth Isichei, ed. *Studies in the History of Plateau State, Nigeria.* 1982; Charles Meek. *The Northern Tribes of Nigeria.* 1969.

B

BA. *See* AMO.

BAAKA. The Baakas are an ethnic group in southern Ethiopia. Most of them are subsistence farmers today.
REFERENCE: M. L. Bender, J. D. Bowen, R. L. Cooper, and C. A. Ferguson, eds. *Language in Ethiopia.* 1976.

BAARAAWAA. *See* BARAWA.

BAATONU. *See* BARIBA.

BAATONUN. *See* BARIBA.

BAN JANJERIN. *See* BILIN.

BABA. *See* BAULE.

BABALIA. The Babalias are a small subgroup of the Bulalas* who live north of Ndjamena in Chad. Their historic center was the now-ruined city of Dal. At the present time, the Babalia have adopted Arabic as their native language.

BABANKI. The Babanki are a subgroup of the Bafut* people of North West Province in Cameroon.

BABEMBA. *See* BEMBA.

BABEMGA. *See* BINGA.

BABENGA. *See* BINGA.

BABIENBA. *See* BEMBA.

BABILE. The Babile are a subgroup of the Afran Qallo,* themselves a sub-group of the Oromo* of Ethiopia. They are primarily Muslims living around the city of Harer who work as sedentary farmers.

BABIMBI. The Babimbi people are an ethnic group living today in southern Cameroon. The speak a Bantu* language and are closely related to the neigh-boring Bakoko* and Bassa* peoples. The collective population of the Bassas, Bakokos, and Babimbis is more than 500,000 people. Although some Babimbis are Christians, most still believe in the tradition that their ancient ancestor, Hil-olumb, emerged from a cave called Ngok Lituba. Most of them still live in rural villages, where they raise yams, maize, cocoyams, and vegetables, although substantial numbers now live in Duala, Edéa, Pouma, and Makak, where they work as laborers, craftsmen, and businessmen. The Babimbis used to live along the coast, where they made their living as subsistence farmers and fishermen, but they were displaced by the Duala* migration and pushed into the interior. During the years of the colonial empires, the Babimbis were fiercely national-istic, resisting the Germans* at every turn. Part of that nationalistic identity came from the efforts of American Presbyterian missionaries who helped educate the Babimbis.
REFERENCES: *African Encyclopedia.* 1974; Mark DeLancey and H. M. Mokeba. *Historical Dictionary of the Republic of Cameroon.* 1990.

BABINGA. *See* BINGA.

BABINKI-TUNGO. The Babinki-Tungo are a subgroup of the Bafut* people of North West Province in Cameroon.

BABIR. *See* BURA.

BABIRWA. *See* BIRWA.

BABOLAONGWE. *See* BOLAONGWE.

BABOLE. The Baboles are a subgroup of the Sanga* peoples of southeastern Cameroon, northern Congo, southern Central African Republic, and northwest-ern Zaire. They interact closely with neighboring Pygmies,* who trade game for Babole agricultural products. The Babole population today is approximately 10,000 people.
REFERENCE: Gordon C. McDonald et al. *Area Handbook for the People's Republic of Congo (Congo Brazzaville).* 1971.

BABOUTE. *See* BAFUT.

BABUISSI. The Babuissi are a linguistic subgroup of the Eshira* people. They live in the upper Nyanga River Basin in Gabon and the Congo Republic. Most of them are small farmers. The Babuissi population today exceeds 20,000 people.

BABUR. *See* BURA.

BABUT. *See* BAFUT.

BACHE. *See* RUKUBA.

BACHEVE. *See* ICHEVE.

BACHIKUNDA. *See* CHIKUNDA.

BACONGO. *See* KONGO.

BADE. The Bades (Beddes, Bedes) can be found today primarily in southern Burkina-Faso and southwestern Niger; smaller groups can be found in northwestern Nigeria and northern Benin. They are part of the larger cluster of Kanuri* peoples of the Bornu State of northeastern Nigeria. Their economy is a complex one, revolving around commerce, home manufacturing, personal services, and agriculture. They farm, raising guinea corn, millet, groundnuts, cattle, sheep, and goats. They also fish in Lake Chad. In recent years, they have begun to produce cotton as a cash crop. The Bades possess small cattle herds, which they contract out to Fulbe* herders. They are a subgroup of the Songhai* peoples of West Africa. They are Muslims of the Maliki school. The Bades are also divided into a number of subgroups based on a powerful sense of kinship. They speak a Chadic language.
REFERENCES: Ronald Cohen. *The Kanuri of Bornu.* 1967; *Language Survey of Nigeria.* 1976; Donald G. Morrison et al. *Black Africa: A Comparative Handbook.* 1989.

BADIARANKE. *See* BADYARAN.

BADIU. The Badius are a peasant people in the interior of São Tiago island in the Cape Verde Islands. They are descendants of runaway slaves who developed a unique identity of their own over the years. Fiercely independent and developing a cultural isolation to match their geographical isolation, the Badius were viewed as an unruly people by Portuguese* colonial administrators. They frequently were the objects of contract labor raids and forced labor programs, which took them to the cacao plantations on São Tome and Principe islands. The Badius speak a language known as Crioulo.

REFERENCES: Richard Lobban and Joshua Forrest. *Historical Dictionary of the Republic of Guinea-Bissau.* 1988; Richard Lobban and Marilyn Halter. *Historical Dictionary of the Republic of Cape Verde.* 1988.

BADJELLI. *See* GELLI and PYGMY.

BADOUMA. *See* BADUMA.

BADUMA. The Badumas are one of the Mbete* peoples of southeastern Gabon and Congo. Their population today exceeds 15,000 people, most of whom are small farmers.

BADYARAN. The Badyaran (Badyaranké, Bajaranke, Badiaranke) are a small ethnic group living along both sides of the border between Guinea and Senegal. Ethnographers traditionally classify them as one of the Tenda* groups, which also includes the neighboring Koñagis,* Basaris,* Bediks,* and Boins.* They are closely related to the Basari and to the Koñagi. The Badyaran are slash-and-burn cultivators who live in twenty villages of from 100 to 500 people each. Their homeland is isolated and one of the least developed economically in the area which is 700 kilometers from Dakar and 250 kilometers from Tambacounda. Roads are poor and often impassable during the rainy season. Unlike surrounding peoples, the Badyaran are subsistence farmers; they do not raise peanuts to sell for cash. They are also known for their skill as beekeepers. Increasingly large numbers of them, however, travel seasonally to towns and cities in search of wage work. They maintain a strong sense of ethnic identity.
REFERENCES: Riall W. Nolan. *Bassari Migrations: The Quiet Revolution.* 1986; William S. Simmons. ''Powerlessness, Exploitation and the Soul-Eating: An Analysis of Badyaranke Witchcraft.'' *American Ethnology* 7 (August 1980): 447–65.

BADYARANKÉ. *See* BADYARAN.

BAFIA. The Bafia live in Central Cameroon in an area bordered to the east by the Mbam River (a Sanaga tributary) and to the west by the Bapé mountains, between 4°35' and 4°32' North and 11°0' and 11°20' East. They are classified as part of the Middle-Cameroon Bantu* group of peoples. The Bafias originated farther to the north and were pushed into their present location by Fulbe* expansion. Theirs is a savanna environment with patches of woodland and gallery forest along water courses. The Bafia call themselves Bekpak and include the Beké and Bekpak subgroups. Both groups speak Rikpak, a Bantu language. They are farmers and fishermen. Their villages stretch along roads and tracks. Their traditional huts are rectangular and have palm-frond roofing. Today, cement houses and corrugated sheet roofs are common, especially in villages near the tarmacked main roads. In Cameroonian history, the most prominent Bafia leaders are Abouem a Tchoyi, Ntang Gilbert, and Bidias a Ngon.

REFERENCES: Mark DeLancey and H. M. Mokeba. *Historical Dictionary of the Republic of Cameroon.* 1990; Olivier P. Gosselain, "Technology and Style: Potters and Pottery Among Bafia of Cameroon." *Man* 27 (1992): 559–86.

BAFOKENG. *See* FOKENG.

BAFRENG. The Bafreng are a subgroup of the Bafut* people of North West Province in Cameroon.

BAFUT. The Bafut (Bute, Bafute, Wute, Mfute) are part of the Tikar* cluster of peoples in Cameroon. They are classified as a "Grassfield" people because of the open vegetational geography of their homeland in the Bamenda highlands of North West Province. The land is very fertile, and most Bafut make their living as farmers, raising maize and a variety of cereals. Like other "Grassfield" peoples, the Bafut speak a Bantu* language and excel in the manufacture of pottery, handicrafts, and metal works. The Bafut social structure is patrilineal with highly centralized political systems. They are divided into the subchiefdoms of Babanki, Babinki-Tungo, Bafreng, Bambui, Bamendankwe, and Bambili, all of whom answer to the Bafut chief, or Fon. In the nineteenth and early twentieth centuries, the Bafuts were decimated in wars with the Fulbes* and by resistance to German colonial authorities. Today, the Bafut population exceeds 35,000 people.
REFERENCES: M. T. Aletum. *Political Conflicts within the Traditional and the Modern Institutions of the Bafut, Cameroon.* 1974; Pat Rizenthaler. *The Fon of Bafut.* 1966.

BAFUTE. *See* BAFUT.

BAGA. The Bagas of Guinea are closely related to the Nalus* and probably originated with them in the Fouta Djallon region. They are scattered along coastal Guinea from Conakry and the Camayenne Peninsula to the Rio Nuñez estuary, which is a distance of approximately 160 miles. Most of the Bagas are farmers and fishermen. They are part of the Western Atlantic cluster of peoples and have a contemporary population of approximately 80,000 people.
REFERENCE: Harold D. Nelson et al. *Area Handbook for Guinea.* 1975.

BAGAFORE. The Bagafores are a small Senegambian* ethnic group living in Guinea, Gambia, Senegal, and Guinea-Bissau. The name "Bagafore" is actually a Soso* term meaning "black Baga," or pagan Bagas. A substantial number of the more than 60,000 Bagafores are Muslims. They are primarily rice farmers. In recent years, large numbers of Bagafores have been assimilated into surrounding Soso populations. Young Bagafore men are especially likely to convert to Islam after marrying Islamic women from other ethnic groups.
REFERENCES: Richard Lobban and Joshua Forrest. *Historical Dictionary of the Republic of Guinea-Bissau.* 1988; Thomas O'Toole. *Historical Dictionary of Guinea.* 1995.

BAGA-MOLOPOLOLE. *See* KWENA.

BAGANDA. *See* GANDA.

BAGA-SECHELE. *See* KWENA.

BAGESHU. *See* GISU.

BAGGARA. The Baggaras—also known as the Seleims, Hawazmas, Mesiriyas, Humrs, Rizeiqat, Ta'aisha, Beni Rashids, Rashaidas, and Habiniyas—are an ethnic group of Arab* descent living in the Darfur and Kordofan regions of Sudan. They are a subgroup of the Juhayna* Arabs. Most of them support themselves economically by herding cattle. During the late nineteenth century, they were major supporters of the Mahdist movement in Sudan.
REFERENCES: Ian Cunnison. *The Baggara Arabs.* 1966; Carolyn Fluehr-Lobban, Richard A. Lobban, Jr., and John Obert Voll. *Historical Dictionary of Sudan.* 1992.

BAGIELLI. *See* GELLI and PYGMY.

BAGIRMI. *See* BARMA.

BAGISH. *See* GISU.

BAGISU. *See* GISU.

BAGO. The Bago people are an ethnic group living today in northern Togo. Their population consists of more than 60,000 people, most of whom are subsistence farmers. They are part of the eastern Grusi* language group.
REFERENCE: Meterwa A. Ourso. "Phonological Processes in the Noun Class System of Lama." *Studies in African Linguistics* 20 (August 1989): 151–78.

BAGOGWE. The Bagogwe are a subgroup of the Tutsi* people of Rwanda. Most of them live in the province of Ruhengeri.

BAGRE. The Bagre are part of the larger Dagari* group.

BAGUIELLI. *See* GELLI and PYGMY.

BAGUIRMI. *See* BARMA.

BAGWAMA. *See* KURAMA.

BAGWERE. *See* GWERE.

BAGYI. *See* GBAGYI.

BAHIMA. *See* HIMA.

BAHLENGWE. *See* HLENGWE.

BAHUMONO. *See* KOHUMONO.

BAHUTU. *See* HUTU.

BAILUNDU. The Bailundus are one of the traditional, autonomous kingdoms and contemporary ethnic subgroups of the Ovimbundu* people of Angola.

BAINOUK. *See* BAÑUN.

BAINUK. *See* BAÑUN.

BAIOTE. *See* BAYOT.

BAIRU. *See* IRU.

BAJA. *See* GBAYA.

BAJAMA. *See* GONGLA.

BAJARANKE. *See* BADYARAN.

BAJU. *See* KAJE.

BAJUN. *See* BAJUNI.

BAJUNI. The Bajuni (Tikuu) are a people of mixed descent—Arab,* Portuguese,* and Somali*—living along the coast of the Lower Juba Region of Somalia, south of Kismayu, and in coastal Kenya. The Bajuni are a Swahili*-speaking people. Their population today is approximately 40,000 people, of whom the vast majority are Muslims. Only about 1,000 of them live on the Bajuni Islands. They make their living raising coconuts, fishing, and exporting mangrove poles.
REFERENCES: Margaret Castagno. *Historical Dictionary of Somalia.* 1975; Bethwell A. Ogot. *Historical Dictionary of Kenya.* 1981.

BAKA. The Baka people today live in far southwestern Sudan and across the border in the Central African Republic and northern Uganda. They are

closely related to the Bongo* people, with whom they share a very similar Nilo-Saharan language and many cultural and economic features. The Bakas are primarily small farmers. The Bakas form part of the larger Moru* cluster of peoples in Sudan.
REFERENCE: Helen C. Metz et al. *Sudan: A Country Study.* 1992.

BAKA. *See* AKA or PYGMY.

BAKAA. *See* KAA.

BAKAHONDE. *See* KAONDE.

BAKALANGA. *See* KALANGA.

BAKANIKI. *See* KANIGUI.

BAKANIQUI. *See* KANIGUI.

BAKAONDE. *See* KAONDE.

BAKELE. *See* KUKELE.

BAKÈLÈ. The Bakèlè—also known historically as the Akèlè, Bongom, and Bougom—are an ethnic group living in Gabon. With a current population of approximately 15,000 people, they are widely dispersed throughout the country, from the Atlantic coast to the interior, although there is some concentration of them in Lambaréné Prefecture in Moyen-Ogooué Province. They were traditionally elephant hunters, selling the ivory tusks through much of the country. They also lived in farming villages, raising several subsistence crops for their own use. From the 1760s to the 1860s, the Bakèlè were very active in the international slave trade as slave raiders, capturing other Africans and selling them to middlemen, who then traded with European slave merchants. They were fierce warriors, but the superior numbers of the expanding Fang* people forced the Bakèlè into the upper Ogooué and Ivindo river systems, where many of them still live. By the 1870s, the Bakèlè were supplying rubber to European rubber traders. At the time of Gabonese independence in 1960, the Bakèlè were the most scattered ethnic group in the country. The Bakèlè living in eastern Gabon are assimilating with the neighboring Bakota* people.
REFERENCES: Henry H. Bucher. *The Mpongwe of the Gabon Estuary: A History to 1860.* 1977; David E. Gardinier. *Historical Dictionary of Gabon.* 1994.

BAKGATLA. *See* KGATLA.

BAKGWATHENG. *See* KGWATHENG.

BAKHAT. The Bakhats, because they speak a Mabang language, are considered to be a subgroup of the Maba* people of Sudan. Ethnologists, however, argue that their unique language and culture imply that they were probably absorbed by the surrounding Maba peoples during the course of the last several centuries. The Bakhats live west of the town of Abéché. Most of them are small farmers, raising cotton, sorghum, millet, and maize.

BAKHAYO. The Bakhayos are a subgroup of the Luhya* people of Kenya and Uganda. They are a Western Bantu* people who live today north of Lake Victoria on both sides of the Kenyan-Ugandan border.

BAKHURUTSHE. *See* KHURUTSHE.

BAKIGA. The Bakiga are a Bantu*-speaking people who are concentrated in southwestern Uganda, northern Rwanda, and eastern Zaire. Their tribal homeland sits on the south shores of Lake Edward.
REFERENCE: Peter Ladefoged, Ruth Glick, and Clive Criper. *Language in Uganda.* 1972.

BAKO. *See* BAYELE.

BAKO. The Bakos are an ethnic group living today in Ethiopia. Ethnologists place them in the Kafa*-Sadama* cluster of Ethiopian peoples.
REFERENCE: M. L. Bender, J. D. Bowen, R. L. Cooper, and C. A. Ferguson, eds. *Language in Ethiopia.* 1976.

BAKOKO. The Bakokos, who are closely related to the Babimbis* and Bassas* of Cameroon, number approximately 150,000 people today and live in southern Cameroon. Most of them still live in rural villages, where they raise yams, maize, cocoyams, and vegetables, although substantial numbers now live in Duala, Edéa, Pouma, and Makak, where they work as laborers, craftsmen, and businessmen. The Bakokos used to live along the coast, where they made their living as subsistence farmers and fishermen, but they were displaced by the Duala* migration and pushed into the interior. During the years of the colonial empires, the Bakokos were fiercely anti-European, and they retain a strong sense of identity today.
REFERENCES: *African Encyclopedia.* 1974; Mark DeLancey and H. M. Mokeba. *Historical Dictionary of the Republic of Cameroon.* 1990.

BAKONGO. *See* KONGO.

BAKONJO. The Bakonjo are a Bantu*-speaking ethnic group who live in southwestern Uganda and across the border in Zaire. Their homeland surrounds the north shore of Lake Edward.

REFERENCE: Peter Ladefoged, Ruth Glick, and Clive Criper. *Language in Uganda.* 1972.

BAKOSSI. The Bakossis are an ethnic group in the Mungo Valley of Cameroon, as well as in Littoral Province and Western Province there. They are part of the larger Bassa*-Bokoko* cluster of Bantu*-speaking peoples. They are concentrated especially in the Meme Division and the subdivisions of Tombel, Bangem, and Nguti. Their neighbors are the Mbos* and Bamilékés.* Their homeland is surrounded by the Kupr and Manengouba mountains. The primary Bakossi subgroup is the Bassossi. Because of their experiences during the colonial period, the Bakossis are known particularly for their dislike of the British.* Most Bakossis work as small farmers, raising cereals, palm oil plants, coffee, and cocoa. In recent years, large numbers of Bakossis have moved to towns and cities in search of work. Their current population exceeds 100,000 people, and their leading political figure has been Albert Ngome Kome.

REFERENCES: Mark W. DeLancey and H. M. Mokeba. *Historical Dictionary of the Republic of Cameroon.* 1990; S. N. Ejedepang-Koge. *The Tradition of a People: Bakossi.* 1971.

BAKOTA. The Bakota, or Koto, are one of the largest ethnic groups in Gabon. They live in northeastern Gabon and across the border in the Congo Republic. Their own historical traditions have them originating at the upper Ivindo River region, near the Singoué and Nona rivers, but, in the nineteenth century, they were driven south and east to their present locations by Bakouélé* invasions. The Bakouélés were themselves fleeing Fang* expansion into their homelands. During the Bakota flight, some of them broke off and headed to the west, where they eventually evolved into the Benga* people of Gabon. Along the way, the Bakota absorbed a number of other peoples. In the 1890s, the Bakota traded ivory, rubber, goats, and chickens to the French* for guns, axes, matches, knives, and fabrics, becoming deeply involved in the local commercial economy. They make their living today as farmers and merchants. The Bakota population today exceeds 20,000 people.

REFERENCES: David E. Gardinier. *Historical Dictionary of Gabon.* 1994; Louis Perrois, "Chronique du pays kota (Gabon)." *Cahiers de l'Office de la Récherche Scientifique et Technique d'Outre Mer* 8 (1970): 15–110.

BAKOUÉLÉ. The Bakouélés (Bakwele) are an ethnic group living today in northeastern Gabon and in the Congo Republic. Some also live in southern Cameroon. The Bakouélés are concentrated in the upper Ivindo River Valley. Their own traditions have them migrating there in the early nineteenth century, fleeing Fang* expansion. During their migrations, they drove out the Bakota.* Bakouélé expansion stopped north of Makokou with the arrival of the

French.* After that, the Bakouélés made their living as subsistence farmers and by trading ivory and rubber for manufactured goods and salt. Most Bakouélés remain small farmers today.
REFERENCES: David E. Gardinier. *Historical Dictionary of Gabon.* 1994; Leon Siroto. "Masks and Social Organization among the Bakwele Peoples of Western Equatorial Africa." Ph.D. dissertation. Columbia University. 1969.

BAKOUKOUYA. The Bakoukouyas are part of the Téké* cluster of peoples in Congo. They live in the grassy savanna plateaus east of Franceville in Haut-Ogooué Province in eastern Gabon and across the border in Congo. They can also be found living on both sides of the Zaire River between Kinshasa and the confluence of the Kasai and Zaire rivers. They planted palm trees after arriving in the region and made their living trading palm oil and raphia fabrics. They also engaged in the slave trade during the eighteenth and nineteenth centuries. Ethnologists believe that the Bakoukouyas originated to the northwest and began their migration to their contemporary homeland in the fifteenth century. Their contemporary population exceeds 150,000 people. Although most Bakoukouyas are settled farmers today, raising manioc and bananas, they still enjoy hunting antelopes, gazelles, and other animals.
REFERENCES: F. Scott Bobb. *Historical Dictionary of Zaire.* 1988; Claude Cabrol and Raoul Lehuard. *La civilisation des peuples batéké.* 1976; David E. Gardinier. *Historical Dictionary of Gabon.* 1994.

BAKPINKA. The Bakpinkas (Iyongiyongs, Uwets) are a small ethnic group living today in the Akampka Division of Cross River State in southern Nigeria. They make their living farming and fishing. The Bakpinka language is in the process of disappearing.
REFERENCE: *Language Survey of Nigeria.* 1976.

BAKUBA. *See* KUBA.

BAKUENA. *See* KWENA.

BAKULUNG. *See* KULUNG.

BAKWÉ. The Bakwé—also known as the Srigbé and Touwé—are one of the Kru* clusters of people in Ivory Coast. The Bakwé are concentrated in the subprefectures of Soubré and San Pedro. They were traditionally subsistence farmers, raising a variety of crops, but, under French* influence in the twentieth century, a substantial number of Bakwé made the transition to commercial farming, particularly coffee and cocoa.
REFERENCE: Robert J. Mundt. *Historical Dictionary of Côte d'Ivoire.* 1995.

BAKWELE. *See* BAKOUÉLÉ.

BAKWENA. *See* KWENA.

BAKWENA-KGABO. *See* KWENA.

BAKWERI. The Bakweri (Bakwiri) are a cluster of peoples living in villages on the slopes and near Mt. Cameroon in South West Province. They arrived in the region as part of a Bantu* migration that began in the early eighteenth century. They are subdivided into the Kpe, Moboko, Isuwu, and Wovea ethnic groups, each with a powerful sense of its own identity. No single political system gives unity to the Bakweri peoples. Because of their location near the coast, the Bakweri were among the first Cameroonians to come into contact with Europeans, and the Bakweri lost much of their land to German* plantation owners in the late nineteenth and early twentieth centuries. In recent years, such groups as the Bakweri Union and the Bakweri Land Claim Committee have tried to recover their lost property. Today, most Bakweris support themselves by working on the palm oil plantations, on oil rigs and in refineries at Cape Limbo, by fishing, and by rice farming. The leading Bakweri politicians in recent Cameroonian history have been E. M. L. Endeley, P. M. Kale, Dorothy Njeuma, and M. N. Luma.
REFERENCE: Mark W. DeLancey and H. M. Mokeba. *Historical Dictionary of the Republic of Cameroon.* 1990.

BAKWIRI. *See* BAKWERI.

BALAABE. *See* YUKUBEN.

BALANTA. *See* BALENTE.

BALANTA-BRASSA. *See* BALENTE.

BALANTÉ. The Balanté people, who today number in excess of 100,000 people, are part of the Jola* cluster of peoples of Senegal. Some Balantés can also be found today living in Guinea-Bissau and The Gambia.

BALE. The term "Bale" refers to the Oromo* people living in Bale Province of Ethiopia. A substantial number of the Bale Oromo are Muslims.

BALEGETE. *See* EVANT.

BALENKE. The Balenkes are a subgroup of the Bongue* people of Equatorial Guinea. The Bongues themselves are considered part of the Ndowe* cluster of peoples in the region.

BALENTE. The Balentes, also known as the Balanta-Brassa and the Balanta, are an ethnic group of approximately 250,000 people living in Guinea-Bissau.

They are the largest ethnic group in the country and enjoy a highly egalitarian social system. Mandinka* expansion drove them to the coastal regions where they now reside. They are especially concentrated in the central-northern area, west of Farim, as well as in the southern coastal area near Catio. The Balentes are non-Muslim rice farmers. They are closely related to the Mancanhas.* Over the centuries, the Balentes learned how to cultivate commercial volumes of rice in their swampy marshland home by building earthen dikes to keep out seawater. Their economy has traditionally revolved around the production of rice, salt, and plam wine, and they remain today skilled commercial farmers. Approximately 10 percent of the Balentes are Muslims.
REFERENCES: Rosemary R. Galli. *Guinea-Bissau.* 1990; Richard Lobban and Joshua Forrest. *Historical Dictionary of the Republic of Guinea-Bissau.* 1988.

BALESE. The Balese are an ethnic group living today in Zaire. They speak a Central Sudanic language, indicating origins to the north; today, they are concentrated in northeastern Zaire, south of the Uele River, with some of them living across the border in Uganda. The Balese are a politically decentralized people. Most of them today are small farmers.
REFERENCE: Irving Kaplan et al. *Zaire: A Country Study.* 1978.

BALETE. *See* LETE.

BALI. The Balis, not to be confused with the Zairean Balis, are a Cameroonian ethnic group who today live in the Bamenda grasslands of North West Province. They can also be found near Bali in the Batta District of Numan Division in Gongola State, Nigeria. During the colonial period, the Balis established close political and military relations with the Germans,* and, as a result, they did not suffer the extensive land losses to Germans that many other Cameroonian groups did. The Balis have a centralized, hierarchical political system headed by a king, or *fon.* They are the only group in the Cameroonian plateau who do not have Tikar* ethnic roots. Most Balis today make their livings as farmers, raising a wide variety of cereals and coffee.
REFERENCE: Mark W. Delancey and H. M. Mokeba. *Historical Dictionary of the Republic of Cameroon.* 1990.

BALI. The Balis, not to be confused with the Cameroonian Balis,* are a Bantu*-speaking people living today in the Haut-Zaire region of northeastern Zaire. Although most Balis still make their living as farmers, raising cassava as a staple, they have become increasingly integrated into the regional commercial economy in recent decades. Large numbers of Balis have moved to the city of Kisangani in search of wage labor.
REFERENCE: Irving Kaplan et al. *Zaire: A Country Study.* 1978.

BALONDE. *See* LUNDA.

BALOUMBOU. *See* LOUMBOU.

BALOUNDOU. *See* LOUMBOU.

BALOZI. *See* LOZI.

BALTAP. *See* MONTOL.

BALUBA. *See* LUBA.

BAMANA. *See* BAMBARA.

BAMANAKAN. *See* BAMBARA.

BAMANGWATO. *See* NGWATO.

BAMBANA. The Bambanas are a subgroup of the Mbete* people of south-eastern Gabon and Congo. The Bambana population today is approximately 20,000 people, most of whom are small farmers.

BAMBARA. The Bambara (Bamana, Banmanan, Bamanakan), who call them-selves the Bamanakan, are a large ethnic group who speak a Manding* language. Their population today exceeds three million people, and they are located throughout Mali as well as in the northern areas of Ivory Coast. They can also be found in Guinea-Bissau. They are the largest ethnic group in Mali, and their language is the lingua franca of the country. Several hundred thousand Bambara are also scattered throughout Guinea, Senegal, and Gambia. They are especially concentrated on the Niger River, from its interior down to Bamako, and on the Bani River in the east to Kaarta in the west. The Bambara constitute 31 percent of the population of Mali and are among the most powerful and influential ethnic groups in the country. Because of the particular soil composition in the savannas where the rural Bambara farm (with heavy clay content), they developed a uniquely cooperative agricultural system, in which whole communities jointly plow, plant, weed, and harvest crops.

During the eighteenth century, there were two Bambara kingdoms in West Africa—the Kingdom of Segu and the Kingdom of Kaarta. A century later, however, in the mid-nineteenth century, a series of militant Muslim revivals overthrew the Bambara kingdoms. Anti-Muslim Bambara warlords resisted the Muslim occupation for the next forty years, but the arrival of the French* in the region eventually led to a Muslim religious triumph. Nonetheless, in 1912, only 3 percent of the Bambara were Muslim. French armies destroyed the Bam-bara warrior class, and the dramatic increase in commercial trade regionally exposed the Bambara to Muslim trading groups. After World War II, resistance to French colonialism often took the form of Muslim revivalism, and the number of Muslim converts grew until the 1980s; at that time, more than 70 percent of the Bambara were followers of Islam, especially the Qadiriyya, Tijaniyya, and Wahhabi denominations.

In recent years, the Bambara have suffered from ecological change and pandemics sweeping through Africa. Drought and overgrazing have badly disrupted the agricultural rhythms of nature in Mali, and the country fell victim to famine in the 1980s. Even more seriously, especially in the long run, is the spread of the AIDS virus into Mali. Although the spread of the virus is not as bad there as it is in Uganda, Mali still suffers from one of the highest infection rates in the world, and the Bambara are certainly not immune to the devastation.

REFERENCES: Jamil Abun-Nasr. *The Tijaniyya: A Sufi Order in the Modern World.* 1967; Jean Bazin. "War and Servitude at Segou." *Economy and Society* 2 (1974): 107–44; Kaba Lansine. *The Wahhabiyya: Islamic Reform and Politics in French West Africa.* 1974; Charles Monteil. *The Bambara.* 1959; Donald R. White. "Manding-Speaking Peoples." In Richard V. Weekes, ed. *Muslim Peoples.* 1984; Dominique Zahan. *The Bambara.* 1974.

BAMBEIRO. The Bambeiros are a subgroup of the Mbundu* peoples of Angola.

BAMBILI. The Bambili are a subgroup of the Bafut* people of North West Province in Cameroon.

BAMBOKO. The Bambokos (Bambuko) are a small Cameroonian ethnic group living near the western border. Some of them can also be found in Bambuka in the Wurkum District in the Muri Division of Gongola State in Nigeria. Most of them make their living as small farmers, urban workers, civil servants, and businessmen. Because of their location on the Atlantic coast, the Bambokos came into contact with German* and British* commercial interests early, which gave them access to economic opportunity and education.

REFERENCE: Harold D. Nelson et al. *Area Handbook for the United Republic of Cameroon.* 1974.

BAMBUI. The Bambui are a subgroup of the Bafut* people of North West Province in Cameroon.

BAMBUKO. *See* BAMBOKO.

BAMBUR. *See* KULUNG.

BAMBUTI. *See* PYGMY.

BAMEND. The Bamend are one of the cluster of Middle-Cameroon Bantu* peoples who live in north-central Cameroon. Most of them make their livings as small farmers and fishermen, although, in recent years, increasing numbers of Bamend men have found work on commercial farms and in the oil fields. The recent emphasis on commercial crops for export—coffee, cocoa, timber, palm oil, and bananas—has actually tended to impoverish most Bamend farmers and has contributed to a decline in their standard of living.
REFERENCE: Mark DeLancey and H. M. Mokeba. *Historical Dictionary of the Republic of Cameroon.* 1990.

BAMENDA. *See* BAMILÉKÉ.

BAMENDANKWE. The Bamendankwe are a subgroup of the Bafut* people of North West Province in Cameroon.

BAMILÉKÉ. The term "Bamiléké" refers to a cluster of Bantu*-speaking people living in Cameroon. Their total population exceeds two million people, constituting approximately 27 percent of the country's population. They are the largest ethnic group in the country. Traditionally, their homeland consisted of grasslands and mountain slopes, where they produced maize, kola nuts, coffee, and pigs. In recent years, because of population growth and the integration of the region into the larger commercial economy, several hundred thousand Bamiléké have moved to towns and cities, especially Duala and Yaoundé, to find work. In the towns and cities, they are known for their skills at running small and large businesses and for their professional abilities. During the years of the French* colonial empire, the Bamiléké were organized into ninety different chiefdoms, including such major subgroups as the Bamiléké proper and the Bamendas, Bamums,* Banens,* Tikars,* Widekums,* Yambassas, and Metas*; the populations ranging from 500 to more than 40,000 people. Today, all of the people of those chiefdoms identify themselves as Bamilékés. During the years of the French colonial empire, the Bamiléké were leaders in the nationalistic rebellion, especially the 1955 uprising that led to Cameroon's independence. Today the Bamiléké are extremely influential in the Cameroonian commercial economy. They are also one of the major constituencies of the Union des Populations du Cameroun (UPC), the fiercely nationalistic political party.
REFERENCES: *African Encyclopedia.* 1974; Mark DeLancey and H. M. Mokeba. *Historical Dictionary of the Republic of Cameroon.* 1990; Harold D. Nelson et al. *Area Handbook for the United Republic of Cameroon.* 1974.

BAMOUM. *See* BAMUM.

BAMUM. The Bamum (Bamoum) are an ethnic group living today in the high grasslands of Cameroon, primarily in West Province around the town of Foum-

ban. The Bamum split off from the Tikar* and migrated to the east about 250
years ago. They are separated from the Bamiléké people by the Noun River,
although they are part of the Bamiléké group of peoples. Their population exceeds 140,000 people, of whom 80 percent are Muslims, although the religion
is a syncretic mix of Islam, Christianity, and indigenous Bamum traditions. The
indigenous Bamum religion, which worships a great god named Yorubang, is
still followed by thousands of people, and this faith has had an impact on Bamum Muslims as well. The Bamum economy revolves around the agricultural
production of maize, millet, vegetables, and coffee.
REFERENCES: *African Encyclopedia.* 1974; Mark DeLancey and H. M. Mokeba.
Historical Dictionary of the Republic of Cameroon. 1990; Claude Tardits. *Le royaume
Bamoum.* 1980; Marcilene K. Wittmer. ''Bamum Village Masks.'' *African Arts* 12 (August 1979): 58–65.

BAMUN. *See* BAMUM.

BANANA. *See* MASSA.

BANDA. The Bandas are one of the major ethnic groups of the Central African
Republic. Their population today exceeds 1.2 million, and they are divided into
a number of subgroups, including the Linda, Kreich, Langba, Yakpa, N'Gao,
Togbo, N'Di, and Dakpa. Their own traditions, confirmed by ethnological and
archaeological research, place their origins in the mountains of Darfur. They
migrated to their present locations in the Central African Republic in the nineteenth century, primarily because they refused to submit to the authority of the
slaving sultans of Wadai and Darfur. They battled the Sabangas* and the Mandijas* during the migration. It was not until the arrival of the Belgians* in 1892
and the French* in 1901 that peace was restored to the region where the Bandas
settled. They are the largest ethnic group in the Central African Republic. They
also live across the border in northernmost Zaire near the Ubangi River and in
Cameroon. Other Bandas can be found scattered throughout Cameroon and
Zaire, as well as in Ghana. The Banda language is of Adamawa-Eastern origin.
REFERENCES: F. Scott Bobb. *Historical Dictionary of Zaire.* 1988; Pierre Kalck.
Historical Dictionary of the Central African Republic. 1992; Pierre Kalck. *Central Af-
rican Republic.* 1993.

BANDA. The Bandas are a major subgroup of the Shona* peoples in Zimbabwe
and Mozambique.

BANDAWA-MINDA. The Bandawa-Minda peoples, also known as the Mindas
or Jinleris, are an ethnic group living today in Nigeria, primarily in the Wurkum
and Lau districts of the Muri Division of Gongola State. They make their livings

raising livestock and managing subsistence farms. The Bandawa-Minda language is part of the Central Jukunoid group of the Benue-Congo family.
REFERENCE: *Language Survey of Nigeria.* 1976.

BANDE. *See* GBANDE.

BANDI. The Bandi (Ghandi) people speak one of the southwestern Mande languages and live in upper Lofa County in Liberia. Their most immediate neighbors are the Kissis,* Mendes,* Golas,* Kuwaas,* and Lomas.* Bandi oral traditions, confirmed by archaeological evidence, have them migrating to their present location from the north and west in the sixteenth century. There is a single Bandi chiefdom today, which is divided into six highly self-conscious clans: the Hasalas, Lukasus, Tahambas, Wanwumas, Wulukohas, and Yawiyasus. The demographic capital of the Bandis is the town of Kolahun. Today the Bandi population of Liberia exceeds 60,000 people.
REFERENCES: D. Elwood Dunn and Svend E. Holsoe. *Historical Dictionary of Liberia.* 1985; Patricia O'Connell. ''Bandi Silver Jewelry.'' *African Arts* 12 (November 1978): 48–51.

BANDIA. The Bandias (Bandiyas) are one of the two major subgroups of the Azandé* people of Zaire. They live near the northern border of Zaire, near the confluence of the Uele and the Ubangi rivers and between the towns of Ango and Bondo. The Bandias speak a Sudanic language that is of Adamawa-Eastern extraction. They are the westernmost of the Azandé peoples. They can also be found in the Central African Republic and Sudan. Most Bandias are subsistence farmers.
REFERENCES: F. Scott Bobb. *Historical Dictionary of Zaire.* 1988; Pierre Kalck. *Central African Republic.* 1993.

BANDIBU. *See* KONGO.

BANDIYA. *See* BANDIA.

BANDJABI. *See* NZABI.

BANDZE. The Bandzes are a subgroup of the Sanga* peoples of southeastern Cameroon, northern Congo, southern Central African Republic, and northwestern Zaire. They are approximately 12,000 Bandzes today. They interact closely with the neighboring Pygmies,* who trade game for Bandze agricultural products.
REFERENCE: Gordon C. McDonald et al. *Area Handbook for the People's Republic of the Congo (Congo Brazzaville).* 1971.

BANE. The Bane (Banen) are a subgroup of the Beti,* one of the dominant ethnic groups in Cameroon. They are part of the larger Fang*-Pahouin* cluster of Bantu*-speaking peoples of Cameroon, Gabon, and Equatorial Guinea. The Bane population today exceeds 250,000 people, most of whom are Roman Catholics. They are primarily farmers, raising cocoa, rice, coffee, groundnuts, cassava, and a variety of other vegetable crops.

BANEN. The Banens are a subgroup of the Bamiléké* peoples of Cameroon. They are concentrated in the northwest corner of the country near the Atlantic Coast. The Banen economy revolves around the agricultural production of maize, millet, vegetables, and coffee.
REFERENCE: Claude Tardits. *Le royaume Bamoum.* 1980.

BANG. *See* MAMBILA.

BANGA. The Banga people (Benga), not to be confused with the Bengas* of Gabon, are an ethnic group living today in Nigeria. They are concentrated in the Zuru-Donko Region of the Juru Division of Sokoto State, where most of them raise livestock and work small farms. The Bangas speak a language that is classified in the Western Plateau group of the Benue-Congo family. Their current population is approximately 25,000 people.
REFERENCE: *Language Survey of Nigeria.* 1976.

BANGALA. The Bangalas are a subgroup of the Mbundu* peoples of Angola.

BANGALA. The Bangalas (Bangis) are a subgroup of the Mbochi* people of eastern Gabon, central Congo, and western Zaire. Their contemporary population exceeds 35,000 people. Although they are increasingly turning to commercial agriculture, the Bangala economy has traditionally revolved around trading and fishing, at which they are highly adept. Their social structure is based on a patrilineal clan structure.
REFERENCES: Gordon C. McDonald et al. *Area Handbook for the People's Republic of the Congo (Congo Brazzaville).* 1971; Donald G. Morrison et al. *Black Africa: A Comparative Handbook.* 1989.

BANGI. *See* BANGALA.

BANGO. The Bangos are a Bantu*-speaking people who live in the upper Lualaba River Valley in north-central Zaire. A riverine people, the Bangos traditionally supported themselves by river-bank farming, fishing, and trading. Many of them still engage in those pursuits.
REFERENCE: Irving Kaplan et al. *Zaire: A Country Study.* 1978.

BANGOLOGA. *See* NGOLOGA.

BANGOU. The Bangou people are part of the larger cluster of Ngbandi* peoples of the Central African Republic and Zaire. They live on the Ubangi River, upstream from Bangui, and are a riverine people. Because of their skills as boatmen, they have been active traders on the Ubangi River; when the French* first arrived in the late nineteenth century, the Bangou served as middlemen between the French and the inland ethnic groups.
REFERENCE: Pierre Kalck. *Central African Republic.* 1993.

BANGU-BANGU. The Bangu-Bangus are one of the subgroups of the Luba* people of Zaire. They are part of the Songye subcluster of the Lubas and live east of the Lualaba River in southeastern Zaire.

BANGUNJI. *See* BANGWINJI.

BANGWAKETSE. *See* NGWAKETSE.

BANGWATO. *See* NGWATO.

BANGWINJI. The Bangwinjis are an ethnic group living today in Nigeria. They are concentrated in the Dadiya District of Gombe Division of Bauchi State, and they speak a language that is part of the Waja* cluster of the Adamawa group. Most Bangwinjis are small farmers.
REFERENCE: *Language Survey of Nigeria.* 1976.

BANHUN. *See* BAÑUN.

BANI SHANGUL. *See* BENI SHANGUL.

BANKAL. The Bankals are one of the Bantu*-speaking peoples of Nigeria. They are classified as part of the Plateau cluster of peoples who occupy central Nigeria. Most Bankals practice subsistence agriculture, raising ginger, millet, guinea corn, beans, and citrus products, and they live in social systems characterized by patrilineal descent and patrifocal residence. In recent years, they have begun migrating to towns and cities looking for work.
REFERENCE: Donald G. Morrison et al. *Black Africa: A Comparative Handbook.* 1989.

BANMANDA. *See* BAMBARA.

BANNA. The Bannas are an ethnic group in southern Ethiopia. They speak an Omotic* language and are divided into two subgroups: the Hamers and the Karos. Most Bannas raise livestock and work as subsistence farmers. Their population today exceeds 18,000 people, the vast majority of whom are Hamers.

REFERENCES: M. L. Bender, J. D. Bowen, R. L. Cooper, and C. A. Ferguson, eds. *Language in Ethiopia.* 1976.

BANTOID. The Bantoid are an ethnic group living today in Nigeria. Their population is approximately 90,000 people, of whom are 45,000 are Muslims. They are largely subsistence farmers.
REFERENCE: Donald G. Morrison et al. *Black Africa: A Comparative Handbook.* 1989.

BANTU. The term ''Bantu'' refers to a large, complex linguistic grouping of peoples in Africa. All Africans—except those speaking a Nilotic,* Cushitic, or Khoisan language—living south of a line from Cameroon in West Africa to Kenya in East Africa, speak a Bantu language. The Bantu languages are themselves part of the larger Nilo-Congo linguistic family. Ethno-archaeologists have located the Bantu origins in eastern Nigeria; their migration to contemporary locations began approximately 2,000 years ago, as they spread south and east along the tributaries of the Congo River. Today, the Northeast Bantu peoples reach as far north as southern Sudan and as far south as South Africa. They were successful because of their skills as ironworkers, which gave them a tremendous advantage over surrounding peoples in terms of weapons and tools. Most Bantu peoples today have preserved their animistic religions, although Muslims have made many converts in coastal East Africa. There are approximately 160 million Bantu-speaking people in Africa today.
REFERENCES: M. C. Guthrie. ''Some Developments in the Prehistory of the Bantu Languages.'' *Journal of African History* 3 (1962): 273–82; M. M. Posnansky. ''Bantu Genesis: Archaeological Reflections.'' *Journal of African History* 9 (1951): 1–11.

BAÑUN. The Bañun (Banyun, Banhun) also known as the Bainuk and Bainunka, were historically the core ethnic group of the great Kasa Kingdom in Senegal from the fifteenth to the eighteenth centuries. When the Portuguese* first arrived in the region of the lower Casamance River region of southern Senegal, the Kasa Kingdom was dominant there. The kingdom fell in power in the eighteenth century because of the increasing military power and political influence of the neighboring Jola* and Manding* peoples. Today, the Bañun in Senegal, Guinea-Bissau, and Gambia are still aware of their identity, although they are rapidly adopting Jola or Manding culture. They are an animistic people known for their skills as weavers and dyers.
REFERENCES: Andrew F. Clark and Lucie Colvin Phillips. *Historical Dictionary of Senegal.* 1994; David P. Gamble. *The Gambia.* 1988.

BANYAI. *See* NYAI.

BANYAMWEZI. *See* NYAMWEZI.

BANYANG. *See* BAYANG.

BANYANKOLE. *See* NYANKORE.

BANYARWANDA. *See* RWANDA.

BANYOMBO. The Banyombos are an ethnic group of approximately 5,000 people living in Rwanda. Most of them are farmers.
REFERENCE: Learthen Dorsey. *Historical Dictionary of Rwanda.* 1994.

BANYORO. *See* NYORO.

BANYUN. *See* BAÑUN.

BANZIRI. The Banziris, who are part of what some people have called the Ubangi cluster of peoples in the Central African Republic, are an ethnic group concentrated at the confluence of the Kouango and the Ubangi rivers. They originated in the Upper Nile region and migrated to their present location beginning in the sixteenth century, displacing in the process several Bantu*-speaking groups. In 1890, the Banziris signed a treaty of protection with the French.* They are today a riverine people, known for their skills as canoemen, fishermen, and small-scale farmers. They are also very influential in the civil service and police force of the Central African Republic.
REFERENCES: Pierre Kalck. *Central African Republic.* 1993; Pierre Kalck. *Historical Dictionary of the Central African Republic.* 1992.

BAOULÉ. *See* BAULE.

BAPEDI. *See* PEDI.

BAPHALENG. *See* PHALENG.

BAPHETLA. *See* PHETLA.

BAPHUTHI. *See* PHUTHI.

BAPINDJI. *See* APINDJI.

BAPOLANE. *See* MAPOLANE.

BAPOUNOU. The Bapounou, or Pounou, are demographically one of the most important ethnic groups in Gabon. They are concentrated in southwestern Gabon, primarily in the mountains and grasslands of the N'Gounié and Nyanga river systems. Bapounou can also be found in the Kibangou District north of the Niari River in the Congo Republic. They have also been known as the Bayaka, which they consider an ethnic slur. Bapounou tradition has them

migrating to their present locations from southern regions in the Congo. During the nineteenth century, the Bapounous were active in the rubber and slave trades. They are closely related to the neighboring Eshira.* Most Bapounou are subsistence farmers, raising manioc, plantains, and a variety of other crops. They are also known for manufacturing a palm-fiber cloth that they trade. The Bapounou population today exceeds 20,000 people.
REFERENCE: David E. Gardinier. *Historical Dictionary of Gabon.* 1994.

BAPUKU. The Bapukus are a subgroup of the Boumba* people of Equatorial Guinea. The Boumbas themselves are part of the larger Ndowe* cluster of peoples.

BAQQARA. *See* BAGGARA.

BARA. The Baras are a Madagascar ethnic group whose population today is approaching 375,000 people. Most of them live in Tulear and Fianarantsoa provinces. They are divided into a number of subgroups. The Barobes live in the valley of the Ihosy River; the Imamonos are concentrated near Andazoabo; and the Vindas are located near the Onilahy River. Other Bara subgroups include the Sautsautas and the Timonjys. In recent years, large numbers of Betsileos* have intermarried with the Baras; from them, the Baras have learned to cultivate rice as a staple and cash crop. Many Baras, however, still loathe agriculture and prefer other forms of work.
REFERENCES: Maureen Covell. *Madagascar: Politics, Economics and Society.* 1987; Harold D. Nelson et al. *Area Handbook for the Malagasy Republic.* 1973.

BARABAIG. The Barabaig are a Tanzanian ethnic group who today number more than 45,000 people. They call themselves the Datog. Their traditional homeland is south of Lake Eyasi, between the cities of Mbulu and Singida in Tanzania. Ethnolinguists classify the Barabaig as being of Nandi* stock, part of the Southern Nilotic* language family. They are a transhumant people, whose entire economy and culture revolve around herding cattle, although they are also known to raise sheep, donkeys, and goats. They must move the cattle frequently in order to find reliable pasture, and milk from the cattle has traditionally provided the Barabaig with their food staple. They mix the milk with blood from a bull and make it into a high-protein paste. Within the last several decades, the Barabaig have also begun to raise small amounts of maize in order to provide a more regular food supply. Historically, the Barabaig were known for their ferocity and their sizable herds of cattle and goats. In recent years, they have come on hard times economically. They were also easily identified by Europeans because of their traditional practice of ritual scarification of the face and earlobes. The droughts that affected East Africa in the late 1980s and early 1990s have had a devastating effect on the Barabaig cattle herds. Today the Barabaig are being assimilated by the Iraqw.*

REFERENCES: G. J. Klima. *The Barabaig: East African Cattle Herders.* 1970; James L. Newman. *The Ecological Basis for Subsistence Change among the Sandawe of Tanzania.* 1970.

BARABRA. The Barabras are a subgroup of the Nubian* people of Sudan and Egypt. Included in the Barabra cluster of peoples are the Kenuzes, Sukkots, and Mahas.*

BARAGUYU. The Baraguyu (Kwavi, Lumbwa, Liokpoli) are closely related to the Masai.* They are often referred to as the "agricultural Masai." They live in the Central Highlands of Tanzania and are considered a Southern Nilotic* people. The main difference between the Masai and the Baraguyu, in terms of economics at least, is that the Baraguyu adopted agriculture in recent years. The Baraguyus are famous for their decorative necklaces and earpieces.
REFERENCES: Laura Kurtz. *Historical Dictionary of Tanzania.* 1978; James L. Newman. *The Ecological Basis for Subsistence Change among the Sandawe of Tanzania.* 1970.

BARAIN. The Barains are one of the Hadjeray* peoples of the mountainous regions of Guéra Prefecture in Chad. They are descended from refugees who were driven into the mountains. They speak a Chadian language and practice the *margai* cult of place and site spirits. In spite of many cultural similarities with such other groups as the Kingas,* Junkuns,* Bidios,* Mogoums,* Sokoros,* Dangaleats,* and Sabas,* the Barains rarely intermarry and maintain a powerful sense of identity.
REFERENCE: Thomas Collelo et al. *Chad: A Country Study.* 1990.

BARAWA. The Barawas (Baaraawaas) are an ethnic group who live today in Nigeria. They are concentrated in the northern reaches of the country, primarily in Bauchi Division of Bauchi State, where they farm and raise livestock. They speak a Chadic language.
REFERENCE: *Language Survey of Nigeria.* 1976.

BARAYA. *See* KURI.

BARBA. *See* BARIBA.

BARBU. *See* BARIBA.

BAREA. The Barea people are one of the subgroups of the Shilluks,* a pre-Nilotic* people of the Sudan.

BAREMBA. *See* LEMBA.

BARESHE. *See* RESHAWA.

BARGU. *See* BARIBA.

BARGWE. *See* BARWE.

BARI. *See* GBARI.

BARI. Not to be confused with the Gbari* (Bari) people of Nigeria, the Baris of Sudan live on the east side of the White Nile River in far southern Sudan, near and across the border with Uganda. The Baris speak a Nilotic* language, although it is a different branch from neighboring Nilotes* in southern Sudan. The Baris are closely related to the Kukus,* Kakwas,* and Mandaris.* The Baris live in the lowlands, where cattle herding is the most productive form of economic support.
REFERENCE: Helen C. Metz et al. *Sudan: A Country Study.* 1992.

BARIA. The Baria are an Ethiopian ethnic group. Approximately 10,000 Barias are Muslims.
REFERENCE: M. L. Bender, J. D. Bowen, R. L. Cooper, and C. A. Ferguson, eds. *Language in Ethiopia.* 1976.

BARIBA. The Bariba (Borgawa), who call themselves the Batonu, Bargu, Barba, Botombu, Batomba, or Batonun, are a major tribal ethnic group of the countries of Benin, Burkina-Faso, Togo, and Nigeria. Perhaps 10,000 of them live in the Cambolé region of Togo. Today there are more than 650,000 members of the group, and they traditionally inhabited the north-central and north-eastern forest and savanna land of Benin. They are especially concentrated around Parakou. Many of them have moved to the major cities of Benin, although they retain powerful elements of traditional culture, including beliefs in supernatural spirits and phenomena. In Nigeria, they can be found in the Gwanara, Ilesha, Okuta, and Yashikira districts of the Borgu Division in Kwara State. Although Bariba tradition traces their origins to the legendary seventh-century Persian warrior Kisra, ethnologists believe the Bariba have roots in the Sudan, because their language carries both Voltaic and Sudanese elements. There are two constituent groups of Bariba. The Busa* people live in the Kwara State of Nigeria, while the Nikki* live in the Department of Borghou in Benin. The Busa population exceeds 95,000 people, while there are more than 550,000 Nikki. Most of the Bariba are farmers, who raise yams, sorghum, millet, corn, rice, peanuts, and beans. Only recently have they begun to abandon hoe agriculture in favor of animal-drawn plows.

The Bariba usually live in concentrated villages; within those villages, they dwell in walled compounds that house several families who are related on a paternal line. There may also be a small farm house a few miles out in the

countryside near their land and herds. Approximately half of the Busa are Muslims, compared with a third of the Nikki who are. The others are for the most part still loyal to indigenous beliefs, which include devotion to ancestors, shamanistic healers, and a belief in a variety of animistic forces. The Bariba have historically been a dominant group wherever they have lived. Neighboring Fulbe* people have generally served the Bariba by raising their cattle herds for them, while the Hausa* are usually merchants and traders supplying the Bariba with goods and services. Both the Fulbe and the Hausa acknowledge Bariba political leadership where they live in close proximity to each other.
REFERENCES: Jacques Maquet. *Civilizations of Black Africa.* 1972; Harold D. Nelson et al. *Area Handbook for Nigeria.* 1972; Carolyn F. Sargent. "Born to Die: Witchcraft and Infanticide in Bariba Culture." *Ethnology* 27 (1988): 79–95.

BARKA. The Barkas are today considered to be one of the Manding* peoples. They speak a Manding language, which is part of the Niger-Congo language family, and they live in Burkina-Faso. The Barka population today numbers more than 240,000 people, of whom nearly a third are Muslims.
REFERENCE: Daniel M. McFarland. *Historical Dictionary of Upper Volta.* 1978.

BARKE. The Barkes (Barkos, Burkunawas, Lipkawas) are a Nigerian ethnic group who live in the Ganjuwa District of the Bauchi Division of Bauchi State. They speak a Chadic language and make their livings as small farmers and herders.
REFERENCE: *Language Survey of Nigeria.* 1976.

BARKO. *See* BARKE.

BARMA. The Barma (Baguirmi) today number approximately 50,000 people and live between Bousso and N'Djamena, between the Bahr Ergig River and the Chari River, in Chad. They speak a Central Sudanese language, which is part of the larger Chari-Nile linguistic family, and most of them function today as poor peasant farmers. They are the descendants of the once-great Bagirmi Empire, which, in the eighteenth century, ruled an area that reached from Bornu to Darfur. Beginning in 1802, the Bagirmi Empire fell under assault from the Islamic armies of Wadai, and the kingdom never managed to regain its political autonomy. In 1897, Bagirmi leaders signed a treaty of protection with the French,* and the kingdom was incorporated into French Equatorial Africa in 1910. Islam first came to the Barma in the sixteenth century. Today, the Barma are devout Muslims, known for avoiding alcohol use, observing Ramadan, reading the Koran, practicing polygyny, making the Haj (pilgrimage) to Mecca if economic resources permit, and saying daily prayers. Some Barma men are members of Sufi brotherhoods. The Barma are also known for their small family size and low fertility rates, probably because of the high age differentials between husbands and wives and the high rates of divorce and sterility from venereal disease. Although the Barma population is approaching 90,000 people, there are also tens of thousands of others—primarily Fulbes,* Kanuris,* Saras,* Massas,* and Niellims*—who have assimilated to one degree or another with the Barma. The Barma divide themselves into two basic groups—the land Barmi, who farm millet, sorghum, beans, sesame, peanuts, and cotton, and the river Barmi, who fish along the Chari and Bahr Ergig rivers.

REFERENCES: Thomas Collelo et al. *Chad: A Country Study.* 1990; S. P. Reyna. "The Costs of Marriage: A Study of Some Factors Affecting Northwest Barma Fertility." Ph.D. dissertation. Columbia University. 1972.

BAROA. *See* SAN.

BAROBE. The Barobes are a subgroup of the Bara* cluster of peoples of the plains of Madagascar.

BAROLONG. *See* ROLONG.

BAROTSE. *See* LOZI.

BAROZWI. *See* ROZVI.

BARUE. *See* BARWE.

BARWE. The Barwes (Barues, Bargwes) are an ethnic group living in the Mtoko and Inyanga districts in Zimbabwe and across the border in Mozambique. Although some ethnologists classify them as a Shona* subgroup, they speak a Bantu* language that is non-Shona in its origins. The Barwe language is very similar to the Nyanja* language spoken north of the Zambezi River. Most Barwes are small farmers. The Barwe population today is approximately 250,000 people.

REFERENCES: Harold D. Nelson et al. *Mozambique: A Country Study.* 1984; R. Kent Rasmussen. *Historical Dictionary of Zimbabwe.* 1994.

BARYA. The Barya are an ethnic group living in Sudan and in the Barentu region of Eritrea near the Sudanese border. They speak a Nilotic* language and make their living as semi-nomadic pastoralists raising cattle. In recent years, increasing numbers of Barya have settled into permanent villages. They were forcibly converted to Islam in the late nineteenth century.

REFERENCE: Chris Prouty and Eugene Rosenfeld. *Historical Dictionary of Ethiopia and Eritrea.* 1994.

BASA. *See* BASSA.

BASAN. The Basans (Bassans) are a subgroup of the Izon* peoples of Rivers State in Nigeria.

BASARE. *See* BASARI.

BASARI. The Basari (Bassari, Basare, Kyamba, Tchamba) are one of the Sudanic peoples who live in northern Togo and across the border in Ghana. Part of the Gurma* cluster of peoples, they are concentrated northwest of Sokodé. The Basari population is approaching 80,000 people. They should not be confused with the Basari* who live along the border between Guinea and Senegal. They also call themselves, and have been known historically, as the Bi-Tchambé (because of their precolonial reputations as metalworkers) or Chamba; they should not be confused with the Chamba of Cameroon. The Basari are animist in their religious loyalties, worshiping the god Bassar, who lives in neighboring Mount Basari. The arrival of the British* and the Germans* broke the monopoly that the Basari had on metallurgy and weapons manufacture, and this situation forced them to make the transition to sedentary agriculture and cattle herding, which characterizes their economy today. Early in the twentieth century, a substantial number of Basari became policemen in the German colonial police force, and the Basari are still overrepresented in police and security forces today.
REFERENCE: Samuel Decalo. *Historical Dictionary of Togo.* 1976.

BASARI. The Basari, not to be confused with the Basari* of Togo and Ghana, are an ethnic group living along the border between Guinea and Senegal. Their population today is approximately 12,000 people, and they are equally divided on both sides of the border. They are among the least Europeanized and least Islamicized peoples in the region. Ethnographers traditionally classify them as one of the Tenda* groups, which also includes the neighboring Koñagi,* Badyaran,* Bedik,* and Boin* groups. They are slash-and-burn cultivators, who live in villages of from 100 to 500 people each. Their homeland is one of the least developed economically in the area. They are 700 kilometers from Dakar and 250 kilometers from Tambacounda. Roads are poor and often impassable during the rainy season. Although nearly 85 percent of Senegalese are Muslims, the Basari remain loyal to their traditional animist faith.
REFERENCES: Riall W. Nolan. *Bassari Migrations: The Quiet Revolution.* 1986; Thomas O'Toole. *Historical Dictionary of Guinea.* 1995.

BASARWA. *See* SAN.

BASEKE. The Basekes are a subgroup of the Bongue* people of Equatorial Guinea. The Bongues themselves are considered part of the Ndowe* cluster of peoples in the region.

BASENGA. *See* DOKO-UYANGA.

BASHAGA. *See* SHAGA.

BASHAR. The Bashars, also known historically as the Bashiris, are a Nigerian ethnic group concentrated in the Wase District of the Langtang Division of Plateau State. Most Bashars are small farmers. They speak a Benue language.
REFERENCE: *Language Survey of Nigeria.* 1976.

BASHIKONGO. *See* SHIKONGO.

BASHIRI. *See* BASHAR.

BASHONA. *See* SHONA.

BASKETO. The Basketos are a small ethnic group living today in southern Ethiopia. Their current population is approximately 17,000 people, most of whom are small farmers and herders. They speak an Omotic* language.
REFERENCE: M. L. Bender, J. D. Bowen, R. L. Cooper, and C. A. Ferguson, eds. *Language in Ethiopia.* 1976.

BASOGA. *See* SOGA.

BASOLONGO. *See* SOLONGO.

BASORONGO. *See* SOLONGO.

BASSA. The Bassa people, not to be confused with the Kruan-speaking Bassas* of Liberia, are an ethnic group living today in southern Cameroon. The speak a Bantu* language and are closely related to the neighboring Bakoko* and Babimbi* peoples. The collective population of the Bassas, Bakokos, and Babimbis is more than 500,000 people. Most of them still live in rural villages, where they raise yams, maize, cocoyams, and vegetables, although substantial numbers now live in Duala, Edéa, Pouma, and Makak, where they work as laborers, craftsmen, and businessmen.
REFERENCES: *African Encyclopedia.* 1974; Mark DeLancey and H. M. Mokeba. *Historical Dictionary of the Republic of Cameroon.* 1990.

BASSA. The Bassa (Basa, Basso, Gbasa) people, not to be confused with the Bantu*-speaking Bassas* of Cameroon, are an ethnic group living primarily in Grand Bassa County in Liberia. They can also be found in Marshall Territory and River Cess Territory in Liberia. They live on the Atlantic coast and are surrounded by the Kpelles,* Manos, Dans,* Wees,* and Krus.* In recent years, there has been a large migration of Bassas from rural areas to Liberian cities. The rural Bassa population exceeds 350,000 people today. Most of them

are small farmers, raising cassava, yams, plantains, and edoes. The Bassas are subdivided into a variety of chiefdoms, with each chiefdom further divided into ethnically distinct clans. In Grand Bassa County, the Bassa clans include the Boe-Glyn, Chan, Doe-Doe, Doe-Gbahn, Dorzohn Goryah, Gbarwein, Gbaryah, Gbor, Gborwein, Gianda, Gogwein, Goingbe, Gorbli, Grand Kola, Hoegbahn, Kabli, Little Kola, Marbli, Marloe, Mehwein, Neekreen, Neepu, New Cess, Nyonniwein, Peter Harris, Seeya, Sewein, Soniwein, Trade Town, Varmbo, Wein, Wen-Gba-Kon, Wensohn, Wrogba, and Zeewein. In Marshall Territory, the Mambam chiefdom includes the following clans: Ganio, Giah, Kafia, Kaba, Kpay, and Zoduan. In the River Cess Territory, the Bassa clans include the Bio/ Wor, Biokwia, Dorgbor/Dowein, Faah, Fenwein, Gbuizohn, Jowein, Kploh, Kporwein, Moweh, Neegban, Timbo, and Zahr-Flahn. Closely related linguistically to the Bassas are the Gbi* and Doru* of southern Nimba County.
REFERENCES: D. Elwood Dunn and Svend E. Holsoe. *Historical Dictionary of Liberia.* 1985; Harold D. Nelson et al. *Liberia: A Country Study.* 1984.

BASSA-KADUNA. The Bassa-Kadunas, also known as the Bassa-Kutas and Gwandara-Bassas, are an ethnic group living today in the Minna Division of Niger State in Nigeria. Their speak a Western Plateau Language, part of the Benue-Congo family. Most Bassa-Kadunas make their living raising livestock and working small farms.
REFERENCE: *Language Survey of Nigeria.* 1976.

BASSA-KOMO. *See* BASSA KWOMU.

BASSA-KUTA. *See* BASSA-KADUNA.

BASSA-KWOMU. The Bassa-Kwomus—also known as the Bassa-Komos, Abachas, and Abatsas—are an ethnic group living today in the Toto and Loko districts of the Nasarwa Division of Plateau State in Nigeria, as well as in the Bassa-Komo, Mozom, and Dekina districts of the Dekina Division in Benue State. They are closely related to the Bassa-Kadunas.* The Bassa-Kwomu population today stands at approximately 130,000 people, most of whom are farmers.
REFERENCE: *Language Survey of Nigeria.* 1976.

BASSAN. *See* BASAN.

BASSANGA. The Bassangas are a subgroup of the Sanga* people.

BASSARI. *See* BASARI.

BASSILA. The Bassilas are a small ethnic group of several thousand people living on both sides of the border in southwestern Togo and southeastern

Ghana, primarily east of Lake Volta. Most Bassilas are small farmers. Ethnologists classify them as one of the Central Togo groups of people.
REFERENCE: Donald G. Morrison et al. *Black Africa: A Comparative Handbook.* 1989.

BASSIMBA. The Bassimba people are an ethnic group living today in central Gabon in West Africa. They speak an Okandé* language and dwell in a heavily forested region, where they fish and farm. The Bassimba population today is perhaps 5,000 people.

BASSO. *See* BASSA.

BASSOSI. The Bassosi are the primary ethnic subdivision of the Bakossi* people of southwestern Cameroon.

BASUTO. *See* SOTHO.

BATA. The Bata people live today in Nigeria and Cameroon. They are concentrated particularly in the Mubi, Adamawa, and Numan divisions of Gongola State in Nigeria. Most Batas make their livings raising livestock and working small subsistence farms. They speak a Chadic language.
REFERENCE: *Language Survey of Nigeria.* 1976.

BATALOTE. *See* TALAOTE.

BATANGA. The Batanga are an ethnic group concentrated in the Kribi region of Cameroon. They are closely related to the Dualas.*

BATAU. The Bataus are a subgroup of the Nupe* peoples of Niger State in Nigeria.

BATAUNG. The Bataungs are a Sotho* clan who trace their origins back to the Rolong people. They live today in Mohale's Hoek District in Lesotho.

BATAWANA. *See* TAWANA.

BATEKE. *See* TÉKÉ.

BATHEPU. *See* THEPU.

BATLOKWA. *See* TLOKWA.

BATONGA. *See* TONGA.

BATONU. *See* BARIBA.

BATONUN. *See* BARIBA.

BATSANGUI. The Batsangui, also known as Tsangui, are an ethnic group living in N'Gounié Province in southeastern Gabon and across the border in the Congo Republic. They speak a Mbete* language and are closely related to the Nzabi* peoples, with whom they live. Most Batsangui are subsistence farmers, raising manioc, plantains, yams, sweet potatoes, taros, and a variety of vegetables.
REFERENCE: David E. Gardinier. *Historical Dictionary of Gabon.* 1994.

BATU. The Batus are an ethnic group living today in Nigeria and Cameroon. They can be found especially in and around the town of Batu in the Tigon District of the Mambilla Division of Gongola State. They are a non-Bantu* people who speak a Bantoid language and are classified with the Tiv*-Bantu group of languages.
REFERENCE: *Language Survey of Nigeria.* 1976.

BATUMA. *See* KURI.

BATUMBUKA. *See* TUMBUKA.

BATURI. The Baturis are one of the two primary subgroups of the Zanaki* people of Tanzania.

BATUTSI. *See* TUTSI.

BATWA. *See* TWA.

BAUCI. *See* BAUSHI.

BAULE. The Baule (Bawle, Baoulé, Ton, Kotoko, Baba, and Po) are a Twi*-speaking group whose Akan* language is part of the Kwa* branch of the Niger-Congo language family. Their population exceeds 1.5 million people and is concentrated in central Ivory Coast, between the Comoé and Bandama rivers. They are one of the major ethnic groups and the most influential people in the country. The Baule are closely related to the Anyi* of Ivory Coast and Ghana. They practice farming and animal husbandry, and their system of social organization is matrilineal. They are subdivided into tribal groups. The Baule are primarily Christians and animists. About 2 percent of them are Sunni Muslims of the Maliki and Shafi schools. Syncretic systems are common among all of their religions. They strongly resisted colonial rule. Since the British* and French* conquests of Ghana, Togo, and Ivory Coast, the Baule have become increasingly Westernized and have viewed themselves as superior to surrounding, non-Akan peoples. Today they make their livings primarily as coffee and cocoa planters.

REFERENCES: Cyprien Arbelbide. *Les Baoulés d'après leurs dictons et proverbes.* 1975; Vincent Guerry. *Life with the Baoule.* 1975.

BAUSHI. The Baushis, also known as the Baucis, Chonges, and Kushis, are an ethnic group living today in Nigeria. Their current population is approximately 10,000 people, and they can be found concentrated in the Kuta and Tegina districts of the Minna Division of Niger State. The Baushi language is part of the Kamuku*-Bassa* group of languages in the Benue-Congo family.
REFERENCE: *Language Survey of Nigeria.* 1976.

BAVARMA. The Bavarmas are a subgroup of the Eshira* peoples of Gabon. They are concentrated along the Gabonese coast, where they live as farmers and fishermen. The Bavarma population today exceeds 20,000 people.

BAVENDA. *See* VENDA.

BAVEYA. The Baveyas are a subgroup of the Okandé* peoples living today in central Gabon in West Africa. Their homeland is a heavily forested region, where they fish and farm. The Baveya population today is perhaps 3,000 people.

BAVOUMBOU. *See* WOUMBOU.

BAVOUNGOU. *See* WOUMBOU.

BAVUMBU. *See* WOUMBOU.

BAWANDJI. The Bawandjis are a subgroup of the Mbete* people of southeastern Gabon and Congo. The Bawandji population today is approximately 20,000 people, most of whom are small farmers.

BAWLE. *See* BAULE.

BAYA. *See* GBAYA.

BAYAKA. *See* AKA and PYGMY.

BAYAKA. *See* BAPOUNOU.

BAYANG. The Bayang (Banyang) are the major ethnic group in the Manyu Division of Cameroon, particularly near the town of Mamfe in South

West Province and across the border in Nigeria. Most of them live in the upper Cross River, which flows into Nigeria. The Bayang are closely related to similar groups in Nigeria. Most Bayang are small farmers engaged in the production of rice, coffee, fruits, palm oil plants, and rubber, as well as cassava as a staple; there are also substantial numbers of craftsmen, small businessmen, and professionals among them. They are divided into fourteen clans, with political authority decentralized at the village level. After years of resistance, the Bayangs fell under German* control in 1909. The Bayang tend to be a well-educated people and very influential in South West Province. Among the most politically powerful Bayang in Cameroon in recent years are Emmanuel Egbe-Tabi, W. N. O. Effiom, M. T. Kima, and S. E. Ncha.
REFERENCE: Mark DeLancey and H. M. Mokeba. *Historical Dictionary of the Republic of Cameroon.* 1990.

BAYEI. *See* YEI.

BAYELE. The Bayeles are a Pygmy* group in Equatorial Guinea who speak a Bujeba* dialect. They are located on the banks of the Río Campo River in northwestern and northeastern Río Muni. In Cameroon, the Bayeles are known as the Gelli.* They call themselves the Bakos.

BAYOT. The Bayots (Baiotes) are a subgroup of the Jola* people of Senegal and Guinea-Bissau. Most Bayos live in the Ziguinchor region of Senegal and around the town of Suzanna in Guinea-Bissau. They are closely related to the Felupes.* Their economy revolves around the production of rice, at which they are highly skilled.

BAYSO. The Baysos are a tiny ethnic group living today in Ethiopia. They speak a Cushitic language, but, since their population is only 600 people, their survival as a conscious ethnic entity is threatened.
REFERENCE: M. L. Bender, J. D. Bowen, R. L. Cooper, and C. A. Ferguson, eds. *Language in Ethiopia.* 1976.

BEAFADA. The Beafadas (Biafada) are one of the dominant ethnic groups in Guinea-Bissau. Their population exceeds 55,000 people, of whom 18,000 are Muslims. Historically, they earned reputations as slave traders who regularly raided coastal ethnic groups to supply slaves to Portuguese* and British* traders. They occupied the Gabu region until the fifteenth century, when Mandinka* expansion drove them toward the coast. The Beafadas violently resisted Portuguese colonial expansion, rising up in rebellion in 1880–1882, 1886, 1900, and 1907–1908. Today, most Beafadas live north of Bambadinca and near Fulacunda and Buba.
REFERENCES: Rosemary Galli. *Guinea-Bissau.* 1990; Richard Lobban and Joshua Forrest. *Historical Dictionary of the Republic of Guinea-Bissau.* 1988.

BEAKA. *See* AKA and PYGMY.

BECHEVE. *See* ICHEVE.

BEDDE. *See* BADE.

BEDE. *See* BADE.

BEDEIRIYA. The Bedeiriyas are one of the Arab* peoples of Sudan. They are part of the larger Kawahla* (Fezara) cluster of Arabic-speaking peoples in the country.

BEDIK. The Bediks are a small ethnic group living along both sides of the border between Guinea and Senegal. Ethnographers traditionally classify them as one of the Tenda* groups, which also includes the neighboring Koñagi,* Basari,* Badyaran,* and Boin* groups. They are slash-and-burn cultivators, who live in villages of from 100 to 500 people each. Their homeland is geographically isolated, so they are subsistence farmers who do not raise crops for market. REFERENCES: Andrew Francis Clark and Lucie Colvin Phillips. *Historical Dictionary of Senegal.* 1994; Jacques Gomila. *Les Bedik.* 1971; Riall W. Nolan. *Bassari Migrations: The Quiet Revolution.* 1986.

BEDJOND. The Bedjond, also known historically as the Mbayé*-Bédiondo and Nangda, are a subgroup of the Sara* people of southern Chad. Most of the more than 40,000 Bedjonds live in and around Bediondo. REFERENCE: Samuel Decalo. *Historical Dictionary of Chad.* 1987.

BEDOUIN. The term ''Bedouin'' is used to describe Arab* peoples whose lifestyle is built around nomadism. Bedouins live in desert regions where the land cannot support permanent settlements. They move constantly, living in tents and raising livestock—primarily donkeys, camels, horses, sheep, and goats. They also carry goods to settlements not connected by adequate roads. The Bedouins are subdivided into tribal groups, and those tribal groups are further subdivided into patrilineal family descent groups. The social structure is patrilineal, patrilocal, and patriarchal. To survive in their harsh world, the Bedouins have developed a culture that places a premium on discipline, group loyalty, and toughness.

BEFUN. *See* ABANYOM.

BEGA. *See* BEJA.

BEIGO. The Beigos are an ethnic group living today in Sudan. They are

part of the Darfur* cluster of peoples concentrated in far west-central Sudan, with some living across the border in Chad. The Beigos raise cattle and farm.
REFERENCE: Donald G. Morrison et al. *Black Africa: A Comparative Handbook.* 1989.

BEIR. The Beir peoples are a cultural and linguistic group of Nilotic* extraction. They are concentrated in a remote frontier region of Sudan and Ethiopia, near the town of Pibor, where they live close to the Sidamo* people. Included in the Beir grouping are the Dinkas* and Nuers.* The Beirs make their living working small farms and herding livestock.
REFERENCE: Carolyn Fluehr-Lobban, Richard A. Lobban, Jr., and John Obert Voll. *Historical Dictionary of Sudan.* 1992.

BEJA. The Beja (Bega) number almost two million people and constitute one of the major ethnic groups of Sudan, Eritrea, and western Ethiopia. Actually, their traditional homeland consists of approximately 110,000 square miles in eastern Sudan and another 20,000 in Eritrea, but the savage civil war in Eritrea in the 1970s and 1980s has driven most of the Eritrean Beja into Sudan. There are also tens of thousands of Beja living in southern Egypt. The Beja are divided into a number of groups and tribes, including the Bisharin,* Hadendowa,* Amarar,* Beni Amer,* Ababda,* Halanga,* Hassanab,* Artiqa,* Kumailab,* Shaiab,* Ashraf,* and Hamran.* The Beja language is one of the Northern Cushitic languages, except for the Beni Amer, a Beja subgroup who speak an Ethio-Semitic language. Those Beja living in the northern region make their living raising camels and sheep, as well as producing grains on a small scale; farther south, they also raise cattle. The Beja living in the Gash and Tokar deltas of the Barka River are commercial and subsistence farmers, raising cotton and grain. Sorghum is the principal grain crop. Less than 10 percent of the Beja have moved to the major cities of the region, particularly to Khartoum, Port Sudan, and Kassala. They are employed primarily by the railroads and on the docks.

The Beja are Muslims, although the pastoral Beja are somewhat perfunctory in their religious devotions. Their indigenous, animistic traditions still have a powerful hold on the people. Rural Beja are characterized by their large crown of curly hair, complete with long ringlets hanging down from the head. The semi-nomadic pastoral herders live in portable, rectangular goat-skin houses, while the sedentary Beja live in permanent, mud-walled homes. In recent years, the Beja have become increasingly integrated into a cash economy, primarily because of the need to pay government taxes. Severe droughts have also damaged their herds of sheep, cattle, and camels, forcing increasingly large numbers of Beja to settle down into permanent farming communities. That process of permanent settlement has a political dimension as well, for more and more Beja are demanding political autonomy for Bejaland within Sudan. Those demands are expressed through a group known as the Beja Congress.
REFERENCES: S. A. el-Arifi. ''Pastoral Nomadism in the Sudan.'' *East African Geo-*

graphical Review 13 (1975): 89–103; Roushdi A. Henin. "Economic Development and Internal Migration in the Sudan." *Sudan Notes and Records* 44 (1963): 100–19; Andrew Paul. *A History of the Beja Tribes of the Sudan.* 1954.

BEKABURUM. *See* KABRÉ.

BEKÉ. *See* BAFIA.

BEKPAK. *See* BAFIA.

BEKWAI. The Bekwais are one of the primary subdivisions of the Asante* people of Ghana.

BEKWARRA. The Bekwarras, also known as the Bekworras and the Yakoros, are an ethnic group living today in Nigeria. They are concentrated demographically in the Ogoja Division of Cross River State. The Bekwarras speak a language that is closely related to the Bendi group of languages in the Benue-Congo family. The Bekwarra population today exceeds 140,000 people.
REFERENCE: *Language Survey of Nigeria.* 1976.

BEKWORRA. *See* BEKWARRA.

BELEGETE. *See* EVANT.

BELEN. *See* BILIN.

BELGIAN. Several thousand ethnic Belgians live in Africa today. During the nineteenth century, King Leopold II of Belgium gained a foothold in what became known as the Congo Free State (Zaire) in south-central Africa. After World War I, when the Allied powers dismembered the German Empire, Belgium was given control over German East Africa (Rwanda-Burundi) as well. All three countries—Zaire, Rwanda, and Burundi—secured their independence in the 1960s, but thousands of ethnic Belgians decided to continue living there. Their descendants and other Belgians now live in those regions of Central and East Africa, where they are concentrated in professional and business concerns.
REFERENCE: James S. Olson. *Historical Dictionary of European Imperialism.* 1991.

BELLA. The Bellas (Bellahs) are a unique ethnic group living today in Burkina-Faso and Niger. Most Bellas make their living as nomadic herdsmen, grazing their cattle in the Béli River area. For centuries, they have functioned as serfs to the more dominant Tuareg* people, among whom they live in the region.
REFERENCES: Samuel Decalo. *Historical Dictionary of Niger.* 1989; Daniel M. McFarland. *Historical Dictionary of Upper Volta.* 1978.

BELLAH. *See* BELLA.

BELLE. *See* KUWAA.

BELLERAMA. *See* KURI.

BEMBA. The Bemba (Awemba, Wemba, Babemba) are one of the largest ethnic groups in Zambia. They are concentrated in the northeastern section of the country and total more than 900,000 people today. They can also be found in southeastern Zaire, with some in Tanzania. They live west of Lake Tanganyika and Lake Mwero. Included in the Bemba cluster of peoples are two other ethnic groups: the Hembas* and the Katangas.* The Bemba language is part of the Bantu* language family, and it is understood throughout Zambia. The Bemba believe they originated in the Katanga region of contemporary Zaire and migrated to Zambia. Their ancestors are the same as those of the Luba* and Lunda* peoples. During the nineteenth century, the Bemba established centralized political control over a large part of Zambia. They are a farming people. Traditionally, because of the poor soil in the region, they relocated their villages every four or five years, but modern fertilizers and crop rotation methods have allowed them to become quite sedentary. They raise maize and millet as staples and cotton as a cash crop. Large numbers of Bemba men also work in the Copperbelt as miners. The Bemba language is a rich one, with its own literature; its best-known writer is Stephen Mpashi. The Bemba are active in interest group politics and played a paramount role in the Zambian independence movement.
REFERENCES: *African Encyclopedia.* 1974; F. Scott Bobb. *Historical Dictionary of Zaire.* 1988; John J. Grotpeter. *Historical Dictionary of Zambia.* 1979; Irving Kaplan et al. *Zambia: A Country Study.* 1979.

BEMBE. The Bembe people, not to be confused with the Bembes* of far eastern Zaire, are one of the subgroups of the Kongo* peoples of Congo, Zaire, and Angola. They are concentrated in southern Congo, northern Angola, and northwestern Zaire. The more than 80,000 Bembes in Congo are concentrated near Mouyondzi in the Bouenza region.

BEMBE. The Bembes, not to be confused with the Kongo* Bembes* of northwestern Zaire and the Congo, are a relatively small ethnic group living in the highlands of eastern Zaire. They live on the northwestern shore of Lake Tanganyika, just south of the Furiiru near the Burundi border. Because of their highland location, the Bembes are able to raise cattle for meat and milk. They also fish the lake and plant small farms.
REFERENCE: Irving Kaplan et al. *Zaire: A Country Study.* 1978.

BEMBO-NGUNI. The Bembo-Ngunis (Embo-Ngunis) are the Northern Nguni* peoples of southern Africa. The Bembo-Ngunis lived for several centuries between Delagoa Bay and the Lubombo Mountains. They gave rise to the Swazi* peoples.

BEMDZABUKO. The Bemdzabukos (Bomdzabukos) constitute one of the major subgroups of the Swazi* people of southern Africa. They consider themselves to be "pure Swazi." The Bemdzabukos are themselves subdivided into the following clans: Mhlanga, Madonsela, Mavuso, Fakude, Hlophe, Mabuza, Simelane, Matsebula, Twala, Ngwenya, Sihlongonyane, Nkonyane, and Manana.
REFERENCE: John J. Grotpeter. *Historical Dictionary of Swaziland.* 1975.

BEN. *See* BENG.

BEN WAIL. The Ben Wails are a subgroup of the Hassaunas,* a large group of ethnic Arabs* living today in Chad.

BENA. *See* YUNGUR.

BENA. The Benas are an ethnic group in Tanzania. Their original tribal homeland was the Iringa Plateau, but, because of increasingly violent feuds with the Hehes,* one group of Benas migrated to the Ulanga Plains. Today, the Benas make their living with mixed agriculture, fishing, and cattle-raising. Some ethnologists include the Sowes* and the Vembas* in the Bena group of peoples. The Bena population today stands at approximately 500,000 people.
REFERENCE: Laura Kurtz. *Historical Dictionary of Tanzania.* 1978.

BENDE. The Bendes are an ethnic group living today in western Tanzania. Most of them are Christians. The Bendes live between Lake Tanganyika and Lake Bukwa. Their population today exceeds 150,000 people, most of whom are farmers raising millet, wheat, coffee, and fruits. They also eat fish from the lakes.
REFERENCE: Laura Kurtz. *Historical Dictionary of Tanzania.* 1978.

BENG. The Beng, also known as the Ben, Ngan, Gan, Nguin, and Ngen, today number approximately 20,000 people and live in Ivory Coast and Burkina-Faso. They speak a language that is part of the Southern Mandé group of the Manding* language family. Most of them live in the subprefecture of M'Bahiakro. The Beng were driven to their present location by the expansion of the Mandinkas* and Akans.* Although the Beng were traditionally hunter-gatherers with some subsistence farming, they have made the transition in the last several decades to commercial agriculture, centered on the production of coffee, rice, and cocoa. Their two groups are separated primarily by geography, with one group living on the savanna and the other in the forest. The Beng maintain strong ties to their indigenous religion, which revolves around the worship of nature, forest ghosts, and ancestors. Some ethnologists consider them a subgroup of the Lobi* people. In recent years, many Beng have converted to Catholicism and Islam.

REFERENCES: Alma Gottlieb. "Cousin Marriage, Birth Order, and Gender: Alliance Models among the Beng of Ivory Coast." *Man* 21 (1987); Alma Gottlieb. "Dog: Ally or Traitor? Mythology, Cosmology, and Society among the Beng of Ivory Coast." *American Ethnologist* 13 (1986): 477–88; Robert J. Mundt. *Historical Dictionary of Côte d'Ivoire.* 1995.

BENGA. The Benga (Bonkoro) are an ethnic group living near Cape Esterias on the northern Atlantic coast of Gabon. They were originally Bakotas.* In the nineteenth century, when the Bakotas fled Fang* expansion, some of them headed west instead of south and east, and the western Bakotas became known as the Benga. Some Benga live on Corsica Island and the coast of Equatorial Guinea. They are part of a larger group of Ndowe* peoples. The Benga became important middlemen in the French* ivory and redwood trade. During the later nineteenth century, Protestant and Roman Catholic missionaries worked with the Benga, but Benga traditionalists eventually saw to their expulsion. The most prominent twentieth-century Bengan in Gabon was François-de-Paul Vané, a prominent Benga nationalist in the 1920s and 1930s. Most Benga today make their living as fishermen.

REFERENCE: David E. Gardinier. *Historical Dictionary of Gabon.* 1994.

BENGA. *See* BANGA.

BENI. The Benis are a subgroup of the Nupe* peoples of Niger State in Nigeria.

BENI AMER. The Beni Amer of Sudan are one of the primary subgroups of the Beja* peoples. Their population today approaches 300,000 people, and they are concentrated in eastern Sudan and northwestern Ethiopia. The Beni Amer living in the northern region of Beni Amer territory have traditionally been camel pastoralists, while the Beni Amer living to the south and east are more likely to raise cattle. Because of the endemic political instability in the area during the last two decades, the Beni Amer living in Eritrea have slowly migrated west with their herds into Sudan. Because of the introduction of a cash economy among them, as well as the expansion of a market system, increasing numbers of Beni Amer in recent years have taken up subsistence agriculture, commercial agriculture, and wage labor in the towns and cities.

The Beni Amer social structure is highly stratified. At the top of the social structure are an elite group who call themselves "true Beni Amer"—or Nabtab. They number approximately 40,000 people and control political and economic decision-making among the entire Beni Amer community. The rest of the population, who constitute a subservient group, are called the Tigre,* or Hedarab.

Although the British* officially abolished such rigid categories in political terms in 1948, the system survived their ban and became part of the system in independent Sudan. It is essentially a feudal system of power. The Beni Amer are also subdivided into hundreds of different groups based on systems of lineage and family loyalties. They are also divided linguistically. The Beni Amer living toward the north are more likely to speak To Bedawie, which is a Cushitic language, as well as some Tigre, which is a Semitic language. The Beni Amer to the south near Kassala and Eritrea are Tigre speakers as well. Arabic is considered a lingua franca in the region.

The Beni Amer are Sunni Muslims, but their conversion is a relatively recent phenomenon. In the nineteenth century, the Arab* missionary Sayyid Muhammed Uthman al-Mirghani brought Islam to the Sudan, and today the vast majority of the Beni Amer are loyal to the Khatmiyya branch of the Muslim Sufi order. During the past several decades, Beni Amir religious practices have become increasingly orthodox in terms of Muslim values.

REFERENCES: Andrew Paul. *A History of the Beja Tribes of the Sudan.* 1954; Andrew Paul. "Notes on the Beni Amer." *Sudan Notes and Records* 31 (1950): 223–45; C. G. Seligman. "Notes on the History and Present Condition of the Beni Amer." *Sudan Notes and Records* 13 (1930): 83–97.

BENI RASHID. *See* BAGGARA.

BENI SHANGUL. The Beni Shanguls (Bani Shanguls) are a subgroup of the Berti* people of Ethiopia. They live in the district of Welega, near the Sudanese border. The Beni Shanguls did not begin converting to Islam until the mid-nineteenth century, so a considerable number of pre-Islamic religious traditions and rituals survive among them. They are a Nilotic* people who have experienced a history of being enslaved by other groups.

BENIM. *See* EDO.

BENU. The Benus are a subgroup of the Nupe* peoples of Niger State in Nigeria.

BERBA. The Berbas are a subgroup of the Somba* people of Benin and Togo. Their contemporary population is approximately 50,000 people, most of whom are farmers raising maize, millet, plantains, and cassava.

BERBER. The Berbers constitute a large ethnic group of more than fifteen million people who live in North Africa, the Sahara Desert, and the Sahel region of West Africa. They have existed as an identifiable ethnic entity for thousands of years, long before Arabs* reached the region. They call themselves Imazighen, which means "free men." Overwhelmingly Muslim in their religious loyalties (Sunni rite and Maliki school), the Berbers are divided into hundreds of tribes, which themselves are subdivided into other groups. In the Western Sahara region of Morocco, the largest Berber group is the Reguibats.* The Ait Waryaghar* are the largest Berber group in Morocco, and the Berrabers* are the second largest. The southernmost of the Berber groups in Morocco is the Shluh.* Dark-skinned Harratine* constitute another Moroccan Berber people. The major Berber group in Algeria is the Kabyles.* The Mzabites* are another Berber people in Algeria. The only Berber group to be truly transnational today is the Tuaregs.* Berbers constitute 34 percent of the population of Morocco, 22 percent of Algeria, 20 percent of Mauritania, 8 percent of Niger, 6 percent of Mali, and 5 percent of Libya. Over the centuries, the Berbers have not developed a strong, centralized political identity, except for the short-lived Republic of the Rif in the 1920s. They have traditionally practiced a transhumant lifestyle, moving their livestock from range to range.

REFERENCES: Robert Montage. *The Berbers.* 1972; William Spencer. ''Berbers.'' In Richard V. Weekes, ed. *Muslim Peoples.* 1984.

BERI. The Beri (Kige) are a large ethnic group who live on the border of Chad and Sudan. They are divided into two basic subgroups—the Zaghawa* and the Bideyat—although both groups identify themselves as Beri. Their total population today exceeds 350,000 people, with the Zaghawa making up approximately 90 percent of that total. In Chad, more than 50,000 of the Zaghawas live in northeastern Wadai Province. They are also present across the border in Darfur Province of Sudan. The Zaghawas are further subdivided into several clans with powerful ethnic identities: Artaj (Unay), Gala, Gurut, Dirong, Kabka, Kigé, Kobé, and Tuer. The Bideyat live north of the Zaghawa in the Ennedi hills of Chad. They are further subdivided into the Borogat to the west and the Bilia to the east. Although most linguists classify the Beri languages with the Saharan branch of the Nilo-Saharan group, others believe that it is Chadic in origin. They are closely related to the Tebu* peoples of the Sahel and Sahara.

In recent decades, the Beri economy has become increasingly complex. For centuries, the Beri were nomadic livestock herders, raising camel, cattle, and sheep, and those pursuits are still central to the lifestyles of many Beri. But today, there are large numbers of Beri who are settled farmers, raising millet, while others are merchants, who trade livestock for manufactured goods. Because of increasing numbers of government jobs and the growing amount of wage labor, the Beri find themselves drawn more and more into a money economy.

Before the arrival of Islam in the seventeenth century, Beri society revolved around clan social systems and a religion oriented toward the god Iru. Islam first reached the Zaghawas in Sudan; there it took deep root and later spread into other Beri groups in Chad. Islam has eroded the power of the clan system, as did the presence of British* political power in Sudan and French* power in Chad. Since the end of the colonial period, more centralized political institutions

in independent Chad and independent Sudan have continued the erosion of clan power.
REFERENCES: H. G. Balfour-Paul. ''A Prehistoric Cult Still Practised in Muslim Darfur.'' *Journal of the Royal Anthropological Institute of Great Britain and Ireland* 86 (1956): 77–86; Marie-José Tubiana. *The Zaghawa from an Ecological Perspective.* 1977.

BERIBERI. *See* KANURI.

BEROM. *See* BIROM.

BERRABER. The Berrabers are one of the main Berber* groups of Morocco. They speak the Taberberit dialect of Tamazight and practice transhumant patterns of livestock production. They also have permanent, fortified villages with communal granaries.

BERTA. *See* BERTI.

BERTI. The Berti are an ethnic group scattered around Sudan and southwestern Ethiopia. A remnant of the Garamantes people, they are closely related to the Zaghawas* and Bideyats. Some ethnologists consider them to be part of the cluster of Shilluk* peoples. Their population today probably exceeds 100,000 people, with the two largest groups concentrated in the Tagabo Hills of northern Darfur Province and in and around Um Keddada and Taweisha in eastern Darfur. Smaller clusters of Berti can be found in El Fasher, Gedaref, Um Ruwaba, and Jazira. The original Berti language was closely related to Zaghawa of the Beris,* but it has died out, being replaced during the twentieth century by Arabic. The Berti live in small, sedentary villages of no more than 100 people and make their living raising millet, sorghum, peanuts, okra, sesame, watermelons, cucumbers, and pumpkins. The Berti living near Taweisha in eastern Darfur Province raise cattle, goats, sheep, and sometimes donkeys, camels, and horses. Because of changing economic patterns in recent years, more and more Berti young men travel seasonally to Libya in search of wage labor jobs. The Berti are Sunni Muslims, but their devotions are lukewarm, at least when compared with many other Muslim groups. They also practice *karama*—the sacrifice of a bull, goat, or lamb to ward off evil or to bring rain and a good harvest. Political power among the Berti was once exercised by *omdas* (or chiefs), but, in recent decades, the Sudanese government has imposed a series of village, division, and regional councils. The *omdas,* however, are still recognized as important judicial officials.
REFERENCES: Carolyn Fluehr-Lobban, Richard A. Lobban, Jr., and John Obert Voll. *Historical Dictionary of Sudan.* 1992; L. T. Holy. *Neighbours and Kinsmen: A Study of the Berti Peoples of Darfur.* 1974; L. T. Holy, ''Gender and Ritual in an Islamic Society: The Berti of Darfur.'' *Man* 23 (September 1988): 469–87.

BERUM. *See* BIROM.

BESOM. The Besoms are a subgroup of the Sanga* peoples.

BET GABRA TARQWE. *See* BILIN.

BET TARQWE. *See* BILIN.

BETA ISRAEL. The Beta Israels, known pejoratively as the Falasha (Felasha) or Kaylas, are Ethiopian Jews. The term ''Falasha'' means ''Black Jews,'' but the Beta Israels consider it a racist reference to them. They call themselves the Bete Israel (House of Israel). Most of them speak Amharic as their first language. In the fifteenth century, when they refused to convert to Christianity, the Amharas* deprived them of their land, so the Beta Israels became craftsmen instead. Their current population is approximately 35,000 people, and they live in the mountains and highlands north of Lake Tana near Gonder in Begemder Province, Ethiopia. They are closely related to the neighboring Agaw* peoples. They are despised by the dominant Amhara people of Ethiopia, and, in the 1980s, a considerable number of Beta Israels emigrated to Israel.
REFERENCE: James Quirin. *The Evolution of Ethiopian Jews: A History of the Beta Israel (Falasha) to 1920.* 1992.

BETANIMENA. The Betanimenas are a subgroup of the Betsimisaraka* people of the eastern coast of Madagascar.

BÉTÉ. The Bétés, also known as the Magwe, Tsien, Bokya, and Kpwe, are an ethnic group in Ivory Coast. They should not be confused with the Bete people of Gongola State in Nigeria. They speak a Kru* language and live in nearly a thousand villages in the region of Saloa, Soubre, and Gagnoa. Their own traditions have them migrating to the region from the west and pushing out the Gagus,* Didas,* and Guros living there. In the nineteenth century, the Bétés resisted the expansion of both the French* commercial economy and the French colonial administration, rebelling for the last time in 1906. Under French tutelage, they then abandoned hunting and gathering for cocoa and coffee farming. In recent years, there has been a substantial migration of Julas* to Bété territory, and many Bétés have migrated to Abidjan. The Bété population today exceeds 600,000 people. Included in the Bété cluster of peoples are the Krus, Didas, Guérés,* Wobés,* Godies,* and Neyos.*
REFERENCES: J. P. Dozon. *Ethnicité et histoire: Productions et métamorphoses sociales chez les Bété de Côte d'Ivoire.* 1981; Robert J. Mundt. *Historical Dictionary of Côte d'Ivoire.* 1995.

BETE. The Betes are a tiny, nearly extinct, ethnic group living today in

Nigeria. Their survivors can be found in Bete town in the Ayikiben District of the Wukavi Division of Gongola State.
REFERENCE: *Language Survey of Nigeria.* 1976.

BETE-BENDI. *See* BETTE-BENDI.

BETI. The Betis believe that they originated farther north and migrated to central and southern Cameroon in the nineteenth century with some of the Fang,* to whom they are closely related. The Bulus,* Banes,* Etons,* and Ewondos* are all subgroups of the Betis. Most Betis live in the Mfoundi, Lekie, Mfou, Nyong So, and Ocean divisions of Centre Province. Today, most Betis are farmers, raising a variety of crops to eat as well as cocoa for sale and export. But large numbers of Betis have also become urbanized—living, working, and going to school in such cities as Yaoundé, Douala, and Mbalmayo. Their population today exceeds 800,000 people. Well-educated and predominantly Roman Catholics (because of their close association with the French* colonial administration), the Betis play an unusually large role in the politics, administration, and educational life of Cameroon. The best known member of the Beti group is the writer Mongo Beti.
REFERENCE: *African Encyclopedia.* 1974.

BETSILEO. The Betsileos are an ethnic group living today in Madagascar. Like the Merinas,* with whom they share many cultural elements, the Betsileos live in the Central Highlands of the island. Their current population exceeds 1.3 million people, and they are divided into four main subgroups: Arindranos, Halanginas, Isandras, and Manadrianas. Most of them are farmers, known for their skill at growing rice in irrigated, terraced fields. In the poorest of soils, they raise cassava. In recent years, increasing numbers of Betsileos have taken to seasonal migration, to work for cash on other farms or in towns and cities. Like the Merinas, they are relatively well-educated and can be found working in government service as well.
REFERENCES: Maureen Covell. *Madagascar: Politics, Economics and Society.* 1987; Harold D. Nelson et al. *Area Handbook for the Malagasy Republic.* 1973.

BETSIMISARAKA. The Betsimisarakas are a large ethnic group living today in Madagascar. With a population of more than 1.5 million people, they are the second largest group on the island. The Betsimisarakas are subdivided into two primary groups—the Betsimisarakas proper and the Betanmenas. They are concentrated in a 400-mile-long belt along the east coast, from the Bay of Antongil in the north to the Manjary River in the south. Betsimisaraka farmers raise coffee and cloves for cash crops, while large numbers of them can also be found working on nearby coffee and vanilla plantations and in graphite mines.

REFERENCES: Maureen Covell. *Madagascar: Politics, Economics and Society.* 1987; Harold D. Nelson et al. *Area Handbook for the Malagasy Republic.* 1973.

BETTE-BENDI. The Bette-Bendis, also known as the Bete-Demdis and the Damas, are an ethnic group living today in Nigeria. They are concentrated in the Obudu Division of Cross River State, where their population exceeds 140,000 people. Most Bette-Bendis are subsistence farmers. Their language is part of the Bendi* group of the Cross River family of Benue-Congo languages. REFERENCE: *Language Survey of Nigeria.* 1976.

BÉTTIÉ. The Béttiés are a subgroup of the Anyis* of Ivory Coast. The Béttiés are overwhelmingly Christian in their religious persuasions.

BEZANOZANO. The Bezanozanos are an ethnic group of Madagascar. Their current population exceeds 100,000 people, most of whom live in the upper and middle Mangoro River Valley between the Merinas* and the Betsimisarakas.* The Merinas conquered them in the eighteenth century. Today they live in close proximity to the Betsimisarakas in Tamatave Province. They raise goats, cattle, and rice.
REFERENCES: Maureen Covell. *Madagascar: Politics, Economics and Society.* 1987; Harold D. Nelson et al. *Area Handbook for the Malagasy Republic.* 1973.

BHEMBE. The Bhembes are one of the clans of the Emakhandzambili,* who themselves are one of the three major subgroups of the Swazi* people of Swaziland.

BIAFADA. *See* BEAFADA.

BIAKA. *See* AKA and PYGMY.

BICHIWA. *See* CHIWA.

BIDEYAT. *See* BERI.

BIDIO. The Bidios (Bidyo) are an ethnic group living in close proximity to the Kinga* people of Chad. Casual observers consider them a Kinga subgroup, although their language is quite distinct. Like Kinga, however, the Bidio language is related to Barma.* The Bidios live in the Hadjeray region of Chad. Their current population exceeds 20,000 people, most of whom make their living as small farmers and by extracting gum arabic from acacia trees.
REFERENCE: Samuel Decalo. *Historical Dictionary of Chad.* 1987.

BIDYO. *See* BIDIO.

BIE. The Bies (Viye, Bihe) are one of the traditional, autonomous kingdoms and contemporary ethnic subgroups of the Ovimbundu* people of Angola.

BIHE. *See* BIE.

BIJAGÓ. The Bijagós—known also as the Bissagos, Bojagos, and Bujagos—are an ethnic group living in Guinea-Bissau. They are concentrated on the islands of the Atlantic Coast; as a result, they have traditionally resented all centralized authority, whether Portuguese,* French,* or contemporary government officials. In 1447, when the Portuguese explorer, Nuno Tristão, tried to conquer the Bijagós, they killed him. The Bijagós rose up in rebellion against the Portuguese in 1900, 1906, 1913–1915, 1917, 1918, 1924, and 1936. Portugal did not consider the Bijagós pacified until 1936. In terms of religion, most Bijagós remain loyal to animist traditions. They have traditionally made their living by farming, fishing, and raiding the settlements of coastal peoples in Guinea-Bissau. They were among the most notorious slave traders in the country, primarily because of their legendary large, ocean-going canoes that were capable of holding up to seventy people. Today, their economy revolves around fishing and the production of palm products.
REFERENCES: Rosemary Galli. *Guinea-Bissau.* 1990; Robert C. Helmholz. "Traditional Bijagó Statuary." *African Arts* 6 (Autumn 1972): 52–57; Richard Lobban and Joshua Forrest. *Historical Dictionary of the Republic of Guinea-Bissau.* 1988.

BILALA. *See* BULALA.

BILE. The Biles (Billes) are an ethnic group living today in Nigeria. They are concentrated in the Degema Local Government Area of River State. They can also be found in the Batta District of the Numan Division in Gongola State. The Biles are part of the larger Ijaw* cluster of peoples. Most of them are subsistence farmers.

BILEN. *See* BILIN.

BILIN. The Bilin (Belen, Bogo) are a people whose homeland for centuries was the Keren region of Eritrea and in Tigray Province, Ethiopia. In recent decades, however, because of savage civil wars and famine in the region, the Bilin, who number approximately 65,000 people, are scattered throughout Eritrea and live in refugee camps in Sudan. They call themselves Bilin and sometimes use the name Gabra Tarqwe Qur. They are a division of the Agaw* people and speak a Central Cushitic language. More than two-thirds of the Bilin are Muslims, while the remainder are Christians—primarily Roman Catholic, but also small groups of Protestants and Ethiopian Orthodox. Their homeland is a high plateau ranging from 3,000 to 6,000 feet in altitude. The Bilin are divided into several subgroups. The largest of these subgroups is the Bet Gabra Tarqwe; they live in the southern portion of the Bilin region. The second group is the Bet Tarqwe, who live in the north. The third, though much smaller group, is the Ban Janjeren, who are being assimilated by the Bet Tarqwe. Each Bilin subgroup is also divided into lineages and sublineages, which are known as *hassat;* each *hassat* has its own territory and hereditary chief. The Bilin are a sedentary people who raise sorghum, barley, maize, wheat, and legumes; they also maintain cattle, goats, camels, and donkeys.

The Bilin homeland was an isolated part of Africa until the completion of the Suez Canal in 1869. England, France, and Italy all competed for power in the region. In the 1930s, Italy employed Bilin troops in its invasion of Ethiopia, but British and Ethiopian forces expelled them from Ethiopia in 1941. Eritrea was attached to Ethiopia in 1952 under a United Nations order, and, in 1962, Ethiopia annexed Eritrea. Until Eritrea achieved independence in 1993, separatist movements in Eritrea have conducted bloody guerrilla campaigns against Ethiopia. During two decades of intermittent warfare, as many as one-half of all Bilin in Eritrea have been displaced and scattered.

REFERENCES: Basil Davidson, Lionel Cliff, and Bereket Selassie. *Behind the War in Eritrea.* 1980; Robert Hertzon. "The Agaw Languages." *Afroasiatic Languages* 3 (1976): 31–45; Werner Munzinger. *On the Customs and Laws of the Bogos.* 1859; Siegfried Nadel. *Races and Tribes of Eritea.* 1944.

BILIRI. *See* TANGALE.

BILLE. *See* BILE.

BIMAL. The Bimals are the largest subclan of the Dir* clan of the Somali* people. Since late in the seventeenth century, they have occupied the town of Merca and its surrounding region. They are primarily pastoralists, although many of them living in the lower Shebelle area are farmers. They also became successful merchants and traders in the nineteenth century, acting as middlemen for interior traders marketing ivory, hides, skins, horses, and slaves. Over the years, they have engaged repeatedly in wars with the Geledi* clan. During the early 1900s, the Bimals violently resisted the imposition of Italian* control over their homeland.

REFERENCE: Margaret Castagno. *Historical Dictionary of Somalia.* 1975.

BIMAWBA. *See* BIMOBA.

BIMOBA. The Bimoba people—also known historically as the Bimawba, B'Moba, Moba, Moare, Mwan, and Moab—are part of the Gurma* cluster of peoples in Ghana and Togo. The Bimoba are one of the Sudanic peoples who live in northern Togo, primarily in the mountainous zone of the Dapango region, as well as west of Sansanne-Mango, in the Northern Region of

Ghana. They are animist in their religious loyalties and make their livings by herding cattle or camels and by subsistence agriculture. Their language is a dialect of Gurma, closely related to the language of the Mossi* in Burkina-Faso. The current Bimoba population exceeds 125,000 people.

REFERENCES: Samuel Decalo. *Historical Dictionary of Togo.* 1976; Daniel M. McFarland. *Historical Dictionary of Ghana.* 1995.

BINAWA. The Binawas, also known as the Bogonas, are a small ethnic group living in Lere District of Saminaka Division of Kaduna State. Their language is part of the Western Plateau cluster of the Benue-Congo family.

REFERENCE: *Language Survey of Nigeria.* 1976.

BINGA. The Western cluster of Pygmies* are sometimes known as the Binga (Babinga, Babenga, Bambenga). They number approximately 35,000 people and live in the northeastern reaches of Congo Republic, southwestern Central African Republic, southern Cameroon, parts of Gabon, and across the Ubangi River in Zaire.

BINI. The Binis, not to be confused with the Binis* of Ivory Coast, are one of the Edo*-speaking peoples of south-central Nigeria. Most Binis today can be found living in and around the cities of Benin, Ojogbo, and Eviakoi.

BINI. The Binis are a subgroup of the Anyis* of Ivory Coast. The Binis are overwhelmingly Christian in their religious persuasions.

BINJI. The Binjis (Mbagani) are one of the subgroups of the Luba* people of Zaire. They are part of the Luba-Kasai subcluster of the Lubas. The Binjis are divided into distinct northern and southern groups and live along the Lualaba River. They are highly decentralized politically.

BINNA. *See* YUNGUR.

BINZA. The Binzas are a small ethnic group in Zaire. They are concentrated north of the Lualaba River in north-central Zaire, south of the Uele River. The region in which they live is heavily forested, and the Binzas make their living raising cassava, bananas, and kolanuts. In recent years, increasing numbers of Binzas have left the forests for work in towns and cities, especially places like Yakoma and Bondo.

REFERENCE: Irving Kaplan et al. *Zaire: A Country Study.* 1978.

BIO/WOR. The Bio/Wors are one of the Bassa* clans living in the River Cess Territory of Liberia.

BIOKWIA. The Biokwias are one of the Bassa* clans living in the River Cess Territory of Liberia.

BIOTU. *See* ISOKO.

BIRA. The Biras are a small ethnic group living on the Ugandan-Zairean border. Most Biras make their living today as small farmers.
REFERENCE: Irving Kaplan et al. *Zaire: A Country Study.* 1978.

BIRI. The Biri people are part of the larger cluster of Azandé* peoples of Sudan.

BIRIFO. *See* BIRIFOR.

BIRIFOR. The Birifors are one of the ''stateless'' peoples who live in northern Ghana, southern Burkina-Faso, and Ivory Coast. They are animist in their religious loyalties and make their livings by herding cattle and by subsistence agriculture, raising millet. They speak one of the Molé-Dagbane* languages. Until 1957, they lived under the administration of what was known as the Northern Territories in the British Gold Coast colony. They are closely related to the Lobis* of Ivory Coast. Today they are concentrated around Namdom in the upper West Region of Ghana.

BIRKED. The Birkeds are a politically prominent ethnic group in Darfur Province of Sudan, with a smaller number of them living across the border in Chad, west of Dar Sila. They are a Nubian* subgroup. They are culturally indistinguishable from the Daju* and speak a language identical to that spoken by the Moubi.*
REFERENCE: Samuel Decalo. *Historical Dictionary of Chad.* 1987.

BIROM. The Biroms—Beroms, Berums, Boroms, Kibbos, Aboros, Gbangs, Afangos, Kibos, and Kibyens—are a people living today in the Jos Plateau of Plateau State of Nigeria. They are concentrated in the Fan, Ropp, Heipang, Riyom, Bachit, Foron, Kuru, Vwang, Du, Gyel, Jos, and Kabong districts of the Jos Division of Plateau State, as well as in the Jema'a District of the Jema'a Division of Kaduna State. The Birom population exceeds 150,000 people. They live in a series of villages where they have made the transition in recent decades to small farming. Hunting, however, has long been of religious and ritual significance to them. The consumption of meat and beer are considered among life's most important activities. Hunting tends to be a communal activity. Most Biroms are subsistence farmers, who produce maize, millet, beans, cassava, and pumpkins on small family plots and raise goats and sheep as well. They are subdivided into three regional identity groups: Western Biroms, Southern Biroms, and Eastern Biroms.

REFERENCES: Samuel Akbapot. "Random Music of Birom." *African Arts* 8 (Winter 1975): 46–47; Charles Meek. *The Northern Tribes of Nigeria.* 1969; *Language Survey of Nigeria.* 1976; Jean-Claude Muller. "Intertribal Hunting Among the Rukuba." *Ethnology* 21 (1982): 203–14.

BIRQID. *See* BIRKED.

BIRU. The Birus are one of the two primary subgroups of the Zanaki* people of Tanzania. See ZANAKI.

BIRWA. The Birwas (Babirwas) are a subgroup of the Tswana* peoples of Botswana, Zimbabwe, and Transvaal in South Africa. Their traditional homeland included the region of eastern Botswana, southwestern Zimbabwe, and northern Transvaal. During the late nineteenth and early twentieth centuries, the Birwas were incorporated in Ngwato state. Most Birwas today are farmers, cattle raisers, and day laborers. The Zimbabwe Birwas live around the Tull River in the southwestern part of the country.
REFERENCES: Fred Morton, A. Murray, and J. Ramsay. *Historical Dictionary of Botswana.* 1989; R. Kent Rasmussen. *Historical Dictionary of Zimbabwe.* 1994.

BISA. *See* BUSANSI.

BISA. The Bisa people of Zambia are part of the larger Bemba* cluster of peoples. With a contemporary population of approximately 140,000 people, the Bisas constitute one of the ten largest ethnic groups in the country. They are concentrated in the central region of east Zambia. The Bemba people conquered the Bisas in the nineteenth century and now live to the north of them. Until that time, the Bisas were a large, powerful people, heavily involved in the ivory, slave, and copper trades. They lost their power to a series of Bemba, Lunda,* and Ngoni* incursions. Today, most Bisas work as small farmers.
REFERENCE: John J. Grotpeter. *Historical Dictionary of Zambia.* 1979.

BISANO. *See* BUSANSI.

BISAPELE. *See* BUSANSI.

BISENI. The Bisenis are a subgroup of the Ijo peoples of Rivers State in Nigeria. *See* IJAW.

BISHARIN. The Bisharin are one of the major subgroups of the Beja* people of Sudan and Eritrea. They speak a Northern Cushitic language and live in a region of approximately 50,000 square miles. That homeland extends from between Mohammed Gol to the Egyptian border on the coast of the Red Sea, then west to the Nile River Valley, and south along the Atbara River Plain. The Bisharin divide themselves into two primary groups. The Um Ali* live in the steppes and deserts of the Atbai subregion, where they work primarily as camel raisers and herders. Two clans of the other group, the Um Nagi,* live close to the Um Ali and herd camels as well. The other clans of the Um Nagi herd camels, sheep, goats, and cattle and farm in the more arable lands south of Sidon.

The Bisharin are Muslims, although the pastoral Bisharin are somewhat perfunctory in their religious devotions. Their indigenous, animistic traditions still have a powerful hold on the people. Rural Bisharin are characterized by their large crown of curly hair, complete with long ringlets hanging down from the head. The semi-nomadic pastoral herders live in portable, rectangular, goat-skin houses, while the sedentary Bisharin live in permanent, mud-walled homes. In recent years, the Bisharin have become increasingly integrated into a cash economy, primarily because of the need to pay government taxes. Severe droughts have also damaged their herds of sheep, cattle, goats, and camels, forcing increasingly large numbers of Bisharin to settle down into permanent farming communities.

REFERENCES: Andrew Paul. *A History of the Beja Tribes of the Sudan.* 1954; S. A. el-Arifi. "Pastoral Nomadism in the Sudan." *East African Geographical Review* 13 (1975): 89–103; Roushdi A. Henin. "Economic Development and Internal Migration in the Sudan." *Sudan Notes and Records* 44 (1963): 100–119.

BISI. *See* PITI.

BISSA. *See* BUSANSI.

BISSAGO. *See* BIJAGÓ.

BITARE. The Bitare people, also known as the Njwandes or Yukutares, live in the Tigon District of the Mambilla Division of Gongola State in Nigeria, as well as across the border in far western Cameroon. Most of them are subsistence farmers who also raise livestock. Their language is part of the Tiv*-Batu* cluster of the Benue-Congo language family.

REFERENCE: *Language Survey of Nigeria.* 1976.

BI-TCHAMBÉ. *See* BASARI.

BITONGA. The Bitongas are one of the two subgroups of the Shope* people of Mozambique.

BLE. The Bles are a small ethnic group living in Blédougou village in the Sindou region of southwest Burkina-Faso. They are a Manding* subgroup who are primarily Muslims. They make their living as farmers, raising corn, rice, sweet potatoes, yams, and peanuts.

REFERENCE: Daniel M. McFarland. *Historical Dictionary of Upper Volta.* 1978.

B'MOBA. *See* BIMOBA.

BOA. The Boas are a very prominent ethnic group living today in Zaire. They are concentrated near Kisangani in Haut-Zaire. The Boas are a patrilineal group that is unusual because they maintain no clan loyalties. Although most Boas are farmers and herdsmen, they do enjoy a diverse economy, with significant numbers of Boas laboring as educated clerks and professionals in northeastern Zairean towns and cities.
REFERENCE: F. Scott Bobb. *Historical Dictionary of Zaire.* 1988.

BOBANGI. *See* BOUBANGUI.

BOBANGUI. *See* BOUBANGUI.

BOBO. At the dawn of the French* colonial period, the Bobo communities near present-day Bobo-Dioulasso, in northwestern Burkina-Faso and across the border in Mali, lived in large, densely settled villages that were loosely confederated by a warrior house but that remained autonomous in internal matters. The market economy changed their matrilineal collectivism. That process gained momentum after the completion of the railroad in Bobo country in 1934. The combined effects of taxation, forced labor, wage work, and a money economy broke the hold of matrilineal corporation elders and increasingly drew the heads of farm production groups into market transactions. Their population today exceeds 230,000 people, of whom nearly 50,000 are Muslims. The Bobos living in Mandiakuy *arrondissement* in Mali are Christians. Most Bobos, however, remain faithful to their traditional animist religion. The Bobos are divided into several subgroups, of which the Bobo-Fing and Bobo-Oulé are the most prominent. The Bobo-Fing (Boua), or "Black Bobo," are concentrated in Burkina-Faso. Also in Burkina-Faso are the Bobo Gbé or Kian (Tian). The Bobo-Oulé (Tara), or "Red Bobo," are primarily in Mali. Very closely related are the Jola Bobo, Niénigé, and Lilas (Kadenba).
REFERENCES: Makir Saul. "Matrilineal Inheritance and Post-Colonial Prosperity in Southern Bobo Country." *Man* 27 (June 1992): 341–67; Makir Saul. "Corporate Authority, Exchange, and Personal Opposition in Bobo Marriages." *American Ethnology* 16 (1989): 58–76.

BOBO-FING. *See* BOBO.

BOBO-GBÉ. *See* BOBO.

BOBO-OULÉ. *See* BOBO.

BODI. The Bodis are a small ethnic group living today in Ethiopia. The Bodis speak a Nilo-Saharan language and live in close proximity to Omotic* peoples. They are primarily plow agriculturalists who also raise cattle. Most of them live in far southwestern Ethiopia.
REFERENCE: Harold D. Nelson et al. *Ethiopia: A Country Study.* 1980.

BODIMAN. The Bodimans are a small Cameroonian ethnic group. Most of them make their living as small farmers, urban and town workers, civil servants, and businessmen. Because of their location on the Atlantic coast, the Bodimans had early contact with German* and British* commercial interests, which gave them access to economic opportunity and education.
REFERENCE: Harold D. Nelson et al. *Area Handbook for the United Republic of Cameroon,* 1974.

BOE-GLYN. The Boe-Glyns are a subgroup of the Bassa* people of Liberia. Most Boe-Glyns live in Grand Bassa County.

BOEM. *See* BUEM.

BOENI. The Boenis are one of the subgroups of the Tenda* people of Guinea. Most Boenis were formerly Basaris* who converted to Islam.

BOFFI. The Boffi are a small ethnic group located in the Boda subprefecture of the Central African Republic.
REFERENCE: Pierre Kalck. *Historical Dictionary of the Central African Republic.* 1992.

BOGGHOM. *See* BOGHOM.

BOGHOM. The Boghoms—Buroms, Burrums, Burmas, Borroms, Boghoroms, Bogghoms, Bohoms, Bokhiyims—are an ethnic group living today in Nigeria. They are concentrated in the Kanam, Wase, and Yergam districts of the Langtang Division in Plateau State. They speak a Chadic language that is closely related to that of the neighboring Ron* peoples. They raise livestock, with some subsistence farming, to support themselves.
REFERENCE: *Language Survey of Nigeria.* 1976.

BOGHOROM. *See* BOGHOM.

BOGO. *See* BILIN.

BOGONA. *See* BINAWA.

BOGUNG. *See* BARIBA.

BOHOM. *See* BOGHOM.

BOIN. The Boins are a small ethnic group living along both sides of the border between Guinea and Senegal. Ethnographers traditionally classify them as one of the Tenda* groups, which also includes the neighboring Koñagis,* Basaris,* Bediks,* and Badyarans.* They are slash-and-burn cultivators who live in villages of from 100 to 500 people each; because of their geographical isolation, the Boins do not really participate in a cash economy.
REFERENCES: Andrew F. Clark and Lucie Colvin Phillips. *Historical Dictionary of Senegal.* 1994; Riall W. Nolan. *Bassari Migrations: The Quiet Revolution.* 1986.

BOJAGO. *See* BIJAGÓ.

BOKHIYIM. *See* BOGHOM.

BOKI. The Bokis are an ethnic group living today in southern Cross River State in Nigeria, as well as across the border in western Cameroon. They are closely related to the Efiks* and Ibibios.* The Boki language is of Bantu* origins. Most Boki farmers raise yams and palm oil. Large numbers of them also work in Nigerian cities. The Boki population today exceeds 350,000 people. *See* BOKYI.
REFERENCE: Donald G. Morrison et al. *Black Africa: A Comparative Handbook.* 1989.

BOKKO. *See* BOKO.

BOKO. The Boko (Bokko) people today are scattered throughout the Borgou Region of northeastern Benin and western Nigeria. In Nigeria, they can be found especially in the Ron, North Sura, and South Sura districts of the Pankshin Division of Plateau State. They speak a Manding* dialect and were historically absorbed culturally by the far more numerous Bariba* people. In Nigeria, they have come under Hausa* cultural influences as well. There are approximately 27,000 Bokos in Benin today. Most of them are small farmers.
REFERENCE: Samuel Decalo. *Historical Dictionary of Benin.* 1994.

BOKOKO. The Bokoko people are an ethnic group living today in southern Cameroon. They speak a Bantu* language and are closely related to the neighboring Bakoko* and Babimbi* peoples. The collective population of the Bassas,* Bakokos, and Babimbis is more than 500,000 people. Although some Bokokos are Christians, most still remain faithful to tribal beliefs. Most Boko-kos live in rural villages where they raise yams, maize, cocoyams, and vegeta-

bles, although substantial numbers now live in centers such as Duala, Edéa, Pouma, and Makak, where they work as laborers, craftsmen, and businessmen.
REFERENCE: *African Encyclopedia.* 1974.

BOKORA. The Bokora are a subgroup of the Karimojon.* They live south of the Jie* in central Karamoja District of Uganda. The Bokora are cattle pastoralists who also raise millet and maize to survive. They speak a language that is part of the Central Paranilotic cluster of languages.

BOKYA. *See* BÉTÉ.

BOKYI. The Bokyis—also known as Bokis,* Nkis, Okiis, Ukis, Nfuas, and Vannerokis—are one of the main ethnic groups in Cross River State of Nigeria. They are concentrated in the Ogoja, Obudu, and Ikom divisions. They can also be found across the border in Cameroon. The Bokyi language is part of the Bendi group in the Benue-Congo family. The Bokyi population exceeds 190,000 people today.
REFERENCE: *Language Survey of Nigeria.* 1976.

BOLAONGWE. The Bolaongwes are a subgroup of the Kgalagadi* people of Botswana.

BOLE. The Boles are a small ethnic group in contemporary Ghana. Most of them work as small farmers and live in and around the town of Bole on the Western Road in the Northern Region. The Boles should not be confused with the Boles* of Bauchi State in Nigeria. The Boles in Ghana are a Guan* people whose population today is approximately 6,000 people.
REFERENCE: Daniel M. McFarland. *Historical Dictionary of Ghana.* 1995.

BOLE. The Boles (Borpikas, Ampikas) are an ethnic group living today in Nigeria. They are concentrated in the Darazo and Kirfi districts of Bauchi Division of Bauchi State and in the Duku, Nafada, Kwami, and Ako districts of Gombe Division in Bauchi State. They speak a Chadic language.
REFERENCE: *Language Survey of Nigeria.* 1976.

BOLEWA. The Bolewas are part of the larger cluster of Kanuri* peoples of Bornu State in northeastern Nigeria. They claim to have originated in Yemen, south of Mecca, and migrated out in the thirteenth century. Their economy is a complex one, revolving around commerce, home manufacturing, personal services, and agriculture. The farmers raise guinea corn, millet, groundnuts, cattle, sheep, and goats. The Bolewas also fish in Lake Chad. In recent years, they have begun to produce cotton as a cash crop. They are Sunni Muslims.
REFERENCES: Ronald Cohen. *The Kanuri of Bornu.* 1967; Donald G. Morrison et al.

Black Africa: A Comparative Handbook. 1989; C. L. Temple, ed. *Notes on the Tribes, Provinces, Emirates and States of the Northern Provinces of Nigeria.* 1967.

BOLGO. The Bolgos are one of the Sudanic peoples living today in Chad and the Central African Republic. Their language is part of the Congo-Kordofanian group. They make their living raising livestock and working small farms. The Bolgo population today exceeds 65,000 people. They were once a mighty commercial empire in what is today southern Chad and the northern Central African Republic. The Bolgos began to decline at the end of the eighteenth century because of wars of extermination with rival groups. Today, they are concentrated in the Ndélé prefecture of the Central African Republic and in Guéra, Salamat, and Moyen-Chari prefectures in Chad.
REFERENCES: Thomas Collelo et al. *Chad: A Country Study.* 1990; Pierre Kalck. *Historical Dictionary of the Central African Republic.* 1992; Donald G. Morrison et al. *Black Africa: A Comparative Handbook.* 1989.

BOLON. The Bolons are a small ethnic group living southwest of Bobo-Dioulasso in Burkina-Faso. They are a Manding* subgroup who make their living raising cotton, millet, and sorghum.
REFERENCE: Daniel M. McFarland. *Historical Dictionary of Upper Volta.* 1978.

BOMA. The Bomas are a Bantu*-speaking people of Zaire. They trace their ethnic origins back to the Tio* Kingdom of the precolonial era. The Bomas are concentrated today in the Mai-Ndombe region along the Zaire River, particularly north of the Kwa/Kasai River.
REFERENCE: F. Scott Bobb. *Historical Dictionary of Zaire.* 1988.

BOMA-MURLE. The Boma-Murles are part of the larger cluster of Murle* peoples living today in Sudan. They are closely related to the Didingas* and to the Beirs.*

BOMBO. The Bombos are a subgroup of the Sanga* peoples of southeastern Cameroon, northern Congo, southern Central African Republic, and northwestern Zaire. They interact closely with neighboring Pygmies,* who trade game for Konambembe* agricultural products.
REFERENCE: Gordon C. McDonald et al. *Area Handbook for the People's Republic of the Congo (Congo Brazzaville).* 1971.

BOMDZABUKO. *See* BEMDZABUKO.

BOMITABA. The Bomitabas are a subgroup of the Sanga* peoples.

BOMOUDI. The Bomoudi people are part of the Bongue* cluster of the Ndowe* peoples of Equatorial Guinea.

BONA. The Bonas are a subgroup of the Anyis* of Ivory Coast. The Bonas are overwhelmingly Christian in their religious persuasion.

BONDEI. The Bondei are a Northeast Bantu*-speaking people of Tanzania; they are part of the larger Shambaa* cluster of peoples. They live in the rich plains between the Usambara Mountains and the Indian Ocean in Tanzania. They are farmers, who raise maize, beans, cassava, cardamom, and bananas. The Bondei are a patrilineal people who are divided among Christian, Muslim, and shamanistic beliefs. Since the 1970s, the Bondei have been affected by the Tanzanian government's program of eliminating the homestead settlement pattern in favor of bringing the Bondei into villages, where public education and health programs can be more effective. The government has also abolished the traditional chiefdoms and is working to integrate the Bondei into the larger body politic. The Bondei population today exceeds 100,000 people.
REFERENCES: S. T. Feierman. *The Shambaa Kingdom.* 1962; Edgar V. Winans. *Shambala: The Constitution of a Traditional State.* 1962.

BONDJO. The Bondjos are a subgroup of the Sanga* peoples.

BONDONGO. The Bondongos are a subgroup of the Sanga* peoples.

BONGO. The Bongos are an African ethnic group living in northwestern Uganda and a small portion of southern Sudan. They are closely related to the Madis* and to the Bakas.* They live on the east side of the Albert Nile River and are surrounded by the Lugbaras* and the Acolis.* East African demographers place their current population at approximately 200,000 people, of whom 40 percent are Muslims. During the nineteenth century, they were badly exploited by Arab* slavers. Their economy revolves around hoe cultivation and livestock raising.
REFERENCE: Carolyn Fluehr-Lobban, Richard A. Lobban, Jr., and John Obert Voll. *Historical Dictionary of Sudan.* 1992.

BONGOM. *See* BAKÈLÈ.

BONGOUM. *See* BAKÈLÈ.

BONGUE. The Bongues are one of the two main clusters of the Ndowe* peoples of Equatorial Guinea. Included in the Bongue grouping are the Bujebas,* Balenkis, Basekes,* Kombes, Bomoudis, Asangons,* and Muikas.

BONGUILI. The Bonguilis are a subgroup of the Sanga* peoples.

BONI. The Bonis are one of the few non-Somali* peoples living today in Somalia. They can also be found in Kenya, primarily between Lamu and the

Somali border. Along with the Rendilles,* they have been called a "Sam-speaking" people by some linguists. They originated in the Ethiopian highlands and migrated toward the Somali coast. The Bonis were traditionally a hunting people, but, by the mid-twentieth century, most of them had made the transition to settled agriculture. Other Bonis became migrant laborers in Somali towns and cities. Ethnic Somalis look down upon the Bonis as an inferior people.

REFERENCES: Helen C. Metz et al. *Somalia: A Country Study.* 1992; Bethwell A. Ogot. *Historical Dictionary of Kenya.* 1981.

BONKORO. *See* BENGA.

BONNY. *See* IBANI.

BONO. *See* ABRON.

BONWIRE. The Bonwires are one of the primary subdivisions of the Asante* people of Ghana.

BOR BELANDA. The Bor Belandas are part of the Western Nilotic* cluster of peoples living today in Sudan. They are Muslims and their economy revolves around the raising of cattle. They are closely related to the Dinkas,* Nuers,* Anuaks,* and Acolis.*

REFERENCE: Donald G. Morrison et al. *Black Africa: A Comparative Handbook.* 1989.

BORAN. The Boran (Borana) are one of the major subgroups of the Oromo* people of Ethiopia, Somalia, and Kenya. They are among the southern cluster of the Oromos in Ethiopia. They live in the arid plains of southern Ethiopia near the Kenya border. They maintain close contacts with other Boran people living in Kenya, as well as with the Boran in Somalia, for the groups cross the border frequently for ritualistic purposes and marriages. Most of the Boran were egalitarian pastoralists, raising cattle, goats, and sheep, but the dessication of Boran land in recent decades has forced them into the business of raising camels. It was not until 1899, under Menelik II, that the Boran were brought under Ethiopian imperial control.

BORANA. *See* BORAN.

BORGAWA. *See* BARIBA.

BORGU. *See* BARIBA.

BORITSU. *See* YUKUBEN.

BORNO. The term ''Borno'' is used in Sudan to refer to immigrants of West African origin, most of whom are ethnic Hausas.*
REFERENCE: Helen C. Metz et al. *Sudan: A Country Study.* 1992.

BORNO. *See* KANURI.

BORNU. *See* KANURI.

BORON. *See* ABRON.

BOROR. The Boror are a small ethnic group of several thousand people living in Mozambique. Most of them are small subsistence farmers who live along the banks of the lower Zambezi River valley. During the late eighteenth and nineteenth centuries, they actively participated in the slave trade, capturing and selling other Africans to Portuguese* traders.
REFERENCE: Mario Azevedo. *Historical Dictionary of Mozambique.* 1991.

BORONG. *See* ABRON.

BORORO. The Bororos (Wodaabe) are a subgroup of the Fulbes* of the Central African Republic, Cameroon, Niger, Nigeria, and Chad. They are a pastoral, cattle-raising people. The Bororos are among the most nomadic people in the region, moving to a new location every few days. They possess a powerful sense of identity and rarely marry outside their own group. Ethnologists disagree on their origins. Some claim the Bororos were once Hausas* in the fourteenth century, who then made the transition to a nomadic lifestyle. Others argue that the Bororos were always Fulbes but that they did not accept the Islamic missionaries who arrived in the Sokoto region early in the 1800s. The Bororos are a nomadic tribe of more than 100,000 people; they herd their cattle over broad stretches of territory in Nigeria and Niger. In recent years, they have experienced extreme poverty and the liquidation of their prized cattle herds because of severe droughts in their homelands.
REFERENCES: Samuel Decalo. *Historical Dictionary of Niger.* 1989; Pierre Kalck. *Historical Dictionary of the Central African Republic.* 1992.

BORPIKA. *See* BOLE.

BORROM. *See* BOGHOM.

BOSHONGO. The Boshongos, also known as the Bushongs, are a subgroup of the Kuba* people of Zaire. The Boshongos live in the Kasai region near Dekese and north of Ilebo. Until the seventeenth century, the Boshongos were primarily fishermen, but, beginning in the 1700s, they began making the transition to farming, learning to raise maize, manioc, and tobacco. With the wealth

that came from agriculture, they became somewhat expansionist and conquered their neighbors, the Luluas* and the Mongos.* Today, most Boshongos are small farmers.
REFERENCES: F. Scott Bobb. *Historical Dictionary of Zaire.* 1988; Jan Vansina. *The Children of Woot: A History of the Kuba People.* 1978.

BOSUME AKYEM. The Bosume Akyem are the smallest subgroup of the Akyem,* a major Akan* group of Ghana. The Bosume Akyem live in eastern Ghana, where they emerged from the Adansi* people. Although most Bosume Akyem are small farmers, they enjoy occupational diversity, ranging from blue-collar to professional jobs. The major Bosume Akyem settlement in Ghana is at Akyem Swedru. Demographers estimate the contemporary Bosume Akyem population at approximately 30,000 people.
REFERENCE: Daniel M. McFarland. *Historical Dictionary of Ghana.* 1995.

BOTOMBU. *See* BARIBA.

BOUA. The Bouas are an ethnic group in Chad whose traditional population center has been located at Korbol. They lived as small farmers and fishermen along the Chari River for centuries, and, when the Baguirmi Kingdom declined in the late eighteenth century, they became prominent in the region. Today, they are distributed along the middle Chari River in Moyen-Chari Prefecture and in central Guéra Prefecture of Chad. The Bouas are known for their extremely powerful sense of identity and for their aggressive suspicion toward outsiders. They are divided into the following subgroups—the Boua proper and the Tounia,* Neilliam, Koke,* and Fanian.*
REFERENCES: Thomas Collelo et al. *Chad: A Country Study.* 1990; Samuel Decalo. *Historical Dictionary of Chad.* 1987.

BOUAKA. The Bouakas are an ethnic group in contemporary Central African Republic. Ethnologists believe that they established themselves at the bend of the Ubangi River around 1830. Closely related to the Gbaya* peoples, they spent much of the nineteenth century fighting various Bantu* groups; in the late 1920s, they rose up in rebellion against the French* empire. Today, they live as small farmers.
REFERENCE: Pierre Kalck. *Historical Dictionary of the Central African Republic.* 1992.

BOUBANGUI. The Boubanguis (Bobangis, Bobanguis) were once a great merchant people who lived in the Central African Republic between the Sangha and Ubangi rivers. In the 1830s, they found themselves battling with the Bouakas,* and later in the century with the Gbayas.* The Boubanguis are a Bantu*-speaking people, who still exhibit commercial skills, although they are not the economically dominant group they once were. They are closely related to the Mbochi* people of Zaire, Congo, and Gabon. They live on the western

bank of the Zaire River and the eastern bank of the Ubangi River, just north of where the two rivers meet in western Zaire. They are a riverine people.
REFERENCES: Pierre Kalck. *Historical Dictionary of the Central African Republic.* 1992; Irving Kaplan et al. *Zaire: A Country Study.* 1978.

BOUBOURI. *See* ADJUKRU.

BOUDOUMA. *See* BUDUMA.

BOULOU. *See* SÉKÉ.

BOUMBA. The Boumbas are a major subgroup of the Ndowe* peoples of Equatorial Guinea. Included in the Boumba cluster are the Bengas* and the Bapukus.*

BOURAKA. The Bourakas are a Sudanic people whom some describe as part of the so-called Ubanguian* group of peoples in the Central African Republic. Their own traditions, confirmed by modern research, place them in the Upper Nile region until the sixteenth century, when they began a migration that brought them to their present location along the Ubangi River between the Bangi bend and the juncture of the Ouellé River and the Mbomou River. They are a riverine people, making their living as fishermen and small farmers. The Bourakas are very influential in the civil service of the Central African Republic.
REFERENCE: Pierre Kalck. *Historical Dictionary of the Central African Republic.* 1992.

BOURANKA. *See* BOURAKA.

BOUSANOU. *See* BUSANSI.

BOUSSANSÉ. *See* BUSANSI.

BOWIRI. *See* BOWLI.

BOWLI. The Bowli people are considered part of the Volta-Togo cluster of ethnic groups in Ghana and Togo. Most of them live east of Lake Volta in Ghana and across the border in Togo. They speak a language known as Bowiri, and most of them make their livings as small farmers and livestock raisers. The Bowli population in Ghana today is approximately 10,000 people.
REFERENCE: Daniel M. McFarland. *Historical Dictionary of Ghana.* 1995.

BOYO. The Boyos are a Bantu*-speaking ethnic group living today in south-eastern Zaire. They live on the western banks of Lake Tanganyika, north of Kalemie. Traditionally, the Boyos have made their living by planting small

farms near the lake and by fishing. In recent years, more and more Boyos have been seeking wage labor in towns and cities.
REFERENCE: Irving Kaplan et al. *Zaire: A Country Study.* 1978.

BOZA. The Boza (Bozo) are considered a fringe Manding* group who trace their tribal origins back to the Mali Empire of the thirteenth century. Their population in Mali today exceeds 55,000 people, virtually all of whom are Muslims. Most of them live along the Niger and Bani rivers, in Mali and Niger, and make their living as fishermen. They move up and down the river seasonally. The Boza living near Mopti are high successful commercial fishermen, using motorized boats and modern refrigeration to export their catch.
REFERENCES: Pascal Imperato. *Historical Dictionary of Mali.* 1986; Donald R. Wright. "Manding-Speaking Peoples." In Richard V. Weekes, ed. *Muslim Peoples.* 1984.

BOZO. *See* BOZA.

BRAME. The Brames are one of the most influential ethnic groups in Guinea-Bissau today. With the development of groundnut plantations in the early twentieth century, the Brames migrated from the interior to Bolama and Galinhas islands, as well as to the Rio Grande de Buba region, to work those plantations. Over time, many Brames came to own smaller plantations of their own, entering the regional commercial economy and the political establishment. Those Brames not owning plantations still make their living as slash-and-burn farmers. Today, the Brames are concentrated especially between Canchungo and Bula on the right side of the Mansoa River. They are closely related to the Papei,* Manjaco,* and Mancanha* peoples. The Brame population today is approximately 50,000 people.
REFERENCES: Rosemary Galli. *Guinea-Bissau.* 1990; Richard Lobban and Joshua Forrest. *Historical Dictionary of the Republic of Guinea-Bissau.* 1988.

BRASS. *See* NEMBA.

BRIGNAN. *See* AVIKAM.

BRIN-SELEKI. The Brin-Selekis are a subgroup of the Jola* peoples of Senegal.

BRITISH. Beginning with their penetration of southern Africa in the eighteenth century, the British steadily expanded their African empire until it included the contemporary nations, or portions thereof, of Sierra Leone, Ghana, Togo, Benin, Nigeria, Botswana, Zambia, South Africa, Zimbabwe, Tanzania, Kenya, Uganda, Sudan, and Egypt. Substantial numbers of English-speaking settlers poured into British Africa, especially in South Africa, Zambia, and Zimbabwe, where they became an influential white minority, active in commerce, civil ad-

ministration, politics, and the professions. Once independence was achieved, the number of ethnic British living in Africa declined, but they have remained a powerful minority in southern Africa. Today, several million people of English descent live in Africa, most of them in Zambia, South Africa, and Zimbabwe, as well as in the major cities of the former British colonies.
REFERENCE: James S. Olson. *Historical Dictionary of European Imperialism.* 1991.

BRON. *See* ABRON.

BRONG. *See* ABRON.

BUBI. The Bubis are the indigenous people of the island of Fernando Po in the country of Equatorial Guinea. Most anthropologists estimate that the Bubis came to Fernando Po in several migrations from Cameroon. They speak a Bantu* language that has four distinct dialects on the island. The Bubis are a monogamous, monotheistic, matrilineal people, whose economy and religion revolve around the cultivation of the yam and the sacred Moka Mountain. Severe epidemics in the nineteenth century reduced their population to only 12,000 people, but, since 1940, it has been on a steady increase. The Bubis resisted Spanish* attempts to impose forced labor on them, and, in 1907, they rose up in rebellion against the empire. In recent years, the Union Bubi, a Bubi political organization, has campaigned for the independence of Fernando Po. During the tyrannical regime of Macias Nguema, the Bubis suffered political repression and atrocities. Most Bubis are Roman Catholics.
REFERENCES: Randall Fegley. *Equatorial Guinea.* 1991; Max Liniger-Goumaz. *Historical Dictionary of Equatorial Guinea.* 1988.

BUDGA. *See* BUDJGA.

BUDJA. *See* BUDJGA.

BUDJGA. The Budjgas (Budgas, Budjas, Budyas) are a Shona* people, who speak a Korekore* dialect and live today in Zimbabwe, primarily in Mtoko District. The Budjgas have been living there for centuries, and they have been governed by paramount chiefs bearing the title of Mutoko. They fiercely resisted Portuguese* incursions from Mozambique in the eighteenth and nineteenth centuries, and, in 1890, they signed a concession with the British South Africa Company. They then promptly resisted paying taxes to the company. The Budjgas possess a strong sense of identity.
REFERENCE: R. Kent Rasmussen. *Historical Dictionary of Zimbabwe.* 1994.

BUDJIA. The Budjia are one of the primary subgroups of the Buduma* people of Chad. They are the dominant Buduma group in the area of Tataverom District and have a population of approximately 14,000 people. Highly ethnocentric, the

Budjia are Muslims in their religious orientation and cattle raisers in their economic life.

BUDU. The Budus are a Bantu*-speaking people who today live in the Haut-Zaire region of Zaire. Although most Budus still make their living as farmers, raising cassava as a staple, they have become increasingly integrated into the regional commercial economy in recent decades. Large numbers of Budus have moved to the city of Kisangani in search of wage labor.
REFERENCE: Irving Kaplan et al. *Zaire: A Country Study.* 1978.

BUDUMA. The Buduma (Boudoumas, Yedinas) are a people living near the islands in Lake Chad in Chad and Nigeria. Their homeland is a region of marshes, reeds, grasses, floating islands, and papyrus. The Buduma call themselves the "Yedina." The Buduma speak a language that ethnolinguists classify as part of the Chadic cluster of languages in the Nilo-Saharan family. Approximately 65,000 Buduma live in Chad; there are another 5,000 Buduma in Niger and 4,000 in Nigeria. They are a fiercely ethnocentric people, known for their suspicion of outsiders, their unwillingness to acculturate to the values and institutions of other groups, and their unwavering tendency to marry endogamously. Because of their habitat, they remain largely outside the reach of centralized political authority in Chad, still running their own political and legal affairs through a traditional chief system. The Buduma economy revolves around cattle and the water level of Lake Chad. When the lake rises and grazing land is reduced, the Buduma tend to rely more heavily on fishing for their livelihood; when water levels fall, the size of their herds increases.

The Buduma are divided into several subgroups. With a population of 27,000 people, the Guria* are the most dominant of the Buduma subgroups. They live in Yakua in the Bol District of Chad and are ruled by the Mehul clan. The Maibuloa* number about 17,000 people and claim to be the direct descendants of Yed, the mythical founder of the Buduma people. The Budjia* total approximately 14,000 people and are concentrated in Tataverom District and in Boso and Ngigimi. The Madjigodjia* have about 10,000 people and live on the islands in western Bol and Tataverom districts. Smaller subgroups, each with several thousand members, are the Ursawa, Siginda, and Media. All of the Buduma subgroups are further divided into powerful clan and lineage systems. After the French* empire was firmly established in Chad, Islamic missionaries managed to get into the region and convert the Buduma. Today, the Buduma are Muslims, but their own indigenous religion—revolving around the worship of the God Kumani—is still active, giving them a syncretic faith.
REFERENCES: Christian Bouquet. "Buduma." In Richard Weekes, ed. *Muslim Peoples.* 1984; J. Chapelle. *Le Peuple Tchadian.* 1981.

BUDYA. *See* BUDJGA.

BUEM. The Buem (Boem) people are part of the Volta-Togo ethnic cluster of peoples who live in the Volta Region of Ghana and across the border in Togo. Most Buems are small farmers. The Buem population of Ghana today exceeds 35,000 people.
REFERENCE: Daniel M. McFarland. *Historical Dictionary of Ghana.* 1995.

BUGABI. The Bugabis are part of a larger Hausa*-Fulbe* cluster of peoples living today in northwestern Nigeria. Some of them can also be found across the border in Niger and in northern Benin. Islam dominates their religious beliefs, and most of them are small farmers and cattle herders.
REFERENCE: Donald G. Morrison et al. *Black Africa: A Comparative Handbook.* 1989.

BUGANDA. *See* GANDA.

BUGI. The Bugis are a people living today in Plateau State in Nigeria. They live in a series of villages where they have made the transition to small farming in recent decades. Hunting, however, has long been of religious and ritual significance to them. The consumption of meat and beer is considered among life's most important activities.
REFERENCE: Jean-Claude Muller. "Intertribal Hunting Among the Rukuba." *Ethnology* 21 (1982): 203–14.

BUILSA. The Builsas, known also as the Builses, Bulses, Kangyagas, and Kanjagas, are a Grusi* people of Ghana and Burkina-Faso. They are concentrated in the Upper Region of Ghana, primarily between the Sisala River and the Great Northern Highway. The language they speak is known as Buli. The Builsas are surrounded by the Mamprusis* to the south, the Kasenas* to the north, the Sasalas* to the west, and the Nankansis to the east. Most Builsas support themselves by raising livestock and working small plots of land. There are approximately 170,000 Builsas living in Ghana today.
REFERENCE: Daniel M. McFarland. *Historical Dictionary of Ghana.* 1995; Daniel M. McFarland. *Historical Dictionary of Upper Volta.* 1978.

BUILSE. *See* BUILSA.

BUJAGO. *See* BIJAGÓ.

BUJEBA. The Bujebas are a subgroup of the Bongue* people of Equatorial Guinea. The Bongues themselves are considered part of the Ndowe* cluster of peoples in the region.

BUJI. The Bujis are a people living today in Plateau State in Nigeria. They live in small villages where they work primarily as subsistence farmers.

The Bujis claim to have origins among the neighboring Ribina* peoples.
REFERENCES: Samuel Akbapot. "Random Music of Birom." *African Arts* 8 (Winter 1975): 46–47; Elizabeth Isichei, ed. *Studies in the History of Plateau State, Nigeria.* 1982; Jean-Claude Muller. "Intertribal Hunting Among the Rukuba." *Ethnology* 21 (1982): 203–14.

BUKUMA. *See* OGBRONUAGUM.

BUKUSU. The Bukusus are a subgroup of the Luhya* people of Kenya and Uganda. They are a Western Bantu* people who live today north of Lake Victoria on both sides of the Kenyan-Ugandan border.

BULALA. Although culturally and linguistically of Arab* origins, the Bulalas (Bilalas) have mixed with a variety of other groups over the centuries. They are concentrated today around Lake Fitri and the city of Yao in Chad. They can also be found in other regions of Chad, including Massakori, oum Hadjer, and in Daza, where they function as nomads. The total number of Bulalas and their associated groups exceeds 500,000 people. Most Bulalas are farmers, raising millet, maize, and cotton. They also raise livestock and fish for a living. They are overwhelmingly Muslims, although pre-Islamic religious rites remain powerful.
REFERENCES: Thomas Collelo et al. *Chad: A Country Study.* 1988; Samuel Decalo. *Historical Dictionary of Chad.* 1987.

BULGEDA. The Bulgedas are a subgroup of the Tebu* people of Chad.

BULLOM. The Bulloms, who are very closely related to the Sherbros,* are an ethnic group located today in Sierra Leone. Their current population is approximately 32,000 people, of whom 80 percent are Muslims. Portuguese* explorers first described the Bulloms in 1507. By the seventeenth century, the Temne* people had expanded to the coast, cutting the Bulloms into two geographical groups. The northern Bulloms retained the name Bullom but began to assimilate into the surrounding Temne and Soso* groups. The southern Bulloms came to be known as the Sherbros.·
REFERENCE: Cyril P. Foray. *Historical Dictionary of Sierra Leone.* 1977.

BULSE. *See* BUILSA.

BULU. The Bulu are an ethnic group living in and around the cities of Sangmelima, Djoum, and Ebolowa in southern Cameroon. They are a subgroup of the Betis,* who are part of the larger Fang*-Pahouin* cluster of peoples. The Bulu population today exceeds 150,000 people. Most of them are farmers,

raising cassava, cocoa, and yams. They speak a Bantu* language (closely related to that of the neighboring Fang and Ewondo* peoples), worship as Christians with strong ties to their traditional religion, and are closely related to the Fangs. Historically, the Bulu were middlemen during the years of the European slave trade, and they resisted German* penetration of their region in the early twentieth century. The Bulu maintain a strong rivalry with neighboring Bamiléké* peoples, which has resulted in periodic civil wars, most recently in 1956. The leading Bulu political figures in Cameroon are Charles Assale and Paul Biya.
REFERENCE: *African Encyclopedia.* 1974.

BUM. *See* MBUN.

BUMAJI. The Bumajis are a relatively small ethnic group living today in Nigeria. They are concentrated demographically in the Obudu Division of Cross River State. Most Bumajis make their living as small subsistence farmers. They speak a Bendi language, part of the Benue-Congo family.
REFERENCE: *Language Survey of Nigeria.* 1976.

BUMO. The Bumos (Bomas) are a subgroup of the Izon* peoples of Rivers State in Nigeria.

BUNGNU. *See* KAMWE.

BUNU. *See* KAMWE.

BUNU. The Bunu Yoruba are one of four Yoruba*-speaking groups that are sometimes referred to as the northeast or O-Kun Yoruba. They live in an area near Lokoja at the confluence of the Niger and Benue rivers of central Nigeria. They have had considerable cultural and historical association with their non-Yoruba neighbors, especially the Ebiras* to the southeast and the Nupes* to the north. Before its incorporation into the Protectorate of Northern Nigeria, established by Great Britain in 1900, the Bunu District consisted of several small kingdoms, each with a large town, ruled by a council of chiefs and a king. The king was selected on a rotational basis from among a group of patricians (patrilineal clans), rather than from a royal clan as in other Yoruba groups. It was a relatively egalitarian system of politics. The Bunu worship *ebora*—amorphous deities associated with various patricians and geographical sites, rather than the hierarchical, personalized deities of other Yorubas. Their economy traditionally revolved around a system in which men raised cotton and sold it to women, who then wove it into cloth. In recent years, the rise of a market economy has brought about a decline in weaving.
REFERENCE: Elisha P. Renne. "Water, Spirits, and Plain White Cloth: The Ambiguity of Things in Bunu Social Life." *Man* 26 (1991): 709–22.

BURA. The Buras (Pabir, Babir, Babur, Kwojeffa) are one of the Plateau Chadic peoples of Nigeria. Their current population exceeds 240,000 people, most of whom are Christians; perhaps one-quarter are Muslims. Traditionally, the Buras lived in walled villages of 100 to 3,000 people and had a decentralized political structure. They live in central Nigeria, east of the Niger River and north of the Benue River, primarily in the Babur, East Bura, West Bura and Askira districts of the Biu Division of Borno State. They are closely related linguistically to the Pabirs.* In the 1980s, many Bura and Pabir leaders tried to bring the two peoples together to decrease their local political differences, but the movement was still-born.
REFERENCES: *Language Survey of Nigeria.* 1976; Helen C. Metz et al. *Nigeria: A Country Study.* 1991.

BURA. The Buras are a subgroup of the Taita* peoples of East Africa, particularly Kenya. They speak a Bantu* language.

BURAK. The Buraks are a very small group of subsistence farmers living today in the Kaltungo area of Tangale-Waja Division of Bauchi State in Nigeria.
REFERENCE: *Language Survey of Nigeria.* 1976.

BURE. *See* DENO.

BURGU. *See* BARIBA.

BURJI. The Burjis are an ethnic group living today in the Marsabit District of the North-Eastern Province of Kenya and in Ethiopia. They originated in the Burji Mountains of Ethiopia, where they lived between Lake Chew Bahir and Lake Abaya and raised cotton and coffee. When Menelik II conquered the Burji between 1890 and 1900, he reduced them to a state of serfdom, so many Burjis fled into Kenya, arriving there between 1906 and 1930. Most Burjis are small farmers. Their Ethiopian population exceeds 20,000 people.
REFERENCES: M. L. Bender, J. D. Bowen, R. L. Cooper, and C. A. Ferguson, eds. *Language in Ethiopia.* 1976; Bethwell A. Ogot. *Historical Dictionary of Kenya.* 1981.

BURKENEJI. *See* SAMBURU.

BURKUNAWA. *See* BARKE.

BURMA. *See* BOGHOM.

BUROM. *See* BOGHOM.

BURRUM. *See* BOGHOM.

BURU. *See* DÉGHA.

BURUNGE. The Burunge (Burungi) are an ethnic group occupying the Central Highlands of Tanzania. They are bordered by the Sandawes* to the west and the Rangis* to the north. Their population exceeds 30,000 people, and they support themselves by raising livestock. Some ethnolinguists classify the Burunge language as part of the Southern Cushitic group, and the Burunge are closely affiliated, culturally and linguistically, with the Iraqws,* Gorowas, Wasis (Sanye*), and Mbugus.* Their neighbors know the Burunge as a shy, somewhat withdrawn people, who have little desire for contact with the outside world.
REFERENCE: James L. Newman. *The Ecological Basis for Subsistence Change among the Sandawe of Tanzania.* 1970.

BURUNGI. *See* BURUNGE.

BUSA. The Busa (Busagwe, Busanse) are part of the larger group of Bariba* people. They number approximately 95,000 people and live primarily in the Kwara State of Nigeria, especially in the Wawa, Busa, Babana, and Yaskikira districts of the Borgu and Gwandu divisions of Sokoto State. Some can also be found in the Department of Borghou in the People's Republic of Benin. Although some Busa have moved to cities in Nigeria and Benin in recent years, taking jobs as civil servants, small businessmen, and craftsmen, most of the Busa are still farmers, who raise yams, sorghum, millet, and corn for their own consumption and rice, peanuts, cotton, and beans as cash crops. The Busa usually live in concentrated villages; within those villages, they dwell in walled compounds that house several families related on a paternal line. They may also have a small farm house a few miles out in the countryside near their land and herds. Approximately half of the Busa are Muslims, and, in recent years, they have become somewhat more devout in their commitment to Islam. The others are for the most part still loyal to their indigenous beliefs, which include devotion to ancestors, shamanistic healers, and a belief in a variety of animistic forces. The Busa have historically been a dominant group wherever they have lived. Neighboring Fulbe* people have generally served the Busa by raising their cattle herds for them, while the Hausas* are usually merchants and traders, supplying the Busa with goods and services. Both the Fulbes and the Hausas acknowledge Busa political leadership where they live in close proximity to each other.
REFERENCES: Jacques Maquet. *Civilizations of Black Africa.* 1972; Harold D. Nelson et al. *Area Handbook for Nigeria.* 1972; Carolyn F. Sargent. "Born to Die: Witchcraft and Infanticide in Bariba Culture." *Ethnology* 27 (1988): 79–95.

BUSAGWE. *See* BUSA.

BUSANGA. *See* BUSANSI.

BUSANSE. *See* BUSA.

BUSANSI. The Busansi (Bisa, Bissa, Boussansé, Bussansi, Busanga, Bouz-antchi, Bousanou) are an ethnic group who live in Burkina-Faso, between Ten-kodogo and the border with Ghana, as well as across the border in northern Ghana, particularly in the northeastern tip of the upper East Region. They can also be found across the border in Togo. They first arrived in the region around 1300. Although they are surrounded by Molé-Dagbane* peoples, who are Mus-lims, the Busansi are considered a Fringe Mandinka* language group, who trace their tribal origins back to the Mali Empire of the thirteenth century. The Busansi were the population base for the first Mossi* state that emerged in Tenkodogo. Most Busansi are small farmers who are known to raise millet, rice, peanuts, and a variety of other crops.
REFERENCE: Donald R. Wright. ''Manding-Speaking Peoples.'' In Richard V. Weekes, ed. *Muslim Peoples.* 1984.

BUSAWA. The Busawas are part of the larger Hausa*-Fulbe* cluster of peoples living today in northwestern Nigeria. Some of them can also be found across the border in Niger and in northern Benin. Islam dominates their religious be-liefs, and most of them are small farmers and cattle herders.
REFERENCE: Donald G. Morrison et al. *Black Africa: A Comparative Handbook.* 1989.

BUSHMEN. *See* SAN.

BUSHONG. *See* BOSHONGO.

BUSOGA. *See* SOGA.

BUSSA. The Bussas are a tiny ethnic group living today in Ethiopia. They speak a Cushitic language and have a current population of approximately 1,500 peo-ple.
REFERENCE: M. L. Bender, J. D. Bowen, R. L. Cooper, and C. A. Ferguson, eds. *Language in Ethiopia.* 1976.

BUSSANSI. *See* BUSANSI.

BUTA-NINGI. The Buta-Ningis are a small ethnic group living today in Ni-geria; they will probably become extinct soon. Their language, which is rapidly disappearing, is part of the Northern group of Plateau languages in the Benue-Congo family. Surviving Buta-Ningis can be found today in the Ningi District of the Bauchi Division of Bauchi State.
REFERENCE: *Language Survey of Nigeria.* 1976.

BUTE. *See* BAFUT.

BUTE. *See* VUTE.

BUZI. *See* NDAU.

BUZZI. *See* LOMA.

BVIRI. The Bviris (Biris) are an ethnic group in southern Sudan who speak a language similar to that of the Azandés.* They live in the region surrounding the city of Wau. Most of them are small farmers who also raise some cattle. The Bviris are closely related to the Ndogos.*
REFERENCE: Helen C. Metz et al. *Sudan: A Country Study.* 1992.

BWA. *See* BOBO.

BWAKA. *See* MBAKA.

BWAL. The Bwals (Bwolls) are a small ethnic group living today in Plateau State in Nigeria. They are closely related to the Dimmuks,* and both groups claim descent from a man known as Dimmuk. They possess a long list of kings and well-developed oral history. Political authority tends to be highly decentralized among the various Bwal villages. Most Bwals are subsistence farmers.
REFERENCE: John Ola Agi. ''The Goemai and Their Neighbors: An Historical Analysis.'' In Elizabeth Isichei, ed. *Studies in the History of Plateau State, Nigeria.* 1982.

BWILE. The Bwiles are a small ethnic group of approximately 15,000 people, living on the eastern shore of Lake Mweru along the northern border of Zambia. They are part of the Bemba* cluster of people. Most Bwiles make their living as fishermen on the lake.
REFERENCE: John J. Grotpeter. *Historical Dictionary of Zambia.* 1979.

BWISI. The Bwisis (Lubwisis) are one of Uganda's more than thirty ethnic groups. They speak a Bantu* language and live in heavily forested regions of the country where they work as subsistence farmers.
REFERENCE: Peter Ladefoged, Ruth Glick, and Clive Criper. *Language in Uganda.* 1972.

BWOLL. *See* BWAL.

BYETRI. *See* MEKYIBO.

C

CAALA. *See* CHALLA.

CABRAI. *See* KABRÉ.

CACONDA. The Cacondas are one of the traditional, autonomous kingdoms and contemporary ethnic subgroups of the Ovimbundu* people of Angola.

CADAU. *See* DOGON.

CAKFEM. *See* CHAKFEM-MUSHERE.

CALABAR. *See* EFIK.

CALA-CALA. *See* LELA.

CALO. The Calo people are an ethnic group living today in northern Togo. Their population consists of more than 60,000 people, most of whom are subsistence farmers. They are part of the eastern Grusi* language group.
REFERENCE: Meterwa A. Ourso. ''Phonological Processes in the Noun Class System of Lama.'' *Studies in African Linguistics* 20 (August 1989): 151–78.

CAMOCHI. The Camochis are a subgroup of the larger Ngangela* cluster of peoples living today in Angola.

CANARY ISLANDER. The Canary Islands are an archipelago in the North Atlantic Ocean, about seventy miles west of the Moroccan coast of Africa. There are seven major islands. The native people of the islands were known as

Guanches, but Spain conquered them in the 1400s and they had become extinct by 1600. The people of the islands are now Spaniards.*

CANGIN. The Cangin are a primary subgroup of the Serer* people of Senegal. There are approximately 15,000 Cangin, and they are divided into the Safen, Ndut, and Non subgroups. Most Cangins live just outside the urban triangle of Dakar, Thies, and Rufisque in Senegal.

CAPE VERDEAN. The people of the Cape Verde Islands today are the products of a process of ethnogenesis over the past 500 years. Portugal claimed the islands in the mid-fifteenth century, and settlers from Portugal began arriving there in the early 1470s. When the Cape Verde islands became involved as transit points for ships engaged in the Atlantic slave trade, large numbers of indigenous Africans from many West African peoples settled there. Over the years, considerable intermarriage occurred between the Portuguese* and the Africans, creating a new ethnic group. Today, Cape Verdeans speak a language known as *crioulo*. Crioulo possesses a Portuguese morphology combined with African phonetic systems and mixtures of Portuguese and African words. The word "crioulo" is sometimes used as a generic reference to Cape Verdean culture. The Cape Verdean population today exceeds 310,000 people.
REFERENCES: Richard Lobban and Marilyn Halter. *Historical Dictionary of the Republic of Cape Verde.* 1988; Caroline Shaw. *Cape Verde.* 1988.

CAPRIVI. The Caprivis are an ethnic group living today in Namibia. In terms of language and culture, they are closely related to the Lozi* people of Zambia. The Caprivi population today is approximately 45,000 people.
REFERENCE: Stanley Schoeman and Elna Schoeman. *Namibia.* 1984.

CARANGA. *See* SHONA.

CARI. The Caris are a subgroup of the Mbundu* peoples of Angola.

CASSANGA. The Cassangas are an ethnic group of the southern Casamance region of Guinea-Bissau. They are closely related to the Bañuns* and Cobianas.* For several centuries, they maintained an independent kingdom at Birkima, and their most prominent historical leader was Kassa-Mansa. Late in the sixteenth century, the Cassangas became active slave hunters and expanded in Bañun territory, assimilating many of them. Today, the Cassangas are known for their skill as weavers and dyers.
REFERENCE: Richard Lobban and Joshua Forrest. *Historical Dictionary of the Republic of Guinea-Bissau.* 1988.

CERDEGUA. The Cerdeguas are one of the Teda* clans of Chad. The

Tedas are a subgroup of the Tebus.* Most Cerdeguas live north of Bardai in Tibesti.

CEWA. *See* CHEWA.

CHABE. The Chabes are one of the many subgroups of the Yoruba* peoples of West Africa. They can be found today especially in southern Benin.

CHAGA. *See* CHAGGA.

CHAGGA. The Chagga (Chaga) people are one of the largest and most highly educated ethnic groups in Tanzania. Their homeland on the slopes of Mt. Kilimanjaro in the northeastern region is known for the fertility of its soil and abundant rainfall. The Chaggas are extremely successful commercial farmers, raising bananas and coffee as their main crops. Their population today exceeds 600,000 people, and more than 80 percent of them are literate. The Chaggas are disproportionately represented among the ruling elites of Tanzania. Some Chaggas can also be found in Kenya.
REFERENCES: Laura Kurtz. *Historical Dictionary of Tanzania.* 1978; Lioba Moshi. "Time Reference Markers in Kiuno Chaga." *Journal of African Languages and Linguistics* 15 (1994): 161–74.

CHAKFEM-MUSHERE. The Chakfem-Musheres are an ethnic group living in the plateau highlands of Plateau State of Nigeria, particularly in the Ron District of the Pankskin Division. They are surrounded ethnically by the Rons* to the north, Mwahavuls* to the east, and Kantanas* to the southwest. Most Chakfem-Musheres are subsistence farmers. Their language is part of the Sura-Gerka group of western Chadic languages.
REFERENCES: John Ola Agi. "The Goemai and Their Neighbors: An Historical Analysis." In Elizabeth Isichei, ed. *Studies in the History of Plateau State, Nigeria.* 1982; *Language Survey of Nigeria.* 1976.

CHAKOSSI. *See* CHOKOSSI.

CHALLA. The Challa, or Caala, were a large ethnic group living at the headwaters of the Koto River before the advent of the Atlantic slave trade. During the centuries of the slave trade, however, the Challa were all but exterminated. By 1950, there were only a few hundred Challa alive, most of whom lived in Bahr-el-Ghazal in the Central African Republic. Today, there are only a few dozen people aware of their Challa ancestry.
REFERENCE: Pierre Kalck. *Historical Dictionary of the Central African Republic.* 1992.

CHAMBA. The Chamba (Chamba-Dakas, Dakas, Samas, Sambas, Tchambas, Tsambas, Jamas, Nakanyares, and Dengs), not to be confused with the

Basari* people of Togo and Ghana who sometimes call themselves Chamba, are an ethnic group living in Nigeria and Cameroon. In Nigeria, they live primarily in Gongola State, especially in the Verre, Wafanga, and Binyeri districts of Adamawa Division, the Leko, Jada, Mbulo, Sugu, Yelwa, and Toungo districts of Ganye Division, and the Dakka, Jalingo, Mutum Biu, Bakundi, and Gassol districts of Muri Division. Their population today is approximately 250,000 people, and about 15 percent of them are Muslims. They are one of the so-called "grasslands" peoples of northwestern Cameroon. Most of them are farmers, raising a variety of cereal crops and vegetables, along with cocoa and coffee in some locations. They are well known regionally for their skill at sculpture, pottery, and metalworking. Closely related are the Chamba-Lekos, who live in Wukari Division of Gongola State.
REFERENCES: Mark W. DeLancey and H. M. Mokeba. *Historical Dictionary of the Republic of Cameroon.* 1990; *Language Survey in Nigeria.* 1976.

CHAMBA. *See* BASARI.

CHAMBA-LEKO. *See* CHAMBA.

CHAM-MWANA. The Cham-Mwanas, also known as the Cham-Mwonas, are a small ethnic group living today in Nigeria. They speak an Adamawa language that is part of the Waja* cluster. Most Cham-Mwanas live in the Cham and Dadiya districts of the Gombe Division of Bauchi State.
REFERENCE: *Language Survey in Nigeria.* 1976.

CHAM-MWONA. *See* CHAM-MWANA.

CHAN. The Chans are a subgroup of the Bassa* people of Liberia. Most Chans live in Grand Bassa County, where they have divided themselves into two distinct groups.

CHANGANE. *See* SHANGAAN.

CHANGE. *See* BAUSHI.

CHARA. The Charas are a tiny ethnic group living today in southern Ethiopia. They speak an Omotic* language and have a population of only 1,500 people, most of whom are herders and subsistence farmers.
REFERENCE: M. L. Bender, J. D. Bowen, R. L. Cooper, and C. A. Ferguson, eds. *Language in Ethiopia.* 1976.

CHARFARDA. The Charfardas are a subgroup of the Daza* people of Chad. They live in the Ouaddai region, where they are nomadic pastoralists raising camels, horses, sheep, and goats.

CHARRA. The Charras (Nfachara) are an ethnic group living today near the Rukubas* and Chawais* in Plateau State of Nigeria. They are primarily a farming people who have only recently made the economic transition away from hunting. Many ethnologists classify them as a dominant subgroup of the Jarawas, or at least a group closely related to the Jarawas (*see* Afusari*). They have tended to intermarry with the Rukuba within recent decades. The Charras are especially concentrated in the Buji District of Plateau State.
REFERENCES: Harold D. Gunn. *Peoples of the Plateau Area of Northern Nigeria.* 1963; Jean-Claude Muller. "Intertribal Hunting Among the Rukuba." *Ethnology* 21 (1982): 203–14.

CHAUCHO. *See* KOTOKOLI.

CHAWAI. The Chawais (Chawe, Chawi, Atsam) are a people living today in the Plateau and Kaduna states of Nigeria. They live in a series of villages where they have made the transition in recent decades to small farming. Hunting, however, has long been of religious and ritual significance to them. The consumption of meat and beer is considered among life's most important activities. Most of them, however, make their real living today as farmers, raising millet, cassava, yams, beans, peas, melons, and pumpkins. They also raise chickens, goats, and sheep. Their population today exceeds 90,000 people.
REFERENCES: *Language Survey of Nigeria.* 1976; Charles Meek. *The Northern Tribes of Nigeria.* 1969; Jean-Claude Muller. "Intertribal Hunting Among the Rukuba." *Ethnology* 21 (1982): 203–14.

CHAWE. *See* CHAWAI.

CHAWI. *See* CHAWAI.

CHAWIA. The Chawias are a subgroup of the Taita* peoples of East Africa, particularly Kenya. They speak a Bantu* language.

CHAWU. The Chawus are a small ethnic group whose contemporary population numbers approximately 50,000 people. Although in recent years many Chawus have made the transition to commercial farming and urban labor, most Chawus continue to live as subsistence farmers and livestock raisers. They live in the lower Zambezi River Valley of Mozambique.
REFERENCE: Mario Azevedo. *Historical Dictionary of Mozambique.* 1991.

CHEKE. *See* GUDE.

CHEKIRI. *See* ITSEKIRI.

CHEREPONG. *See* KYEREPONG.

CHESSU. The Chessus are a relatively small Nigerian ethnic group. They speak a Bantu* language and live on the southwestern edge of the Jos Plateau in Plateau State. Their most immediate ethnic neighbors are the Rindres (Nunkus*), Arums,* Turkwans,* Kantanas,* and Ninzams.* Most Chessus are subsistence farmers who raise millet, guinea corn, maize, and a variety of other products.
REFERENCE: Elizabeth Isichei, ed. *Studies in the History of Plateau State, Nigeria.* 1982.

CHEWA. The Chewas (Chuas, Achewa, Ancheya, Masheba, Cewas) are the largest ethnic group in Malawi and the third largest in Zambia. Their 1993 population exceeded 2,000,000 people. One of every five Chewas is Muslim. In addition to living in Malawi, they can be found in eastern Zambia and central Mozambique. They speak a Bantu* language called Chinyanja or Chichewa. Included in the Chewa cluster of peoples are the Nyanja, Maganja, Chipeta* (Achipeta), Ambo,* and Ngoni* (Angoni). The Chewa peoples were part of the Kalonga Muzura state in the seventeenth century, when they were called the Maravi. Invading Nguni* warriors conquered the Maravi in the nineteenth century, but the Nguni adopted the Chewa language and culture. The Yao* people regularly enslaved the Chewas. British* and Portuguese* missionaries converted most Chewas to Christianity during the colonial era. They were hurt badly in the 1930s when they were forcibly moved to special reserves for Africans. Although large numbers of Chewa men work in major coastal cities, most Chewas are farmers raising maize, beans, and rice. The drought in Malawi in the 1980s severely affected their standard of living.
REFERENCES: *African Encyclopedia.* 1974; John J. Grotpeter. *Historical Dictionary of Zambia.* 1979; Kenji Yoshida. ''Masks and Secrecy Among the Chewa.'' *African Arts* 26 (April 1993): 34–45.

CHIBAK. *See* KYIBAKU.

CHIBBUK. *See* KYIBAKU.

CHICUMA. The Chicumas are a subgroup of the Ovimbundu* people of Angola.

CHICUNDA. *See* CHIKUNDA.

CHIKUNDA. The Chikundas (Cikunda, Bachikunda, Chicunda) first emerged as an ethnic group in the early nineteenth century in the lower Zambezi River Valley of Mozambique, where they lived on great Portuguese* estates and worked as hunters and slavers. They are concentrated in the lower Zambezi River Valley, Chire, and Luanga; several thousand also live in extreme northern Zimbabwe, around the Hunyani River. Chikundas can also be found in Zambia.

They hunted ivory to trade with the Portuguese, and they were known for their warrior values. The Chikundas played a leading role in the slave trade, adapting quickly to the technology of guns and capturing Chewa,* Tonga,* and Nsenga* peoples to sell as slaves to the Portuguese. The Chikundas are a relatively small ethnic group by East African standards, with a population of several hundred thousand people. The Chikundas speak a Nsenga, or Sena language, which is part of the larger Bantu* cluster.
REFERENCES: *African Encyclopedia.* 1974; R. Kent Rasmussen. *Historical Dictionary of Zimbabwe.* 1994.

CHILALA. *See* LELA.

CHILENDJE. The Chilendjes are a major subgroup of the Shona* peoples of Zimbabwe and Mozambique.

CHIMAHUTA. The Chimahutas are a subgroup of the Makonde* peoples.

CHIP. The Chip (Ship) people live today in the Zangon Katab District of Kachia Division of Kaduna State in Nigeria. They speak a Chadic language and make their living as small farmers and herders.
REFERENCE: *Language Survey of Nigeria.* 1976.

CHIP. The Chips live in Plateau State, Nigeria, and are closely related to the Dokos,* Mwahavuls,* and Kofyars.* Like other peoples in the region, they are subsistence farmers, raising millet, maize, guinea corn, beans, and livestock. Their village political system is decentralized. The Chips are surrounded by the Tals,* Ngas,* Kofyars, Mwahavuls, and Dokos.
REFERENCE: John Ola Agi. "The Goemai and Their Neighbors: An Historical Analysis." In Elizabeth Isichei, ed. *Studies in the History of Plateau State, Nigeria.* 1982.

CHIPANGO. *See* PODZO.

CHIPETA. The Chipeta, also known as the Achipeta, are a subgroup of the Chewa* people of Malawi, eastern Zambia, and central Mozambique. The Chipeta population today exceeds 350,000 people, most of whom are sedentary farmers, raising maize, beans, and rice. They are predominantly Roman Catholics.

CHIRE. The Chire are a major subgroup of the Maravi* people of Mozambique.

CHIRUMBA. The Chirumbas are a major subgroup of the Shona* peoples of Zimbabwe and Mozambique.

CHIRWARE. The Chirwares are a major subgroup of the Shona* peoples of Zimbabwe and Mozambique.

CHISINGA. The Chisingas (Cishinga) are a Zambian ethnic group whose population today is over 100,000 people. They live between the Lundas* and the Bembas,* north of Lake Bangweulu. Over the years, the Chisingas have been conquered by the Lundas and often subject to Arab* slaving raids. Most Chisingas make their livings today as small farmers.
REFERENCE: John J. Grotpeter. *Historical Dictionary of Zambia.* 1979.

CHIVI. The Chivis are a subgroup of the Karanga* people, who are part of the Shona* cluster of peoples in Zimbabwe.

CHIWA. The Chiwa, also known as the Bichiwa, are an ethnic group in Gabon. They have been celebrated in Gabonese history because of the resistance they put up to the French* in the Ogooué River region in the late nineteenth century. Their own oral traditions claim common origins with the Ngumba people and then a descent from the north along the Ivindo River. Although ethnologists classify them as a Fang* people, they claim they are more closely related to the Ngumba and the Bakouélé.* In 1893, when the Société Commerciale, Industriele et Agricole du Haut-Ogooué secured its protectorate concession in Gabon, the Chiwa were living at the junction of the Ivindo and Ogooué rivers, but the company forced their relocation because it wanted their land. Today the Chiwa live in several villages on the Ogooué River, downstream from the Booué River in Gabon.
REFERENCE: David E. Gardinier. *Historical Dictionary of Gabon.* 1994.

CHIWERE. The Chiweres are a subgroup of the Ngoni* people of Malawi.

CHIYAKA. The Chiyakas are one of the traditional, autonomous kingdoms and contemporary ethnic subgroups of the Ovimbundu* people of Angola.

CHOA. The Choas are a major subgroup of the Shona* peoples of Zimbabwe and Mozambique.

CHOA. The Choa, not to be confused with the Choa* people of Mozambique, are a subgroup of the Arabic people of Cameroon and Nigeria. Most of them live in northern Cameroon between Fort Foreau and Mora. The Choa crossed the Chari and Logone rivers and entered Cameroon beginning two centuries ago. They entered Nigeria at approximately the same time. They are primarily cattle raisers. The Choa are strict Muslims.
REFERENCE: Harold D. Nelson et al. *Area Handbook for the Republic of United Cameroon.* 1974.

CHOBBA. *See* KILBA.

CHOKFEM. *See* CHAKFEM-MUSHERE.

CHOKOBO. The Chokobos—also known as Azoras, Izoras, and Cikobus—are a relatively small ethnic group living today in the Jere District of Jos Division of Plateau State in Nigeria. Their population numbers several thousand people, most of whom are subsistence farmers. Their language is classified with the Northern Jos group of the Western Plateau cluster in the Benue-Congo family.
REFERENCE: *Language Survey of Nigeria.* 1976.

CHOKOSI. *See* CHOKOSSI.

CHOKOSSI. The Chokossi (Chakossi, Kyokosi, Kyokoshi, Tschokossi, Tyo-kossi) are an Akan* ethnic group living in the Sansanné-Mango and Dapango regions of Togo and in Ghana. They claim Manding* origins, arriving in their current location after a migration in the late eighteenth century, traveling from Ivory Coast through Ghana and Burkina-Faso. Their language is a Baule* dialect loaded with Mande expressions. They call themselves the Anoufou (Anufo). They are closely related to the Anyi*-Baules, Sefwis,* and Aowins.* Before the arrival of the German* empire, the Chokossi were known for their own kingdom, with its capital in Sansanné-Mango, and for their reputation as warriors and mercenaries who could often be found in the service of the Dogambas* and Konkombas.* They at first resisted the German military conquest but then joined the German military units in the conquest of neighboring regions. Today, the Chokossi population is approaching 50,000 people, of whom perhaps a third are Muslims.
REFERENCE: Samuel Decalo. *Historical Dictionary of Togo.* 1976; Daniel M. Mc-Farland. *Historical Dictionary of Ghana.* 1995.

CHOKWE. The Chokwes (Kioko, Cokwe, Tschokwe, Quioco) are a Bantu* ethnic group living today in the Katanga, Kasai, and upper Kwango and Kasai river regions of Zaire and Angola, as well as in Zambia. Until the mid-1800s, the Chokwes were a matrilineal society of semi-nomadic hunters living in north-eastern Angola. Their homeland was the savanna. In the eighteenth century, the expansion of the Chokwe empire began in earnest as Chokwe traders spread throughout the Lunda* empire, selling slaves, rubber, wax, and tusks. Through marriage and conquest in the nineteenth century, the Chokwes absorbed most of the other ethnic groups between the Kwango River and the Kubango and Kunene rivers. Chokwe expansion toward Zambia was stopped in the 1890s. They became an important group in the Shaba region of southeastern Zaire. Most Chokwes are now farmers, but many have also gravitated to industrial and mining jobs in the Shaba copper belts.

REFERENCES: F. Scott Bobb. *Historical Dictionary of Zaire.* 1988; Susan H. Broadhead. *Historical Dictionary of Angola.* 1992; John J. Grotpeter. *Historical Dictionary of Zambia.* 1979; Irving Kaplan et al. *Zaire: A Country Study.* 1978; Reinhald Kauenhoven-Janzen. "Chokwe Thrones." *African Arts* 14 (May 1981): 69–74.

CHOMA-KARIM. The Choma-Karims—also known historically as the Shomohs, Shomongs, Kiyus, Nuadhus, Karims, and Kirims—speak a Jukunoid* language of the Benue-Congo family. Most of them are small farmers, living in the Muri, Wurkum, Lau, Gassol, and Jalingo districts of Muri Division in Gongola State, Nigeria.
REFERENCE: *Language Survey of Nigeria.* 1976.

CHONA. *See* SHONA.

CHONYI. The Chonyis are part of the Mijikenda* cluster of people of coastal Kenya and Tanzania. Most of them are farmers, raising maize, millet, sheep, and goats, while others are laborers on sugar cane, sisal, and cotton plantations.

CHOPE. *See* SHOPE.

CHOPI. *See* SHOPE.

CHOPI-BITONGA. *See* SHOPE.

CHUA. *See* CHEWA.

CHUABO. The Chuabo (Maganja) are a small ethnic group of several thousand people living in Mozambique. Most of them are small subsistence farmers who live along the banks of the lower Zambezi River Valley. During the late eighteenth and nineteenth centuries, they actively participated in the slave trade, capturing and selling other Africans to Portuguese* traders.
REFERENCE: Mario Azevedo. *Historical Dictionary of Mozambique.* 1991.

CHUKA. The Chukas are a Bantu*-speaking people who are a subgroup of the Meru* cluster of peoples in Kenya and Tanzania.

CHUMBURUNG. The Chumburungs are an ethnic group living today in central-eastern Ghana. Most of them are subsistence farmers. Their population today exceeds 22,000 people. The Chumburung language is part of the Guan* subgroup of the Volta-Comoe group.
REFERENCE: Keith Snider. "Apocope, Tone and the Glottal Stop in Chumburung." *Journal of African Languages and Linguistics* 8 (October 1986): 133–44.

CIKOBU. *See* CHOKOBO.

CIKUNDA. *See* CHIKUNDA.

CISHINGA. *See* CHISINGA.

CLELA. *See* LELA.

COBIANA. The Cobianas are an ethnic group of the southern Casamance region of Guinea-Bissau. They are closely related to the Bañuns* and Cassangas.* For several centuries, they were part of the independent Cassanga kingdom at Birkima, and their most prominent historical leader was Kassa-Mansa. Late in the sixteenth century, the Cobianas became active slave hunters. Today, the Cobianas are mostly small farmers.
REFERENCE: Richard Lobban and Joshua Forrest. *Historical Dictionary of the Republic of Guinea-Bissau.* 1988.

COCOLI. *See* LANDOMA.

COKWE. *See* CHOKWE.

COLOURED. The term "Coloured" has been used for more than a century in southern Africa to denote people who possess mixed blood ancestry—primarily through the union of English men with African women, usually women of Khoisan-speaking groups. The term "Coloured" was also used to describe the offspring of mixed Indian*-Khoisan unions. During the decades of apartheid in what is today South Africa, Zambia, and Zimbabwe, Coloureds occupied a middle position in the social hierarchy, well below whites but above full-blooded black Africans. The triumph of independence in Zambia and Zimbabwe and of black majority rule in South Africa during the past twenty years has liberated the large group of Coloureds from white dominance in those three countries.
REFERENCE: Amry Vandenbosch. *South Africa and the World: The Foreign Policy of Apartheid.* 1970.

COMOROS. The Comoros Islands are a volcanic archipelago located in the Indian Ocean between Mozambique and Madagascar. Centered at the crossroads of the Indian Ocean, the islands were originally settled by a mixed group of African Bantus,* Malayo-Indonesians, and Arabs.* Most of these people were converted to Islam by Arab missionaries in the fifteenth and sixteenth centuries. Madagascar slavers almost depopulated the islands in the eighteenth century, carrying Comoros Islanders to Madagascar, Mauritius, and Reunion. The islands eventually came under the control of the French* empire, and they be-

came independent in 1975. The population of the islands today exceeds 475,000 people.
REFERENCE: Frederica M. Bunge. *Indian Ocean: Five Island Countries.* 1982.

COMPA. *See* ABURÉ.

CONGO. *See* KONGO.

CONGOE. The term Congoe, or Congoe Recaptives, refers to the people of Liberia who descend from individuals captured on slave ships in the 1820s and 1830s. In 1807, the United States Constitution had outlawed the international slave trade. Thereafter, American naval ships plying the coast of West Africa sometimes boarded illegal slave ships, seized their slave cargoes, and resettled the freed people in Liberia, the region where the American Colonization Society was also repatriating freed U.S. blacks. Most of the recaptured people came from the Congo River area, and they became known as "Congoe Recaptives." Congoe settlements appeared all along the Liberian coast, from Robertsport to Harper. Many of those settlements have retained a distinct sense of identity.
REFERENCE: D. Elwood Dunn and Svend H. Holsoe. *Historical Dictionary of Liberia.* 1985.

CONGOE RECAPTIVE. *See* CONGOE.

CONHAQUE. *See* KONHAQUE.

CONIAGUI. *See* KOÑAGI.

COTOCOLI. *See* KOTOKOLI.

CRAU. *See* KRU.

CROPHY. *See* AGAVE.

CWA. *See* TWA.

D

DABA. The Dabas are a non-Fulbe,* non-Muslim ethnic group of northern Cameroon, a subgroup of the Kirdis.* They arrived there while fleeing the Fulbe slave traders in the lowlands. The Dabas are farmers who raise crops in terraced, hillside fields. Most Dabas live in the Bénoué, Margui-Wandala, and Diamaré departments of Cameroon. The Daba population today exceeds 55,000 people.
REFERENCES: Ruth Leinhardt and Ursula Wiesemann. "La Modalité du vera daba." *Journal of African Languages and Linguistics* 8 (April 1986): 41–63; Harold D. Nelson et al. *Area Handbook for the Republic of United Cameroon.* 1974.

DABIDA. The Dabidas are a subgroup of the Taita* peoples of East Africa, particularly Kenya. They speak a Bantu* language.

DADIYA. The Dadiyas, also known as the Nda Dias and Boleris, are a small ethnic group living today in the Dadiya District of the Gombe Division of Bauchi State in Nigeria. They speak an Adamawa language and make their livings as small farmers.
REFERENCE: *Language Survey of Nigeria.* 1976.

DADJO. *See* DAJU.

DAFFO-BATURA. The Daffo-Baturas are an ethnic group living today in the Ron and Monguna districts of the Pankshin Division of Plateau State in Nigeria. They speak a Chadic language that is closely related to that of the Ron* people. Most Daffo-Baturas are small farmers.
REFERENCE: *Language Survey of Nigeria.* 1976.

DAFI. The Dafi (Dafing, Southern Marka) are considered a Fringe Manding* group, who trace their tribal origins back to the Mali Empire of the thirteenth century. Other ethnic groups identified them as "Black Lips" because of the cosmetic practice of Dafi women to dye their lips blue. They live today in Mali and Burkina-Faso where they pursue a nomadic, pastoral lifestyle. They first began to arrive in the region with the decline of the Songhai* Empire in the seventeenth century. The Dafi population is estimated at 175,000 people today, of whom 75 percent are Muslims.

REFERENCES: Daniel M. McFarland. *Historical Dictionary of Upper Volta.* 1978; Donald R. Wright. "Manding-Speaking Peoples." In Richard V. Weekes, ed. *Muslim Peoples.* 1984.

DAFING. *See* DAFI.

DAGABA. *See* DAGARI.

DAGABAA. *See* DAGARI.

DAGANA. The Daganas are a subgroup of the Hassaunas,* a large group of ethnic Arabs* living today in Chad.

DAGARA. *See* DAGARI.

DAGARI. The Dagari (Dagara, Dagaba, Dagarte, Dagati, Dagate, Dagabaa) are considered one of the stateless Molé-Dagbane* peoples of West Africa. More specifically, they are concentrated in the northeast corner of Ghana, primarily in the Upper Region-West, between the Black Volta River and Kulpawn, and across the border in Burkina-Faso, especially between Diébougou and Boura. They can also be found in Ivory Coast. Their population exceeds 500,000 people. Most of them are settled farmers, raising millet and a variety of other crops. The main Dagari settlement is at Han, Ghana.

REFERENCES: Jack Goody. *Death, Property and the Ancestors: A Study of Mortuary Customs of the LoDagaba of West Africa.* 1962; Daniel M. McFarland. *Historical Dictionary of Ghana.* 1995.

DAGARTE. *See* DAGARI.

DAGATE. *See* DAGARI.

DAGEL. The Dagels are one of the major subgroups of the Tama*-speaking people of Chad; Tama is a Waddian language. Most Dagels live in settled villages where they have learned to rotate crops, which allows them to farm the arid Sahel region. Most of them can be found living in Biltine Prefecture in southeastern Chad.

REFERENCE: Thomas Collelo et al. *Chad: A Country Study.* 1990.

DAGILA. *See* KURI.

DAGOMBA. *See* DOGAMBA.

DAHALO. The Dahalos are a small ethnic group living in the lower Tana River Valley in Kenya. They were traditionally a hunting and gathering people, but that way of life has largely disappeared; the Dahalos now make their living as laborers and small farmers. Although their original language had the familiar clicks of more southerly groups, they adopted the Dahalian tongue from Cushitic speakers.
REFERENCE: Bethwell A. Ogot. *Historical Dictionary of Kenya.* 1981.

DAHOMEAN. *See* FON.

DAIR. The Dair are one of the non-Arabic Nuba* peoples of Kordofan Province of Sudan. Most of them are farmers, raising sorghum, cotton, and peanuts through rainfall agricultural techniques in the granite inselbergs of the central Nuba Mountains. They are mostly Muslim in their religious loyalties.

DAJA. *See* DAJU.

DAJU. The Daju (Dadjo) are a people of western Sudan and eastern Chad. Approximately 80,000 Dajus live in Sila Province, while another 50,000 are in Wadai and Guerra. They call themselves ''Koska.'' There are also approximately 50,000 Dajus living in Darfur Province and in southern Kordofan in Sudan. Scholars disagree about the classification of the Daju language, some believing that it is Nilo-Saharan while others claim it is Nubian.* Some argue that Daju must be classified by itself. Arabic is rapidly replacing Daju as the primary language among the people. The vast majority of the Daju are sedentary farmers who raise millet, sorghum, and corn. Some Daju own cattle but allow them to be controlled by nomadic Arab* herders, who are also allowed to graze their animals on Daju land. This arrangement gives the Daju fertilizer for their fields. The Daju are Sunni Muslims who follow the Maliki school, although they are not known as being particularly devout. Daju society is divided into tribes that are further subdivided into patrilineal clans. Among their neighbors and former French* colonial administrators, the Daju are known as a politically volatile, warlike people, whose mountainous homeland has made them especially difficult to control.
REFERENCES: Henri Berre. ''Daju.'' In Richard V. Weekes, ed. *Muslim Peoples.* 1984; Carolyn Fluehr-Lobban, Richard A. Lobban, Jr., and John Obert Voll. *Historical Dictionary of Sudan.* 1992.

DAKA. *See* CHAMBA.

DAKARKARI. *See* LELA.

DAKKA. *See* DIRIM.

DAKKARARI. *See* LELA.

DAKPA. The Dakpas are a subgroup of the Banda* people of the Central African Republic. The French* conducted nearly genocidal wars of conquest against them between 1897 and 1901. Their current population exceeds 175,000 people.

DALATAWA. The Dalatawas (Dalatoas) are a subgroup of the Kanembus* who live in and around Mao in the Kanem Prefecture of Chad. They are descendants of the Bornu army that invaded the region in the mid-seventeenth century.

DALATOA. *See* DALATAWA.

DALLA. *See* KURI.

DALOL. The Dalols, with a population of approximately 150,000 people, are a major clan of the Issa* people of the Horn of Africa.

DALONG. *See* PAI.

DAMA. *See* BETTE-BENDI.

DAMARA. The Damara people of Namibia are a unique ethnic group whose roots are non-Bantu* and who today speak either a Herero* language or a Nama* language. The contemporary population of the Damara people exceeds 100,000 people, most of whom are farmers.
REFERENCES: Reginald Green, Marja-Liisa Kiljunen, and Kimmo Kiljunen. *Namibia: The Last Colony.* 1981; Stanley Schoeman and Elna Schoeman. *Namibia.* 1984.

DAMBI. The Dambis are a subgroup of the Taita* peoples of East Africa, particularly Kenya. They speak a Bantu* language.

DAMBOMO. *See* SHAKÉ.

DAN. The Dan—also known as Yacouba, Mebe, Samia, and Gyo (Gio)—are a Manding*-speaking group of people who today are concentrated in Ivory Coast, especially in the departments of Man, Danané, and Biankouma. There are also smaller clusters of Dan people across the border in Liberia, primarily in Nimba County near the town of Tapita. Their population today exceeds

350,000 people. Today, the Dan live in close proximity to the Guérés,* Wobés,* and Touras.* They speak a language that is part of the Mande-fu branch of the Manding language group. Although many Dan resisted the overtures of Islamic missionaries from the Mali Empire in the fifteenth and sixteenth centuries, a substantial number eventually became Muslims. The Dan are primarily sedentary farmers who raise high-altitude rice, kola nuts, peanuts, cotton, millet, rice, goats, chickens, and a variety of fruits. Traditionally, they have exchanged these goods for fish. Today, large numbers of Dan men travel seasonally to work as lumberjacks, stevedores, and domestics. The Dan in Liberia are subdivided into four distinct chiefdoms. The Gio chiefdom consists of the Doe, Gbear, and Gblor clans. The Boe-Quella chiefdom consists of the Boe and Quella clans. The Gbehlay-Geh chiefdom consists of the Gbehlay, Kpiarplay, Slalay, Solay, and Zor clans. The Butulu, Gbao, Gbor, Yarlay, and Zoe clans make up the last chiefdom.

REFERENCES: Eberhard Fischer. "Dan Forest Spirits: Masks in Dan Villages." *African Arts* 11 (January 1978): 16–23; Alain Marie. "Parenté, échange matrimonial et récriprocité: Essay d'interprétation à partir de la société Dan et de quelques autres sociétés de Côte d'Ivoire." *L'Homme* 12 (1972), Number 3: 6–46; Number 5:5–36; Donald R. White. "Manding-Speaking Peoples." In Richard V. Weekes, ed. *Muslim Peoples.* 1984.

DANAGLA. The Danaglas are probably of Nubian* extraction, although they have been thoroughly Arabized in recent centuries. They live in the Dongola region of Sudan. Historically, the Danaglas have enjoyed a reputation as skilled merchants and traders. Today, they are classified as a subgroup of the Jaaliyin* Arabs* of Sudan.

REFERENCE: Carolyn Fluehr-Lobban, Richard A. Lobban, Jr., and John Obert Voll. *Historical Dictionary of Sudan.* 1992.

DANAKIL. *See* AFAR.

DANGALEAT. The Dangaleats are one of the Hadjeray* peoples of the mountainous regions of Guéra Prefecture in Chad. They are descended from refugees who were driven into the mountains. They speak a Chadic language and practice the *margai* cult of place and site spirits. In spite of many cultural similarities with such other groups as the Kingas,* Dionkors (Junkun*), Bidios,* Mogoums,* Sokoros,* Barains,* and Sabas,* the Dangaleats rarely intermarry and maintain a powerful sense of identity.

REFERENCE: Thomas Collelo et al. *Chad: A Country Study.* 1990.

DANGME. *See* ADANGBE.

DANKYIRA. *See* DENKYIRA.

DANSHI. The Danshis are a subgroup of the Gezawa* people of northern Nigeria.

DARAMDÉ. The Daramdés are a subgroup of the Maba* people of Sudan. Most Daramdés function in servile positions relative to the Mabas.

DARASA. The Darasas are an ethnic group living among the Oromos* and Sadamas* in southwestern Ethiopia. Most of them are egalitarian pastoralists and subsistence farmers who raise maize and millet.
REFERENCE: M. L. Bender, J. D. Bowen, R. L. Cooper, and C. A. Ferguson, eds. *Language in Ethiopia.* 1976.

DARFUR. The term ''Darfur'' is sometimes used as a generic reference to the ethnic groups living in Darfur Province in western Sudan. Included in this cluster are the Fur,* Masalit,* Daju,* and Zaghawa.*

DARI. The Daris are an ethnic group living on the plains of northern Cameroon and southern Chad. In Chad, they can be found primarily in Mayo-Kebbi Prefecture. Ethnologists assign them a Nilotic* origin, arguing that they came to Chad up the Chari River about two centuries ago. Most of them are farmers, raising groundnuts and cotton for commercial sale. In recent years, periodic droughts in the Cameroonian and Chadian plains have badly damaged the Dari economy. They are actually a subgroup of the Kirdi* peoples. Their population today is approximately 25,000. Like other groups on the plains, they have avoided having much contact with missionaries and government officials, preferring their own cultural isolation and animist religion. They fish, farm, and herd on the floodplains of the Chari River. They are closely related to the Moussey,* Marba,* and Massa* peoples, who speak Massa languages.
REFERENCES: Thomas Collelo et al. *Chad: A Country Study.* 1990; Samuel Decalo. *Historical Dictionary of Chad.* 1987; François Dumas-Champion. ''Le rôle social et rituel du bétail chez les Massa du Tchad.'' *Africa* 50 (1980): 161–81.

DAROD. The Darod are one of the six primary clans of the Somali* people of Somalia. Like all Somalis, they claim their descent from Samaale, the mythical founder of the entire ethnic group. Also, like all other Somalis, they speak the Somali language and are Sunni Muslims. The vast majority of the Darod, except those who work in the major cities, are nomadic herders, who raise camels, sheep, and cattle. The Darod ethnic group, however, is subdivided into thousands of sub-clans and sub-sub-clans, and individual Darod feel far more loyalty to their local clan than to any larger collectivity. Most Darod are concentrated in northern Somalia, primarily in the Bari and Nugal regions, as well as in parts of the Mudugh, Tug Dheer, Sanaag, and Lower Juba regions. They can also be found in the Ogaden and Harar regions of Ethiopia and in the North-Eastern

Region of Kenya. Their current population exceeds 2.2 million people. They both farm and raise cattle or camels.

During the late 1980s and early 1990s, hundreds of thousands of Darod faced starvation because of the famine and civil war in Somalia. Political instability became endemic as centralized authority broke down in the face of severe clan and sub-clan rivalries. Somalia essentially became a no-man's-land of misery and suffering, with no single individual or group enjoying enough power to impose any order. In 1991, many Darod joined with the Issaqs,* the major clan in northern Somalia, and declared their independence from Somalia, establishing the country of Somaliland. Their rebellion, however, failed to secure recognition from the international diplomatic community.
REFERENCES: Margaret Castagno. *Historical Dictionary of Somalia.* 1975; *New York Times,* October 4, 1992.

DASENECH. *See* DASSANETCH.

DASS. The Dasses are an ethnic group living today approximately ten miles northeast of the Jos Plateau in Plateau State in northwestern Nigeria. They are surrounded ethnically by the Zaris,* Jarawas (Afusari*), Zeems,* and Polcis.* Most Dasses are subsistence farmers.
REFERENCE: Elizabeth Isichei, ed. *Studies in the History of Plateau State, Nigeria.* 1982.

DASSA. The Dassas are one of the many subgroups of the Yoruba* peoples of West Africa. They can be found today especially in southern Benin.

DASSANETCH. The Dassanetch (Dasenech) are an ethnic group of approximately 25,000 people who live north of Lake Turkana on both sides of the Omo River in southwestern Ethiopia. Their economy today is based on pastoral animal husbandry and flood-retreat cultivation. The Dassanetch are divided into several tribal groupings; within those tribal groupings are loose clan systems. Those clan systems, however, are relatively weak, for they own no land, control no resources, have no internal systems of political organization, and do not place any real value on endogamy. The basic social unit is the extended household, composed of a man, his wife or wives, and their children.
REFERENCE: Uri Almagor. "Alternation Endogamy in the Dassanetch Generation–Set System." *Ethnology* 22 (1983): 93–108.

DAURAWA. The Daurawas are a subgroup of the Hausa* peoples of Nigeria.

DAYE. The Dayes are one of the large subgroups of the Sara* people of Chad. The Dayes number more than 50,000 people today and live on the middle Man-

doul River and in the Moissala District. They have been completely assimilated by the Saras, though their dialect remains distinct.
REFERENCE: Samuel Decalo. *Historical Dictionary of Chad.* 1987.

DAZA. The Daza are a subgroup of the Dazaga,* who are themselves a subgroup of the Tebu* peoples of the Sahel and Saharan regions of Niger and Chad. In Chad, the Daza can be found in Borkou Subprefecture and Kanem Prefecture, between the Tibesti Mountains and Lake Chad. In Niger, they live in Manga and Kaouar. The Daza population makes up the largest of the Tebu subgroups, numbering more than 200,000 people who are divided into patrilineal clans. They are known for their commercial skills, although most Daza are nomadic pastoralists, who move herds of camels, horses, sheep, and goats between clan-owned wells in the Sahel. The Daza live in loaf-shaped mat tents. They are devout Muslims. The Daza maintain control of the Aza,* another Tebu subgroup, who work as blacksmiths and slaves. The Daza are themselves divided into a number of subgroups, including the Kredas of Bahr el Ghazal, the Charfardas* of Ouaddai, the Kecherdas* and Djagadas* of Kanem, the Dozas,* Anakazas,* Kokordas,* Kamadjas,* and Noarmas* of Borkou, and the Ounias,* Gaedas,* and Erdihas* of Ennedi.
REFERENCE: Thomas Collelo et al. *Chad: A Country Study.* 1988.

DAZAGA. The Dazagas are a subgroup of the Tebu,* a large ethnic group of the Sahel and Saharan regions of Niger, Chad, Sudan, and southern Libya. The Dazaga population exceeds 220,000 people today, and their language is the lingua franca of the region. The Dazaga tend to be concentrated in the Sahel of Niger and Chad. They are themselves subdivided into four groups—Dazas,* Azas,* Dowazas,* and Wajungas*—which are further divided into patrilineal clans. Most Dazaga raise cattle and camels, moving their herds between clan-owned wells in the Sahel. They are overwhelmingly Muslim. During the 1980s and early 1990s, the Dazaga economy suffered badly from droughts in the Sahel, forcing Dazaga men to move seasonally to towns and cities in search of work and to leave women and children with the herds for extended periods.
REFERENCES: Catherine Baroin. "Effets de la colonisation sur la société traditionnelle Daza." *Journal des Africanistes* 47 (1977): 123–39; Kim Kramer. "Tebu." In Richard V. Weekes, ed. *Muslim Peoples.* 1984.

DEBBA. The Debbas are a subgroup of the Maba* people of Sudan.

DEFAKA. The Defakas, also known as the Afakanis, are a small ethnic group in Rivers State, Nigeria. They are concentrated near Nkoro and Iwoma villages in Opobo Division. Although the Defakas have many linguistic similarities to the Ijaws,* they are not technically a subgroup. Most Defakas are subsistence farmers.

REFERENCE: E. J. Alagoa and Tekena N. Tamuno. *Land and People of Nigeria: Rivers State.* 1989.

DEFORO. The Deforos are one of the Habé* peoples. They live north of the Mossi* people along the border of Mali and Burkina-Faso. Most of them are farmers, raising sorghum, peanuts, millet, and cotton.
REFERENCE: Daniel M. McFarland. *Historical Dictionary of Upper Volta.* 1978.

DEGEMA. The Degemas, also known as the Atalas, are a small ethinc group living today in the Kalabari Division of Rivers State in Nigeria. Ethnolinguists classify their language as part of the Edo* group of the Kwa* family. Most Degemas are small farmers.
REFERENCE: *Language Survey of Nigeria.* 1976.

DÉGHA. The Dégha (Déya, Buru, Mofo, Dyoma) are a Voltaic people living in the subprefecture of Bondoukou in Ivory Coast. In terms of their population, which today is estimated at perhaps 20,000 people, they are a small group, living in only ten villages. Like most Voltaic peoples, the Dégha support themselves by herding cattle and raising millet and cassava in subsistence gardens.
REFERENCE: Robert J. Mundt. *Historical Dictionary of Côte d'Ivoire.* 1995.

DEHOXDE. *See* DGHWEDE.

DEI. The Dei (Dey) people live in Bomi County, Liberia. They speak a Kruan* language. In the nineteenth century, when the American Colonization Society began settling African Americans in Liberia, the Dei were among the first to meet the new colonists. The Dei constitute one chiefdom, which is composed of the Bulugba, Deigbo, Gbaavon, and Zoo clans. Their rural population today exceeds 10,000 people, most of whom are farmers. There are also substantial numbers of Dei living and working in Monrovia.
REFERENCES: D. Elwood Dunn and Svend E. Holsoe. *Historical Dictionary of Liberia.* 1985; Harold D. Nelson et al. *Liberia: A Country Study.* 1984.

DEKKA. The Dekkas are a subgroup of the Maba* people of Sudan.

DELO. The Delo people are an ethnic group living today in northern Togo. Their population consists of more than 60,000 people, most of whom are subsistence farmers. They are part of the eastern Grusi* language group.
REFERENCE: Meterwa A. Ourso. ''Phonological Processes in the Noun Class System of Lama.'' *Studies in African Linguistics* 20 (August 1989): 151–78.

DEMA. The Dema are a small ethnic group of several thousand people living in Mozambique. Most of them are small subsistence farmers who live along the

banks of the lower Zambezi River. During the late eighteenth and nineteenth centuries, they actively participated in the slave trade, capturing and selling other Africans to Portuguese* traders.
REFERENCE: Mario Azevedo. *Historical Dictionary of Mozambique.* 1991.

DEMBO. *See* NDEMBU.

DENDI. The Dendis (Dandis, Dandawas), not to be confused with the Dendis* of the Central African Republic, are an ethnic group of approximately 100,000 people. They are concentrated in the northern reaches of the Republic of Benin, as well as in Togo, Niger, and Nigeria. They speak a Songhai* language and know of their origins in the great Songhai Empire of the sixteenth century, when they were actually a Mende* group. Centuries ago, as merchants, they migrated throughout the Niger River Valley, establishing themselves along caravan routes where they could sell their goods and services. Today, they continue to work as merchants and itinerant traders, although large numbers of Dendis also work as subsistence farmers, raising maize, millet, manioc, and plantains. The Dendis are a subgroup of the Songhai people of West Africa. They are particularly concentrated in Parakou, Djougou, Kandi, and Nikki in Benin. They are over-whelmingly Muslim and indistinguishable from surrounding Bariba* Muslims.
REFERENCE: Samuel Decalo. *Historical Dictionary of Benin.* 1994.

DENDI. The Dendi people are part of the Ngbandi* group of people in the Central African Republic. They live on the banks of the Ubangi River, upstream from Bangi. The Dendis are a riverine people. Because of their skills as boatmen, they have been active traders on the Ubangi River, and, when the French* first arrived in the late nineteenth century, the Dendis served as middlemen between the French and the inland ethnic groups. In recent years, Dendis have found a prominent place in the police and civil service of the Central African Republic.
REFERENCE: Pierre Kalck. *Central African Republic.* 1993.

DENG. *See* CHAMBA.

DENKERA. *See* DENKYIRA.

DENKYERA. *See* DENKYIRA.

DENKYIRA. The Denkyira (Dankyira, Denkera, Denkyera, Kankyira) are one of the major ethnic subdivisions of the Akan* people. They are concentrated demographically along the border between the Western and Central regions of southern Ghana. The Akan state was supreme in the region until 1701, when Osei Tutu of the Asante* conquered them. The Denkyira rebelled against the

Asante in 1711, but they were crushed and never recovered from the Asante conquest. The contemporary Denkyira population is approximately 85,000 people.

DENO. The Deno people, also known as the Bures, speak a language that is classified as part of the Bole*-Tangale* group of Chadic languages. Their population today exceeds 20,000 people, most of whom live in Ganjuwa District of the Bauchi Division of Bauchi State in Nigeria.
REFERENCE: *Language Survey of Nigeria.* 1976.

DENYA. The Denyas, also known as the Anyang people, are a small ethnic group of approximately 15,000 people who live today in the forests of the Akwaya Subdivision and the Mamfe Central Subdivision of Manyu Prefecture in the Southwest Province of Cameroon. Most of them live near the Mamyu River and in Mamfe Town, and, from there, westward toward the Nigerian border. Denyas can also be found across the border in eastern Nigeria. They are divided into a number of clan subgroups, including the Takamandas, Bitiekus, Bashos, and Kendems, which enjoy their own dialects. Most Denyas are subsistence farmers.
REFERENCE: Samson Negbo Abangma. *Modes in Denya Discourse.* 1987.

DERA. The Dera (Deru, Kanakuru) people live in the Shani and Shellem districts of the Numan Division in Gongola State in Nigeria. Most of them are subsistence farmers. The Deras speak a Chadic language that is part of the Bole*-Tangale* group.
REFERENCE: *Language Survey of Nigeria.* 1976.

DERESA. The Deresas are part of the larger cluster of Omotic* peoples in Ethiopia. They live near the Gofas,* although they are surrounded by Oromic peoples, in southern Ethiopia. Most Deresas are hoe cultivators, who raise ensete or other grain products. They also practice animal husbandry. They have retained many elements of their indigenous religions. Their contemporary population exceeds 325,000 people. The Deresas speak a Cushitic language.
REFERENCES: M. L. Bender, J. D. Bowen, R. L. Cooper, and C. A. Ferguson, eds. *Language in Ethiopia.* 1976; Harold D. Nelson et al. *Ethiopia: A Country Study.* 1980.

DEY. *See* DEI.

DÉYA. *See* DÉGHA.

DGHWEDE. The Dghwedes—also known historically as the Hudes, Johodes, Dehoxdes, Tghuades, Toghwedes, Traudes, Azaghwanas, Wa'as, and Zaghmanas—are an ethnic group of approximately 60,000 people living in Nigeria. They are concentrated in the East Gwoza District of Borno State, where

they work as subsistence farmers. They speak a Chadic language that is part of the Mandara* group.
REFERENCE: *Language Survey of Nigeria.* 1976.

DHOPADHOLA. The Dhopadholas are an ethnic group living today in Uganda. They speak a Western Nilotic* language and are concentrated in the north-central region of the country, north of Lake Kyoga and northeast of Lake Albert. Most of them are small farmers and cattle raisers.
REFERENCE: Peter Ladefoged, Ruth Glick, and Clive Criper. *Language in Uganda.* 1972.

DIAKHANKÉ. *See* JAHANKA.

DIALONKE. The Dialonke, not to be confused with the term "Dialonke," which sometimes refers to the Yalunka,* are a Manding*-speaking people of Mali. Their contemporary population is approximately 150,000 people, and about half of them are Muslims.
REFERENCES: Pascal Imperato. *Historical Dictionary of Mali.* 1986; Donald G. Morrison et al. *Black Africa: A Comparative Handbook.* 1989.

DIALONKE. *See* YALUNKA.

DIAN. *See* DYAN.

DIANKHANKE. *See* JAHANKA.

DIANNE. *See* DYAN.

DIAWARA. The Diawara are an ethnic group living today in Mali, particularly in the *cercles* of Nioro and Nara. They speak the Sarakolé (Soninké*) language, but they are not of Sarakolé descent. They have simply acculturated to the more numerous Sarakolé people, by whom they are surrounded. Diawara legend has them descending from one Daman Guille, to whom the Sarakolé also are connected. The Diawara population is approximately 100,000, almost all of whom are Muslims.
REFERENCE: Pascal Imperato. *Historical Dictionary of Mali.* 1986.

DIDA. The Didas are an ethnic group living just west of the Baule* in Ivory Coast, especially in the south-central part of the country near the towns of Lakota, Divo, Guitry, and Grand Lahou. They are part of the Kru* cluster of peoples. The Didas resisted the economic and political intrusions of the French* empire and violently resisted French colonial administration until 1918, surrendering after a nine-year-long battle. The Didas did not become part of the larger commercial economy of Ivory Coast until after World War II, when commercial agriculture slowly penetrated their region. Their current population is approximately 120,000 people, divided into the following subgroups: Divo, Yo-koboué, Maké, and Lozoua.

REFERENCES: Monni Adams and T. Ross Holdcroft. "Dida Women's Raffia Cloth from Côte d'Ivorie." *African Arts* 25 (July 1992): 42–51; Robert E. Handloff et al. *Côte d'Ivoire: A Country Study.* 1990.

DIDINGA. The Didingas are a relatively small ethnic group of perhaps 40,000 people living in southeastern Sudan. They speak an eastern Sudanic language. Some can also be found across the border in Ethiopia as well as in northern Kenya. The Didingas have frequently been in conflict with neighboring groups because of economic pressures on the southern Sudanic environment. Some ethnologists classify them with the Murle* peoples.

REFERENCES: B. A. Lewis. *The Murle: Red Chiefs and Black Commoners.* 1972; Helen C. Metz et al. *Sudan: A Country Study.* 1992.

DIGHIL. *See* DIGIL.

DIGIL. The Digils (Dighils) are one of the six primary clans of the Somali* people of Somalia. They are closely related to the Rahanwayns.* Like all Somalis, they claim descent from Samaale, the mythical founder of the entire ethnic group. Also like all other Somalis, they speak the Somali language and are Sunni Muslims. Some Digils are nomadic herders, who raise camels, sheep, and cattle, but most of them are farmers. The Digil ethnic group, however, is subdivided into thousands of sub-clans and sub-sub-clans, and individual Digils feel far more loyalty to their local clan than to any larger collectivity of people. Most Digils are concentrated in northwestern Somalia.

During the late 1980s and early 1990s, hundreds of thousands of Digils faced starvation because of the famine and civil war in Somalia. Political instability became endemic as centralized authority broke down in the face of severe clan and sub-clan rivalries. Somalia essentially became a no-man's-land of misery and suffering, with no single individual or group enjoying enough power to impose any order. In 1991, many Digils joined the Somali National Alliance, a group headed by General Mohammed Farrah Aidid, a member of the Hawiye* clan. Even the intervention of United Nations troops in 1992 did not perma-nently restore stability to the region. Like millions of other Somalis, the Digils faced catastrophe.

REFERENCES: Margaret Castagno. *Historical Dictionary of Somalia.* 1975; *New York Times,* October 4, 1992; Helen C. Metz et al. *Somalia: A Country Study.* 1992.

DIGO. The Digos are part of the Nyika* group of the Mijikenda* cluster of Northeast Bantu*-speaking peoples who today live in Tanzania near the Kenya border, on the coastal strip of Kenya along the Indian Ocean. The Digos are farmers who raise rice, maize, cassava, and coconuts. They also supply palm oil for the palm wine industry. They are nominally Sunni Muslims of the Shafi school, and their social system is based on patrilineal descent. Generally, the surrounding Swahili*-speaking people of Kenya and Tanzania look down upon the Digos as an inferior group. The Digo population today is approximately 75,000 people.

REFERENCES: P. B. Bostock. *The Peoples of Kenya.* 1967; Bethwell A. Ogot. *Historical Dictionary of Kenya.* 1981.

DILLING. The Dilling are one of the non-Arabic Nubian* peoples of Kordofan Province in Sudan. Most of them are rainfall farmers, raising sorghum, cotton, and peanuts through rainfall agricultural techniques in the granite inselbergs of the southern Nuba Mountains. They are Muslim, Christian, and animist in their religious loyalties, although Islam has been gaining ground during the past thirty years.

DIME. The Dimes are a tiny Ethiopian ethnic group who live in the southern reaches of the country. They speak an Omotic* language and make their living as herders and small farmers. The Dime population today exceeds 2,500 people.

REFERENCE: M. L. Bender, J. D. Bowen, R. L. Cooper, and C. A. Ferguson, eds. *Language in Ethiopia.* 1976.

DIMMUK. The Dimmuks (Doemaks) are a small ethnic group living today in Plateau State in Nigeria. They are closely related to the Namus* and Bwals.* All three groups claim descent from a man known as Dimmuk. They possess a long list of kings and a well-developed oral history. Political authority tends to be highly decentralized among the various Dimmuk villages. Most Dimmuks are subsistence farmers.

REFERENCE: John Ola Agi. ''The Goemai and Their Neighbors: An Historical Analysis.'' In Elizabeth Isichei, ed. *Studies in the History of Plateau State, Nigeria.* 1982.

DINDJE. The Dindjes are a subgroup of the Sara* people of Chad. Today, the Dindjes are devout Muslims known for avoiding alcohol use, observing Ramadan, reading the Koran, practicing polygyny, making the Haj (pilgrimage) to Mecca if economic resources permit, and saying daily prayers. Some Dindje men are members of Sufi brotherhoods. They are also known for their small family size and low fertility rates, probably because of the high age differential between husbands and wives and the high rates of divorce and sterility from venereal disease. The Dindje population is approaching 90,000 people.

DINGI. *See* DUNGU.

DINKA. Today there are more than 1.5 million people who identify themselves

as Dinkas. They are concentrated in Upper Nile Province in Sudan, especially in northern Bahr al Ghazal and south and west of the White Nile. Some ethnologists divide the Dinkas into twenty-five self-conscious subgroups. Their economy and religious life revolve around herding cattle. During the dry season, the Dinkas move their herds about to find pasture; during the wet season, to avoid Nile River flooding, they settle in villages away from the river where they raise millet. Their diet consists largely of milk and millet. The Dinkas speak a Nilotic* language and are divided into dozens of subgroups with little centralized direction, although the need for dry-season grazing forces cooperation on the Dinka subtribes. During times of drought, there have often been bloody battles between Dinkas and Atuots* over grazing lands. Prior to the introduction of centralized administrative and police services in southern Sudan, the Dinka practiced bridewealth in their cattle camps. The Dinkas have been known for the ferocity of their resistance to British* and Arab* political and cultural intrusions. The most prominent Dinka leaders in recent Sudanese history have been William Deng, Francis Deng, and Abel Alier.
REFERENCES: *African Encyclopedia.* 1974; Carolyn Fluehr-Lobban, Richard A. Lobban, Jr., and John Obert Voll. *Historical Dictionary of Sudan.* 1992.

DIOLA. *See* JOLA.

DIONGOR. *See* JUNKUN.

DIONKOR. *See* JUNKUN.

DIPA. *See* KWENI.

DIR. The Dir are one of the six primary clans of the Somali* people of Somalia. Like all Somalis, they claim descent from Samaale, the mythical founder of the entire ethnic group. Also like all other Somalis, they speak the Somali language and are Sunni Muslims. The vast majority of the Dir, except for those who work in the major cities, are nomadic herders, who raise camels, sheep, and cattle. The Dir ethnic group, however, is subdivided into thousands of sub-clans and sub-sub-clans, and individual Dir feel far more loyalty to their local clan than to any larger collectivity of people. Most Dir are concentrated in northwestern Somalia. The Gadabursi subclan of the Dir live in the Northern Region, while the Bimals can be found in the region of Merca. Many ethnologists consider the Issas* in Djibouti to be a Dir clan. The Dir in northern Somalia raise camels, while those to the south raise cattle.

During the late 1980s and early 1990s, hundreds of thousands of Dir faced starvation because of the famine and civil war in Somalia. Political instability became endemic as centralized authority broke down in the face of severe clan and sub-clan rivalries. Somalia essentially became a no-man's-land of misery and suffering, with no single individual or group enjoying enough power to

impose any order. In 1991, many Dir joined the Somali National Alliance, a group headed by General Mohammed Farrah Aidid, a member of the Hawiye* clan. Even the intervention of United Nations troops in 1992 did not permanently restore stability to the region. Like millions of other Somalis, the Dir faced catastrophe.
REFERENCES: Margaret Castagno. *Historical Dictionary of Somalia.* 1975; *New York Times,* October 4, 1992.

DIRIM. The Dirims, also known as the Dakkas, are an ethnic group of approximately 35,000 people living in Nigeria. They tend to be concentrated in the Toungo District of the Danye Division, as well as in the Gashaka, Mambilla, and Muri divisions of Gongola State. The Dirims speak a language that is grouped with Sama in the Adamawa family.
REFERENCE: *Language Survey of Nigeria.* 1976.

DIRIYA. *See* DIRYA.

DIRONG. *See* BERI.

DIRYA. The Dirya people, also known historically as the Diriyas, Sagos, and Tsagos, are a small ethnic group of approximately 10,000 people living in Nigeria. They are concentrated in the Ningi and Ganjuwa districts of the Bauchi Division of Bauchi State. Most of them are subsistence farmers. They speak a Chadic language.
REFERENCE: *Language Survey of Nigeria.* 1976.

DIULA. *See* JOLA.

DIVO. The Divos are one of the subgroups of the Dida* peoples of Ivory Coast.

DJADNE. The Djadnes are a subgroup of the Djoheina,* themselves a large Arab* subgroup in Chad.

DJAGADA. The Djagadas are a subgroup of the Daza* people of Chad. Most of the Djagadas live in the Kanem region, where they are primarily nomadic pastoralists, raising camels, sheep, goats, and sometimes horses.
REFERENCE: Thomas Collelo et al. *Chad: A Country Study.* 1990.

DJALLONKE. *See* YALUNKA.

DJALONKE. *See* YALUNKA.

DJATSI. The Djatsis are a subgroup of the Lendu* people of Zaire.

DJEBERTI. *See* JABARTI.

DJEM. The Djems are an ethnic group living in southern Cameroon, northern Equatorial Guinea, and northern Gabon. They are a subgroup of the Betis,* who are part of the larger Fang*-Pahouin* cluster of peoples. The Djem population today exceeds 150,000 people. Most of them are farmers, raising cassava, cocoa, and yams. They speak a Bantu* language with strong ties to neighboring Fang and Ewondo* peoples, worship as Christians with strong ties to their traditional religion, and are closely related to the Fangs. Historically, the Djems were middlemen during the years of the European slave trade; they resisted German* penetration of their region in the early twentieth century. The Djems also maintain a strong rivalry with neighboring Bamiléké* peoples.
REFERENCE: Donald G. Morrison et al. *Black Africa: A Comparative Handbook.* 1989.

DJEMA. The Djemas are a subgroup of the Maba* people of Sudan.

DJERMA. *See* ZERMA.

DJIMINI. The Djimini are an ethnic group of the Voltaic cluster of peoples in Ivory Coast. Their language is closely related to that of the neighboring Senufos.* The Djimini homeland is south of the Senufos, between the Comoé and Nzi rivers and the towns of Kong and Satama-Sokoura. During the late 1800s, the Djimini were decimated by the expansion of Samory Toure's Mandinka* empire. During that holocaust, more than one-third of all Djimini were killed. Another third were drafted into Toure's army, and a third fled to Anyi* and Baluyé territory. Not until after the defeat of Samory Toure did the repopulation of Djimini villages begin. Today, most Djimini are small farmers, raising a variety of crops.
REFERENCES: Robert J. Mundt. *Historical Dictionary of Côte d'Ivoire.* 1995; Ellen Suthers. ''Perception, Knowledge and Divination in Djimini Society, Ivory Coast.'' Ph.D. dissertation. University of Virginia. 1987.

DJIOKO. The Djiokos are a subgroup of the Sara* people of Chad.

DJIRI. *See* LOPA.

DJOHEINA. The Djoheina, or Eastern Arabs, are a major Arab* subgroup in the country of Chad. Their total population today exceeds 1.75 million people, most of whom are nomadic pastoralists and small farmers. The Chadian Djoheina are divided into the following subgroups: Hemat, Salamat, Rachid, Myssirie, Djadne, Khozzam, and Rizegat.

DJONGOR. *See* JUNKUN.

DLADLA. The Dladlas are one of the clans of the Emafikamuva* people, who themselves are one of the three major subgroups of the Swazi* people of Swaziland.

DODO. The Dodos (Dodoth, Dotho) live in the semi-arid plateau in Uganda, more particularly in the region bordering on Sudan and Kenya. They speak a language that is part of the Central Paranilotic cluster of languages. The Dodo economy revolves around transhumant pastoralism, with the men raising cattle and the women trying to raise sorghum and millet. Of all of Uganda's ethnic groups, they are among the least developed and the least acculturated to Western technologies. Although their economy has an important agricultural component (sorghum and maize), their religion and culture revolve around cattle herding. Because of severe droughts in northeastern Africa during the 1980s and early 1990s, the Dodos have faced dire economic circumstances.
REFERENCE: K. S. Gourlay. "The Practice of Cueing Among the Karimojon of North-East Uganda." *Journal of Ethnomusicology* 16 (May 1972): 240–46.

DODOTH. See DODO.

DOE. The Doe people are an ethnic group living today in Tanzania. Some ethnologists include them as part of the Zigalu* cluster of peoples. The Doe population exceeds 20,000 people.

DOE-DOE. The Doe-Does are a subgroup of the Bassa* people of Liberia. Most Doe-Does live in Grand Bassa County.

DOE-GBAHN. The Doe-Gbahns are a subgroup of the Bassa* people of Liberia. Most Doe-Gbahns live in Grand Bassa County.

DOEMAK. See DIMMUK.

DOGAMBA. The Dogambas (Dagomba) are one of the larger of the Molé-Dagbane* group of peoples. Their population in the early 1990s was estimated at more than 450,000 people. Approximately 60 percent of all Dogambas are Muslims. Most Dogambas are small farmers, raising millet and yams in northern Ghana and Togo. In the mid-1500s, King Na Louro established their kingdom in what is today Yendia, Ghana, driving the Konkomba* into Togo. German* troops conquered the Yendi* in 1884, effectively separating these Dogambas from the Dogamba in Gold Coast. After the Germans were expelled from Togo in 1914, the British* secured a mandate over the region, bringing the Yendi and Togolese Dogambas together again. Most of them are farmers, raising millet, sorghum, and beans.
REFERENCE: Phyllis Ferguson. "Patterns of Succession to High Office in Dagomba."

In Michael Crowder and Obaro Ikime. *West African Chiefs: Their Changing Status Under Colonial Rule and Independence.* 1970.

DOGO. The Dogos are one of the major subgroups of the Ngambaye* people of Chad. The Ngambayes are themselves a subgroup of the Saras.*

DOGON. The Dogon people, also known as the Habé and Cadau, today number more than 350,000 and are scattered across the highlands of the Bandiagara escarpment in central Mali and in the *cercles* of Koro, Bankass, Bandiagara, and Douentza. They live in hundreds of distinct villages. Because of the topography of their homeland, isolated in the valleys and high plateaus of the escarpment, the Dogon have been relatively little affected by modern society. The cliffs of the escarpment have protected the Dogon from invaders since the fifteenth century. They are simply too isolated, even from one another, a fact that is evident in that they speak more than thirty-five dialects. Although some Dogon do a little hunting, the people are primarily farmers, raising millet as their staple crop. Since World War I, when the French* controlled Mali as part of French West Africa, the Dogon have also raised onions as a cash crop.

Muslim and Christian missionaries work among the Dogon, but their success in making converts has been slow in recent years. Approximately 35 percent of the Dogon are Muslim and about 10 percent are Christians, but the majority of the Dogon remain loyal to their indigenous, animist religion, which places great spiritual significance on the many caves dotting the cliff landscapes. The Dogon bury their dead there. They believe that the environment, especially the baobab tree, is full of spiritual beings who must be appeased. The community calendar is replete with religious festivals and rituals designed to guarantee the renewal of the world in its eternal cycles.

REFERENCES: Helen Loup. ''Dogon Figure Styles.'' *African Arts* 22 (November 1988): 44–51; David Roberts. ''Below the Cliff of Tombs: Mali's Dogon.'' *National Geographic* 178 (1990): 100–128; Tito Spini and Sandro Spini. *Togu Na: The African Dogon: ''House of Men, House of Words.''* 1977.

DOKA. The Doka people live in Dajura District of Kachia Division in Kaduna State, Nigeria, and are closely related to the Chips,* Mwahavuls,* Chakfem-Mushere,* and Kofyars.* They are divided into two subgroups—the Jortus and the Jaghnins. Like other savanna peoples in the region, they are subsistence farmers, raising millet, maize, guinea corn, beans, and livestock. Their village political systems are decentralized.

REFERENCE: John Ola Agi. ''The Goemai and Their Neighbors: An Historical Analysis.'' In Elizabeth Isichei, ed. *Studies in the History of Plateau State, Nigeria.* 1982.

DOKO. *See* DOKOA.

DOKOA. The Dokoas (Dokos) are a subgroup of the formerly powerful Sa-

banga* peoples of Zaire and the Central African Republic. Their population in the nineteenth century exceeded 10,000 people, and they were prominent on the Ubangian Plateau. Most Dokoas today have adopted the Banda* language and are assimilating with the Banda people. They can be found today living along the Zaire River in western and northwestern Zaire and across the border in the Congo.
REFERENCES: Pierre Kalck. *Historical Dictionary of the Central African Republic.* 1992; Irving Kaplan et al. *Zaire: A Country Study.* 1978.

DOKO-UYANGA. The Doko-Uyangas (Dokl-Uyangas, Dosangas, Basangas, Ikos) are an ethnic group living the Akamkpa Division of Cross River State in Nigeria. They are primarily subsistence farmers.
REFERENCE: *Language Survey of Nigeria.* 1976.

DOM. *See* ABRON.

DOMBE. The Dombes are one of the traditional, autonomous kingdoms and contemporary ethnic subgroups of the Ovimbundu* people of Angola.

DOMPAGO. The Dompagos, a Voltaic people of northern Benin and Togo, are a subgroup of the Kilangas.* Their current population exceeds 200,000 people, most of whom are farmers.

DON. *See* SAMOGHO.

DONDO. The Dondo (Badondo) people are one of the subgroups of the Kongo* peoples of Congo, Zaire, and Angola. They are concentrated in southern Congo, northern Angola, and northwestern Zaire. The more than 25,000 Dondos in Congo are concentrated in the Mindouli District.

DONG. The Dongs are a small ethnic group living today in the Binyeri District of the Adamawa Division of Gongola State in Nigeria. They speak an Adamawa language and make their livings as small farmers and herders.
REFERENCE: *Language Survey of Nigeria.* 1976.

DONGIRO. The Dongiros (Donyiro) are an ethnic group in East Africa who speak a Central Paranilotic language. They live in southern Sudan near the Uganda border. The Dongiros pursue a pastoral lifestyle, with the women and children living in permanent villages and the men leaving home seasonally to take cattle to pastures. The cattle provide them with milk, blood, and hides. Dongiro women work agricultural plots and raise millet, maize, cow peas, and some tobacco. Because of the droughts that have hit the region in the 1980s and early 1990s, the Dongiros have faced what can be called at best a very marginal living. Their traditional religion and culture revolve around cattle.
REFERENCE: John Lamphear. *The Traditional History of the Jie of Uganda.* 1976.

DONGUENA. The Donguenas are part of the larger cluster of Nyaneka-Humbe* peoples of southwestern Angola.

DONYIRO. *See* DONGIRO.

DOOKA. *See* GBAYA.

DORAI. The Dorais are a subgroup of the Gezawa* people of northern Nigeria.

DORGBOR/DOWEIN. The Dorgbor/Doweins are one of the Bassa* clans living in the River Cess Territory of Liberia.

DORIA. *See* KURI.

DOROBE. The Dorobes, also known as the Lorobos, are subgroup of the Fulbe* people. They tend to be found especially in the Wuli, Kantora, and Fuladu regions of Gambia. Like other Fulbes, they are cattle herders, but, even among Fulbes, they are known for being unusually mobile in their lifestyle and extremely conservative in their traditions.

DOROBE. *See* DOROSIE.

DOROBO. The Dorobos (Ndorobos, Nderebes) are a hunting and foraging tribe living today amidst the Masai* people of Tanzania and Kenya. The two groups maintain a symbiotic relationship. The Dorobos supply honey and game meat to the Masai, who provide iron work and cereals to the Dorobos. Some ethnologists believe that the Dorobos have their origins in San* culture, but they speak a Para-Nilotic language. The Dorobos live on meat, honey, roots, berries, and tubers. Their population today is approximately 35,000 people.
REFERENCES: Laura Kurtz. *Historical Dictionary of Tanzania.* 1978; Bethwell A. Ogot. *Historical Dictionary of Kenya.* 1981.

DOROSIE. The Dorosie (Dorossie, Dorobe) people, not to be confused with the Dorobes* of Gambia, are a subgroup of the Lobi* people of Burkina-Faso. They are concentrated west of Gaoua, around Lakosso.

DOROSSIE. *See* DOROSIE.

DORU. The Doru people are closely related to the Bassa* people of Liberia because they speak a Bassa language. They live in the southern part of Nimba County in Liberia and interact closely with the Gbuizohns, Joweins, and

Mowehs, three of the Bassa clans. Most of the Dorus, whose population is approximately 3,000 people, are subsistence farmers.
REFERENCE: D. Elwood Dunn and Svend E. Holsoe. *Historical Dictionary of Liberia.* 1985.

DORZE. The Dorze people live in a very small, fifteen-square-mile area of the Gemu-Gofa highlands of Ethiopia. They speak a Sadama* dialect and have a contemporary population of approximately 23,000 people. They are famous for their basket-shaped, woven bamboo houses and for their skill as weavers. The Dorzes who have migrated to Ethiopian cities maintain a powerful sense of Dorze identity and return home annually for the Mesqel Day festival.
REFERENCE: Chris Prouty and Eugene Rosenfeld. *Historical Dictionary of Ethiopia and Eritrea.* 1994.

DORZOHN GORYAH. The Dorzohn Goryahs are a subgroup of the Bassa* people of Liberia. Most Borzohn Goryahs live in Grand Bassa County.

DOSANGA. *See* DOKO-UYANGA.

DOTHO. *See* DODO.

DOUALA. *See* DUALA.

DOUROU. The Dourou are an ethnic group of approximately 50,000 people who live today between the towns of Garoua and Ngaoundéré in Cameroon. They speak an Adamawa language and are divided in their religious loyalties among Muslim, Christian, and indigenous traditions. They prefer the summits of the hills of river valleys for their homes.
REFERENCE: Harold D. Nelson et al. *Area Handbook for the United Republic of Cameroon.* 1974.

DOWAYO. *See* DOYAYO.

DOWAZA. The Dowazas are a subgroup of the Dazagas,* themselves a subgroup of the Tebu* peoples of the Sahel and Sahara regions in Niger, Chad, and Sudan. Dowazas speak the Dazaga language and live in the pastures and oases south of the Tibesti Mountains in northwestern Chad. They prefer to live in towns rather than as nomadic pastoralists, maintaining their herds of cattle and camels outside their primary settlements. Because they live in permanent homes—usually stone houses—the Dowazas have been deeply influenced by Islamic and French* culture. The Dowaza population is approximately 10,000 people.

DOYAYO. The Doyayos (Dowayos) are an ethnic group living today in and

around Poli in the Department of Benue in northern Cameroon. Their language is part of the Adamawa-Eastern family, which is part of the larger Niger-Congo group. Most Doyayos are farmers who raise guinea corn, peanuts, cotton, and kapok.
REFERENCE: Elisabeth Wiering and Marinus Wiering. *The Doyayo Language.* 1994.

DOZA. The Dozas are a subgroup of the Daza* people of Chad. Most Dozas live in the Borkou Subprefecture where they are nomadic pastoralists raising goats, sheep, camels, and sometimes horses.
REFERENCE: Thomas Collelo et al. *Chad: A Country Study.* 1990.

DRAWA. The Drawas are a subgroup of the Shilha* people, who themselves are one of the Berber* peoples of Morocco.

DUAISH. The Duaishes are one of the Moor* subgroups living today in Mauritania.

DUALA. The Dualas (Doualas) are an ethnic group of approximately 120,000 people living in and around the city of Douala on the Atlantic coast of Cameroon. Approximately four centuries ago, they migrated to their present location from Zaire. They believe they descend from the Mbedi and Ewala peoples and are closely related to the Batangas* of the Kribi region and the Bakweris* of western Cameroon. They were among the first Cameroonian people to meet and interact with Europeans, and they became active middlemen in the Atlantic slave trade during the seventeenth and eighteenth centuries. During the century of French* administration, the Dualas became one of the most educated and acculturated groups in Cameroon. The Duala language is closely related to Lingala.* In recent years, the Dualas have lost of their economic influence, although Duala culture remains extremely powerful in Cameroon. Duala is the Christian lingua franca among coastal peoples. The leading Duala politicians in Cameroon include Soppo Priso, Betote Akwa, and Sengat Kuo.
REFERENCES: *African Encyclopedia.* 1974; Mark DeLancey and H. M. Mokeba. *Historical Dictionary of the Republic of Cameroon.* 1990.

DUGUSA. *See* DUGUZA.

DUGUZA. The Duguza people, also known as the Dugusas, are a group of several thousand people living today in the Jema'a District of the Bauchi Division of Bauchi State in Nigeria. Their language is classified as part of the Northern Jos group of the Benue-Congo family.
REFERENCE: *Language Survey of Nigeria.* 1976.

DUKA. The Duka people, who have also been called Hunes and Ethuns, are an ethnic group of approximately 80,000 people who live in Nigeria. They can be

found in the Kontagora Division of Niger State, the Kuyambana District of Sokoto Division, Yauri Division, and in the Rijau District of the Zura Division of Sokoto State. Their language is part of the Benue-Congo family.
REFERENCE: *Language Survey of Nigeria.* 1976.

DUKAWA. *See* DUKKAWA.

DUKKAWA. The Dukkawas are part of the larger Hausa*–Fulbe* cluster of peoples living in the Yauri Division of Sokoto State in Nigeria. They make their living as farmers and fishermen. Actually, they are hoe cultivators, raising millet and guinea corn in the highlands and onions along the river. In addition, they raise maize, groundnuts, sweet potatoes, beans, okra, cassava, and tobacco. Hunting remains culturally important to Dukkawa men. Islam came to them via traders, Hausa administrators, and traveling *mullahs.* More than two-thirds of the Dukkawas are now Muslims; their language is part of the Benue-Congo branch of the Niger-Congo linguistic family. Because of the completion of the Kainji Dam Project in 1968, many of them were forced to relocate off their islands and river banks into larger settlements, where government schools, jobs, and health facilities are accelerating their acculturation and assimilation.
REFERENCES: Ceslaus Prazan. *The Dukkawa of Northwest Nigeria.* 1977; Frank A. Salamone. ''All Resettled at Kainji?'' *Intellect* (1977): 231–33.

DULBU. The Dulbus are a small ethnic group that is now bordering on extinction as a distinct cultural entity. They live in the Jungur District of Bauchi Division of Bauchi State in Nigeria. Their language is classified as part of the Jarawan Bantu* group of the Benue-Congo family.
REFERENCE: *Language Survey of Nigeria.* 1976.

DUMA. The Dumas, also known as Vadumas, are a subgroup of the Karanga* people of Zimbabwe. They are concentrated between Fort Victoria and Chipinga.

DUMBUSEYA. The Dumbuseyas are a Shona* people living today in Zimbabwe. Their origins as an ethnic group are relatively recent, since they appear to have coalesced from a number of refugee Shona groups fleeing Ngoni* attacks in the 1830s. There are a number of Ngoni elements in Dumbuseya culture, indicating that some Ngonis must have settled with them as well. Since the mid-nineteenth century, the Dumbuseyas have lived near present-day Shabani, where they work as farmers and laborers.
REFERENCE: R. Kent Rasmussen. *Historical Dictionary of Zimbabwe.* 1994.

DUMPO. The Dumpos, who are also known as the Kugulos and Kaalas, are a subgroup of the Guan* people who live among the Abron* in Ghana.

DUNGAL. The Dungals are an ethnic group living in close proximity to the Kinga* people of Chad. Casual observers consider them a Kinga subgroup, although their language is quite distinct. Like Kinga, however, the Dungals' language is related to Barma.* The Dungals live in the Hadjeray region of Chad. Their current population exceeds 20,000 people, most of whom make their living as small farmers and by extracting gum arabic from acacia trees.
REFERENCE: Samuel Decalo. *Historical Dictionary of Chad.* 1987.

DUNGI. *See* DUNGU.

DUNGU. Dungu (Dungi, Dingi, Dwingi, Dunjawa) people live today in the Lere District of the Saminaka Division of Kaduna State in Nigeria. The use of their native language is rapidly declining.
REFERENCE: *Language Survey of Nigeria.* 1976.

DUNJAWA. *See* DUNGU.

DUROP. *See* KOROP.

DURUMA. The Durumas are one of the Nyika* peoples, who are part of the Mijikenda* cluster of people, of coastal Kenya and Tanzania. Most of them are farmers, raising maize, millet, sheep, and goats, while others are laborers on sugar cane, sisal, and cotton plantations.

DURU-VERRE. The Duru-Verres (Verre, Vere, Were) are a small ethnic group in contemporary Cameroon and in Gongola State in Nigeria. They are a sub-division of the Baya-Mbun* cluster of peoples in the western reaches of the Central African Republic and in eastern Cameroon. Their population today is around 35,000 people, a third of whom are Muslims. The others practice Christianity and/or a variety of tribal animist faiths. The conversion of the Duru-Verres to Islam began early in the 1800s, when Fulbe* and Hausa* groups established trading relationships with them. Christian missionaries first reached them in the 1920s. Traditional beliefs in ancestor worship and witchcraft still exist, but they are losing ground. Duru-Verre society is organized around patrilineal clans. People live in nuclear or extended family compounds consisting of mud-walled houses protected by a fence or wall. They practice slash-and-burn agriculture and concentrate on producing maize and cassava, which they consume themselves and market for cash. They have learned how to raise cattle for their Fulbe neighbors.
REFERENCES: Philip Burnham. *Opportunity and Constraint in a Savanna Society.* 1980; Philip Burnham. ''Regroupement and Mobile Societies: Two Cameroon Cases.'' *Journal of African History* 16 (1975): 577–94.

DUWUD. The Duwuds are a black ethnic group living in southwestern Libya.

Ethnologists have not been able to identify their origins. The Duwuds are concentrated near the salt lakes of the western Fezzan region, where they live primarily off the meat of red crayfish. They are despised by Arab* groups in the area.
REFERENCE: Robert Bruce St. John. *Historical Dictionary of Libya.* 1991.

DWABEN. The Dwabens (Juabens) are one of the primary subdivisions of the Asante* people of Ghana.

DWANWO. The Dwanwos are a small ethnic group whose contemporary population numbers approximately 50,000 people. In recent years, many Dwanwos have made the transition to commercial farming and urban labor, but most Dwanwos continue to live as subsistence farmers and livestock raisers. They live in the lower Zambezi River Valley of Mozambique.
REFERENCE: Mario Azevedo. *Historical Dictionary of Mozambique.* 1991.

DWINGI. *See* DUNGU.

DYALONKÉ. *See* YALUNKA.

DYAN. The Dyans (Dian, Dianne, Janni) are one of the Lobi* subgroups of Burkina-Faso. They are concentrated in and around the towns of Boromo, Ouahabou, and Hounde in the Centre-Ouest Department. Most of the Dyans are small farmers, raising millet, cotton, sorghum, and peanuts.

DYE. The Dyes are a subgroup of the Somba* people of Benin and Togo. Their contemporary population is approximately 50,000 people, most of whom are farmers, raising maize, millet, plantains, and cassava.

DYOLA. *See* JOLA.

DYOMA. *See* DÉGHA.

DYULA. *See* JULA.

DZA. *See* JANJO.

E

EBE. The Ebes are a subgroup of the Nupe* peoples of Niger State in Nigeria.

EBENA. *See* YUNGUR.

EBINA. *See* YUNGUR.

EBIRA. The Ebiras (Igbirra, Igbira, Edbira, Egbura) are a Nigerian ethnic group. Their current population is approximately 375,000 people, of whom one in four is Muslim. They can be found in the Akoko-Edo Division of Bendel State; in the Gadabuke, Toto, and Umaisha districts of the Nasarawa Division of Plateau State; and in the Kogi and Igbirra divisions of Kwara State. They speak a Nupe* language. Their region is characterized by open woodlands with rocky hills, upon which the Ebiras have traditionally built their villages for protection. Another group of Ebiras live north of the confluence of the Niger and Benue rivers. They are subdivided into six patrilineal clans (patriclans). They trace their origins to the confluence of the Niger and Benue rivers in what used to be Northern Nigeria.
REFERENCES: *Language Survey of Nigeria.* 1976; A. Oyewole. *Historical Dictionary of Nigeria.* 1987; John Picton. ''Masks and the Igbira.'' *African Arts* 7 (Spring 1974): 38–41.

EBRIÉ. The Ebriés, also known as the Kyaman, Gbon, Tchrimbo, and Ebu, are an ethnic group concentrated in Abidjan Department in Ivory Coast. Ethnolinguists classify them as one of the Lagoon peoples, and Ebrié Lagoon is named after them. The Ebriés probably arrived in the coastal region in the eighteenth century, pushed there by Anyi* expansion. They have always had a highly decentralized political system and a social structure dominated by age grade societies. Because of vast immigration into the Abidjan region, the Ebriés have become a minority, but they still maintain a distinct sense of identity. They are Christians and are highly integrated into the commercial economy and modern society.

REFERENCES: Robert E. Handloff et al. *Côte d'Ivoire: A Country Study.* 1990; Robert J. Mundt. *Historical Dictionary of Côte d'Ivoire.* 1995.

EBU. *See* EBRIÉ.

ECHIRA. *See* ESHIRA.

ECHTOUKA. The Echtoukas are one of the subgroups of the Izarguien* people, who themselves are a subgroup of the Tekna* people of Western Sahara in what is today southern Morocco.

EDDA. The Eddas are one of the many subgroups of the Igbo* people, an ethnic group of nearly fifteen million people living today in southern and southeastern Nigeria.

EDERGUIA. The Ederguias are the oldest of the Teda* clans in Tibesti, Chad.

EDIBA. *See* KOHUMONO.

EDIENE. The Edienes are a subgroup of the Ibibio* peoples of Nigeria.

EDIONG. The Ediongs are a subgroup of the Ibibio* peoples of Nigeria.

EDO. The Edo (Binis, Oviedos, Oviobos, Benims) people are one of the primary ethnic communities in Bendel State in Nigeria. They are especially concentrated in the Benin East and Benin West divisions. During and after the fifteenth century, the Edos maintained a powerful kingdom there and in Benin. Although Yorubans* claim that the Edos are offshoots of them, the two languages are mutually unintelligible. There are a number of Edo subgroups, including the Etsakos, Emais, Okpes, Ishans, Owans, Sobos, Kukurukus, Ishans, and Urhobos. Their language is classified as one of the Kwa* languages. Today the Edos have a population of approximately 800,000 people.

REFERENCES: Robert De la Burde. "Ancestral Ram's Heads of the Edo-Speaking Peoples." *African Arts* 6 (Autumn 1972): 29–34; A. Oyewole. *Historical Dictionary of Nigeria.* 1987.

EDWISO. *See* EJISO.

EFE. The Efe are a subgroup of the Mbutis, themselves a subgroup of the Pygmies.* The Efe live in the northeastern portion of the Ituri forest in Zaire. REFERENCE: Roy Richard Grinker. ''Images of Denigration: Structuring Inequality between Foragers and Farmers in the Ituri Forest of Zaire.'' *American Ethnology* 17 (February 1990): 111–30.

EFFIDUASE. The Effiduases are one of the primary subdivisions of the Asante* people of Ghana.

EFIK. The Efik people live in Cross River State in Nigeria, particularly in the Calabar and Akamkpa divisions. They can also be found across the border in Cameroon. In terms of their language and culture, they are closely related to the Ibibios.* Historically, the Efiks have made their living as fishermen and traders on the Cross River. During the seventeenth, eighteenth, and nineteenth centuries, the Efiks played central roles in the European slave and palm oil traffic. They organized themselves into family trading houses that competed with one another for business. Each head of a commercial house was called an *etubon;* the *etubons* selected the *obong,* who dominated commercial activities in a city, such as Calabar. Within Efik society, prominent individuals joined the Ekpe society, which had a powerful influence on local affairs. Today, the Efiks are highly influential in Calabar.
REFERENCES: *African Encyclopedia.* 1974; *Language Survey of Nigeria.* 1976.

EFUTOP. The Efutops, also known as Ofutops and Agbaragbas, are an ethnic group living today in the Ikom Division of Cross River State in Nigeria. Most of them are subsistence farmers. They have a population today of approximately 35,000 people. Efutops speak a Bantu* language.
REFERENCE: *Language Survey of Nigeria.* 1976.

EFUTU. The Efutus (Afutu, Fetu, Futu) are a subgroup of the Guan* peoples of Ghana. They have been concentrated in the Central Region, especially near Cape Coast where the town of Efutu is located today. Although the Efutus were originally a Guan people, they have been classified with the Fante* because of the expansion of the Fantes into the region and the process of assimilation that has occurred. There are approximately 80,000 Efutus living in Ghana today.
REFERENCE: Daniel M. McFarland. *Historical Dictionary of Ghana.* 1995.

EGA. The Egas, also known as the Dies, are part of the Lagoon cluster of peoples of Ivory Coast. They are concentrated in the subprefectures of Guitry and Fresco. Like the other peoples of the southeast coast and lagoons of Ivory Coast, they practice cash-crop farming and engage in the production and trade of palm oil. Some Egas still fish as well to provide themselves with a protein source. They are part of the larger Akan* culture group.
REFERENCE: Robert J. Mundt. *Historical Dictionary of Côte d'Ivoire.* 1995.

EGBA. The Egbas (Egbado) are a subgroup of the Yoruba* people of Nigeria. They were the first Yorubas to have contact with Christian missionaries; because of that, Western cultural influences spread to the rest of Yorubaland from the Egba center in Abeokuta. The Egba kingdom maintained its independence from the British* until 1914. Today, most Egbas are farmers or, because of their proximity to Lagos, businessmen and professionals. They reside primarily in Ogun State.
REFERENCE: A. Oyewole. *Historical Dictionary of Nigeria.* 1987.

EGBADO. *See* EGBA.

EGBIRA. *See* EBIRA.

EGBURA. *See* EBIRA.

EGEDE. *See* IGEDE.

EGGAN. The Eggans (Eggon, Egon, Mada Eggon, Megong) are one of the Bantu*-speaking peoples of Nigeria. They are classified as part of the Plateau cluster of peoples who occupy north-central Nigeria. They can be found particularly in the Assaiko District of the Lafia Division and the Eggon District of the Akwanga Division of Plateau State. Most Eggans practice subsistence horticulture, raising ginger, millet, guinea corn, beans and citrus products. They live in social systems characterized by patrilineal descent and patrifocal residence. In recent years, they have begun migrating to towns and cities looking for work.
REFERENCES: *Language Survey of Nigeria.* 1976; Donald G. Morrison et al. *Black Africa: A Comparative Handbook.* 1989.

EGGEDE. *See* IGEDE.

EGGON. *See* EGGAN.

EGHAGI. The Eghagis are a subgroup of the Nupe* peoples of Niger State in Nigeria.

EGON. *See* EGGAN.

EGUAFO. The Eguafos were once a powerful people in Ghana. Part of the Guan* cluster of peoples, they were known to seventeenth- and eighteenth-century Europeans as the Comany or Great Komenda. They were concentrated near Shama at the mouth of the Pra River on the coast. From that point,

they played key roles in the gold and slave trades. During the nineteenth century, the Eguafos were overwhelmed by the Fante* expansion to the coast, becoming a Fante subgroup in spite of their Guan heritage.
REFERENCE: Daniel M. McFarland. *Historical Dictionary of Ghana.* 1995.

EGUN. The Eguns, also known as Gus and Aladas, are one of the Ewe* peoples of Nigeria. They can be found today living in the Badagry Division of Lagos State, as well as across the border in Benin.

EHOTILE. *See* MEKYIBO.

EHOUÉ. The Ehoués are one of the subgroups of the Ewe* cluster of peoples in Togo, Benin, and Ghana in West Africa.

EIBE. *See* EWE.

EJAGHAM. The Ejaghams (Ekois) are an ethnic group living today in southern Cross River State in Nigeria, as well as across the border in western Cameroon. In Nigeria, they can be found concentrated in the Akamkpa, Ikom, and Calabar divisions of Cross River State. They are closely related to the Efiks* and Ibibios.* The Ejagham language is of Bantu* origins. Most of the Ejaghams are farmers, raising yams and palm oil. Large numbers of them also work in Nigerian cities. The Ejagham population today exceeds 400,000 people.
REFERENCES: *Language Survey of Nigeria.* 1976; Donald G. Morrison et al. *Black Africa: A Comparative Handbook.* 1989.

EJISO. The Ejisos (Edwisos) are one of the primary subdivisions of the Asante* people of Ghana.

EKAJUK. The Ekajuks (Akajuks) are an ethnic group living today in Nigeria, primarily in the Ogoja Division of Cross River State. They speak a Bantu* language.
REFERENCE: *Language Survey of Nigeria.* 1976.

EKEKETE. The Ekeketes are a subgroup of the Ovimbundu* peoples of Angola.

EKET. The Ekets (Ekits) are an ethnic group living in Eket Division of Cross River State in Nigeria. They speak a language closely related to that of the neighboring Efik* and Ibibio* peoples.
REFERENCES: *Language Survey of Nigeria.* 1976; Donald G. Morrison et al. *Black Africa: A Comparative Handbook.* 1989.

EKIT. *See* EKET.

EKITI. The Ekitis are one of the major subgroups of the Yoruba* people of Nigeria. Most Ekitis live today in the northern reaches of Ondo State and in south-central Kwara State in western Nigeria.

EKKPAHIA. The Ekkpahias are one of the many subgroups of the Igbo* people, an ethnic group of nearly fifteen million people living today in southern and southeastern Nigeria.

EKOI. *See* EJAGHAM.

EKOKOMA. *See* MBEMBE.

EKPETIAMA. The Ekpetiamas are a subgroup of the Izon* people of Rivers State in Nigeria.

EKPEYE. The Ekpeye people are an ethnic group of approximately 80,000 people living today in the Ahoada and Ogba-Egbema divisions of Rivers State in Nigeria. They speak a Kwa* language.
REFERENCE: *Language Survey of Nigeria.* 1976.

EKUMFI. The Ekumfis are a subgroup of the Fante* peoples of southern Ghana. They are concentrated along the Ghanaian coast in the Central Region, west of the town of Winneba. Most Ekumfis make their living as fishermen.
REFERENCE: Daniel M. McFarland. *Historical Dictionary of Ghana.* 1995.

EKUMURU. *See* KOHUMONO.

EKURI. *See* NKUKOLI.

EL-BEYED. The El-Beyeds are a subgroup of the Mejat* people of Western Sahara in what is today Morocco. They are primarily a fishing people.

EL-BOIHAT. *See* LEBOUIHAT.

ELEME. The Eleme people are an ethnic group living today in the Tai-Eleme Division of Rivers State in southeastern Nigeria. They are a farming and fishing people of the Niger Delta. The contemporary Eleme population exceeds 200,000 people. Their language is part of the larger Benue-Congo family.
REFERENCE: Suanu M. Ikoro. "Numeral Classification in Kana." *Journal of African Languages and Linguistics* 15 (1994): 7–28.

EL-FAARIS. The El-Faaris are a subgroup of the Oulad Tidrarin* people of southern Morocco.

ELGEYO. *See* KEYO.

EL-GHERRABA. The El-Gherrabas are a subgroup of the Souaad people, who are part of the Reguibat* es-Sahel ethnic group in Western Sahara.

EL-GRONA. The El-Gronas are a subgroup of the Mejat* fishing people of Western Sahara.

EL-GUERAH. The El-Guerahs are one of the three subgroups of the Izarguien* people, who are part of the Ait Jmel* cluster of the Tekna* peoples of Western Sahara in what is today Morocco.

ELGUMI. *See* ITESO.

ELMOLO. The Elmolos are a tiny ethnic group living on the southeastern shores of Lake Turkana in Kenya. Their population is fewer than one thousand people. Most ethnologists believe they are descended from the Rendilles.* Although the original Elmolo language has Cushitic roots, today most of them are Maa-speakers. The Elmolos make their entire living off the fish of Lake Turkana.
REFERENCE: Bethwell A. Ogot. *Historical Dictionary of Kenya.* 1981.

ELOYI. The Eloyis—also known as Afos, Epes, Ahos, Afus, and Afaos—are a Nigerian ethnic group. They can be found today living in the Agatu District of the Oturkpo Division of Benue State, as well as in the Doma District of the Lafia Division and the Nasarwa, Loko, and Ago districts of the Nasarwa Division in Plateau State. They can also be found in Kwara State. Their language is part of the Benue-Congo family. They trace their origins to the confluence of the Niger and Benue rivers in what used to be Northern Nigeria. They have long been a farming people, but, in recent decades, because their region has been integrated into a larger commercial economy, large numbers of Eloyis are working for wages and experiencing occupational diversity.
REFERENCES: *Language Survey of Nigeria.* 1976; Donald G. Morrison et al. *Black Africa: A Comparative Handbook.* 1989; A. Oyewole. *Historical Dictionary of Nigeria.* 1987.

EMAFIKAMUVA. The Emafikamuvas are one of the three major subgroups of the Swazi* people of Swaziland. They are known as the "latecomers," since they arrived in Swaziland after the Swazis had already settled there. At the time, the Emafikamuvas were fleeing Zulu* expansion. They were incorporated into Swazi ethnic culture, but they are still not considered to be real Swazis by many Swazis. The Emafikamuvas are composed of the following major clans: Nkambules, Manyatsis, Nhlengetfwas, Mtsettfwaa, Hlatshwako, Tselas, Masukus, Dladlas,* Vilakatis, and Masilelas.
REFERENCE: John J. Grotpeter. *Historical Dictionary of Swaziland.* 1975.

EMAI. The Emais, sometimes called the Ivbiosakons, are a subgroup of the Edo* peoples of Nigeria. They can be found living in the Owan, Akoko-Edo, Ishan, East Benin, and West Benin divisions of Bendel State. Their population today is approaching 200,000 people.

EMAKHANDZAMBILI. The Emakhandzambilis are one of the three major subgroups of the Swazi* people of Swaziland. They are of Ngoni* or Sotho* origins and were living in the area when it was invaded by Sobhuza I and his followers in the early nineteenth century. Over time, they were absorbed by the Swazi peoples, although even today they are still not considered to be ''true Swazis,'' like the Bemdzabakos. The Emakhandzambilis are subdivided into many clans, including the Gama, Magagula, Maziya, Kubonye, Mnisi, Maphosa, Gwebu, Shabanga, Tabetse, Sifundza, Malindza, Bhembe, Shabalala, Mncina, Makhubu, Mashinini, Msimango, Motsa, Mahlangu, Zwane, Shongwe, Thabede, and Ngcomphalala.
REFERENCE: John J. Grotpeter. *Historical Dictionary of Swaziland.* 1975.

EMANE. The Emane people, also known historically as the Amanas, live today in Obudu Division of Cross River State, Nigeria. Their non-Bantu* language is part of the Tiv*-Batu* group.
REFERENCE: *Language Survey of Nigeria.* 1976.

EMBO-NGUNI. *See* BEMBO-NGUNI.

EMBU. The Embus are an ethnic group living in the Embu District of the Eastern Province of Kenya. They speak a Central Bantu* language and are closely related to the Kikuyus* and Merus.* The Mbweres are an Embu subgroup. Originally a hunting and gathering people, they have made the transition in the last several centuries to agriculture, raising millet, sorghum, arrowroot, cassava, sugar cane, bananas, maize, coffee, tea, and pyrethrum. The Embus also raise cattle, goats, and sheep. Their current population exceeds 175,000 people.
REFERENCE: Bethwell A. Ogot. *Historical Dictionary of Kenya.* 1981.

EMORO. *See* LEMORO.

ENCASSAR. *See* SEFWI.

ENENGA. The Enenga are a Myènè-speaking people who today live around Lake Zilé, between Lambaréné Island and the junction of the N'Gounié River in the Atlantic coastal area of Gabon. They lost their original language and adopted Myènè during the decades of their descent down the Ogooué River.

By 1910, their original language was gone. During the nineteenth century, the Enenga dominated trade on the middle Ogooué River and the N'Gounié River, trading for slaves from the Adouma* and Okandé* peoples and shipping them downstream. Today, most Enenga are small farmers. The Enenga have flocked to Protestant and Catholic missionary schools, converted to various Christian sects, and become extremely influential in Gabonese commercial and administrative life, even though their contemporary population numbers only several thousand people.
REFERENCE: David E. Gardinier. *Historical Dictionary of Gabon.* 1994.

ENGLISH. *See* BRITISH.

ENNEDI. The Ennedi are an ethnic group of approximately 10,000 people living in the Ennedi mountains of northeastern Chad. Their social system is characterized by its subdivision into patrilineal clans. They make their living from very small-scale agriculture and from raising camels and goats. The Ennedi are 100 percent Muslims, converted long ago during the Arab* conquest of the region. The Ennedi language is part of the Nilo-Saharan family, and they are closely related to the Tebu* peoples of the region.
REFERENCE: Kim Kramer. ''Tebu.'' In Richard V. Weekes, ed. *Muslim Peoples.* 1984.

EOTILE. *See* MEKYIBO.

EOUTILÉ. *See* MEKYIBO.

EPE. *See* ELOYI.

EPHE. *See* EWE.

EPIE. The Epies (Epie-Atissa) are a relatively small ethnic group living today in Nigeria. They are concentrated in the Yenagoa Division of Rivers State. They are an Edo* people. *See* EDO.

EPIE-ATISSA. *See* EPIE.

ERAKWA. *See* ERUWA.

ERDIHA. The Erdihas are a subgroup of the Daza* people of Chad. Most Erdihas live in the Ennedi region where they are nomadic pastoralists, raising goats, sheep, camels, and sometimes horses.
REFERENCE: Thomas Collelo et al. *Chad: A Country Study.* 1988.

ERENGA. The Erenga are one of the Tama*-speaking peoples of Sudan and Chad. They live on the Sudanese side of the border and are closely, even inti-

mately, related to the Asungor* who live across the border in Chad. The Erenga population today is approximately 35,000 people, most of whom are settled pastoralists, raising cattle, camels, and goats and practicing small-scale subsistence agriculture. The main Erenga commercial and marketing centers are the towns of Sirba, Abu Suruj, Tendelti, and El Geneina. The Erenga are overwhelmingly Muslim; their social structure is further subdivided into such powerful clan systems as the Shali, Awra, and Girga.
REFERENCE: Paul Doornbos. ''Tama-Speaking Peoples.'' In Richard V. Weeks, ed. *Muslim Peoples.* 1984.

ERGUIBAT. *See* REGUIBAT.

EROHWA. *See* ERUWA.

ERUWA. The Eruwas (Erohwas, Erakwas, Arokwas) are one of the Edo* peoples of Nigeria. They live in Isoko Division of Bendel State.

ESA. The Esa people live in Bendel State in Nigeria. They are closely related to the neighboring Edo* people. Both groups make their living raising yams, cassava, and oil palm products, as well as by fishing. In recent years, the Esas have increasingly mixed with the Edo, Ijaw,* and Itsekiri* peoples of the region, but they still maintain a distinct sense of identity.
REFERENCES: *African Encyclopedia.* 1974; Donald G. Morrison et al. *Black Africa: A Comparative Handbook.* 1989; A. Oyewole. *Historical Dictionary of Nigeria.* 1987.

ESAN. The Esans (Ishans, Anwains) are one of the Edo* peoples of Nigeria. They can be found in the Ishan, East Benin, Agbor, and Aniocha divisions of Bendel State. The Esan population today exceeds 600,000 people.

ESANGUI. The Esanguis are a subgroup of the Fang* people of Equatorial Guinea. They are the dominant political group in the country, primarily because the Obiang and Nguema families, which have largely monopolized political power in the country since 1968, are Esanguis.

ESELA. The Eselas are a subgroup of the Mbundu* peoples of Angola.

ESHIELU. *See* ISHIELU.

ESHIRA. The Eshiras are a cluster of peoples who live today in coastal Gabon. Their current population exceeds 200,000 people and includes such subgroups as the Eshiras proper and the Bapounous,* Ngowés,* Bavarmas,* Woumbous,* Baloumbous, Babuissis,* and Massangos.*
REFERENCES: David E. Gardinier. *Historical Dictionary of Gabon.* 1994; Donald G. Morrison et al. *Black Africa: A Comparative Handbook.* 1989.

ESHIRA. The Eshira (Echira, Shira) people live in Ogooué-Maritime Province of Gabon, primarily on the Ofoubou River and the Rembo N'Komi River near Fernan Vaz Lagoon. They arrived there in the eighteenth century, fleeing war with the Bakèlès.* They were widely known for the tobacco they raised and for their fine manufactured cloth, known as *raphia.* The Eshiras were devastated by smallpox epidemics in 1865 and again in 1898. In the twentieth century, cheap British textiles destroyed the Eshira *raphia* industry. Today, most Eshiras are small farmers.
REFERENCE: David E. Gardinier. *Historical Dictionary of Gabon.* 1994.

ESSOUMA. The Essoumas are part of the Lagoon cluster of peoples of Ivory Coast. They are concentrated in the subprefecture of Adiaké and Aboisso. Like the other peoples of the southeast coast and lagoons of Ivory Coast, they practice cash-crop farming and engage in the production and trade of palm oil. Some Essoumas still fish as well to provide themselves with a protein source. They are part of a large Akan* culture group.
REFERENCE: Robert J. Mundt. *Historical Dictionary of Côte d'Ivoire.* 1995.

ETCHE. The Etches are one of the many subgroups of the Igbo* people, an ethnic group of nearly fifteen million people living today in southern and southeastern Nigeria.

ETHUN. *See* DUKA.

ETIEN. *See* GANAWURI.

ETKYWA. *See* ICEN.

ETOI. The Etois are a subgroup of the Ibibio* peoples of Nigeria.

ETON. The Etons are an ethnic group living in southern Cameroon, northern Equatorial Guinea, and northern Gabon. They are a subgroup of the Betis,* who are part of the larger Fang*-Pahouin* cluster of peoples. The Eton population today exceeds 200,000 people. Most of them are farmers, raising cassava, cocoa, and yams. They speak a Bantu* language similar to the neighboring Fang and Ewondo* peoples, worship as Christians with strong ties to their traditional religion, and are closely related to the Pahouins. Historically, the Etons were middlemen during the years of the European slave trade; they resisted German* penetration of their region in the early twentieth century. The Etons also maintain a strong rivalry with neighboring Bamiléké* peoples.
REFERENCE: Donald G. Morrison et al. *Black Africa: A Comparative Handbook.* 1989.

ETSAKO. The Etsakos are a subgroup of the Edo* people of Bendel State in Nigeria.

ETSU. The Etsus, also known as the Ati or Atti, are a small ethnic group who are part of the Guan* cluster of peoples. They are concentrated north of the Fante* peoples of the Central Region of Ghana. The Etsus were among the first Ghanians contacted by Europeans in the sixteenth century. Today, most of them live and work as small farmers.
REFERENCE: Daniel M. McFarland. *Historical Dictionary of Ghana.* 1995.

ETULO. The Etulos—also known as the Utors, Eturos, and Turumawas—are an ethnic group living today in Kwara State in Nigeria. Etulos can especially be found in the Shitive and Nyam Atsor districts of Katsina Ala Division of Benue State. They trace their origins to the confluence of the Niger and Benue rivers in what used to be Northern Nigeria. Most of them are farmers. Their language is part of the Idoma* group.
REFERENCES: Donald G. Morrison et al. *Black Africa: A Comparative Handbook.* 1989; A. Oyewole. *Historical Dictionary of Nigeria.* 1987.

ETUMTAK. *See* UTUGWANG.

ETURO. *See* ETULO.

EVALUE. The Evalues are an Akan* people who today live in southwestern Ghana and across the border in Ivory Coast. During the nineteenth century, the Evalues, like the Nzimas,* to whom they are closely related, became important traders between interior tribes and English sailors. That practice came to an end in 1898, when French* merchants got the French colonial administration, in Ivory Coast at least, to tax Evalue merchants heavily and put them out of business. Similar discriminatory taxation policies drove Evalue merchants out of the timber business. During the early years of the French empire, a substantial number of Evalues received French educations, giving rise to a small Evalue professional class in Ghana today. Most Evalues are small farmers. The Evalue population in Ghana today is approximately 5,000 people.

EVANT. The Evant people, also known as Ovandes, Avandes, Balegetes, and Belegates, are a Nigerian ethnic group with strong connections to the Tiv* people. Evants can be found today living in the Obudu Division of Benue State.
REFERENCE: *Language Survey of Nigeria.* 1976.

EVE. *See* EWE.

EVEGBÉ. The term ''Evegbé'' refers to the language spoken by the Ewe* people of West Africa. The three most important Ewe dialects are Anlo,* which is spoken by the Anlo Ewe of Ghana; Gé, which is spoken by the Mina

Ewe of Togo; and Ouatchi,* spoken by the Ouatchi Ewe who live along the coast and in Atakpamé.
REFERENCE: Samuel Decalo. *Historical Dictionary of Togo.* 1976.

EVÉIA. The Evéia people of Gabon are concentrated along the middle N'Gounié River region near Fougamou in N'Gounié Province. They are part of the Okandé* linguistic family. Their own traditions place them near the Atlantic Ocean before the slave trade drove them inland. During the nineteenth century, they migrated into the Ogooué Valley near Lambaréné to escape attacks from the Fangs* and Balèlès. Later they migrated up the N'Gounié River. Today, they make their living as small farmers and fishermen.
REFERENCE: David E. Gardinier. *Historical Dictionary of Gabon.* 1994.

EWE. The Ewe (Ehoué, Eibe, Ephe, Krepe) are one of the dominant ethnic groups of Togo, Benin, and Ghana in West Africa. They are a cluster of Adja* clans who speak the Evegbé* language. The Ewe population today is approaching two million people. It includes the Ewe proper as well as the Anlo,* Krepi,* Ho, Ouatchi,* Mina,* Maxe, Ge, Fon,* Adja* (Aja), and other groups. Anlo is the main literary dialect of the Ewe. They are closely related to the Fon. Their own traditions trace their origins back to Oyo, Nigeria, from where they began their thirteenth-century migration to their present regional location. They are the most highly educated people in the region and the most politically influential. The Ewe are primarily Christian in their religious loyalties, and they are concentrated demographically in southeastern Ghana, southwestern Benin, and southern Togo. Ewe farmers raise maize, millet, manioc, and plantains. In recent years, they have also started producing rice and cocoa.

Among the Ewe, the centralized power of chiefs has traditionally been weak, and the authority of more than 120 sub-clans has been stronger. During the colonial period, pan-Ewe movements developed in Gold Coast and French Togo, but, even after independence, they remained administratively separated. Although the Ewe failed in their attempts to create an all-Ewe political entity, they remain today the dominant group in politics, administration, and civil service in Togo, Benin, and Ghana.
REFERENCES: *African Encyclopedia.* 1974; David Locke. "Eve Dance Drumming." *Journal of Ethnomusicology* 26 (1981): 217–46; Daniel M. McFarland. *Historical Dictionary of Ghana.* 1995; Diedrich Westermann. *A Study of the Ewe Language.* 1930.

EWONDO. The Ewondos are a subgroup of the Betis* (themselves part of the Fang*-Pahouin* conglomeration of peoples), one of the dominant ethnic groups in Cameroon. It is not uncommon for some people to refer to the entire Fang-Pahouin group as Ewondos, primarily because Ewondo has become a lingua franca for them. The Ewondo population today exceeds 250,000 people, most of whom are Roman Catholics. They are scattered across Centre, South, and East provinces in Cameroon. The most prominent Ewondos in Cameroonian

history are André Fouda and Charles Atangana. The Ewondos are engaged in a variety of occupations, although most of them raise rice, cocoa, groundnuts, coffee, palm oil, and timber.
REFERENCE: Mark DeLancey and H. M. Mokeba. *Historical Dictionary of the Republic of Cameroon.* 1990.

EWUTRE. *See* MEKYIBO.

EYAN. The Eyans are an ethnic group living in northeastern Uganda, on the southeastern slopes of Mt. Orom. They speak a language that ethnologists classify as Central Paranilotic. The Eyan economy is a mixed one. Eyan men spend most of their time herding cattle, which provide milk, blood, and hides for the Eyan lifestyle. Eyan women spend much of their time trying to raise crops in what can be an inhospitable environment; they focus their farming on raising millet, maize, cow peas, and tobacco.
REFERENCE: John Lamphear. *The Traditional History of the Jie of Uganda.* 1976.

EYLE. The Eyles are one of the few non-Somali* peoples living today in Somalia. The Eyles were traditionally a hunting people, but, by the mid-twentieth century, most of them had made the transition to settled agriculture. Other Eyles had become migrant laborers in Somali towns and cities. Ethnic Somalis look down upon the Eyles as an inferior people.
REFERENCE: Helen C. Metz et al. *Somalia: A Country Study.* 1992.

EZEKWE. *See* UZEKWE.

EZIAMA. The Eziamas are one of the many subgroups of the Igbo* people, an ethnic group of nearly fifteen million people living today in southern and southeastern Nigeria.

EZZA. The Ezzas are one of the many subgroups of the Igbo* people southern and southeastern Nigeria.

F

FAAH. The Faahs are one of the Bassa* clans living in the River Cess Territory of Liberia.

FA'AWA. *See* PA'A.

FACHARA. *See* CHARA.

FAJELU. *See* POJULU.

FAKARA. *See* CHARA.

FAKKAWA. The Fakkawas can be found today in southern Burkina-Faso, southwestern Niger, northwestern Nigeria, and northern Benin. Smaller groups can be found in northern Ghana and Ivory Coast. Most of them live in villages where they are subsistence farmers. They possess small cattle herds, which they contract out to Fulbe* herders. The Fakkawas are a subgroup of the Songhai* peoples of West Africa. They are Muslims of the Maliki school. The Fakkawas are also divided into a number of subgroups based on a powerful sense of kinship.
REFERENCE: Donald G. Morrison et al. *Black Africa: A Comparative Handbook.* 1989.

FAKUDE. The Fakudes are one of the major clans of the Bemdzabuko* division of the Swazi* people of Swaziland.

FALASHA. *See* BETA ISRAEL.

FALI. The Fali people of Cameroon and southeastern Nigeria have a current population of approximately 95,000 people. Of that total, more than 80 percent

are Muslims. The rest of the Fali are Roman Catholics, Protestants, animists, or syncretic combinations of all three. They are known as the Fali in Nigeria and the Bana in Cameroon. In Nigeria, they can be found especially in the Mubi District of the Mubi Division of Gongola State. Most Fali live near Garova in Cameroon. The Fali in the hills remain loyal to traditional ways, but those on the plains—perhaps one-third of all Fali—are adapting to the larger commercial society. They arrived there escaping Fulbe* slave traders in the lowlands. The Fali are farmers who raise crops in terraced, hillside fields.
REFERENCES: *Language Survey of Nigeria.* 1976; Harold D. Nelson et al. *Area Handbook for the United Republic of Cameroon.* 1974.

FAN. *See* FANG.

FANG. The Fangs (Fans, Fanwes, Mfangs, Mpangwes) are one of the major subgroups of the Pahouin* people of Cameroon, Equatorial Guinea, and Gabon. Their population exceeds 100,000 people today and includes such subgroups of its own as the Ntumus* and Mvaes.*

FANG-PAHOUIN. The term ''Fang-Pahouin'' is used as a generic reference for several ethnic groups living between Douala, Cameroon, and Libreville, Gabon. Included in this cluster are Fangs,* Betis,* Ewondos,* Ntumus,* Banens,* Mvaes,* and Fonds,* Etons,* Makas,* and Bulus.* They all speak closely-related Bantu* languages. *See* PAHOUIN.

FANIAN. The Fanians (Manas) are a subgroup of the Boua* people, who live along the middle Chari River in the Moyen-Chari Prefecture of Chad. Fanians can also be found in central Gueré Prefecture. The Fanians arrived in the Chari Valley long before the Saras* did. Over the centuries, they were victimized by Barma* slave traders, although the Fanians themselves often enslaved the Neilliam. Most Fenians today are small farmers, raising millet, sorghum, and cotton. Their population today is fewer than 5,000 people.
REFERENCE: Thomas Collelo et al. *Chad: A Country Study.* 1988.

FANTE. The Fante (Fanti, Fantyn) are a Twi-speaking group whose Akan* language is part of the Kwa* branch of the Niger-Congo language family. They are the dominant ethnic group in the coastal area of the Central Region in Ghana. They are closely related to the Asantes,* even though they often joined the British* in fighting the Asante Confederacy in the nineteenth century. Traditionally, most Fante were fishermen and farmers. The Fante practice farming and animal husbandry today. Their system of social organization is matrilineal, and they are subdivided into tribal groups. The Fante are Christians, Muslims, and animists, with syncretic systems common among them. Most Fante Muslims follow the Sunni school of the Maliki tradition; a minority of Fante Muslims adhere to the Shafi rite. Since the European conquest of Ghana, Togo, and Ivory

Coast, the Fante have become increasingly Westernized and view themselves as superior to surrounding, non-Akan peoples. African demographers place the contemporary Fante population at approximately 1,700,000 people. Of that total, only 2 percent are Muslims; the remainder are either Christians or loyal to traditional Fante beliefs.

REFERENCES: James Anquandah. ''State Formation Among the Akan of Ghana.'' *Sankofa, The Journal of Archaeological and Historical Studies* 1 (1975): 47–57; J. B. Christiansen. *Double Descent Among the Fante.* 1954; E. T. Meyerowitz. *Akan Traditions of Origins.* 1952.

FANWE. *See* FANG.

FEBE. *See* JULA.

FEDIJA. The Fedija are a subgroup of the Nubians.* Traditionally, they lived several hundred miles from Aswan on the Nile, and the original floodings of Nubian land because of Aswan Dam construction in 1897, 1912, and 1927 did not affect them. They farmed land near the Sudanese border until the 1960s, when the Aswan High Dam project flooded their homelands and forced their relocation.

FELASHA. *See* BETA ISRAEL.

FELLANI. *See* FULBE.

FELLATA. The term ''Fellata'' is used in Sudan to refer to Muslims of West African origins. Throughout the rest of West Africa, the term is often used to refer to people of Fulbe* extraction.

FELOUP. *See* FLUP.

FELUPE. The Felupes are a Senegambian people living today in Guinea-Bissau. They are concentrated particularly in the northwestern corner of Guinea-Bissau, south of the Casamance River and north of the Cacheu River, extending all the way to the coast. They are widely known in the region for their skill as rice farmers using flood irrigation techniques. The Felupes are closely related to the Balantes* and Bayot.* During the colonial period, they earned a reputation as a fiercely proud people, rebelling against the Portuguese* in 1878, 1901, 1903, and 1915.

REFERENCE: Richard Lobban and Joshua Forrest. *Historical Dictionary of the Republic of Guinea-Bissau.* 1988.

FEM. *See* FYAM.

FENWEIN. The Fenweins are one of the Bassa* clans living in the River Cess Territory of Liberia.

FERA. The Feras are a subgroup of the Grusi* people of Ghana. In particular, the Feras live along the border of Burkina-Faso and in the Upper Region of Ghana.

FERNANDINO. The term ''Fernandino'' is used to describe the mixed, creole population of Fernando Po in Equatorial Guinea. The indigenous population of the island of Fernando Po—the Bubis*—refused to cooperate in Spanish plantation projects, and Spain then imported workers from Liberia, Sierra Leone, and Nigeria. Over the years, these workers and their offspring mixed into a new group known as Fernandinos. During the twentieth century, the Fernandinos became an educated and politically influential group in Equatorial Guinea, although they have been oppressed under the recent regime of Macías Nguema. REFERENCE: Max Liniger-Goumaz. *Historical Dictionary of Equatorial Guinea.* 1988.

FERTIT. *See* MABA.

FESEREK. *See* AFUSARI.

FETRA. *See* KURI.

FETU. *See* EFUTU.

FEZERE. *See* AFUSARI.

FIER. *See* FYER.

FILALA. The Filala people are a small tribe in Western Sahara who are defined as *chorfas*—people descended directly from the Prophet Mohammed. They are known for their spirituality. They have also been known for the high number of scholars among them and their respect for learning. The traditional Filala homeland is near Hagounia in the El-Gaada region. There are three Filala subgroups: the Oulad Sidi Ahmed Filalis, the Ahel Ben Mehdis, and the Ahel Faki Ben Salahs. REFERENCE: Tony Hodges. *Historical Dictionary of Western Sahara.* 1982.

FILIYA. *See* PERO.

FINGO. *See* MFENGU.

FIPA. The Fipas are an ethnic group living today in Tanzania and Zambia. They are of mixed heritage (Bantu* and Hamiti), and most of them are Chris-

tians. The Fipas live between Lake Tanganyika and Lake Bukwa. Their population today exceeds 150,000 people, most of whom are farmers, raising millet, wheat, coffee, and fruits. They also fish the lakes for protein. The Fipas are a matrilineal people. Local people recognize the Fipas for their metalworking skills.
REFERENCES: John J. Grotpeter. *Historical Dictionary of Zambia.* 1979; Laura Kurtz. *Historical Dictionary of Tanzania.* 1978.

FIRDU. The Firdu are a subgroup of the Fulbe* people of Gambia.

FITI. *See* SURUBU.

FIZERE. *See* AFUSARI.

FLUP. The Flups, also known as the Feloups, are a subgroup of the Jola.* Most Flups live near Usuy (Oussouye) in Senegal.

FOGNY. *See* KUJAMAAT.

FOKENG. The Fokeng (Bafokeng) are a subgroup, or, more exactly, a chiefdom, of the Sotho* people of Lesotho and South Africa. The Sothos regard them as the first of the Sotho peoples to occupy present-day Lesotho. They also consider the Fokeng dialect to be the purest form of the Sotho language.

FON. The term "Fon" refers to a large cluster of more than three million people living today in the Republic of Benin, with some scattered in Nigeria, Togo, and Ghana. Included in the Fon cluster of peoples are the Fon proper as well as the Mahis,* Agonlinus,* Gouns,* Guemenus,* Tofinus,* Adja*-Wachis, Aizos,* Minas,* Baribas,* Sombas,* Berbas,* Natimbas,* Niendés,* Woabas,* Sorubas,* Dyes,* Kilingas, Dompagos,* Pila-Pilas,* and Yorubas.*
REFERENCE: Donald G. Morrison et al. *Black Africa: A Comparative Handbook.* 1989.

FON. The Fon (Dahomeans, Fonn), who number more than one million people, are the largest ethnic group in the Republic of Benin. They live in the southern third of the country and make their living as farmers, raising maize, millet, manioc, and plantains. They can also be found in Togo, primarily in the Atakpamé region. They speak a Ewe* dialect. Historically, they were the core ethnic group of the precolonial Kingdom of Dahomey, and their state, with its capital at Abomey, Benin, is well-organized and powerful. Today, the Fon play a leading role in the economic and political life in Benin, occupying the most powerful positions in the civil service and professions. The leading Fon in mod-

ern history is Justin Ahomadégbé. The Fon are divided into such subgroups as
the Fon proper as well as the Mahi* and Agonlinu.*
REFERENCES: *African Encyclopedia.* 1974; Samuel Decalo. *Historical Dictionary of Benin.* 1987.

FOND. The Fond are an ethnic group living in southern Cameroon, northern
Equatorial Guinea, and northern Gabon. They are a subgroup of the Betis,* who
are part of the larger Fang*-Pahouin* cluster of peoples. The Fond population
today exceeds 150,000 people. Most of them are farmers, raising cassava, cocoa,
and yams. They speak a Bantu* language, with strong ties to neighboring Fang
and Ewondo* peoples, and worship as Christians with strong ties to their traditional religion. Historically, the Fond were middlemen during the years of the
European slave trade; they resisted German* penetration of their region in the
early twentieth century. They also maintain a strong rivalry with neighboring
Bamiléké* peoples.
REFERENCE: Donald G. Morrison et al., *Black Africa: A Comparative Handbook.* 1989.

FONGORO. The Fongoro call themselves the Gelege; they are also known as
the Kole. The Fongoro live in the hilly region along the border between Chad
and Sudan. It is an extremely isolated region, largely because of the devastations
of the tsetse fly, the poor soil, and the inadequate sources of water. Some Fongoro raise small amounts of sorghum, but most of them live by hunting and
gathering. There is more farming and less isolation in the southern reaches of
the Fongoro region, primarily because the environment is more hospitable. Since
the eighteenth century, the Fongoro have been pushed into their remote homeland by Arab* and Fur* expansion. The Fongoro ruling dynasty has disintegrated, and the Fongoro are in a state of rapid assimilation with the Fur. In fact,
substantial numbers of Fongoro now live among the Fur in towns and cities and
are virtually indistinguishable from them. The Fongoro language, which is Central Sudanic in its origins, is nearly extinct. The Fongoro are Muslims. Their
current population is approximately 2,000 people.
REFERENCE: Paul Doornbos. ''Fongoro.'' In Richard V. Weekes, ed. *Muslim Peoples.*
1984.

FONI. *See* PA'A.

FONN. *See* FON.

FONO. The Fono are a subgroup of the Songhai* people of West Africa. More
particularly, they live in the upper lake districts of central Mali.

FOQRA. The Foqras are a subgroup of the Reguibat* ech-Charg people of
Western Sahara in what is today Morocco. They are divided into the following
subgroups: Ahel Ahmed Ben Lahsen, Ahel Lemjed, Ahel Taleb Hamad, Rema,

Lemnasra, Seddagha, and Oulad Sidi M'hamed. There are approximately 1,800 Foqra today; about 600 of them live near Mahbes. The Foqras are a nomadic people, whose range has included the region of Saguia el-Hamra.
REFERENCE: Tony Hodges. *Historical Dictionary of Western Sahara.* 1982.

FOUIKAT. The Fouikats are a small ethnic group who make their living as fishermen on the coast of Western Sahara. They claim to be descended from Moussa Ibn Fouikat. The Fouikats are divided into four subgroups: the Ahel Chehebs, the Ahel Abdahous, the Aila Ould Saids, and the Ahel Lagoueyeds. Before the arrival of the French* and Spanish* in the late nineteenth century, the Fouikats paid tribute to the Izarguiens.*
REFERENCE: Tony Hodges. *Historical Dictionary of Western Sahara.* 1982.

FOULA. The Foulas (Foula Djallons) are a subgroup of the Fulbe* people of Guinea in West Africa.

FOULA DJALLON. *See* FOULA.

FOULACOUNDE. *See* FULBE.

FOULAH. *See* FULBE.

FOULBE. *See* FULBE.

FOULSE. *See* FULSE.

FRA. *See* FRA-FRA.

FRA-FRA. The Fra-Fra (Fra) are part of the larger Molé-Dagbane* cluster of peoples in northern Ghana and the immediately surrounding region, particularly east of Léo. They are especially concentrated in the eastern portion of the Upper Region of Ghana, east of Bolgatanga near the border with Burkina-Faso. Most of the Fra-Fra raise cattle and work small plots of land. The Fra-Fra population in Ghana today is approximately 300,000 people. Some ethnologists include the Grusis,* Nabdams, Kusasis,* and Talensis* within a Fra-Fra cluster of peoples.
REFERENCES: Meyer Fortes. "Some Aspects of Migration and Mobility in Ghana." *Journal of Asian and African Studies* 6 (1971): 1–20; Fred T. Smith. "Symbols of Conflict and Integration in Frafra Funerals." *African Arts* 21 (November 1987): 46–51.

FRENCH. Tens of thousands of ethnic French live in Africa today, the vast majority of them in the former colonies of the French empire. In the 1830s, after a dispute between the ruler of Algiers and the French consul there, French troops occupied Algeria, and it soon evolved into a French colony. France went

on to establish a protectorate over Tunisia in 1881 and over much of Morocco in 1904. By that time, the scramble for Africa, in which the European empires tried to carve out spheres of influence, was under way. By the early 1900s, France had established the colonies of French West Africa (Benin, Burkina-Faso, Ivory Coast, Guinea, Mali, Mauritania, Niger, and Senegal), French Equatorial Africa (Gabon, Middle Congo, Ubangi-Shari, and Chad), and Madagascar. During the twentieth century, all of these colonies gained their independence, but a small residue of highly influential ethnic French settlers, and their descendants, remained there. Today they constitute the French community in Africa.
REFERENCE: James S. Olson, ed. *Historical Dictionary of European Imperialism.* 1991.

FULA. *See* FULBE.

FULANI. *See* FULBE.

FULBE. The Fulbes (Fula, Fulfulde, Fullah, Fulani, Foulbe) are the world's largest community of nomadic herders. Their original home was between the Senegal River Valley and eastern Guinea. They began an eastward expansion beginning in the twelfth century. Converted at an early date to Islam, they played an important role in spreading the new religion across West Africa. Early in the 1800s, they conquered the emirates of Adamawa, Bauchi, Daura, Gombe, Hadeija, Ilorin, Kano, Katsina, Kasaure, Misau, Nupe, Zaria, Jama'are, and Kontagora. Their capital was at Sokoto. Between 1900 and 1910, however, the British* conquered the Fulbe empire.

Totaling as many as seventeen million people (eight million who still live as herders), they herd cattle and sheep across a wide region of West Africa, from the Atlantic coast of Senegal in the west past Lake Chad in the east. They are found in large numbers in northern Nigeria, Mali, Niger, Guinea, Cameroon, Burkina-Faso, and Gambia. There are also smaller groups of Fulbes in a number of other countries, such as Benin, Ghana, Sierra Leone, and Guinea-Bissau. They call themselves the Fulbe, although they are also known as the Peul, Fulani, Hilani, Fula, and Fulata. They speak a language that is part of the Niger-Congo language family. Fulbe is closely related linguistically to Wolof,* Serer,* and Temne.* More than 95 percent of the Fulbes are Muslims.

The Fulbes are divided into a number of different subcultures. The Bororos* are Fulbes who remain completely loyal to the nomadic lifestyle. They raise large herds of cattle on the open savannas. Another Fulbe subculture is the Fulbe Ladde (Bush Fulani, Fulbe Na'i, Cattle Fulani). They are no longer permanently nomadic because they raise crops seasonally to supplement their diets. The Fulbe Wodabe of Senegal, or "Red Fulbe," whose skin color tends to be lighter than their darker neighbors, even copper-colored, are a distinct group. The Fulbe Mbalu are also known as the Sheep Fulani because their livelihood is derived completely from raising sheep. The Fulbe Siire, also known as the Town Fulani, are people who no longer have cattle herds and work for cash in West African towns and cities. The Dorobe* (Lorobo) are an extremely mobile group of Fulbes who live in Wuli, Kantora, and Fuladu in Gambia. They are conservative and highly traditional in their approach to the outside world. The Firdus are a Fulbe group, known for their trading skills, who today live primarily in West African cities. The Laubes are Fulbes who have acquired an ethnic identity as professional woodworkers who make canoes, wooden statues, and wooden bowls. Finally, the elite Fulbes, who are highly educated and dominate political, legal, and cultural life, are known as Toroobe. During the 1980s and 1990s, many Fulbes fell victim to the savage drought that hit the Sahel in West Africa, destroying range grasses and thus the cattle and sheep herds.

REFERENCES: C. T. Edwensi. *Burning Grass: A Story of the Fulani of Northern Nigeria.* 1962; C. Edward Hopen. "Fulani." In Richard V. Weekes, ed. *Muslim Peoples.* 1984; John Paden. *Religion and Culture in Kano.* 1973; Emily A. Schultz, ed. *Image and Reality in African Interethnic Relations: The Fulbe and Their Neighbors.* 1980.

FULERU. The Fulerus are a small ethnic group who live today near the town of Bukavu in the eastern highlands of Zaire. Most of them are subsistence farmers.

REFERENCE: F. Scott Bobb. *Historical Dictionary of Zaire.* 1988.

FULFULDE. *See* FULBE.

FULILWA. The Fulilwas are a subgroup of the Tumbuka* cluster of peoples living today primarily in Malawi.

FULLAH. *See* FULBE.

FULSE. The Fulse (Foulse) are one of the indigenous peoples of Burkina-Faso in West Africa. They are part of the larger Ninisi* (Tinguimbissi) cluster of ethnic groups. The Fulses are widely known among the other people of the region for their skill as blacksmiths and potters. They are concentrated in central Burkina-Faso, especially in Center-West Department.

REFERENCE: Daniel M. McFarland. *Historical Dictionary of Upper Volta.* 1978.

FUNG. *See* FUNGOR.

FUNGOR. The Fungors (Fungs) are one of the non-Arabic Nuba* peoples of Kordofan Province of Sudan. Most of them are farmers, raising sorghum, cotton, and peanuts through rainfall agricultural techniques in the granite inselbergs of the Nuba Mountains. They are Muslim in their religious loyalties.

FUNGWE. The Fungwes are part of the Tumbuka* cluster of peoples living today in northern Malawi, primarily between Lake Nyasa and the Zam-

bian border, south of the Tanzanian border. Some Fungwes can also be found in Zambia and Tanzania. The Fungwe population today exceeds 40,000 people. They speak a language closely related to that of the Tongas.* The Fungwe economy still revolves around the production of maize, sorghum, and millet.
REFERENCES: *African Encyclopedia.* 1974; John J. Grotpeter. *Historical Dictionary of Zambia.* 1979; Donald G. Morrison et al. *Black Africa: A Comparative Handbook.* 1989.

FUNJ. *See* FUNGOR.

FUR. The Fur (Keira) live in western Sudan, primarily in the Darfur area. Their population today is approaching 800,000 people. They speak a language that is part of the Nilo-Saharan language family. Beginning in the seventeenth century, the Fur empire controlled the western Sudan, but they fell under the control of the Anglo-Egyptian Sudan in the late nineteenth and early twentieth centuries. They are Sunni Muslims loyal to the Maliki tradition, but Fur religious devotions are not as intense as those of other Muslim groups; many Fur are only nominally Muslim. Most of the Fur people are subsistence farmers, who raise millet, tomatoes, and chili peppers. In recent years, however, commercial agriculture has become increasingly important, with Fur farmers securing cash through the production of peanuts, onions, wheat, mangos, oranges, okra, tobacco, sesame, and sugar cane. In addition to being gradually incorporated into the larger cash economy, the Fur also find themselves being increasingly acculturated to Arab* values.
REFERENCES: I. T. Cunnison and W. L. James. *Essays in Sudan Ethnography.* 1972; Gunnar Haaland. "Fur." In Richard V. Weekes, ed. *Muslim Peoples.* 1984; R. S. O'Fahey. *State and Society in Dar Fur.* 1980; R. S. O'Fahey. "Slavery and the Slave Trade in Dar Fur." *Journal of African History* 14 (1973): 29–43.

FURIIRU. The Furiiru people are a subgroup of the Kivu* peoples of Zaire. They live in the highlands of east-central Zaire, south of Lake Kivu, and near the Rwandan and Burundi borders. They can also be found in Rwanda and Burundi. The Furiirus speak a Bantu* language and make their living as farmers who also raise cattle for milk and meat. Historically, the Furiirus once enjoyed their own highly centralized state. During the genocidal civil war in Rwanda in 1994, the Furiirus were overrun by refugees fleeing the violence.
REFERENCE: Irving Kaplan et al. *Zaire: A Country Study.* 1978.

FURU. The Furus are a subgroup of the Mbochi* people of eastern Gabon and central Congo. Their contemporary population exceeds 35,000 people. Although they are increasingly turning to commercial agriculture, the Furu economy has traditionally revolved around trading and fishing, at which they are highly adept. Their social structure is based on a patrilineal clan structure.
REFERENCES: Donald G. Morrison et al. *Black Africa: A Comparative Handbook.*

1989; Gordon C. McDonald et al. *Area Handbook for the People's Republic of the Congo (Congo Brazzaville).* 1971.

FUTANKOBE. *See* TUKULOR.

FUTU. *See* EFUTU.

FWE. The Fwe people are part of the larger cluster of Tonga* peoples in Zambia and Zimbabwe.

FYAM. The Fyams—also known as Pyams, Pyems, Paiems, Fems, Pems, and Gyems—are an ethnic group living today in Gindiri, North Sura, and Kadun districts of Pankshin Division of Plateau State in Nigeria. Their population today exceeds 25,000 people, most of whom are small farmers. The Fyams claim to have broken off years ago from the Ron* people, their neighbors in the region. REFERENCES: Harold D. Gunn. *The Peoples of the Plateau Area of Nigeria.* 1953; *Language Survey of Nigeria.* 1976.

FYER. The Fyers (Fiers) are a relatively small ethnic group living today primarily in the Fier, North Sura, and South Sura districts of the Pankshin Division of Plateau State, Nigeria. They speak a Chadic language. REFERENCE: *Language Survey of Nigeria.* 1976.

G

GA. The Ga, sometimes called Gamashie, are a subgroup of the Mina,* themselves a Ewe* group in the southern reaches of Ghana, Benin, and Togo. They are primarily a coastal and urban people, with many making their living as fishermen. Most of the approximately 50,000 Ga people have adopted the Ouatchi* language as their primary tongue, although it is heavily mixed with Ga vocabulary. They are closely related to the Adangbe.*
REFERENCE: Diana Azu. *The Ga Family and Social Change.* 1974.

GAALIN. *See* JAALIYIN.

GA'ANDA. The Ga'andas (Mokars) are a subgroup of the Mangbetu* people of Zaire and Nigeria. In Nigeria, they can be found in the Ga'anda District of Adamawa Division of Gongola State. Their current population in Nigeria is approximately 30,000 people.

GA-ANDANGME. The Ga-Andangme are a large ethnic group in Ghana. Their current population exceeds 1,300,000 people. Less than 2 percent of the Ga-Andangmes are Muslims. Today they are concentrated in Accra, Osu, Labadi, Nungua, Teshi, and Tema in Ghana. Their own traditions have them migrating to the Accra Plains from Nigeria in the sixteenth century under the leadership of Okai Koi. They are a patrilineal society whose traditional economy revolved around fishing. They were also active, because of their location along the coast, as commercial traders with Europeans.
REFERENCE: Daniel M. McFarland. *Historical Dictionary of Ghana.* 1995.

GABBRA. *See* GABRE.

GABIBI. The Gabibi, also known as the Gabibi Arbi, are a subgroup of the

Songhai* people of West Africa. More particularly, the Gabibi live north of Gao along the Niger River in Mali.

GABIBI ARBI. *See* GABIBI and SONGHAI.

GABLAI. The Gablais are a small ethnic group of approximately 35,000 people living in Chad. They speak a Chadic language and are concentrated in Tandjilé Prefecture. Their language represents a transition between Massa* and Sara.* Most Gablais are herdsmen, day laborers, and small farmers raising millet, maize, and cotton.
REFERENCES: Thomas Colello et al. *Chad: A Country Study.* 1988; Samuel Decalo. *Historical Dictionary of Chad.* 1987.

GABRE. The Gabre (Gabbra), who are also known as the Garre, are one of the major subgroups of the Oromo* people of Ethiopia. They are among the southern cluster of the Oromos and live east of Lake Turkana. They can also be found in the Marsabit District in northeast Kenya. Traditionally, the Gabre were nomadic camel herders, and many of them remain egalitarian pastoralists today.

GABRI. The Gabris are a relatively small ethnic group living today in the Tandjilé Prefecture of Chad. They speak a Chadic language that is linguistically transitional between Sara* and Massa.* Most Gabris are small farmers and herdsmen.
REFERENCE: Thomas Collelo et al. *Chad: A Country Study.* 1988.

GADE. The Gades (Gedes) are one of the Bantu*-speaking peoples of Nigeria. They are classified as part of the Plateau cluster of peoples who occupy central Nigeria. They can be found primarily in the Gadabuka and Loko districts of the Nasarwa Division of Plateau State. Most Gades practice subsistence horticulture, raising ginger, millet, guinea corn, beans, and citrus products. They live in social systems characterized by patrilineal descent and patrifocal residence. In recent years, they have begun migrating to towns and cities looking for work.
REFERENCES: *Language Survey of Nigeria.* 1976; Donald G. Morrison et al. *Black Africa: A Comparative Handbook.* 1989.

GAEDA. The Gaedas are a subgroup of the Daza* people of Chad. Most Gaedas live in the Ennedi region, where they are nomadic pastoralists, raising goats, sheep, camels, and sometimes horses.
REFERENCE: Thomas Collelo et al. *Chad: A Country Study.* 1988.

GAGON. *See* GAGU.

GAGOU. *See* GAGU.

GAGU. The Gagu (Gagon) are an ethnic group of south-central Ivory Coast. Ethnologists believe they were the first ethnic group to occupy the region in the Department of Oumé. The earliest anthropological reports of the Gagu indicated that they were shorter in stature than surrounding peoples, which has led to some speculation that they also have pygmoid roots. The fact that they supplemented their farming by a persistent hunting and gathering culture, as well as their tendency to make clothing out of bark, has reinforced that conclusion. In recent years, the Gagu have become increasingly acculturated to the Guros; most Gagu now speak Guro as their first language. The Gagu population today is approximately 25,000 people.
REFERENCES: Robert E. Handloff et al. *Côte d'Ivoire: A Country Study.* 1988; Bohumil Holas. *Le Gagou: Son Portrait Culturel.* 1975; Robert J. Mundt. *Historical Dictionary of Côte d'Ivoire.* 1995.

GAKI. The Gakis are an ethnic group living today southwest of Mount Kenya in Kenya in East Africa. They are closely related to the Kikuyu* and Meru* peoples. Some ethnologists consider them a Kikuyu subgroup. Most of them are subsistence farmers.
REFERENCE: W. H. Whiteley. *Language in Kenya.* 1974.

GALA. *See* BERI.

GALA. The Galas are a Tanzanian ethnic group and are often included by ethnologists in the larger Nyamwezi* cluster of peoples.

GALAGANZA. The Galaganzas are a Tanzanian ethnic group and are often included by ethnologists in the larger Nyamwezi* cluster of peoples.

GALAMBE. *See* GALAMBI.

GALAMBI. The Galambis (Galembes, Galambes) are a small ethnic group living today in Nigeria. They are classified ethnolinguistically with the Bole*-Tangale* group of Chadic languages. Most Galambis live in the Galembi District of the Bauchi Division of Bauchi State.
REFERENCE: *Language Survey of Nigeria.* 1976.

GALAVDA. *See* GLAVUDA.

GALEMBE. *See* GALAMBI.

GALLA. *See* OROMO.

GALLAO. *See* KURI.

GALLINA. The Gallinas are a small subgroup of the Vai* people of Sierra Leone.

GALOA. The Galoa people, who are also known as the Galwa, are an ethnic group who speak a Myènè language and live today in Ogooué-Maritime Province in western Gabon. Before they arrived at their present location in the nineteenth century, the Galoas lived around Lakes Onangué, Ezanga, and Oguemoue and downstream along the Ogooué. During much of the nineteenth century, they fell under the rule of the Enengas,* not really gaining their independence until the 1870s. They subsequently cooperated closely with British,* German,* and French* trading firms in the area. Not surprisingly, Galoa land became the staging area for European penetration of the Ogooué River Valley in the 1870s and 1880s. The Galoas flocked to Protestant and Catholic missionary schools, converted to various Christian sects, and became extremely influential in Gabonese commercial and administrative life, even though their contemporary population numbers only several thousand people.
REFERENCES: David E. Gardinier. *Historical Dictionary of Gabon.* 1994; Paul Pounah. *La récherche du Gabon traditionnel: hier Edongo, aujourd'hui Galwa.* 1975.

GALWA. *See* GALOA.

GAMASHIE. *See* GA.

GAMA. The Gamas are one of the clans of the Emakhandzambili,* who themselves are one of the three major subgroups of the Swazi* people of Swaziland.

GAMBAYE. *See* NGAMBAYE.

GAMBO. The Gambos are part of the larger cluster of Nyaneka*-Humbe peoples of southwestern Angola.

GAMO. *See* GAMU.

GAMO. *See* NGAMO.

GAMU. The Gamu (Gamo), or Gamu-Gofa, people speak an Omotic* language and inhabit the highland area south of Lake Abaya in the Rift Valley of southern Ethiopia. Generally, they live in isolated mountain groups divided by deep valleys. Historically, the Gamus have used the valley floors for grazing, while the mountainsides have been intensively terraced to raise ensete, barley, and maize. Gamu population density is quite high—from 550 to 2,600 people per square mile—and their total population in the late 1980s was approaching 400,000 people. The Gamus are for the most part confined to their current region. Expansion to the north is limited by the presence of the Wolayta (Welamo*) and Borodda peoples, while inhospitable malarial lowlands lie to the west, south, and east. The Gamus are divided into forty territories called *dere;* the *dere* are further divided into districts called *betante* and neighborhoods called *guta.* The Gamus are also divided into powerful family clan systems, and they tend to marry endogamously within a *dere.*

The Gamu social system is highly authoritarian and stratified. Land ownership is controlled by patrilineal inheritance, in which a father bequeaths half of his property to the eldest son and divides the other half among his other sons. Slaves and artisans are not allowed to own land. Each *dere, betante,* and *guta* supports a political assembly, which is used to discuss matters of common concern and settle disputes revolving around cultivation, irrigation, and family issues. Landless people are not allowed to participate.

REFERENCE: John Hamer. ''Hierarchy, Equality, and Availability of Land Resources: An Example from Two Ethiopian Ensete Producers.'' *Ethnology* 25 (1986): 215–28.

GAN. *See* BENG.

GANA. The Ganas are a subgroup of the Tshu-Kwe* peoples, themselves a subgroup of the San* people of Botswana.

GANAWURI. The Ganawuris (Aten, Ten, Etien, Jal, and Niten) are an ethnic group living in the grassy savannas and volcanic hills of the southern region of the state of Kaduna in Nigeria, primarily in the Moroa District of the Jema'a Division. They can also be found in the Jal District of the Jos Division in Plateau State. Between 1810 and 1833, the Ganawuris fell under Fulbe* influence when the Emir of Jema'a conquered them for plunder and slaves; then from 1847 to 1854, the Emir of Zaria did the same. After the imposition of British* authority in the Ganawuri area, the slave raids and plunder-taking gradually declined. The Ganawuris practice subsistence horticulture, raising ginger, millet, guinea corn, beans, and citrus products. Their population today is approximately 18,000 people.

REFERENCES: Elizabeth Isichei, ed. *Studies in the History of Plateau State, Nigeria.* 1982; *Language Survey of Nigeria.* 1976; Carol V. McKinney. ''A Linguistic Shift in Kaje, Kagoro, and Katab Kinship Terminology.'' *Ethnology* 22 (1983): 281–95.

GANDA. The Ganda are a Bantu*-speaking people who call their language Kiganda. They constitute one of the major ethnic groups of Uganda, especially in southern and central Uganda, and their current population totals nearly three million people. They can also be found across the border in Kenya and Tanzania. The Ganda trace their heritage back to the ancient and powerful Kingdom of Buganda, which thrived from the fourteenth to the nineteenth centuries in the region of Lake Victoria, Lake Edward, Lake Albert, and Lake Kygoa. British* rule of the Ganda was formalized in 1894 and continued until Ugandan independence in the 1960s. The capital of Uganda is Kampala, which lies within the Ganda cultural region. The Ganda are the most highly educated ethnic group in Uganda and dominate the professions, education, and government civil service. Gandan farmers raise bananas as a staple and raise coffee, cotton, and tea as cash crops.

Approximately 20 percent of the Ganda are Muslims—Sunnis of the Shafi school. Swahili* and Arab* traders from East Africa penetrated the region in the mid-nineteenth century and converted large numbers of Gandas, although their conversion was quite superficial; the Ganda were geographically isolated and so their contacts with Muslim traders were relatively infrequent. Those traders also brought a written language—Arabic—to the region, as well as wheat and rice farming. Perhaps 60 percent of Ganda are Christians. Protestant missionaries came to Uganda in 1877, and Catholic missions were established in 1879. Christianity became the primary religion of the Ganda once the British established their formal control in the 1890s. The remaining 20 percent are loyal to traditional, animistic Gandan rituals.

REFERENCES: M.S.M. Kiwanuka. *A History of Buganda from the Foundation of the Kingdom to 1900.* 1971; D. A. Low. *Buganda in Modern History.* 1971; Arye Oded. "Ganda." In Richard V. Weekes, ed. *Muslim Peoples.* 1984; M. L. Pirouet. "Religion in Uganda Under Amin." *Journal of Religion in Africa* 11 (1980): 13–29.

GANDA. The Gandas, not to be confused with the Ganda* of Uganda, are one of the traditional, autonomous kingdoms and contemporary ethnic subgroups of the Ovimbundu* people of Angola.

GANGUELA. *See* NGANGELA.

GANIO. The Ganios are a clan with the chiefdom of Mambahn, a subgroup of the Bassa* people of Liberia. Most Ganios live in the Marshall Territory of Liberia.

GANMU. *See* MONA.

GARAP. The Garaps are one of the constituent groups of the Kim* confederation in Chad.

GARJAK. The Garjaks are a major subdivision of the Nuer* people of Southern Sudan. They are concentrated in the Nasser District.

GARJOK. The Garjoks are a major subdivision of the Nuer* people of Southern Sudan. They are concentrated in the Nasser District.

GARO. The Garo are a Muslim subgroup of the Sadama* people of southwestern Ethiopia.

GARRE. *See* GABRE.

GAWAMA'A. The Gawama'as are an ethnic group included in the larger cluster of Kawahlas,* who themselves are members of the Juhayna* Arabs* of Sudan.

GAWEIR. The Gaweirs are a major subdivision of the Nuer* people of Southern Sudan. They are concentrated in the Fanjak District.

GAWWADA. The Gawwadas are an Ethiopian ethnic group whose language is part of the Cushitic family. The Gawwadas are divided into three subgroups: the Gawwada proper, the Gobezes, and the Werizes. Most Gawwadas are small farmers. Their population today exceeds 60,000 people.
REFERENCE: M. L. Bender, J. D. Bowen, R. L. Cooper, and C. A. Ferguson, eds. *Language in Ethiopia.* 1976.

GBAGYI. The Gbagyi (Bagyis) are a primary subgroup of the Gbari* people of Nigeria. They are concentrated in the states of Niger, Plateau, Kaduna, and Kwara. The Gbagyi themselves are highly divided into subgroups based on dialect and cultural differences. The Gbagyi languages are all part of the Benue-Plateau division of the Niger-Congo language family. There are two primary divisions among the Gbagyi. The Gbagyi Ngenge live in the state of Plateau and number as many as 250,000 people, about 10 percent of whom are Muslims; the rest are Christians and animists. The Gbagyi Yamma number approximately 125,000 people and live in the states of Niger and Kwara; about half of them are Muslims. Because of a long history of persecution at the hands of Hausas* and Fulbes,* the Gbagyi have acquired a common Gbagyi identity. The Hausas and Fulbes derisively call them "Gwari," which means slave. Most Gbagyi, except those who have left to work in the cities, are subsistence farmers. In recent years, the Gbagyi have undergone forced resettlement because of the construction of the new Nigerian capital at Abuja, an event the Gbagyi see as part of a Hausa-Fulbe conspiracy against them.
REFERENCES: Harold D. Gunn. *Peoples of the Plateau Area of Nigeria.* 1953; Charles K. Meek. *The Northern Tribes of Nigeria.* 1969; Malam Shuaibu Na'ibi and Alhaji Hassan. *Gwari, Gade, and Koro Tribes.* 1969; Frank A. Salamone. "Gbagyi." In Richard V. Weekes, ed. *Muslim Peoples.* 1984.

GBAGYI NGENGE. *See* GBAGYI.

GBAGYI YAMMA. *See* GBAGYI.

GBAN. *See* GAGU.

GBANDA. *See* AVIKAM.

GBANDE. The Gbandes (Bandes) are a small Liberian ethnic group. Their current population is estimated at 60,000 people, and approximately 10 percent of them are Muslims. The Lokos* of Sierra Leone are an offshoot of the Gbandes. The civil war in Liberia in the late 1980s and early 1990s badly disrupted the Gbande lifestyle.
REFERENCE: Harold D. Nelson et al. *Liberia: A Country Study.* 1984.

GBANG. *See* BIROM.

GBANRAIN. The Gbanrains are a subgroup of the Izon* peoples of Rivers State in Nigeria.

GBANZIRI. The Gbanziris are a Ubangian* group who live in the Ubangi River Valley of the Central African Republic and across the river in Zaire. They are a riverine people, known for their skill as canoemen and fishermen. Before the arrival of the French* in the late nineteenth century, the Gbanziris were commercial traders moving up and down the tributaries of the Ubangi River system. Their language gradually became the lingua franca of the entire Ubangi-Shari region, including contiguous areas of Chad and Middle Congo.
REFERENCES: Pierre Kalck. *Historical Dictionary of the Central African Republic.* 1992; Donald G. Morrison et al. *Black Africa: A Comparative Handbook.* 1989.

GBARI. The Gbaris (Gwaris, Agbaris, Gwalis, Gbagyis,* Gwarris Baris) are one of the hundreds of ethnic groups in Nigeria. Their current population is approximately 500,000 people; of that total, more than a third are Muslims. They are concentrated in Niger State, particularly in the Minna and Abuja divisions. They can also be found in Kaduna and Plateau states. The Gbaris trace their origins to Bornu. Most of the Gbaris are small farmers.
REFERENCES: *Language Survey of Nigeria.* 1976; A. Oyewole. *Historical Dictionary of Nigeria.* 1987.

GBARWEIN. The Gbarweins are a subgroup of the Bassa* people of Liberia. Most Gbarweins live in Grand Bassa County.

GBARYAH. The Gbaryahs are a subgroup of the Bassa* people of Liberia. Most Gbaryahs live in Grand Bassa County.

GBASA. *See* BASSA.

GBAYA. The Gbaya (Baja, Baya) are an ethnic group of more than 1.2 million people who live in the western reaches of the Central African Republic and in eastern Cameroon. Some can also be found in Gongola State in Nigeria. Perhaps 20 percent of the Gbaya are Muslims. The others practice Christianity or a variety of tribal animist faiths. The conversion of the Gbaya to Islam began early in the 1800s when Fulbe* and Hausa* groups established trading relationships with them. Christian missionaries first reached the Gbaya in the 1920s. Today, Christianity, which is preferred over Islam by those Gbaya with Western educations and by Gbaya women, is gaining ground. Traditional beliefs in ancestor worship and witchcraft still exist, but they are losing ground. The Gbaya are subdivided into a number of subgroups, including the Gbaya Bouli, Gbaya Kaka, Gbaya Bokoto, Gbaya Bodomo, Gbaya Yaiyuwe, Gbaya Lai, Gbaya Dooka, and Gbaya Kara. Gbaya society is organized around patrilineal clans. People live in nuclear or extended family compounds, consisting of mud-walled houses protected by a fence or wall. They practice slash-and-burn agriculture and concentrate on producing maize and cassava, which they consume themselves and market for cash. They have learned how to raise cattle for their Fulbe* neighbors.
REFERENCES: Philip Burnham. "Gbaya." In Richard V. Weekes, ed. *Muslim Peoples.* 1984; Philip Burnham. *Opportunity and Constraint in a Savanna Society.* 1980; Philip Burnham. "Regroupement and Mobile Societies: Two Cameroon Cases." *Journal of African History* 16 (1975): 577–94.

GBAYA BODOMO. *See* GBAYA.

GBAYA BOKOTO. *See* GBAYA.

GBAYA BOULI. *See* GBAYA.

GBAYA DOOKA. *See* GBAYA.

GBAYA KAKA. *See* GBAYA.

GBAYA KARA. *See* GBAYA.

GBAYA LAI. *See* GBAYA.

GBAYA YAIYUWE. *See* GBAYA.

GBHU. *See* NINZAM.

GBI. The Gbi people are closely related to the Bassa* people of Liberia and speak a Bassa language. They live in the southern part of Nimba County in Liberia and interact closely with the Gbuizohn, Jowein, and Moweh, three of

the Bassa clans. Most of the Gbis, whose population is approximately 3,000 people, are subsistence farmers.
REFERENCE: D. Elwood Dunn and Svend E. Holsoe. *Historical Dictionary of Liberia.* 1985.

GBON. *See* EBRIÉ.

GBOR. The Gbors are a subgroup of the Bassa* people of Liberia. Most Gbors live in Grand Bassa County.

GBORWEIN. The Gborweins are a subgroup of the Bassa* people of Liberia. Most Gborweins live in Grand Bassa County.

GBUGBLA. *See* PRAMPRAM.

GBUIZOHN. The Gbuizohns are one of the Bassa* clans living in the River Cess Territory of Liberia.

GCALEKA. The Gcaleka people are a highly independent subgroup of the Xhosa* people in southeastern Cape Province of South Africa.

GE. *See* GA.

GEDE. *See* GADE.

GEIRIKU. The Geirikus are a subgroup of the Kavanga* people of Namibia.

GELEBDA. *See* GLAVUDA.

GELEDI. The Geledi are one of the subclans of the Rahanwayn* clan, a major constituent group of the Somali* people of Somalia. The Geledi arrived in the Shebelle River area in the seventeenth century. Although they were farmers and merchants at the time, they adapted quickly to the local cattle economy. They controlled the caravan routes from the interior to Mogadishu and taxed those doing business on the routes. They thereby became one of the most powerful of the Somali clans. The Geledi have had a longstanding and usually violent rivalry with the Bimals.*
REFERENCE: Margaret Castagno. *Historical Dictionary of Somalia.* 1975.

GELEGE. *See* FONGORO.

GELLI. The Gelli (Bagielli, Badjelli, Baguielli) are part of the Western cluster of Pygmies.* They number approximately 2,500 people and live on the Atlantic coast near Kribi in Cameroon and in Río Muni in Equatorial Guinea.

GELOWAR. The term ''Gelowar'' is sometimes used to describe the largest and most politically organized subgroups of the Serer* in Senegal. The term is derived from the surname of the ruling family of the kingdoms of Siin and Saalum.

GEMASAKUN. *See* SUKUR.

GEMU-GOFA. *See* GOFA.

GENGISTA. The Gengistas are a subgroup of the larger Ngangela* cluster of peoples living today in Angola.

GENGLE. The Gengles (Wegeles) live in the Mayo Belwa District in the Bauchi Division in Bauchi State, Nigeria. They speak an Adamawa language.
REFERENCE: *Language Survey of Nigeria.* 1976.

GERA. The Geras are one of the major subgroups of the Oromo* people of Ethiopia. They should not be confused with the Geras* of Nigeria.

GERA. The Geras are an ethnic group living today in the Galembi and Ganjuwa districts of the Bauchi Division of Bauchi State in Nigeria. They speak a Chadic language that is part of the Bole*-Tangale* group. Most of the more than 28,000 Geras are subsistence farmers and livestock raisers.
REFERENCE: *Language Survey of Nigeria.* 1976.

GERAGE. *See* GURAGE.

GERAWEGE. *See* GURAGE.

GEREMA. *See* GERUMA.

GERKA. *See* YIWOM.

GERKAWA. The Gerkawas are one of the Bantu*-speaking peoples of Nigeria. They are classified as part of the Plateau cluster of peoples who occupy central Nigeria. Most of them live in Plateau State. The Gerkawas have resulted from a mixture of Jukun,* Gomei,* and Montol* peoples. They are bordered to the north by the Yergan* peoples. Most Gerkawas practice subsistence horticulture, raising ginger, millet, guinea corn, beans, and citrus products. They live in social systems characterized by patrilineal descent and patrifocal residence. In recent years, they have begun migrating to towns and cities looking for work.

REFERENCE: Elizabeth Isichei, ed. *Studies in the History of Plateau State, Nigeria.* 1982.

GERMA. *See* GERUMA.

GERMAN. Because Germany did not complete its process of national unification until late in the nineteenth century, it was also late in developing a colonial empire. Beginning in the 1880s, however, Germany participated in the "scramble for Africa" and established a colonial presence in German West Africa (Togo and Cameroon), German South West Africa (Namibia), and German East Africa (Rwanda and Burundi). After its defeat in World War I, Germany lost all of those colonies. Nevertheless, thousands people of German descent still live in Africa, primarily in the former German colonial possessions.
REFERENCE: James S. Olson, ed. *Historical Dictionary of European Imperialism.* 1991.

GERUMA. The Gerumas (Geremas, Germas) are an ethnic group living today in the Jama'a, Zungur, and Ganjuwa districts of the Bauchi Division of Bauchi State in Nigeria. They speak a Chadic language that is part of the Bole*-Tangale* group. Most of the more than 10,000 Gerumas are subsistence farmers and livestock raisers.
REFERENCE: *Language Survey of Nigeria.* 1976.

GESERA. *See* PYGMY.

GESHU. *See* GISU.

GEWARA. The Gewaras are a Plateau Chadic people of Nigeria. Their current population is approximately 90,000 people, of whom about 10 percent are Muslims.
REFERENCE: Donald G. Morrison et al. *Black Africa: A Comparative Handbook.* 1989.

GEWO. *See* GUÉRÉ.

GEZAWA. The Gezawas, also known as the Zarandawas, are a Bantu*-speaking people whose territorial homeland in recent decades has been in Bauchi Province in the Plateau region of northern Nigeria. They claim to be descendants of Bornu, with Arab* roots, but they have tended to keep their distance from Islam, though Islamic conversions have increased in recent decades. The Gezawas are subdivided into the following groups, based on village residence: the Zuls, Doreis, Danshes, Tulais, and Kayauris. Most Gezawas are subsistence farmers who raise maize, millet, guinea corn, and beans.
REFERENCE: Harold D. Gunn. *Peoples of the Plateau Area of Northern Nigeria.* 1963.

GEZIRA. The Gezira—also known as the Messellimiyas, Halawins, and Rufa'as—are a subgroup of the Juhayna* Arabs* of the Sudan.

GHANDI. *See* BANDI.

GHIZZI. *See* KISSI.

GHOTUO. The Ghotuo people are a Nigerian ethnic group. They are concentrated in the Owan and Akoko-Edo divisions of Bendel State. The Ghotuo population is approximately 35,000 people. They are classified as an Edo* people.

GHULFAN. The Ghulfan are one of the non-Arabic Nuba* peoples of Kordofan Province of Sudan. Most of them are farmers, raising sorghum, cotton, and peanuts through rainfall agricultural techniques in the granite inselbergs of the northern Nuba Mountains. They are mostly Muslim in their religious loyalties.

GIAH. The Giahs are a clan with the chiefdom of Mambahn, a subgroup of the Bassa* people of Liberia. Most Giahs live in the Marshall Territory of Liberia.

GIANDA. The Giandas are a subgroup of the Bassa* people of Liberia. Most Giandas live in Grand Bassa County.

GIBE. The Gibes are an Ethiopian group who are part of the larger Kafa*-Sadama* cluster of peoples.
REFERENCE: M. L. Bender, J. D. Bowen, R. L. Cooper, and C. A. Ferguson, eds. *Language in Ethiopia.* 1976.

GIDICHO. The Gidichos are a subgroup of the Koyra* peoples of Ethiopia.

GIDOLE. The Gidole people are an Ethiopian ethnic group whose language is part of the Cushitic family. Most Gidoles are subsistence farmers, whose population today is approximately 7,000 people.
REFERENCE: M. L. Bender, J. D. Bowen, R. L. Cooper, and C. A. Ferguson, eds. *Language in Ethiopia.* 1976.

GIGUCHI. The Giguchis are an ethnic group living today southwest of Mount Kenya in Kenya. They are closely related to the Kikuyu* and Meru* peoples. Most of them are subsistence farmers.
REFERENCE: W. H. Whiteley. *Language in Kenya.* 1974.

GIKIKUYU. *See* KIKUYU.

GIMA. The Gimas are a subgroup of the Jaaliyin* Arabs* of Sudan.

GIMBA. The Gimbas are a subgroup of the Taita* peoples of East Africa, particularly Kenya. They speak a Bantu* language.

GIMIRA. The Gimira people live south of Kefa in Ethiopia. In 1935, their population numbered more than 100,000 people, but they have suffered so horribly from slave raids and attacks from Oromo* and Amhara* groups that their contemporary population is only about 40,000 people. They are divided into two primary subgroups: the Tolus and the Dizus.
REFERENCES: W. T. Lange. *Gimira, Remnants of a Vanishing Culture.* 1975; Chris Prouty and Eugene Rosenfeld. *Historical Dictionary of Ethiopia and Eritrea.* 1994.

GIMR. The Gimr are one of the seven Tama*-speaking peoples of Sudan and Chad. They live on the Sudan side of the Sudanese-Chadian border in a region known as Dar Gimr. It is a bleak area in terms of natural resources—sandy, hilly, and short of rainwater and ground moisture. The only agriculture possible is dry farming, which the Gimr use to produce millet and a few other crops. Because of economic conditions in the region, there has been a steady out-migration of Gimr. Today, thousands of Gimr can also be found in Southern Darfur Province in Sudan, as well as in the city of Darfur and the Nile Valley. Their population today exceeds 50,000 people. The Gimr have lost the use of their own Tama language and speak Arabic.

Historically, the Gimr were situated between the Sultanate of Wadai and the Sultanate of Darfur. From the early 1700s to 1874, they were tributaries to the Wadai sultanate. That ended when the Turko-Egyptian Sudan conquered the region in 1874. They then paid tribute to the Turks until 1882 when the Mahdist rebellion deposed them. Between 1880 and 1910, the Gimr suffered at the hands of succeeding armies—the Mahdists, Masalits,* Furs,* and French.* In 1924, negotiations between the French and the British* resulted in Dar Gimr becoming part of the Anglo-Egyptian Sudan. The British then incorporated the Gimr ruling families into their own judiciary and administrative structure. The vast majority of the Gimr are Muslims.
REFERENCE: Paul Doornbos. ''Tama-Speaking Peoples.'' In Richard V. Weekes, ed. *Muslim Peoples.* 1984.

GIO. *See* DAN.

GIRIAMA. *See* GIRIYAMA.

GIRIYAMA. The Giriyamas (Giriama, Giryama) are part of the Nyika* group of the Mijikenda* cluster of Northeast Bantu*-speaking peoples who today live

in the coastal lowlands of Kenya along the Indian Ocean. The Giriyamas are farmers who raise rice, maize, cassava, and coconuts. They also supply palm oil for the palm wine industry. Their social system is based on patrilineal descent. Generally, the surrounding Swahili*-speaking people of Kenya and Tanzania look down upon the Giriyamas as an inferior group. East African demographers estimate the Giriyama population at approximately 550,000 people. Of that total, about 10 percent are Sunni Muslims; the rest are either Christians or adherents of Giriyama animism.
REFERENCE: Cynthia Brantley. ''An Historical Perspective on the Giriama and Witchcraft Control.'' *Africa* 49 (1979): 112–33.

GIRYAMA. *See* GIRIYAMA.

GISHU. *See* GISU.

GISIGA. *See* GUIZIGA.

GISSI. *See* KISSI.

GISU. The Gisu (Geshu, Bagisu, Bageshu, Bagish, Lamasaba, Masaba, Sokwia, Gishu) are Bantu*-speaking farmers living on the slopes and foothills of Mount Elgon in eastern Uganda. They are a patrilineal people. The Gisu population today exceeds 800,000 people, most of whom are Christians, Gisu animists, or a syncretic mix of both; only 5 percent of the Gisu are Muslims. Included in the Gisu cluster of peoples are the Samias* and the Nyoles.* The western slopes of Mount Elgon are well-watered, and the Gisus raise millet, bananas, corn, coffee, and cotton.
REFERENCE: Susan Heald. ''Joking and Avoidance, Hostility and Incest: An Essay on Gisu Moral Categories.'' *Man* 25 (1990): 377–92.

GLANDA. *See* GLAVUDA.

GLAVDA. *See* GLAVUDA.

GLAVUDA. The Glavudas (Glandas, Glavdas, Gelebdas) are one of the Bantu*-speaking peoples of Nigeria. They are classified as part of the Plateau cluster of peoples who occupy central Nigeria, primarily in the East Gwoza District of Borno State. Most Glavudas practice subsistence horticulture, raising ginger, millet, guinea corn, beans, and citrus products. They live in social systems characterized by patrilineal descent and patrifocal residence. In recent years, they have begun migrating to towns and cities looking for work. Their population today exceeds 70,000 people.
REFERENCES: *Language Survey of Nigeria.* 1976; Donald G. Morrison et al. *Black Africa: A Comparative Handbook.* 1989.

GOBAWEYN. The Gobaweyns are a small ethnic group living in Somalia and are concentrated in the Juba River area near Lugh. They make their living as farmers and nomadic hunters. The Gobaweyns speak a Bantu* language and were already living in the region before the Somali* migrations.
REFERENCE: Margaret Castagno. *Historical Dictionary of Somalia.* 1975.

GOBEZE. The Gobezes are a subgroup of the Gawwada* people of Ethiopia.

GOBIR. *See* GOBIRWA.

GOBIRWA. The Gobirwas (Gobir) are a subgroup of the Hausa* people of Niger and Nigeria. Some ethnologists trace their origins to Egypt, while others argue that the Gobirwas are the result of a mixing of Tebu* and Semitic cultures. They first arrived in the Bilma region of what is today Niger in the seventh century, where they settled among existing Hausa communities. They fell under considerable Tebu pressure after the twelfth century, and, in the nineteenth century, they were conquered by the Fulbes.* Most Gobirwas today live in southern Niger and northern Nigeria, from Maradi to Madaoua.
REFERENCE: Samuel Decalo. *Historical Dictionary of Niger.* 1989.

GODIÉ. The Godié are an ethnic group in Ivory Coast. They are part of the Kru* cluster of peoples and are often classified as part of the Didas,* to whom they are closely related. The Godié are concentrated in and around the town of Lakota.

GOEMAI. *See* GOMEI.

GOFA. The Gofa (Gemu-Gofa) people are an ethnic group living today in Ethiopia. They are part of the Omotic* cluster of peoples in southern Ethiopia. The Gofas plant ensete and other grains and practice animal husbandry for a living. They have remained loyal to their indigenous religious traditions. Their population today exceeds 300,000 people. Some ethnologists put them in the Welamo* cluster of dialects.
REFERENCES: M. L. Bender, J. D. Bowen, R. L. Cooper, and C. A. Ferguson, eds. *Language in Ethiopia.* 1976; Harold D. Nelson et al. *Ethiopia: A Country Study.* 1980.

GOGO. The Gogo are a Bantu*-speaking people living in the central highlands of Tanzania. The are closely related linguistically to the Turus.* The Gogo population today exceeds 600,000 people, and they are known for the process through which they have adopted Masai* customs. The Gogo economy revolves around livestock, especially cattle; they are semi-nomadic, moving the herds seasonally in search of range grasses and water. The Gogo are also known

for their resistance to modern technology and social change. Many of them still live in their traditional flat, mud-roofed houses.
REFERENCE: James L. Newman. *The Ecological Basis for Subsistence Change among the Sandawe of Tanzania.* 1970.

GOGWEIN. The Gogweins are a subgroup of the Bassa* people of Liberia. Most Gogweins live in Grand Bassa County.

GOINGBE. The Goingbes are a subgroup of the Bassa* people of Liberia. Most Goingbes live in Grand Bassa County.

GOKANA. The Gokana people are an ethnic group living today in the Bori Division of Rivers State in Nigeria. They are a farming and fishing people of the Niger Delta. The contemporary Gokana population exceeds 300,000 people. Their language is part of the Ogoni group of the Benue-Congo family.
REFERENCES: Suanu M. Ikoro. ''Numeral Classification in Kana.'' *Journal of African Languages and Linguistics* 15 (1994): 7–28; *Language Survey of Nigeria.* 1976.

GOLA. The Gola people of Liberia and Sierra Leone speak a Mel language. They are linguistically related to the Kissis.* Although large numbers of the Liberian Golas have migrated to towns and cities in recent years in search of work, more than 100,000 of them still live in four counties: Lofa County, Grand Cape Mount County, Bomi County, and Montserrado County. During the era of the Atlantic slave trade, the Golas were widely known for their role as middlemen, transferring captured Africans from inland areas to the coastal Vais,* who then sold them to Europeans. There are two Gola chiefdoms in Lofa County. The Kongbaa chiefdom is composed of the Gboba Nenge clan, the Tungele clan, and the Zui clan, while the Gorje chiefdom includes the Gbama and Yangaya clans. In Grand Cape Mount County, there are also two Gola chiefdoms. The Pokpa chiefdom includes the Dagole, Dazambo, Kposo, Semavule, and Sokpo clans, and the Gola Kone chiefdom consists of Dablo, La, and Mana clans. There is only one Gola chiefdom in Bomi County. The Lofa-Gola chiefdom there is composed of the Boj, Gbor, Gobla, Kpo, Mana, Senje, and Te clans. In Montserrado County, there are two Gola chiefdoms. The Ding chiefdom is built around the Ding, Markoi, Mein, and Nyein clans, while the Todi chiefdom possesses the Fanse, Kpo, and Plimu clans. Most rural Golas are subsistence farmers. The Sierra Leone Golas are concentrated in a small region of Kenema and Pujehun provinces.
REFERENCES: D. Elwood Dunn and Svend E. Holsoe. *Historical Dictionary of Liberia.* 1985; Irving Kaplan et al. *Area Handbook of Sierra Leone.* 1976; Harold D. Nelson et al. *Liberia: A Country Study.* 1984.

GOLLE. The Golle are a subgroup of the Zerma,* themselves a subgroup of the Songhai* people of West Africa. They live in far western Niger.

GOMA. The Gomas, originally a Sadama* people of Ethiopia, have all but been transformed into an Oromo* subgroup in the past three centuries. They speak the Metcha dialect of Oromo and live in Gemu-Gofa Province in Ethiopia. Most Gomas live as settled farmers who raise maize, coffee, and cotton.

GOMANI. The Gomanis are a subgroup of the Ngoni* people of Malawi.

GOMEI. The Gomei (Goemai, Groemai, Ankwai, Ankwe) people of Plateau State in Nigeria live in close relationship to the Jukuns,* their neighbors to the south, and to the Ngas,* their neighbors to the north. They can be found particularly in the Shendam, Gerkawa, and Namu districts of the Shendam Division; the Resettlement District of the Langtang Division; and the Assaiko District of the Lafia Division. They practice subsistence horticulture, raising ginger, millet, guinea corn, beans, and citrus products. They live in social systems characterized by patrilineal descent and patrifocal residence. In recent years, they have begun migrating to towns and cities looking for work.
REFERENCES: Elizabeth Isichei, ed. *Studies in the History of Plateau State, Nigeria.* 1982; *Language Survey of Nigeria.* 1976.

GOMLA. *See* GONGLA.

GOMOA. The term ''Gomoa,'' also Gomua, is used to describe a group of Akan* people who live in the Winneba region of contemporary Ghana. They are surrounded by the Ga* and the Fante.* The Gomoas have also been known historically as the Akramans.

GOMUA. *See* GOMOA.

GONGLA. The Gonglas (Gomlas, Bajamas, Jarengs) are a relatively small ethnic group living today in the Jereng District of the Adamawa Division of Gongola State in Nigeria. They speak an Adamawa language.
REFERENCE: *Language Survey of Nigeria.* 1976.

GONGYA. *See* GONJA.

GONJA. The Gonja (Gongya) are a bilateral ethnic group living in northern Ghana and across the border in Ivory Coast, especially in the subprefectures of Bondoukou and Mankono. Those living in Ghana are located primarily in the western reaches of the Northern Region. They are part of the larger cluster of Guan* peoples. Ethnologists believe they migrated to their current homeland from Mali in the seventeenth century. They were conquered by the Asante* in the eighteenth century and then by the British* and French* in the nineteenth century. Most of the Gonjas are small farmers.

REFERENCES: E. C. Goody. "The Fostering of Children in Ghana: A Preliminary Report." *Ghana Journal of Sociology* 2 (1966): 26–33; E. C. Goody. "Kinship Fostering in Ghana: Deprivation or Advantage?" In P. M. Meyer, ed. *Socialization: The Approach from Social Anthropology.* 1970.

GOR. The Gor (Gore) people are a major subgroup of the Mbaye* people of Chad; they have also been known as the Mbaye-Doba. Although Gor history is characterized by frequent slave raids by Fulbes* and Barmas,* they have survived and progressed. Gor territory in the Logone-Orientale and Moyen-Chari prefectures has undergone rural economic development and modernization in recent decades, and a good number of the more than 75,000 Gor have achieved important positions in the Chadian government and military.
REFERENCE: Samuel Decalo. *Historical Dictionary of Chad.* 1987.

GORBLI. The Gorblis are a subgroup of the Bassa* people of Liberia. Most Gorblis live in Grand Bassa County.

GORENSI. *See* GRUSI.

GORISE. *See* GRUSI.

GOSHA. The Gosha people are part of the Eastern Hamatic cluster of peoples who live today in far northwestern Kenya, southern Ethiopia, and eastern Somalia. They speak a Somali* language and have a current population of approximately 60,000 people. The Goshas are a pastoral people who also cultivate small plots of land.
REFERENCE: Donald G. Morrison et al. *Black Africa: A Comparative Handbook.* 1989.

GOUIN. The Gouin (Guin, Mbwen, Kpen) are a Voltaic people living in the subprefecture of Ferkéssédougou, north of the city, in Ivory Coast and in Haut-Bassins Department in western Burkina-Faso. In terms of their population, which today is estimated at perhaps 60,000 people, they are a small group, living in several dozen villages. Like most Voltaic peoples, the Gouin support themselves by herding cattle and raising millet, cassava, and yams in subsistence gardens (sometimes corn and rice as well for commercial sale). They are considered to be Senufo* people.
REFERENCES: Daniel M. McFarland. *Historical Dictionary of Upper Volta.* 1978; Robert J. Mundt. *Historical Dictionary of Côte d'Ivoire.* 1995.

GOULA. *See* GULA.

GOULA IRO. *See* GULA.

GOULAYE. The Goulayes are one of the major subgroups of the Sara* people of Chad. They are concentrated in the Moyen-Chari prefecture, especially in the Lai District. The Goulaye population today exceeds 130,000 people, many of whom have been converted to Christianity by Western missionaries.
REFERENCE: Samuel Decalo. *Historical Dictionary of Chad.* 1987.

GOUN. The Goun speak an Adja* language and are considered part of the larger Fon* or Ewe* cluster of peoples in Benin. Their population today is approximately 140,000 people, and they are concentrated in the Kétou-Porto Novo regions of Benin. They remain the dominant political group in Porto Novo. Their most prominent modern leader has been Sourou-Migan Apithy. The Goun are divided into such subgroups as the Goun proper and the Guemenus and Tofinus. They make their living fishing in the Atlantic coastal areas where they are concentrated.

GOUNDA. The Goundas are one of the primary subgroups of the Teda* people, who themselves are a branch of the Toubou (Tebu*). The Goundas live in the Tibesti region of Chad, the Fezzan region of Libya, and in East Niger.

GOURMA. *See* GURMA.

GOURMANTCHÉ. *See* GURMA.

GOURO. *See* KWENI.

GOUROUNSI. *See* GRUSI.

GOVA. The Gova are various small Shona* group of several thousand people living in Mozambique and Zimbabwe. Most of them are small subsistence farmers who live along the banks of the lower Zambezi River. During the late eighteenth and nineteenth centuries, they actively participated in the slave trade, capturing and selling other Africans to Portuguese* traders. They actually derive from several unrelated Shona groups. The Gova branch of the Korekores* lives in the Zambezi Valley. The Gova subgroup of the Zezuru* lives north of Salisbury in Mazoe District. The Karanga Gova are located in the Selukwe District of Zimbabwe.
REFERENCES: Mario Azevedo. *Historical Dictionary of Mozambique.* 1991; R. Kent Rasmussen. *Historical Dictionary of Zimbabwe.* 1994.

GOVERA. The Goveras are a subgroup of the Karanga* people, who are part of the Shona* cluster of peoples in Zimbabwe. They are concentrated near Chirumanzu.

GOW. The Gow are a subgroup of the Songhai* people of West Africa. More particularly, they live in the grasslands of Anzourou and the hills of Hombori in central Mali.

GOWA. The Gowa (Goba) people are part of the larger Tonga* cluster of peoples in Zambia.

GRAND KOLA. The Grand Kolas are a subgroup of the Bassa* people of Liberia. Most Grand Kolas live in Grand Bassa County.

GREBO. The Grebos are part of the Kru* cluster of peoples in Ivory Coast. Most of them live in Sassandra Department there. There are also some Grebos in Liberia, concentrated in Maryland, Grand Gedeh, and Sinoe counties. They are subdivided into several dozen subgroups, each of which consists of a number of chiefdoms and clans. They have traditionally farmed their land and raised plantains, bananas, rice, and sugar cane. They are also known for their skill in distilling sugar cane into a rum known regionally as "cane juice." Today, the Grebo population exceeds 300,000 people.
REFERENCES: D. Elwood Dunn and Svend E. Holsoe. *Historical Dictionary of Liberia.* 1985; Mario Meneghini. "The Grebo Mask." *African Arts* 8 (Autumn 1974): 36–39; Robert J. Mundt. *Historical Dictionary of Cote d'Ivoire.* 1995.

GREEK. There are more than 500,000 people of Greek descent living today in Africa. The vast majority of them—more than 375,000—are in Egypt, primarily in Alexandria, with some in Cairo as well. The Greeks have been a distinct minority in Alexandria since the time of Alexander the Great, and they have maintained a distinct sense of linguistic, cultural, and religious identity separate from Muslim Egyptians.
REFERENCES: Arthur Goldschmidt. *Historical Dictionary of Egypt.* 1994; Helen C. Metz et al. *Egypt: A Country Study.* 1991.

GRIQUA. The Griquas are a unique ethnic group of southern Africa. They are the result of a recent process of ethnogenesis involving the mixing of Khoi-khois,* San,* and European peoples. At the present time, the Griqua population is approximately 9,000 people. Traditionally, they were cattle herders. Early in the 1800s, they migrated north from the Cape Colony to Namaqualand, and from there, east to Griqualand West and the Orange Free State. In the 1860s, another group of Griquas migrated to Transkei. During their migrations, they were repeatedly driven from their land by invading groups of Boer farmers. The Boers also used Griqua soldiers to fight the Sotho* and Ndebele* peoples. In South Africa, the Griquas are classified as part of the Coloured* population, even though they maintain a distinct sense of identity. They can also be found today in Zimbabwe.

REFERENCES: *African Encyclopedia.* 1974; R. Kent Rasmussen. *Historical Dictionary of Zimbabwe.* 1994.

GRUNSHI. *See* GRUSI.

GRUNSI. *See* GRUSI.

GRUSI. The Grusi proper (Grunsi, Grussi, Gorise, Gurense, Grunshi, Gurinse, Gurunsi, Gourounsi), sometimes called Nankansi, are part of the larger Grusi cluster of peoples, the largest of the Molé-Dagbane* peoples of northern Ghana and southern Burkina-Faso. They are sometimes identified as the Awuna* or the western Kasena. They are surrounded by the Mo,* Nunuma,* Kasena,* and Sasala* peoples, who are sometimes considered to be Grusi subgroups. There are two Grusi subgroups, the Feras and the Nagwas. Most Grusis are small farmers, raising millet, yams, and various other crops, and their primary settlement is in Pina. Their total population in the region exceeds 500,000 people.
REFERENCES: J. T. Bendor-Samuel. "The Grusi Sub-Group of the Gur Languages." *Journal of West African Languages* 2 (1965): 47–55; Daniel M. McFarland. *Historical Dictionary of Ghana,* 1995; Fred T. Smith. "Earth, Vessels, and Harmony among the Gurensi." *African Arts* 22 (February 1989): 60–65.

GRUSSI. *See* GRUSI.

GU. *See* EGUN.

GUAN. The Guans (Guang, Gwan) were among the first settlers of Ghana and consist of the Kyerepongs* (Cherepong, Kyerepon), Lartes* (Larteh, Late), Efutus,* Krakyes* (Krachi), Anums,* Awutus,* Atwodes* (Achode, Atyoti), Gonjas,* Salagas,* Buems,* Likpes,* Nkonyas,* Ntwumuru* (Nchumuru), Kpesi* (Kpeshi), Senyas* (Beyna Bereku), Santrofokis,* Boles,* and Bowiris (Bowli*) groups. Their contemporary population is more than 600,000 people, of whom approximately 10 percent are Muslims. Today they live in the great curve from Gonja in the Northern Region of Ghana to Krakeye and Larteh in the Eastern Region, and to Senya Bereku and Efutu in the Central Region. Their language is closely related to Akan.* Except for the Gonjas, most Guan peoples live in scattered enclaves among the Akan, Ga-Adangme,* and Ewe* peoples.
REFERENCE: Daniel M. McFarland. *Historical Dictionary of Ghana.* 1995.

GUANG. *See* GUAN.

GUBA. *See* GUBI.

GUBAWA. The Gubawas are a subgroup of the Maouri* people of Niger. They are essentially a hunting people who are making the transition to stockbreeding and farming.

GUBI. The Gubis (Gubas) are a small ethnic group living today in the Zungur District of the Bauchi Division in Bauchi State, Nigeria. They speak a Jarawan Bantu* language.
REFERENCE: *Language Survey of Nigeria.* 1976.

GUDE. The Gudes (Chekes, Mapudas, Shedes, Tchades, Mapodis, and Mubis) are one of the peoples of Nigeria. Gudes can be found in the Uba District of Borno State and the Mubi District of the Mubi Division of Bauchi State. They also live across the border in Cameroon. Most Gudes practice subsistence horticulture, raising ginger, millet, guinea corn, beans, and citrus products. They live in social systems characterized by patrilineal descent and patrifocal residence. In recent years, they have begun migrating to towns and cities looking for work. They have a population today of approximately 100,000 people.
REFERENCES: *Language Survey of Nigeria.* 1976; Donald G. Morrison et al. *Black Africa: A Comparative Handbook.* 1989.

GUDU. The Gudus (Gutus) live in the Song District of the Adamawa Division of Gongola State in Nigeria. They are a small ethnic group of several thousand people who speak a Chadic language.
REFERENCE: *Language Survey of Nigeria.* 1976.

GUDUF. The Gudufs (Yaghwatadaxas, Afkabiyes, Yawotataxas, Gudupes) are an ethnic group living today in the East Gwoza District of Borno State in Nigeria. They speak a Chadic language that is classified with the Mandara* group. The Guduf population today stands at approximately 65,000 people.
REFERENCE: *Language Survey of Nigeria.* 1976.

GUDUPE. *See* GUDUF.

GUEMENU. The Guemenus are a subgroup of the Goun* peoples of Benin, who themselves are part of the larger Fon* or Ewe* cluster of peoples. Some Guemenus can also be found in Togo and Ghana.

GUÉRÉ. The Guérés, also known as Gewos and Wé, are an ethnic group concentrated in the Department of Guiglo in Ivory Coast. They are part of the Kru* cluster of peoples there. The Guérés living in Liberia are known as the Kran (Krahn). They are closely enough related to the Wobé* of Ivory Coast to be included with them in many ethnographies of the region; the religious beliefs and customs of both groups are very similar. But, like the neighboring Dan* people, they also maintain age-group classification systems in their social structure. Up to about thirty years ago, the Guérés were all subsistence farmers, raising rice and manioc, but most of them have now made the transition to the larger commercial economy. Large numbers of Guérés have also been recruited to work in police forces around the country. The Guéré population is approximately 200,000 people today.

REFERENCES: Monni Adams. "Women's Art as Gender Strategy among the Wè of Canton Boo." *African Arts* 26 (October 1993): 32–43; Robert E. Handloff et al. *Côte d'Ivoire: A Country Study.* 1988; S. E. Holsoe and Joseph Lauer. "Who Are the Kran/ Guere and the Gio/Yacouba? Ethnic Identifications along the Liberia-Ivory Coast Border." *African Studies Review* 19 (1976): 139–49.

GUÉREP. The Guéreps are one of the constituent groups of the Kim* confederation in Chad.

GUERZÉ. *See* KPELLE.

GUHAYNA. *See* JUHAYNA.

GUIDAR. The Guidars are a small ethnic group of approximately 70,000 people living in Chad and Cameroon. They speak a Chadian language and are concentrated in Tandjilé Prefecture in Chad and in Bénoué Department in Cameroon. Their language represents a transition between Massa* and Sara.* Most Guidars are herdsmen, day laborers, and small farmers, raising millet, maize, and cotton.

REFERENCES: Thomas Collelo et al. *Chad: A Country Study.* 1988; Samuel Decalo. *Historical Dictionary of Chad.* 1987; Harold D. Nelson et al. *Area Handbook for the United Republic of Cameroon.* 1974.

GUIN. *See* GOUIN.

GUIZAGA. *See* GUIZIGA.

GUIZIGA. The Guizigas (Guizagas) are a subgroup of the Kirdi* peoples of northern Cameroon, southwestern Chad, and southeastern Nigeria. Most of them are small farmers, raising crops on terraced, hillside farms in the Mandara Mountains. They produce millet, groundnuts, cotton, and cattle. They resisted Islamic missionaries and remained loyal to the cult of the ancestors, a ritual central to their religious beliefs. The Guizigas are concentrated in the western reaches of Diamaré Department, near Méri and Maroua. Their contemporary population exceeds 80,000 people.

REFERENCE: Harold D. Nelson et al. *Area Handbook for the United Republic of Cameroon.* 1974.

GUJI. The Guji (Gugi) are one of the major subgroups of the Oromo* people of Ethiopia. They are among the southern cluster of the Oromos there. They are also divided into northern and southern subgroups; the northern Guji are known as the Jamjam. Most of the Guji are egalitarian pastoralists and subsistence farmers, raising maize and millet, who live east of Lake Abaya in southwestern Ethiopia.

GULA. The Gulas (Goula) are one of the Sudan peoples living today in Chad and the Central African Republic. They tend to be concentrated in southern Chad, where they make their living raising livestock and working small farms. The Gula population today exceeds 75,000 people. They were once a mighty commercial empire in that region. Their language preceded Arabic as the commercial lingua franca of north-central Africa. The Gula empire began to decline at the end of the eighteenth century because of wars of extermination with rival groups. Today, there are two small groups of people—the Gula Koumra and the Gula Médé—who survived these onslaughts. They are concentrated in the Ndélé prefecture of the Central African Republic and in Guéra, Salamat, and Moyen-Chari prefectures in Chad.
REFERENCES: Thomas Collelo et al. *Chad: A Country Study.* 1988; Pierre Kalck. *Historical Dictionary of the Central African Republic.* 1992; Donald G. Morrison et al. *Black Africa: A Comparative Handbook.* 1989.

GULE. The Gule people are one of the subgroups of the Shilluks,* a pre-Nilotic* people of the Sudan.

GULUD. The Guluds are one of the Nuba* peoples of Sudan.

GUMA. The Guma are one of the major subgroups of the Oromo* people of Ethiopia.

GUMUZ. The Gumuz are an ethnic group living in Sudan and far western Ethiopia. They speak a Nilotic* language and make their living as semi-nomadic pastoralists, raising cattle, and as plow agriculturalists. By the early 1990s, the Gumuz population had reached 70,000 people.
REFERENCES: *African Encyclopedia.* 1974; Harold D. Nelson et al. *Ethiopia: A Country Study.* 1980.

GUN. *See* GOUN.

GUNGANCI. *See* RESHAWA.

GUNGAWA. *See* RESHAWA.

GUR. *See* MOLÉ-DAGBANE PEOPLES.

GURA. *See* GURE-KAHUGU.

GURAGE. The Gurage (Gerawege, Gerage) are a Semitic-language people who live in the southwestern reaches of Shoa Province in Ethiopia. They are divided into fourteen distinct subgroups. Their particular homeland is bordered by Lake Zway to the east and the Awash River to the west. Approximately one-third of the 2.5 million Gurage are Muslims, while the rest are divided equally between Christians and traditional animists, who worship the god Waq. Those Gurage who are Muslims have been so since the thirteenth century, and they actively proselytize among other Ethiopians. They are a settled people who make their living raising ensete as a staple and cattle where suitable rangeland exists. The western Gurage, whose soil base is quite poor, rely almost exclusively on the ensete, while the eastern Gurage are also able to raise grain crops. They live in densely populated communal villages.
REFERENCES: William A. Shack. *The Gurage: A People of the Ensete Culture.* 1966; William A. Shack and Elliott P. Skinner. *Gods and Heroes: Oral Traditions of the Gurage of Ethiopia.* 1974.

GURE-KAHUGU. The Gure-Kahugus—also known historically as the Guras, Kafugus, Kagus, Kapugus, Igbiris, Agaris, Agbiris, and Aniragos—are an ethnic group living today in the Lere District of the Saminaka Division of Kaduna State in Nigeria. Their language is classified as part of the Western Plateau group of the Benue-Congo family.
REFERENCE: *Language Survey of Nigeria.* 1976.

GURIA. The Guria are one of the primary subgroups of the Buduma* people of Chad. They are the dominant Buduma group in the area of Bol District and have a population of approximately 27,000 people. Highly ethnocentric, the Guria are Muslims in their religious orientation and cattle raisers in their economic life.

GURKA. *See* YIWOM.

GURMA. The term ''Gurma'' is used to refer to a cluster of peoples who live in northeastern Ghana near the Togo border and in southern Burkina-Faso, between the Mossi region and the Niger River. The Gurmas living in Togo are concentrated in Sansanné-Mango and in Dapango. Their population is estimated at more than one million people. Included in the Gurma classification are the Basari* (Basares), Bimobas* (Bimawba, Bmoba, Moab, Moba), Konkombas* (Komba), Gourmantchés (Gurma proper), Kyambas (Tchamba), and Pilapilas.* Most of the Gurmas make their living as small farmers and pastoralists. Gurmas can also be found in northern Benin.
REFERENCES: Daniel M. McFarland. *Historical Dictionary of Ghana.* 1995; Daniel M. McFarland. *Historical Dictionary of Upper Volta.* 1978.

GURMANA. The Gurmana people live today in Kurmin Gurmana District of the Minna Division of Niger State in Nigeria. Their language is part of the Kamuku*-Bassa* group of the Benue-Congo family.
REFERENCE: *Language Survey of Nigeria.* 1976.

GURMANCHE. *See* GURMA.

GURO. *See* KWENI.

GURREH. The Gurreh people are part of the Eastern Hamatic cluster of peoples who live today in far northwestern Kenya, southern Ethiopia, and eastern Somalia. They speak a Somali* language and have a current population of approximately 60,000 people. The Gurrehs are a pastoral people who also cultivate small plots of land.
REFERENCE: Donald G. Morrison et al. *Black Africa: A Comparative Handbook.* 1989.

GURRUM. The Gurrums are a people living today in Plateau State in Nigeria. They live in a series of villages where they have made the transition in recent decades to small farming. Hunting, however, has long been of religious and ritual significance to them. They are closely related—religiously, culturally and linguistically—to the Ribina* peoples.
REFERENCES: Harold Good. *The Peoples of the Plateau Region of Northern Nigeria.* 1963; Jean-Claude Muller. "Intertribal Hunting Among the Rukuba." *Ethnology* 21 (1982): 203–14.

GURUKA. The Gurukas are a Tanzanian ethnic group whom ethnologists sometimes include in the Safwa* cluster of peoples.

GURUNSE. *See* GRUSI.

GURUNSHI. *See* GRUSI.

GURUNSI. *See* GRUSI.

GURUNTUM-MBAARU. The Guruntum-Mbaaru people, also known as Gurutums, are a Chadic-speaking people who live today in Nigeria. They tend to be concentrated in the Duguri, Galembi, and Fali districts of the Bauchi Division of Bauchi State. Most of them are small farmers and herders.
REFERENCE: *Language Survey of Nigeria.* 1976.

GURUT. *See* BERI.

GURUTUM. *See* GURUNTUM-MBAARU.

GUSII. The Gusii (Kissi) are an ethnic group of approximately one million people living primarily in Nyanza Province in southwestern Kenya, especially in the highlands east of Lake Victoria. They speak a Bantu* language and are closely related to the Luhyas* and Kikuyus.* They first emerged as a conscious ethnic entity in the mid-eighteenth century. During the nineteenth century, they suffered from slave raids at the hands of the Nandi* and Kipsigi* peoples. In the twentieth century, they have made the transition from cattle herding to sedentary farming, in which they raise pyrethrum, tea, millet, maize, cassava, bananas, and cattle. Their population is growing rapidly today, and their economy is diversifying.
REFERENCES: *African Encyclopedia.* 1974; R. Thomas Hakansson. ''The Detachability of Women: Gender and Processes of Change Among the Gusii of Kenya.'' *American Ethnology* 21 (August 1994): 516–37; Bethwell A. Ogot. *Historical Dictionary of Kenya.* 1981.

GUSU. The Gusu people live on the northern edge of the Jos Plateau in Plateau State, Nigeria. They are surrounded ethnically by the Hausas* to the north and east, Jeres* to the west, and Ribinas* to the south. Most Gusus today are farmers, raising subsistence amounts of millet, maize, and guinea corn; they have completed the transition from hunting only in recent decades.
REFERENCE: Elizabeth Isichei, ed. *Studies in the History of Plateau State, Nigeria.* 1982.

GUTU. *See* GUDU.

GWA. *See* MBATTO.

GWA. The Gwa people, not to be confused with the Gwas (Mbattos*) of Ivory Coast, are a small ethnic group living today in the Lame District of the Bauchi Division of Bauchi State. They number several thousand and speak a language that is classified as part of the Jarawan Bantu* group.
REFERENCE: *Language Survey of Nigeria.* 1976.

GWALI. *See* GBARI.

GWAN. *See* GUAN.

GWANDARA. *See* GWANDARI.

GWANDARA-BASSA. *See* BASSA-KADUNA.

GWANDARI. The Gwandaris are one of the Plateau Chadic peoples of Nigeria. Their current population is approximately 35,000 people, of whom about one-third are Muslims. They speak a Hausa* language. Most Gwandaris live in the

Eggon and Mada districts of the Akwanga Division; the Obi and Assaiko districts of the Lafia Division; the Kokona, Keffi, Uke, Karu, and Karshi districts of the Keffi Division; and the Nasarwa District of Nasarwa Division, all in Plateau State. They can also be found today in the Kagargo District of Kaduna State and the Abuja and Bauri districts of the Abuja Division of Niger State. They were a dominant political group in the region for many years. Their most immediate neighbors today are the Eggans,* Alagos, and Migilis.* Today, most Gwandaris are subsistence farmers.
REFERENCES: *Language Survey of Nigeria.* 1976; A. Chukwudi Unomah. "The Gwandara." In Elizabeth Isichei, ed. *Studies in the History of Plateau State, Nigeria.* 1982.

GWARI. *See* GBARI.

GWARRI. *See* GBARI.

GWEBU. The Gwebus are one of the clans of the Emakhandzambili,* who themselves are one of the three major subgroups of the Swazi* people of Swaziland.

GWEDJI. *See* DIDA.

GWEMBE. The Gwembes are a subgroup of the Tonga* people of Zambia. They live in the Gwembe Valley. During the twentieth century, they have been known for their resistance to European economic development schemes because of the threat they posed to traditional lifestyles. In 1908, the Gwembes rose up against the British South African Company to protest the imposition of taxes; in the 1950s, they fought against the Kariba Dam, which flooded Lake Kariba and much of their homeland. Today, many Gwembes make their living as fishermen on Lake Kariba.
REFERENCE: John J. Grotpeter. *Historical Dictionary of Zambia.* 1979.

GWERE. The Gweres (Lugwere, Bagwere) are a Bantu*-speaking people who today live in eastern Uganda and across the border in western Kenya. Their immediate neighbors are the Karimojons,* Itesos,* Sogas,* and Gisus.* They are primarily farmers who raise millet, coffee, corn, bananas, and cotton. The Gweres have struggled for years to come out from under the cultural and economic domination of the neighboring Gisus.
REFERENCE: Rita M. Byrnes et al. *Uganda: A Country Study.* 1990.

GWI. The Gwis are a subgroup of the Tshu-Kwe* peoples, themselves a subgroup of the San* people of Botswana.

GWOMO. *See* JANJO.

GWOMU. The Gwomu are a small ethnic group who today are concentrated in the Wurkum District of the Muri Division of Gongola State in Nigeria. They speak an Adamawa language.
REFERENCE: *Language Survey of Nigeria.* 1976.

GWONG. *See* KAGOMA.

GWORAM. *See* ROBA.

GYAAMEN. *See* GYAMEN.

GYAMAN. *See* GYAMEN.

GYAMEN. The Gyamens (Gyaamen, Gyaman, Jaman) are a subgroup of the Abrons,* an Akan* group of Ghana and Ivory Coast. The Gyamens had their own kingdom in the late 1600s and early 1700s, but they were conquered by the Asantes* in 1740, freeing themselves in 1875 only to confront European domination. The main Gyamen settlement is at Bonduku in Ivory Coast.
REFERENCE: Daniel M. McFarland. *Historical Dictionary of Ghana.* 1995.

GYEM. *See* FYAM.

GYO. *See* DAN.

GYONG. *See* KAGOMA.

H

HA. The Ha are a large ethnic group in contemporary Tanzania. They are concentrated between Lake Tanganyika and Lake Victoria. There are more than 1.5 million Ha people today. Although some of them work as migrant and seasonal laborers on large commercial farms or in Dar es Salaam and Tanga, most of the Ha people prefer a traditional lifestyle in which they raise cattle, honey, and tobacco. Included in the Ha group of people, according to many ethnologists, are the Jijis* and the Vinzas.*
REFERENCE: Laura Kurtz. *Historical Dictionary of Tanzania.* 1978.

HABAB. The Hababs are one of the three subdivisions of the Bet Asgede people of Ethiopia. In the nineteenth century, they adopted Islam and the Tigre language of the Tigre* people, over whom they presided as feudal lords. Most Hababs are nomadic pastoralists.

HABASH. The so-called Habash people of Somalia are the non-Somali* inhabitants of the coastal and riverine regions. They are descended from the pre-Somali, indigenous inhabitants of Somalia, from escaped slaves who made their way into the region during the eighteenth and nineteenth centuries, or from slaves freed by the British* during the antislavery campaigns. Included in the Habash cluster of peoples are the Eyles,* Bonis,* Bajunis,* and Amaranis.* Although some of the Habash people still hunt for a living, most of them are farmers and laborers.
REFERENCE: Helen C. Metz et al. *Somalia: A Country Study.* 1992.

HABÉ. The term "Habé" is used by some ethnologists to describe a cluster of non-Fulbe* people of Burkina-Faso. Included in the cluster are the Bobos,* Dogons,* Tombos,* and related groups living south of the Cliffs of Bandiagara.
REFERENCE: Daniel M. McFarland. *Historical Dictionary of Upper Volta.* 1978.

HABINIYA. *See* BAGGARA.

HACO. The Hacos are a subgroup of the Mbundu* peoples of Angola.

HADDAD. The Haddad are a unique African ethnic group. Their population numbers more than 250,000 people, and they are scattered throughout the African Sahel, in Chad, Nigeria, and Sudan. Almost all of the Haddad work as blacksmiths, speaking the languages of the people they serve, and they are universally despised by other groups. They are usually forbidden to own land or water rights, and they are rigidly segregated in their living arrangements. Other groups will not intermarry with them or even, in many instances, touch them. For their part, the Haddad look upon outsiders with scorn, since they have adopted a sense of superiority about themselves. Only recently, as cheap imported tools and weapons have undermined the Haddad economy, have the Haddad begun to consider occupational changes. Because of that, there are increasing numbers of Haddad living in the towns of western Sudan in close proximity to other groups. The Haddad are Muslims.
REFERENCES: Paul Doornbos. "Haddad." In Richard V. Weekes, ed. *Muslim Peoples.* 1984; Johannes Nicolaisen. "The Haddad—A Hunting People in Chad." *Folk* 10 (1968): 91–109.

HADDIYA. *See* HADIYA.

HADENDIWA. *See* HADENDOWA.

HADENDOWA. The Hadendowa (Hadendiwa) are one of the major Beja* groups of Sudan. With a population exceeding 600,000 people, the Hadendowa are the largest of the Beja groups. They live north of Eritrea, between the hill country bordering the Red Sea and the Atbara River. Beja tribesmen have been in the region for more than four thousand years, but the Hadendowa did not emerge as a self-conscious ethnic group until the sixteenth century. During the late 1800s, the Hadendowa led a brave resistance movement against domination by the Egyptians and the British.* They were led by Muhammad Ahmad el Mahdi. Their resistance, combined with their huge crowns of fuzzy hair characteristic of many Beja groups, inspired a number of poems by Rudyard Kipling, who admired their ferocious resistance to imperial rule.

The Hadendowa live in a political system in which large patrilineal clans are subdivided into segmentary patrilineages called *bedanas.* Each *bedana* owns its own grazing lands and water sites. Each *bedana* is also divided into sublineages, known as *hissas.* The Hadendowa speak a Northern Cushitic language, as do other Beja groups, and they have traditionally been a pastoral people, wandering in groups of one to twelve families in search of pasture for their sheep, goat,

or camel herds. Their traditional housing consists of rectangular, portable dwellings woven from goat hair. The Hadendowa live primarily on dairy products, particularly cow's milk, as well as on meat from slaughtered stock and small amounts of grain. They raise sorghum in wadi beds, planting just after rain storms but not tending until harvest. In regions where government irrigation projects exist, increasingly large numbers of Hadendowa are settled farmers, raising cotton and other crops for commercial markets. The Hadendowa are Muslims, but their religious life still has elements of pre-Islamic custom.
REFERENCES: S. A. el-Arifi. ''Pastoral Nomadism in the Sudan.'' *East African Geographical Review* 13 (1975): 89–103; Andrew Paul. *A History of the Beja Tribes of the Sudan.* 1954.

HADEYA. *See* HADIYA.

HADIMU. The Hadimus are considered by some to be indigenous to Tanzania, but they are actually a subgroup of the Shirazi* people. They are of mixed ethnic origins, having evolved from various ethnic groups who migrated to the island of Zanzibar. Until the early 1800s, the Hadimus were concentrated on the fertile, western portions of the island, but they then migrated to the east and south. In 1865, Sultan Majid forced the Hadimu into an uneasy union with the Tumbatus. The Hadimus became the dominant group.
REFERENCE: Laura Kurtz. *Historical Dictionary of Tanzania.* 1978.

HADIYA. The Hadiya (Haddiya) are a subgroup of the Sadama* people of Shewa Province in southwestern Ethiopia. They speak an eastern Cushitic language and are Muslims. Most Hadiyas make their living raising ensete. Their population today exceeds one million people.

HADJERAI. *See* HADJERAY.

HADJERAY. The term ''Hadjeray'' (Hadjerai) is a collective reference to several groups of people in Chad—Dajus,* Kingas,* Junkun,* Dangaleats,* Mogoums,* Sokoros,* Sabas,* Barains,* Bidios,* and Yalnas*—who live in the hilly region between Mongo and Melfi in Guéra Prefecture of south-central Chad. There is little political connection among the various groups. They are united by common beliefs in *margais*—invisible spirits who live in natural geological formations and control the elements. Even though most Hadjerays converted to Islam during the colonial era, the margai beliefs survived. Most Hadjerays are small farmers. Their population today exceeds 150,000 people. The Hadjerays are widely known for their fierce sense of independence.
REFERENCES: Samuel Decalo. *Historical Dictionary of Chad.* 1987; Jean-François Vincent. *Le Pouvoir et le Sacré chez les Hadjerjay du Tchad.* 1975.

HADYA. *See* HADIYA.

HADZA. The Hadza (Hadzapi, Kindiga, Tindiga) are an ethnic group living near Lake Eyasi in Tanzania. Their economy revolves around hunting and gathering, primarily wild berries, roots, baobab fruit, honey, and game meat. Their population today is fewer than 1,000 people. Traditionally, they have been associated with San* and Khoikhoi* groups because of their use of click sounds in their language. More recently, ethnolinguists have classified the Hadza in the Afro-Asiatic linguistic family. Until very recently, the Hadza did not cultivate crops or maintain livestock. They have resisted attempts by the Tanzanian government to settle them in permanent villages.

REFERENCES: Nicholas Burton Jones, Kristen Hawks, and Patricia Draper. "Foraging Returns of Kung Adults and Children: Why Didn't Kung Children Forage?" *Journal of Anthropological Research* 50 (Fall 1994): 217–48; James L. Newman. *The Ecological Basis for Subsistence Change among the Sandawe of Tanzania.* 1970.

HADZIPI. *See* HADZA.

HAKO. The Hakos are a subgroup of the Mbundu* people of north-central Angola.

HALANGA. The Halanga are a small, surviving subgroup of the larger group of Beja* peoples in Sudan. They were originally not part of the Beja group, but, in the nineteenth and twentieth centuries, they gradually fell within a Beja cultural orbit. The Halanga live on the Red Sea coastal plain south of Port Sudan.

REFERENCES: Carolyn Fluehr-Lobban, Richard A. Lobban, Jr., and John Obert Voll. *Historical Dictionary of Sudan.* 1992; Andrew Paul. *A History of the Beja Tribes of the Sudan.* 1954.

HALAWIN. *See* GEZIRA.

HALFAWI. The Halfawis are a subgroup of the Nubian* people of Sudan.

HAM. *See* HYAM.

HAMAJ. The Hamaj people of Sudan predate the arrival of the Arabs* and the Fungor* peoples in the area. Some ethnologists consider them part of the Shilluk* cluster of peoples. They live south of Sennar in the Blue Nile region near the frontier with Ethiopia. Their language is part of the Koman branch of the Sudan linguistic family. During the eighteenth century, the Hamaj played key roles in the powerful Fung Sultanate, but the sultanate disintegrated in the late eighteenth and early nineteenth centuries. Today, most Hamaj are small farmers and herders.

REFERENCE: Carolyn Fluehr-Lobban, Richard A. Lobban, Jr., and John Obert Voll. *Historical Dictionary of Sudan.* 1992.

HAMAR. The Hamars are an ethnic group included in the larger cluster of Kawahlas,* who themselves are members of the Juhayna* Arabs* of Sudan.

HAMBUKUSHU. *See* MBUKUSHU.

HAMER. The Hamers are a subgroup of the Banna* peoples of Ethiopia.

HAMID. The Hamids are an ethnic group included in the larger cluster of Kawahlas,* who themselves are members of the Juhayna* Arabs* of Sudan.

HAMRAN. The Hamran are a small, surviving subgroup of the larger group of Beja* peoples in Sudan. They are concentrated on the north bank of the Setit River, a good deal south of Kassala.
REFERENCES: Carolyn Fluehr-Lobban, Richard A. Lobban, Jr., and John Obert Voll. *Historical Dictionary of Sudan.* 1992; Andrew Paul. *A History of the Beja Tribes of the Sudan.* 1954.

HANDA. The Handas are part of the larger cluster of Nyaneka-Humbe* peoples of southwestern Angola.

HANGAZA. The Hangazas are a Tanzanian ethnic group whom some ethnologists include in the Subi* group of people. The Hangaza population today is approximately 110,000 people.

HANHA. The Hanhas (Hanya) are one of the traditional, autonomous kingdoms and contemporary ethnic subgroups of the Ovimbundu* people of Angola.

HANYA. *See* HANHA.

HAOUSSA. *See* HAUSA.

HARARI. The Harari (Hareri) are a unique Ethiopian ethnic group. From the sixteenth to the early twentieth centuries, Hararis isolated themselves behind the walls of the city of Harer, a Sunni Muslim enclave. The city is located in the Ethiopian highlands, approximately halfway to the Red Sea. Because of their urban background, the Harari are known for their mercantile skills. They speak an Ethiopian Semitic language that is distantly related to Gurage,* but the vast majority of Harari also speak other languages as well. They marry endogamously most of the time and discourage social contacts with non-Harari people. The Harari consider themselves superior to surrounding ethnic groups, and their widespread property ownership gives them the economic means to sustain that social perspective. Beginning in 1948, after Ethiopia restored its control over the city, some Harari began leaving Harer, heading for places like Addis Ababa and Dire Dawa to engage in trade. After the Ethiopian Revolution of 1974, the out-migration vastly accelerated. When the government passed the Rural Properties Act of 1975, prohibiting individual landholdings in excess of twenty-five acres, the Harari lost much of their land to Oromo* tenants. In addition, the Urban Property Act that same year limited the number of urban properties that any individual could own. Both laws devastated the Harari economy. Today there are approximately 40,000 Harari, but only a few thousand of them still live in the city. The majority are now in Addis Ababa.

REFERENCES: Peter Koehn and Sidney Waldron. *Afocha: A Link Between Community and Administration in Harar, Ethiopia.* 1978; Wolf Leslau. *Ethiopians Speak: Studies in Cultural Background I. Harari.* 1965; Sidney Waldron. ''Harari.'' In Richard V. Weekes, ed. *Muslim Peoples.* 1984.

HARATHIN. *See* HARRATINE.

HARATIN. *See* HARRATINE.

HARERI. *See* HARARI.

HARRATIN. *See* HARRATINE.

HARRATINE. The Harratines are a black ethnic group living in Morocco, Libya, and Mauritania. A widely held belief is that the Harratines are descendants of African slaves brought from south of the Sahara to work in desert oases. Other ethnologists claim that the Harratines descend from sub-Saharan Africans who migrated north to escape the desert and ended up paying tribute to Arab* and Berber* nomads. In many of the oases of southern Morocco, the population is of mixed African and Shluh* Berber ancestry. Even though they are legally free, the Harratines still occupy subservient positions in Moroccan society. Most of them are farm laborers and domestic servants. In urban areas, they live in the worst slums. Harratines are Muslims.

REFERENCE: Harold D. Nelson et al. *Morocco: A Country Study.* 1985.

HASALA. The Hasalas are one of the clans of the Bandi* chiefdom of Lofa County in Liberia.

HASSANAB. The Hassanab are a small, surviving subgroup of the larger group of Beja* peoples in Sudan. They were originally not part of the Beja group, but, in the nineteenth and twentieth centuries, they gradually fell within the Beja cultural orbit. They live on the Red Sea coastal plain south of Port Sudan.

REFERENCES: Carolyn Fluehr-Lobban, Richard A. Lobban, Jr., and John Obert Voll. *Historical Dictionary of Sudan.* 1992; Andrew Paul. *A History of the Beja Tribes of the Sudan.* 1954.

HASSANIYA. The Hassaniyas are one of the main subgroups of the Jaaliyin* Arabs* of Sudan.

REFERENCE: Phillip Chiviges Naylor and Alf Andrew Heggoy. *Historical Dictionary of Algeria.* 1994.

HASSAUNA. The Hassaunas (Shuwas or Western Arabs) are a major subgroup of the Arab* people of Chad, where their population today exceeds 1.75 million people. Most of them are nomadic pastoralists and small farmers. The Hassaunas are subdivided into the following groups: Assales, Daganas, Oulad Meharebs, Oulad Mansours, and Ben Wails.

HASSUNA. *See* HASSAUNA.

HAUSA. The Hausas include a huge collection of linguistically related people who are scattered across West Africa. Their population exceeds forty-five million people, although the vast majority of them live in northern Nigeria and southern Niger. They can also be found in northern Ghana, Benin, Chad, and Sudan. They are the largest Muslim group in sub-Saharan Africa. At the present time, anthropologists argue that there are too many internal cultural differences among various Hausa peoples to call them a single ethnic group. In fact, it is not at all uncommon for people to call themselves Fulbe*-Hausa or Kanuri*-Hausa because of the intermarriage that has occurred. Nonetheless, because of modern communications and the tendency of non-Hausa people to identify them as a single group, that sense of ethnicity is slowly developing. The Hausas are divided into many subgroups, such as the Daurawas, Gobirs,* Kanawas, Katsenawas, Kebbawas, Zamfaras, Zazzagawas, and Auyokawas of Nigeria.

Central to Hausa identity is being Muslim. Traders from Sudan and the Arab* countries first brought Islam to the Hausa in the fourteenth century, and they converted to it, especially to the Maliki school of the Sunni faith. Although most Hausas are settled farmers, raising millet, corn, rice, yams, peanuts, and tobacco, they are also known as excellent traders, who are characterized by their gowns and embroidered caps. In recent years, Hausa farmers have also started raising cotton and groundnuts. The long dry season, which runs from November to May, provides the opportunity to travel to look for work or commercial opportunities. Finally, the Hausa language, which is spoken in Nigeria and Niger, as well as in parts of Ghana, Ivory Coast, Sudan, Burkina-Faso, Benin, and Togo, is a unifying force; it is part of the Chadic branch of the Afro-Asiatic linguistic family. It has a rich tradition in oral literature; written Hausa, using the Arabic script, was developed several years ago. The best-known contemporary Hausa writer is Alhaji Abubakar Imam.

REFERENCES: Jerome H. Barkow. "Hausa." In Richard V. Weekes, ed. *Muslim Peoples.* 1984; Gretchen Didoff. *Katsina: Profile of a Nigerian City.* 1970; Polly Hill. *Rural Hausa: A Village and a Setting.* 1972; Madauci Ibrahim, Yahaya Isa, and Bello Daura. *Hausa Customs.* 1968; Ahmed Yusuf. "A Reconsideration of Urban Conceptions: Hausa Urbanization and the Hausa Rural-Urban Continuum." *Urban Anthropology* 3 (1974): 200–221.

HAVU. The Havus are a subgroup of the Kivu* peoples of Zaire. They live in the highlands of east-central Zaire, near Lake Kivu and the Rwandan border. The Havus speak a Bantu* language and make their livings as farmers who also raise cattle for milk and meat. During the genocidal civil war in Rwanda in 1994, the Havus were overrun by refugees fleeing the violence.
REFERENCE: Irving Kaplan et al. *Zaire: A Country Study.* 1978.

HAWARA. The Hawara people are part of the larger cluster of Berber* peoples in Sudan.

HAWAWIR. The Hawawir people are part of the larger cluster of Berber* peoples in Sudan.

HAWAZMA. *See* BAGGARA.

HAWIYA. *See* HAWIYE.

HAWIYE. The Hawiyes are one of the six primary clans of the Somali* people of Somalia. Like all Somalis, they claim descent from Samaale, the mythical founder of the entire ethnic group. Also like all other Somalis, they speak the Somali language and are Sunni Muslims. The vast majority of the Hawiyes, except for those who work in the city of Mogadishu, are nomadic herders who raise camels, sheep, and cattle. The vast majority of the Hawiyes are concentrated in Mogadishu and its environs. The Hawiye ethnic group, however, is subdivided into thousands of sub-clans and sub-sub-clans, and individual Hawiyes feel far more loyalty to their local clan than to any larger collectivity. The Hawiyes are found in the Galguduud Region of Somalia, as well as in the Hiran, Central, Lower Shebelle, and Lower Juba regions. They are also across the border in Ethiopia and in the North-Eastern Region of Kenya. The Hawiye population exceeds 800,000 people.

During the late 1980s and early 1990s, hundreds of thousands of Hawiyes faced starvation because of the famine and civil war in Somalia. Political instability became endemic as centralized authority broke down in the face of severe clan and sub-clan rivalries. Somalia essentially became a no-man's-land of misery and suffering, with no single individual or group enjoying enough power to impose any order. The Hawiyes control Mogadishu, but even there they are engaged in a civil war between the sub-clans. Mohammed Ali Mahdi from one sub-clan calls himself the interim president of Somalia, while General Mohammed Farrah Aidid, a Soviet-trained military officer, heads the so-called Somali National Alliance. Although Aidid's control in 1993 was more extensive than Mahdi's, it too was tenuous.
REFERENCES: Margaret Castagno. *Historical Dictionary of Somalia.* 1975; *New York Times,* October 4, 1992.

HAYA. The Haya are Bantu*-speaking people whose staple food is the banana. They drink banana beer, but raise coffee for a cash crop. The Haya kingdoms were abolished in 1962. The Haya number approximately 1.2 million people and are concentrated in the lakes region of northern Tanzania. Before the colonial period, they formed powerful kingdoms, which today have left them with a hierarchically organized social and political system. The traditional homeland of the Haya is the western shore of Lake Victoria, where the land is fertile. Their homes are characterized by beehive-shaped huts with grass roofs. They also raise some cattle.
REFERENCES: Robert G. Carlson. "Banana Beer, Reciprocity, and Ancestor Propitiation Among the Haya of Bukoba, Tanzania." *Ethnology* 29 (1990): 297–313; Brad Weiss. "Plastic Teeth Extraction: The Iconography of Haya Gastro-Sexual Affliction." *American Ethnology* 19 (August 1992): 531–52.

HEBA. *See* KILBA.

HEDARAB. *See* BENI AMER.

HEHE. The Hehe are an ethnic group living in the Iringa region of south-central Tanzania. They speak a Bantu* language and support themselves by sedentary farming and raising cattle. Until 1850, the Hehe were divided into more than thirty highly independent groups, but the great chief Muyugumba united the Hehe peoples in the nineteenth century. Between 1878 and 1883, the Hehe conquered the Ngonis* and took control of the region, confining the Ngonis to the area adjacent to Lake Malawi. Muyugumba's son Mkwawa defeated the German* advance at Iringa in 1891. The Hehes were not pacified until the end of the century. Today the Hehe population is approximately 550,000 people. The Hehe are especially known in Tanzania for their powerful influence on the national police force.
REFERENCES: *African Encyclopedia.* 1974; Laura Kurtz. *Historical Dictionary of Tanzania.* 1978.

HEIBAB. The Heibabs are one of the Nuba* peoples of Sudan.

HEMAT. The Hemats are a subgroup of the Djoheina,* themselves a large Arab* subgroup in Chad.

HEMBA. The Hembas (Bahemba) are one of the groups in the Bemba* cluster of peoples in northeastern Zaire and northern Zambia. They can also be found in Tanzania. They live west of Lake Tanganyika and Lake Mweru, as well as along the Zairean-Zambian border south of Lake Mweru and several hundred miles north on the Lualaba River. The Hemba language is part of the Bantu* language family, and it is understood throughout Zambia. The Hembas believe they originated in the Katanga region of contemporary Zaire and migrated to

Zambia. Their ancestors are the same as those of the Luba* and Lunda* peoples. They are a farming people. Traditionally, because of the poor soil in the region, they have relocated their villages every four or five years, but modern fertilizers and crop rotation methods have allowed them to become quite sedentary. They raise maize and millet as staples and cotton as a cash crop. Large numbers of Hemba men also work in the Copperbelt as miners. Some ethnologists classify them as part of the Luba cluster of peoples.

REFERENCES: *African Encyclopedia.* 1974; Thomas D. Blakely and Pamela A. R. Blakely. "So'o Masks and Hemba Funerary Festivals." *African Arts* 21 (November 1987): 30–38; F. Scott Bobb. *Historical Dictionary of Zaire.* 1988; Irving Kaplan et al. *Zaire: A Country Study,* 1978.

HENGA. The Hengas are part of the Tumbuka* cluster of peoples living today in northern Malawi, primarily between Lake Nyasa and the Zambian border, south of the Tanzanian border. Some Hengas can also be found in Zambia and Tanzania. The Henga population today exceeds 35,000 people. They speak a language closely related to that of the Tongas.* The Henga economy revolves around the production of maize, sorghum, and millet.

REFERENCES: *African Encyclopedia.* 1974; John J. Grotpeter. *Historical Dictionary of Zambia.* 1979; Donald G. Morrison et al. *Black Africa: A Comparative Handbook.* 1989.

HERA. The Heras, also known as Vaheras, are a Shona*-speaking people who live today in Zimbabwe. Ethnologists classify the Heras as a subgroup of the Zezurus,* but some Heras believe their origins are actually with the Karangas.* Most Heras live in the Mount Hedza region of Zimbabwe where they were close to the Njanjas.* They enjoy a reputation as skilled ironworkers.

REFERENCE: R. Kent Rasmussen. *Historical Dictionary of Zimbabwe.* 1994.

HERERO. The Hereros (Ovahereros) are a large group of people who today live in Botswana, Angola, and Namibia. They were traditionally a nomadic and semi-nomadic people who herded cattle and were isolated by the harsh geography of their homeland. As a result, the Hereros remained relatively free of slave traders during the eighteenth and nineteenth centuries, as well as out of touch with the commercial economic changes occurring throughout much of southern Africa. They generally resisted the attempts of colonial authorities—whether German,* Portuguese,* or British*—to subdue them. During the late nineteenth century, German colonial soldiers exterminated as many as 70 percent of the entire Herero population, which sent the survivors fleeing from what was then German South Africa into what is today Botswana and Transvaal. Today, most Hereros are small farmers, urban laborers, and pastoralists. They are divided into a number of subgroups, including the Hereros proper, the Mbanderos, and the Kaokabanders, who themselves are subdivided into the Himbas and Tjimbas.

REFERENCES: Susan H. Broadhead. *Historical Dictionary of Angola.* 1992; Carlos

Estermann. *The Ethnography of Southwestern Angola III: The Herero People.* 1981; Reginald Green, Marja-Liisa Kiljunen, and Kimmo Kiljunen. *Namibia: The Last Colony.* 1981.

HIGGI. The Higgis (Kipsikis) are one of the Bantu*-speaking peoples of Nigeria. They are classified as part of the Plateau cluster of peoples who occupy central Nigeria. Most Higgis practice subsistence horticulture, raising ginger, millet, guinea corn, beans, and citrus products. They live in social systems characterized by patrilineal descent and patrifocal residence. In recent years, they have begun migrating to towns and cities looking for work.
REFERENCE: Donald G. Morrison et al. *Black Africa: A Comparative Handbook.* 1989.

HIGI. *See* KAMWE.

HIGIDI. *See* LEGBO.

HIJI. *See* KAMWE.

HIMA. The Himas (Bahimas)—not to be confused with the Tutsi* Himas of Rwanda and Burundi—are one of the two subgroups of the Nyankore,* Nyoro,* and Toro* peoples of Uganda. They are known for their tall stature. During the years of British* authority, from 1901 to 1962, most Himas converted to Protestantism. They have formed an aristocracy in the region, dominating the more populous but also more subservient Iru* people. The Himas today total more than 100,000 people, most of whom are farmers, raising millet, plantains, coffee, tea, and cotton.

HIMA. The Himas—not to be confused with the Himas* of the Nyankores* of Uganda—are one of the two primary subgroupings of the Tutsi* people of Burundi. The other subgroup—the Abanyaruguru—looks down upon the Himas. The Himas themselves are divided into thirty identifiable family lineages. They are a small group of people with Nilotic* roots. The Himas tend to be a nomadic, traveling through northern and northeastern Rwanda and across the border in Zaire.
REFERENCES: Richard F. Nyrop et al. *Rwanda: A Country Study.* 1989; Warren Weinstein. *Historical Dictionary of Burundi.* 1976.

HIMBA. The Himbas are a subgroup of the Kaokabanders, themselves a subgroup of the Herero* people of Namibia and Angola.

HINGA. The Hingas are part of the larger cluster of Nyaneka-Humbe* peoples of southwestern Angola.

HLATSHWAKO. The Hlatshwakos are one of the clans of the Emafikamuva*

people, who themselves are one of the three major subgroups of the Swazi*
people of Swaziland.

HLENGUE. *See* HLENGWE.

HLENGWE. The Hlengwes (Bahlengues, Hlengues) are a Bantu*-speaking
people who are classified as part of the Tsonga* cluster of peoples in southeastern Zimbabwe, southern Mozambique, and northern Transvaal. During the
nineteenth century, the Hlengwes paid tribute to the Gaza state, and they acquired some Gaza cultural elements from them. Most Hlengwes today are small
farmers, workers, and cattle raisers.
REFERENCES: R. Kent Rasmussen. *Historical Dictionary of Zimbabwe.* 1994; Harold
D. Nelson et al. *Zimbabwe: A Country Study.* 1982.

HLOPHE. The Hlophes are one of the major clans of the Bemdzabuko* division of the Swazi* people of Swaziland.

HO. The Ho are a subgroup of the Ewe* peoples of southeastern Ghana. They
are concentrated near the town of Ho in the Volta Region of Ghana and across
the border in Togo.

HOEGBAHN. The Hoegbahns are a subgroup of the Bassa* people of Liberia.
Most Hoegbahns live in Grand Bassa County.

HOLLI. The Hollis are one of the many subgroups of the Yoruba* peoples of
West Africa. They can be found today especially in southern Benin.

HOLO. The Holos are a subgroup of the Mbundu* peoples of Angola.

HOLOHOLO. The Holoholos are an ethnic group living along the central shore
of Lake Tanganyika in western Tanzania. Most Holoholos make their living
fishing, farming, and raising cattle. Some ethnologists classify them as a Bemba*
group.
REFERENCE: Laura Kurtz. *Historical Dictionary of Tanzania.* 1978.

HONA. *See* HWANA.

HOROM. The Horoms are an ethnic group living today in the Richa and Tof
districts of the Pankshin Division of Plateau State in Nigeria. Most of them are
small farmers. They speak a language that is part of the Eastern Plateau cluster
of the Benue-Congo family.
REFERENCE: *Language Survey of Nigeria.* 1976.

HOTTENTOT. The term ''Hottentot'' is a common but pejorative reference to
Khoikhoi* people.
REFERENCE: R. Kent Rasmussen. *Historical Dictionary of Zimbabwe.* 1994.

HOVA. *See* MERINA.

HUAMBO. The Huambos (Wambos) are one of the traditional, autonomous kingdoms and contemporary ethnic subgroups of the Ovimbundu* people of Angola. With a population today of more than 600,000 people in Namibia, they are the dominant ethnic group there, where they live in the northern region bordering Angola and are known as Ambos.*

HUDE. *See* DGHWEDE.

HUELA. *See* HWELA.

HUM. The Hum (Humbe) people live today in southwestern Zaire and northern Angola. They are a riverine people living near the Kwango River. There they fish, plant, and trade goods—occupations they have pursued there for centuries. Most Hums live in and around Popokabaka.
REFERENCE: Irving Kaplan et al. *Zaire: A Country Study.* 1978.

HUM. *See* HYAM.

HUMBE. *See* HUM.

HUMR. *See* BAGGARA.

HUNDE. The Hundes are a subgroup of the Kivu* peoples of Zaire. They live in the highlands of east-central Zaire, near Lake Kivu and the Rwandan border. They can also be found in Rwanda and southwestern Uganda. The Hundes speak a Bantu* language and make their living as farmers who also raise cattle for milk and meat. During the genocidal civil war in Rwanda in 1994, the Hundes were overrun by refugees fleeing the violence.
REFERENCE: Irving Kaplan et al. *Zaire: A Country Study.* 1978.

HUNGU. The Hungus are a subgroup of the Mbundu* people of north-central Angola.

HUNGWE. *See* MANHICA.

HURUTSHE. The Hurutshes (Barutshes) are a subgroup of the Tswana* people of Botswana today. They developed from another Tswana subgroup—the Kwena.* Most Hurutshes today live in Transvaal, South Africa, and in Botswana. Most Botswana Hurutshes are descendants of those who left Transvaal in the 1850s. Others left in the 1950s, when South African police were harassing

them. The Hurutshes are further divided into such subgroups as the Mokubidu, who live in Kweneng District, and the Manyana, who live in the Southern District.
REFERENCE: Fred Morton, A. Murray, and J. Ramsay. *Historical Dictionary of Botswana.* 1989.

HUSAYNAT. The Husaynats are a subgroup of the Jaaliyin* Arabs* of Sudan.

HUTU. The Hutus, also known as Abahutus, Bahutus, and Wakhutus, are the dominant ethnic group in Rwanda and Burundi in East Africa. Their population numbers more than six million people, and they speak a Bantu* language. Their religious loyalties are divided. Approximately half of the Hutus are Roman Catholics, while the others remain loyal to indigenous religious traditions. In the fifteenth century, the Hutus came under the domination of the Tutsis,* but in Rwanda that domination ended late in the 1950s when the Hutus rose up in rebellion against the Tutsis. That rebellion turned violent in 1959, driving more than 200,000 Tutsis out of the country. Belgian* officials sided with the majority Hutus, and, in 1962, when Rwanda gained its independence, the Hutus were in complete control. The Tutsis retained their dominance in Burundi after independence in 1962. The Hutu-Tutsi rivalry festered during the 1960s, 1970s, and 1980s, periodically erupting into violence. In 1994, a new civil war in Rwanda resulted in the deaths of more than 500,000 people.

In Burundi, the Tutsis remained in control. In 1965, a Hutu rebellion there failed, and, in the process, thousands of Hutus, especially intellectuals, were slaughtered. The failed rebellion left Burundi under complete Tutsi control. In the early 1970s, another Tutsi-Hutu civil war erupted in Burundi. In the fighting, nearly 3,000 Tutsis died, but more than 200,000 Hutus were killed and another 100,000 fled. During the early 1990s, the power struggle began to devastate Burundi. The violence forced more than 700,000 people—Hutus and Tutsis— to flee Burundi for Rwanda, Tanzania, and Zaire. Today, there are approximately 300,000 Tutsis living in Rwanda and surrounding countries. The political and ethnic rivalry between the Hutus and Tutsis is the dominant theme of Rwanda and Burundi politics. In Rwanda in 1994, more than 500,000 people were slaughtered in a Hutu-Tutsi civil war.
REFERENCES: *African Encyclopedia.* 1974; Warren Weinstein. *Historical Dictionary of Burundi.* 1976.

HWANA. The Hwana people, also known as Honas and Hwonas, are a Nigerian ethnic group. Their language is part of the Tera group of Chadic languages, and they are concentrated in Ga'anda District of Adamawa Division of Gongola State. Most of them are subsistence farmers and herders.
REFERENCE: *Language Survey of Nigeria.* 1976.

HWASO. *See* KPAN.

HWAYE. *See* KPAN.

HWELA. The term "Hwela" (Huela, Vuela, Weela) is used to refer to a group of Jula* farmers who live along the Black Volta River in Ghana.

HWONA. *See* HWANA.

HYAM. The Hyams (Hams, Hums, Jabas) are part of a larger Hausa*-Fulbe* cluster of peoples living in northwestern Nigeria. The Hyams are concentrated in the Zangon Katab districts of the Kachia Division and the Jema'a and Kwoi districts of the Jema'a Division in Kaduna State. Some of them can also be found across the border in Niger and in northern Benin. A strong Muslim component dominates their religion. Most of them are small farmers and cattle herders. Traditionally, the Hyams lived in conical houses with grass-thatched roofs, and they hunted. In the twentieth century, they have turned to agriculture, growing corn and millet, as well as producing ginger and palm oil for cash. Ethnolinguists classify their language with the Eastern Plateau languages of the Benue-Congo family.
REFERENCES: *Language Survey of Nigeria.* 1976; Donald G. Morrison et al. *Black Africa: A Comparative Handbook.* 1989.

I

IAMBI. The Iambis are a Bantu*-speaking people of the Central Highlands of Tanzania. They are surrounded by the Irambas,* Isanzus,* Barabaigs,* and Turus.* Most of them are settled farmers raising grains—sorghum, maize, and millet—for subsistence, as well as several cash crops. Like the Irambas, to whom they are most closely related, the Iambis are Sunni Muslims of the Shafi school. In recent years, they have found themselves forced to abandon their isolated homestead settlements as part of the government's *ujamaa* program, which has moved them into larger villages where educational and medical facilities are better. The Iambi population in Tanzania today exceeds 50,000 people.
REFERENCES: E. R. Danielson. "Brief History of the Waniramba People Up to the Time of the German Occupation." *Tanganyika Notes and Records* 56 (1961): 67–68; E. R. Danielson. "Proverbs of the Waniramba Peoples of East Africa." *Tanganyika Notes and Records* 47–48 (1957): 187–97; J. Spencer Trimingham. *Islam in East Africa.* 1964.

IBAMI. *See* AGOI.

IBANI. The Ibanis are one of the many ethnic groups living in Rivers State, Nigeria. They are concentrated particularly in the Bonny Local Government Area. Ethnolinguists classify them as part of the larger cluster of Ijaw* peoples. The Ibanis are primarily subsistence farmers.
REFERENCE: E. J. Alagoa and Tekena N. Tamuno. *Land and People of Nigeria: Rivers State.* 1989.

IBARAPA. The Ibarapas are one of the main subgroups of the Yoruba* people. Most Ibarapas live around Eruwa and Igbo-Ora in southwestern Oyo State in western Nigeria.

IBENO. *See* IBINO.

IBESIKPO. The Ibesikpos are a subgroup of the Ibibio* peoples of Nigeria.

IBIAKU. The Ibiakus are a subgroup of the Ibibio* peoples of Nigeria.

IBIBIO. The Ibibio people live in the southern reaches of Cross River State in Nigeria, primarily in the Opobo, Itu, Uyo, Etiman, Oron, Ikot Ekpene, and Eket divisions. In terms of language and culture, they are closely related to the Efiks.* Their social structure has traditionally been highly decentralized, with family groups and villages dominant. Each village had its *Ekpo* society, a secret religious and social organization that was designed to appease ancestors, conduct the rituals necessary to bring good fortune to the group, and make major community decisions. Most Ibibios are farmers who raise yams and palm oil products. In recent years, however, increasing numbers of Ibibios have moved to such cities as Uyo, Ikot Ekpene, and Itu looking for work. The Ibibios are subdivided into dozens of subgroups, including the Iwawas, Ndikpos, Okus, Offots, Etois, Ibesikpos, Uruans, Nsits, Imans, Ubiums, Nung Ndems, Oniongs, Ikonos, Edienes, Itaks, Ibionos, Itams, Ayadeghes, Ideres, Ikpanjas, Ikas, Ikpas, Ukpums, Ibaikus, Ikpes, Odots, and Ediongs. Their current population is well in excess of 1.2 million people.
REFERENCES: *African Encyclopedia.* 1974; Daryll Forde and G. I. Jones. *The Ibo and Ibibio-Speaking Peoples of South-Eastern Nigeria.* 1950; A. Oyewole. *Historical Dictionary of Nigeria.* 1987.

IBIE. The Ibies are a subgroup of the Edo* peoples of south central Nigeria.

IBINO. The Ibinos (Ibunos, Ibenos) live today in the Eket and Oron divisions of Cross River State, Nigeria. Their language falls within the larger Benue-Congo family.
REFERENCE: *Language Survey of Nigeria.* 1976.

IBIONO. The Ibionos are a subgroup of the Ibibio* peoples of Nigeria.

IBO. *See* IGBO.

IBOLO. The Ibolos are one of the main subgroups of the Yoruba.* Most Ibolos are concentrated in eastern Oyo State and southern Kwara State in western Nigeria.

IBUKWO. *See* KPAN.

IBUNO. *See* IBINO.

IBUT. *See* JIDDA-ABU.

ICEN. The Icen people—also known historically as the Ichens, Itchens, Kentus, Kyatos, Etkywas, and Nyidus—speak a central Jukunoid language and live to-day in Nigeria. They are concentrated in the Ichen District of the Mambilla District of Gongola State, as well as in the Gayam, Gindin Dutse, Likam, and Suntai districts of the Wukari Division of Gongola State.
REFERENCE: *Language Survey of Nigeria.* 1976.

ICHAKIRI. *See* ITSEKIRI.

ICHEN. *See* ICEN.

ICHEVE. The Icheves (Utses, Utsers, Utseus, Becheves, and Bacheves) live in the Obudu Division of Cross River State in Nigeria. Most of them are subsis-tence farmers who are closely related to the Tiv* people.
REFERENCE: *Language Survey of Nigeria.* 1976.

ICIBAK. *See* KYIBAKU.

ID AHMED. The Id Ahmeds are a subgroup of the Ait Atman* people of Western Sahara. The Ait Atman are themselves a subgroup of the Tekna* peo-ples.

ID BRAHIM. The Id Brahims are a subgroup of the Ait Atman* people of Western Sahara. The Ait Atman are themselves a subgroup of the Tekna* peo-ples.

ID DAOUD OU ABDALLAH. The Id Daoud Ou Abdallahs are a subgroup of the Ait Lahsens* of Western Sahara in what is today Morocco.

IDAISA. The Idaisas are one of the main subgroups of the Yoruba.* Although most Yorubans live in Nigeria, the Idaisas migrated westward several centuries ago. Today, they live in central Benin, near the towns of Savalou and Dassa-Zoume.

IDAKHO. The Idakhos are a subgroup of the Luhya* people of Kenya and Uganda. They are a Western Bantu* people who today live north of Lake Vic-toria on both sides of the Kenya-Uganda border.

IDERE. The Ideres are a subgroup of the Ibibio* peoples of Nigeria.

IDOMA. The Idomas are a large Nigerian ethnic group. Their current population exceeds 400,000 people, and they are one of the dominant ethnic groups in southeastern Nigeria, where they are concentrated just east of the confluence of the Benue and Niger rivers, especially in the Oturkpo Division of Benue State. Included within the Idoma orbit of ethnic groups are the Igalas,* Aragos, Afus, and Igbirras. Most Idomas are small farmers, but, since they live in a region that has become highly commercialized, their own economy is becoming increasingly diversified. Although a few Idomas are Muslims, most remain loyal to their traditional religious faith.
REFERENCES: Sidney L. Kasfir. "Anjenu: Sculpture for Idoma Water Spirits." *African Arts* 15 (August 1982): 47–51; *Language Survey of Nigeria.* 1976; Donald G. Morrison et al. *Black Africa: A Comparative Handbook.* 1989.

IDOMA-NOKWU. *See* ALAGOA.

IDON. The Idons, also known as the Idongs and the Igongs, are a people living in the Kajuru District of the Kachia Division of Kaduna State in Nigeria. Their language is part of the Eastern Plateau cluster of Benue-Congo languages.
REFERENCE: *Language Survey of Nigeria.* 1976.

IDUWINI. The Iduwinis are a subgroup of the Izon* peoples of Rivers State in Nigeria.

IFE. The Ifes are one of the main subgroups of the Yoruba.* Although most Yorubans live in Nigeria, some Ifes migrated westward several centuries ago. Today, they live in eastern Togo and Western Benin, near the towns of Atakpame, Djakoulou, and Kpesi. Other Ifes can be found in southeastern Oyo State in Nigeria.

IFONYIM. The Ifonyims are one of the main subgroups of the Yoruba* people of Nigeria. Most Ifonyims can be found today living east of the Weme River in Benin and along the Benin-Nigerian border in western Ogun State in Nigeria.

IFUNUBWA. *See* MBEMBE.

IGABO. *See* ISOKO.

IGALA. The Igalas (Igaras) are one of the ethnic groups of Nigeria. With a population of as many as one million people, they are one of the larger ethnic groups in the country. The Igalas can be found concentrated in the Dekina, Idah, and Ankpa divisions of Benue State, as well as in the Anambra Division of Anambra State and the Ishu Division of Bendel State. Although most

Igalas are small farmers, they value education highly and are enjoying increasing occupational diversity.

REFERENCES: Roger de la Burde. ''Ancestral Ram's Heads of the Edo-Speaking Peoples.'' *African Arts* 6 (Autumn 1972): 29–34; *Language Survey of Nigeria.* 1976.

IGARA. *See* IGALA.

IGBEDE. The Igbedes are one of the primary subgroups of the Yoruba* people of Nigeria. Most Igbedes live today in eastern Kwara state in western Nigeria.

IGBIRA. *See* EBIRA.

IGBIRI. *See* GURE-KAHUGU.

IGBIRRA. *See* EBIRA.

IGBO. The Igbo, also known as Ibo, are one of the three dominant ethnic groups of Nigeria. Their population is nearly 15 million people, most of whom live in the Anambra and Imo states. They can also be found across the border in southern Cameroon, having moved there during the British* mandate period, and in Ghana. The population density there is the highest in West Africa. The Igbo can also be found in Mid-Western State, Rivers State, and other regions. The Igbo have occupied this homeland for more than a thousand years. Their language is classified as one of the Kwa* languages of the Niger-Congo linguistic family. Most Igbo are farmers, raising yams, cocoyams, maize, and cassava; they also produce palm oil products. Although many Igbo are Christians, the traditional belief in Chukwu Okike, the great creator god, is still intact, as is a worshipful respect for dead ancestors and the mysterious forces of nature. The Igbo fiercely resisted the expansion of the British empire until 1929; after the unification of Nigeria, they spread throughout the country as traders, civil servants, teachers, and professionals. The Igbo were targeted during the Biafran civil war in 1966. The Igbo social system is patrilineal, and they are divided into many subgroups, including the Abadja,* Abaja,* Abam,* Alensaw,* Aro,* Awhawfia,* Awhawzara,* Awtanzu,* Edda,* Ekkpahia,* Etche,* Eziama, Ezza,* Ihe, Iji, Ika, Ikwerri, Ikwo, Ishielu, Isu, Isu-Ochi, Ndokki, Ngbo, Ngwa, Nkalu, Nkanu, Okoba, Onitsha, Oratta, Oru, Owerri, Ubani, and Ututu.

REFERENCES: *African Encyclopedia.* 1974; Mary S. Duru. ''Continuity in the Midst of Change: Underlying Themes in Igbo Culture.'' *Anthropological Quarterly* 5 (January 1983): 1–9; Daryll Forde and G. I. Jones. *The Ibo and Ibibio-Speaking Peoples of South-Eastern Nigeria.* 1950; A. Oyewole. *Historical Dictionary of Nigeria.* 1987.

IGBO IMABAN. *See* LEGBO.

IGBOMINA. The Igbominas are one of the primary subgroups of the Yoruba* people of Nigeria. Most Igbominas live today in central Kwara state in western Nigeria.

IGDALEN. The Igdalens are a subgroup of the Tuareg* people of Niger and Mali. Known for their religious piety and honesty, the Igdalens are essentially religious groups attached to various Tuareg clans. Ethnologists place their origins in Morocco and their arrival in the Air region of Niger before the eleventh century.

IGEDE. The Igede (Igedde) people, also known as the Egede (Eggede), live primarily in the Eggede, Ito, Worku, and Oturkpo districts of the Oturkpo Division in Benue State in Nigeria. Some can also be found in the Ogoja Division of Cross River State. They are concentrated north of the Middle Cross River, just bordering the tropical forest. The Igede population today exceeds 250,000 people, most of whom are farmers living in scattered villages. Many ethnologists have classified them with their northern neighbors, the Idomas,* but their language and culture are distinct. They trace their origins to the confluence of the Niger and Benue rivers in what used to be Northern Nigeria. Although most Igedes remain small farmers, they live in a region which has been assimilated into a larger commercial economy, bringing about increasing amounts of wage labor and occupational diversification.
REFERENCES: *Language Survey of Nigeria.* 1976; Robert W. Nicholls. "Igede Funeral Masquerades." *African Arts* 17 (May 1984): 70–76; A. Oyewole. *Historical Dictionary of Nigeria.* 1987.

IGEMBI. The Igembis are a Bantu*-speaking people who are a subgroup of the Meru* cluster of peoples in Kenya and Tanzania.

IGOJI. The Igojis are a Bantu*-speaking people who are a subgroup of the Meru* cluster of peoples in Kenya and Tanzania.

IGONG. *See* IDON.

IGUTA. *See* NARAGUTA.

IHANZU. The Ihanzu are a Bantu*-speaking people of the Central Highlands of Tanzania. They maintain a powerful sense of ethnic identity and make their living as small farmers.
REFERENCE: J. Spencer Trimingham. *Islam in East Africa.* 1964.

IHE. The Ihes are one of the many subgroups of the Igbo* people, an ethnic group of nearly fifteen million people living today in southern and southeastern Nigeria.

IJAW. The Ijaw (Ijo) people live in Rivers and Bendel states, Nigeria. Much of their land is located in the Niger Delta and consists of mangrove swamps and farmland. Since the region is crisscrossed by many creeks and rivers, fishing has always been important to the Ijaws. They also produce salt and are known for their trading abilities. During the centuries of the Atlantic slave trade, the Ijaws regularly served as middlemen in the traffic. Ijaw tradition has them moving from the east and north to their present homeland in the fifteenth century, but their language does not resemble other Nigerian languages in the region; ethnologists believe they may have arrived in the area long before the other groups. The Ijaws are divided into a number of subgroups, including the Ibani* (Bonny), Okrika,* Kalabari,* Nemba (Brass), Akassa,* and Defaka.* During the past thirty years, Ijaw life has been transformed by the discovery of vast reserves of oil and natural gas in their region. This development has provided large numbers of well-paying jobs, as well as the instant incorporation of the region into the larger commercial economy of Nigeria.
REFERENCES: *African Encyclopedia.* 1974; A. Oyewole, *Historical Dictionary of Nigeria.* 1987.

IJEBU. The Ijebus are a subgroup of the Yoruba* peoples of Nigeria. Along with the Egbas,* another Yoruba subgroup, the Ijebus constitute the majority population of Ogun State. During the last several centuries, because of their location near Lagos and the Atlantic coast, the Ijebus played the role of commercial middlemen between European traders and interior ethnic groups. Their defeat at the hands of the British* in 1892 marked the beginning of British domination of Yorubaland.
REFERENCE: A. Oyewole. *Historical Dictionary of Nigeria.* 1987.

IJEKIRI. *See* ITSEKIRI.

IJEMU. The Ijemus are one of the primary subgroups of the Yoruba* people of Nigeria. Most Ijemus live today in eastern Kwara state in western Nigeria.

IJESU. The Ijesus are one of the main subgroups of the Yoruba* people of Nigeria. Most Ijesus today live near the town of Ilesa in southeastern Oyo State, as well as in western Ondo State, in western Nigeria.

IJI. The Ijis are one of the many subgroups of the Igbo* people, an ethnic group of nearly fifteen million people living today in southern and southeastern Nigeria.

IJO. *See* IJAW.

IK. The Ik people, also known as the Tuesos, are one of Uganda's approxi-

mately thirty ethnic groups. They speak an Eastern Nilotic* language and live in the northeast part of the Karamoja region. Their population today is approximately 5,000 people, most of whom are subsistence farmers.
REFERENCE: Peter Ladefoged, Ruth Glick, and Clive Criper. *Language in Uganda.* 1972.

IKA. The Ikas are one of the many subgroups of the Igbo* people, an ethnic group of nearly fifteen million people living today in southern and southeastern Nigeria.

IKALE. The Ikales are one of the primary Yoruba* subgroups in Nigeria. Most of them live today near the town of Okitipupa in southern Ondo State of western Nigeria.

IKAN. *See* UKAAN.

IKELAN. *See* BELLA.

IKIBIRI. The Ikibiris are a subgroup of the Izon* peoples of Rivers State in Nigeria.

IKIRI. The Ikiris are one of the primary subgroups of the Yoruba* people of Nigeria. Most Ikiris live today in eastern Kwara state in western Nigeria.

IKIZU. The Ikizus are a small ethnic group living today in Tanzania. They speak a Bantu* language and have a population of approximately 30,000 people, most of whom are subsistence farmers.
REFERENCES: Iriving Kaplan et al. *Tanzania: A Country Study.* 1978; Edgar C. Polomé and C. P. Hill. *Language in Tanzania.* 1980.

IKO. *See* DOKO-UYANGA.

IKOBA. *See* BAKOTA.

IKOLU. *See* IKULU.

IKOMA. The Ikomas are a small ethnic group living today in Tanzania. They speak a Bantu* language and have a population of approximately 15,000 people, most of whom are subsistence farmers.
REFERENCE: Edgar C. Polomé and C. P. Hill. *Language in Tanzania.* 1980.

IKONGO. The Ikongos are a subgroup of the Tanala* peoples of Madagascar.

IKONO. The Ikonos are a subgroup of the Ibibio* peoples of Nigeria.

IKPA. The Ikpas are a subgroup of the Ibibio* peoples of Nigeria.

IKPAN. *See* KPAN.

IKPANJA. The Ikpanjas are a subgroup of the Ibibio* peoples of Nigeria.

IKPE. The Ikpes are a subgroup of the Ibibio* peoples of Nigeria.

IKPESHI. The Ikpeshis are a small group of people who speak an Edo* language. They live in Etsako Division of Bendel State in Nigeria.

IKU-GORA-ANKWA. The Iku-Gora-Ankwas are one of the Eastern Plateau peoples who live in the Kachia District of the Kachia Division of Kaduna State in Nigeria. Their language is part of the Benue-Congo family.
REFERENCE: *Language Survey of Nigeria.* 1976.

IKULU. The Ikulus are an ethnic group of approximately 25,000 people who live in the Zangon Matab District of the Kachia Division in Kaduna State, Nigeria. They are one of the Eastern Plateau peoples who speak a Benue-Congo language.
REFERENCE: *Language Survey of Nigeria.* 1976.

IKWERRI. The Ikwerris are one of the many subgroups of the Igbo* people, an ethnic group of nearly fifteen million people living today in southern and southeastern Nigeria.

IKWO. The Ikwos are one of the many subgroups of the Igbo* people of southern and southeastern Nigeria.

ILA. The Ilas are an ethnic group living in the Kafue valley in southern Zambia. Their current population exceeds 70,000 people. Like their neighbors, the Tongas,* they originated in the Lake Tanganyika region and migrated southwestward. The Ilas have a matrilineal descent system but a patrilineal residence pattern. The traditional Ila economy has revolved around raising cattle, with beef and milk products central to their diet. Fishing and hunting have also been important. Some people classify them as part of the Bantu* Botatwe group. In recent years, the tsetse fly infestation has reduced the cattle herds and forced the Ilas into a more sedentary agricultural lifestyle. Included in the Ila cluster of peoples are the Ilas proper, Leyas, Subiyas,* Totelas,* Lumbus, and Lundwes.
REFERENCES: *African Encyclopedia.* 1974; John J. Grotpeter. *Historical Dictionary of Zambia.* 1979.

ILAJE. The Ilajes are one of the primary Yoruba* subgroups in Nigeria. They live today primarily on the coast in southern Ondo State of western Nigeria.

ILALANGINA. The Ilalanginas are a subgroup of the Betsileo* peoples of the central plateau of Madagascar.

ILEME. *See* UNEME.

ILLABAKAN. The Illabakans are an important clan of the Tuaregs* in Niger. They are a nomadic people whose range consists of the region between Tahoua and Agadez.

IMAJEREN. The Imajerens are a noble clan of the Tuaregs* of Niger and Mali. They constitute the Tuareg warrior aristocracy.

IMAMONO. The Imamonos are a subgroup of the Bara* cluster of peoples of the plains of Madagascar.

IMAN. The Imans are a subgroup of the Ibibio* peoples of Nigeria.

IMENTI. The Imentis are a Bantu*-speaking people who are a subgroup of the Meru* cluster of peoples in Kenya and Tanzania.

IMERINA. *See* MERINA.

IMGANGALA. The Imgangalas are a subgroup of the Mbundu* people of north-central Angola. During the Portuguese conquest of Angola, the Imgangalas often allied themselves with the Europeans in attacking neighboring ethnic groups.

IMILANGA. The Imilangas are part of the larger cluster of Luyana* peoples of Zambia. The Luyanas are part of the Lozi* group. Their contemporary population exceeds 8,000 people.

IMOUZOURAG. The Imouzourags are one of the primary Tuareg* clans of Niger and Mali.

IMRAD. The Imrads are considered the second-ranking noble clan of the Tuaregs* of Mali and Niger.

IMRAQUEN. The Imraquens are one of the Moorish* subgroups living today in Mauritania.

INADIN. The Inadins are a clan among the Tuaregs.* They are primarily silversmiths who travel from one Tuareg encampment to another to work their craft.

INAMWANGA. *See* NAMWANGA.

INCHAZI. *See* RUKUBA.

INDIAN. With the decline of the East African slave trade in the nineteenth century and the formal prohibition of slavery, the need for cheap labor in East Africa and South Africa increased steadily. Plantation owners and industrialists met these needs by importing workers from India. The migration of Indians continued during most of the twentieth century. Of the Indians who settled in Africa, approximately 70 percent are Hindus and 20 percent are Muslims. They have tended to be concentrated in especially large numbers in the coastal cities of South Africa and in the countries of East Africa. In spite of ethnic, religious, and linguistic differences, they are a rather cohesive community. In South Africa, their population in 1990 exceeded 825,000 people.
REFERENCE: Christopher Saunders. *Historical Dictionary of South Africa.* 1983.

INEME. *See* UNEME.

INESLEMEN. The Ineslemen are a religious class among the Tuaregs* of Mali and Niger. Because they are highly respected as a sacerdotal caste, they are not required to work and instead live off the contributions of other clans to their upkeep.

INGASSANA. *See* INGESSANA.

INGESSANA. The Ingessana are a pre-Nilotic people of the Sudan who are part of the Shilluk* cluster of ethnic groups. They were driven into the hills of their present location between the White Nile and Blue Nile rivers in eastern Sudan by the expansion of neighboring ethnic groups. Like other groups straddling the Ethiopian-Sudanese border, the Ingessana have been victimized over the years by Arab* slavers and ethnic conflict with Arabs from northern Sudan. The contemporary civil war in Sudan has been very hard on the Ingessana.
REFERENCE: Helen C. Metz et al. *Sudan: A Country Study.* 1992.

INGWE. *See* NGWOI.

INJOUREN. The Injourens are a subgroup of the Ait Lahsens* of Western Sahara in what is today Morocco.

INKASSAR. *See* SEFWI.

INYIMA. *See* LENYIMA.

IRAMBA. The Irambas are a prominent Bantu*-speaking people who live in Central Tanzania. Included in the Iramba cluster of peoples are the Irambis and the Izanzus. Their particular Bantu language is known as Kiniramba. The majority of the Irambas living in rural areas are hoe farmers, raising sorghum, millet, maize, cattle, sheep, and goats. A few of the Irambas also raise peanuts and castor oil plants as cash crops. The political system of the Irambas revolves around independent councils of elders in each village or general settlement area. Until the early 1970s, most Irambas lived in isolated homestead settlements in the miyombo bush country of the north or the thorn scrub region of the south. In 1974, Tanzania officially launched its *ujamaa* program, gathering the Irambas into larger villages where education, commercial agriculture, and political control would be easier to implement. Islam first reached the Irambas in the nineteenth century when slave traders came into central Tanzania; today more than half of the Irambas identify themselves as Muslims—Sunni Muslims of the Shafi school. Nevertheless, strong elements of their traditional animist faith—particularly worship at rain shrines—survives, and relatively few people conduct their daily Islamic prayers or observe Ramadan.
REFERENCES: E. R. Danielson. "Brief History of the Waniramba People Up to the Time of the German Occupation." *Tanganyika Notes and Records* 56 (1961): 67–68; E. R. Danielson. "Proverbs of the Waniramba Peoples of East Africa." *Tanganyika Notes and Records* 47–48 (1957): 187–97; J. Spencer Trimingham. *Islam in East Africa.* 1964.

IRAMBI. The Irambis are a Bantu*-speaking people living today in Central Tanzania. They are included by many ethnologists in the Iramba*' group of peoples.

IRAQW. The Iraqw are a people of the Central Highlands of Tanzania in East Africa. They are concentrated in the Mbulu and Hanang districts, and their population is approximately 250,000 people. They are bordered by Ngorongoro Crater National Park to the north, the Great Rift Valley to the east, the Serengeti Plain to the west, and dry bush savanna to the south. The Iraqw's most immediate neighbors are the Masai* to the east; the Tatogas and Hadsas (Hatsa) to the west; the Irambas,* Ihanzus, Irangis, Turus,* and Gogos* to the south; and the Gorowas and Alagwas to the southeast. There is considerable controversy on how to classify the Iraqw language, since they are descendants of Cushitic, Nilotic,* Bantu, and Khoisan peoples. The Iraqw economy is largely a subsistence one, in which they raise maize, millet, cattle, sheep, and goats. The Iraqw are known for their suspicion and hostility toward Swahili*-speaking government officials in Tanzania; their belief in egalitarianism has led to territorial expansion and geographic segmentation. Most Iraqw remain loyal to traditional

religious beliefs that revolve around the immortality of individual souls, their eternal residence in the Iraqw homeland, and a cosmos dominated by Lo'a, a good spirit, and Netlangw, a bad spirit.
REFERENCE: Robert Thornton. *Space, Time, and Culture among the Iraqw of Tanzania.* 1980.

IRÉBU. The Irébus are a subgroup of the Mbochi* people of eastern Gabon, central Congo, and western Zaire. Their contemporary population exceeds 30,000 people. Although they are increasingly turning to commercial agriculture, the Irébu economy has traditionally revolved around trading and fishing, at which they are highly adept. Their social structure is based on a patrilineal clan structure.
REFERENCES: Donald G. Morrison et al. *Black Africa: A Comparative Handbook.* 1989; Gordon C. McDonald et al. *Area Handbook for the People's Republic of the Congo (Congo Brazzaville).* 1971.

IRHOBO. *See* ITSEKIRI.

IRIGWE. The Irigwe (Rigwes, Aregwes, Nnerigwes, Miangos, Kwals, Nyangos, Kwolls, and Kwans) are an African ethnic group numbering approximately 21,000 people. They are a hunting group and live in dozens of villages roughly twenty-five miles southeast of Jos, the capital city of Plateau State in Nigeria. Hunting, an exclusively masculine activity, has great religious and tribal significance for the Irigwe. The consumption of meat and beer is considered among life's most important activities. Historically, the Irigwe practiced ritualized forms of cannibalism and head-hunting, but those have declined dramatically in recent years. The Irigwe do not speak the languages of their neighbors, nor do they allow their children to intermarry. Today, most of them are farmers, with millet their primary crop.
REFERENCES: Harold D. Gunn. *The Peoples of the Plateau Area of Nigeria.* 1953; *Language Survey of Nigeria.* 1976; Jean-Claude Muller. ''Intertribal Hunting Among the Rukuba.'' *Ethnology* 21 (1982): 203–14.

IRU. The Irus are a subgroup of the Nyankores,* Toros,* and Nyoros,* who are Bantu*-speaking people of Uganda. The Iru population today is approaching one million people, most of whom are Roman Catholics and raise cattle for a living. Although they are the largest of the two Nyankore subgroups, they have traditionally been subservient to the dominant, aristocratic Hima.*

IRWANA. The Irwanas are a Tanzanian ethnic group and are often included by ethnologists in the larger Nyamwezi* cluster of peoples.

ISA. The Isas are one of the main subgroups of the Yoruba* people. Although most Yorubans live in Nigeria, the Isas migrated to the west several centuries ago. Today, they live in western Benin, near the town of Bante, with some of them across the border in Togo.

ISALA. *See* SASALA.

ISANDRA. The Isandras are a subgroup of the Betsileo* peoples of the central plateau of Madagascar.

ISANZU. The Isanzu are a Bantu*-speaking people of the Central Highlands of Tanzania. They are surrounded by the Irambas,* Iambis,* Hadzas,* Barabaigs,* and Iraqws,* and their homeland borders the southern tip of Lake Eyasi. The Isanzus raise grain crops as well as peanuts and castor oil crops for cash; they also raise cattle, goats, and sheep. The most recent change in the Isanzu lifestyle is the result of the Tanzanian government's *ujamaa* program. In order to provide educational and medical facilities to the Isanzu, the government has worked to end their lifestyle in scattered homesteads and to relocate them into more demographically concentrated villages. The Isanzu population today is approximately 30,000 people.
REFERENCES: E. R. Danielson. "Brief History of the Waniramba People Up to the Time of the German Occupation." *Tanganyika Notes and Records* 56 (1961): 67–68; E. R. Danielson. "Proverbs of the Waniramba Peoples of East Africa." *Tanganyika Notes and Records* 47–48 (1957): 187–97; J. Spencer Trimingham. *Islam in East Africa.* 1964.

ISEKIVI. *See* ITSEKIRI.

ISELEMA. *See* ITSEKIRI.

ISHAAK. *See* ISSAQ.

ISHAK. *See* ISSAQ.

ISHAN. *See* ESAN.

ISHERIFEN. The Isherifens are Tuareg* clans who claim direct descent from the Prophet Muhammad.

ISHIELU. The Ishielus (Eshielus) are one of the many subgroups of the Igbos* an ethnic group of nearly fifteen million people living today in southern and southeastern Nigeria.

ISOKO. The Isokos, also known as Urhobos, Biotus, Igabos, and the pejorative Sobos, live in the northwest fringe of the Niger River Delta in Nigeria, especially in the Isoko and Eastern Urhobo divisions of Bendel State. They are divided into sixteen clans. They are closely related to the neighboring Urhobo*

people. Both groups make their living raising yams, cassava, and palm oil products, as well as by fishing. In recent years, the Isokos have increasingly mixed
with the Edo,* Ijaw,* and Itsekiri* peoples of the region, but they still maintain
a distinct sense of identity. The primary Isoko settlements in Nigeria can be
found in Oleh and Ozoro. Their population today exceeds 250,000 people.
REFERENCES: *African Encyclopedia.* 1974; *Language Survey of Nigeria.* 1976; A. Oyewole. *Historical Dictionary of Nigeria.* 1987; Philip M. Peek. ''Isoko Sacred Mud Sculpture.'' *African Arts* 9 (July 1976): 34–39.

ISSA. The Issa people are considered a subgroup of the Dir* of Somalia, Ethiopia, and Djibouti. With a current population of approximately 150,000 people,
they constitute one-third of the population of Djibouti. They can also be found
in the Northern Region of Somalia and near Harer in Ethiopia. They are primarily cattle herders. The Issas are concentrated in the southern one-third of
Djibouti, especially below the Gulf of Tadjoura and east of the Djibouti-Addis
Ababa railway. There are also about 50,000 Issas in Somalia and perhaps
250,000 in Ethiopia. Several thousand can be found in Eritrea. They have a
highly egalitarian form of social organization revolving around clan systems
(these are divided into clans and sub-clans). The largest Issa clan is the Abgal,
which accounts for about 75 percent of all Issas in the Horn of Africa. The
Abgals are further subdivided into the Yonis-Moussa, Saad-Moussa, Mamassan,
and Ourweiné sub-clans. The Dalol clan is divided into the Fourlaba, Horoneh,
Walaldon, and Wardick sub-clans. They are overwhelmingly Muslims. Issa culture, which places high value on livestock, individual bravery, and the nomadic
lifestyle, remains intact in rural areas.
REFERENCES: Margaret Castagno. *Historical Dictionary of Somalia.* 1975; Peter J.
Schraeder. *Djibouti,* 1991.

ISSAQ. The Issaqs (Ishaak, Ishak) are one of the six primary clans of the
Somali* people of Somalia. Like all Somalis, they claim descent from Samaale,
the mythical founder of the entire ethnic group. Also like all other Somalis, they
speak the Somali language and are Sunni Muslims. Most Issaqs, except those
who work in the major cities, are nomadic herders who raise camels, sheep, and
cattle. The vast majority of the Issaqs are concentrated in northern Somalia. The
Issaq ethnic group, however, is subdivided into thousands of sub-clans and sub-
sub-clans, and individual Issaqs feel far more loyalty to their local clan than to
any larger collectivity. The Issaqs live primarily in the Tug Dheer, Sanaag, and
Hargeisa regions of northern Somalia. Some can also be found in the Haud
region of Ethiopia. Their current population is approximately 700,000 people.
    During the late 1980s and early 1990s, hundreds of thousands of Issaqs faced
starvation because of the famine and civil war in Somalia. Political instability
became endemic as centralized authority broke down in the face of severe clan
and sub-clan rivalries. Somalia essentially became a no-man's-land of misery

and suffering, with no single individual or group enjoying enough power to impose any order. In 1991, the Issaqs, with the support of some Darods,* another major clan in northern Somalia, declared their independence from Somalia, establishing the country of Somaliland. Their rebellion, however, failed to secure recognition from the international diplomatic community.
REFERENCE: *New York Times,* October 4, 1992.

ISSENYE. The Issenye people live in northwestern Tanzania, primarily along the southwestern shore of Lake Victoria. They raise cattle and farm, using the manure to keep their soil productive. They are also known for their skill as fishermen.
REFERENCE: Laura Kurtz. *Historical Dictionary of Tanzania.* 1978.

ISSIA. *See* KURI.

ISSONGO. The Issongos are a Bantu*-speaking people living today in the southwestern reaches of the Central African Republic. Most Issongos are small farmers who live in a close symbiotic relationship with neighboring Aka* pygmies, whom they call the Babinga.
REFERENCE: Pierre Kalck. *Central African Republic.* 1993.

ISSUKA. The Issukas are a subgroup of the Luhya* people of Kenya and Uganda. They are a Western Bantu* people who live today north of Lake Victoria on both sides of the Kenyan-Ugandan border.

ISU. The Isus are one of the many subgroups of the Igbo* people, an ethnic group of nearly fifteen million people living today in southern and southeastern Nigeria.

ISU-OCHI. The Isu-Ochis are one of the many subgroups of the Igbo* people of southern and southeastern Nigeria.

ISUWU. The Isuwus are a subgroup of the Bakweri* peoples of Cameroon. They live in villages on the slopes and near Mt. Cameroon in South West Province. They arrived in the region as part of a Bantu* migration beginning in the early eighteenth century. Because of their location near the coast, the Isuwus were among the first Cameroonians to come into contact with Europeans, and they lost much of their land to German* plantation owners in the late nineteenth and early twentieth centuries. In recent years, such groups as the Bakweri Union and the Bakweri Land Claim Committee have tried to recover Isuwu property. Today, most Isuwus support themselves by working on the palm oil plantations, oil rigs, and refineries at Cape Limbo, as well as by fishing and rice farming.

REFERENCE: Mark W. DeLancey and H. M. Mokeba. *Historical Dictionary of the Republic of United Cameroon.* 1990.

ITAK. The Itaks are a subgroup of the Ibibio* peoples of Nigeria.

ITALIAN. Tens of thousands of people of Italian descent live in Africa today, most of them in the countries that were once Italian colonies. Beginning in 1911, Italy conquered much of what is today Libya, taking the region from Ottoman control. By the 1930s, more than 100,000 Italians had settled in Libya. Since Libyan independence was declared, the number of Italians living in Libya has declined, but the Italian community there is substantial. In 1935, when Italy declared protectorates over Italian East Africa (Somalia and Ethiopia), several thousand Italians relocated there. Although Allied armies regained control of the region early in World War II, some Italians remained behind, and they still live there.
REFERENCE: James S. Olson. *Historical Dictionary of European Imperialism.* 1991.

ITAM. The Itams are a subgroup of the Ibibio* peoples of Nigeria.

ITCHEN. *See* ICEN.

ITESEN. The Itesens are a Tuareg* clan who today live in the Madaoua area where they have all but assimilated into the Kel Grass people.

ITESO. The Itesos (Wamias, Elgumis, Itesyo) are an East African ethnic group living in the dry plateaus of northeastern Uganda and in the Busia District of the Western Province in Kenya. The Itesos pursue a pastoral lifestyle, with the women and children living in permanent villages and the men leaving home seasonally to take cattle to pastures. The cattle provide the Itesos with milk, blood, and hides. Iteso women cultivate agricultural plots and raise millet, maize, cow peas, and some tobacco. Because of the droughts that have hit the region in the 1980s and early 1990s, the Itesos have faced what can be called at best a very marginal living. Their traditional religion and culture revolve around cattle. They speak a Central Paranilotic language. Their most immediate neighbors are the Karimojons,* Bagisus (Gisu*), Bagweres, and Basogos.
REFERENCES: Rita M. Byrnes et al. *Uganda: A Country Study.* 1990; John Lamphear. *The Traditional History of the Jie of Uganda.* 1976; Bethwell A. Ogot. *Historical Dictionary of Kenya.* 1981.

ITESYO. *See* ITESO.

ITSEKIRI. The Itsekiris (Isekivi, Ishekiris, Shekiris, Chekiris, Jekois, Ijekiris, Jekiris, Ichakiris, Iweres, Irhobos, Warris, and Iselema-Otus) are an ethnic group living today on the western side of the Niger River delta in Bendel

State in Nigeria. They are concentrated in the Warri and West Benin divisions. During the centuries of the Atlantic slave trade, the Itsekiri Kingdom was a major participant in the slave traffic, securing slaves from interior groups and selling them to Europeans. Today, the Itsekiris speak a Yoruba* dialect. Their homeland has been greatly influenced in recent years by the discovery of oil and natural gas.
REFERENCES: *Language Survey of Nigeria.* 1976; A. Oyewole. *Historical Dictionary of Nigeria.* 1987.

ITSHA. The Itshas are one of the many subgroups of the Yoruba* peoples of West Africa. They can be found especially in southern Benin.

ITTU. The Ittu are a major subgroup of the Oromo* peoples of Ethiopia. Most of the Ittus are Sunni Muslims who live near the city of Harer. They work as sedentary farmers.

IVBIE. The Ivbie people, whose population totals approximately 45,000 people, live in the Etsako and Akoko-Edo divisions of Bendel State in Nigeria. They speak an Edo* language.

IWA. The Iwa (Mashukulumbwe) people today number about 45,000 and live in the northeastern corner of Zambia. They speak a Mambwe* language. Traditionally, the Iwas raised cattle along the Chambeshi River, east of the Bemba* people. In the early 1920s, Jehovah's Witnesses converted substantial numbers of Iwas.
REFERENCE: John J. Grotpeter. *Historical Dictionary of Zambia.* 1979.

IWAWA. The Iwawas are a subgroup of the Ibibio* peoples of Nigeria.

IWERE. *See* ITSEKIRI.

IYALA. *See* YALA.

IYEKHEE. *See* YEKHEE.

IYEMBI. The Iyembis are a relatively small ethnic group living today in Zaire. They are located near the Lokoro River and Lake Ndombe in west-central Zaire. The Iyembis make their living by fishing on the river and the lake and by planting subsistence crops. Many Iyembis can be found in the towns of Inongo and Kiri.
REFERENCE: Irving Kaplan et al. *Zaire: A Country Study.* 1978.

IYONGIYONG. *See* BAKPINKA.

IZANZU. The Izanzus are a Bantu*-speaking people living today in central Tanzania. They are included by many ethnologists in the Iramba* group of peoples.

IZAREK. *See* AFUSARI.

IZARGUIEN. The Izarguiens are the largest subgroup of the Tekna* people of southwest Morocco and Western Sahara. They were traditionally a nomadic people, herding heir livestock between pastures along the coast between Oued Draa and Boujdour. The Izarguiens are themselves subdivided into three self-conscious groups: the Echtouka, El-Guerah, and Aid Said. By the late nineteenth century, the Izarguiens were actively trading with European merchants on the coast. Today, the Izarguiens are the leading element in the Ait Jmel* confederacy. Most Izarguiens have settled as merchants in small towns in Western Sahara and southern Morocco. Their population today is approximately 10,000, most of whom live in El-Ayoun.
REFERENCE: Tony Hodges. *Historical Dictionary of Western Sahara.* 1982.

IZON. The Izon people live in Rivers State, Nigeria, especially in the Yenagoa Local Government Area and the Sagbama Local Government Area. They are considered to be part of the larger cluster of Ijaw* peoples. Some Izons can also be found in Bendel and Ondo states in Nigeria. The Izons are divided into a number of subgroups, including the Bumo, Taarakiri, Oporoma, Olodiama, Basan, Apoi, Ikibiri, Ogboin, Ekpetiama, Kolokuma, Gbanrain, Kabou, Tungbo, Oiyakiri, Kumbo Mein, and Iduwini. Most Izons are subsistence farmers.
REFERENCE: E. J. Alagoa and Tekena N. Tamuno. *Land and People of Nigeria: Rivers State.* 1989.

IZORA. *See* CHOKOBO.

J

JAALIYIN. The Jaaliyins (Gaalin) are an Arabic group of people who claim direct descent from the Prophet Mohammed in Arabia. They live between southern Nubia and the Gezira in Sudan. Some ethnologists consider them actually to be an arabized group of Nubians.* The Jaaliyins who have mixed with Danaglas* in the region have become known as Jellabas,* a people of great mercantile skills in the Nile Valley. Today, Jaaliyins are commonly found among successful businessmen and merchants in Sudan. The Jaaliyins are subdivided into a number of subgroups, including the Danaglas, Hassaniyas, Kawahlas,* Gimas, and Husaynats. The Jaaliyin Arab* population in Sudan today exceeds 1.5 million people.

REFERENCE: Carolyn Fluehr-Lobban, Richard A. Lobban, Jr., and John Obert Voll. *Historical Dictionary of Sudan.* 1992.

JABA. *See* HYAM.

JABARA. *See* JABARTI.

JABARTI. The Jabarti (Jabara, Jeberti, Jiberti, Djeberti) are a Tigrinya*-speaking people who live in the city of Amhara, Ethiopia, and Eritrea. Their population today is approaching 250,000 people, and they are overwhelmingly Sunni Muslims of the Hanafi school. They are very devout in their Muslim faith, avoiding contact with Christians whenever possible. Jabarti living in the countryside are farmers who raise maize, millet, barley, and wheat as staple crops, as well as peas, onions, cabbage, beans, cattle, sheep, goats, horses, donkeys, chickens, bees, and camels. Those Jabarti living in Amhara are confined to the poorest section of the city and the lowest-paying jobs, primarily because Christians dominate the political and economic life of the city. That economic

reality made most Jabarti strong supporters of the Eritrean separatist movement in the 1970s and 1980s.
REFERENCES: Thomas R. DeGregori and Richard V. Weekes. "Jabartis." In Richard V. Weekes, ed. *Muslim Peoples.* 1984; S. F. Nadel. *Races and Tribes of Eritrea.* 1944; William A. Shack. *The Central Ethiopians: Amhara, Tigrina and Related Peoples.* 1974.

JACK-JACK. *See* ALLADIAN.

JAGHNIN. The Jaghnins are a subgroup of the Doka* peoples of Nigeria.

JAHAANKÉ. *See* JAHANKA.

JAHANKA. The Jahankas (Jahanke, Jahaanké, Jaxanke, Diakhanké, Tubacaye) are a group of clans who are descended from the Soninké* people. They live in what are known as "Jahanke villages" in Gambia and Senegal, with a few of them across the border in Guinea. They dwell among the much larger Mandinka* population and speak Mandinka, although, privately, many Jahankas still speak Azer, the Soninké language. They are an extremely devout Muslim people—Sunnis following the Maliki school—with large numbers of adult men pursuing clerical careers. They are highly educated, but, because they attend Islamic schools, they are less likely than other people in the Senegambia region to speak English or French. They claim to be intellectually descended from Al-Hajj Salim Suwarti, the great fifteenth-century West African cleric. The Jahanka Muslim tradition eschews the notion of *jihad,* or holy war, in favor of pacifism; they feel no need to convert others to Islam. They also retain the knowledge and practice of Suwarian magical rituals. Today there are approximately 60,000 Jahankas, living in approximately sixty-five villages. Given their respect for education and scholarship, the Jahankas are also known for their success in commerce and the professions. Only in recent years, when urbanization accelerated dramatically, has the Jahanka population become more dispersed and the pressures of modernization more acute.
REFERENCES: Lamin O. Sanneh. *The Jahanka: The History of an Islamic Clerical People of the Senegambia.* 1979; Lamin O. Sanneh. "Slavery, Islam and the Jahanke People of West Africa." *Africa* 46 (1976): 80–95; Donald R. Wright. "Jahanka." In Richard V. Weekes, ed. *Muslim Peoples.* 1984.

JAHANKE. *See* JAHANKA.

JAKU. The Jakus live in the Galembi District of the Bauchi Division of Bauchi State in Nigeria. Their language is classified with the Jarawan Bantu* group.
REFERENCE: *Language Survey of Nigeria.* 1976.

JAL. *See* GANAWURI.

JALLONKÉ. *See* YALUNKA.

JALONCA. *See* YALUNKA.

JALONKÉ. *See* YALUNKA.

JALUNKA. *See* YALUNKA.

JAMA. *See* CHAMBA.

JAMALA. The Jamalas—also known as the Kababishes and Shukriyas—are a subgroup of the Juhayna* Arabs* of Sudan.

JAMAN. *See* GYAMEN.

JAMAT. The Jamat, also known as Ayamat, are a subgroup of the Jola* people. Most Jamats live near Efok and Yutu in Senegal.

JAMJAM. *See* GUJI and OROMO.

JANJERO. The Janjero are one of the subgroups of the Sadama* people of southwestern Ethiopia. Their current population is approximately 2,000 people.

JANJI. The Janji people live today in northwestern Nigeria, as well as in southern Niger and northeastern Benin. In Nigeria, they can be found in the Rukuba District of the Jos Division of Plateau State. Most of them are Muslim farmers and cattle herders.
REFERENCES: *Language Survey of Nigeria.* 1976; Donald G. Morrison et al. *Black Africa: A Comparative Handbook.* 1989.

JANJO. The Janjo people, also known as Jenjos, Jens, Dzas, Gwomos, and Karenjos, are a Nigerian ethnic group. They are concentrated in the Wurkum District of the Muri Division of Gongola State. The Janjos speak an Adamawa language and have a current population of approximately 25,000 people.
REFERENCE: *Language Survey of Nigeria.* 1976.

JANNI. *See* DYAN.

JARA. The Jaras (Jeras) are a small ethnic group living today in Nigeria, particularly in the Yamaltu District of the Gombe Division of Bauchi State

and the Tera District of the Biu Division of Borno State. Their language is part of the larger Tera* group of Chadic languages.
REFERENCE: *Language Survey of Nigeria.* 1976.

JARAWA. *See* AFUSARI.

JARENG. *See* GONGLA.

JARI. *See* AFUSARI.

JAXANKE. *See* JAHANKA.

JEBEL. *See* MILERI.

JEBERTI. *See* JABARTI.

JEKIANG. The Jekiangs are a major subdivision of the Nuer* people of southern Sudan. They are concentrated in the Nasser District.

JEKIRI. *See* ITSEKIRI.

JEKOI. *See* ITSEKIRI.

JELLABA. The Jellabas are a unique people living in eastern Chad and Sudan. They are of Sudanese Nilotic* extraction, and, since the eighteenth century, they have lived in the region, serving as traders and commercial middlemen working the trade routes between Darfur, Ouadai, and Baguirmi. They are of mixed Jaaliyin* and Danagla* extraction.
REFERENCES: Samuel Decalo. *Historical Dictionary of Chad.* 1987; Carolyn Fluehr-Lobban, Richard A. Lobban, Jr., and John Obert Voll. *Historical Dictionary of Sudan.* 1992.

JEN. *See* JANJO.

JENA. The Jenas are a subgroup of the Karanga* people, who are part of the Shona* cluster of peoples in Zimbabwe.

JENG. *See* NZANGI.

JENGE. *See* NZANGI.

JENHA. The Jenha are a subgroup of the Ahel Brahim Ou Daouds, themselves a subgroup of the Reguibat* ech-Charg people of Western Sahara in what is today Morocco. They are a nomadic people with a population of approximately

1,500, most of whom migrate along the Western Sahara-Mauritanian border close to Ain Ben Tili and Tifarity.

JENJI. *See* JANJI.

JENJO. *See* JANJO.

JERA. *See* JARA.

JERAWA. *See* AFUSARI.

JERE. The Jeres, closely related to the Jerawas, are an ethnic group living today north of the Jos Plateau in Plateau State in northwestern Nigeria. They are surrounded ethnically by the Jarawas, Afusaris,* Hausas,* Amos,* Bujis,* and Gusus.* Most Jeres are subsistence farmers who still hunt when they can to supplement their diets.
REFERENCE: Elizabeth Isichei, ed. *Studies in the History of Plateau State, Nigeria.* 1982.

JEW. *See* BETA ISRAEL.

JIBANA. The Jibanas are part of the Mijikenda* cluster of people of coastal Kenya and Tanzania. Most of them are farmers, raising maize, millet, sheep, and goats, while others are laborers on sugar cane, sisal, and cotton plantations.

JIBERTI. *See* JABARTI.

JIDDA-ABU. The Jiddas-Abus, also known as Ibuts and Nakares, are a small ethnic group, confined today largely to the Wamba District of the Akwanga Division of Plateau State in Nigeria. Their language is part of the Benue group of the Benue-Congo family.
REFERENCE: *Language Survey of Nigeria.* 1976.

JIE. The Jie live in the semi-arid plateau in Uganda, particularly in Jie County, an area of 1,300 square miles, in the Karamoja District of Uganda, the region bordering Sudan and Kenya. They are surrounded by the Dodos,* Bokora* Karimojons,* Matheniko Karimojons, the eastern Acolis,* Labwors,* Nyakwais,* and Turkanas.* The Jie population today exceeds 40,000 people. Ethnolinguists classify the Jie as part of the Central Paranilotic cluster of languages. Their economy revolves around transhumant pastoralism, with the men raising cattle and the women trying to raise sorghum and millet. To a much lesser extent, Jie women also raise groundnuts, maize, pumpkins, sweet potatoes, cow peas, and tobacco. Of all of Uganda's ethnic groups, the Jie are among the

least developed and the least acculturated to Western technologies. Their religion and culture revolve around cattle. Milk, often mixed with the blood of bulls, is as important to the Jie diet as grains are. The Jie live in permanent villages that are occupied year-round by women and children who do most of the farming. Each homestead in that village is surrounded by walls made up of interwoven branches. Jie men leave those villages seasonally to find pasture for the cattle herds. Because of severe droughts in northeastern Africa during the 1980s and early 1990s, the Jie have faced dire economic circumstances.
REFERENCES: K. S. Gourlay. ''The Practice of Cueing Among the Karimojon of North-East Uganda.'' *Journal of Ethnomusicology* 16 (May 1972): 240–46; John Lamphear. *The Traditional History of the Jie of Uganda.* 1976.

JIJI. The Jijis are part of the Interlacustrine Bantu* cluster of peoples living in Tanzania. They live in northwestern Tanzania and southwestern Uganda and are often included in the Ha* cluster of peoples. There are more than 12,000 Jiji people today.

JILEK. The Jileks are a major subdivision of the Atuot* people of the southern Sudan.

JIMA. The Jimas are a subgroup of the Oromo* people of Ethiopia.

JIMBIN. The Jimbins are a small ethnic group of approximately 3,500 people who live today in the Ganjuwa District of the Bauchi Division of Bauchi State in Nigeria.
REFERENCE: *Language Survey of Nigeria.* 1976.

JIMI. The Jimis are a tiny ethnic group, almost extinct today as an identifiable social entity, who live in the Ganjuwa District of the Bauchi Division of Bauchi State in Nigeria. They speak a Chadic language.
REFERENCE: *Language Survey of Nigeria.* 1976.

JINGA. The Jingas are a subgroup of the Mbundu* people of north-central Angola.

JINLERI. *See* BANDAWA-MINDA.

JIRU-KIR. The Jiru-Kir people, who are also known as the Zhirus, Ataks, Wiyaps, and Kirs, are a Jukunoid ethnic group who live today in the Jalingo District of the Muri Division of Gongola State in Nigeria. Most of them are subsistence farmers and migrant workers.
REFERENCE: *Language Survey of Nigeria.* 1976.

JITA. The Jitas live south of Lake Victoria in northern Tanzania and

just across the border in Burundi. For centuries, they maintained a feudal system for control of the land, with tenants owing allegiance to feudal lords; in recent years, they have made the transition to commercial agriculture, with peasants renting land from landlords. The Jitas have a patrilineal social system. They raise cattle, cotton, and rice. They are closely related culturally and linguistically to the Sukumas* and Kereres.* The Jita population of Tanzania today exceeds 150,000 people.
REFERENCE: Laura Kurtz. *Historical Dictionary of Tanzania.* 1978.

JIYE. The Jiyes are an ethnic group in East Africa who speak a Central Nilotic* language. They live in southern Sudan near the Uganda border. The Jiyes pursue a pastoral lifestyle, with the women and children living in permanent villages and the men leaving home seasonally to take the cattle to pastures. The cattle provide the Jiyes with milk, blood, and hides. Jiye women work agricultural plots and raise millet, maize, cow peas, and some tobacco. Because of the droughts that hit the region in the 1980s and early 1990s, the Jiyes have faced what can be called at best a very marginal living. Their traditional religion and culture revolve around cattle.
REFERENCE: John Lamphear. *The Traditional History of the Jie of Uganda.* 1976.

JJU. *See* KAJE.

JOHODE. *See* DGHWEDE.

JOLA. The Jolas (Diula, Yola, Dyola) are a major ethnic group in southwestern Senegal. Their total population exceeds 700,000, with approximately 140,000 in the Lower Casamance area of Senegal, 500,000 more scattered through Senegal, and as many as 70,000 in Guinea Bissau and Gambia. Others live in Mali and Burkina-Faso. The Jolas are divided into a complex variety of subgroups based on linguistic and ethnic patterns. Ethnolinguists classify them as one of the Bak group of the West Atlantic language family. The Jolas make their living through wet rice agriculture in the wet lowlands and tidal streams of the coastal area and through raising peanuts in the drier forests. Traditionally, the Jolas lived in extended families, but the expansion of the commercial economy in Senegal has undermined village-wide property models in favor of nuclear families. Increasing numbers of the Jolas are leaving their villages for wage labor in the cities.

Ethnologists have identified three basic Jola groupings. The Jolas of Kasa, south of the Casamance River, have been more geographically isolated than other Jolas and therefore more successful in maintaining their traditional cultural institutions. Islam never reached them, and, although Roman Catholic missionaries baptized many of them, the indigenous religious practices survived. The religion is animistic and revolves around shrines that the Jolas call *sinaati.* In the regions of Fogny, Combo, and Boulouf north of the Casamance River, most

Jolas are Muslims, primarily because the French* colonial administration succeeded in building good roads throughout the region beginning in the 1890s;
this situation permitted Muslim missionaries and traders to reach the area. Much
farther to the east, along the Soungrougrou River, the Jolas are assimilating to
Mendé* cultural and agricultural practices. Many Jolas have also abandoned
their own language. Today, more than half of all Jolas are Muslims.

REFERENCES: Frances Anne Leary. "Islam, Politics, and Colonialism: A Political History of Islam in the Casamance Region of Southwestern Senegal, 1850–1914." Ph.D.
dissertation. Northwestern University. 1970; Peter Mark. "Diola." In Richard V. Weekes, ed. *Muslim Peoples.* 1984; Louis V. Thomas. "The Cosmology of the Diola." In
Meyer Fortes and George Dieterlen, eds. *African Systems of Thought.* 1965.

JOLA-BOBO. *See* BOBO.

JOLA-HAER. The Jola-Haers are a subgroup of the Jola* people. Most Jola-
Haers live in Kabrus, Senegal.

JOLOF. *See* WOLOF.

JOMVU. The Jomvus are a Swahili*-speaking people who today live in Kenya.

JONAM. The Jonams are an ethnic group living today in Uganda. They speak
a Nilotic* language and are concentrated in the north-central region of the country, north of Lake Kyoga and northeast of Lake Albert. Most Jonans are small
farmers. Ethnologists include them in the Luo* cluster of peoples.

JORTO. *See* JORTU.

JORTU. The Jortus (Jortos) are a subgroup of the Doka* peoples of Plateau
State in Nigeria. They live particularly in the Shendam District of Shendam
Division.

JOWEIN. The Joweins are one of the Bassa* clans living in the River Cess
Territory of Liberia.

JSOKO. The Jsoko people live in Bendel State in Nigeria. They are closely
related to the neighboring Edo* people. Both groups make their living raising
yams, cassava, and palm oil products and by fishing. In recent years, the Jsokos
have increasingly mixed with the Edo, Ijaw,* and Itsekiri* peoples of the region,
but they still maintain a distinct sense of identity.

REFERENCES: *African Encyclopedia.* 1974; Donald G. Morrison et al. *Black Africa: A
Comparative Handbook.* 1989; A. Oyewole. *Historical Dictionary of Nigeria.* 1987.

JU. The Ju people are a very small ethnic group living today in the Jungur District of the Bauchi Division in Bauchi State in Nigeria. They speak a Chadic language.
REFERENCE: *Language Survey of Nigeria.* 1976.

JU LUO. *See* JUR.

JUABEN. *See* DWABEN.

JUABLIN. The Juablins are a subgroup of the Anyis* of Ivory Coast. The Juablins are overwhelmingly Christian in their religious persuasion.

JUBU. The Jubus are one of the Bantu*-speaking peoples of Nigeria. They are classified as part of the Plateau cluster of peoples who occupy central Nigeria. Most Jubus practice subsistence horticulture, raising ginger, millet, guinea corn, beans, and citrus products. They live in social systems characterized by patrilineal descent and patrifocal residence. In recent years, they have begun migrating to towns and cities looking for work.
REFERENCE: Donald G. Morrison et al. *Black Africa: A Comparative Handbook.* 1989.

JUHAYNA. The Juhaynas are a large group of Arabs* in the Sudan, Chad, and Libya. They claim descent from Arabs who colonized the Nile Valley during the past millenium. They tend to be a nomadic people who herd camels in the dry regions and the eastern grasslands and cattle in the western savannas. Some of the Juhaynas in the river valleys are farmers. Included among the Juhaynas are the Baggaras,* Jamalas,* and Geziras.
REFERENCE: Carolyn Fluehr-Lobban, Richard A. Lobban, Jr., and John Obert Voll. *Historical Dictionary of Sudan.* 1992.

JUKUN. The Jukuns are one of the many ethnic groups living today in northern Nigeria in the Benue River Valley. They can be found especially in the Makurdi Division of Benue State; the Langtang and Lafia divisions of Plateau State; and the Wukari and Muri divisions of Gongola State. Hausa* mythology traces their origins to Yemil, east of Mecca, in what is today Saudi Arabia. They are also called the Kororofa, because the man who led them to Nigeria in ancient times was named Kororofa. They are considered a warlike people by their neighbors, and they brought many of them under domination before the arrival of the Fulbes* in the nineteenth century.
REFERENCES: R. C. Abraham. *The Tiv People.* 1933; *Language Survey of Nigeria.* 1976; A. Oyewole. *Historical Dictionary of Nigeria.* 1987.

JULA. The Julas—also known as the Dyula, Diula, Wangara, Joola, Juula, Va, Febe, and Kangah—are one of the Manding*-speaking ethnic groups of West Africa. It is important to distinguish them from the Jolas,* who are a

Senegambian* people. Although their population is difficult to estimate, ethnologists suspect that it exceeds two million people. The term "Dyula" in Manding refers to an individual skilled at trade and business, but its specific ethnic designation refers to a people who today live in the northeastern and northern sections of Ivory Coast, in southwestern Burkina-Faso, and across the border in Ghana, Guinea-Bissau, and Mali. In Ghana, they are known as the Wangara people. All but perhaps 10,000 Julas are Muslims. Jula is a Manding language, itself part of the larger Niger-Congo language family. Thanks to their historic skill as traders, the Julas were responsible for carrying Manding institutions throughout West Africa, especially Islam, Arabic, weaving, and mosque architecture based on sun-dried bricks and projecting timbers. The Julas are a patrilineal people who still practice polygamy, even though current legislation in Ivory Coast prohibits the practice. Education for young people is based on a Koran curriculum. The Julas are extremely suspicious of the secular education provided by the government because they view it as a threat to Islamic values.
REFERENCES: Carlton Dodge. *Papers on the Manding.* 1971; Kathryn Green. "Dyula." In Richard V. Weekes, ed. *Muslim Peoples.* 1984; Robert E. Handloff et al. *Côte d'Ivoire: A Country Study.* 1990; Robert Launay. *Traders without Trade: Responses to Change in Two Dyula Communities.* 1982; Nehemia Levtzion. *Muslims and Chiefs in West Africa.* 1968.

JUNKUN. The Junkun—also known as the Diongor, Djongor, and Dionkor— are an ethnic group living in close proximity to the Kinga* people of Chad. Casual observers consider them a Kinga subgroup, although their language is quite distinct; like Kinga, however, it is related to Barma.* The Junkun live in the Hadjeray* region of Chad. Their current population exceds 20,000 people, most of whom make their living as small farmers and by extracting gum arabic from acacia trees. *See* JUKUN.
REFERENCE: Samuel Decalo. *Historical Dictionary of Chad.* 1987.

JUR. The Jurs (Ju Luos) are part of the Western Nilotic* cluster of peoples living today in Sudan. They are Muslims whose economy revolves around the raising of cattle. The Jurs are closely related to the Dinkas,* Nuers,* Anuaks,* and Acolis.*
REFERENCE: Donald G. Morrison et al. *Black Africa: A Comparative Handbook.* 1989.

JUULA. *See* JULA.

K

KAA. The Kaa (Bakaa) people are an offshoot of the Rolong* people who settled in the Shoshong Hills in Botswana in the early eighteenth century. The Ngwato* people brought them under control during the late eighteenth and early nineteenth centuries. In 1848, their leader, Mosinyi, led them in flight away from the Ngwato to the control of the Kwenas,* and, a half century later, they began to fragment into separate groups. The Kaa then emerged as a distinct people in the Shoshong region.
REFERENCE: Fred Morton, A. Murray, and J. Ramsay. *Historical Dictionary of Botswana.* 1989.

KAALA. *See* DUMPO.

KABA. The Kabas are a clan within the chiefdom of Mambahn, a subgroup of the Bassa* people of Liberia. Most Kabas live in the Marshall Territory of Liberia. They should not be confused with the Kabas* of Chad, who are a subgroup of the larger Sara* people.

KABA. The Kabas, not to be confused with the Kabas* of Liberia, are a subgroup of the Sara.* They should also not be confused with the Sara-Kabas of Chad. The Kabas are concentrated near Sarh, in the Moyen-Chari District, and across the border in the Central African Republic. Over the years, the Kabas have been the objects of slave raids from surrounding groups. Most Kabas are sedentary farmers, raising a variety of crops for food and cotton for cash. During the rainy season, they are active fishermen. The current Kaba population exceeds 45,000 people, with about 15,000 of them in Chad and 30,000 in the Central African Republic.
REFERENCE: Samuel Decalo. *Historical Dictionary of Chad.* 1987.

KABABISH. The Kababishes are a group of Arabs* from the Juhayna* cluster. They are a camel-herding people who live west of the Nile River in the northern Kordofan and Darfur regions of Sudan. Opponents of the Mahdist movement in the nineteenth century, they possess a powerful sense of independence and self-reliance. The Kababishes have played important roles in recent Sudanese politics. Among the most prominent Sudanese leaders of Kababish descent is Ali al-Tom.
REFERENCES: Talal Asad. *The Kababish Arabs,* 1970; Carolyn Fluehr-Lobban, Richard A. Lobban, Jr., and John Obert Voll. *Historical Dictionary of Sudan.* 1992.

KABENDE. The Kabendes are part of the larger cluster of Aushi* peoples in Zambia. The contemporary Kabende population exceeds 40,000 people.

KABILA. *See* LUBILA.

KABIYE. The Kabiye people are an ethnic group living today in northern Togo. Their population consists of more than 60,000 people, most of whom are subsistence farmers. They are part of the eastern Grusi* language group.
REFERENCE: Meterwa A. Ourso. ''Phonological Processes in the Noun Class System of Lama.'' *Studies in African Linguistics* 20 (August 1989): 151–78.

KABKA. *See* BERI.

KABLI. The Kablis are a subgroup of the Bassa* people of Liberia. Most Kablis live in Grand Bassa County.

KABONGO. The Kabongos are a subgroup of the Sanga* peoples of southeastern Cameroon, northern Congo, southern Central African Republic, and northwestern Zaire. They interact closely with neighboring Pygmies,* who trade game for Kabongo agricultural products.
REFERENCE: Gordon S. McDonald et al. *Area Handbook for the People's Republic of Congo (Congo Brazzaville).* 1971.

KABOU. The Kabous are a subgroup of the Izon* peoples of Rivers State in Nigeria.

KABRA. The Kabras are a subgroup of the Luhya* people of Kenya and Uganda. They are a Western Bantu* people who live today north of Lake Victoria on both sides of the Kenyan-Ugandan border.

KABRÉ. The Kabré (Cabrai, Bekaburum, Kabure, Kaure) are one of the Sudanic peoples who live in northern Togo. In recent decades, large numbers of Kabré have also migrated to Central Togo. Until the seventeenth century,

they were spread over a much broader area, well into Benin, but expansion of
the Baribas* drove the Kabrés to their present location. Today they are concentrated in the Centrale region of northern Togo, a mountainous zone, although
there are smaller clusters of Kabré near Atakpamé in the Plateaux region;
French* and German* authorities during the colonial period encouraged relocation there. The Kabré population today exceeds 450,000 people. Perhaps
120,000 Kabré live in the Plateaux region, with more migrating there because
soil erosion on the volcanic lands of the Centrale region. They call themselves
the Lan-mba, or Lama. The primary Kabré subgroups are the Kabré proper and
the Losso,* Lambas,* Tambermas, Mossis,* and Logbas.* They are primarily
animist in their religious loyalties. Most Kabré are small farmers, although, since
the colonial period, they have had an unusually large representation in the military and police forces of Togo.
REFERENCES: Charles D. Piot. ''Wealth Production, Ritual Consumption, and Center/
Periphery Relations in a West African Regional System.'' *American Ethnology* 19 (February 1992): 34–52; Raymond Verdier. ''Ontology of the Judicial Thought of the Kabré
of Northern Togo.'' In Laura Nader, ed. *Law in Culture and Society.* 1969.

KABURE. *See* KABRÉ.

KABYLE. The Kabyles are the major Berber* subgroup in Algeria. They live
in and around the large mountain block of Djurdjura, which has been difficult
for conquerors to invade; this has made for an extremely strong sense of Kabyle
identity. The Kabyles are sedentary farmers who terrace their fields on the sides
of mountains. Their houses, made of stone with red tile roofs, are placed on
mountain ridges above their fields. The social structure and political system are
village oriented.

KACHAMA. The Kachamas are a tiny ethnic group living today in southern
Ethiopia. They speak an Omotic* language and make their living as subsistence
farmers. The Kachama population in Ethiopia is under 1,000 people.
REFERENCE: M. L. Bender, J. D. Bowen, R. L. Cooper, and C. A. Ferguson, eds.
Language in Ethiopia. 1976.

KACHE. *See* KAJE.

KADARA. Approximately 400 years ago, the Kadaras (Kaduros, Adaras) lived
in the area of Kufena Rock near Zaria City, but they gradually moved south
during those years, scattering out over approximately 3,000 square miles in the
Kajuru and Kacia districts of the Zaria emirate and in Adunu in Niger State in
Nigeria. They have been subject to Muslim domination by neighboring Kanuri,*
Hausa,* and Fulbe* peoples. The Kadaras have paid tribute, in the form of
slaves and produce, to those tribes for the last two centuries, and especially
since the slave raids of 1894 when Emir Yero of Zaria devastated them.

Before their migration south from Kufena, the Kadaras were adept at making pottery, smelting iron, raising cattle, and producing grains. Today the Kadara social organization revolves around exogamous localized patrilineages. Their animist religion focuses on a belief in Onum, a God-creator whom they associate with the sun.

After the imposition of British* authority in the Kadara area, the slave raids and plunder-taking gradually declined. The Kadaras practice subsistence horti-culture, raising ginger, millet, guinea corn, beans, and citrus products. They live in social systems characterized by patrilineal descent and patrifocal residence. They have accepted public school programs and are Christians. Most Kadaras today can be found in the Minna Division of Niger State and the Kajuru, Kachia, and Chikun districts of the Kachia Division of Kaduna State. Their current population exceeds 90,000 people.

REFERENCES: Carol V. McKinney. "A Linguistic Shift in Kaje, Kagoro, and Katab Kinship Terminology." *Ethnology* 22 (1983): 281–95; M. G. Smith. "Cosmology, Prac-tice, and Social Organization Among the Kadara and Kagoro." *Ethnology* 21 (January 1982): 1–20.

KADARU. The Kadarus are a subgroup of the Nubian* people of the Sudan.

KADENBA. *See* BOBO.

KADIANGA. Today, the Kadianga are considered to be a subgroup of the Maba* people of Sudan. Ethnologists, however, argue that, because of their unique language and culture, they were probably absorbed by the surrounding Maba peoples during the course of the last several centuries.

KADJIDI. The Kadjidis are a small ethnic group whose history has been marked by their long-term enslavement to the Kanembus* of Chad and the Kanuris* of Bornu in Nigeria. They are a subservient group in Chad, living among the Kanembus but rarely intermarrying with them. They live in a con-dition of quasi-peonage. The Kadjidis make their living herding Zebu* cattle.

REFERENCE: Samuel Decalo. *Historical Dictionary of Chad.* 1987.

KADO. The Kado are a subgroup of the Zermas,* themselves a subgroup of the Songhai* people. They are concentrated in the westernmost provinces of Niger and in eastern Mali in West Africa. Originally located in the Yatenga area of Burkina-Faso, they had to migrate to escape Mossi* expansion.

KADUGLI. The Kaduglis are a subgroup of the Nuba* peoples of Sudan.

KADURU. The Kadurus are one of the non-Arabic Nuba* peoples of

Kordofan Province of Sudan. Most of them are farmers, raising sorghum, cotton, and peanuts through rainfall agricultural techniques in the granite inselbergs of the western Nuba Mountains. They are primarily Muslim in their religious loyalties.

KAFA. The Kafas are an ethnic group living today in Ethiopia. Ethnologists place them in the Kafa-Sadama* cluster of Ethiopian peoples.
REFERENCE: M. L. Bender, J. D. Bowen, R. L. Cooper, and C. A. Ferguson, eds. *Language in Ethiopia.* 1976.

KAFFIR. The term "Kaffir" has its origins in the Arabic word *kafir,* which means "non-believer." Portuguese* explorers began using it as a reference to native Africans, because they mistakenly believed it meant "black people." In nineteenth-century South Africa, the word Kaffir was applied to all Bantu* speaking people. Today, the word has highly pejorative implications.
REFERENCE: R. Kent Rasmussen. *Historical Dictionary of Zimbabwe.* 1994.

KAFIA. The Kafias are a clan with the chiefdom of Mambahn, a subgroup of the Bassa* people of Liberia. Most Kafias live in the Marshall Territory of Liberia.

KAFUGU. *See* GURE-KAHUGU.

KAGOMA. The Kagomas (Agomas, Gwongs, Gyongs) are part of a larger Hausa* Fulbe* cluster of peoples living today in northwestern Nigeria. Most of them live in the Jema'a District of the Jema'a Division of Kaduna State. The Kagoma population today exceeds 50,000 people. They are surrounded by the Yeskwa,* Mada,* Kaje,* and Jaba peoples. Some of them can also be found across the border in Niger and in northern Benin. Islam dominates their religious beliefs. Most of them are small farmers and cattle herders; they are considered highly skilled as farmers.
REFERENCES: *Language Survey of Nigeria.* 1976; C. L. Temple, ed. *Notes on the Tribes, Provinces, Emirates and States of the Northern Provinces of Nigeria.* 1967.

KAGORO. The Kagoros are an ethnic group living in the grassy savannas and volcanic hills of the southern region of the state of Kaduna in Nigeria and in the Karta region of Mali. They call themselves the Agorok. Their language is part of the Benue-Congo subsection of the Niger-Congo family. The Kagoros are among the more technologically primitive African peoples. Anthropologists estimate that they were a true Stone Age culture until approximately 250 years ago. The Kagoros believe that they originated on the Jos Plateau and then migrated to southern Kaduna state. Historically, the Kagoros were frequently subservient to the Hausa* and Fulbe* peoples, who often raided them to take plunder, collect taxes, and secure slaves. They managed to maintain a degree of independence, however, by fleeing to the highlands for protection. The ancestors of the Kagoros were the Ankwei. Around 1750, the Ankwei began absorbing refugees from the Kagomas,* Katabs,* Kajes,* Kaninkwoms, Kafanchans, and other local tribes fleeing from Fulbe slave traders. These refugees coalesced into a group known as the Kpashan, who became second-class citizens in Kagoro society. After the imposition of British* authority in the Kagoro area, the slave raids and plunder-taking gradually declined. The Kpashans remained second-class citizens in Kagoro society because the Ankwei would not let them participate in major religious and political ceremonies.

The Kagoros practice subsistence horticulture, raising ginger, millet, guinea corn, beans, and citrus products. They live in social systems characterized by patrilineal descent and patrifocal residence. They have accepted public school programs and are Christians and Muslims.

REFERENCES: Carol V. McKinney. "A Linguistic Shift in Kaje, Kagoro, and Katab Kinship Terminology." *Ethnology* 22 (1983): 281–95; M. G. Smith. "Cosmology, Practice, and Social Organization Among the Kadara and Kagoro." *Ethnology* 21 (January 1982): 1–20.

KAGU. See GURE-KAHUGU.

KAGULU. *See* KAGURU.

KAGURU. The Kaguru (Kagulu) are one of the individual groups in the Zaramo* cluster of the Northeast Bantu*-speaking people of East Africa. They live in the mountainous highlands of coastal Tanzania where most of them function as hoe farmers, producing maize, beans, vegetables, cardamom, bananas, sorghum, and casava; they also raise sheep, goats, and poultry. During the nineteenth century, the Kaguru were for the most part left alone because of their geographic isolation. The lowland Zaramo peoples were more vulnerable. Most Kaguru today live in small, plastered houses with thatched roofs, although a few still reside in the traditional round house, which is thatched all the way to the ground. Although a majority of Kaguru were once Muslims, various Christian groups have established missions in the Tanzanian highlands, and today only one in three Kaguru is still Muslim. Even those are considered to be only marginally loyal, confining their religious observances to fasting at Ramadan, taking on Arab names, and wearing the white skull cap.

Since the mid-1970s, the Kaguru have been dramatically affected by the Tanzanian government's *ujamaa* policy, which is designed to gather rural people out of their scattered homestead settlements into more concentrated villages where public education and public health campaigns can be more effective. Rates of malaria and schistosomiasis are relatively high among Kaguru, and only improved public health programs can alleviate the crisis. The Kaguru people have also been affected in recent years by the East African drought, as well as by the threat of the human immunodeficiency virus and the disease of AIDS,

although their geographic isolation in the highlands has provided some protection. Their current population is approximately 250,000 people.
REFERENCE: L. W. Swantz. *Ritual and Symbol in Transitional Zaramo Society.* 1970.

KAIBI. *See* KAIVI.

KAIVI. The Kaivi (Kaibi) people are a small ethnic group living today in the Haura District of the Saminaka Division of Kaduna State in Nigeria. Their language is classified with the Western Plateau group in the Benue-Congo family.
REFERENCE: *Language Survey of Nigeria.* 1976.

KAJE. The Kaje (Kajji, Kache, Jju, Baju) are an ethnic group living in the grassy savannas and volcanic hills of the southern region of the state of Kaduna in Nigeria, especially in the Zangon Katab District, as well as in the Jema'a and Kagoro districts of the Jema'a Division in Kaduna State. They call themselves the Bajju. Their language is part of the Benue-Congo subsection of the Niger-Congo family. The Kaje believe that they originated in Miango on the Jos Plateau. Between 1810 and 1833, the Kaje fell under Fulbe* influence when the Emir of Jema'a conquered them for plunder and slaves; from 1847 to 1854, the Emir of Zaria did the same. After the imposition of British* authority in the region, the slave raids and plunder-taking gradually declined. The Kaje practice subsistence horticulture, raising ginger, millet, guinea corn, beans, and citrus products. They live in social systems characterized by patrilineal descent and patrifocal residence. They have accepted public school programs and are Christians. Their population today exceeds 100,000 people.
REFERENCE: Carol V. McKinney. "A Linguistic Shift in Kaje, Kagoro, and Katab Kinship Terminology." *Ethnology* 22 (1983):281–95.

KAJJI. *See* KAJE.

KAKA. The Kaka are an important subgroup of the Gbaya* people of the Central African Republic. They emerged in the nineteenth century after a mixing of Batas* and various Bantu*-speaking groups.

KAKABA. *See* KAMKAM.

KAKONDE. The Kakondes are a subgroup of the Ovimbundu* peoples of Angola.

KAKONGO. The Kakongos are today classified as part of the larger Lunda*-Chokwe* cluster of peoples living in central Angola. Most Kakongos are small farmers.

KAKWA. The Kakwas are an ethnic group living today in northeastern Zaire and southern Sudan, as well as in western Uganda. They speak an eastern Sudanic language, although they are of Nilotic* origin. The Kakwas are primarily subsistence farmers who live in a very remote, isolated part of the country, especially the highlands where cattle production is difficult. They are closely related to the Kukus,* Mandaris,* and Baris.* During the 1970s, Idi Amin, a Kakwa, imposed his dictatorial rule on Uganda. East African demographers place the Kakwa population at approximately 75,000 people in Uganda, of whom roughly 10,000 are Muslims. Most Kakwas are farmers who raise corn, millet, potatoes, and cassava.
REFERENCES: F. Scott Bobb. *Historical Dictionary of Zaire.* 1988; Rita M. Byrnes et al. *Uganda: A Country Study.* 1990; Helen C. Metz et al. *Sudan: A Country Study.* 1992.

KALA. The Kala people live today in western Zaire, primarily north of the Kasai River in the vicinity of the Lukenie River and the towns of Oshwe and Dekese. They are surrounded by the Panga,* Titu,* Ooli,* and Ndengese* peoples. Most Kalas are small farmers.
REFERENCE: Irving Kaplan et al. *Zaire: A Country Study.* 1978.

KALABARI. The Kalabaris are a subgroup of the Ijaw* people of Nigeria. They live today in Rivers State in Nigeria. Traditionally, their homeland has been on the islands of the delta of the Niger River, where they earned their reputation as traders. Today they can be found concentrated in Buguma, Abonnema, Tombia, Bakana, and Port Harcourt, where they enjoy jobs in the professions, civil service, and business community. Kalabari is the lingua franca of the region, used on radio and television.
REFERENCE: Joanna B. Eicher and Tonya V. Erekosima. "Kalabari Funerals: Celebration and Display." *African Arts* 21 (November 1987): 38–45.

KALAKA. *See* KALANGA.

KALANGA. The Kalangas (Kalakas, Bakalangas, Vakalangas), are one of the major subgroups in the Shona* cluster of peoples in northeastern Botswana, western Zimbabwe, and Mozambique. They have been in the region for at least a thousand years. Most of them are farmers, raising cattle, millet, maize, pumpkins, and yams. The Kalangas are the largest non-Tswana*-speaking people in Botswana. During the past century, they have absorbed a number of peoples with Pedi,* Tswana, and Sotho* origins. During the colonial period, the Kalanga became widely known in southern Africa for their belief in egalitarian nationalism and ethnic separatism. They tend to be highly resentful of Tswana dominance of their homeland. The major Kalanga subgroups are the Nanzwas and the Lilimas.
REFERENCE: Fred Morton, A. Murray, and J. Ramsay. *Historical Dictionary of Botswana.* 1989.

KALENJIN. The Kalenjins are a group of approximately two million people who live today primarily in Rift Valley Province of Kenya. Ethnologists believe that they originated in the area between Lake Turkana and the southern Ethiopian highlands around one thousand years ago, when they emerged as an identifiable ethnic group. Their language is part of the Highland, or Southern, branch of the Nilotic* languages. Included in the Kalenjin cluster of peoples are the Kipsigis,* Nandis,* Teriks* (Nyang' oris), Keyos,* Tugens, Marakwets, Pokots,* Sabaots* (Kony, Pok, and Bungomeks), Sebeis,* and Okieks.* Most Kalenjins are small farmers and cattle raisers.
REFERENCE: Bethwell A. Ogot. *Historical Dictionary of Kenya.* 1981.

KALIA. *See* KURI.

KALLAMEIDA. *See* KURI.

KALLE. The Kalle are a subgroup of the Zerma,* themselves a subgroup of the Songhai* people of West Africa. They live in far western Niger.

KALUKEMBE. The Kalukembes are a subgroup of the Ovimbundu* peoples of Angola.

KALUNDWE. The Kalundwes are a subgroup of the Luba*-Katanga* cluster of peoples in the Shaba region of southeastern Zaire.

KAM. The Kam people constitute a small ethnic group living today in the Bakundi District of the Muri Division of Gongola State in Nigeria. They speak an Adamawa language.
REFERENCE: *Language Survey of Nigeria.* 1976.

KAMADJA. The Kamadja are an ethnic group of approximately 5,000 people who live in Chad. They are a subgroup of the Dazas.* For much of their recent history, they served as slaves to the Tebu.* Today, the Kamadja live among the Tebu in quasi-peonage, tending the palm groves in the oases. The Kamadja have a strong sense of identity and do not intermarry with the Tebu. Most Kamadja live in the Borkou Subprefecture.
REFERENCES: Thomas Collelo et al. *Chad: A Country Study.* 1988; Samuel Decalo. *Historical Dictionary of Chad.* 1987.

KAMANGA. The Kamangas are part of the Tumbuka* cluster of peoples living today in northern Malawi, primarily between Lake Nyasa and the Zambian border, south of the Tanzanian border. Some Kamangas can also be found in Zambia and Tanzania. The Kamanga population today exceeds 40,000 people. The economy still revolves around the production of maize, sorghum, and millet.

REFERENCES: *African Encyclopedia.* 1974; John J. Grotpeter. *Historical Dictionary of Zambia.* 1979; Donald G. Morrison et al. *Black Africa: A Comparative Handbook.* 1989.

KAMANTAM. The Kamantams (Kamantons, Angans) are an ethnic group living today in the Zangon Katab District of the Kachia Division of Kaduna State in Nigeria. Most of the more than 15,000 Kamantams make their living as subsistence farmers. Their language is classified with the Eastern Plateau group of the Benue-Congo family.
REFERENCE: *Language Survey of Nigeria.* 1976.

KAMANTON. *See* KAMANTAM.

KAMAYA. The Kamaya are a lower caste among the Teda* and Daza* peoples of Chad. They are the children of freed Aza* slaves.

KAMBA. The Kambas, not to be confused with the Kambas* of Zaire, Congo, and Angola, are one of Kenya's primary ethnic groups. They have traditionally lived east of Nairobi, especially in the Machakos and Kitui districts in Eastern Province. In the eighteenth century, they migrated from the Mount Kilimanjaro region to their present location. A small number of them can also be found in Tanzania. They speak a Central Bantu* language and have a current population of more than two million people. Although many Kambas have become Christians, their traditional religion, which revolves around a variety of spirits and a single, all-powerful god, remains vital in the lives of most Kambas. The traditional Kamba economy was agricultural, with Kamba farmers raising millet, sweet potatoes, and legumes. They also were skilled traders, serving as middlemen between the coastal and the internal highland economies. Today, many Kambas have settled in urban areas throughout Kenya where they work at a variety of jobs.
REFERENCES: *African Encyclopedia.* 1974; Bethwell A. Ogot. *Historical Dictionary of Kenya.* 1981.

KAMBA. The Kambas are an ethnic subgroup of the Kongo* peoples of Congo, Zaire, and Angola. Most of the Kambas, who number more than 35,000 people in Congo, are concentrated near Madingou in the Niari Valley of Congo and across the border as well.

KAMBARI. *See* KAMBERI.

KAMBATA. *See* KEMBATTA.

KAMBATTA. *See* KEMBATTA.

KAMBE. The Kambes are part of the Mijikenda* cluster of people of coastal Kenya and Tanzania. Most of them are farmers, raising maize, millet, sheep, and goats, while others are laborers on cashew, sugar cane, sisal, and cotton plantations.

KAMBERI. The Kamberis (Kambari) are an ethnic cluster of people who live in the Kwara, Niger, and Sokoto states of Nigeria. Their population today probably exceeds 750,000 people, of whom perhaps 75,000 are Muslims. The vast majority of Kamberis remain loyal to their traditional animist religion, although Christians and especially Muslims continue to make important inroads. They speak a language that linguists classify as part of the Plateau division of the Benue-Congo languages in the Niger-Congo family. The Kamberis are considered to be the best farmers in Nigeria, raising guinea corn, millet, dry rice, and sorghum, and hiring Fulbes* to run their cattle herds. They are also willing to experiment with new crops and innovative agricultural techniques. Although they are surrounded by the more numerous Hausa* people, the Kamberis have maintained a distinct sense of ethnic identity.
REFERENCES: Frank A. Salamone. ''Children's Games as Mechanisms for Easing Ethnic Tensions.'' *Anthropos* 74 (1979): 201–10; Frank A. Salamone. ''Dukawa-Kamberi Relations of Privileged Familiarity.'' *Ethnicity* 6 (1979): 123–36; Frank A. Salamone. ''Kamberi.'' In Richard V. Weekes, ed. *Muslim Peoples.* 1984.

KAMI. The Kamis are one of the individual groups in the Zaramo* cluster of the Northeast Bantu*-speaking people of East Africa. They live in the coastal lowlands of Tanzania, where most of them do hoe farming, producing maize, sorghum, and rice; they also raise sheep, goats, and poultry. During the nineteenth century, the Kamis were victimized by the East African slave trade, and, in response, they built fortified villages protected by stockades. In the twentieth century, those settlement patterns gave way to the homestead system in which rural Kamis scattered out more widely. They live in mud-and-wattle homes characterized by high, thatched, cone-shaped roofs (those thatched roofs are giving way today to tin roofs). The vast majority of Kamis are Muslims, although they are considered to be only marginally loyal, confining their religious observances to fasting at Ramadan, taking on Arab names, and wearing the white skull cap. Like many other Tanzanian rural groups, they have been affected by government relocation policies.
REFERENCE: L. W. Swantz. *Ritual and Symbol in Transitional Zaramo Society.* 1970.

KAMKAM. The Kamkams, also known historically as Kakabas, Bunus, and Bungus, are a small ethnic group of several thousand people living today in the Mambilla District of the Mambilla Division of Gongola State in Nigeria. They can also be found across the border in western Cameroon. Their language is part of the Kamberi* group of languages.
REFERENCE: *Language Survey of Nigeria.* 1976.

KAMO. The Kamo (Kamu) people live today in the Kaltungo and West Tangale districts of the Gombe Division of Bauchi State, Nigeria. They are part of the Waja* group of Adamawa languages.
REFERENCE: *Language Survey of Nigeria.* 1976.

KAMU. *See* KAMO.

KAMUKU. The Kamuku people, whose population today exceeds 35,000 people, live in the Sokoto and Zura divisions of Sokoto State in Nigeria, as well as in the Birnin Gwari Division of Kaduna State and the Kontagora and Minna divisions of Niger State. Their language is grouped with the Kamuku-Bassa* group of Western Plateau languages in the Benue-Congo family.
REFERENCE: *Language Survey of Nigeria.* 1976.

KAMWE. The Kamwes (Higis, Hijis) are an ethnic group primarily concentrated today in the Michika and Madagali districts of the Mubi Division of Gongola State in Nigeria. They can also be found across the border in western Cameroon. Most of them are subsistence farmers. Their current population is approaching 250,000 people. They speak a Chadic language.
REFERENCE: *Language Survey of Nigeria.* 1976.

KANA. The Kana (Khana, Ogoni) people are an ethnic group living today in the Ogoni Region of southeastern Nigeria, primarily in the Khana, Bori, and Tai-Eleme divisions of Rivers State. They are a farming and fishing people of the Niger Delta. The contemporary Kana population exceeds 300,000 people.
REFERENCE: Suanu M. Ikoro. "Numeral Classification in Kana." *Journal of African Languages and Linguistics* 15 (1994): 7–28.

KANAKURU. *See* DERA.

KANAM. *See* KOENOEM.

KANAM. The Kanams are one of the Bantu*-speaking peoples of Nigeria. They are classified as part of the Plateau cluster of peoples who occupy central Nigeria. Most Kanams live in Plateau State and are the result of the mixing of Gomei* Tal,* and Piapung* peoples. They are bordered to the north by the Yergan* peoples and to the west by the Ngans (Beng*). Most Kanams practice subsistence horticulture, raising ginger, millet, guinea corn, beans, and citrus products. They live in social systems characterized by patrilineal descent and patrifocal residence. In recent years, they have begun migrating to towns and cities looking for work.
REFERENCE: Elizabeth Isichei, ed. *Studies in the History of Plateau State, Nigeria.* 1982.

KANAWA. The Kanawas are a subgroup of the Hausa* peoples of Nigeria.

KANEMBU. The Kanembus (Kanuri,* Bornu, Borno, Beriberi) live in Kanem Province in Chad. They are concentrated on the northern shore of Lake Chad and in and around the city of Mao. The Kanembu region then extends north to Chitati and south into northern Nigeria and Niger. They are closely related to the Tebu* groups of the Sahel and Sahara. Today, the number of Kanembus exceeds 300,000 people. The Kanembu language is part of the cluster of Eastern Saharan languages. The Kanembus claim that they originated with Tubba Lawal, an Arab* leader who was converted to Islam by the Prophet Mohammed. Between the eighth and thirteenth centuries, the Kanembus built a great empire in central, sub-Saharan Africa; their decline began in the fourteenth century. They were, and are today, devout Sunni Muslims whose children avoid the French*-speaking public schools for private Islamic educations. Most Kanembus are members of the Tijaniyya and Qadiriyya Sufi orders. The Kanembus are divided into dozens of subgroups based on lineages; those groups include the Dalatoa around Mao, the Kadjiji around Bol, the Ngigim near Dininentchi, the Ngaltuku near Ngelea, the Kubri near Liwa, the Tumagri near Ngigmi in Niger, and the Magimi across the border in Nigeria.

Most Kanembus are farmers and herders. Those living in the northern reaches of Kanembu territory are a semi-nomadic people, herding their cattle to pasture, while the central and southern Kanembus are settled farmers, raising livestock and millet. The Kanembus living near Lake Chad are also fishermen. Because of the isolation of the region and the lack of good roads, the Kanembu economy remains highly localized.

REFERENCES: Christian Bouquet. "Kanembu." In Richard V. Weekes, ed. *Muslim Peoples.* 1984; Thomas Collelo et al. *Chad: A Country Study.* 1988; *Language Survey of Nigeria.* 1976.

KANGAH. *See* JULA.

KANGYAGA. *See* BUILSA.

KANIGUI. The Kanigui, also known historically as the Akanigui and the Bakaniki, are a Mbete*-speaking people who live northwest of Franceville in Gabon. The Kanigui were driven to their present location by the Mbochi* people of the Middle Congo. Today, most Kanigui are small farmers.

REFERENCE: David E. Gardinier. *Historical Dictionary of Gabon.* 1994.

KANIOKA. The Kaniokas are a subgroup of the Luba* people of Zaire. They are part of the Luba-Shaba subcluster.

KANJAGA. *See* BUILSA.

KANKYIRA. *See* DENKYIRA.

KANTANA. The Kantanas are a relatively small Nigerian ethnic group. They speak a Bantu* language and live on the southwestern edge of the Jos Plateau in Plateau State. Their most immediate ethnic neighbors are the Rindres, Chessus,* Turkwans,* Arums,* and Ninzams.* Most Kantanas are subsistence farmers who raise millet, guinea corn, maize, and a variety of other products.
REFERENCE: Elizabeth Isichei, ed. *Studies in the History of Plateau State, Nigeria.* 1982.

KANTANA. *See* MAMA.

KANUFI. The Kanufis are a small ethnic group living today in the Jema'a District of Jema'a Division of Kaduna State in Nigeria.
REFERENCE: *Language Survey of Nigeria.* 1976.

KANUMA. *See* KUNAMA.

KANURI. The Kanuri (Beriberi, Bornu, Borno, Kanembu) are a people who live south and west of Lake Chad in the Bornu state of Nigeria. They can also be found across the border in Niger, where they are known as Bornuans. They are closely related to the Kanembu* of Chad. The major Kanuri settlement in Nigeria is the city of Maiduguri. They speak a language that is classified as part of the Nilo-Saharan linguistic family. Anthropologists estimate that the Kanuri population is approaching five million people, with the vast majority of them in Nigeria. There are also scattered Kanuri groups living in neighboring countries where they have moved looking for work. Trans-Saharan traders first brought Islam to the Kanuri in the eleventh century, and the conversion process was complete by the fifteenth century. They have a tradition of centralized political authority, and, in the fourteenth, fifteenth, and sixteenth centuries, the Bornu, or Kanuri, empire was a major power in West Africa.

Today, the Kanuri are devout Sunni Muslims whose social life revolves around the Islamic religious calendar. They are known to practice polygyny. Most Kanuri are members of the Tijaniyya order of the Sufi brotherhood. The Kanuri economy is a complex one, revolving around commerce, home manufacturing, personal services, and agriculture. Kanuri farmers raise guinea corn, millet, groundnuts, cattle, sheep, and goats. Recently, they have introduced the production of cotton as a cash crop. They also fish in Lake Chad.
REFERENCES: Ronald Cohen. *Dominance and Defiance: A Study of Marital Instability in an Islamic African Society.* 1971; Ronald Cohen. *The Kanuri of Bornu.* 1967; John P. Hutchison. "Aspects of Kanuri Syntax." Ph.D. dissertation. Indiana University. 1976; David H. Spain. "Kanuris." In Richard V. Weekes, ed. *Muslim Peoples.* 1984.

KANYAWA. *See* KARIYA.

KAO. The Kao are one of the non-Arabic Nuba* peoples of Kordofan Province of Sudan. Most of them are farmers, raising sorghum, cotton, and peanuts through rainfall agricultural techniques in the granite inselbergs of the eastern Nuba Mountains. They are Muslim, Christian, and animist in their religious loyalties, although Islam has been gaining ground in the past thirty years.

KAOKABANDER. The Kaokabanders are a subgroup of the Herero* peoples of Namibia and Angola. The Kaokabanders are divided into two subgroups of their own: the Himbas and the Tjimbas.

KAONDE. The Kaonde (Bakahonde, Bakaonde, Kaundi, Kunda) are a major ethnic group in North-West Province of Zambia and in the Haut-Shaba region of northeastern Zaire. They live at the headwaters of the Lualaba River. Their current population exceeds 250,000 people. Many anthropologists consider them to be a subgroup of the Kongos.* They originated in the Katanga region of Zaire, and they are related closely to the Luba* people. They speak a Bantu* language. During the years of the African slave trade, the Kaonde frequently found themselves victimized by the Lundas,* who raided them regularly for slaves. Today, most Kaonde work as farmers, raising sorghum and maize. They burn shrubs and branches before the rainy season and plant their crops in the ashes; they also plant near rivers and streams after burning reeds and grass. Urbanization in Africa in recent decades, however, has brought thousands of Kaonde to cities in search of work.
REFERENCES: *African Encyclopedia.* 1974; F. Scott Bobb. *Historical Dictionary of Zaire.* 1988; John J. Grotpeter. *Historical Dictionary of Zambia.* 1979.

KAPSIGI. *See* KAPSIKI.

KAPSIKI. The Kapsikis (Kapsigis) are a non-Fulbe,* non-Muslim ethnic group of northern Cameroon, a subgroup of the Kirdis.* They arrived in the region escaping Fulbe slave traders in the lowlands. The Kapsikis are farmers who raise crops in terraced, hillside fields. Most Kapsikis can be found living near Mokolo, but several thousand of them are across the border in Nigeria. The current Kapsiki population exceeds 50,000 people.
REFERENCE: Harold D. Nelson et al. *Area Handbook for the United Republic of Cameroon.* 1974.

KAPUGU. *See* GURE-KAHUGU.

KARA. The Kara are one of the subgroups of the Gbayas.* They live in the Central African Republic and southwestern Chad. They speak a Sudanic language. The Karas were once a larger, more concentrated people, but slave-

raiding in the nineteenth century dispersed them and reduced their population dramatically. The most visible Kara group today is located in Birao. They should not be confused with the Kara* people of Tanzania.
REFERENCE: Pierre Kalck. *Historical Dictionary of the Central African Republic.* 1992.

KARA. The Karas, not to be confused with the Karas* of the Central African Republic, are a unique ethnic group living near Lake Victoria in northern Tanzania. They are known for their skill as farmers, even though the soil of their region is poor. The Karas till the land continually in a crop-and-cattle system, through which the cattle keep the soil fertilized. The Karas believe in individual property ownership, which is quite unusual for African peoples.
REFERENCE: Laura Kurtz. *Historical Dictionary of Tanzania.* 1978.

KARABORO. The Karaboros (Karakoras) are an ethnic group whom anthropologists classify as part of the larger cluster of Senufo* peoples of West Africa. The Karaboros are concentrated along the border of northern Ivory Coast and southwestern Burkina-Faso, particularly where the Komnoé River crosses the frontier. Most of them are small farmers, raising corn, rice, yams, peanuts, sesame, and sweet potatoes.
REFERENCE: Daniel M. McFarland. *Historical Dictionary of Upper Volta.* 1978.

KARAIKARAI. *See* KARAKARE.

KARAKARE. The Karakares, also known as Kerekeres and Karaikarais, are an ethnic group of approximately 80,000 people who live today in Potiskum and Fika districts of the Fika Division of Bornu State in Nigeria, as well as in the Dagauda and Jalam districts of the Katagum Division of Bauchi State. They speak a Chadic language.
REFERENCE: *Language Survey of Nigeria.* 1976.

KARAKORA. *See* KARABORO.

KARAMOJONG. *See* KARIMOJON.

KARANGA. Today, the Karangas are considered to be a subgroup of the Maba* people of Sudan. Ethnologists, however, argue that their unique language and culture indicate that they were probably absorbed by the surrounding Maba peoples during the course of the last several centuries. Most Karangas today live in the highlands north of Abéché, where they work as small farmers. *See* SHONA.

KARANGA. The Karangas (Vakaranga), not to be confused with the Karanga* who are a subgroup of the Mabas* of Chad, are a subgroup of the Shona* of

Zimbabwe and Mozambique. They are the "Southern Shonas." Most of them are farmers, raising cattle, millet, maize, pumpkins, and yams. The Karanga language is spoken by about one-third of all Shona peoples, and they are concentrated in a very compact region of Zimbabwe—between Gwkelo in the northwest, Bikita in the northeast, Chiredzi in the southeast, and West Nicolson in the southwest. The Karangas are divided into such subgroups as the Maris, Goveras, Dumas, Govas, Jenas, and Nyubis.
REFERENCE: R. Kent Rasmussen. *Historical Dictionary of Zimbabwe.* 1994.

KARBO. The Karbos are one of the many ethnic groups in Chad. Virtually all of the 40,000 or so Karbos are Muslims. They are part of the larger Nilotic* cluster of Chadian peoples. Most Karbos make their living as small farmers, laborers, and semi-nomadic and nomadic pastoralists.
REFERENCES: Pierre Hugot. *Le Tchad.* 1965; J. C. Lebeuf. *Afrique Centrale.* 1972; Donald G. Morrison et al. *Black Africa: A Comparative Handbook.* 1989.

KAREKARE. The Karekares are part of the larger cluster of Kanuri* peoples of the Bornu State of northeastern Nigeria. Their economy is a complex one, revolving around commerce, home manufacturing, personal services, and agriculture. The farmers raise guinea corn, millet, groundnuts, cattle, sheep, and goats. In recent years, they have begun to produce cotton as a cash crop. They also fish in Lake Chad. They are Sunni Muslims.
REFERENCES: Ronald Cohen. *The Kanuri of Bornu.* 1967; Donald G. Morrison et al. *Black Africa: A Comparative Handbook.* 1989.

KARENJO. *See* JANJO.

KARFA. The Karfas (Kerifa) are a subgroup of the Ron* people of the Mama District of the Akwanga Division of Plateau State in Nigeria.

KARIA. *See* KURI.

KARIMOJON. Most Karimojon live in the semi-arid plateau in Uganda, particularly in the region bordering on Sudan and Kenya. Other Karimojon live across the border in northwestern Kenya and southern Sudan. They are divided into a number of subgroups, such as the Bokora Karimojon, the Pei Karimojon, and the Matheniko Karimojon of Uganda. Their economy revolves around transhumant pastoralism, with the men raising cattle and the women trying to raise sorghum and millet. Of all of Uganda's ethnic groups, they are among the least developed and the least acculturated to Western technologies. Their entire life—economy, religion, and culture—revolves around cattle. Because of the severe droughts in northeastern Africa during the 1980s and early 1990s, the Karimojon have faced dire economic circumstances. Included in the Karimojon cluster of

Ugandan peoples are the Tesos,* Dodos,* Jies,* Tepeths,* Nyakwais,* and Kak-
was.*
REFERENCES: Rita M. Byrnes et al. *Uganda: A Country Study.* 1990; K. S. Gourlay.
"The Practice of Cueing Among the Karimojon of North-East Uganda." *Journal of
Ethnomusicology* 16 (May 1972): 240–46.

KARIMOJONG. *See* KARIMOJON.

KARIYA. The Kariyas, also known as Kanyawas and Lipkawas, are a small
ethnic group of approximately 5,000 people living today in the Ganjuwa District
of the Bauchi Division of Bauchi State in Nigeria. They speak a Chadic language.
REFERENCE: *Language Survey of Nigeria.* 1976.

KARO. The Karos are a subgroup of the Banna* people of Ethiopia.

KARURA. The Karuras are an ethnic group living today southwest of Mount
Kenya in Kenya in East Africa. They are closely related to the Kikuyu* and
Meru* peoples. Most of them are subsistence farmers.
REFERENCE: W. H. Whiteley. *Language in Kenya.* 1974.

KASENA. The Kasenas (Kassenas) are one of the Grusi* peoples of northern
Ghana and southern Burkina-Faso. They are concentrated in the Upper Region
of Ghana, primarily in the Paga and Navrongo areas; others live across the
border from Paga in Burkina-Faso. During the decades of the Zerma* slave
raids, the Kasenas were among the most devastated of the regional ethnic groups.
Most of them now are small farmers, raising millet, yams, and a variety of other
crops. The population of Kasena people in Ghana today is approximately 90,000
people.
REFERENCES: Daniel M. McFarland. *Historical Dictionary of Ghana.* 1995; Daniel M.
McFarland. *Historical Dictionary of Upper Volta.* 1978.

KASHAF. The Kashafs are a Nubian* subgroup. They are the descendants of
Turkish soldiers who were stationed along the southern Sudan frontier during
the Ottoman era. Many soldiers married Nubian women and remained in the
area, where they became a land-owning elite often resented by other Nubians.
See NUBA.

KASHMÉRÉ. Today, the Kashmérés are considered to be a subgroup of the
Maba* people of Sudan. They speak a Mabang language and live in the highlands north of Abéché. Ethnologists, however, argue that their unique language
and culture indicate that they were probably absorbed by the surrounding Maba
peoples during the course of the last several centuries.

KASIGAU. The Kasigaus are a subgroup of the Taita* peoples of East Africa, particularly Kenya. They speak a Bantu* language.

KASSENA. *See* KASENA.

KATAB. The Katabs are an ethnic group living in the grassy savannas and volcanic hills of the southern region of the state of Kaduna in Nigeria, primarily in the Jema'a and Kachia divisions. They call themselves the Atyap. Their language is part of the Benue-Congo subsection of the Niger-Congo family. The Katabs believe that they originated near Zaria. Between 1810 and 1833, the Katabs fell under Fulbe* influence when the Emir of Jema'a conquered them for plunder and slaves; from 1847 to 1854, the Emir of Zaria did the same. After the imposition of British* authority in the Katab area, the slave raids and chaos gradually declined. The Katabs practice subsistence horticulture, raising ginger, millet, guinea corn, beans, and citrus products. They live in social systems characterized by patrilineal descent and patrifocal residence. They have accepted public school programs and are Christians.
REFERENCE: Carol V. McKinney. "A Linguistic Shift in Kajè, Kagoro, and Katab Kinship Terminology." *Ethnology* 22 (1983): 281–95.

KATANGA. The Katangas are one of the groups in the Bemba* cluster of peoples in northeastern Zaire and northern Zambia. They live west of Lake Tanganyika and Lake Mwero. The Katanga language is part of the Bantu* language family and is understood throughout Zambia. The Katangas believe that they originated in the Katanga region of contemporary Zaire and migrated to Zambia. Their ancestors are the same as those of the Luba* and Lunda* peoples. They are a farming people. Traditionally, because of the poor soil in the region, they relocated their villages every four or five years, but modern fertilizers and crop rotation methods have allowed them to become quite sedentary. They raise maize and millet as staples and cotton as a cash crop. Large numbers of Katanga men also work in the Copperbelt as miners.
REFERENCES: *African Encyclopedia.* 1974; F. Scott Bobb. *Historical Dictionary of Zaire.* 1988.

KATLA. The Katlas are a subgroup of the Nuba* peoples of Sudan.

KATSENAWA. The Katsenawas are a subgroup of the Hausa* peoples of Nigeria.

KAUMA. The Kaumas are part of the Mijikenda* cluster of people of coastal Kenya and Tanzania. Most of them are farmers, raising maize, millet, sheep, and goats, while others are laborers on sugar cane, sisal, and cotton plantations.

KAUNDI. *See* KAONDE.

KAURE. *See* KABRÉ.

KAVANGA. The Kavangas are an ethnic group living today in Namibia. Their current population exceeds 100,000 people, and they are divided into several subgroups, including the Kwangaris, Mbukushus, Kwangalis, Sambyus, Mbunzas, and Geirikus. Most Kavangas work today as small farmers. They can also be found in Angola.
REFERENCE: Stanley Schoeman and Elna Schoeman. *Namibia.* 1984.

KAWAHLA. The Kawahlas are considered one of the major subgroups of the Arab* people in Sudan. The Kawahlas are part of the larger cluster of Jaaliyin* Arab peoples. They should not be confused with the larger Kawahla* cluster of Arabic peoples, who are part of the Juhayna* cluster. They are divided into thirteen subgroups of their own, most of them located north and west of Khartoum and south of Khartoum to north of Kusti. Those Kawahlas north and west of Khartoum have tended to be a pastoral people, while those to the south have been settled agriculturalists. The Kawahlas are Muslims.
REFERENCE: Helen C. Metz et al. *Sudan: A Country Study.* 1991.

KAWAHLA. The Kawahlas (Fezara) are a cluster of Juhayna* Arabs* living today in Sudan. Included in the Kawahla cluster are the Kawahlas proper, as well as the Hamids, Mamars, Bedeiriyas, and Gawama'as.

KAYAURI. The Kayauris are a subgroup of the Gezawa* people of northern Nigeria.

KAYLA. *See* BETA ISRAEL.

KAZEMBE. The Kazembes are an ethnic group living today in the Haut-Shaba region of Zaire and across the border in Zambia. They are closely related to the Lunda.* During the eighteenth and nineteenth centuries, the Kazembes were very active as middlemen in the East African ivory trade, but today most of them are farmers.
REFERENCE: F. Scott Bobb. *Historical Dictionary of Zaire.* 1988.

KEAKA. The Keakas are a small ethnic group living today in the Cross River region of Nigeria, where most of them labor as small farmers. Their neighbors in the region include Ekois (Ejaghams*), Ibibios,* Anangs,* and Widekums.*
REFERENCE: Keith Nicklin. "Nigerian Skin-Covered Masks." *African Arts* 7 (Spring 1974): 8–15.

KEBBAWA. The Kebbawas are a subgroup of the Hausa* peoples of Nigeria.

KEBU. The Kebu are one of the prominent ethnic groups in central Togo. They practice a traditional animist religion. They should not be confused with the Kebu* people of Uganda. Like most other peoples in the region, the Kebu are subsistence farmers.
REFERENCE: Samuel Decalo. *Historical Dictionary of Togo.* 1976.

KEBU. The Kebu people are one of the thirty or so ethnic groups living today in Uganda. They speak a Sudanic language and tend to reside in the northern reaches of the country, where most of them are subsistence farmers and livestock raisers.
REFERENCE: Peter Ladefoged, Ruth Glick, and Clive Criper. *Language in Uganda.* 1972.

KECHERDA. The Kecherdas are a small ethnic group living in the Moussoro region of Kanem in Chad and in the Kaouar region of Niger. They are a Tebu* subgroup. Today, they have mixed extensively with the Dazas,* having adopted the Daza language as well, although they maintain a distinct sense of identity. Most Kecherdas are small farmers and herders.
REFERENCE: Samuel Decalo. *Historical Dictionary of Chad.* 1987; Samuel Decalo. *Historical Dictionary of Niger.* 1989.

KEDI. The Kedi are one of the ethnic groups of Uganda in East Africa. Their population today exceeds one million people, of whom approximately 10 percent are Muslims. They are a Bantu*-speaking people who today live in eastern Uganda and across the border in western Kenya. Their immediate neighbors are the Karimojon,* Itesos,* Sogas,* and Gisus.* They are primarily farmers who raise millet, coffee, corn, bananas, and cotton. The Kedi have struggled for years to come out from under the cultural and economic domination of the neighboring Gisus.
REFERENCE: Rita M. Byrnes et al. *Uganda: A Country Study.* 1990.

KEDJIM. The Kedjims are an ethnic group living today in Cameroon. Most of the more than 30,000 Kedjims are subsistence farmers occupying two villages— Kedjim Keku and Kedjom Ketinguh—in the Northwest Province.
REFERENCE: Susan Diduk. ''Twins, Ancestors, and Socio-Economic Change in Kedjim Society.'' *Man* 28 (September 1993): 551–72.

KEFA. *See* KEFICHO.

KEFICHO. The Kefichos (Kefas) are a prominent ethnic group in Kefa Province, Ethiopia. They are closely related to the Mochas.* The Kefichos are part of the larger Omotic* cluster of peoples and possess a strong sense of ethnic identity. Ethnologists believe they migrated to the region from the Damot highlands, first enslaving and then assimilating the original inhabitants. In the sixteenth century, the region came under Oromo* control. The Kefichos are known for their skill as coffee producers. Their population today exceeds 125,000 people.

REFERENCES: Harold D. Nelson et al. *Ethiopia: A Country Study.* 1980; Chris Prouty and Eugene Rosenfeld. *Historical Dictionary of Ethiopia and Eritrea.* 1994.

KEGUEME. *See* SERER.

KEIGA-GIRRU. The Keiga-Girrus are one of the Nuba* peoples of Sudan.

KEIRA. *See* FUR.

KEIYU. *See* KEYO.

KEMBATA. *See* KEMBATTA.

KEMBATTA. The Kembattas (Kambattas, Kambatas) are one of the subgroups of the Sadama* people of southwestern Ethiopia. They are actually of mixed Sadama and Amhara*-Tigre* descent. Although they are nominally Christians, they still practice a number of Cushitic rites. Their population today exceeds 300,000 people, including the Timbaros and Alabas, whom some consider to be their subgroups.

KEMNANT. The Kemnant people are a subgroup of the Agaw* people of central and northern Ethiopia. Most of them are farmers today, raising millet, coffee, and castor oil plants.

KENEDOUGOU. *See* SENUFO.

KENGA. *See* KINGA.

KENGA. *See* SHANGAWA.

KENGAWA. The Kengawa—also known as the Kiengawa, Kyengawa, and Tienga—are an ethnic group living in northwestern Nigeria. They are surrounded by Hausas,* who tend to control political and economic life. The Kengawa speak a language in the Niger-Benue division of the Niger-Congo linguistic family. The Kengawa claim descent from the legendary Kisra, who opposed Islam until the Prophet Mohammed defeated him in battle. They were part of the Songhay Empire by the thirteenth century, and remained so until the

Moroccan invasions of the sixteenth century. During those invasions, the Kengawa relocated to Yauri in Sokoto State, and, during the slave raids of the nineteenth century, they found refuge in the hinterland. The Kengawa make their living as farmers, raising vegetables on the Niger River banks and millet and guinea corn in the highlands. They also fish and are known for their commercial skills. Nearly half of all Kengawa are Sunni Muslims of the Maliki school.

REFERENCES: Jonathan Jeness. *Fishermen of the Kainji Basin.* 1970; Frank Salamone. *Gods and Goods in Africa.* 1974; Frank Salamone. ''Shangawa.'' In Richard V. Weekes, ed. *Muslim Peoples.* 1984.

KENTU. *See* ICEN.

KENUZ. The Kenuz are a Nubian* subgroup who lived close to Aswan. They are the descendants of the Beni Kanz, an Arab* people, who intermarried with Nubians beginning in the thirteenth century. The building of the Aswan Dam in the 1890s and early 1900s forced their resettlement, but the Kenuz have maintained a sense of Kenuz, as well as Nubian, identity, even though they are now living in Egyptian cities.

KENYANG. The Kenyangs are a relatively small ethnic group living today in the forests of the Manyu Prefecture of Southwest Province in Cameroon. They can be found along the north bank of the headwaters of the Cross River, east of Mamfe Town. Their most immediate ethnic neighbors are the Mundanis,* Ngwois,* Menkas,* Denyas,* and Ejaghams.* Most Kenyangs are subsistence farmers.

REFERENCE: Samson Negbo Abangma. *Modes in Denya Discourse.* 1987.

KENYI. The Kenyis (Lukenyis) are one of the more than thirty ethnic groups living today in Uganda. They speak a Bantu* language and live in the heavily forested regions of central Uganda. Most Kenyis are subsistence farmers.

REFERENCE: Peter Ladefoged, Ruth Glick, and Clive Criper. *Language in Uganda.* 1972.

KERA. The Keras are an ethnic group of approximately 30,000 people who are concentrated east and south of Lake Tikun in Chad.

REFERENCE: Samuel Decalo. *Historical Dictionary of Chad.* 1987.

KERANG. *See* ANGA.

KEREKERE. *See* KARAKARE.

KERERE. The Kereres (Kerewe) live south of Lake Victoria in northern Tanzania. For centuries, they maintained a feudal system in control of the land, with

tenants owing allegiance to feudal lords, but, in recent years, they have made the transition to commercial agriculture, with peasants renting land from landlords. The Kereres maintain a patrilineal social system and raise cattle, cotton, and rice. They are closely related, culturally and linguistically, to the Sukumas* and Jitas.* Some ethnologists include the Redis with the Kerere cluster. The Kerere population exceeds 100,000 people today.
REFERENCE: Laura Kurtz. *Historical Dictionary of Tanzania.* 1978.

KEREWE. *See* KERERE.

KERIFA. *See* KARFA.

KETE. The Ketes are one of the subgroups of the Luba* peoples of Zaire. They are part of the Luba-Kasai subcluster of the Lubas.

KETEUN. *See* UTUGWANG.

KETU. The Ketus are one of the many subgroups of the Yoruba* peoples of West Africa. Most Ketus can be found today living east of the Weme River in Benin and along the Benin-Nigerian border in western Ogun State in Nigeria.

KEYO. The Keyos (Elgeyos, Keiyus) are an ethnic group of approximately 150,000 people who live on a narrow strip of land on the western bank of the Kerio River in the Elgeyo-Marakwet District in Kenya. Many also live in the highlands, where they are known for their skill with irrigation. Most Keyos are small farmers, growing maize, groundnuts, coffee, and wheat and raising cattle, goats, and sheep.
REFERENCE: Bethwell A. Ogot. *Historical Dictionary of Kenya.* 1981.

KGAFELA KGATLA. The Kgafela Kgatlas are a branch of the Kgatla* people, who are a subgroup of the Tswana* people of Botswana. The Kgafelas are the easternmost branch of those people. They first emerged as an identifiable ethnic group in the late seventeenth century when they split off from the Mosetlha Kgatlas in the western Transvaal. During the mid-nineteenth century, they came under increasing pressure from Boer settlers, who demanded their land and labor. During the late nineteenth century, they relocated to what is today Botswana. Today, Kgafela Kgatlas can be found in both the Transvaal in the Union of South Africa and in Botswana. Most of them are members of the Dutch Reformed Church.
REFERENCE: Fred Morton, A. Murray, and J. Ramsay. *Historical Dictionary of Botswana.* 1989.

KGALAGADI. The Kgalagadis (Bakgalagadis) are a large cluster of ethnic

groups who speak a Sotho*-Tswana* language but are not considered to be a subgroup of the Tswana people of Botswana. The Kgalagadis are concentrated in the western reaches of the Southern and Kweneng districts. They are divided into the following subgroups: Kgwatheng (BaKgwatheng), Ngologa (Ba-Ngologa), Bolaongwe (BaLaongwe), Phaleng (BaPheleng), and Shaga (Ba-Shaga). In the nineteenth century, most of the Kgalagadis were hunters, supplying food to the traders on the Trans-Kgalagadi desert trade routes; in the twentieth century, they have made the transition to cattle herding, usually for Tswana owners. Their remote location near the Kgalagadi Desert left the Kgal-agadi largely untouched during the colonial period, at least from tax collectors and the intrusions of the European imperial apparatus, although they remained largely under Tswana domination. It was not until the 1930s that the Kgalagadis entered the commercial economy as migrant laborers and came under govern-mental administrative influence. In the 1950s, under the leadership of Tumello Puleng, the Kgalagadis began to assert themselves to break away from Tswana control. Today, they have achieved a degree of cultural independence through separate churches, local economic development, and party politics in Botswana.
REFERENCE: Fred Morton, A. Murray, and J. Ramsay. *Historical Dictionary of Botswana.* 1989.

KGATLA. The Kgatlas (Bakgatlas) are one of the major subgroups of the Tswana* people of Botswana.

KGWATHENG. The Kgwathengs are a subgroup of the Kgalagadi* people of Botswana.

KHANA. *See* KANA.

KHASONKA. The Khasonka (Khassonkés) are a Manding*-speaking people whose language is actually considered part of the Fringe Manding cluster of Manding languages. Most Khasonka are settled farmers who raise rice and pea-nuts. They live in and around Khaso on the upper Senegal River near Kayes in far western Mali, especially in the *cercles* of Kayes, Bafoulabé, and Kita. They are also some Khasonka living across the border in southern Mauritania and in eastern Senegal. The Khasonka are Muslims who believe that they have Fulbe* ethnic origins. Their population today exceeds 100,000 people.
REFERENCE: Carleton T. Hodge, ed. *Papers on the Manding.* 1971.

KHASSONKÉ. *See* KHASONKA.

KHAYO. The Khayos are a subgroup of the Luhya* people of Kenya and Uganda. They are a Western Bantu* people who live today north of Lake Victoria on both sides of the Kenyan-Ugandan border.

KHOI. *See* KHOIKHOI.

KHOIKHOI. The Khoikhois are a pastoral people living today in South Africa. They became known as Hottentots to whites in the seventeenth and eighteenth centuries (today, the term "Hottentot" is considered an ethnic slur). Ethnologists place Khoikhoi origins near northern Botswana, but, more than a thousand years ago, the Khoikhoi added cattle to their hunting-and-gathering economy and slowly migrated south to the Orange River and beyond. Smallpox epidemics in 1713, 1735, and 1767 killed most Khoikhois. Eventually, the survivors evolved into the "Coloured"* population of South Africa. As late as 1995, some 50,000 Khoikhois still survived in Namibia. Few Khoikhois currently live in South Africa.
REFERENCES: Richard Elphick. *Khoikhoi and the Founding of White South Africa.* 1985; Isaac Schapera. *The Khoisan Peoples of South Africa: Bushmen and Hottentots.* 1930; Jiro Tanaka. *The San, Hunter-Gatherers of the Kalahari.* 1980.

KHOISAN. The term "Khoisan" refers to a language group in southern Africa that includes the San* people and the Khoikhoi.*

KHOLIFA. The Kholifas are a minor subgroup of the Temne* people of Sierra Leone.

KHOZZAM. The Khozzams are a subgroup of the Djoheina,* themselves a large Arab* subgroup in Chad.

KHURUTSHE. The Khurutshes (Bakhurutshes) are a subgroup of the Hurutshes,* who are themselves a subgroup of the Tswana* people of Botswana. At the beginning of the nineteenth century, they were living in northeast Botswana. The Ndebeles* conquered them early in the 1840s; twenty years later, they fled to Shoshong and came under Ngwato* influence. Rauwe, a Khurutshe leader, took his people back to the northeast in the 1890s and launched an independent Khurutshe church, which was absorbed by the Anglicans early in the twentieth century.
REFERENCES: Fred Morton, A. Murray, and J. Ramsay. *Historical Dictionary of Botswana.* 1989.

KHUTE. The Khutes are a subgroup of the Tshu-Kwe* peoples, themselves a subgroup of the San* people of Botswana.

KIAN. *See* BOBO.

KIBALA. The Kibalas are a subgroup of the Mbundu* peoples of Angola.

KIBALLO. The Kiballos (Kiwollos) are a small ethnic group living today in the grassy savannas and volcanic hills of the southern region of the state of Kaduna in Nigeria and in the Karta region of Mali. They are surrounded by the Konos* to the north, the Kuramas* to the south and east, and the Hausas* to the east. They make their living in a mixed economy of subsistence agriculture and livestock raising.
REFERENCE: Elizabeth Isichei, ed. *Studies in the History of Plateau State, Nigeria.* 1982.

KIBBO. *See* BIROM.

KIBET. The Kibets are one of the major subgroups of the Tama*-speaking people of Chad. Tama is a Waddian language. Most Kibets live in settled villages where they have learned to rotate crops, a practice that allows them to farm the arid Sahel region. Most of them can be found living in Biltine Prefecture in southeastern Chad.
REFERENCE: Thomas Collelo et al. *Chad: A Country Study.* 1988.

KIBO. *See* BIROM.

KIBSI. The Kibsis are one of the most ancient peoples of Burkina-Faso. They are part of the larger Ninisi* cluster of peoples. The Kibsis lived in the Yako region before Mossi* immigrants displaced them. Some Kibsis migrated northward to the Bandiagara area where they have mixed with the Dogons.* Those who retreated to the south eventually became known as the Kipirsi,* or Kõ, people. Most Kibsis are farmers, raising millet as a staple and onions as a cash crop.
REFERENCE: Daniel M. McFarland. *Historical Dictionary of Upper Volta.* 1978.

KIBULA. The Kibulas are a subgroup of the Ovimbundu* peoples of Angola.

KIBYEN. *See* BIROM.

KIGA. The Kigas (Rukiga) are an ethnic group living today in northern Rwanda and southern Uganda. They have traditionally made their living through fishing and subsistence farming. The devastating ethnic holocaust in Rwanda in 1994 sent many Kigas fleeing into southern Uganda. They are a patrilineal people.
REFERENCE: Jim Freedman. "Joking, Affinity, and the Exchange of Ritual Services among the Kiga of Northern Rwanda." *Man* 12 (April 1977): 154–65.

KIGE. *See* BERI.

KIKUK. *See* KYIBAKU.

KIKUYU. The Kikuyus (Gikikuyus) are one of the main ethnic groups in Kenya. Traditionally, the Kikuyu homeland was in the highlands north of Nairobi, toward Mt. Kenya, and, although they are still concentrated there, they have also settled throughout the country. They speak a Bantu* language and have a contemporary population of nearly four million people. Traditional Kikuyu society was patrilineally organized, with extended family homesteads and frequent polygyny. More recently, neolocal, nuclear families are to be found. The Kikuyus are widely recognized as a driving, opportunistic, and industrious people. Their economy has revolved around the agricultural production of maize, coffee, tea, pyrethrum, and potatoes, as well as subsistence animal husbandry. Families within the village own and work farmland within walking distance of their homes. Large urban areas are near, so many Kikuyus also engage in wage labor and produce cash crops. Kikuyus played a central role in the movement to achieve independence from Great Britain and in the Mau Mau movement of the 1950s. They are also prominent in the Kenyan African National Union today.
REFERENCES: *African Encyclopedia.* 1974; Bethwell A. Ogot. *Historical Dictionary of Kenya.* 1981.

KILA. The Kilas are a small group of ethnically distinct people living in the Mambilla District of the Mambilla Division of Gongola State in Nigeria. They speak a non-Bantu* language that is closely related to the Mambilla-Vute group.
REFERENCE: *Language Survey of Nigeria.* 1976.

KILANG. The Kilangs, who live along the southern border of Chad, are one of the major subgroups of the Ngambaye* people of Chad. The Ngambayes are themselves a subgroup of the Saras.*

KILANGA. The Kilangas are part of the larger Bariba* cluster of peoples in northern Benin and Togo. Some Kilangas can also be found today in Ghana. They come from Voltaic origins. The Kilanga population today exceeds 250,000 people, most of whom are small farmers. The Kilangas are divided into two subgroups of their own: the Dompagos* and the Pila-Pilas.* The Dompagos are by far the larger of the subgroups.
REFERENCE: Donald G. Morrison et al. *Black Africa: A Comparative Handbook.* 1989.

KILBA. The Kilba people, also known historically as Hebas and Chobbas, are an ethnic group of approximately 125,000 people living in the Kilba District of the Adamawa Division of Gongola State in Nigeria. They speak a Chadic language.
REFERENCE: *Language Survey of Nigeria.* 1976.

KILENGI. The Kilengis are part of the larger cluster of Nyaneka*-Humbe peoples of southwestern Angola.

KILINDE. The Kilinde people are an ethnic group living today in Tanzania. Some ethnologists include them as part of the Zigalu* cluster of peoples.

KILLAKADA. *See* KURI.

KIM. There are approximately 15,000 people in Chad today who are identified as Kim people. They originated with the confederation of four city-states along the Logone River, between Bongor and Lai. Included in the confederation were the Kossopes, Guéreps, Garaps, Kolops, and Kolobos. Collectively, they were known as Kims. Kims can also be found in Ndjamena and Bongor. Since the 1940s, the Kims have come under the influence of Protestant missionaries working out of Nigeria, and their educational levels have risen dramatically.
REFERENCE: Samuel Decalo. *Historical Dictionary of Chad.* 1987.

KIMBU. The Kimbu people of central Tanzania are a Bantu*-speaking group. They first arrived in their contemporary homeland in the late nineteenth century when they were fleeing the slave trade. They are concentrated in Iseke, which is located outside of Kwa Mtoro. Their population today is approximately 75,000 people.
REFERENCE: James L. Newman. *The Ecological Basis for Subsistence Change among the Sandawe of Tanzania.* 1970.

KINDIGA. *See* HADZA.

KINGA. The Kingas (Kenga) are a collection of closely related ethnic groups, including the Kinga proper, who live in the hills of the Hadjeray region, near Mongo and Melfi, in Chad. Their language closely resembles that of the Barmas.* They originated to the east, in the Darfur region of Sudan, in the fifteenth century, moving west to Hadjeray. They make their living as farmers and by tapping the acacia trees for gum arabic. Although the Kingas are nominally Muslims, they remain very loyal to many pre-Islamic rites, including the worship of *margai* spirits. The current Kinga population exceeds 30,000 people, although another 100,000 people—from such groups as the Junkuns,* Dungals,* and Bidios*—live in close proximity with them.
REFERENCE: Samuel Decalo. *Historical Dictionary of Chad.* 1987.

KINGA. The Kingas are a Tanzanian ethnic group who are included in the Nyasa* cluster of peoples. Their Tanzanian population is approximately 140,000 people today.

KINGOLO. The Kingolos are a subgroup of the Ovimbundu* peoples of Angola.

KINKOMBA. The Kinkomba are one of the Molé-Dagbane* peoples of northern Ghana.
REFERENCE: David Tait. *The Kinkomba of Northern Ghana.* 1961.

KINONGO. *See* KONONGO.

KINUGY. *See* KINUKU.

KINUKA. *See* KINUKU.

KINUKU. The Kinukus, who are also known as Kinugys and Kinukas, are a tiny ethnic group living in the Kauru District of the Saminaka Division of Kaduna State in Nigeria.
REFERENCE: *Language Survey of Nigeria.* 1976.

KIOKO. *See* CHOKWE.

KIONG. The Kiong (Akoiyang, Akayon, Okoyong, and Okonyong) people are an ethnic group living today in the Calabar and Akamkpa divisions of Cross River State in Nigeria. Their language, today spoken by only a handful of elderly Kiongs, is part of the Cross River group of Benue-Congo languages.
REFERENCE: *Language Survey of Nigeria.* 1976.

KIPIRSI. The Kipirsi (Kõ) are one of the autochthonous peoples of Burkina-Faso. They are part of the larger Ninisi* cluster of peoples. The Kipirsi lived in the Yako region before Mossi* immigrants displaced them. Some Kipirsi migrated northward to the Bandiagara area, where they have mixed with the Dogons.* Those who retreated to the south eventually became known as the Kipirsi, or Kõ, people. The language they speak is known as Kõ. The Kipirsi live in the Kipirsi Mountain region. Frequently enslaved by neighboring Mossi and Zerma* peoples, they submitted to the French* in 1897 for protection.
REFERENCE: Daniel M. McFarland. *Historical Dictionary of Upper Volta.* 1978.

KIPSIGI. The Kipsigis have a population of nearly one million people and live in the western highlands of Kenya. They are one of the Kalenjin* peoples. Cattle were central to the traditional Kipsigi economy, but, in recent years, the Kipsigis have started raising maize and tobacco on large commercial farms and moving to towns and cities for work and business opportunities. The Kipsigis had a reputation as fierce, skilled warriors who regularly raided neighboring Masais,* Luos,* and Gusiis* for cattle. The arrival of British* military force in the region

in 1905 ended those raids. The Kipsigis call their language Kalenjin, which is also spoken by the neighboring Nandi* people.
REFERENCE: *African Encyclopedia.* 1974.

KIPUNGU. The Kipungus are part of the larger cluster of Nyaneka*-Humbe peoples of southwestern Angola.

KIR. *See* JIRU-KIR.

KIRA. *See* SITI.

KIR-BALAR. The Kir-Balar people are a small ethnic group living today in the Zungur District of the Bauchi Division of Bauchi State in Nigeria. They speak a Chadic language.
REFERENCE: *Language Survey of Nigeria.* 1976.

KIRDI. The term ''Kirdi'' has long been used to refer to the non-Fulbe,* non-Muslim, non-Christian peoples of northern Cameroon, southeastern Nigeria, and southwestern Chad. Included in the group are the Kapsikis,* Tupurs,* Falis,* Dabas,* Mofus,* Matakams,* Mandaras,* Guizigas,* Musgus,* Mundangs,* and Massas.* In the process of avoiding Fulbe domination, large numbers of Kirdis sought refuge in the hills, mountains, and isolated valleys of the region. Because of their isolation, the Kirdi lifestyle has remained remarkably stable. Those Kirdis still in close contact with Fulbes function as Fulbe slaves. Fulbes despise the Kirdis. Most Kirdis are small farmers, raising various cereals, cattle, and groundnuts.
REFERENCES: Mark DeLancey and H. M. Mokeba. *Historical Dictionary of the Republic of Cameroon.* 1990.

KIRFI. The Kirfi speak a Chadic language and live today in the Kirfi Division of the Bauchi Division of Bauchi State, Nigeria. Most of them are subsistence farmers who also raise livestock.
REFERENCE: *Language Survey of Nigeria.* 1976.

KIRIKJIR. *See* LOPA.

KISA. The Kisas are a subgroup of the Luhya* people of Kenya and Uganda. They are a Western Bantu* people who today live north of Lake Victoria on both sides of the Kenyan-Ugandan border.

KISAMA. The Kisamas are a subgroup of the Mbundu* people of north-central Angola.

KISHAMBA. The Kishambas are a subgroup of the Taita* peoples of East Africa, particularly Kenya. They speak a Bantu* language.

KISI. *See* KISSI.

KISII. *See* GUSII.

KISSANJE. The Kissanjes are a subgroup of the Ovimbundu* peoples of Angola.

KISSI. The Kissis (Kisi) are a West African ethnic group living today in the region where the frontiers of Liberia, Sierra Leone, and Guinea meet. The majority of the Kissis live in Guinea, especially in the Guéckédou and Kissidougou administrative regions; it is a densely forested area. Kissi traditions trace their origins to the Upper Niger region before the seventeenth century. There they lived in the southern part of Fouta Djallon until the Yalunkas* drove them out. After 1600, they migrated to the west, displacing the Limbas* during their migration. They then found themselves frequently under attack from the Korankos.* The Kissis then began intensive cultivation of millet, but, to do so, they deforested the region, which still shows the effects of their economic decision. In the nineteenth century, they made the transition to rice cultivation. They are concentrated in the border regions connecting the three countries. Their population exceeds 525,000 people, most of whom are Christians, Kissi animists, or a syncretic combination of both religions. A small minority of the Kissis, perhaps 9 percent of them, are Muslims. The Kissis speak a Mel language. Most Kissis are subsistence farmers or urban laborers. In Sierra Leone, they are coming under increasing Mendé* cultural influence.
REFERENCES: D. Elwood Dunn and Svend E. Holsoe. *Historical Dictionary of Liberia.* 1985; Cyril P. Foray. *Historical Dictionary of Sierra Leone.* 1977; Thomas O'Toole. *Historical Dictionary of Guinea.* 1987.

KITATA. The Kitatas are a subgroup of the Ovimbundu* peoples of Angola.

KITIMI. The Kitimi people, whom ethnolinguists classify with the Western Plateau group of the Benue-Congo language family, are a small ethnic group living in the Kauru District of the Saminaka Division of Kaduna State in Nigeria. Their population is under 5,000 people.
REFERENCE: *Language Survey of Nigeria.* 1976.

KITTA. *See* LOTSU-PIRI.

KITUBA. The term ''Kituba'' is used to refer to a Bakongo dialect of the Kongo* language that is used as a lingua franca in eastern Zaire and parts of the Central African Republic.

KITURIKA. The Kiturikas are a Tanzanian ethnic group whom some ethnologists classify in the Yao* cluster of peoples.

KIVU. The so-called Kivu peoples are a cluster of ethnic groups living today in Zaire. Included in the Kivu cluster are the Furus,* Havus,* Hundes,* Nyangas,* Rwandas,* Shis,* and Yiras.* There are more than three million Kivu people living in Zaire today.
REFERENCE: Donald G. Morrison et al. *Black Africa: A Comparative Handbook.* 1989.

KIWOLLO. *See* KIBALLO.

KIYAKA. The Kiyakas are an ethnic group living today in southwestern Zaire and northern Angola. They speak a Bantu* language and support themselves as subsistence farmers.
REFERENCE: Lukowa Kidima. ''Object Agreement and Topicality Hierarchies in Kiyaka.'' *Studies in African Linguistics* 18 (August 1987): 174–209.

KLOLI. *See* KROBOU.

KÕ. *See* KIPIRSI.

KOALIB. The Koalibs are one of the Nuba* peoples of Sudan.

KOBCHI. The Kobchis are one of the Bantu*-speaking peoples of Nigeria. They are classified as part of the Plateau cluster of peoples who occupy central Nigeria. Most Kobchis practice subsistence agriculture, raising ginger, millet, guinea corn, beans, and citrus products. They live in social systems characterized by patrilineal descent and patrifocal residence. In recent years, they have begun migrating to towns and cities looking for work.
REFERENCE: Donald G. Morrison et al. *Black Africa: A Comparative Handbook.* 1989.

KOBE. *See* BERI.

KODIA. *See* KOTROHOU.

KODOI. The Kodois (Kodoy) are a subgroup of the Maba* people of Chad. They are located in the hilly area of Abéché in Ouadai.

KODOY. *See* KODOI.

KOENOEM. The Koenoems, also known as Kanams,* speak a Chadic

language and are concentrated today in the Chip and South Sura districts of Pankshin Division of Plateau State in Nigeria.
REFERENCE: *Language Survey of Nigeria.* 1976.

KOFYAR. The Kofyars live in Plateau State, Nigeria—primarily in the Kofyar, Dimmukl, Shendam, and Namu districts of the Shendam Division. They are closely related to the Chips,* Mwahavuls,* Chokfiems (Chakfem-Musheres*) and Dokos.* They are divided into two subgroups—the Jortus and the Jaghnins. Like other savanna peoples in the region, they are subsistence farmers, raising millet, maize, guinea corn, beans, and livestock. Their village political systems are decentralized.
REFERENCES: John Ola Agi. ''The Goemai and Their Neighbors: An Historical Analysis.'' In Elizabeth Isichei, ed. *Studies in the History of Plateau State, Nigeria.* 1982; *Language Survey of Nigeria.* 1976.

KOHUMONO. The Kohumonos—also known historically as the Ekumurus, Bahumonos, and Edibas—are an ethnic group of approximately 45,000 people who live today in the Ediba District of the Obubra Division of Cross River State in Nigeria. Their language is classified as one of the Cross River languages of the Benue-Congo family.
REFERENCE: *Language Survey of Nigeria.* 1976.

KOKE. The Kokes are a subgroup of the Boua* people, who live along the middle Chari River in the Moyen-Chari Prefecture of Chad. Kokes can also be found in central Guéré Prefecture. The Kokes arrived in the Chari Valley long before the Saras* did. Most Kokes today are small farmers, raising millet, sorghum, and cotton. Their population is fewer than 5,000 people.
REFERENCE: Thomas Collelo et al. *Chad: A Country Study.* 1988.

KOKOFU. The Kokofus are one of the primary subdivisions of the Asante* people of Ghana.

KOKOLI. *See* LANDOMA.

KOKORDA. The Kokordas are a subgroup of the Daza* people of Chad. Most Kokordas live in the Borkou Subprefecture, where they are nomadic pastoralists raising goats, sheep, camels, and sometimes horses.
REFERENCE: Thomas Collelo et al. *Chad: A Country Study.* 1988.

KOLA. *See* KURI.

KOLE. *See* FONGORO.

KOLELA. *See* LELA.

KOLOBO. The Kolobos are one of the constituent groups of the Kim* confederation in Chad.

KOLOKUMA. The Kolokumas are a subgroup of the Izon* peoples of Rivers State in Nigeria.

KOLOLO. The Kololos (Bakololos) are a subgroup of the Fokeng Sothos,* some of whom can be found today in Botswana and Zambia. They are widely known in southern Africa for their reputations in the nineteenth century as cattle thieves. Today, most of them raise cattle of their own or work as migrant laborers.
REFERENCE: Fred Morton, A. Murray, and J. Ramsay. *Historical Dictionary of Botswana.* 1989.

KOLOP. The Kolops are one of the constituent groups of the Kim* confederation in Chad.

KOM. The Koms are today considered a subgroup of the Tikar* peoples of the Bamenda highlands of North West Province in Cameroon. They are classified as part of the Middle-Cameroon Bantu* group of peoples. The Koms originated farther to the north and were pushed into their present location by Fulbe* expansion. It is a savanna environment, with patches of woodland and gallery forest along water courses. The Koms are farmers and fishermen. Their villages stretch along roads and tracks. Traditional huts are rectangular and have palm-frond roofing. Today, cement houses and corrugated sheet roofs are common, especially in villages near the tarmacked main roads. Unlike most Tikar groups, the Koms are a matrilineal society.
REFERENCE: Mark W. DeLancey and H. M. Mokeba. *Historical Dictionary of the Republic of Cameroon.* 1990.

KOMA. The Koma people of Ethiopia, not to be confused with the Komas* of Zambia, are considered by ethnologists to be a Nilotic* group who are part of the Beni-Sciangul cluster. Most of them are nomadic pastoralists. They are subdivided into regional groups—northern, southern, and central. The Koma population today is approximately 10,000 people.
REFERENCE: M. L. Bender, J. D. Bowen, R. L. Cooper, and C. A. Ferguson, eds. *Language in Ethiopia.* 1976.

KOMA. The Komas are part of the larger cluster of Luyana* peoples of Zambia. The Luyanas are part of the Lozi* group.

KOMA. The Koma (Kuma) people, who should not be confused with the Komas* of either Ethiopia or Zambia, are a small ethnic group concentrated

today in the Koma Yomni District of the Ganye Division of Gongola State in Nigeria and across the border in Cameroon. They speak an Adamawa language.
REFERENCE: *Language Survey of Nigeria.* 1976.

KOMBA. *See* KONKOMBA.

KO-MENDE. The Ko-Mende are one of the three major subgroups of the Mendé.* They live in the forests of south-central Sierra Leone. *See* MENDÉ.

KOMO. The Komos are a Bantu*-speaking people living today in the Haut-Zaire region of northeastern Zaire. Although most Komos still make their living as farmers, raising cassava as a staple, they have become increasingly integrated into the regional commercial economy in recent decades. Large numbers of Komos have moved to the city of Kisangani in search of wage labor.
REFERENCE: Irving Kaplan et al. *Zaire: A Country Study.* 1978.

KOMONO. The Komonos are considered one of the stateless Molé-Dagbane* peoples of West Africa. They can be found in Ghana, Ivory Coast, and Burkina-Faso. Most Komonos are settled farmers, raising millet and a variety of other crops. They are classified as part of the larger cluster of Lobi* peoples.

KOÑAGI. The Koñagi (Coniagui) people are a small ethnic group living along both sides of the border between Guinea, Senegal, and Guinea-Bissau. Ethnologists consider them among the original inhabitants of the region. They are closely related to the Basari* people of Senegal. Ethnographers traditionally classify them as one of the Tenda* groups, which also includes the neighboring Badyaran,* Basari, Bedik,* and Boin* groups. As early as the seventeenth century, the Koñagis were widely scattered and sparsely settled throughout eastern Senegal, but they suffered from slaving expeditions and wars of conquest by the Mandinkas,* Fulbes,* and Tukulors.* Over the next several centuries, most Koñagis were assimilated or destroyed by those groups. Today, however, a remnant of the Koñagis still survives. They are concentrated in southeastern Senegal and across the border in northern Guinea. They are slash-and-burn cultivators who live in villages of from 100 to 500 people each. Their homeland is isolated and one of the least developed economically in the area—700 kilometers from Dakar and 250 kilometers from Tambacounda. Roads are poor and often impassable during the rainy season. Unlike surrounding peoples, the Koñagis are subsistence farmers; they do not raise peanuts to sell for cash. Increasingly large numbers of them, however, travel seasonally to towns and cities in search of wage work.
REFERENCES: Andrew F. Clark and Lucie Colvin Phillips. *Historical Dictionary of Senegal.* 1994; Monique de Lestrange. *Les Coniagui et les Bassari.* 1955; Riall W. Nolan. *Bassari Migrations: The Quiet Revolution.* 1986.

KONAMBEMBE. The Konambembes are a subgroup of the Sanga* peoples of southeastern Cameroon, northern Congo, southern Central African Republic, and northwestern Zaire. They interact closely with neighboring Pygmies,* who trade game for Konambembe agricultural products.
REFERENCE: Gordon S. McDonald et al. *Area Handbook for the People's Republic of the Congo (Congo Brazzaville).* 1971.

KONDA. The Konda people are a Zairean ethnic group who live north of Lake Ndombe in the western part of the country. Most Kondas are small farmers who also engage in seasonal labor in such cities and towns as Bikoro, Ingende, and Mbandaka.
REFERENCE: Irving Kaplan et al. *Zaire: A Country Study.* 1978.

KONGO. The Kongos (Bakongos, Bandibu, Congos, Bacongos, Koongos) are the largest ethnic group in Zaire. Substantial numbers of Kongos also live in southern Congo and northern Angola near the Atlantic coast. The Kongo language, part of the Bantu* family, is spoken in eastern Zaire, northern Angola, and parts of Congo and the Central African Republic. During the late European Middle Ages, the Kongo established a powerful kingdom in central Africa. The state of Kongo existed south of the Zaire River by 1300; by 1500, there were other Kongo states—Loango, Ngoyo, and Kakongo—north of the river. Each Kongo king was known as a *manicongo*. During the sixteenth century, Portuguese* missionaries reached the Kongo, and, in the 1530s, the *manicongo* Mbembe-a-Nzinga converted to Catholicism. The presence of the Portuguese empire, as well as the growing international slave trade, destabilized the Kongo states and sent them into decline. In the late nineteenth century, the Kimbanguism movement—a syncretic mix of Christian and animistic rituals—emerged and led the resistance to the Belgian* empire. The Kongos generally resisted both the Belgian and Portuguese empires and were finally brought under European control only in the early 1900s. In the twentieth century, the *Association des Bakongo* continued the resistance until Zaire achieved its independence. Other Kongo political organizations, like the Frente Naconal de Libertacão de Angola (FNLA), represented an anti-white, anti-Portuguese ethnonationalism in Angola that played a key role in that country's war of national liberation from 1961 to 1974.

Today, the Kongo population exceeds five million people. Most of them are farmers, raising cassava, bananas, palm oil, sweet potatoes, maize, coffee, and cocoa. Large numbers of Kongos also work in a variety of occupations in the towns and cities of the region. They are divided into a number of distinct subgroups, including the Solongos,* Muskikongos, Sossos, Yakas,* Woyos, Kongo Lalis, Kougnis, Sundis, Zombos, Ntandus, Vilis, Kambas, Dondos,* and Yombes.* Because of their long contact with European educational systems, the Kongos tend to be influential in professional, commercial, and administrative life.

REFERENCES: *African Encyclopedia.* 1974; John K. Thornton. *The Kingdom of Kongo: Civil War and Transition, 1641–1718.* 1983; Jacques Valdy. *Bakongo.* 1955.

KONGO-SUNDI. The Kongo-Sundis are a subgroup of the Kongo* people of Zaire and Angola.

KONGURAMA. *See* KURI.

KONHAQUE. The Konhaques (Conhaques) are a cluster of Senegambian* peoples who began arriving on the coast of what is today Guinea-Bissau in the fifteenth century. During the migration to the region, they acquired a number of Mandinka* cultural characteristics. Today, most Konhaques live in the hills of southeastern Guinea-Bissau and in the Madina Boé area.
REFERENCE: Richard Lobban and Joshua Forrest. *Historical Dictionary of the Republic of Guinea-Bissau.* 1988.

KONIANKE. The Koniankes live in West Africa, particularly in Sierra Leone, Liberia, and Guinea. They speak a Mandé language, trace their origins to the thirteenth-century Mali Empire, and believe they first arrived in Guinea and Sierra Leone around 1600. The Koniankes have earned a reputation as excellent soldiers. Most of them are small farmers who raise millet, rice, peanuts, and a variety of other crops. Most of them remain loyal to animist traditions, although perhaps a third are Muslims.
REFERENCES: Cyril P. Foray. *Historical Dictionary of Sierra Leone.* 1977; Donald G. Morrison et al. *Black Africa: A Comparative Handbook.* 1989; Donald R. Wright. "Manding-Speaking Peoples." In Richard V. Weeks, ed. *Muslim Peoples.* 1984.

KONIÉRÉ. Today, the Koniérés are considered to be a subgroup of the Maba* people of Sudan. Ethnologists, however, argue that their unique language and culture indicate that they were probably absorbed by the surrounding Maba peoples during the course of the last several centuries. The Koniérés live east of the town of Abéché.

KONKOMBA. The Konkombas (Komba) are one of the Sudanic peoples who live in northern Togo, northern Ghana, and Burkina-Faso. They are included in the Gurma* cluster of peoples. In Togo, they are particularly concentrated along the Oti River, north of the Basari* and in between the Bimoba* and Chokossi* peoples. They speak a dialect of the Gurma language. Estimates of the Konkomba population vary widely, from 70,000 to 250,000 people. The Konkomba social structure is characterized by powerful, parochial ethnic loyalties to clans; intraclan fissures into new clans are common, as are interclan rivalries and warfare. Unable to unite among themselves, they have been pawns in the ethnic struggles of the region. In the sixteenth century, the Dogambas* established their capital city, Yendi, on Konkomba land and drove the Konkombas out. In the late eighteenth century, the Chokossis, who were migrating out of Ivory Coast through Ghana and Burkina-Faso, displaced the Konkombas again. During the colonial period, the Konkombas staged violent uprisings against the French* and the Germans,* the most broadly based rebellions in 1897–1898, 1923, and 1935–1936. Most Konkombas today are small farmers. The Konkombas are mortal enemies with the Nanumbas, and hostilities between the two peoples resulted in hundreds of deaths in 1981.

REFERENCES: Samuel Decalo. *Historical Dictionary of Togo.* 1976; Daniel M. Mc-Farland. *Historical Dictionary of Ghana.* 1995; Mary Steele and Gretchen Weed. *Collected Field Reports on the Phonology of Konkomba.* 1966.

KONO. The Kono people of Sierra Leone, Ivory Coast, Guinea, and Liberia speak a language closely related to Manding.* Some ethnolinguists consider them a Fringe Manding group. Their own traditions claim that they were once a powerful people in Guinea and Mali—the same people as the Vai* (Gallinas). During their migration from the interior of Guinea toward the Atlantic coast, one group stopped and settled in 2,000 square miles of mountainous territory in what is today the Kono District in the Eastern Province of Sierra Leone. Smaller numbers of Konos can be found in Guinea and Liberia. The other group continued to the Atlantic Coast, settling in what is today far southern Sierra Leone and the adjacent coastal areas of Liberia. There they became known as the Vai or Gallinas. Until the establishment of British* colonial rule, the Konos experienced considerable violence at the hands of the Mendés.* They have a social system based on patrilineal descent. They are mostly subsistence farmers. They have been a very politically active group in Sierra Leone ever since 1955, when Tamba S. Mbriwa founded the Kono Progressive Movement to protest the alienation of Kono land to mining companies retrieving diamonds. The Kono population today exceeds 250,000 people.

REFERENCES: Cyril A. Foray. *Historical Dictionary of Sierra Leone.* 1977; Donald R. Wright. "Manding-Speaking Peoples." In Richard V. Weekes, ed. *Muslim Peoples.* 1984.

KONO. The Konos (Konu, Kwono) are a small ethnic group living today in the grassy savannas and volcanic hills of the southern region of the state of Kaduna in Nigeria and in the Karta region of Mali. They are surrounded by Hausas* and Kuramas.* They make their living in a mixed economy of subsistence agriculture and livestock raising. Their population is approximately 6,000 people.

REFERENCE: Elizabeth Isichei, ed. *Studies in the History of Plateau State, Nigeria.* 1982.

KONONGO. The Konongos (Kinongo) are an ethnic group living in Tanzania. More particularly, they are concentrated demographically east of Lake Tanganyika in the Rukwa and Tabora regions. They are related to the Kimbus*

and Yanzis.* Most Konongos are farmers. Their population today is approximately 50,000 people.
REFERENCE: Laura Kurtz. *Historical Dictionary of Tanzania.* 1978.

KONOSARALA. *See* SITI.

KONSO. The Konsos, with a population of approximately 75,000 people, live in the Gemu-Gofa region of Ethiopia. They speak a Cushitic language, closely related to Oromo,* and are divided into nine subgroups. The Amharas* conquered them late in the nineteenth century, and the two groups still carry powerful resentments toward one another. Amharas look down upon the Konsos as an inferior group. The Konsos are known for their skill in building terraced farms near their hillside homes. Most of them remain loyal to their indigenous religious faith, which revolves around the worship of a male sky god. The Konsos are known for their walled communities, which house approximately 1,500 people.
REFERENCES: C. R. Hallpike. *The Konso of Ethiopia.* 1972; Harold D. Nelson et al. *Ethiopia: A Country Study.* 1980; Chris Prouty and Eugene Rosenfeld. *Historical Dictionary of Ethiopia.* 1981.

KONTA. The Kontas are an Ethiopian ethnic group who speak an Omotic* language and live south of Jima in southern Ethiopia. They are hoe cultivators who raise ensete and a variety of other grains. They also practice animal husbandry. Most Kontas have remained loyal to their indigenous religion. Some ethnologists place them in close cultural association with the Kullos.* Together, the Konta-Kullo population is approximately 100,000 people.
REFERENCE: Harold D. Nelson et al. *Ethiopia: A Country Study.* 1980.

KONU. *See* KOMO.

KONYAKA. The Konyaka people of northwestern Ivory Coast trace their origins back to the great Mali Empire of the thirteenth century. Beginning in the sixteenth century, their ancestors migrated southwest and eventually arrived at their present location. The Konyakas speak a Manding* language, which some ethnolinguists identify as being Fringe Manding. Most of the Konyakas are subsistence farmers. There are also Konyakas living across the border in southern Mali and eastern Guinea.
REFERENCE: Donald R. Wright. "Manding-Speaking Peoples." In Richard V. Weekes, ed. *Muslim Peoples.* 1984.

KOONGO. *See* KONGO.

KORANKO. The Korankos (Kourankos, Kurankos) live in West Africa, particularly in Sierra Leone, Liberia, and Guinea. Their population in the early

1990s was estimated at 270,000 people, approximately one-third of whom are Muslims. They are a branch of the Mandinkas* who trace their origins back to the thirteenth-century Mali Empire and who first arrived in Guinea and Sierra Leone around 1600. They drove the Limbas* and Konos* out of the northern areas of what is today the Koinadugu District in Sierra Leone, but they then faced hostile attacks themselves from the Yalunkas.* The Korankos are subdivided into such powerful clans as the Sisi, Fula, Kuruma, Kagbo, Kwaite, Mara, Toli, Fona, and Dau. The Korankos have earned a reputation as excellent soldiers. Most Kurankos are small farmers who raise millet, rice, peanuts, and a variety of other crops. The Korankos today are concentrated in the southern reaches of Koinadugu District and the northern portion of the Onkolili District in the Northern Province of Sierra Leone. They can also be found in the Kissidougou region of Guinea. Most of them remain loyal to animist traditions.
REFERENCES: Cyril P. Foray. *Historical Dictionary of Sierra Leone.* 1977; Donald R. Wright. "Manding-Speaking Peoples." In Richard V. Weekes, ed. *Muslim Peoples.* 1984.

KOREKORE. The Korekore are a subgroup of the Shonas* of Zimbabwe and Mozambique. They constitute the "Northern Shona" cluster of peoples. The Korekore language is spoken south of the Zambezi River, from Lake Kariba in the west to the point where the Mazoe River exits Zimbabwe in the east. The Korekores are bordered on the south by the Zezurus.* Perhaps 15 percent of the Shonas in Zimbabwe speak a Korekore dialect. The main subgroups of the Korekore are the Tavaras, Budjgas, Shangwes, Nyungwes, Pfungwes, and Tandes. Most of them are farmers, raising cattle, millet, maize, pumpkins, and yams.
REFERENCE: R. Kent Rasmussen. *Historical Dictionary of Zimbabwe.* 1979.

KORING. *See* ORING.

KORO. The Koros are one of the Bantu*-speaking peoples of Nigeria. They are classified as part of the Plateau cluster of peoples who occupy central Nigeria, primarily in the Minna Division of Niger State, the Kwoi District of the Jema'a Division and the Kagoro District of the Kachia Division, in Kaduna State. Most Koros practice subsistence horticulture, raising ginger, millet, guinea corn, beans, and citrus products. They live in social systems characterized by patrilineal descent and patrifocal residence. In recent years, they have begun migrating to towns and cities looking for work.
REFERENCES: *Language Survey of Nigeria.* 1976; Donald G. Morrison et al. *Black Africa: A Comparative Handbook.* 1989.

KOROBAT. The Korobats are an ethnic group classified as part of the larger Hawawir cluster of Berber* peoples in Sudan.

KOROKORO. *See* POKOMO.

KOROM BOYE. *See* KULERE.

KOROP. The Korops, also identified as Durops and Ododops, live in the Akamkpa and Galabar divisions of Cross River State in Nigeria, as well as across the border in Cameroon. They speak a Cross River language in the Benue-Congo family.
REFERENCE: *Language Survey of Nigeria.* 1976.

KOROROFA. *See* JUKUN.

KOSA. The Kosas are one of the major subgroups of the Oromo* people of Ethiopia.

KOSANKE. The Kosankes are one of the Manding*-speaking peoples of Mali who trace their origins to the great Mali kingdom of the thirteenth century. Today, they are primarily a nomadic, pastoral people, herding cattle in their traditional homeland. Drought in recent years has badly damaged the Kosanke economy. West African demographers place their current population at approximately 80,000 people, of whom perhaps a third are Muslims.
REFERENCE: Donald R. Wright. "Manding-Speaking Peoples." In Richard V. Weekes, ed. *Muslim Peoples.* 1984.

KOSSA. *See* MENDÉ.

KOSSEDA. The Kossedas are one of the subgroups of the Teda* people of Chad. The Tedas are themselves a branch of the Tebu* people.

KOSSOP. The Kossops are one of the constituent groups of the Kim* confederation in Chad.

KOTA. *See* BAKOTA.

KOTE. The Kotes are a small ethnic group living today in Zaire. They tend to be concentrated in the northwestern region of Zaire, south of the Zaire River and south of the city of Basankusu. Most Kotes are small farmers and wage laborers.
REFERENCE: Irving Kaplan et al. *Zaire: A Country Study.* 1978.

KOTO. The Kotos (Bakota, Bandjambi, Ikota) are a cluster of ethnic groups living today in Gabon, primarily in the northeastern part of the country. They can also be found across the border in Cameroon. Their combined population today exceeds 125,000 people, and they are divided into the following

subgroups: Bakotas, Mahongwes, Shakes, Dambomos, Shamayes, Mindassas, Voumbous, and Mahouins.
REFERENCE: Donald G. Morrison et al. *Black Africa: A Comparative Handbook.* 1989.

KOTOKO. The Kotokos are an ethnic group of approximately 90,000 people. More than half of them live in Cameroon, with the remainder equally divided between Chad and Nigeria. They are subdivided into a number of clans, all of whom look to the legendary Sao as their common ancestor. They are closely related to the Budumas* of Lake Chad. In the fifteenth century, the Kotoko state reached across northern Nigeria and Cameroon. Ethnologists classify the Kotokos as a riverine townspeople because they are concentrated along the Logone River between Bongor and Kusseri, the Chari River south of Lake Chad, and the Makari, Mani, Kusseri, Logone-Birni, and Logone-Gana rivers. They live in fortified towns surrounded by high walls along those rivers. Their language is part of the Chadic group of the Nilo-Saharan family. For centuries, they were vassals to the Kanuris* of the Bornu Empire, who began converting them to Islam in the eighteenth century. Pre-Islamic beliefs in water and riverine spirits still survive, however. Traditionally, the Kotokos were fishermen, hunters, horticulturalists, and craftsmen, but, in recent years, they have begun working as merchants and commercial livestock raisers. Throughout the region, they have been known for their skill as fishermen who use large butterfly nets. Some of the wealthier Kotoko families also own cattle. The growing commercial economy is undermining traditional Kotoko kinship groups.
REFERENCES: Christian Bouquet. "Kotoko." In Richard V. Weekes, ed. *Muslim Peoples.* 1984; Harold M. Nelson et al. *Area Handbook for the United Republic of Cameroon.* 1974.

KOTOKO. The term "Kotoko," not to be confused with the Kotoko* peoples of Cameroon, Chad, and Nigeria, is used in Ivory Coast to refer to the Anyi* people.

KOTOKOLI. The Kotokolis (Cotocolis, Tems, Chauchos, Tembas, Timns) are a West African ethnic group. They are concentrated in Ghana and Togo and number approximately 350,000 people. More than 80 percent of the Kotokolis are Muslims. They originated as a confederation of Gurma* chiefdoms who settled near Sokodé in the seventeenth and eighteenth centuries. They probably came from the area of contemporary Burkina-Faso to the north. The conversion to Islam came from Chokossi* merchants in the nineteenth century. To rid himself of Muslim influences, Chief Uro Djobo acquiesced to a German* protectorate in 1880. In spite of that, the Islamic conversions continued. The Kotokoli speak the Tem language and are most properly known as the Temba.
REFERENCE: Donald G. Morrison et al. *Black Africa: A Comparative Handbook.* 1989.

KOTOKU AKYEM. The Kotoku Akyems are a subgroup of the Ak-

yems,* a major Akan* group of Ghana. They live in the Eastern Region of Ghana, near the Birim River, where they emerged from the Adansi* people. The chief Kotoku Akyem settlement in Ghana today is the city of Jedem. Although most Kotoku Akyems are small farmers, they enjoy occupational diversity, from blue-collar to professional jobs. Their population today exceeds 100,000 people.
REFERENCE: Daniel M. McFarland. *Historical Dictionary of Ghana.* 1995.

KOTOPO. The Kotopo people—also known as Potopos, Potopores, and Pataporis—live in the Toungo District of the Ganye Division of Gongola State in Nigeria, as well as across the border in western Cameroon. They speak an Adamawa language and make their living as small farmers.
REFERENCE: *Language Survey of Nigeria.* 1976.

KOTROHOU. The Kotrohou (Kodia) are one of the Kru* clusters of people in Ivory Coast. The Kotrohous are concentrated in the subprefectures of Guitry, Gresco, and Grand-Lahou. They were traditionally subsistence farmers, raising a variety of crops, but, under French* influence in the twentieth century, a substantial number of Kotrohous made the transition to commercial farming, particularly coffee and cocoa.
REFERENCE: Robert J. Mundt. *Historical Dictionary of Côte d'Ivoire.* 1995.

KOUAYA. *See* KWAYA.

KOUEN. *See* KWENI.

KOUENI. *See* KWENI.

KOUGNI. The Kougnis people are one of the subgroups of the Kongo* peoples of Congo, Zaire, and Angola. They are concentrated in southern Congo, northern Angola, and northwestern Zaire. The more than 40,000 Kougnis in Congo are concentrated in the regions of Dolisie and Loudima.

KOUKA. The Koukas are a subgroup of the Lisis,* a cluster of ethnic groups in Chad. Demographers place the Kouka population today at approximately 60,000 people, virtually all of whom are Muslims. They share judicial institutions and intermarry regularly with the Bulala* and Medogo* people. They are located mainly between Ati and Oum Hadjer in the Batha Prefecture. About 10,000 Koukas live on the east side of Lake Chad, where they intermingle with the Bulalas.
REFERENCE: Samuel Decalo. *Historical Dictionary of Chad.* 1987.

KOUMRA. *See* GULA.

KOURANKO. *See* KORANKO.

KOURI. The Kouri people speak a Chadic language, closely related to Buduma,* and live today on the southern shores of Lake Chad in Chad and across the border in Nigeria. They are devout Muslims who consider themselves direct descendants of Yemenese immigrants to the region. They work as farmers, herdsmen, and merchants. The Kouris are known for grazing their cattle on the islands of Lake Chad during the dry season but entrusting them to the care of Kanembu* herders during the rainy season.
REFERENCE: Thomas Collelo et al. *Chad: A Country Study.* 1988.

KOUROUMBA. *See* KURUMBA.

KOURTEY. The Kourtey are a subgroup of the Zermas,* themselves a subgroup of the Songhai* peoples of West Africa. They live on the banks of the Niger River and on islands between Niamey and Say in far western Niger. In recent years, they also have been migrating downstream along the Niger River into Benin. They emerged in a process of ethnogenesis as the result of the intermarriage of Dendis* and Fulbes.* They make their living as fishermen.

KOUSSASSI. *See* KUSASI.

KOUYA. The Kouyas are one of the Kru* clusters of people in Ivory Coast. They are concentrated in the subprefecture of Vavoua. They were traditionally subsistence farmers, raising a variety of crops, but, under French influence in the twentieth century, a substantial number of Kouyas made the transition to commercial farming, particularly coffee and cocoa.
REFERENCE: Robert J. Mundt. *Historical Dictionary of Côte d'Ivoire.* 1995.

KOUYOU. *See* KUYU.

KOUZIÉ. The Kouziés are one of the Kru* clusters of people in Ivory Coast. The Kouziés are concentrated in the subprefecture of Buyo. Most Kouziés are subsistence farmers.
REFERENCE: Robert J. Mundt. *Historical Dictionary of Côte d'Ivoire.* 1995.

KOVU. The Kovus are a subgroup of the Alladian* people of Ivory Coast.

KOYAM. The Koyams are a tiny, almost extinct ethnic group living near Illela in Niger. They originated in the Kanem region of Chad but were driven and devastated by Tebu* warriors, reducing them to only a small remnant of their former numbers. The few remaining Koyams farm and raise cattle. Some of them can also be found across the border in northeastern Nigeria.
REFERENCE: Samuel Decalo. *Historical Dictionary of Niger.* 1989.

KOYRA. The Koyras are a tiny ethnic group living today in southern Ethiopia. The Gidichosa are one of their subgroups. The Koyras speak an Omotic* language and work as subsistence farmers. Their current population is approximately 7,000 people.
REFERENCE: M. L. Bender, J. D. Bowen, R. L. Cooper, and C. A. Ferguson, eds. *Language in Ethiopia.* 1976.

KPA-MENDE. The Kpa-Mende are one of the three major subgroups of the Mendé.* They live in the coastal bush of south-central Sierra Leone.

KPAN. The Kpans—also identified during the past century as the Kpantens, Ikpans, Akpanzhis, Kpanzons, Abakans, Kpwates, Hwayes, Hwasos, Nyatsos, Nyonyos, Yordas, and Ibukwos—are a Nigerian ethnic group who speak a Jukunoid language in the Benue-Congo family. They are concentrated in the Lehen District of the Mambilla Division of Gongola State, as well as in the Likam, Gindin Dutse, Gayan, Suntai, Wukari, and Kato Bahga districts of the Wukari Division, also in Gongola State.
REFERENCE: *Language Survey of Nigeria.* 1976.

KPANTEN. *See* KPAN.

KPANZON. *See* KPAN.

KPATILI. *See* PATRI.

KPAY. The Kpays are a clan with the chiefdom of Mambahn, a subgroup of the Bassa* people of Liberia. Most Kpays live in the Marshall Territory of Liberia.

KPE. The Kpes are a subgroup of the Bakweri* peoples of Cameroon. They live in villages on the slopes and near Mt. Cameroon in South West Province. They arrived in the region as part of a Bantu* migration beginning in the early eighteenth century. Because of their location near the coast, the Kpes were among the first Cameroonians to come into contact with Europeans. The Kpe lost much of their land to German* plantation owners in the late nineteenth and early twentieth centuries. In recent years, such groups as the Bakweri Union and the Bakweri Land Claim Committee have tried to recover Kpe property. Today, most Kpes support themselves by working on the palm oil plantations, oil rigs, and refineries at Cape Limbo, as well as by fishing and rice farming.
REFERENCE: Mark W. DeLancey and H. M. Mokeba. *Historical Dictionary of the Republic of Cameroon.* 1990.

KPELLE. The Kpelle (Pele, Guerzé) are a Manding*-speaking people who today live in Liberia, Guinea, and Sierra Leone. In Liberia, they are concentrated in Bong County but can also be found in Gibi Territory, Bomi County, and Lofa County. They migrated to the region from Guinea beginning in the sixteenth century. They are closely related linguistically to the Mendés* of Sierra Leone. Today, the Kpelles constitute Liberia's largest ethnic group, with a rural population exceeding 270,000 people. In Guinea, they are known as the Guerzé (Nguerze, Ngere) and live mainly in the Nzérékoré administrative region. Their language is one of the Mande-fu cluster of the Manding group. Like other Manding people, they trace their history, through oral traditions, back to the thirteenth-century Mali Empire. They believe that, after the disintegration of the empire, they migrated southwest to Liberia. Most Kpelles are small farmers, raising rice, millet, and peanuts.
REFERENCES: David Dalby. "Distribution and Nomenclature of the Manding People and their Language." In Carlton T. Hodge. *Papers on the Manding.* 1971; William P. Murphy. "The Rhetorical Management of Dangerous Knowledge in Kpelle Brokerage." *American Ethnology* 8 (November 1981): 667–85; Thomas O'Toole. *Historical Dictionary of Guinea.* 1987.

KPEN. *See* GOUIN.

KPESHI. *See* KPESI.

KPESI. The Kpesis (Kpeshis) are one of the Guan* peoples of Ghana. Most Kpesis live along the coast of the Accra Plains in the Tema area.

KPLOH. The Kplohs are one of the Bassa* clans living in the River Cess Territory of Liberia.

KPOKPO. *See* AIZI.

KPONG. The Kpongs are one of the subgroups of the Adangbe* peoples of the Accra Plain and coastal inselbergs of southeastern Ghana. Most of them make their living as small farmers.

KPORWEIN. The Kporweins are one of the Bassa* clans living in the River Cess Territory of Liberia.

KPWATE. *See* KPAN.

KPWE. *See* BÉTÉ.

KRACHI. *See* KRAKYE.

KRAHN. *See* WEE and GUÉRÉ.

KRAKYE. The Krakyes, also known as the Krachis, are one of the Guan* peoples of Ghana. Most of them are small farmers and fishermen who live on the peninsula between the main Volta River and the Oti arm of Lake Volta. The primary Krakye settlement in Ghana is Kete-Krakye. Their population today exceeds 40,000 people.
REFERENCE: Daniel M. McFarland. *Historical Dictionary of Ghana.* 1985.

KRAN. The term ''Kran'' is frequently used to refer to the Wè-speaking people of Liberia. They used to be classified as Guéré.

KRAO. *See* KRU.

KRAU. *See* KRU.

KREDA. The Kredas are one of the subgroups of the Daza* people of Chad. Most Kredas live in the Bahr al Ghazal region of Chad.

KREICH. The Kreich were once an ethnic group who dominated much of the Ubangian Plateau of what is today the eastern Central African Republic. They can also be found across the border in the western Sudan. They speak a Nilo-Saharan language. Their own traditions place their origins in the Nile Basin before their migration to the Ubangian Plateau. Today, the surviving Kreich have adopted Banda* as their primary language and are rapidly assimilating into the Banda group.
REFERENCE: Pierre Kalck. *Historical Dictionary of the Central African Republic.* 1992.

KREISH. *See* KREICH.

KREPE. *See* KREPI.

KREPI. The Krepis (Krepe, Peki) are one of the Ewe* peoples of southeastern Ghana and southwestern Togo. They are concentrated in the Volta Region of Ghana between Ho and Asikuma. Their chief settlement is at Peki. The Krepis came under Danish control in the early 1800s, English control in 1850, German* control in the 1880s, and English control again in 1914. Most of them live as small farmers and fishermen.
REFERENCE: Daniel M. McFarland. *Historical Dictionary of Ghana.* 1995.

KRIM. The Krims are one of West Africa's smaller ethnic groups. They live in Sierra Leone and number no more than 15,000 people. They are closely related to the Sherbro* and call themselves the Kim. Many anthropologists consider them a subgroup of the Sherbro. The Krims occupy about 600 square miles of territory in the Pujehm and Bonthe districts, and they can also be found on twenty-five miles of coastline southeast of the Sherbro, where they form an ethnic buffer between the Sherbro and the Vais.* They are being assimilated rapidly by the Mendés.* About 40 percent of Krims are Muslims; the others are equally divided between Christians and animists. Most Krims are farmers and fishermen who speak a Bullom* dialect.

REFERENCE: Cyril P. Foray. *Historical Dictionary of Sierra Leone.* 1977.

KRIO. The term ''Krio'' is used in Sierra Leone to refer to a people of racially mixed origins. Most Krios live in the Freetown area. In 1787, a group of about 400 former slaves, who had been living in abject poverty in Great Britain, were resettled in Freetown. Five years later, another 1,000 freed slaves joined them. These former slaves had fought for the British* during the American Revolution and had been freed as a reward for their services. They tried to live for a while in Nova Scotia but could not adjust to the region. In 1800, another 500 people, mostly Maroons from Jamaica, moved to Freetown. These three groups became known as The Settlers and formed the core group of the Krios, or Creoles. Between 1807, when Great Britain prohibited the slave trade, and 1800, another 74,000 people who had been taken off illegal slave ships were settled in Free-town. For many years, the later arrivals mixed with The Settlers and became known as Krios. They were also joined by several thousand Yorubas* from Nigeria, who maintained a separate identity and were known as Akus.* The Krios are the most Westernized and highly educated people in Sierra Leone and tend to dominate political and economic life. Their current population exceeds 150,000 people.

REFERENCES: Margaret Binns and Tony Binns. *Sierra Leone.* 1992; Irving Kaplan et al. *Area Handbook for Sierra Leone.* 1976.

KROBO. *See* KROBOU.

KROBOU. The Krobous (Krobo, Kloli) are part of the Lagoon cluster of peoples of Ivory Coast and Ghana. Ethnologists consider them a subgroup of the Adangbes.* They are concentrated in the Department of Agboville in Ivory Coast and in Odumasi, Kpong, and Akuse in Ghana. Like the other peoples of the southeast coast and lagoons of Ivory Coast and Ghana, they practice cash-crop farming and engage in the production and trade of palm oil. Some Krobous still fish as well, to provide themselves with a protein source. They are part of a large Akan* culture group. The Krobou population in Ghana today exceeds 325,000 people.

REFERENCES: Robert J. Mundt. *Historical Dictionary of Cote d'Ivoire.* 1995; Louis Wilson. ''The Evolution of Krobo Society.'' Ph.D. dissertation. University of California, Los Angeles. 1980.

KRONG. The Krong people of Sudan have a population today of approximately 15,000 people.
REFERENCE: Gerrit J. Dimmendaal. "Krongo." *Journal of African Languages and Linguistics* 9 (October 1987): 161–77.

KROO. *See* KRU.

KROU. *See* KRU.

KRU. The term "Kru" refers to a language group found today in southwest Ivory Coast and southern Liberia. Some Krus are also living in Ghana. They tend to live on the Atlantic coast where they make their living as fishermen and subsistence farmers. Included in the Kru cluster are Krus* proper, Bétés,* Niabouas,* Niédébouas,* Kwayas,* Kouziés,* Didas,* Kotrohous,* Wobés,* Guérés,* Bakwés,* Ubis,* and Neyos.* Renowned for their seafaring abilities, the Krus today remain a coastal people or live near the docks of Freetown where they work on ships or as longshoremen.
REFERENCES: Robert J. Mundt. *Historical Dictionary of Côte d'Ivoire.* 1995; Elizabeth Tonkin. "Jealousy Names, Civilised Names: Anthroponomy of the Jlao Kru of Liberia." *Man* 15 (December 1980): 163–64.

KRU. The Kru (Krao, Crau, Nana, Krou, Krumen, Grebo, Wané) proper are an ethnic group of the Kru* language cluster in the coastal region of Sassandra Department of Ivory Coast and across the border in Liberia. Kru migrants can also be found in Sierra Leone. Scholars believe they arrived in the coastal region only 200 years ago. For several generations, Kru men served as sailors on European vessels plying the major trade routes between Europe and India. A number of these Kru seamen traveled widely around the world. In spite of that experience, the Kru were slow to adapt to commercial and social change. In 1915, Kru leaders in Liberia launched a bloody but unsuccessful rebellion against the American-supported government in Monrovia. Large numbers of Krus are Harrists—members of a religious group that preaches the Protestant doctrine of one William Harris, a missionary in Ivory Coast in the early twentieth century, along with traditional animist beliefs.
REFERENCE: Bohumil Holas. "Krou Popular Traditions in the Ivory Coast." In A. Bharati, ed. *The Realm of the Extra-Human: Ideas and Actions.* 1976; Suzanne Lafage. *Traditions Krou.* 1980.

KUA. The Kuas, including the Kua proper and the southern Kua, are subgroups of the Tshu-Kwe* peoples, themselves a subgroup of the San* people of Botswana.

KUALUTHI. The Kualuthis are a subgroup of the Ambos* of Namibia.

KUAMBI. The Kuambis are a subgroup of the Ambos* of Namibia.

KUANYAMA. The Kuanyamas are a subgroup of the Ambos* of Namibia. *See* KWANYAMA.

KUBA. The Kuba (Bakuba) are the dominant ethnic group in south-central Zaire. Included in the Bakuba group are the Leele* and Njembe* peoples. They are closely related to the Sakata* and Ngongo* peoples. All of them speak Bantu* languages. In the sixteenth century, the Kuba lived in the lower reaches of the Zaire River system, but they fled to the Kasai region, fleeing the cultural and political influence of the Portuguese* and the vicious attacks of the Yaka* people. By the mid-1600s, a powerful Kuba state that controlled the trade routes in central Africa had emerged. In rural areas, most Kuba are farmers, raising maize, millet, and cassava. In towns and cities, large numbers of Kuba work in a variety of occupations. They are also known for their tapestries and wood carvings. The Kuba have played a significant role in recent Zairean politics. For a short time in 1961, they established the state of South Kasai, which temporarily seceded from the country.
REFERENCES: *African Encyclopedia.* 1974; Jan Vansina. *The Children of Woot: A History of the Kuba People.* 1978.

KUBA. *See* KUBI.

KUBI. The Kubi people, also known locally as Kubas, are a small ethnic group living today in the Ganjuwa District of the Bauchi Division of Bauchi State in Nigeria. They speak a Chadic language.
REFERENCE: *Language Survey of Nigeria.* 1976.

KUBONYE. The Kubonyes are one of the clans of the Emakhandzambili,* who themselves are one of the three major subgroups of the Swazi* people of Swaziland.

KUBRI. *See* KANEMBU.

KUCHE. *See* RUKUBA.

KUDA-CHAMO. The Kuda-Chamos are a very small ethnic group living today in the Ningi District of the Bauchi Division of Bauchi State in Nigeria. Their language is classified with the Western Plateau group of Benue-Congo languages, but relatively few Kuda-Chamos still speak it.
REFERENCE: *Language Survey of Nigeria.* 1976.

KUDAWA. The Kudawas are part of a larger Hausa*-Fulbe* cluster of peoples living today in northwestern Nigeria. Some of them can also be found

across the border in Niger and in northern Benin. Islam dominates their religious beliefs, and most of them are small farmers and cattle herders. During the past fifty years, the Kudawas adopted Hausa as their primary language, largely abandoning their indigenous tongue. That trend accompanied the adoption of Islam.
REFERENCES: Donald G. Morrison et al. *Black Africa: A Comparative Handbook.* 1989; C. L Temple, ed. *Notes on the Tribes, Provinces, Emirates and States of the Northern Provinces of Nigeria.* 1967.

KUEK. The Kueks are a major subdivision of the Atuot* people of the southern Sudan.

KUENA. *See* KWENA.

KUGAMA. The Kugama people, also known as the Wegams, are a small ethnic group concentrated largely in the Wafanga District of the Adamawa Division of Gongola State in Nigeria. Their language is part of the Yandang* group of Adamawa languages.
REFERENCE: *Language Survey of Nigeria.* 1976.

KUGBO. The Kugbo people are an ethnic group concentrated today in the Abua-Odual, Ogbia, and Brass divisions of Rivers State in Nigeria. Most of them are subsistence farmers. Their language is classified in the Cross River group of the Benue-Congo family.
REFERENCE: *Language Survey of Nigeria.* 1976.

KUGULO. *See* DUMPO.

KUJAMAAT. The Kujamaat, also known historically as the Fogny, are a subgroup of the Jolas*—the northernmost Jola group. The vast majority of them live on the southern coast of Senegal along the Casamance River. They usually live in villages of under 1,000 people. Late in the nineteenth century, the Kujamaat region was invaded by Manding* warriors intent on converting the Kujamaat to Islam, but the invasion was aborted by the arrival of the French.* The Manding missionary effort then assumed more peaceful forms and was successful, converting most Kujamaat to Islam. With the arrival of the French, the Kujamaat began making the adjustment to larger forms of political organization and a commercial economy, especially peanut farming. Today the Kujamaat number approximately 220,000 people.
REFERENCE: Judith T. Irvine and David Sapir. "Musical Style and Social Change Among the Kujamaat Diola." *Journal of Ethnomusicology* 20 (January 1986): 67–86.

KUKA. The Kukas are one of the subgroups of the Lisis* of Chad. They are a Nilotic* people who today make a living as nomadic and semi-nomadic pastoralists, although many are also farming.

KUKELE. The Kukeles, also known to historians as the Bakeles and Ukeles, are an ethnic group of approximately 125,000 people living in Nigeria and Cameroon. In Nigeria, they can be found in the Ogoja Division of Cross River State and the Ishielu Division of Anambra State. Large numbers of Kukeles are Christians.
REFERENCE: *Language Survey of Nigeria.* 1976.

KUKU. The Kukus are an ethnic group living today in northeastern Zaire and southern Sudan, as well as in western Uganda. They speak an eastern Sudanic language, although they are of Nilotic* origin. The Kukus are primarily subsistence farmers who live in a very remote, isolated part of the country. They are closely related to the Kakwas,* Mandaris,* and Baris.* Most Kukus live in the highland areas where raising cattle is difficult, so they are small farmers instead.
REFERENCES: F. Scott Bobb. *Historical Dictionary of Zaire.* 1988; Helen C. Metz et al. *Sudan: A Country Study.* 1992.

KUKURUKU. The Kukuruku people live in Bendel State in Nigeria. They are closely related to the neighboring Edo* people. Both groups make their living raising yams, cassava, and palm oil products, as well as by fishing. In recent years, the Kukurukus have increasingly mixed with the Edo, Ijaw,* and Itsekiri* peoples of the region, but they still maintain a distinct sense of identity. They can be found especially between the towns of Auchi and Irrua. The term "Kukuruku" is considered pejorative by many people today, who prefer the use of the term "northern Edo people."
REFERENCES: *African Encyclopedia.* 1974; Robert De la Burde. "Ancestral Ram's Heads of the Edo-Speaking Peoples." *African Arts* 6 (Autumn 1972): 29–34; Donald G. Morrison et al. *Black Africa: A Comparative Handbook.* 1989; A. Oyewelo. *Historical Dictionary of Nigeria.* 1987.

KUKWE. The Kukwes are a Tanzanian ethnic group whom some ethnologists include in the Nyakyusa* cluster of peoples.

KULAMO. *See* KULANGO.

KULANGO. The Kulango—also known as the Koulango, Kulamo, Lorhon, Nkoramfo, Ngwela, and Babé—are a Voltaic people living in northeastern Ivory Coast in the departments of Bouna and Bondoukou and in far southwestern Burkina-Faso. They are closely related to the nearby Lobi* people and have a population today of approximately 65,000. The Kulango migrated to the Ivory Coast and Burkina-Faso from points east several centuries ago. They came under the domination of the Abron* in the seventeenth century and remained under their suzerainty until the rise of the French* empire in the late 1800s.

In spite of vigorous attempts by Jula merchants-missionaries, the Kulango have resisted converting to Islam.

REFERENCES: Robert E. Handloff et al. *Côte d'Ivoire: A Country Study.* 1990; Robert J. Mundt. *Historical Dictionary of Côte d'Ivoire.* 1995.

KULERE. The Kulere people, also known historically as the Korom Boyes and Tofs, live in Nigeria, particularly in the Kamwai, Richa, and Tof districts of the Pankshin Division of Plateau State. Many people consider them to be a subgroup of the Rons.*

REFERENCE: *Language Survey of Nigeria.* 1976.

KULLO. The Kullos are an Ethiopian ethnic group who speak an Omotic* language and live between the Konsos* and Welamos* in southern Ethiopia. They are hoe cultivators who raise ensete and a variety of other grains. They also practice animal husbandry. Most Kullos have remained loyal to their indigenous religion.

REFERENCE: Harold D. Nelson et al. *Ethiopia: A Country Study.* 1980.

KULTU. *See* MABA.

KULUNG. The Kulungs (Bakulungs, Bamburs, Wurkums) are a Nigerian people who speak a Jarawan Bantu* language of the Benue-Congo family. The Kulungs can be found concentrated near Gada Mayo in the Kinda Kuvyo District of the Wukari Division of Gongola State, as well as in the Lau and Wurkum districts of the Muri Division of Gongola State. Most Kulungs are subsistence farmers.

REFERENCE: *Language Survey of Nigeria.* 1976.

KULYA. *See* KURIA.

KUMA. *See* KOMA.

KUMAILAB. The Kumailab are a small, surviving subgroup of the larger group of Beja* peoples in Sudan. They were originally not part of the Beja group, but, in the nineteenth and twentieth centuries, they gradually fell within a Beja cultural orbit. They live on the Red Sea coastal plain south of Port Sudan.

KUMAM. *See* KUMAN.

KUMAN. The Kumans (Kumam) are an ethnic group living today in Uganda. They speak a Western Nilotic* language and are concentrated in the north-central region of the country, north of Lake Kyoga and northeast of Lake

Albert. Most Kumans are small farmers. Ethnologists include them in the Luo*
cluster of peoples.

KUMASE. *See* KUMASI.

KUMASI. The Kumasis (Kumases) are one of the primary subdivisions of the
Asante* people of Ghana.

KUMBA. The Kumbas, also known as the Sates and Yofos, are a Nigerian
ethnic group living today in the Mayo Belwa District of the Adamawa Division
of Gongola State in Nigeria. Their language is classified with the Yandang*
cluster of Adamawa languages.
REFERENCE: *Language Survey of Nigeria.* 1976.

KUMBO MEIN. The Kumbo Meins are a subgroup of the Izon* peoples of
Rivers State in Nigeria.

KUMRA. The Kumras are a subgroup of the Sara* people of Chad. Like other
Sara peoples, many of them, in spite of powerful proseletyizing efforts by Muslim and Christian missionaries, remain loyal to their animist traditions.

KUNAMA. The Kunama (Kunema) are an ethnic group living in Sudan and in
the Barentu region of Eritrea near the Sudanese border. They speak a Nilotic*
language, follow a matrilineal descent system, and make their living as pastoralists, raising cattle. About 30 percent of the Kunama are Roman Catholics and
Protestants, primarily because of European missionaries who came to the area
in the late 1930s. Their contemporary population exceeds 60,000 people. Included among the Kunama is a small subgroup, the Ilits.
REFERENCES: *African Encyclopedia.* 1974; Chris Prouty and Eugene Rosenfeld.
Historical Dictionary of Ethiopia and Eritrea. 1994.

KUNDA. *See* KAONDE.

KUNDA. The Kundas, not to be confused with the Kaondes,* are a small ethnic
group living in southeastern Zambia. Their current population is approximately
125,000 people. They have their origins in the Congo and became part of the
Bemba* migration to Zambia. The Kundas also have strong cultural connections
with the Bisas* and the Ushis. They have a matrilineal descent system and speak
a Nyanja* language.
REFERENCES: John J. Grotpeter. *Historical Dictionary of Zambia.* 1979; Sirarpi Ohannessian and Mubanga E. Kashoki. *Language in Zambia.* 1978.

KUNDU. The Kundus are an ethnic group who live near the Kondas*

north of Lake Ndombe in western Zaire. The Kundus can be found in and around the cities of Bikoro, Ingende, and Mbandaka. They are farmers and wage workers.
REFERENCE: Irving Kaplan et al. *Zaire: A Country Study.* 1978.

KUNEMA. *See* KUNAMA.

KUNFEL. The Kunfels are an ethnic group living today in Ethiopia. They speak a Central Cushitic language and are closely related to the Agaw* peoples. The Kunfels are concentrated west of Lake Tana near the Sudanese border in western Ethiopia. The Kunfel population today exceeds 3,000 people, most of whom are small farmers and cattle raisers who remain loyal to their traditional religious beliefs. Some Kunfels are loyal to the Ethiopian Orthodox Church, a Christian organization.
REFERENCE: Harold D. Nelson et al. *Ethiopia: A Country Study.* 1980.

KUNG. The Kung (Zhu, Xhu) people are an African ethnic group concentrated in western Botswana. Within the last twenty to thirty years, the Kung San* of the Kalahari Desert have found themselves in the midst of a transition from a nomadic hunting-and-gathering culture to a settled farming and stock-raising society. Some of the Kung are farther along the path to economic modernization than others. Those in the Kalahari region have gone through much of the transition, while the Kung along the Namibia-South Africa border remain in a hunting-gathering economic mode.
REFERENCE: Patricia Draper and Elizabeth Cashdan. ''Technological Change and Child Behavior among the !Kung.'' *Ethnohistory* 27 (1988): 339–66.

KUNIKE. The Kunikes are a prominent subgroup of the Temne* people of Sierra Leone.

KUPSABINY. The Kupsabiny people are one of the more than thirty ethnic groups of Uganda. They speak an Eastern Nilotic* language and live in northern Uganda. Their economy revolves around transhumant pastoralism, with the men raising cattle and the women trying to raise sorghum and millet. Of all of Uganda's ethnic groups, the Kupsabiny are among the least developed and the least acculturated to Western technologies. Their entire life—economy, religion, and culture—revolves around cattle. Because of severe droughts in northeastern Africa during the 1980s and early 1990s, the Kupsabiny have faced dire economic circumstances.
REFERENCES: Peter Ladefoged, Ruth Glick, and Clive Criper. *Languages in Uganda.* 1972.

KUPTO. The Kuptos people live in the Nafada District of the Gombe

Division of Bauchi State in Nigeria. They speak a Chadic language and make their living raising subsistence crops and livestock.
REFERENCE: *Language Survey of Nigeria.* 1976.

KURA. *See* KURI.

KURAMA. The Kuramas—also known historically as the Tikurimis, Bagwa-mas, Ruramas, and Akurumis—are a small ethnic group living today in the grassy savannas and volcanic hills of the southern region of the state of Kaduna in Nigeria and in the Karta region of Mali. They are surrounded by the Konos* and Kiballos* to the west, the Katabs* and Chawas to the south, and the Amos* and Rukubas* to the east. The Kuramas migrated to their present location in the Jere District early in the twentieth century, coming from the Zaria area. They make their living in a mixed economy of subsistence agriculture and livestock raising. Their lifestyle closely resembles that of the neighboring Hausas.* Until recently, the Kuramas married endogamously or to Azuras.* They have a population of approximately 9,000 people.
REFERENCES: Harold D. Gunn. *The Peoples of the Plateau Area of Nigeria.* 1953; Elizabeth Isichei, ed. *Studies in the History of Plateau State, Nigeria.* 1982.

KURANKO. *See* KORANKO.

KURFEI. *See* KURFEY.

KURFEY. The Kurfeys (Kurfei, Soudié) are a subgroup of the Hausa* people in Niger. They established villages north of Tahoua along major fault lines, where they could easily defend themselves from attackers. Most Kurfeys raise cattle and farm.
REFERENCE: Samuel Decalo. *Historical Dictionary of Niger.* 1989.

KURI. The Kuri are a small ethnic group of approximately 14,000 people who live on islands and peninsulas in the eastern reaches of Lake Chad, all within the country of Chad. Their roots are similar to those of the Kanembus,* although the Kuri today speak a language called Yedina, which is a Buduma* dialect. The Kuri are divided into five subgroups—Kalia, Kura, Medis, Ngadji, and Yakudi. Those primary subgroups are further divided into a series of clans: the Bodalla, Kola, Yerima, Tcharigiria, Marcudia, Baraya, Karia, Killakada, Gallao, Mullumtchilloum, and Wadjirima. There are five Kura clans: Dagila, Tojima, Doria, Maradalla, and Kallameida. The two Medis clans are the Fetra and Dalla. There are five Ngadji clans: Issia, Batuma, Bellerama, Tchukulia, and Kongur-ama. Finally, the four Yakudi clans are the Mallumia, Kallamia, Kanoa, and Kwallia. The Kuri are Sunni Muslims.

The Kuri are known as an economically adaptable people. They fish, manage gardens, and raise a renowned cattle breed known as ''Kuri cattle.'' After the

rise in the water level of Lake Chad in 1956, they learned how to manufacture polders to make their lands more fertile for farming. Because of their small population, the loss of their original language, and the fact that they are surrounded by the vastly more numerous Budumas, the Kuri are likely to disappear as a self-conscious ethnic group in the next several decades.
REFERENCE: Christian Bouquet. "Kuri." In Richard V. Weekes, ed. *Muslim Peoples.* 1984.

KURIA. The Kuria (Kuriya) people, also known as the Kulya or Tende, live in northwest Tanzania and in the South Nyanza District of western Kenya. They claim to have originated in the Elgon Region of Eastern Uganda and migrated to Kenya and Tanzania between 1500 and 1900. They are concentrated on the east side of Lake Victoria in the North Mara District of the Mara Region. Most Kurias are farmers who specialize in the production of millet, maize, bananas, and tobacco; they also raise cattle. Kurias play a very prominent role in Tanzanian police forces as well. The Kuria population in Kenya today exceeds 100,000 people.
REFERENCES: Laura Kurtz. *Historical Dictionary of Tanzania.* 1978; Bethwell A. Ogot. *Historical Dictionary of Kenya.* 1981.

KURIYA. *See* KURIA.

KURTEY. The Kurteys are an ethnic group in Niger and Mali who represent a fusion of Songhais,* Zermas,* and Fulbes.* Fulbes first arrived in what is today Niger around 1750 under the leadership of Chief Maliki. By 1820, they had settled on the river on islands near Tillabéry and Niamey. There they mixed with the Sorkos and Kados, adopted the local culture and languages, and evolved into a distinct group. They dominated the Niger River region before the arrival of the French.* Today, they raise river rice, millet, tobacco, and cattle. They are also skilled fishermen. Large numbers of Kurteys today are seasonal laborers who spend long stretches of time working in Ghana.
REFERENCE: Samuel Decalo. *Historical Dictionary of Niger.* 1989.

KURUMBA. The Kurumba (Akurumba, Kouroumba) are one of the autochthonous peoples of Burkina-Faso. They are part of the larger Ninisi* cluster of peoples in the central part of the country. Several centuries ago, the Kurumba enjoyed their own political kingdom, which went by the name of Louroum, but it declined under attack from the expanding Mossis.* Today, they are primarily small farmers, living in the Liptako, Djilgodji, and Yatenga areas.
REFERENCE: Daniel M. McFarland. *Historical Dictionary of Upper Volta.* 1978.

KUSAE. *See* KUSASI.

KUSAI. *See* KUSASI.

KUSASE. *See* KUSASI.

KUSASI. The Kusasi (Koussassis, Kusae, Kusai, Kusase) speak one of the Molé-Dagbane* languages and live in the northeast corner of Ghana and in Burkina-Faso. They live along the White Volta River near the town of Gambaga. Most of them are settled farmers, whose population is approaching 270,000 people; they raise sorghum and millet. Until 1957, they lived under the administration of what was known as the Northern Territories in the British Gold Coast colony.
REFERENCE: Daniel M. McFarland. *Historical Dictionary of Ghana.* 1995.

KUSHE. *See* BAUSHI.

KUSHI. *See* BAUSHI.

KUSU. The Kusus are a Bantu*-speaking people who live today along the Lomami River in the western Kivu Region of Zaire. They are concentrated between Kimombo and Lubao. Some ethnologists classify them as part of the Mongo* cluster of Zairean peoples. Once the same people as the Tetelas,* the Kusus came under the influence of Arab* traders while the Tetelas resisted Arab cultural domination. Today, most Kusus wear Arab dress, speak Swahili,* and pledge allegiance to Islam. Belgian* authorities in the early twentieth century placed the Kusus in Kivu Province and the Tetelas in Lasai Province.
REFERENCE: F. Scott Bobb. *Historical Dictionary of Zaire.* 1988.

KUTED. The Kuted people, also known over the years as the Kutevs, Kuteps, Mbarikes, and the pejorative Zumpers (Jompres), live in the Likam and Ayikiben districts of the Wukari Division of Gongola State in Nigeria. Their language is classified as one of the Jukunoid group in the Benue-Congo family.
REFERENCE: *Language Survey of Nigeria.* 1976.

KUTEP. *See* KUTED.

KUTEV. *See* KUTED.

KUTIN. The Kutins are a tiny ethnic group living today in the Binyari District of the Adamawa Division of Gongola State in Nigeria. They speak a language that is classified with the Adamawa languages.
REFERENCE: *Language Survey of Nigeria.* 1976.

KUTU. The Kutu are one of the individual groups in the Zaramo* cluster of the Northeast Bantu*-speaking people of East Africa. They live in the coastal lowlands of Tanzania where most of them work as hoe farmers, producing maize, sorghum, and rice, and raising sheep, goats, and poultry. During the nineteenth century, the Kutu were victimized by the East African slave trade; in response, they built fortified villages protected by stockades. In the twentieth century, those settlement patterns gave way to a homestead system in which rural Kutu scattered out more widely. They live in mud-and-wattle homes characterized by high, thatched, cone-shaped roofs; those thatched roofs are giving way today to tin roofs. The vast majority of the Kutu are Muslims, although they are considered to be only marginally loyal, confining their religious observances to fasting at Ramadan, taking on Arab names, and wearing the white skull cap. Still, several Kutu villages have schools where children study the Koran. The Kutu population is approximately 35,000 people today.

Since the mid-1970s, the Kutu have been dramatically affected by the Tanzanian government's *ujamaa* policy, which is designed to gather rural people from their scattered homestead settlements into more concentrated villages, so that public education and public health campaigns can be more effective. Rates of malaria and schistosomiasis are high among the Kutu, and only improved public health programs can alleviate the crisis. The Kutu people have also been affected in recent years by the East African drought of the late 1980s and early 1990s and by the threat of the human immunodeficiency virus (HIV) and the disease of AIDS.

REFERENCES: L. W. Swantz. *Ritual and Symbol in Transitional Zaramo Society.* 1970.

KUTUMBAWA. The Kutumbawas are a relatively small ethnic group living today in northwestern Nigeria, primarily in Plateau State. They are part of the larger Abakwariga* cluster of Hausa*-speaking peoples, which also includes the Gwandaris* and the Maguzawas.* Most Kutumbawas are subsistence farmers.
REFERENCES: A. Chukwudi Unomah. "The Gwandara Settlements of Lafia to 1900." In Elizabeth Isichei, ed. *Studies in the History of Plateau State, Nigeria.* 1982.

KUTURMI. The Kuturmis (Adas) are part of a larger Hausa*-Fulbe* cluster of peoples living today in northwestern Nigeria, primarily in the Kachia District of the Kachia Division of Kaduna State, where their population exceeds 12,000 people. Some of them can also be found across the border in Niger and in northern Benin. Islam dominates their religious beliefs, and most of them are small farmers and cattle herders.
REFERENCES: *Language Survey of Nigeria.* 1976; Donald G. Morrison et al. *Black Africa: A Comparative Handbook.* 1989.

KUWAA. The Kuwaas, sometimes known as the Belles, are a Kruan-speaking people of Liberia. Most of them live in Lofa County, on the edge of the national forest, and work as subsistence farmers and laborers. They are subdivided into two prominent clans—the Battis and the Lobaizus. Their contemporary population is approximately 10,000 people.

KWALLA									319

REFERENCES: D. Elwood Dunn and Svend H. Holsoe. *Historical Dictionary of Liberia.* 1985; Harold D. Nelson et al. *Liberia: A Country Study.* 1984.

KUYU. The Kuyus (Kouyous) are a subgroup of the Mbochi* people of eastern Gabon, central Congo, and western Zaire. They are especially concentrated in the Congolese Basin of northern Congo, a region criss-crossed by countless rivers. They spend time in the dense forests as well as the steppes in the area. Their contemporary population exceeds 40,000 people. Although they are increasingly turning to commercial agriculture, the Kuyu economy has traditionally revolved around trading and fishing, at which they are highly adept. Their social structure is based on a patrilineal clan structure. The Kuyus have played significant roles in Congolese politics in recent years, because of the control they exercise in the armed forces of the country.
REFERENCES: Anne-Marie Bénézeck. ''So-Called Kuyu Carvings.'' *African Arts* 22 (November 1988): 52–59; Gordon C. MacDonald et al. *Area Handbook for the People's Republic of the Congo (Congo Brazzaville).* 1971.

KUZAMANI. The Kuzamanis (Rishuwas) are one of the Western Plateau peoples of central Nigeria. They can be found today living in the Kaduna State. The Kuzamani population is approximately 3,000 people.
REFERENCES: *Language Survey of Nigeria.* 1976.

KWA. The term ''Kwa'' is used to describe a cluster of West African languages, including Akan,* Guan,* Ewe,* Ga,* and Adangbe.*
REFERENCES: Daniel M. McFarland. *Historical Dictionary of Ghana.* 1995.

KWA. The Kwa people of Nigeria live primarily in the Bachama District of the Numan Division of Gongola State.
REFERENCES: *Language Survey of Nigeria.* 1976.

KWABZAK. *See* TAL.

KWAHU. The Kwahu (Akwahu, Kwawu, Quahoe) are one of the major ethnic subdivisions of the Akan* people. They are concentrated at the junction between the Eastern Region, the Brong-Ahafo Region, and the Asante* Region of eastern Ghana. The Kwahu population in Ghana today is approximately 275,000 people.

KWAL. *See* IRIGWE.

KWALLA. The Kwallas are an ethnic group living today in Plateau State, Nigeria. Their ancestors were Dimmuk* peoples who then mixed with a variety of other ethnic groups. Most Kwallas are subsistence farmers. They are

surrounded demographically by the Gomeis,* Mirriams,* Dimmuks, and Kofyars.*
REFERENCES: John Ola Agi. "The Goemai and Their Neighbors: An Historical Analysis." In Elizabeth Isichei, ed. *Studies in the History of Plateau State, Nigeria.* 1982.

KWALLIA. *See* KURI.

KWAMI. The Kwamis (Kwoms) are a Nigerian ethnic group whose language
is classified as part of the Bole-Tangale* group of Chadic languages. Most
Kwamis live in the Kwami District of the Gombe Division of Bauchi State,
where they farm and raise livestock.
REFERENCES: *Language Survey of Nigeria.* 1976.

KWAN. *See* IRIGWE.

KWANDI. The Kwandis are part of the larger cluster of Luyana* peoples of
Zambia. The Luyanas are part of the Lozi* group. The number of Kwandis in
Zambia today exceeds 20,000 people.

KWANGA. The Kwangas (Kwangwas, Makwangas) are a group of approximately 100,000 people who live today in southwestern Zambia. They speak a
Luyana* language and are closely related to the Lozis.* Today, the Kwangas
are concentrated in the heavy forests of the Mongu-Lealui District where they
farm and fish near the many lakes dotting the region.
REFERENCES: John J. Grotpeter. *Historical Dictionary of Zambia.* 1979.

KWANGALI. *See* KWANGARI.

KWANGARI. The Kwangaris are a subgroup of the Kavanga* people of Namibia.

KWANKA. The Kwankas are an ethnic group living today northeast of the Jos
Plateau in Plateau State in northwestern Nigeria, primarily in the Lere District
of the Bauchi Division of Bauchi State and in the Kaduna and Pankshin districts
of the Pankshin Division of Plateau State. They are surrounded ethnically by
the Sayas,* Ngas,* and Fyams.* Most Kwankas are subsistence farmers.
REFERENCES: Elizabeth Isichei, ed. *Studies in the History of Plateau State, Nigeria.*
1982; *Language Survey of Nigeria.* 1976.

KWANKUA. The Kwankuas are part of the larger cluster of Nyaneka-Humbe*
peoples of southwestern Angola.

KWANYAMA. The Kwanyamas are one of the Ambo* peoples of Angola.
They are the southernmost of the Ambos. During the late eighteenth and early

nineteenth centuries, the Kwanyama Kingdom was powerful in what is known as the Namibe hinterland, and the Kwanyamas fiercely resisted the expansion of Portuguese* imperial authority. They were not conquered until 1915. Traditionally, the Kwanyamas were pastoralists and hunters on the flood plain of the Kuvelai River. Many of them still raise cattle for a living, although increasing numbers are also farming and searching for work in towns and cities.
REFERENCES: Susan H. Broadhead. *Historical Dictionary of Angola.* 1992.

KWARA. The Kwara people are a subgroup of the Agaw* people of central and northern Ethiopia. Most of them are farmers today, raising millet, coffee, and castor oil plants.

KWARRA. *See* MAMA.

KWATAMA. The Kwatamas are part of a larger Hausa*-Fulbe* cluster of peoples living today in northwestern Nigeria. Some of them can also be found across the border in Niger and in northern Benin. Islam dominates their religious beliefs, and most of them are small farmers and cattle herders.
REFERENCES: Donald G. Morrison et al. *Black Africa: A Comparative Handbook.* 1989.

KWAVI. *See* BARAGUYU.

KWAWU. *See* KWAHU.

KWAYA. The Kwaya, not to be confused with the Kwaya* people of Tanzania, are one of the Kru* peoples of the Ivory Coast. They are a small group, numbering perhaps 15,000 people, and they live in the south-central region of Ivory Coast, especially in the Vavoua area. Most of them are small farmers and workers.

KWAYA. The Kwayas are an ethnic group living today in Tanzania. Some ethnologists include them as part of the Jiji* group of people. Others see them as an independent people. The Kwaya population today is approximately 90,000 people.

KWE. *See* DIDA.

KWENA. The Kwena (Bakwena, Kuena, Bakuena) are a subgroup (more exactly, a chiefdom) of the Tswana* people of Botswana, Lesotho, and South Africa. They are considered the royal clan of Lesotho, and are known as the "people of the crocodile." The Ngwatos,* Ngwaketses,* and Twananas all recognize their Kwena ethnic roots. The Kwena have existed as a series of identifiable ethnic groups for several centuries, but it was not until the leadership of Sechele I in the nineteenth century that they coalesced into a more unified cluster. Their power declined after 1870, primarily because of the increasing power of the Ngwatos and Kgatlas.* They were unable to resist British* expansion in the 1880s and 1890s. During the 1890s, they became subject to the Hut Tax, fell victim to epidemic diseases, and became a nation of migrant laborers. The Kwena economy remains largely underdeveloped today.

REFERENCES: Gordon Haliburton. *Historical Dictionary of Lesotho.* 1977; Fred Morton, A. Murray, and J. Ramsay. *Historical Dictionary of Botswana.* 1989.

KWENI. The Kweni (Koueni), also known as the Guro (Gouro), Lo, Dipa, and Kouen, are a Manding*-speaking people who today live in Ivory Coast, primarily in the west-central region of the country in Bouaflé and Zuénoula departments. The Kweni are bordered by the Bétés* to the west and the Baules* to the east. Their language is one of the Mande-fu cluster of the Manding group. They should not be confused with the Lo* people of Nigeria. They are a patrilineal people. The Kweni population today exceeds 220,000 people. Like other Manding peoples, they trace their history, through oral traditions, back to the thirteenth-century Mali Empire. They believe that, after the disintegration of the empire, they migrated southwest to Ivory Coast, probably escaping Mandinka* expansion. Most Kweni are small farmers, raising rice, millet, and peanuts. The Kweni farmers living in southern Ivory Coast also raise palm oil plants and kola trees.

REFERENCES: David Dalby. "Distribution and Nomenclature of the Manding People and Their Language." In Carlton T. Hodge. *Papers on the Manding.* 1971; Arian Deluz. *Organisation sociale et tradition orale: Les Gouro de Côte d'Ivoire.* 1970; Robert J. Mundt. *Historical Dictionary of Côte d'Ivoire.* 1995.

KWERE. The Kwere are one of the individual groups in the Zaramo* cluster of the Northeast Bantu*-speaking people of East Africa. They live in the coastal lowlands of Tanzania where most of them work as hoe farmers, producing maize, sorghum, and rice, and raising sheep, goats, and poultry. During the nineteenth century, the Kwere were victimized by the East African slave trade; in response, they built fortified villages protected by stockades. In the twentieth century, those settlement patterns gave way to a homestead system in which rural Kwere scattered out more widely. They live in mud-and-wattle homes characterized by high, thatched, cone-shaped roofs; those thatched roofs are giving way today to tin roofs. The vast majority of the Kwere are Muslims, although they are considered to be only marginally loyal, confining their religious observances to fasting at Ramadan, taking on Arab* names, and wearing the white skull cap. There are approximately 80,000 Kwere people today.

REFERENCES: J. L. Brain. "The Kwere of the Eastern Province." *Tanganyika Notes and Records* 58–59 (1962): 231–41; L. W. Swantz. *Ritual and Symbol in Transitional Zaramo Society.* 1970.

KWESE. The Kweses are a small ethnic group of the Pande* cluster of peoples living between the Kwilu and Kasai rivers in the Bandundu region of Zaire. They can also be found in the Kasai Occidental region. Most Kweses are small farmers.
REFERENCE: F. Scott Bobb. *Historical Dictionary of Zaire.* 1988.

KWOJEFFA. *See* BURA.

KWOLL. *See* IRIGWE.

KWOM. *See* KWAMI.

KWONO. *See* KONO.

KYAMAN. *See* EBRIÉ.

KYAMBA. *See* BASARI.

KYATO. *See* ICEN.

KYEDYE. The Kyedyes are a subgroup of the Nupe* peoples of Niger State in Nigeria.

KYENGA. *See* SHANGAWA.

KYEREPON. *See* KYEREPONG.

KYEREPONG. The Kyerepong, also known as the Cherepong and Kyerepon, are one of the Guan* peoples of Ghana. Most of them live and work as small farmers in the Eastern Region, and they are particularly concentrated in the Akuapem Hills near Adukrom. The Kyerepong population in Ghana today is approximately 90,000 people.
REFERENCE: Daniel M. McFarland. *Historical Dictionary of Ghana.* 1995.

KYIBAKU. The Kyibakus (Chibaks, Icibaks, Chibbuks, and Kikuks) are one of Nigeria's ethnic groups. They can be found in the Margi District of the Borno

Division of Borno State, where they farm and raise livestock. The Kyibakus speak a Chadic language.
REFERENCE: *Language Survey of Nigeria.* 1976.

KYOKOSHI. *See* CHOKOSSI.

KYOKOSI. *See* CHOKOSSI.

KYOKOSSI. *See* CHOKOSSI.

L

LAA. *See* SANYE.

LAAMANG. The Laamangs are a Chadic-speaking people who are concentrated today in the Madagali District of the Mubi Division in Gongola State, Nigeria, as well as in the West Goza District of Borno State in Nigeria. Laamangs can also be found across the border in Cameroon.
REFERENCE: *Language Survey of Nigeria.* 1976.

LABWOR. The Labwor people live in the Central Karamoja District of northeastern Uganda. They are especially concentrated along the Loyoroit River and in the Labwor Hills. The Labwors speak a language that ethnolinguists classify as part of the Lwo group of dialects. For centuries, the Labwors have been pastoralists, living a semi-nomadic lifestyle, the men herding their cattle seasonally in search of pasture and the women remaining in permanent villages raising maize, millet, gourds, sweet potatoes, goats, beans, and peanuts. A number of Labwor men have achieved great wealth as traders. Even though their economy is a mixed one, the Labwor religion and culture revolve around cattle. Like other pastoral peoples in East Africa in the 1980s and early 1990s, the Labwors have suffered because of the persistent droughts there.
REFERENCES: Rita M. Byrnes et al. *Uganda: A Country Study.* 1990; John Lamphear. *The Traditional History of the Jie of Uganda.* 1976.

LAHOU. *See* AVIKAM.

LAIAICHA. The Laiaichas are a subgroup of the Reguibat* people of Western Sahara in what is today Morocco. They are divided into two subgroups themselves—the Ahel Belal and the Ahel Beilal. The Laiaicha population today exceeds 2,000 people, most of whom live settled lives in small towns in Western

Sahara, particularly in El-Ayoun. A substantial number of Laiaichas still pursue nomadic lifestyles, especially in southeast Western Sahara and across the border in Mauritania.
REFERENCE: Tony Hodges. *Historical Dictionary of Western Sahara.* 1982.

LAK. The Laks are a major subdivision of the Nuer* people of southern Sudan. They are concentrated on Zeraf Island in the Fanjak District.

LAKA. The Lakas (Laus, Lao Habes) are a subgroup of the Ngambaye* people, who were once a large and powerful ethnic group in northern Cameroon, southern Chad, western Central African Republic, and northern Zaire. Some can also be found in Borno State in Nigeria. For centuries, with the linguistically related Mbuns,* they dominated the Adamawa region, battling periodically against Fulbe* slave raiders. Those slave raids continued into the early twentieth century. During the late nineteenth and early twentieth centuries, the Lakas fiercely resisted German* and French* colonization efforts, suffering military defeat and population decline in the process. They are a Bantu* people. In Zaire, the Lakas strongly supported the Kwilu Rebellion in the mid-1960s. Still suspicious of the central government of Zaire, they live as small farmers.
REFERENCES: F. Scott Bobb. *Historical Dictionary of Zaire.* 1988; Thomas Collelo et al. *Chad: A Country Study.* 1988; Pierre Kalck. *Historical Dictionary of the Central African Republic.* 1992; Pierre Kalck. *Central African Republic.* 1993.

LAKUNDWE. The Lakundwes are a subgroup of the Luba* people of Zaire. The Lakundwes are part of the Luba-Shaba subcluster of the Lubas.

LALA. The Lalas live in central Zambia, south and east of the Congo Pedicle and west of the Luangwa River. They are the descendants of several ethnic groups that migrated there from Zaire. Like many Zambian ethnic groups, they follow a matrilineal descent system. They are also one of the major Kongo* subgroups in Zaire. Although they practice a system of shifting agriculture, the Lalas are also known for their skill as craftsmen in copper and iron-working. Their current population exceeds 175,000 people. In recent decades, drought and poor agricultural practices have destroyed large volumes of topsoil in Lala land, forcing many Lalas to move to towns and cities to work for wages.
REFERENCES: *African Encylopedia.* 1974; John J. Grotpeter. *Historical Dictionary of Zambia.* 1979.

LALA. *See* ROBA.

LALAWA. *See* LELA.

LALI. The Lalis (Laris, Balilis) are one of the Kongo* peoples of Zaire, Congo, and Angola. Most of the Lalis, whose population today exceeds 500,000 people,

can be found living in the Atlantic coastal regions of those countries. Although today they are part of the Kongo cluster, ethnologists believe that the Lalis are actually of Téké* ethnic extraction. The Lalis are one of the dominant groups in contemporary Congo because their homeland is in and around Brazzaville, the capital of the country.
REFERENCE: Virginia Thompson and Richard Adloff. *Historical Dictionary of the People's Republic of the Congo.* 1984.

LALLA. *See* ROBA.

LAMA. The Lama people are an ethnic group living today in northern Togo. Their population consists of more than 60,000 people, most of whom are subsistence farmers. They are part of the eastern Grusi* language group.
REFERENCE: Meterwa A. Ourso. "Phonological Processes in the Noun Class System of Lama." *Studies in African Linguistics* 20 (August 1989):151–78.

LAMBA. The Lamba are one of the major subgroups of the Kabré* peoples of the Centrale and Plateaux regions of contemporary Togo. They should not be confused with the Lambas* of Zaire and Zambia.

LAMBA. The Lambas are an ethnic group living in the southeasternmost tip of Zaire and across the border in Zambia. They tend to be concentrated in and around the towns of Sakania in Zaire and Chingola and Kitwe in Zambia, south and west of the Congo Pedicle in the Copperbelt, although Lambas are scattered throughout the region. Most Lambas are small farmers and laborers. Their social system is patrilineal and matrilocal. In the 1970s, the Lambas bitterly protested that the Zambian government was ignoring economic development in their homeland. In Zambia, the Lamba population exceeds 125,000 people.
REFERENCES: John J. Grotpeter. *Historical Dictionary of Zambia.* 1979; Irving Kaplan et al. *Zaire: A Country Study.* 1978.

LAMBYA. The Lambyas are a small ethnic group of several thousand people who live in the northeastern corner of Zambia and across the border in Tanzania. They are related culturally and politically to the Ngondes.* Most Lambyas are small farmers today. Some ethnologists include the Malilas, Ndalis, Tambos,* and Wandyas as Lambya groups. The number of Lambya in Tanzania exceeds 30,000 people.
REFERENCE: John J. Grotpeter. *Historical Dictionary of Zambia.* 1979.

LAME. The Lames are a Jarawan Bantu* people living today in the Lame District of the Bauchi Division of Bauchi State in Nigeria.
REFERENCE: *Language Survey of Nigeria.* 1976.

LAMJA. The Lamjas are one of Nigeria's many ethnic groups. They speak an Adamawa language and live today primarily in the Jereng and Binyeri districts of the Adamawa Division of Gongola State.
REFERENCE: *Language Survey of Nigeria.* 1976.

LANDOMA. The Landomas (Landoumans, Landumas, Landoumas, Cocolis, Kokolis, Tyopis, and Tiapis) are a small Senegambian* ethnic group living near the town of Catio in southern Guinea-Bissau and inland from the Nalus* between the Rio Nuñez and the Fatala River estuary, west of Gaoual on the border with Guinea-Bissau. They are an offshoot of the Bijagos* and live in the coastal region near the mouth of the Geba River. The Landomas in Guinea-Bissau are surrounded by the Nalus.* Along with other ethnic groups in the region, the Landomas are skilled rice farmers. They speak a Baga* dialect. The Landomas first arrived in the region in the fifteenth century. Most of them today are small farmers. In recent decades, the Landomas have been increasingly assimilated by the surrounding Soso* peoples.
REFERENCES: Richard Lobban and Joshua Forrest. *Historical Dictionary of the Republic of Guinea-Bissau.* 1988; Thomas O'Toole. *Historical Dictionary of Guinea.* 1987.

LANDOUMA. *See* LANDOMA.

LANDOUMAN. *See* LANDOMA.

LANDUMA. *See* LANDOMA.

LANGA. The Langas are a relatively small ethnic group living today in the Kasai Orientale region of central Zaire. Most of them live west of the Lualaba River. Their homeland is a heavily forested region where they support themselves by raising cassava, bananas, and kola nuts. They should not be confused with the Langa* people of Ethiopia.
REFERENCE: Irving Kaplan et al. *Zaire: A Country Study.* 1978.

LANGA. The Langas are a tiny ethnic group living today in Ethiopia. They speak a Nilo-Saharan language and make their living as pastoralists. The current Langa population in Ethiopia exceeds 2,500 people.
REFERENCE: M. L. Bender, J. D. Bowen, R. L. Cooper, and C. A. Ferguson, eds. *Language in Ethiopia.* 1976.

LANGBA. The Langbas are a subgroup of the Banda* peoples of the Central African Republic. Their population is approximately 175,000 people.

LANGI. *See* LANGO.

LANGO. The Langos (Langi) are an East African ethnic group living in central

and northern Uganda, primarily east of the Nile River. They are surrounded by the Acolis,* Karimojons,* and Gandas,* and they have developed a close relationship with the Acolis in recent decades. Some historians believe the Langos split off from the Karimojon about 500 years ago. The Langos speak a language that is part of the Western Nilotic* group. Until the nineteenth century, the Lango economy revolved around the production of cattle, but the rinderpest infestation destroyed the herds and forced the Lango into sedentary agriculture. Today most of the more than 750,000 Langos are farmers, raising millet, sorghum, cassava, sesame, sweet potatoes, and cotton.
REFERENCES: *African Encyclopedia.* 1974; Rita M. Byrnes et al. *Uganda: A Country Study.* 1990.

LANGUDA. *See* LONGUDA.

LANGULO. *See* SANYE.

LAO HABE. *See* LAKA.

LARI. *See* LALI.

LARO. *See* LARU.

LARTE. The Lartes, also known as the Late and the Lartehs, are one of the Guan* peoples of Ghana. Their current population exceeds 30,000 people, most of whom are concentrated in and around the town of Larte in the Akuapem area of the Eastern Region.
REFERENCE: Daniel M. McFarland. *Historical Dictionary of Ghana.* 1995.

LARTEH. *See* LARTE.

LARU. The Larus (Laros) are a Nigerian ethnic group with a contemporary population of approximately 5,000 people. Most Larus live in the Busa and Wawa districts of the Borgu Division of Kwara State. They speak one of the Western Plateau languages in the Benue-Congo family.
REFERENCE: *Language Survey of Nigeria.* 1976.

LATE. *See* LARTE.

LATUKA. The Latukas are an Eastern Nilotic* people who live today in southern Sudan near the Uganda border. They pursue a pastoral lifestyle, raising cattle for milk, blood, and hides. Latuka women produce millet, maize, cow peas, and some tobacco. Recent droughts in the region have devastated the Latuka economy.

REFERENCES: John Lamphear. *The Traditional History of the Jie of Uganda.* 1976; Donald G. Morrison et al. *Black Africa: A Comparative Handbook.* 1989.

LAU. *See* LAKA.

LAU. The Laus are a major subdivision of the Nuer* people of southern Sudan. They are concentrated in Abwong District.

LAUBE. The Laube are a Fulbe* subgroup living in Gambia. They speak a Wolof* language and are widely known in the region for their skill as woodworkers. Laube canoes, wooden statues, and wooden bowls are highly valued in the region.

LEBANESE. Tens of thousands of people of Lebanese extraction live today in the major urban centers of Africa, particularly in countries that used to be part of the French* empire, such as Senegal, Chad, and Mali. They began arriving in Africa in the 1890s, but their immigration accelerated between World War I and World War II, when Lebanon was a French protectorate. The Lebanese tend to constitute a commercial elite, working as middlemen between ethnic Africans and the world economy.
REFERENCE: Harold D. Nelson et al. *Area Handbook for Senegal.* 1982.

LEBOU. *See* LEBU.

LEBOUIHAT. The Lebouihats, also known as the El-Boihats, are one the major subgroups of the Reguibat* people of Western Sahara in what is today Morocco. Their population exceeds 10,000 people. About half of the Lebouihats live settled lifestyles in El-Ayoun and Smara; the rest are nomadic herders, wandering over a broad range of territory from Boudjour in the west to Housa in the east. The Lebouihat themselves are divided into subgroups that include the Ahel Daddah, Ahel Qadi, Ahel Haioun, Ahel Aidi Ahmed Ben Yahya, Lemrasguia, and Ahel Sidi Abdallah Ben Mousa.
REFERENCE: Tony Hodges. *Historical Dictionary of Western Sahara.* 1982.

LEBU. The Lebu (Lebou) people are an ethnic group that originally inhabited the Cape Verde peninsula of western Senegal. They speak the Wolof* language but maintain a powerful sense of Lebu ethnic identity. The Lebus fiercely resisted first Portuguese* and then French* colonization efforts, and it was not until 1897 that they finally agreed to French control. The city of Dakar on the Cape Verde peninsula soon became the political and commercial center of French West Africa. Many Lebus managed to secure title to their lands there, and, as Dakar developed, they became wealthy because of their urban real estate assets. Today, the Lebus are among the most politically and economically in-

fluential groups in Senegal. The Lebus have largely been converted to Islam. Today there is a high rate of intermarriage between Wolofs and Lebus.
REFERENCES: Andrew F. Clark and Lucie Colvin Phillips. *Historical Dictionary of Senegal.* 1994; Harold D. Nelson et al. *Area Handbook for Senegal.* 1974.

LEELE. The Leeles are part of the Bakuba (Kuba*) cluster of peoples in south-central Zaire. In rural areas, most Leeles are farmers, raising maize, millet, and cassava. In towns and cities, large numbers of Leeles work in a variety of occupations. Leele social structure has been distinct from that of surrounding peoples because women were allowed to take more than one husband.

LEGA. The Lega people speak a Bantu* language and live in Zaire. They live east of the Lualaba River in east-central Zaire, up to points near the borders of Rwanda and Burundi. A few Legas lived across the border until the civil wars in Rwanda erupted in 1994. The Legas have a strong sense of ethnic identity, forged even more deeply during the ethnic battles in eastern Zaire during the 1960s. Most Legas are small farmers. They are known for their skill at carving ivory, bone, and wood.
REFERENCES: Daniel Biebuyck. "Sculpture from the Eastern Zaire Forest Region." *African Arts* 9 (January 1976): 8–14; Irving Kaplan et al. *Zaire: A Country Study.* 1978.

LEGBO. The Legbos, also known over the years as the Agbos, Igbo Imabans, Agbos, and Higidis, live today in the Afikpo Division of Imo State and the Obubra Division of Cross River State in Nigeria. Their population exceeds 50,000 people.
REFERENCE: *Language Survey of Nigeria.* 1976.

LELA. The Lelas are an ethnic group living today in southern Burkina-Faso, southwestern Niger, northwestern Nigeria, and northern Benin. Smaller groups can be found in Ivory Coast. Historically, they have been known by a variety of names, including Dakarkaris, Dakkararis, Lalawas, Clelas, Chilalas, Kolelas, and Cala-Calas. They are classified as one of the Western Plateau peoples in the Benue-Congo language family. Most of the more than 200,000 Lelas in Nigeria live in the Kontagora Division of Niger State and the Zuru Division of Sokoto State. They reside in villages where they are subsistence farmers. They possess small cattle herds that they contract out to Fulbe* herders. The Lelas are a subgroup of the Songhai* peoples of West Africa. They are Muslims of the Maliki school and support themselves through farming and soldering.
REFERENCES: Allen Bassing. "Grave Monuments of the Dakarkari." *African Arts* 6 (Summer 1973): 36–39; *Language Survey of Nigeria.* 1976.

LELA. *See* LELE.

LELAU. The Lelaus are a relatively small ethnic group living today in the Wurkum District of the Muri Division of Gongola State in Nigeria. They speak an Adamawa language.
REFERENCE: *Language Survey of Nigeria.* 1976.

LELE. Not to be confused with the Leles* of Burkina-Faso, Chad, and Zaire, the Leles are a small ethnic group living today in the Kissidougou region of Guinea, near and across the Sierra Leone border. They have resided in the area for the past three centuries. Today, the Leles of Sierra Leone and Guinea are being absorbed ethnically by the surrounding Manding* and Kissi* peoples. The Leles speak a Malinké language.
REFERENCE: Thomas O'Toole. *Historical Dictionary of Guinea.* 1987.

LELE. The Leles are a small ethnic group of approximately 40,000 people living south of Kélo in Chad. They speak a Chadic language and are concentrated in Tandjilé Prefecture. Their language represents a transition between Massa* and Sara.* Most Leles work as herdsmen, day laborers, and small farmers, raising millet, maize, and cotton.
REFERENCES: Thomas Collelo et al. *Chad: A Country Study.* 1988; Samuel Decalo. *Historical Dictionary of Chad.* 1987.

LELE. There is another group of people who use the term "Lele" to describe themselves. They live in Tenado Department, west of Koudougou, among the Kipirsi,* between the Black Volta River and the Red Volta River in Burkina-Faso. They are part of the larger Grusi* cluster of ethnic groups in the region. Most of them are farmers.
REFERENCES: Jean-Paul Bourdier and Trinh T. Minh-Ha. "The Architecture of a Lela Compound." *African Arts* 16 (1982): 68–72, 96; Daniel M. McFarland. *Historical Dictionary of Upper Volta.* 1978.

LELE. The Leles, not to be confused with the Leles of Chad or of Burkina-Faso, are a small and very independent ethnic group in Zaire. They are one of the Kuba* peoples and live in the lower Kasai region. During the late nineteenth and twentieth centuries, the Leles offered fierce resistance to the imposition of the Belgian* colonial empire in the Belgian Congo. Today, most Leles are small farmers.
REFERENCES: F. Scott Bobb. *Historical Dictionary of Zaire.* 1988; Mary Douglas. *The Lele of the Kasai.* 1963.

LEMBA. The Lembas are a Bantu*-speaking people who live today in the Katanga region of southeastern Zaire. Some Lembas can also be found across the border in Zambia. Most Lembas make their living as small farmers, although, in recent decades, more and more of them have moved to cities and

towns looking for wage labor. The major urban center for the Lemba people is
Lubumbasha.
REFERENCE: Irving Kaplan et al. *Zaire: A Country Study.* 1978.

LEMBA. The Lembas (Valembas, Rembas, Barembas) are a relatively small
but influential Zimbabwean ethnic group. They are concentrated in the Belingwe
region and are closely associated with the Vendas.* The Lembas speak a Shona*
language. Although the Lembas are not Muslims, they appear to exhibit a number of Muslim cultural traits. Most Lembas are small farmers, craftsmen, potters,
weavers, and merchants.
REFERENCE: R. Kent Rasmussen. *Historical Dictionary of Zimbabwe.* 1994.

LEMBWE. Like the Lembas, the Lembwes are a Bantu*-speaking people living
in the Katanga region of Zaire. Most Lembwes live to the north and east of the
Lembas, closer to the city of Kasenga and the Luaplula River. Most Lembwes
are small farmers raising cassava and a variety of other crops.
REFERENCE: Irving Kaplan et al. *Zaire: A Country Study.* 1978.

LEMIAR. The Lemiars are a small ethnic group of Western Sahara in what is
today Morocco. They traditionally made their living as fishermen along the
northern Atlantic coast and paid tribute for protection to the Izarguiens.* The
Lemiars are subdivided into the Ahel Sidi Amar, the Ahel Brahim, and the Ahel
Ahmed.
REFERENCE: Tony Hodges. *Historical Dictionary of Western Sahara.* 1982.

LEMORO. The Lemoro people—also identified over the years as the Limorros,
Emoros, Anemoros, and Anowurus—are a Nigerian people. They speak a
Northern Jos language of the Benue-Congo family and can be found primarily
in the Leme District of the Bauchi Division of Bauchi State, as well as in the
Jere District of the Jos Division of Plateau State.
REFERENCE: *Language Survey of Nigeria.* 1976.

LEMRASGUIA. The Lemrasguias are a subgroup of the Lebouihat* people of
Western Sahara.

LEMTOUNA. The Lemtounas are one of the Moor* subgroups living today in
Mauritania.

LENDO. The Lendo people of Zaire are concentrated in the western part of the
country, especially in the vicinity of the Lokoro River upstream from Lake
Ndombe and around the city of Lokolama. Most Lendos are small farmers.
REFERENCE: Irving Kaplan et al. *Zaire: A Country Study.* 1978.

LENDU. The Lendu people of northeastern Zaire live on the western shore of Lake Albert, where they farm and fish. The region is characterized by excellent soil, which makes their farming activities profitable and allows for a relatively dense population. Some Lendus can also be found across the border in Uganda. The Lendus are considered to be part of the Lugbara* cluster of peoples. They are divided into three subgroups of their own: the Pitsi, the Djatsi, and the Tatsis. Their language is part of the Sudanic group.

REFERENCES: Irving Kaplan et al. *Zaire: A Country Study.* 1978; Constance Lojenga. "The Secret Behind Vowelless Syllables in Lendu." *Journal of African Languages and Linguistics* 11 (October 1989): 115–26.

LENGE. *See* LENJE.

LENGOLA. The Lengolas are a Bantu*-speaking people who live today on both sides of the Lualaba River in east-central Zaire. The Lengolas have traditionally been a riverine people whose livelihood came from fishing, trading, and riverbank farming. Most Lengolas still pursue this traditional lifestyle, although more and more are seeking work in cities and towns.

REFERENCES: Daniel Biebuyck. "Sculpture from the Eastern Zaire Forest Region." *African Arts* 9 (January 1976): 8–14; Irving Kaplan et al. *Zaire: A Country Study.* 1978.

LENJE. The Lenjes (Lenges) are a Bantu*-speaking people of south-central Zambia. They are closely related to the Ilas,* Tongas,* Totelas,* and Salas.* The Lenjes have a contemporary population of approximately 150,000 people. Most Lenjes are small farmers.

REFERENCE: John J. Grotpeter. *Historical Dictionary of Zambia.* 1979.

LENYIMA. The Lenyima people have also been known historically as the Anyimas and Inyimas. They speak a Cross River language in the Benue-Congo language family and live primarily in the Obubra Division of Cross River State, Nigeria.

REFERENCE: *Language Survey of Nigeria.* 1976.

LESE. The Lese people are an ethnic group living today in the Ituri Forest of Zaire, where they support themselves as subsistence farmers and as foragers.

REFERENCE: Roy Richard Grinker. "Images of Denigration: Structuring Inequality Between Foragers and Farmers in the Ituri Forest of Zaire." *American Ethnology* 17 (February 1990): 111–30.

LETE. The Letes (Baletes, Bamaletes) are a subgroup of the Tswana* people of Botswana. They are actually of Nguni* origins and live today primarily in and around Ramotswa in the Southeast District. They split away from Ndebeles* under the leadership of Malete and settled among Tswana groups in the Transvaal. Within a few decades, they had rapidly assimilated Tswana culture,

including the Tswana language. The British* settled them in Lete Reserve in the 1890s. Large numbers of the Letes are Lutherans.
REFERENCE: Fred Morton, A. Murray, and J. Ramsay. *Historical Dictionary of Botswana.* 1989.

LEYA. The Leyas are an ethnic group living today in Zambia. They are part of the larger cluster of Ila* peoples in the southwestern region of the country. The Leya population today exceeds 10,000 people.

LEYIGHA. Leyigha people—also referred to by others as the Asigas, Ayigas, and Yighas—are a Nigerian ethnic group who live in the Obubra Division of Cross River State. Their population today is approximately 13,000 people, most of whom are farmers.
REFERENCE: *Language Survey of Nigeria.* 1976.

LGOUACEM. *See* REGUIBAT.

LHENGWE. *See* HLENGWE.

LIA. The Lias are a subgroup of the Mongo* people of Zaire. The Lias are concentrated between the Tshuapa and the Lomami rivers in the southeastern reaches of the Equateur Region. The fact that they are, linguistically and culturally, the most distinct of the Mongo subgroups indicates a recent period of independence from them. Most Lias are small farmers and laborers.
REFERENCE: F. Scott Bobb. *Historical Dictionary of Zaire.* 1988.

LIANGULO. *See* SANYE.

LIBIDE. The Libides are an ethnic group in Ethiopia. They are considered a subgroup of the Sadama* peoples and have a population today that exceeds 600,000 people.

LIBO. The Libo people are a small, Adamawa-speaking ethnic group living today in the Shellum and Mbula districts of the Adamawa Division of Gongola State, Nigeria.
REFERENCE: *Language Survey of Nigeria.* 1976.

LIBOLO. The Libolo are a subgroup of the Mbundu* people of north-central Angola.

LIBTAKO. *See* LIPTAKO.

LIDADSA. The Lidadsas are a major subgroup of the Oulad Tidrarins* of Western Sahara.

LIGBI. The Ligbis (Ligby) are a subgroup of the Julas.* For centuries, they enjoyed a reputation as skilled merchants trading along the Black Volta River in Ghana, where they specialized in trading kola nuts and gold. When that trade declined in the nineteenth century, the Ligbis turned to farming. Today, there are descendants of the Ligbis living among the Abron west of Wenchi in Ghana.
REFERENCE: Daniel M. McFarland. *Historical Dictionary of Ghana.* 1995.

LIGBY. *See* LIGBI.

LIKOUALA. *See* LIKUBA.

LIKPE. By Ghanian standards, the Likpes are a very small group of Central Togo peoples who live in the Volta Region of Ghana, east of Lake Volta, and across the border in Togo. Most of them are small farmers. Their current population is approximately 15,000 people.
REFERENCE: Daniel M. McFarland. *Historical Dictionary of Ghana.* 1995.

LIKUBA. The Likubas (Likwala, Likoualas) are a subgroup of the Mbochi* peoples of eastern-central Congo and northwestern Zaire. They are a riverine people who dwell on the banks of the Congo, Likouala, and Kuyu rivers. As protection from flooding, Likuba villages are built on elevated ground. Individual sections of the rivers are parceled out to individual families for use, and the Likubas support themselves by fishing, boatbuilding, and trading. The Likuba population today is in a state of decline because of high mortality rates, low fertility rates, and migration to the cities.
REFERENCE: Gordon C. McDonald et al. *Area Handbook for the People's Republic of the Congo (Congo Brazzaville).* 1971.

LIKWALA. *See* LIKUBA.

LILA. *See* BOBO.

LILIMA. The Lilimas are a subgroup of the Kalanga* people of Zimbabwe and Botswana.

LILSE. The Lilses, also known as Lyelas, are one of the oldest ethic groups in Burkina-Faso. They are part of the Ninisi* cluster of peoples and live in the Center-West Department. They are surrounded by the Samos* to the north, the Dafis* to the west, and the Mossis* to the east, between the Black Volta River and the Red Volta River. Most Lilses today are farmers, raising millet and sorghum.
REFERENCE: Daniel M. McFarland. *Historical Dictionary of Upper Volta.* 1978.

LIMA. The Limas are a subgroup of the Bemba* people of Zambia. Their current population is about 45,000 people, and they live in central Zambia, along and west of the southern Copperbelt. Most Limas today are small farmers, miners, and laborers.
REFERENCE: John J. Grotpeter. *Historical Dictionary of Zambia.* 1979.

LIMBA. There are approximately 600,000 Limbas in West Africa. Approximately 90 percent of them live in Sierra Leone, primarily between the Little Scarcies and Rokel rivers in the Kambia, Bombali, Koinadugu, and Tonkolili districts of the Northern Province, although recent migrations to the area of Freetown have somewhat dispersed them. The rest are in Guinea. Just over 70 percent of the Limbas are Sunni Muslims. Their conversion to Islam was a phenomenon of the late nineteenth century when the Mandinka* conqueror, Samory Touré, took control of Limba territory. Other Limbas are Christians or followers of traditional animist rituals. The Limbas are divided into five subgroups: Tonkos, Biriwas, Wara Waras,* Safrokos, and Selas. Ethnolinguists classify the Limba language as part of the Mel cluster of the Niger-Congo family. Most Limbas are farmers who raise rice, peanuts, and cassava. They also supply fruits and vegetables to the urban market in Freetown and are palm wine tappers. The Wara Waras raise some cattle. Most Limba children attend Islamic schools, which helps prevent too much Westernization. In recent years, however, Protestant missionary groups from the United States have converted substantial numbers of Limbas.
REFERENCES: R. C. Finnegan. *Limba Stories and Storytelling.* 1967; R. C. Finnegan. *Survey of the Limba of Sierra Leone.* 1965; C. Magbaily Fyle. "Limba." In Richard V. Weekes, ed. *Muslim Peoples.* 1984; W. S. Hart. "Limba Funeral Masks." *African Arts* 22 (November 1988): 60–67; K. P. Moseley. "Land, Labour and Migration: The Saffroko Limba Case." *Africana Research Bulletin* 8 (1978): 14–44; Simon Offenberg. "The Beaded Bands of Bafoeda." *African Arts* 25 (April 1992): 64–75.

LIMORRO. *See* LEMORO.

LINDA. The Lindas are a subgroup of the Banda* peoples of the Central African Republic. Their population is approximately 160,000 people.

LINDIRI. *See* NUNKU.

LINGA. The Lingas are a subgroup of the Mbochi* people of eastern Gabon, central Congo, and western Zaire. Their contemporary population exceeds 25,000 people. Although they practice some small-scale agriculture, the Lingas usually support themselves by fishing and trading. Their social structure is based on a patrilineal clan structure.
REFERENCES: Donald G. Morrison et al. *Black Africa: A Comparative Handbook.*

1989; Gordon C. MacDonald et al. *Area Handbook for the People's Republic of the Congo* (*Congo Brazzaville*). 1971.

LINGALA. Lingala, a Bantu* language, is spoken today by millions of people in Zaire. It is the country's main language. Originally, the language was spoken only in the middle Zaire River Valley, but, during the colonial era, large numbers of Lingalas joined the Belgian* army and carried the language all over the country.
REFERENCE: *African Encyclopedia.* 1974.

LIOKPOLI. *See* BARAGUYU.

LIPKAWA. *See* KARIYA.

LIPTAKO. The Liptakos, also known as the Libtako, live in the northeastern Dori region of Burkina-Faso. Their homeland is a vast, dry plain. After being under Fulbe* and Gurma* domination for centuries, the Liptakos acquiesced to French* authority by treaty in 1891. During the early 1970s, the Liptakos were devastated by droughts that all but destroyed the pastoral economy of the Sahel. Most Liptakos today make their living raising cattle, although some are engaged in the production of sorghum and millet.
REFERENCE: Daniel M. McFarland. *Historical Dictionary of Upper Volta.* 1978.

LISAWAN. The Lisawans are a subgroup of the Tuareg* people of Mali and Niger.

LISI. The Lisis are an ethnic group made up of approximately 135,000 people in Chad. Virtually all Lisis are Muslims. They are divided into a number of subgroups, including the Bulalas,* Kukas, Midogos, and Abusemens.* The Lisis are a Nilotic* people who today make a living as nomadic and semi-nomadic pastoralists, although many also farm today. In the northern regions of Chad, the Lisis harbor deep resentments toward Arabs,* whom they consider snobbish and ethnocentric.
REFERENCE: Donald G. Morrison et al. *Black Africa: A Comparative Handbook.* 1989.

LITTLE KOLA. The Little Kolas are a subgroup of the Bassa* people of Liberia. The Little Kolas live in Grand Bassa County.

LO. *See* KWENI.

LO. *See* LOBI.

LO. The Lo people, not to be confused with the Lo or Kweni people of Ivory Coast, are a small Nigerian ethnic group who live in the Wurkum Dis-

trict of the Muri Division of Gongola State. They speak an Adamawa language.
REFERENCE: *Language Survey of Nigeria.* 1976.

LO DAGABA. The Lo Dagabas are a subgroup of the Lobi* people of Ghana, Ivory Coast, and Burkina-Faso.

LOBALA. The Lobalas are a ethnic group living today in Zaire and the Congo. They are located on both sides of the Ubangi River in northwestern Zaire and northeastern Congo. The Lobalas are a riverine people who have traditionally supported themselves by planting small gardens on the river banks, fishing, and trading up and down the Zaire and Ubangui rivers.
REFERENCE: Irving Kaplan et al. *Zaire: A Country Study.* 1978.

LOBER. *See* LOBI.

LOBI. The Lobi (Lo, Lober) live east of the Senufos,* along the borders of northwestern Ivory Coast and northeastern Ghana, and in Burkina-Faso, primarily between the Black Volta River and the White Volta River. Most ethnologists believe that they began arriving in their present homeland late in the eighteenth century after migrating from Ghana. France annexed Lobi land in 1897 and suppressed the subsequent rebellion in 1903. The Lorhon, Téuessué, Touna, Tounbé, Miwo, Lo Dagaba, Lowili, and Yagala (Yangala) are so closely related to the Lobis that most ethnologists consider them to be Lobi subgroups. Other Lobi subgroups include the Dorosie* (Dokhosie), Dyan* (Dian), Gan, Kulango,* Tusyan,* and Vifye. Near the end of the eighteenth century, because of pressure from Mamprusis,* Dogambas,* and Gonjas,* the Lobi migrated to their present location. At the time, they were primarily hunters and gatherers. During the years of the French* and British* empires, Europeans had little contact with the Lobi, and the Lobi migration continued during the colonial period as they moved into Burkina-Faso. There are more Lobi in Burkina-Faso today than in Ivory Coast. They are animist in their religious loyalties and make their living herding cattle or camels and raising cotton, peanuts, and millet. They speak one of the Molé-Dagbane* languages. The Lobi population is approximately 500,000 people.
REFERENCES: Barbara L. Hagaman. "Beer and Matriliny: The Power of Women in a West African Society." Ph.D. dissertation. Northeastern University. 1977; Robert E. Handloff et al. *Côte d'Ivoire: A Country Study.* 1988.

LOGBA. The Logba are one of the major subgroups of the Kabré* peoples of the Centrale and Plateaux regions of contemporary Togo and Ghana. Most of them live in the mountains of southeastern Ghana and southwestern Togo. The Logba population in Ghana today is approximately 5,000 people.

LOGIT. The Logits are an ethnic group living today in southeastern Sudan and across the border in Uganda. They are part of the Eastern Nilotic* group of peoples in the region. Like other Nilotic peoples, they raise cattle to supply their need for milk, blood, and hides. They also farm.
REFERENCE: Donald G. Morrison et al. *Black Africa: A Comparative Handbook.* 1989.

LOGO. The Logos are an ethnic group living today in northeastern Zaire, with some also scattered in western Uganda. They speak an eastern Sudanic language, although they are of Nilotic* origin. The Logos are primarily subsistence farmers who live in a very remote, isolated part of the country.
REFERENCE: F. Scott Bobb. *Historical Dictionary of Zaire.* 1988.

LOGOLI. The Logolis of western Kenya are a Bantu*-speaking people. The primary domestic group is the patrilineally extended family homestead, but this grouping has become more attenuated under the pressure of increasing population. Polygyny is rare. Although the Logolis practice both horticulture and animal husbandry, their high population density has led to a loss of grazing land and a decline in herds and herding activities. A number of the Logolis engage in wage labor.
REFERENCE: Robert L. Munroe and Ruth H. Munroe. "Land, Labor, and the Child's Cognitive Performance Among the Logoli." *American Ethnology* 4 (May 1977): 309–20.

LOI. The Lois are a subgroup of the Mbochi* people of eastern Gabon, central Congo, and western Zaire. Their contemporary population exceeds 30,000 people. Although they are increasingly turning to commercial agriculture, the Loi economy has traditionally revolved around trading and fishing, at which they are highly adept. Their social structure is based on patrilineal clans.
REFERENCES: Donald G. Morrison et al. *Black Africa: A Comparative Handbook.* 1989; Gordon C. MacDonald et al. *Area Handbook for the People's Republic of the Congo (Congo Brazzaville).* 1971.

LOKE. The Loke people, frequently referred to as the Lokos, Yakurrs, Yakos, and Ugeps, are a Nigerian ethnic group who speak a Cross River language of the Benue-Congo family. They are located in the Obubra Division of Cross River State. The Loke population today exceeds 140,000 people.
REFERENCE: *Language Survey of Nigeria.* 1976.

LOKELE. The Lokeles are a relatively small ethnic group living in Zaire. Most Lokeles are concentrated on the west bank of the Lualaba River, downriver from the city of Bumba. As a riverine people, they have traditionally supported themselves by fishing, planting gardens on river banks, and trading. Today, more and more Lokeles are seeking wage labor in the towns and cities of north-central Zaire.
REFERENCE: Irving Kaplan et al. *Zaire: A Country Study.* 1978.

LOKKO. *See* LOKO.

LOKO. *See* LOKE.

LOKO. The Lokos (Lokko) are an ethnic group of Sierra Leone. Their population today exceeds 120,000 people, of whom more than a third are Muslims; the rest are Christians and animists. The contemporary religious trend, however, is increased conversions to Islam. The Lokos occupy five chiefdoms in the Port Loko and Bombali districts of the Northern Province of Sierra Leone. Lokos can also be found around Bradford and Rotifunk in the Southern Province. They are closely related to the Mendés* and Gbandes.* In fact, most Lokos living in Freetown designate themselves as Temnes.* Sometime in the fifteenth century, the Lokos split away from the Gbande and came under Mendé influence.
REFERENCES: Cyril P. Foray. *Historical Dictionary of Sierra Leone.* 1977; Irving Kaplan et al. *Area Handbook for Sierra Leone.* 1976.

LOKOYA. The Lokoyas are an ethnic group living today in southeastern Sudan and across the border in Kenya. They are closely related to such groups as the Logits,* Latukas,* Kukus,* and Toposas.* They raise cattle and work small farms.
REFERENCE: Donald G. Morrison et al. *Black Africa: A Comparative Handbook.* 1989.

LOKUKOLI. *See* NKUKOLI.

LOLOBI. The Lolobis are a very small group of Central Togo peoples who live in the Volta Region of Ghana, east of Lake Volta, and across the border in Togo. Most of them are small farmers. In Ghana, the number of Lolobi people is approximately 6,000.
REFERENCE: Daniel M. McFarland. *Historical Dictionary of Ghana.* 1995.

LOMA. The Loma (Toma, Lorma, Buzzi) are a Manding*-speaking people who today live in Liberia, Guinea-Bissau, and Guinea. Most Loma live in Lofa County, Liberia. Those living in Guinea and Guinea-Bissau are known as Tomas. The Loma in Guinea live east of the Kissis* in the Macenta administrative district. Their language is one of the Mande-fu cluster of the Manding group. Like other Manding peoples, they trace their history, through oral traditions, back to the thirteenth-century Mali Empire. They believe that, after the disintegration of the empire, they migrated southwest to Liberia. Most Loma are small farmers, raising rice, millet, and peanuts, although substantial numbers have moved to towns and cities to work as wage laborers. The Loma population today exceeds 100,000 people.

LOMATWA

REFERENCES: David Dalby. "Distribution and Nomenclature of the Manding People and their Language." In Carlton T. Hodge. *Papers on the Manding*. 1971; Donald R. Wright. "Manding-Speaking Peoples." In Richard V. Weekes, ed. *Muslim Peoples*. 1984; Thomas O'Toole. *Historical Dictionary of Guinea*. 1987.

LOMATWA. The Lomatwas are a subgroup of the Luba* people of Zaire. They are part of the Luba-Shaba subcluster of Luba peoples.

LOMBI. The Lombis are a Bantu*-speaking people living today in the Haut-Zaire region of northeastern Zaire. Although most Lombis still making their living as farmers, raising cassava as a staple, they have become increasingly integrated into the regional commercial economy in recent decades. Large numbers of Lombis have moved to the city of Kisangani in search of wage labor.
REFERENCE: Irving Kaplan et al. *Zaire: A Country Study*. 1978.

LOMWE. The Lomwe (Acilowe, Alomwe, Nguru) people of southern Malawi, southern Tanzania, and northern Mozambique are closely related to the Yaos.* Today they constitute approximately 20 percent of the total population of Malawi, where they are concentrated in Thyolo and Chiradzulu districts of the Southern Region. The total Lomwe population in all three countries today exceeds two million people. The Lomwes call their language Chilomwe. Their social structure and system of matrilineal descent are so close to those of the Yaos and Nyanjas* that a good deal in intermarriage is taking place today. Most Lomwes are small farmers and migrant laborers.
REFERENCES: Cynthia Crosby. *Historical Dictionary of Malawi*. 1980; Harold D. Nelson et al. *Area Handbook for Malawi*. 1975.

LONGUDA. The Longudas (Langudas, Nungudas, Nunguras, Nungurabas) are a Nigerian people who speak an Adamawa language. They have a population of more than 50,000 people, most of whom are Christians and live in the Waja and Cham districts of the Gombe Division of Bauchi State and in the Longuda District of the Numan Division of Gongola State.
REFERENCE: *Language Survey of Nigeria*. 1976.

LOPA. The Lopas are a small ethnic group of approximately 5,000 people living today in the Agwarra District of the Borgu Division of Kwara State in Nigeria.
REFERENCE: *Language Survey of Nigeria*. 1976.

LOPAWA. The Lopawas are part of the larger Hausa*-Fulbe* cluster of peoples living in the Yauri Division of Sokoto State in Nigeria. They make their living as farmers and fishermen; they are mainly hoe cultivators, raising millet and Guinea corn on the highlands and onions along the river. The Muslim religion came to them via traders, Hausa administrators, and traveling *mullahs*.

More than two-thirds of the Lopawas are Muslims. Their language is part of the Benue-Congo branch of the Niger-Congo linguistic family. Because of the completion of the Kainji Dam Project in 1968, many of them were forced to relocate off their islands and river banks into larger settlements where government schools, jobs, and health facilities are accelerating their acculturation and assimilation.

REFERENCE: Frank A. Salamone. "All Resettled at Kainji?" *Intellect* (1977): 231–33.

LOQA. The Loqa are a subgroup of the Zermas,* themselves a subgroup of the Songhai* people of West Africa. They live in far western Niger.

LORHON. *See* KULANGO.

LORHON. The Lorhon are a subgroup of the Lobi* people of Ivory Coast, Ghana, and Burkina-Faso.

LORMA. *See* LOMA.

LOROBO. *See* DOROBO and FULBE.

LOSSO. The Losso people are one of the subgroups of the Kabré* peoples in northern Togo. Their current population is approximately 160,000 people, most of whom live in the Lama Kara region and the Sansanné-Mango region. Some have also migrated recently toward Atakpamé. They are known for their palm plantations.

LOTSU-PIRI. The Lotsu-Piri people, also known as the Kittas, are an ethnic group whose language is part of the Adamawa family. More than 8,000 Lotsu-Piris live today in the Bachama District of the Numan Division of Gongola State in Nigeria.

REFERENCE: *Language Survey of Nigeria.* 1976.

LOUMBOU. The Loumbous, also known as the Baloumbous, are an ethnic group living in Nyanga Province in southwest Gabon and in Cameroon, particularly in Neme Department. Their own oral traditions trace Loumbou origins to what is today Point-Noire in the Congo Republic, but they migrated to Gabon over the course of several centuries. Historically, the Loumbous on the Atlantic coast collected salt from saltwater and traded it with interior ethnic groups. By the late fifteenth century, with the arrival of the Portuguese,* the Loumbous entered into the ivory, beeswax, slave, and redwood trades. From the late eighteenth century through much of the nineteenth century, the Loumbous came under the domination of the Vili* Kingdom of Loango. By the late nineteenth and early twentieth centuries, the Loumbous were trading rubber with the

Europeans. Today, most Loumbous are small farmers, merchants, and traders. Their current population exceeds 25,000 people.
REFERENCE: David E. Gardinier. *Historical Dictionary of Gabon.* 1994.

LOUNDA. *See* LUNDA.

LOVALE. *See* LUVALE.

LOVEDU. The Lovedu are a group of more than 175,000 people who live primarily in the northern Transvaal in South Africa. They are linguistically related to the Shona* and Sotho* peoples, but their material culture and social organization resemble that of the Venda.* In the nineteenth century, the Lovedu, because of their strong internal unity, resisted the expansion of Boer and British* power, becoming one of the last indigenous peoples in South Africa to be brought under European control. Their sense of identity remains powerful today.
REFERENCE: *African Encyclopedia.* 1974.

LOWIILI. The Lowiili are one of the "stateless" peoples who live in northern Ghana. They are animist in their religious loyalties and make their living herding cattle and in subsistence agriculture, raising millet. They speak one of the Molé-Dagbane* languages. Until 1957, they lived under the administration of what was known as the Northern Territories in the British* Gold Coast colony. Many ethnologists consider them a subgroup of the Lobis.*
REFERENCE: Jack Goody. *The Social Organization of the Lo Willi.* 1956.

LOZI. The Lozis (Barotse, Barutse, Barotze, Marotse, Balozi, Rotse, Rozi) are an ethnic group in Zambia and Botswana. They can also be found in the Caprivi region of Namibia. They number approximately 300,000 people today, of whom one-sixth are Muslims. Their economy revolves around fishing and the production of maize and cattle. They live in villages constructed on higher ground near a river; during the dry season, they migrate down to the low floodplain to plant their crops in the rich soil. They first emerged as a self-conscious ethnic group in the seventeenth century, the result of the fusion of more than twenty groups. In 1840, the Kololos* conquered the Lozis, but the Lozis won back their independence in 1870 under Sipopa. Sipopa was succeeded as leader of the Lozis by Lewanika, who, in 1890, ceded the mineral rights of his territory to the British* in return for their assistance in resisting combined Portuguese*-Ndebele* attacks on them. The Lozis managed to maintain a strong sense of ethnic identity during the years of British colonial administration. The Lozis speak a Bantu* language. The Lozis are a dominant ethnic group because of the power of their language, because of the stability of their chieftainship, and because they interacted successfully with the British early in the colonial period.
REFERENCES: *African Encyclopedia.* 1974; D. F. Gowlett. "The Parentage and De-

velopment of Lozi." *Journal of African Languages and Linguistics* 11 (October 1989): 127–49; John J. Grotpeter. *Historical Dictionary of Zambia.* 1979; Fred Morton, A. Murray, and J. Ramsay. *Historical Dictionary of Botswana.* 1989.

LOZOUA. The Lozoua are a subgroup of the Dida* people of Ivory Coast.

LUAC. The Luacs are a major subdivision of the Atuot* people of southern Sudan.

LUANGO. The Luangos are a subgroup of the Mbundu* peoples of Angola.

LUANO. The Luano people are one of the smaller ethnic groups in Zambia. Their population today is approximately 10,000 people. They live in south-central Zambia, east of Lusaka. Most Luanos are small farmers.
REFERENCE: John J. Grotpeter. *Historical Dictionary of Zambia.* 1979.

LUAPALA. The Luapalas are a cluster of peoples in Zambia, Angola, and Zaire, who include the Lundas,* Chisingas,* Shilas,* and Bwiles.*
REFERENCE: Donald G. Morrison et al. *Black Africa: A Comparative Handbook.* 1989.

LUBA. The Lubas (Balubas) are one of the major ethnic groups of Zaire. Their population today exceeds four million people, of whom about 12 percent are Muslims. The rest are Christians or faithful to traditional Luba beliefs and rituals. Lubas can also be found in Zambia. They extend from the Kasai River and Mbuji-Mayi in the west to the Lualaba and Luffira rivers near the towns of Bukavu and Bulundi in the southeast. Their social system is patrilineal. Most Lubas still work as fishermen and farmers, raising maize and millet, but Lubas also dominate the mining and industrial economy of Katanga Province. Luba states emerged as early as the eight century; in the sixteenth and seventeenth centuries, the Luba state grew rich from the trade in ivory and slaves. Traditionally, the Lubas have dominated their neighbors, the culturally and religiously related Lundas.* Lubas helped to crush the Lunda rebellion in Zaire in 1961–1962.

The Luba Kingdom first appeared in the fifteenth century. It began to decline in the late nineteenth century because of the expansion of the Chokwe* empire. When Belgian* colonial authority extended into what is today southern and eastern Zaire in the twentieth century, the Lubas resisted ferociously, acquiring a reputation as a violent, dissenting group. They are a highly independent, ethnocentric people. Ethnologists divide the Lubas into a variety of subgroups. The Luba-Shaba cluster includes the Kaniokas, Kalundwes, and Lomotwas, while the Luba-Kasai cluster is composed of the Luluas,* Lundas, Binjis,* Mputus, and North Ketes. The Songwe* cluster includes the Bangu-Bangus* and Hembas.*

REFERENCES: *African Encyclopedia.* 1974; F. Scott Bobb. *Historical Dictionary of Zaire.* 1988; William Burton. *Luba Religion and Magic in Custom and Belief.* 1961.

LUBA-KASAI. The Luba-Kasais are one of the subclusters of the Luba* people of Zaire. Included in the Luba-Kasai cluster are the Luluas,* Lundas,* Binjis,* Mputus, and North Ketes. They are concentrated in the southern savannas of Zaire, east of the middle Kasai River.

LUBALE. *See* LUVALE.

LUBA-SHABA. The Luba-Shabas are one of the subclusters of the Luba* people of Zaire. Included in the Luba-Shaba cluster are the Kaniokas, Kalundwes, and Lomotwas.

LUBILA. The Lubilas, who have also been known over the years as the Ojors and the Kabilas, are a Nigerian ethnic group. They speak a language that is classified with the Delta Cross group of Benue-Congo languages. They live today in and around Ojo Nkomba and Ojo Akangba in the Akamkpa Division of Cross River State.

REFERENCE: *Language Survey of Nigeria.* 1976.

LUCAZI. *See* LUCHAZI.

LUCHATZE. *See* LUCHAZI.

LUCHAZI. The Luchazis (Lucazi, Luchatzes) are one of the subgroups of the eastern Ngangela* people of Angola and northwestern Zambia. In Zambia, their population exceeds 60,000 people. They are closely related to the Chokwes* and Luvales.*

LUENA. *See* LWENA.

LUENA. *See* LUVALE.

LUGBARA. The Lugbaras are an ethnic group living in southern Sudan, northwestern Uganda, and northeastern Zaire. They occupy the treeless plateau highlands between the Congo River and the Nile. Many Lugbaras also live in the city of Arua on the Uganda-Zaire border. Their most immediate neighbors are the Madis,* Alurs,* and Kakwas.* The Lugbaras speak a language that is part of the Central Sudanic cluster of languages. Within the Lugbara language are such dialects as Terego and Aringa. Their economy revolves around agriculture because of the excellent soil in the region; they raise millet, corn, cassava, sorghum, legumes, and a variety of root crops. The Lugbaras are also known for their skill in animal husbandry. Included in the Lugbara cluster of peoples are the Lugbaras proper, the Madis and the Lendus.*

REFERENCES: F. Scott Bobb. *Historical Dictionary of Zaire.* 1988; Rita M. Byrnes et al. *Uganda: A Country Study.* 1990; Irving Kaplan, et al. *Zaire: A Country Study.* 1978; Peter Ladefoged, Ruth Glick, and Clive Criper. *Language in Uganda.* 1972.

LUGULU. *See* LUGURU.

LUGURU. The Luguru (Lugulu) are one of the individual groups in the Zaramo* cluster of the Northeast Bantu*-speaking peoples of East Africa. They live in the mountainous Uluguri highlands of coastal Tanzania, especially near Morogoro, where most of them work as hoe farmers, producing maize, beans, vegetables, cardamom, bananas, sorghum, and cassava; they also raise sheep, goats, and poultry. During the nineteenth century, the Luguru were for the most part left alone because of their geographic isolation. The lowland Zaramo peoples were more vulnerable. Most Luguru today live in small, plastered houses with thatched roofs, although a few still reside in traditional round houses thatched all the way to the ground. Because of the Arab* slave trade and commercial contacts, the Luguru converted to Islam, and today more than 85 percent of Luguru are Sunni Muslims of the Shafi school. Even those are considered to be only marginally loyal, confining their religious observances to fasting at Ramadan, taking on Arab names, and wearing the white skull cap. Christian Luguru, converted by the Holy Ghost fathers, tend to be in the highlands. The Luguru population today exceeds 425,000 people.

REFERENCES: J. L. Brain. ''Symbolic Rebirth: The Mwali Rite Among the Luguru of East Tanzania.'' *Africa* 48 (1978): 176–88; James Christensen. ''Luguru Verbal Art.'' *African Arts* 16 (February 1983): 68–69, 94–96; L. W. Swantz. *Ritual and Symbol in Transitional Zaramo Society.* 1970; Roland Young and Henry Fosbrooke. *Land and Politics Among the Luguru of Tanganyika.* 1960.

LUHYA. The Luhyas—also known as the Luyia or Abaluyia—constitute one of the three main ethnic groups of Kenya in East Africa. Their current population exceeds 2.5 million people, most of whom live in Western Province. Ethnologists believe that they migrated from Uganda to Kenya beginning in the fifteenth century. They speak a Bantu* language similar to those spoken in eastern Uganda. A highly decentralized people dominated by seventeen clans, the Luhya had a difficult time resisting slave and cattle raids in the nineteenth century. In the northern reaches of Western Province, where the climate is dry, the Luhya raise cattle; to the south, they are more likely to be farmers, raising millet and maize. In recent years, increasing numbers of young Luhya men have gone to work on large commercial farms or to the cities for wage labor. The primary Luhya subgroups are the Isukkas, Idakhos, Kabras, Nyalas, Tsotsos, Wangas, Maramas, Kisas, Nyores, Margolis, Tirikis, Bakhayos, Tachonis, Marachs, Sam-

ias, and Bukhusus. All Luhya are classified as part of the Western Bantu, or
Kavirondo, cluster of East African peoples.
REFERENCES: *African Encyclopedia.* 1974; Gerard Dalish. ''Reduction Phenomena in
Luyia.'' *Studies in African Linguistics* 17 (August 1986): 155–76.

LUIMBE. The Luimbes are an ethnic group living today in Zaire. Their current
population exceeds 300,000 people. They are considered to be part of the Ngangela* cluster of peoples.

LUKASU. The Lukasus are one of the clans of the Bandi* Chiefdom of Lofa
County in Liberia.

LUKOLWE. *See* MBWELA.

LUKPA. The Lukpas are people living today in northern Togo. Their population
consists of more than 60,000 people, most of whom are subsistence farmers.
They are part of the eastern Grusi* language group.
REFERENCE: Meterwa A. Ourso. ''Phonological Processes in the Noun Class System
of Lama.'' *Studies in African Linguistics* 20 (August 1989): 151–78.

LULUA. The Luluas are an ethnic group in Zaire who have only recently
emerged from the Luba* people, their immediate ethnic ancestors. The Luluas
are concentrated in the Lulua River Valley in northwestern Katanga, between
the Lulua and Kasai rivers. Some can also be found across the border in northern
Angola. During the period of Belgian* imperial rule, the Luluas became rich
and powerful under the leadership of Chief Mukenge Kalamba, who encouraged
his people to acculturate to European ideas and to accommodate themselves to
the European economy. Belgian authorities cultivated the Luluas as a means of
countering the highly independent Lubas. In 1959, the Luluas called for Zairean
autonomy but not independence, while the Lubas demanded independence. In
the process, the Luluas became prominent in commercial endeavors and in public administration. They remain a very influential subgroup of the Luba people.
Civil war erupted between the Luluas and Lubas in 1959 and 1960.
REFERENCES: *African Encyclopedia.* 1974; F. Scott Bobb. *Historical Dictionary of
Zaire.* 1988.

LULUBA. The Lulubas are an Eastern Nilotic* people who live today in southern Sudan near the Uganda border. They pursue a pastoral lifestyle, raising cattle
for milk, blood, and hides. Luluba women produce millet, maize, cow peas, and
some tobacco. Recent droughts in the region have devastated the Luluba economy. Their current population is approximately 10,000 people.
REFERENCES: John Lamphear. *The Traditional History of the Jie of Uganda.* 1976;

Torben Andersen. "An Outline of Lulubo Phonology." *Studies in African Linguistics* 18 (April 1987): 39–65.

LUMBO. The Lumbos are one of the major subgroups of the Ovimbundu* peoples of Angola.

LUMBU. The Lumbus are an ethnic group living today in Zambia. They are part of the larger cluster of Ila* peoples in the southwestern region of the country. *See* LEYA and TONGA.

LUMBWA. *See* BARAGUYU.

LUNDA. The Lunda (Alund, Arundes, Balondes, Loundas, Valundas, Malhundos, Luntus, Ruunds) people of the southern Shaba region of Zaire, northern Zambia, and eastern Angola have traditionally been dominated politically by the neighboring Lubas,* to whom they are culturally and linguistically related. The Lundas enjoyed one of the most powerful states in Central Africa during the sixteenth and seventeenth centuries, which explains their spread throughout a broad region today. During the eighteenth century, they expanded because of the salt, ivory, copper, and slave trades, but their decline set in during the nineteenth century. Like the Lubas, the Lundas are primarily maize and millet farmers, but they also work in the mining and industrial economy of Katanga Province. After World War II, the Lundas formed CONAKAT, a powerful political organization headed by Moise Tshombe in Zaire. Its main purpose was to oppose the ascendancy of Luba and Chokwe* politicians. The Lundas opposed colonial rule, and, once independence came, they opposed the central government. In fact, in 1961–1962, after Zaire achieved its independence from Belgium, the Lundas played a key role in the unsuccessful rebellion to secede from Zaire; the rebellion was crushed. During the 1970s and early 1980s, Lunda guerrillas operating out of Angola frequently attacked Zaire. The Lundas are sometimes considered part of the Mawika* cluster of peoples.
REFERENCES: *African Encyclopedia.* 1974; F. Scott Bobb. *Historical Dictionary of Zaire.* 1988; Philip De Boek. "Of Trees and Kings: Politics and Metaphor Among the Alund of Southwestern Zaire." *American Ethnology* 21 (August 1994): 451–73; John J. Grotpeter. *Historical Dictionary of Zambia.* 1979; Irving Kaplan et al. *Zaire: A Country Study.* 1978.

LUNDWE. The Lundwes are an ethnic group living today in Zambia. They are part of the larger cluster of Ila* peoples in the southwestern region of the country.

LUNGU. The Lungu people of Nigeria should not be confused with the Lungus* of Zaire and Zambia. The Nigerian Lungus have also been referred to as Ungus and Adongs. Most of the more than 6,000 Lungus are farmers

living in the Kwoi District of the Jema'a Division in Kaduna State. Their language is one of the Eastern Plateau languages of the Benue-Congo family.
REFERENCE: *Language Survey of Nigeria.* 1976.

LUNGU. The Lungus are a small ethnic group living today near the Bembas* and Kazembes* near Lake Tanganyika in Zaire. They can also be found along the southern reaches of Lake Tanganyika in northeastern Zambia. Their population today exceeds 100,000 people. The Lungu language is part of the Mambwe* group of languages, although many Lungus speak Bemba. They are divided into two groups. The northern Lungus, who probably have origins in East Africa, have a patrilineal descent system and make their living fishing and growing rice and cassava. The southern Lungus are farmers who raise millet and have a matrilineal descent system. In regions free of the tse-tse fly, the Lungus raise cattle.
REFERENCES: F. Scott Bobb. *Historical Dictionary of Zaire.* 1988; John J. Grotpeter. *Historical Dictionary of Zambia.* 1979.

LUNTO. The Luntos are a subgroup of the Luba-Kasai grouping of Luba* peoples in southeastern Zaire.

LUO. The Luo (Lwoo) are one of the main ethnic groups of Kenya. They are concentrated in southwestern Kenya and across the border in Uganda and Tanzania. Some can also be found in southern Sudan. The combined population of Luos in Kenya, Uganda, and Tanzania today is approximately 2.7 million people. The traditional Luo economy revolved around the production of maize, millet, cassava, and sesame; they supplemented their diet by hunting and fishing. They also maintained a few cattle and lived in traditional homes characterized by surrounding hedges of prickly plants. In recent years, the Luos have turned to cotton production to generate cash. Large numbers of Luo men now work in Nairobi and Mombasa, where they are known for their mercantile skills. The Luo speak a Nilotic* language closely related to that of the Acolis* of Uganda and the Shilluks* of Sudan. They probably migrated to southwestern Kenya from southern Sudan more than four centuries ago. That expansionist migration stopped only when the Luos confronted the British* in the late nineteenth century. Included in the Luo cluster of peoples are the Langos,* Acolis, Alurs,* Padholas,* Kumans,* Jonams, and Paluos.
REFERENCES: Carolyn Fluehr-Lobban, Richard A. Lobban, Jr., and John Obert Voll. *Historical Dictionary of Sudan.* 1992; Pascal James Imperato. ''Luo Shields from Tanzania.'' *African Arts* 16 (November 1982): 72–77; Laura Kurtz. *Historical Dictionary of Tanzania.* 1978; Stefano Santandrea. *The Luo of the Bahr El Ghazal.* 1968.

LUPA. *See* LOPA.

LURI. The Luri people speak a Chadic language and live today in the Zungur District of the Bauchi Division of Bauchi State in Nigeria.
REFERENCE: *Language Survey of Nigeria.* 1976.

LUSOGA. *See* SOGA.

LUVALE. The Luvale (Lovale, Lubale, Luena) people are a matrilineal ethnic group living today in Western and Northwestern provinces in Zambia. They are one of the prominent ethnic groups of northwestern Zambia. Luvales can also be found in northeastern Angola and southern Zaire, although the Zambian Luvales should be distinguished today from the Luvales of Angola. They migrated to Zambia from Zaire and Angola in the seventeenth century. Luvale tradition has them descending from the Lunda* people of Katanga, Zaire, who were led to Zambia in the seventeenth century by Chinyama. Their traditional economy was a mixed one, involving hunting, fishing, and the agricultural production of maize and millet. They raised cassava to trade for cattle with the Lozis.* They also engaged in long-distance ivory and metal trading. The Luvale are part of a larger cluster of people known as the Mawikas,* which includes the Lundas, Nkoyas,* and Mbowes.* The contemporary Luvale population is approximately 300,000 people.
REFERENCES: *African Encyclopedia.* 1974; John J. Grotpeter. *Historical Dictionary of Zambia.* 1979; Anita Spring. ''Faith and Participation in Traditional versus Cosmopolitan Medical Systems in Northwest Zambia.'' *Anthropological Quarterly* 53 (April 1980): 130–41.

LUVALE. The Luvales are one of the subgroups of the eastern Ngangela* people of Angola.

LUYANA. The Luyanas are part of the larger Barotse, or Lozi,* cluster of peoples living today in Botswana, Angola, and Zambia. Most Luyanas work as small farmers and wage laborers. Included in the Luyana cluster of peoples are the Kwangwas, Kwandis, Komas,* Nyengos, Simaas, Mwenyis, Imilangus, Mashis,* Mbukushus,* Ndundulus, and Lyuwas.*
REFERENCE: Donald G. Morrison et al. *Black Africa: A Comparative Handbook.* 1989.

LUYIA. *See* LUHYA.

LWENA. The Lwenas are one of the subgroups of the eastern Ngangela* people of Angola.

LWOO. *See* LUO.

LYASE-NE. *See* BANGA.

LYELA. *See* LILSE.

LYUWA. The Lyuwas are part of the larger cluster of Luyana* peoples of Zambia. The Luyanas are part of the Lozi* group.

M

MA. The Mas, who are called Mano by the neighboring Bassa* people, are a Manding*-speaking group who today live in Liberia, Guinea-Bissau, and Guinea. Their language is one of the Mande-fu cluster of the Manding group. Most of the more than 140,000 Mas live in Nimba County, Liberia. Like other Manding people, the Mas trace their history, through oral traditions, back to the thirteenth-century Mali Empire. They believe that, after the disintegration of the empire, they migrated southwest to Liberia. Most Mas are small farmers, raising rice, millet, and peanuts.

REFERENCES: David Dalby. "Distribution and Nomenclature of the Manding People and Their Language." In Carlton T. Hodge. *Papers on the Manding.* 1971; Thomas O'Toole. *Historical Dictionary of Guinea.* 1987; Donald R. Wright. "Manding-Speaking Peoples." In Richard V. Weekes, ed. *Muslim Peoples.* 1984.

MAALE. The Maale are an ethnic group of approximately 30,000 people who live today along the southern perimeter of the high plateau of Ethiopia. The Maales are divided into the following chiefdoms, each with a strong sense of identity: Lemo, Ginte, Goddo, Bio, Shabo, Jato, Gollo, Bala, Bunka, Bunati, Gero, Irbo, and Makana. Until the mid-nineteenth century, all of southern Ethiopia was quite independent of the north, and the Maales enjoyed complete independence. At the head of their society was a ritual king, known as the *kati*, whom the Maales believed to be responsible for maintaining the health and prosperity of the country. The *kati* did this through a system of rituals devoted to his own ancestors. At the end of the nineteenth century, however, southern Ethiopia was conquered by the north, and the Maales were integrated into a larger political entity. That put them under the domination of the Amhara* people of Shewa. Amhara rule was quite indirect, with the Maale's own chiefs acting as imperial agents. Most Maales today work as peasant farmers and herders.

REFERENCE: Donald L. Donham. "An Archaeology of Work Among the Maale of Ethiopia. *Man* 29 (March 1994): 147–60.

MAAQUIL. The Maaquils are one of the Moor* subgroups living today in Mauritania.

MAASI. *See* MASAI.

MABA. The Maba (Fertit, Mandala, Wadain) are a Sunni Muslim people (Maliki school) who live in Wadai Province in the Republic of Chad. They speak a language called Bora Mabang, which is part of the larger Nilo-Saharan linguistic family. They number approximately 230,000 people, of whom perhaps 10 percent live across the border in Sudan. They are divided into a variety of subgroups, all of whom consider themselves Maba and who intermarry with individuals who also speak Bora Mabang. The Kodoi, Awlad Jema, Madaba, Debba, Dekker, Djema, Abissa, Malanga, Mandala, and Madanga are all primary Maba subgroups. Another cluster of Maba subgroups consists of people who assimilated to the Maba during the last several centuries. They include the Marfa,* Karanga,* Kashméré, Koniéré, and Kadianga. Finally, the Daramdé (Kultu) are a special caste of hunters, potters, and blacksmiths who occupy subservient positions in Maba society.

The Maba converted to Islam in the seventeenth century, and the Maba Sultanate dominated eastern Chad throughout the nineteenth century. France conquered the Maba in 1911. During the next seven years, more than half of the Maba population succumbed to disease and war. The Maba region remained a neglected outpost in the French Equatorial empire.

The Maba live in a Sahelian environment where they raise sorghum, millet, maize, peanuts, cattle, sheep, and goats. Most Mabas live in villages with between 200 and 1,500 people. Beginning in 1965, the Maba joined other central Chadian groups in rebeling against the government of François Tombalaye. They formed the Chadian Liberation Front, but the ensuing civil war, which has lasted on and off ever since, has proved devastating to Maba economic and social life.
REFERENCES: Torben Andersen. "Aspects of Mabaan Tonology." *Journal of African Languages and Linguistics* 13 (April 1993): 183–204; Samuel Decalo. "Chad, the Roots of Centre-Periphery Strife." *African Affairs* 79 (1980): 490–509; John A. Works, Jr. "Maba." In Richard V. Weekes, ed. *Muslim Peoples.* 1984.

MABO-BARKUL. The Mabol-Barkuls are one of the Eastern Plateau peoples of Nigeria. They live today in the Richa and Tof districts of the Pankshin Division of Plateau State.
REFERENCE: *Language Survey of Nigeria.* 1976.

MABUZA. The Mabuzas are one of the major clans of the Bemdzabuko* division of the Swazi* people of Swaziland.

MACHINGA. The Machingas are an ethnic group in Tanzania whom many ethnologists include in the Yao* cluster of peoples. Their contemporary population is approximately 35,000 people.

MACONDE. *See* MAKONDE.

MACUA-LOMWE. The Macua-Lomwe (Mukwa, Lomwe, Lomue), also known as the Alolo and Makwa, are the largest ethnic group in Mozambique; their contemporary population exceeds five million people. They are concentrated primarily in the lower Zambezi River Valley, in Niassa and Cabo Delgafo provinces, and along parts of the northeast coast of the Indian Ocean. They are a matrilineal people. During the past four centuries, the Macua-Lomwe have become converts to Islam. The Macua form the larger of the groups, constituting more than two-thirds of the entire Macua people. They live primarily north of the Ligonha River and along the coast. Most Lomwe live south of the river and in the interior. Over the centuries, the Macua and Lomwe have been members of shifting political coalitions based on their subdivision into chiefdoms. Still, their sense of ethnic identity has not been highly centralized. Historically, identity tended to revolve around village clusters. The Macua-Lomwe living near the coast came under the influence of Islam sooner, while those in the interior resisted conversion.
REFERENCES: Mario Azevedo. *Historical Dictionary of Mozambique.* 1991; Harold D. Nelson et al. *Mozambique: A Country Study.* 1984.

MADA. The Madas, also known as Yiddas, are one of the Bantu*-speaking peoples of Nigeria. They are classified as part of the Plateau cluster of peoples who occupy central Nigeria, primarily in the Jema'a District of the Jema'a Division of Kaduna State and the Mada District of the Akwanga Division of Plateau State. They are surrounded by the Yeskwas,* Kagomas,* and Kajes* to the west, the Kagoros* to the north, the Eggans* to the south, and the Nunkus* and Ninzams* to the east. Most Madas practice subsistence horticulture, raising ginger, millet, guinea corn, beans, and citrus products. They live in social systems characterized by patrilineal descent and patrifocal residence. In recent years, they have begun migrating to towns and cities looking for work.
REFERENCES: Elizabeth Isichei, ed. *Studies in the History of Plateau State, Nigeria.* 1982; Donald G. Morrison et al. *Black Africa: A Comparative Handbook.* 1989.

MADABA. The Madabas are one of the main subgroups of the Maba* people of Sudan.

MADA-EGGON. *See* EGGAN.

MADANGA. The Madangas are one of the main subgroups of the Maba* people of Sudan.

MADI. The Madi are an East African ethnic group living in northwestern Uganda and a small portion of southern Sudan. They live on the east side of the Albert Nile River and are surrounded by Lugbaras* and Acolis.* The Madi are closely related to the Bongo* and Moru* peoples. East African demographers place their current population at approximately 200,000 people, of whom 40 percent are Muslims. Some ethnologists include them in the Lugbara group. During the nineteenth century, they were badly exploited by Arab* slavers. Their economy revolves around hoe-cultivation and livestock raising. Within the Madi grouping in Uganda are the Okollos, Ogokos, Moyos, and Oyuwis, who speak a Madi dialect.

REFERENCES: Rita M. Byrnes et al. *Uganda: A Country Study.* 1990; Carolyn Fluehr-Lobban, Richard A. Lobban, Jr., and John Obert Voll. *Historical Dictionary of Sudan.* 1992; Peter Ladefoged, Ruth Glick, and Clive Criper. *Language in Uganda.* 1972; Helen C. Metz et al. *Sudan: A Country Study.* 1992.

MADJIGODJIA. The Madjigodjia are one of the primary subgroups of the Buduma* people of Chad. They are the dominant Buduma group in the islands of the western Bol District and of the Tataverom District in Chad. They have a population of approximately 10,000 people. Highly ethnocentric, the Madjigodjia are Muslims in their religious orientation and cattle raisers in their economic life.

MADJINGAYE. The Madjingaye people are a subgroup of the Sara* people of Chad. The Madjingayes are found concentrated in the Koumra and Sarh regions of the Moyen-Chari Prefecture. They consider themselves to be the purest group, ethnically and linguistically, in the Sara cluster. The Madjingayes, a highly homogeneous people, first migrated to the region in the seventeenth century; over the next two centuries, they were subject to devastating slave raids by outsiders. Although Catholic and Protestant missionaries have worked among the Madjingayes for decades, they have had little impact. The contemporary Madjingaye population exceeds 100,000 people.

REFERENCE: Samuel Decalo. *Historical Dictionary of Chad.* 1987.

MADONSELA. The Madonselas are one of the major clans of the Bemdzabuko* division of the Swazi* people of Swaziland.

MAGA. *See* MAHA.

MAGAGULA. The Magagulas are one of the clans of the Emakhandzambili* peoples, who themselves are one of the three major subgroups of the Swazi* people of Swaziland.

MAGANGA. The Maganga (Makanga) are a subgroup of the Chewa* peoples of Malawi, eastern Zambia, and central Mozambique. They are also known in

Mozambique as Chuabo. Their current population exceeds 300,000 people, most of whom are Roman Catholics. The Maganga economy revolves around the production of maize, beans, and rice. They are concentrated in the lower Zambezi River Valley.

MAGIMI. *See* KANEMBU.

MAGORAWA. The Magorawas (Magori) are an ethnic group located today in the Ader region of Niger. They originated in Bilma and migrated, because of Tuareg* pressures, in the eighth century. In the intervening centuries, the Magorawas have fought repeatedly and successfully to maintain their independence from the Tuaregs.
REFERENCE: Samuel Decalo. *Historical Dictionary of Niger.* 1989.

MAGORI. *See* MAGORAWA.

MAGU. The Magu people, sometimes called the Mvanips, speak a language classified with the Bole-Tangale* group of the Benue-Congo family. They can be found today concentrated in the Mambilla District of the Mambilla Division of Gongola State in Nigeria.
REFERENCE: *Language Survey of Nigeria.* 1976.

MAGUZAWA. The Maguzawas are a relatively small ethnic group living today in northwestern Nigeria, primarily in the Plateau State. They are part of the larger Abakwariga* cluster of Hausa*-speaking peoples, which also includes the Gwandaris* and the Kutumbawas.* Most Maguzawas are subsistence farmers.
REFERENCE: A. Chukwudi Unomah. ''The Gwandara Settlements of Lafia to 1900.'' In Elizabeth Isichei, ed. *Studies in the History of Plateau State, Nigeria.* 1982.

MAGWE. *See* BÉTÉ.

MAHA. *See* MAHASI.

MAHA. The Maha (Maka, Maga) people, not to be confused with the Nubian* (Mahasis*) of Sudan, are a Nigerian ethnic group. They can be found living in the Gujba District of the Borno Division of Borno State. Most of them are small farmers.
REFERENCES: *Language Survey of Nigeria.* 1976.

MAHAFALI. *See* MEHAFALY.

MAHAMID. *See* RIZEGAT.

MAHARGE. *See* RIZEGAT.

MAHASI. The Mahasi (Maha) are a subgroup of the Nubians.* Traditionally, they lived several hundred miles from Aswan on the Nile, and the original floodings of Nubian land because of Aswan dam construction in 1897, 1912, and 1927 did not affect them. They farmed land near the Sudanese border until the 1960s, when the Aswan High Dam project flooded their homelands and forced their relocation.

MAHI. The Mahi are an ethnic group living in Togo and Benin. They speak a Twi language and are part of the Ewe* cluster of peoples. Historically, the Mahi emerged from a fusion of Adja* and Nagot* peoples and founded the Savalou Kingdom. The Mahi, who have traditionally been slaves to the Fon* people, are concentrated in Togo in the Atakpamé region, arriving in 1854 after having migrated there from the Allada and Savalou regions of what was then the Kingdom of Dahomey. In Benin, they are concentrated north of Abomey between the Ouémé River and the Dassa hills. The Mahi maintain allegiance to the Savalou royal family. Their current population is approximately 100,000 people. Ethnologists today classify them as a Fon subgroup.
REFERENCE: Samuel Decalo. *Historical Dictionary of Benin.* 1987.

MAHINDO. The Mahindo are a small ethnic group of several thousand people living in Mozambique. Most of them are small subsistence farmers who live and work along the banks of the lower Zambezi River. During the late eighteenth and nineteenth centuries, they actively participated in the slave trade, capturing and selling other Africans to Portuguese* traders.
REFERENCE: Mario Azevedo. *Historical Dictionary of Mozambique.* 1991.

MAHLANGU. The Mahlangus are one of the clans of the Emakhandzambili* peoples, who themselves are one of the three major subgroups of the Swazi* people of Swaziland.

MAHON. The Mahons are a Manding*-speaking people who live today in northwestern Ivory Coast and southern Mali. Large numbers of the Mahons are Muslims. They make their living working small farms and raising cattle. The Mahon population is approximately 150,000 people.
REFERENCE: Donald G. Morrison et al. *Black Africa: A Comparative Handbook.* 1989.

MAHONGWÉ. The Mahongwés are a Bakota*-speaking people who live in Ogooué-Ivindo Province in northeast Gabon. They are concentrated in the southern portion of Mékambo Prefecture. Before Poupou's War in the nineteenth century, the Mahongwés lived at the junction of the Ivindo and Mouniangui rivers, but the war drove them upstream to the northeast, where most of them live and work today as small farmers.
REFERENCE: David E. Gardinier. *Historical Dictionary of Gabon.* 1995.

MAHOUIN. Like the Mahongwés,* the Mahouins are part of the larger Bakota,* or Kota, cluster of peoples of northeastern Gabon. Some of them can also be found in Cameroon. Most of the Mahouins are small farmers.

MAI. The Mai people are today classified as part of the larger Lunda*-Chokwe* cluster of peoples living in central Angola. Most Mais are small farmers.

MAIBULOA. The Maibuloa are one of the primary subgroups of the Buduma* people of Chad. They have a population of approximately 17,000 people. Highly ethnocentric, the Maibuloa are Muslims in their religious orientation and cattle raisers in their economic life. They claim to be the direct descendants of Yed, the mythical founder of the Buduma people.

MAIOMBE. *See* MAYOMBE.

MAJANG. The Majangs are a small ethnic group living today in southwestern Ethiopia. They speak a language that is part of the Nilo-Saharan linguistic family. Their social system revolves around decentralized lineages and clans, and they make their living as hoe cultivators and cattle raisers.
REFERENCE: Harold D. Nelson et al. *Ethiopia: A Country Study.* 1980.

MAJI. The Majis are an ethnic group living today in Ethiopia. Some ethnologists place them in the Kafa*-Sadama* cluster of Ethiopian peoples, while others classify them as one of the Omotic* peoples. They live in far southwestern Ethiopia, near the Sudanese border, where they make a living raising ensete and other grain crops, as well as raising some cattle. The Majis are surrounded by various Nilo-Saharan groups, including the Bodis,* Majangs,* and Kiskenas. The Maji population in Ethiopia today exceeds 22,000 people.
REFERENCE: M. L. Bender, J. D. Bowen, R. L. Cooper, and C. A. Ferguson, eds. *Language in Ethiopia.* 1976; Harold D. Nelson et al. *Ethiopia: A Country Study.* 1980.

MAKA. The Makas are an ethnic group living in southern Cameroon, northern Equatorial Guinea, and northern Gabon. They are a subgroup of the Betis,* who are part of the larger Fang*-Pahouin* cluster of peoples. The Maka population today exceeds 150,000 people. Most of them are farmers, raising cassava, cocoa, and yams. They speak a Bantu* language (with strong ties to neighboring Fang and Ewondo* peoples), worship as Christians with strong ties to their traditional religion, and are closely related to the Fangs. Historically, the Makas were middlemen during the years of the European slave trade. They resisted German* penetration of their region in the early twentieth century. The Makas also maintain a strong rivalry with neighboring Bamiléké* peoples.
REFERENCE: Donald G. Morrison et al. *Black Africa: A Comparative Handbook.* 1989.

MAKA. *See* MAHA.

MAKANGA. *See* MAGANGA.

MAKATE. The Makates are a major subgroup of the Shona* peoples of Zimbabwe and Mozambique.

MAKÉ. The Maké are one of the subgroups of the Dida* people of Ivory Coast.

MAKERE. The Makeres are a Bantu*-speaking people who live today in northeastern Zaire. Their immediate neighbors are the Azandes,* Abarambos,* and Boas,* who live in the heavily forested region south of the Uele River. The Makeres support themselves through agriculture, raising cassava, bananas, and several other crops.
REFERENCE: Irving Kaplan et al. *Zaire: A Country Study.* 1978.

MAKHUBU. The Makhubus are one of the clans of the Emakhandzambili* peoples, who themselves are one of the three major subgroups of the Swazi* people of Swaziland.

MAKOA. The Makoas are an ethnic group living today in Madagascar. They are widely dispersed among the Sakalavas* in the northern reaches of the island. Their contemporary population is approximately 150,000 people. They are the most African of any of the ethnic groups in Madagascar because they are the descendants of slaves brought to the island from East Africa by Arab* traders. They maintain a strong sense of ethnic identity and have as little contact with non-Makoas as possible.
REFERENCES: Maureen Covell. *Madagascar: Politics, Economics and Society.* 1987; Harold D. Nelson et al. *Area Handbook for the Malagasy Republic.* 1973.

MAKOMA. The Makomas are an ethnic group living in Zambia. Their population exceeds 15,000 people today, most of whom are subsistence farmers.
REFERENCE: Sirarpi Ohannessian and Mubanga E. Kashoki. *Language in Zambia.* 1978.

MAKONDE. The Makonde (Maconde) are a large ethnic group of approximately 1.3 million people who live primarily in southeastern Tanzania, with smaller groups in Malawi and northern Mozambique. Included in the Makonde group of people are the Matambwes* and the Mawis. Their social system is matrilineal. Ethnically and linguistically, they are closely related to the neighboring Makua* and Mwere* peoples. They make their living as hoe agriculturalists, raising millet and sorghum as their staples. Although they also raise cattle and goats, livestock are not central to their economy. In recent decades, substantial numbers of Makonde have migrated to such cities as Lilongwe, Tete, Morogoro, and Dar es Salaam to work as wage laborers. Approximately 80 percent of the Makondes are nominal Sunni Muslims. The rest are nominal Christians or faithful to the indigenous Makonde religion. Many ethnologists consider them a subgroup of the Yaos,* but they are culturally independent from all other groups. During Mozambique's war of national liberation against the Portuguese* in the 1960s and early 1970s, the Makonde played a central role in FRELIMO (Mozambique Liberation Front).

REFERENCES: Mario Azevedo. *Historical Dictionary of Mozambique.* 1991; Laura Kurtz. *Historical Dictionary of Tanzania.* 1978.

MAKOU. *See* MAKU.

MAKOULA. The Makoulas, who live in Bao, Krim-Krim, and Dadjilé in Chad, are one of the major subgroups of the Ngambaye* people. The Ngambayes are themselves a subgroup of the Saras.*

MAKU. The Maku are a subgroup of the Mbochi* people of eastern Gabon, central Congo, and western Zaire. Their contemporary population exceeds 30,000 people. Although they are increasingly turning to commercial agriculture, the Maku economy has traditionally revolved around trading and fishing, at which they are highly adept. Their social structure is based on a patrilineal clan structure.

REFERENCES: Donald G. Morrison et al. *Black Africa: A Comparative Handbook.* 1989; Gordon C. MacDonald et al. *Area Handbook for the People's Republic of the Congo (Congo Brazzaville).* 1971.

MAKUA. The Makua are a large ethnic group of approximately 4.7 million people who live primarily in Tanzania, with smaller groups in Malawi and Mozambique. They make their living as hoe agriculturalists, raising millet and sorghum as their staples. In recent decades, substantial numbers of Makuas have migrated to major cities to work as wage laborers. Many ethnologists consider them a subgroup of the Yao.*

MAKWA. The Makwas are a subgroup of the Mbochi* people of the Congolese Basin of northern Congo, a region of steppes and swampy forests.

MALAKOTE. *See* WELWAN.

MALANGA. The Malangas are one of the main subgroups of the Maba* people of Sudan.

MALAWI. *See* MARAVI.

MALE. The Male people are a small ethnic group living today in southern Ethiopia. They speak an Omotic* language and make their living raising livestock and working as subsistence farmers. The Male population is approximately 15,000 people.
REFERENCES: M. L. Bender, J. D. Bowen, R. L. Cooper, and C. A. Ferguson, eds. *Language in Ethiopia.* 1976; Harold D. Nelson et al. *Ethiopia: A Country Study.* 1980.

MALELE. The Maleles are a Bantu*-speaking people living today in the Haut-Zaire region of northeastern Zaire. Although most Maleles still making their living as farmers, raising cassava as a staple, they have become increasingly integrated into the regional commercial economy in recent decades. Large numbers of Maleles have moved to the city of Kisangani in search of wage labor.
REFERENCE: Irving Kaplan et al. *Zaire: A Country Study.* 1978

MALENI. *See* SHAGAWU.

MALETE. The Maletes (Bamaletes) are a subgroup of the Tswana* people of Botswana in southern Africa. They speak a Bantu* language and make their living as farmers and livestock raisers.
REFERENCE: John A. Wiseman. *Botswana.* 1992.

MALHOUNDO. *See* LUNDA.

MALIGO. The Maligos are a small group of people living in the far southern reaches of Angola. They speak a Khoisan language. Khoisan peoples were the original inhabitants of the region, but, by the sixteenth century, Bantu* immigrants had absorbed or displaced most of them. Some of the original Khoisan peoples still survive, and the Maligos are one of them. The Maligos live in the semi-arid steppes of far southern Angola. Although increasing numbers of them are farming and seeking day labor in towns and cities, some Maligos still adhere to their traditional foraging lifestyle.
REFERENCE: Susan H. Broadhead. *Historical Dictionary of Angola.* 1992.

MALILA. The Malilas are an ethnic group living today in Tanzania. They are part of the Rukwa cluster of peoples and are closely associated with the Lambyas.* Their current population is approximately 40,000 people.

MALINDZA. The Malindzas are one of the clans of the Emakhandzambili* peoples, who themselves are one of the three major subgroups of the Swazi* people of Swaziland.

MALLUMIA. *See* KURI.

MALO. The Malos are a subgroup of the Welamo* peoples of Ethiopia. They have a population of approximately 6,000 people.

MAMA. The Mamas (Kwarras, Kantanas) are a Jarawan Bantu* people who live in the Mama District of the Akwanga Division in Plateau State, Nigeria.
REFERENCE: *Language Survey of Nigeria.* 1976.

MAMBAHN. The Mambahns are a subgroup of the Bassa* people of Liberia. Actually, the Mambahns are a chiefdom in Liberia, with the following clans as members: Ganios, Giahs, Kafias, Kabas, Kpays, and Zoduans. The Mambahns live in Marshall Territory in Liberia.

MAMBARI. The term "Mambari" is used in southern Africa to refer to traders and merchants of mixed Portuguese* and African descent who traded with the Lozis,* Makololos, Lambas,* Luvales,* Kaondes,* Tongas,* Ilas,* and Lundas* in Angola and Zambia. The term is also sometimes used to refer to the Ovimbundus* of Angola.
REFERENCE: John J. Grotpeter. *Historical Dictionary of Zambia.* 1979.

MAMBERE. *See* MAMBILA.

MAMBILA. The Mambila people, also known historically as the Mambillas, Mamberes, Bangs, Nor Tagbos, and Tongbos, are a Nigerian and Cameroonian people. In Nigeria, they can be found concentrated in the Mambilla, Tigon, and Gashaka districts of the Mambilla Division of Gongola State. They have a population of approximately 165,000 people, equally divided between Nigeria and Cameroon. The Mambila language is part of the Mambila-Vute* group of the Benue-Congo family.
REFERENCE: *Language Survey of Nigeria.* 1976.

MAMBILLA. *See* MAMBILA.

MAMBU. *See* MAMVU.

MAMBWE. The Mambwes are one of the major ethnic groups living in Zambia today. They can also be found in Tanzania. Approximately 70,000 people are of Mambwe descent, but another 250,000 people speak the Mambwe language as their first language, including the Lungus,* Tambos,* and Namwangas.* The Mambwes are descended from the Lungu people. Most Mambwes are farmers who raise a variety of crops, including cotton. They are known as excellent farmers because of their tradition of using grass to fertilize their land. The Mambwes also raise cattle. There are more than sixty separate Mambwe clans. During the twentieth century, the Jehovah's Witnesses converted large

numbers of Mambwes to their version of Christianity. Most Mambwes live in northeastern Zambia near the Tanzanian border. Included in the Mambwe cluster are the Winamwanges* and the Wiwas.*
REFERENCE: John J. Grotpeter. *Historical Dictionary of Zambia.* 1979.

MAMPONG. The Mampongs are one of the primary subdivisions of the Asante* people of Ghana.

MAMPRUSE. *See* MAMPRUSI.

MAMPRUSI. The Mamprusis (Mampruli, Mampruse, Mamprussi) are a group of more than 120,000 people who speak a Molé-Dagbane* language and live in northern Ghana, particular near the border between the Northern Region and the Upper East Region, and in Burkina-Faso. Their major villages are Gambaga and Naleregu. They are primarily a settled farming people. The Mamprusi Kingdom was founded in the late fourteenth century by Gweba of Pusiga, but the dynasty declined in the eighteenth century. They signed a treaty of friendship with the British* in 1894.
REFERENCES: S. D. Brown. *Ritual Aspects of Mamprusi Kinship.* 1975; S. D. Brown. "Horse, Dog, and Donkey: The Making of a Mamprusi King." *Man* 27 (March 1992): 71–90.

MAMPRUSSI. *See* MAMPRUSI.

MAMVU. The Mamvus are a major ethnic group in Zaire and Mozambique. There are scattered Mamvus living in Uganda and Sudan. Most Zairean Mamvus live in Haut-Zaire between Isiro and the border with Sudan and Uganda. The Mamvus in Mozambique live in the lower Zambezi River Valley. They speak a Bantu* language. The Mamvus never developed a highly centralized state and remain today a very decentralized people. Most Mamvus are small farmers and urban laborers. Their contemporary population numbers approximately 50,000 people. Although many Mamvus have made the transition to commercial farming and urban labor in recent years, most Mamvus continue to live as subsistence farmers and livestock raisers.
REFERENCES: Mario Azevedo. *Historical Dictionary of Mozambique.* 1991; F. Scott Bobb. *Historical Dictionary of Zaire.* 1988.

MANA. *See* FANIAN.

MANADRIANA. The Manadrianas are a subgroup of the Betsileo* peoples of the central plateau of Madagascar.

MANAMA. The Manamas are one of the major clans of the Bemdzabuko* division of the Swazi* people of Swaziland.

MANASIR. The Manasirs are the product of ethnogenesis between the Arab*
and the Nubian* peoples of Sudan. Their population today numbers more than
one million people, most of whom are small farmers and workers living in north-
central Sudan. Virtually all of them are Muslims.
REFERENCE: Donald G. Morrison et al. *Black Africa: A Comparative Handbook.* 1989.

MANBETU. *See* MANGBETU.

MANCANHA. The Mancanhas are part of the Senegambian* cultural group of
the Niger-Congo linguistic family. They are closely related to the Balentes* and
live in Guinea-Bissau. Mandinka* expansion drove them to the coastal regions
where they now reside. They are non-Muslim rice farmers. Over the centuries,
the Mancanhas have learned how to cultivate commercial volumes of rice in
their swampy marshland home by building earthen dikes to keep out seawater.
Their economy has traditionally revolved around the production of rice, salt,
and palm wine. They remain skilled commercial farmers today.
REFERENCES: Rosemary R. Galli. *Guinea-Bissau.* 1990; Richard Lobban and Joshua
Forrest. *Historical Dictionary of the Republic of Guinea-Bissau.* 1988.

MANDALA. *See* MABA.

MANDARA. The Mandaras (Wandalas, Ndaras) are a Muslim ethnic group
living in the Mandara Hills of northern Cameroon. They live north of the Matakams* between Mora and Mokolo. They can also be found across the border
in Borno State, Nigeria. For several centuries, they enjoyed the power that comes
from a highly centralized state, but that power no longer exists. Most Mandaras
are farmers, raising groundnuts and cotton for commercial sale. In recent years,
periodic droughts in the Cameroon plains have badly damaged the Mandara
economy. They are considered a subgroup of the Kirdi* peoples. Unlike most
other peoples of the hill country in the region, they accepted Islam, which has
helped them establish close associations with local Arabs.* There are small
mosques in most Mandara villages. They wear the traditional Muslim robe and
amulets. The Mandara population exceeds 35,000 people.
REFERENCES: Harold D. Nelson et al. *Area Handbook for the United Republic of
Cameroon.* 1974; C. L. Temple, ed. *Notes on the Tribes, Provinces, Emirates and States
of the Northern Provinces of Nigeria.* 1967.

MANDARI. The Mandaris of Sudan live on the east side of the White Nile
River in far southern Sudan, near and across the border with Uganda. They
speak a Nilotic* language, although it is a different branch from that of the
neighboring Nilotes* in southern Sudan. The Mandaris are closely related to the
Kuku,* Kakwa,* and Bari* peoples. The Mandaris live in the lowlands, where
cattle herding is the most productive form of economic support.
REFERENCE: Helen C. Metz et al. *Sudan: A Country Study.* 1992.

MANDE. *See* MANDING.

MANDE-TAN. *See* VAI.

MANDIJA. The Mandijas (Mandja, Mandjia) are a subgroup of the Gbayas*
of the Central African Republic. During the nineteenth century, they expanded
triumphantly onto the Ubangian plateau. They accepted a French* protectorate
in 1892, but they soon found themselves being exploited as porters supplying
the French army in Chad. They experienced a severe population decline because
of disease and famine. In 1903, the Mandijas rose in rebellion against the French,
who crushed the uprising with a vengeance. Their population currently exceeds
160,000 people.
REFERENCE: A. M. Vergiat. *Moeurs et coutumes des Mandjia.* 1981.

MANDING. The term ''Manding'' (Mandingue, Mandingo, Mande) refers to a
large linguistic group in West Africa. The Manding languages are part of the
larger Niger-Congo language family. The term itself comes from French* colonial officials who used ''Mandingue'' because Manden on the upper Niger
River is the heartland of the Manding peoples. Ethnolinguists divide Manding
speakers into two large clusters. The Mande-tan group includes the Mandinka,*
Bambara,* and Jula* peoples, who generally are the more northerly Manding
peoples. The Mande-fu group are more southerly and include the Sosos,* Yalunkas,* Mendés,* Lokos,* Kpelles,* Lomas,* Manos, Dans,* and Kwenis.* There
are dozens of other groups whose languages are closely related to Manding.
Most Manding speakers today live in Gambia, Burkina-Faso, Ivory Coast,
Guinea, Sierra Leone, Mali, Guinea-Bissau, Benin, Liberia, Mauritania, and
Ghana. Their population exceeds thirteen million people. The Manding-speaking
ethnic groups all trace their origins to the great Mali Empire, whose center was
on the upper Niger River. They were a trading people who converted to Islam
and reached their zenith in the thirteenth century. Manding-speaking people then
spread west and southwest into West Africa. Today, most of the Manding speakers are settled farmers, raising millet, rice, peanuts, or cotton.
REFERENCES: Guy Atkins, ed. *Manding: Focus on African Civilization.* 1972; Nehemiah Levtzion. *Ancient Ghana and Mali.* 1971; Donald R. White. ''Manding-Speaking
Peoples.'' In Richard V. Weekes, ed. *Muslim Peoples.* 1984.

MANDINGO. *See* MANDINKA.

MANDINGUE. *See* MANDING.

MANDINKA. The Mandinkas (Maninka, Mandinko, Mandingo, and Malinké)
are a Manding*-speaking people who today live in an area that includes southern
Ghana, northwestern Ivory Coast, Sierra Leone, northern Liberia, Gambia,
Guinea, Senegal, and the region of Manden on the border of Mali and Guinea-

Bissau. The Mandinkas constitute 40 percent of the population of Gambia. They can also be found in the Casamance region of Senegal. They are primarily farmers, who trace their origins back to the great thirteenth-century Mali Empire. Most Mandinkas are Muslims, although there are sizable Christian and animist minorities. They did not begin adopting Islam in large numbers until the late nineteenth century. In Ivory Coast, they are often referred to as Julas,* only because of their Muslim faith. Their social structure is patrilineal, patriarchal, and polygynous. They live in small, compact villages, composed of homes with mud walls and thatched roofs. Their population today exceeds four million people. In many West African countries, the Mandinkas have become powerful merchants, civil servants, and religious leaders.

REFERENCES: Guy Atkins, ed. *Manding: Focus on African Civilization.* 1972; Pascal J. Imperato. "Bambara and Malinke Ton Masquerades." *African Arts* 13 (August 1980): 47–55; Nehemiah Levtzion. *Ancient Ghana and Mali.* 1971; Donald R. White. "Manding-Speaking Peoples." In Richard V. Weekes, ed. *Muslim Peoples.* 1984.

MANDINKE-MORI. The Mandinke-Moris are a subgroup of the Mandinka* people of West Africa. They are distinguished by their occupation as merchants. Historically, the Mandinke-Moris dominated the trade routes in the Senegambia region, and, in the process, they acquired a distinct ethnic identity based on their occupation. In Gambia, Ghana, and Senegal today, the Mandinke-Moris retain that occupational identity.

REFERENCE: Andrew F. Clark and Lucie Colvin Phillips. *Historical Dictionary of Senegal.* 1981.

MANDINKO. *See* MANDINKA.

MANDJA. *See* MANDIJA.

MANDJIA. *See* MANDIJA.

MANDYAKO. *See* MANJACO.

MANE. The Mane people live today in Guinea-Bissau. They are a tiny ethnic group of only 4,000 people, virtually all of whom are Muslims.

REFERENCE: Donald G. Morrison et al. *Black Africa: A Comparative Handbook.* 1989.

MANG. The Mangs, who live in Bébélum and Bénoyé in Chad, are one of the major subgroups of the Ngambaye* people. The Ngambayes are themselves a subgroup of the Saras.*

MANGA. The Manga people of Niger, Nigeria, and Chad speak a Kanuri* language and live east of Zinder and north of Gouré, between Mounio and the Komadougou River in Niger, and in the Zungur District of the Bauchi Division

of Bauchi State in Nigeria. Their current population is approaching 200,000
people. Many Mangas consider themselves part of the Kanuri people, and their
languages are mutually intelligible. Historically, they never established centralized political states and, as a result, fell under Fulbe* control. Today, most
Mangas raise cattle and farm. For years, they have been intermarrying with the
Kanuris.
REFERENCES: Samuel Decalo. *Historical Dictionary of Niger.* 1989; Helen C. Metz et
al. *Nigeria: A Country Study.* 1991; C. L. Temple, ed. *Notes on the Tribes, Provinces,
Emirates and States of the Northern Provinces of Nigeria.* 1967.

MANGBETU. The Mangbetus (Manbetu) are a Sudanic people living today in
Zaire and Nigeria. They straddle the border zone of forests and savannas in
northwestern Zaire. They are divided into a number of subgroups, including the
Ga'andas* and Benas.* Their language is classified by ethnolinguists as part of
the central Sudanic cluster, but there is diversity there too, since the Ga'anda
speak a Chadic language and the Benas an Adamawa language. They migrated
from Sudan to the northern and northeastern Congo Basin in the late seventeenth
and early eighteenth centuries. Today, they live near Poko, Isiro, and Rungu, in
Zaire, between the Ituri and the Uelé rivers. The Mangbetus have absorbed a
number of surrounding ethnic groups during the past century. Historically, the
Mangbetus established centralized states and had a social structure clearly divided between aristocrats and commoners. They are closely related to the Mamvus.*
REFERENCES: F. Scott Bobb. *Historical Dictionary of Zaire.* 1988; Irving Kaplan et
al. *Zaire: A Country Study.* 1978; Enid Schildkront, Jill Hellman, and Curtis Kera.
''Mangbetu Pottery.'' *African Arts* 22 (February 1989): 38–47.

MANGONI. *See* NGONI.

MANGUTU. The Mangutus are an ethnic group in Zaire, with scattered members of the group living in Uganda and Sudan. Most Zairean Mangutus live in
Haut-Zaire, between Isiro and the border with Sudan and Uganda. They speak
a Bantu* language. Most of them are small farmers and urban laborers. Their
contemporary population numbers approximately 60,000 people. Most Mangutus continue to live as subsistence farmers and livestock raisers. Some ethnologists cluster them with the Mamvus.*
REFERENCES: F. Scott Bobb. *Historical Dictionary of Zaire.* 1988; Donald G. Morrison
et al. *Black Africa: A Comparative Handbook.* 1989.

MANHICA. The Manhicas (Manyica) are a major subgroup of the Shona*
peoples of Zimbabwe and Mozambique. The Manhicas of Zimbabwe are concentrated in the Makoni, Inyanga, and Umtali districts, while those in Mozambique live south of the Pungwe River. They are descended from the Rodzi
people, who defeated the original inhabitants of the region, the Wazamoi.

The Atewes* are closely related to the Manhicas. There are two primary Manhica dialects—Manhica proper, spoken in the Mutasa kingdom, and Maungwe (Hungwe), spoken in the Makoni kingdom.

REFERENCES: Mario Azevedo. *Historical Dictionary of Mozambique.* 1991; R. Kent Rasmussen. *Historical Dictionary of Zimbabwe.* 1994; Harold D. Nelson et al. *Zimbabwe: A Country Study.* 1982.

MANIANKA. *See* SENUFO.

MANICA. *See* MANHICA.

MANIGIRI. The Manigiris are one of the many subgroups of the Yoruba* peoples of West Africa. They can be found today especially in Benin, around the town of Bassila, and across the border in Togo.

MANIGRI. *See* MANIGIRI.

MANIKA. *See* MANHICA.

MANINKA. *See* MANDINKA.

MANJA. The Manjas are an ethnic group living today in the Central African Republic. They originated centuries ago in the larger Gbaya* group but broke away from them and evolved a separate identity. Today, the Manjas are concentrated in the center of the country, especially in the town of Bangui, where they constitute one of the major ethnic groups.

REFERENCE: Pierre Kalck. *Central African Republic.* 1993.

MANJACO. The Manjaco (Mandyako, Manjago) people are one of the ethnic groups of Senegal, Guinea-Bissau, and Gambia. Their current population exceeds 115,000 people. They are closely related to the Brames,* Mancanhas,* and Papeis.* Most of them are Christians or Manjaco animists, while approximately 5,000 are Muslims. Their language is part of the Niger-Congo family. Most Manjacos live south of the Cacheu River and north of the Mansoa River. Between 1878 and 1891, the Manjacos put up fierce resistance to Portuguese* expansion. Most of them are either small farmers, primarily raising rice, or urban workers, although a considerable number still work on the groundnut plantations.

REFERENCES: David P. Gamble. *The Gambia.* 1989; Richard Lobban and Joshua Forrest. *Historical Dictionary of the Republic of Guinea-Bissau.* 1988.

MANJAGO. *See* MANJACO.

MANKOYO. *See* NKOYA.

MANO. *See* MA.

MANON. *See* MA.

MANYA KROBO. The Manya Krobos are a subgroup of the Adangbe* people of Ghana. They live on the Volta Plains, with their major settlement at Odumasi.

MANYAI. *See* NYAI.

MANYANKA. The Manyanka are a Manding*-speaking people, whose language is actually considered part of the Fringe Manding cluster of Manding languages. Most Manyanka are settled rice and peanut farmers living in eastern Sierra Leone and across the border in southwestern Guinea and northwestern Ivory Coast. They are a patrilineal, patriarchal people who are mostly Muslim in their religious orientation. Like other Manding peoples, they trace their origins back to the great thirteenth-century Mali Empire.
REFERENCE: Carleton T. Hodge, ed. *Papers on the Manding.* 1971.

MANYATSI. The Manyatsis are one of the major clans of the Emafikamuva* people, who themselves are one of the three major subgroups of the Swazi* people of Swaziland.

MANYEMA. The Manyema are an ethnic group of Kenya and Tanzania. They speak a Bantu* language. Their contemporary population in Tanzania exceeds 60,000 people, most of whom are subsistence farmers.
REFERENCE: Edgar C. Polomé and C. P. Hill. *Language in Tanzania.* 1980.

MANYIKA. The Manyika are one of the major subgroups in the Shona* cluster of peoples in Zimbabwe and Mozambique. Most of them are farmers, raising cattle, millet, maize, pumpkins, and yams.

MAO. The Mao people of Ethiopia are of Nilotic* extraction. Most Maos make their livings as nomadic and semi-nomadic pastoralists, although, in recent years, more and more of them are becoming settled farmers or urban workers. Their current population exceeds 18,000 people.
REFERENCES: M. L. Bender, J. D. Bowen, R. L. Cooper, and C. A. Ferguson, eds. *Language in Ethiopia.* 1976; Harold D. Nelson et al. *Ethiopia: A Country Study.* 1980.

MAOURI. The Maouri group can be found in the Dallol Maouri Valley of Niger. They are an animistic people still loyal to their indigenous religious traditions and rituals. They speak a Hausa* dialect. They are divided into two subgroups: the Arewa and the Gubawa. Most Maouris farm and raise cattle.
REFERENCE: Samuel Decalo. *Historical Dictionary of Niger.* 1989.

MAPHOSA. The Maphosas are one of the clans of the Emakhandzambili*
peoples, who themselves are one of the three major subgroups of the Swazi*
people of Swaziland.

MAPODI. *See* GUDE.

MAPOLANE. The Mapolanes are a Lesotho ethnic group who migrated to their
present homeland from the Tugela Valley beyond the Drakensberg Mountains.
There they settled among Phetlas* and Phuthis.* Moorosi, the Phuthi ruler,
united them. Together, the three peoples are today known as Phuthis. They are
concentrated today in the Quthing, Qacha's Nek, and Mohale's Hoek districts
of Lesotho.
REFERENCE: Gordon Haliburton. *Historical Dictionary of Lesotho.* 1977

MAPUDA. *See* GUDE.

MARACH. The Marachs are a subgroup of the Luhya* people of Kenya and
Uganda. They speak a Western Bantu* language and live today north of Lake
Victoria on both sides of the Kenyan-Ugandan border.

MARADALLA. *See* KURI.

MARAGOLI. The Maragolis are a subgroup of the Luhya* people of Kenya
and Uganda. They speak a Western Bantu* language and live today north of
Lake Victoria on both sides of the Kenyan-Ugandan border.

MARAIT. *See* MARARI.

MARAKWET. The Marakwets live in the southwestern highlands of Kenya,
near Lake Victoria. They are a subgroup of the Kalenjin* cluster of peoples.
The Marakwets enjoyed a reputation as fierce, skilled warriors who regularly
raided neighboring Masais,* Luos,* and Gusiis* for cattle. The arrival of British* military force in the region in 1905 ended those raids. They are also known
for their skills as irrigation farmers who live in the cliffs of the Cherangany
Hills. They call their language Kalenjin, which is also spoken by the neighboring
Kipsigi* people.

MARAMA. The Maramas are a subgroup of the Luhya* people of Kenya and
Uganda. They live north of Lake Victoria on both sides of the Kenyan-Ugandan
border.

MARANSI. The Maransi are an ethnic group living near Djibo, Aribinda, and Dori in Burkina-Faso.
REFERENCE: Donald G. Morrison et al. *Black Africa: A Comparative Handbook.* 1989.

MARARI. The Mararis (Mararits, Maraits) are one of the Tama*-speaking peoples of Sudan and Chad. They are very closely related to the neighboring Abu Charibs (Abu Sharibs*). They live mostly on the Chad side of the border, and their population today is approximately 20,000 people, most of whom are settled pastoralists, raising cattle, camels, and goats; they also do small-scale subsistence agriculture. Marari traditions place their origins with the Tunjurs,* migrants from Sudan. The main Marari settlement is Mabrone. They consider themselves descendants of a mixture of Asungors* and Tunjurs.
REFERENCES: Thomas Collelo et al. *Chad: A Country Study.* 1988; Paul Doornbos. "Tama-Speaking Peoples." In Richard V. Weekes, ed. *Muslim Peoples.* 1984.

MARARIT. *See* MARARI.

MARAVE. *See* MARAVI.

MARAVI. The Maravi (Marave) people gradually began leaving the Congo in the sixteenth century, under the leadership of one Karongo; they migrated in a southeasterly direction to their present location in Mozambique. Today, their homelands in Mozambique are in the north, near Lake Nyasa, and in the east, along the Luanga River in Tete Province. They can also be found in Malawi and eastern Zambia. There are a number of major subgroups of the Maravi, including the Nyanjas* of Lake Nyasa, the Chewas* of Capoche and Angonia, the Tsengas of Tete District, and the Chires, Mutararas, Chipetas,* Zimbas, and Makangas. Today, the Maravi population is approximately 300,000 people, most of whom are small farmers.
REFERENCES: Mario Azevedo. *Historical Dictionary of Mozambique.* 1991; G. T. Nurse. "Moiety Endogamy and Anthropometrical Variation Among the Maravi." *Man* 12 (December 1977): 397–404.

MARBA. The Marbas are an ethnic group of southern Chad. They are closely associated with the Massa* and Moussey* peoples, making their living as stockbreeders and fishermen along the Logone River. The Marbas have maintained a high degree of isolation, avoiding contact with missionaries and officials of the government. Most of them are illiterate and remain loyal to their animist religion. They can be found in the Tandjilé Prefecture. Their current population exceeds 50,000 people.
REFERENCE: Samuel Decalo. *Historical Dictionary of Chad.* 1987.

MARBLI. The Marblis are a subgroup of the Bassa* people of Liberia. Most Marblis live in Grand Bassa County.

MARCUDIA. *See* KURI.

MARDOLA. The Mardolas are one of the main subgroups of the Maba* people of Sudan.

MARFA. Today, the Marfas are considered to be a subgroup of the Maba* people of Sudan. Ethnologists, however, argue that their unique language and culture indicate that they were probably absorbed by the surrounding Maba peoples during the course of the last several centuries. Most Marfas can be found today living in the highlands north of Abéché.

MARGI. The Margi are one of the Plateau Chadic peoples of Nigeria. They are concentrated in the Madagali, Michika, Mubi, and Mbani districts of the Mubi Division of Gongola State and the Margi District of the Borno Division of Borno State. Their contemporary population is approximately 200,000 people, about 10 percent of whom are Muslims.
REFERENCE: *Language Survey of Nigeria.* 1976.

MARI. The Maris (Vamari, Mhari) are a subgroup of the Karangas,* who are themselves a Shona* people of Zimbabwe. Most Maris live near Chivi.

MARKA. The term "Marka" is often used as a synonym for the Soninke* people of Mali and Burkina-Faso. These "Markas" should not be confused with the Marka* people of Mali, a distinct ethnic group.

MARKA. The Markas are an ethnic group living primarily in the Ségou region of Mali and in the Dafina area of Burkina-Faso. They are descended from Soninkes* who arrived there several centuries ago, probably migrating west from the Ghana Empire. When Bambaras* later arrived in the area, the Markas adopted Bambara customs and the Bambara language, although they still maintain a distinct sense of identity. The Markas did not, however, adopt the animist religion of the Bambaras; they remained loyal to Islam. Most Markas are traders and farmers, although a substantial number have moved in recent years to Bamako and to coastal areas in search of work.
REFERENCE: Pascal Imperato. *Historical Dictionary of Mali.* 1977.

MARLOE. The Marloes are a subgroup of the Bassa* people of Liberia. Most Marloes live in Grand Bassa County.

MAROTSE. *See* LOZI.

MARROMEU. *See* PODZO.

MARTA. The Martas are an ethnic group in Ethiopia.
REFERENCES: M. L. Bender, J. D. Bowen, R. L. Cooper, and C. A. Ferguson, eds. *Language in Ethiopia.* 1976; Harold D. Nelson et al. *Ethiopia: A Country Study.* 1980.

MARUNGA. The Marungas are a major subgroup of the Shona* peoples of Zimbabwe and Mozambique.

MARYA. The Maryas are one of the principal ethnic groups of the Hamasen District in the central region of Eritrea. The Marya population today exceeds 25,000 people, all of whom claim descent from a Sahlo warrior who lived in the fourteenth century. The Maryas played a central role in the Eritrean secessionist movement and Ethiopian civil war in the 1970s. Although the region itself is officially Christian, most Maryas are Muslims, having converted to Islam early in the nineteenth century.
REFERENCE: Chris Prouty and Eugene Rosenfeld. *Historical Dictionary of Ethiopia and Eritrea.* 1994.

MASA. *See* MASSA.

MASABA. *See* GISU.

MASAI. The Masai (Maasai) are a cattle-keeping society of East Africa, concentrated primarily in Kenya. Ethnolinguists identify them as a Nilo-Hamitic people. They live in the Great Rift Valley of northern Tanzania and southern Kenya. Their current population is approximately 250,000 people. The Masai economy depends completely on cattle production, although they also keep goats and sheep. The Masai abhor other occupations and spend their time moving their herds seasonally in search of good pasture, living in their traditional huts surrounded by fences of thornbushes. Cattle play a key role in Masai religious life as well. From the time of earliest contact, Western missionaries, explorers, and researchers have universally described the ferocity and endurance of the Masai. Such Westerners explained the Masai proclivity toward cattle raids and warfare as an innate characteristic. Even neighboring African tribes respected the Masai tendency toward violence, bravery, aggressiveness, and endurance. More recent research has attributed Masai aggressiveness to the use of drug stimulants designed to increase their endurance during cattle raids and lion hunts. Only since the 1970s have significant numbers of Masai begun to settle down into a farming lifestyle.
REFERENCES: A. C. Lehmann and L. J. Mihalyi. "Aggression, Bravery, Endurance, and Drugs: A Radical Re-Evaluation and Analysis of the Masai Warrior Complex." *Ethnology* 21 (October 1982): 335–48; Thomas Spear and Richard Waller, eds. *Being Masai: Ethnicity and Identity in East Africa.* 1993.

MASALAT. *See* MASALIT.

MASALIT. The Masalit (and the very closely related Masalat) are an ethnic group of approximately 330,000 people who are concentrated in the Dar Masalit District of Northern Darfur Province in Sudan and across the border in the Adre District of Chad. Another 25,000 Masalit live farther west in the Oum Hadjer-Am Dam region of Chad. Tens of thousands of other Masalit have migrated in recent years to points in eastern Sudan, such as Khartoum and Gedaref-Kassala. Most Masalit live as nuclear families, in villages composed of conical wood and thatch houses. They speak a language that is part of the Maba* division of the Nilo-Saharan linguistic family. Most Masalits are bilingual in Masalit and Arabic. Tribal tradition places their origins in Tunisia in North Africa, from where they migrated through Chad to Sudan. Most Masalit are small farmers, raising millet and peanuts. In the southern reaches of Masalit territory, the farmers also raise sorghum, okra, sesame, mangoes, and coriander. In recent years, increasingly large numbers of Masalit young men have taken to seasonal migration to towns and cities in eastern Sudan where they labor for cash. Although there are still elements of pre-Islamic religious rituals in Masalit culture, the people are becoming increasingly orthodox in their religious devotions. Their conversion to Islam began in the seventeenth century when traveling holy men reached the Masalit communities. In the early 1990s, the Masalit were in a state of warfare with the neighboring Fur* peoples of Sudan.
REFERENCES: M. L. Bender, ed. *Peoples and Cultures of the Ethio-Sudan Borderlands.* 1981; Helen C. Metz et al. *Sudan: A Country Study.* 1992; Dennis Tully. ''Masalit.'' In Richard V. Weekes, ed. *Muslim Peoples.* 1984.

MASHASHE. The Mashashes are part of the larger cluster of Lunda* peoples of Zambia. Their current population is approximately 2,500 people.

MASHEBA. *See* CHEWA.

MASHI. The Mashis are a small ethnic group of approximately 10,000 people who live today in the extreme southwestern region of Zambia. They can also be found across the border in southeastern Angola. They speak a Luyana* language. Most of the Mashis are farmers.
REFERENCE: John J. Grotpeter. *Historical Dictionary of Zambia.* 1979.

MASHININI. The Mashininis are one of the clans of the Emakhandzambili* peoples, who themselves are one of the three major subgroups of the Swazi* people of Swaziland.

MASHONA. *See* SHONA.

MASHUKULUMBWE. *See* IWA.

MASILELA. The Masilelas are one of the major clans of the Emafikamuva*

people, who themselves are one of the three major subgroups of the Swazi*
people of Swaziland.

MASINA. The Masina are a nomadic, pastoral people of Burkina-Faso.
REFERENCE: Donald G. Morrison et al. *Black Africa: A Comparative Handbook.* 1989.

MASOUFA. The Masoufas are one of the Moor* subgroups living today in
Mauritania.

MASSA. The Massas (Banana) are an ethnic group living on the plains of
northern Cameroon and southern Chad. In Chad, they can be found primarily
in Mayo-Kebbi Prefecture. In Cameroon, their administrative and geographic
center is located in Yagoua. Ethnologists assign them a Nilotic* origin, arguing
that they came to Chad up the Chari River about two centuries ago. Most of
them are farmers, raising groundnuts and cotton for commercial sale. In recent
years, periodic droughts in the Cameroonian and Chadian plains have badly
damaged the Massa economy. They are actually a subgroup of the Kirdi* peoples. Their population today is approximately 150,000 people. Like other groups
on the plains, they have avoided much contact with missionaries and government
officials, preferring their own cultural isolation and animist religion, which revolves around Olona, the rain god. They fish, farm, and herd on the floodplains
of the Chari River. They are closely related to the Moussey,* Marba,* and Dari*
peoples, who speak Massa languages, and to the Tupuris.*
REFERENCES: Samuel Decalo. *Historical Dictionary of Chad.* 1987; François Dumas-
Champion. ''Le rôle social et rituel du bétail chez les Massa du Tchad.'' *Africa* 50
(1980): 161–81; Harold D. Nelson et al. *Area Handbook for the United Republic of
Cameroon.* 1974.

MASSANGO. The Massangos, also known as the Sangous or Sangos, are
closely related, linguistically and in terms of their oral traditions, with the
Eshira* people. The Massangos live primarily in the forested mountains of
N'Gounié Province of south-central Gabon, particularly between the Ogoulou
and Offoué rivers. Originally, the Massangos and Eshiras were one people, but
they split in two when the Eshiras migrated toward the coast. The Massango
economy in the eighteenth and nineteenth centuries revolved around the slave,
palm cloth, iron, and weapons trades, which they gave to the Bapounous* in
return for salt. Between 1917 and 1919, the Massangos, under the leadership of
Mayambo, rebelled against the French* colonial empire. Although the French
crushed the rebellion, nationalistic sentiment has remained strong among the
Massangos.
REFERENCE: David E. Gardinier. *Historical Dictionary of Gabon.* 1995.

MASUKU. The Masukus are one of the major clans of the Emafikamuva* people, who themselves are one of the three major subgroups of the Swazi* people of Swaziland.

MATABA. The Matabas are today classified as part of the larger Lunda*-Chokwe* cluster of peoples living in central Angola. Most Matabas are small farmers.

MATABELE. *See* NDEBELE.

MATAKAM. The Matakams are a non-Fulbe,* non-Muslim, non-Christian ethnic group of northern Cameroon. They can also be found in the Central Gwoza District of Borno State in Nigeria. Their population is approximately 200,000 people. They arrived there fleeing Fulbe slave traders in the lowlands. The Matakams are farmers who raise crops in terraced, hillside fields. They are a subgroup of the Kirdi* peoples. The Matakams live primarily around the city of Mokolo in the Mandara Hills in a densely settled region. They maintain a patrilineal, patrilocal social structure. Most Matakams remain loyal to a number of ingidenous religious traditions, resisting Islam.
REFERENCES: *Language Survey of Nigeria.* 1976; Harold D. Nelson et al. *Area Handbook for the United Republic of Cameroon.* 1974.

MATAMBWE. The Matambwes are a Bantu*-speaking people who live today in Tanzania. They are included in the Makonde* group of peoples.

MATENGO. The Matengos are a Tanzanian ethnic group who are included in the Nyasa* cluster of peoples. Their contemporary population is approximately 100,000 people.

MATHENIKO. The Matheniko are a subgroup of the Karimojon.* They live southeast of the Jie* in the central Karamoja District of Uganda. The Matheniko are cattle pastoralists, who also raise millet and maize to survive. They speak a language that is part of the Central Paranilotic cluster of languages.

MATSEBULA. The Matsebulas are one of the major clans of the Bemdzabuko* division of the Swazi* people of Swaziland.

MATUMBI. The Matumbis are an East African people who are part of the Ngindo* cluster of the Northeastern Bantu* language group of East Africa. Most of the Matumbis are rice farmers who raise this cash crop in the fertile, damp floodplains of the Kilombero and Rufiji rivers in Tanzania. They also raise poultry and goats. The Matumbis trace their descent through male lines. They are primarily Muslim in their religious orientation, but they generally do not observe Ramadan or many other Islamic rituals. The wearing of a white skull cap and the adoption of an Arab* name are the only religious requirements

they regularly fulfill. Like other Tanzanians, the Matumbis have been dealing with the government's *ujamaa* program since the mid-1970s. The policy is designed to alter the traditional homestead settlement pattern in favor of establishing village clusters where public education and public health campaigns can be more successful. Their Tanzanian population exceeds 100,000 people today.
REFERENCE: A. R. W. Crosse-Upcott. "Male Circumcision Among the Ngindo." *Journal of the Royal Anthropological Institute* 89 (1959): 169–89.

MATUMBI-NDENDEHULE. *See* MATUMBI.

MATUMBOKA. *See* TUMBUKA.

MAUKA. The Mauka people of northwestern Ivory Coast trace their origins back to the great Mali Empire of the thirteenth century. Beginning in the sixteenth century, their ancestors migrated southwest and eventually arrived at their present location. The Mauka speak a Manding* language that some ethnolinguists identify as being Fringe Manding. Most of the Mauka are subsistence farmers. There are also some Mauka living across the border in southern Mali and eastern Guinea.
REFERENCE: Donald R. Wright. "Manding-Speaking Peoples." In Richard V. Weekes, ed. *Muslim Peoples.* 1984.

MAUNGWE. The Maungwes are a subgroup of the Manhica* people of Zimbabwe.

MAURE. *See* MOOR.

MAURITIAN. On the island of Mauritius in the Indian Ocean, there are approximately 240,000 people of mixed African, Malagasay, Indian, Chinese, and European ancestry. During the colonial period, British,* French,* and Dutch officials imported African slaves to work the island's sugar plantations. The descendants of these slaves mixed with other settlers to the island, creating a creole, mixed population. Most of the Mauritian Creoles work as fishermen, small farmers, factory workers, and mechanics.
REFERENCE: Lindsay Riviere. *Historical Dictionary of Mauritius.* 1982.

MAVIA. The Mavia (Mawia) people are a subgroup of the Makonde* people of Mozambique and Tanzania. The Mavias live primarily south of the Rovuma River on the Mavia Plateau. During the nineteenth and early twentieth centuries, the Mavias suffered from Arab* and Nguni* slave raids. Today, the Mavias support themselves as farmers, fishermen, and hunters. Most of them are Muslims. The Mavia population in Tanzania today is approximately 40,000 people.

MAVONDE. The Mavondes are a major subgroup of the Shona* peoples of Zimbabwe and Mozambique.

MAVUSO. The Mavusos are one of the major clans of the Bemdzabuko* division of the Swazi* people of Swaziland.

MAWANDA. The Mawandas are a Tanzanian ethnic group whom some ethnologists classify as part of the Rufiji* cluster of peoples.

MAWIA. *See* MAVIA.

MAWIKA. The term ''Mawika'' is used in Zaire to refer to a group of peoples that includes the Luvale,* Lunda,* Nkoya,* and Mbowe* groups.
REFERENCE: Donald G. Morrison et al. *Black Africa: A Comparative Handbook.* 1989.

MAXE. The Maxe are an ethnic group of Ewe*-speaking people who live in Benin, where they work as farmers raising millet, maize, rice, and cocoa.

MAYGA. The Mayga are a subgroup of the Songhai* peoples of Mali. They claim to be descendants of the ancient Askia, a Songhai nobility group.

MAYO. The Mayos are a subgroup of the Tenda* people of Guinea. Like the Boenis,* they are probably Basari* people who converted to Islam.

MAYOMBE. The Mayombes (Maiombes) are part of the larger cluster of Kongo* peoples. They can be found today living in the mountain forests of Cabinda in Angola as well as in Zaire. Most of them are small farmers. The Mayombes in Zaire became politically active as part of the Alliance of Bakongo, but the Mayombes in Cabinda have been active in the Cabinda separatist movement—the Alliance of Mayombe.
REFERENCE: Thomas Collelo et al. *Angola: A Country Study.* 1989.

MAZIYA. The Maziyas are one of the clans of the Emakhandzambili* peoples, who themselves are one of the three major subgroups of the Swazi* people of Swaziland.

MBA. The Mbas are a Bantu*-speaking people living today in the Haut-Zaire region of northeastern Zaire. Although most Mbas still making their living as farmers, raising cassava as a staple, they have become increasingly integrated into the regional commercial economy in recent decades. Large numbers of Mbas have moved to the city of Kisangani in search of wage labor.
REFERENCE: Irving Kaplan et al. *Zaire: A Country Study.* 1978.

MBADZO. The Mbadzos are an ethnic group whose contemporary population

numbers approximately 50,000 people. Although, in recent years, many Mbadzos have made the transition to commercial farming and urban labor, most Mbadzos continue to live as subsistence farmers and livestock raisers. They live in the lower Zambezi River Valley of Mozambique.
REFERENCE: Mario Azevedo. *Historical Dictionary of Mozambique.* 1991.

MBAI. *See* MBAYE.

MBAKA. The Mbakas are a subgroup of the Mbundu* people of Angola.

MBAKA. The Mbakas, also known as the Bwakas and Ngbakas, are an ethnic group living near Lobaye in the Central African Republic and Zaire. In Zaire, they are concentrated in the northwest corner of the country along the Ubangi River near the town of Zongo. Most Mbakas still residing along the river make their living as fishermen. They have played a key role in the history of the Central African Republic. In 1890, the Mbakas entered into a long-term political relationship with the French* that placed them in powerful positions in the colonial administrative structure. Many key leaders in the recent history of the Central African Republic—Barthelemy Boganda, David Dacko, and Jean-Bedel Bokassa—are members of the Mbaka group. The Mbaka population today exceeds 200,000 people.
REFERENCES: Pierre Kalck. *Historical Dictionary of the Central African Republic.* 1992; G. V. Sévy. *Terre Ngbaka.* 1972.

MBAKA-MANDIJA. The Mbaka-Mandija people are the result of recent ethnogenesis between the Bantu*-speaking Mbakas* and the Gbaya*-speaking Mandjias* of the Central African Republic. They live in and around Lobaye, where most of them work as small farmers, raising cacao, peppers, and kola nuts.
REFERENCE: Pierre Kalck. *Historical Dictionary of the Central African Republic.* 1992.

MBALA. The Mbalas are a Bantu*-speaking ethnic group living between the Kwango and Kasai rivers in the western part of southern Zaire. Their language is related to that spoken by the Kongo* people. Most Mbalas can be found near the town of Kikwit along the Kwilu River, where they are small farmers and urban laborers. Although the Mbalas have frequently opposed the dictates of the central government in Zaire, they are also suspicious of political initiatives by neighboring groups, especially the Pandes* and the Mbuns.* Their political structure is highly decentralized.
REFERENCE: F. Scott Bobb. *Historical Dictionary of Zaire.* 1988.

MBALANTU. The Mbalantus are a subgroup of the Ambos* of Namibia.

MBALE. The Mbales are a subgroup of the Taita* peoples of East Africa, particularly Kenya. They speak a Bantu* language.

MBAMBA. *See* OBAMBA.

MBANDERO. The Mbanderos are a subgroup of the Herero* people of Namibia and Angola.

MBANDJA. *See* MBANZA.

MBANE. The Mbanes are a subgroup of the larger Ngangela* cluster of peoples living today in Angola.

MBANJA. *See* MBANZA.

MBANZA. The Mbanzas, also known as the Mbanjas (Mbandja), are a relatively large ethnic group in Zaire. They speak Banda,* which is classified as an Adamawa-Eastern language. Most Mbanzas are small farmers, living between the Zaire and the Ubangi rivers in the Equateur Region of Zaire. Their contemporary population probably exceeds 500,000 people. Like other ethnic groups in the region, they do not have well-defined geographic boundaries. Mbanza communities are dispersed throughout far northwestern Zaire.
REFERENCES: F. Scott Bobb. *Historical Dictionary of Zaire.* 1988; Irving Kaplan et al. *Zaire: A Country Study.* 1978.

MBAOUA. The Mbaouas, who live along the Logone River in Chad, are one of the major subgroups of the Ngambaye* people. The Ngambayes are themselves a subgroup of the Saras.*

MBARIKE. *See* KUTED.

MBATTO. The Mbattos—also known as the Gwas—are part of the Lagoon cluster of peoples of Ivory Coast. They should not be confused with the Gwa* people of Nigeria. They are concentrated in the subprefecture of Bingerville. Like the other peoples of the southeast coast and lagoons of Ivory Coast, they practice cash-crop farming and engage in the production and trade of palm oil. Some Mbattos still fish as well, to provide themselves with a protein source. They are part of a large Akan* culture group.
REFERENCE: Robert J. Mundt. *Historical Dictionary of Côte d'Ivoire.* 1995.

MBAYE. The Mbayes (Mbai) are a subgroup of the Sara* peoples of Chad. They live primarily in southern Chad, particularly in the Doba and Moissala regions of Logone Orientale Prefecture. They are probably of Nilotic* origins, and their language has some affinities with dialects spoken in the Bahr-el-Ghazal

region of Sudan. Historically, the Mbayes have been terrorized by Fulbe* and Barma* slave raiders. Today, the Mbaye population exceeds 60,000 people. The Mbayes have played very influential roles in the government and military of Chad.
REFERENCE: Samuel Decalo. *Historical Dictionary of Chad.* 1987.

MBE AFAL. *See* UTUGWANG.

MBÉDÉ. The Mbédé are one of the largest ethnic groups in Gabon in West Africa. Their contemporary population exceeds 250,000 people.
REFERENCE: David E. Gardinier. *Gabon.* 1992.

MBEERE. The Mbeeres (Mbere) are an ethnic group of approximately 60,000 people who live today in the Embu District of the Eastern Province of Kenya. The region is not very fertile, so the Mbeeres depend more on animal husbandry, primarily the raising of goats and cattle, than on farming. When and where agriculture is possible, the Mbeeres raise cotton, tobacco, millet, maize, cassava, and bananas. They are also known for their skill as beekeepers.
REFERENCE: Bethwell A. Ogot. *Historical Dictionary of Kenya.* 1981.

MBELWE. The Mbelwes are a subgroup of the Ngoni* people of Malawi.

MBEMBE. The Mbembes (Tigongs), who should not be confused with the Mbembes* of Cross River State in Nigeria, are an ethnic group living today in the Mambilla and Tigon districts of the Mambilla Division of Gongola State in Nigeria, as well as across the border in western Cameroon. They are closely related to the Efiks* and Ibibios.* Most of them are farmers, raising yams and palm oil. Large numbers of them also work in Nigerian cities. The Mbembe population today exceeds 350,000 people.
REFERENCES: *Language Survey of Nigeria.* 1976; Donald G. Morrison et al. *Black Africa: A Comparative Handbook.* 1989.

MBEMBE. The Mbembes—identified also as the Okams, Oderigas, Wakandes, Ifunubwas, Ekokomas, and Ofunobwans—are a Nigerian ethnic group concentrated in the Izi Division of Ananbra State and the Obubra and Ikom divisions of Cross River State in Nigeria. They speak a Bantu* language and make their living primarily as small farmers.
REFERENCE: *Language Survey of Nigeria.* 1976.

MBERE. *See* MBEERE.

MBESA. The Mbesas are a relatively small ethnic group living in Zaire. Most Mbesas are concentrated on the west bank of the Lualaba River, up river from

the city of Bumba. As a riverine people, they have traditionally supported themselves by fishing, planting gardens on the river banks, and trading. Today, more and more Mbesas are seeking wage labor in towns and cities of north-central Zaire.
REFERENCE: Irving Kaplan et al. *Zaire: A Country Study.* 1978.

MBETE. The Mbetes (Mbetis) are a large cluster of peoples living today in southeastern Gabon and southwestern Congo. Their population exceeds 250,000 people. Included in the Mbete cluster are the Bandjabis, Badumas, Ambambas, Bambanas,* Mindoumous, Bakaniquis, Batsanguis,* and Bawandjis.* Most of the Mbetes are small farmers.
REFERENCE: Donald G. Morrison et al. *Black Africa: A Comparative Handbook.* 1989.

MBETI. *See* MBETE.

MBEUR. The Mbeurs are one of the major subgroups of the Ngambaye* people of Chad. The Ngambayes are themselves a subgroup of the Saras.*

MBIMOU. The Mbimous are a Bantu*-speaking people of the Central African Republic and northern Congo. They live in the Upper Sangha region of the equatorial rain forest in the southwestern reaches of the Central African Republic. The Mbimous were once a much larger group, but, beginning in 1908, they suffered badly from epidemics of sleeping sickness, which still afflict them today. They are a subgroup of the Sangas.*
REFERENCE: Pierre Kalck. *Historical Dictionary of the Central African Republic.* 1992.

MBIRE. The Mbires are a subgroup of the Zezuru* peoples of Zimbabwe.

MBO. The Mbos, not to be confused with the Mbos* of Zaire, are an ethnic group of approximately 50,000 people living on the Atlantic coast of Cameroon. Roughly four centuries ago, they migrated to their present location from Zaire. They believe they are descended from the Mbedi and Ewala peoples and are closely related to the Batangas* of the Kribi region and the Bakweris* of western Cameroon. They were among the first Cameroonian people to meet and interact with Europeans, and they became active middlemen in the Atlantic slave trade during the seventeenth and eighteenth centuries. During the century of French* administration, the Mbos became one of the most educated and acculturated groups in Cameroon. The Mbo language is closely related to Lingala.* In recent years, the Mbos have lost much of their economic influence.
REFERENCES: *African Encyclopedia.* 1974; Mark DeLancey and H. M. Mokeba. *Historical Dictionary of the Republic of Cameroon.* 1990.

MBO. The Mbos, not to be confused with the Cameroonian Mbos,* are

an ethnic group living today in the forests of northeastern Zaire. The Mbos can be found especially in the vicinity of Bafwasende. Most Mbos are small farmers.
REFERENCE: Irving Kaplan et al. *Zaire: A Country Study.* 1978.

MBOCHI. The Mbochis are a cluster of closely related ethnic groups living today in central Congo, western Zaire, and eastern Gabon in West Africa. They speak a Bantu* language. Ethnologists believe that they migrated from the west bank of the Congo River, pushing north to the confluence of the Sangha, Likouala, and Congo rivers and eventually as far north as the present-day Central African Republic, where they are known as the Bobanguis. Today, most of the Mbochi groups are concentrated in the Cuvette and Likoula regions of Congo. Although they are farmers, the Mbochis are also known for their skill as traders and fishermen. Their social structure is based on patrilineal clans. The major Mbochi subgroups include the Bangis, Bongalas, Mbochis proper, Kuyus,* Makus,* Makwas, Furus,* Irébus,* Likubas,* Lingas,* Lois,* Mbokos,* Ngirils,* and Likoualas. The total population of the Mbochi peoples exceeds 250,000 people today.
REFERENCES: Donald G. Morrison et al. *Black Africa: A Comparative Handbook.* 1989; Gordon C. McDonald et al. *Area Handbook for the People's Republic of the Congo (Congo Brazzaville).* 1971.

MBOI. The Mbois (Mboires, Mboyis) speak an Adamawa language and live in the Song District of the Adamawa Division of Gongola State in Nigeria.
REFERENCE: *Language Survey of Nigeria.* 1976.

MBOIRE. *See* MBOI.

MBOKO. The Mbokos are a subgroup of the Mbochi* peoples. Although many Mbokos are turning to commercial agriculture or day labor to earn a living, their traditional economy has revolved around fishing and trading, in which they still engage today. The Mbokos population today exceeds 30,000 people in the Republic of the Congo.
REFERENCE: Gordon C. McDonald et al. *Area Handbook for the People's Republic of the Congo (Congo Brazzaville).* 1971.

MBOLE. The Mbole people live south of the Middle Zaire River and west of the Lokmani River in Zaire. They are fishermen and farmers, raising cassava, bananas, and kola nuts. The Mboles speak a Mongo* language, which is part of the larger Bantu* linguistic family. The Mbole are considered to be part of the forest culture.
REFERENCE: Daniel Biebuyck. "Sculpture from the Eastern Zaire Forest Region." *African Arts* 9 (January 1976): 8–15.

MBOLOLO. The Mbololos are a subgroup of the Taita* peoples of East Africa, particularly Kenya. They speak a Bantu* language.

MBONDO. The Mbondos are one of the major subdivisions of the Mbundu* people of Angola.

MBOSHI. *See* MBOCHI.

MBOUM. *See* MBUN.

MBOWE. The Mbowe people are an ethnic group in Zaire and Zambia. They are part of the Mawika* cluster of peoples in the region. Most of them are small farmers. There are approximately 14,000 Mbowes in Zambia.
REFERENCE: John J. Grotpeter. *Historical Dictionary of Zambia.* 1979.

MBOYI. *See* MBOI.

MBUBE. *See* UTUGWANG.

MBUGU. The Mbugus are an ethnic group who arrived in Tanzania beginning in the seventeenth century. They were a non-Bantu* people then speaking a Cushitic language. The Mbugus settled in the Pare mountain region. Since that time, the Mbugus have become thoroughly Bantu-ized and assimilated by the Pare* people.
REFERENCE: Laura Kurtz. *Historical Dictionary of Tanzania.* 1978.

MBUGWE. The Mbugwe are a prominent, Bantu*-speaking people who live in central Tanzania. They are surrounded by the Iraqws* and live east and south of Lake Manyara. Most Mbugwe living in rural areas are hoe farmers, raising sorghum, millet, maize, cattle, sheep, and goats. The Mbugwe political system revolves around independent councils of elders in each village or general settlement area. Until the early 1970s, most of the Mbugwes lived in isolated homestead settlements, but, in 1974, Tanzania officially launched its *ujamaa* program, gathering the Mbugwe into larger villages where education, commercial agriculture, and political control would be easier to implement.

Islam first reached the Mbugwe in the nineteenth century when slave traders came into central Tanzania. Today, more than half of the Mbugwe identify themselves as Sunni Muslims of the Shafi school. But strong elements of their traditional animist faith—particularly worship at rain shrines—survive, and relatively few people conduct their daily Islamic prayers or observe Ramadan.
REFERENCES: E. R. Danielson. "Brief History of the Waniramba People Up to the Time of the German Occupation." *Tanganyika Notes and Records* 56 (1961): 67–68; E. R. Danielson. "Proverbs of the Waniramba Peoples of East Africa." *Tanganyika Notes and Records* 47–48 (1957): 187–97; J. Spencer Trimingham. *Islam in East Africa.* 1964.

MBUI. The Mbuis are a subgroup of the Ovimbundu* peoples of Angola.

MBUJA. The Mbujas are a small ethnic group in Zaire. They are concentrated north of the Lualaba River in north-central Zaire, south of the Uele River. The region in which they live is heavily forested, and the Mbujas make their living raising cassava, bananas, and kola nuts. In recent years, increasing numbers of Mbujas have left the forests for work in towns and cities, especially places like Yakoma and Bondo.
REFERENCE: Irving Kaplan et al. *Zaire: A Country Study.* 1978.

MBUKUSHU. The Mbukushus (Hambukushus) are an ethnic group with origins in the middle Zambezi River Valley. Before the nineteenth century, they lived in northern Ngamiland in Botswana and across the border in Angola. During the mid-nineteenth century, they came under Tawana* control. In the late 1960s and early 1970s, substantial numbers of Mbukushus fled Angola for Botswana to escape the civil wars and wars of national liberation there. They can also be found in Namibia. Some ethnologists classify the Mbukushus as one of the Kavanga* peoples.
REFERENCES: Fred Morton, A. Murray, and J. Ramsay. *Historical Dictionary of Botswana.* 1989; Stanley Schoeman and Ellen Schoeman. *Namibia.* 1984.

MBULA-BWAZZA. The Mbula-Bwazza people are a Jarawan Bantu* people who live in Nigeria. They can be found especially in the Girei District of the Adamawa Division of Gongola State, as well as in the Bachama, Shellem, and Mbula districts of the Numan Division in Gongola. Their population stands today at approximately 35,000 people.
REFERENCE: *Language Survey of Nigeria.* 1976.

MBUM. *See* MBUN.

MBUN. The Mbuns were once a large and powerful ethnic group in northern Cameroon, southern Chad, and western Central African Republic. For centuries, they dominated the Adamawa region, battling periodically against Fulbe* slave raiders. Those slave raids continued into the early twentieth century. During the late nineteenth and early twentieth centuries, the Mbuns fiercely resisted German* and French* colonization efforts, suffering military defeat and population decline in the process. Today, the Mbuns are a small ethnic group in province in western Cameroon and across the border in the Central African Republic. In recent decades, the Mbuns have come under the influence of Protestant missionaries. Their population today is approaching 800,000 people, of whom half are Muslims. They are a Bantu* people. In Zaire, the Mbuns strongly supported the Kwilu Rebellion in the mid-1960s. Still suspicious of the central

government of Zaire, they now live as small farmers. In Cameroon, they are concentrated in the highlands of the Adamawa massif.
REFERENCES: F. Scott Bobb. *Historical Dictionary of Zaire.* 1988; Pierre Kalck. *Historical Dictionary of the Central African Republic.* 1992; Pierre Kalck. *Central African Republic.* 1993.

MBUNDA. The Mbundas are one of the eastern Ngangela* ethnic groups in Angola and Zambia. Their population in Zambia exceeds 75,000 people. Along with surrounding groups in Zambia and Zaire, they are sometimes referred to collectively as the Balovales. They have a highly decentralized political system. Most Mbundas are farmers who raise cassava, millet, and yams.
REFERENCE: John J. Grotpeter. *Historical Dictionary of Zambia.* 1979.

MBUNDU. The Mbundus are a people living today in north-central Angola, particularly in Luanda, Bengo, Malanje, North Kwanza, and South Kwanza provinces in the Kwanza River Valley. Their population today exceeds 2.5 million people, which constitutes one-quarter of the total population of Angola. The Mbundus speak a Bantu* language known as Kimbundu. The Kimbundu language is divided into two large subgroups: Ambundu and Awkauanda. The Mbundus are divided into a number of subgroups, including the Kisamas, Libolos, Hakos, Ndembus, Hungos, Jingas, Mbakas, Bangalas, Holos, Mbondos, Munungos, Kibalas, Luangos, Ntemas, Punas, Caris, Bambeiros, Hacos, Eselas, Shinjes, Songos, Imgangalas, Ndongos, Mdakas, and Dembos.

Ethnohistorians believe the Mbundus arrived at their present location in the sixteenth century, migrating from central and east-central Africa. Before the arrival of the Portuguese,* the Mbundus were farmers, craftsmen, and traders. They were politically organized into several kingdoms. Beginning in the sixteenth century, the Mbundus had extensive contact with Portuguese traders and colonial administrators; by the mid-seventeenth century, most Western Mbundus were under Portuguese control. The Portuguese had their deepest impact in this region of Angola. During the nineteenth century, the expansion of the sugar and coffee plantations resulted in the alienation of Mbundu land.

In the twentieth century, a significant number of Mbundus became commercial farmers or well-educated businessmen. They also played a key role in the battle to expel the Portuguese in the 1950s and 1960s, finally achieving their goal of independence in 1972. The Mbundus were the main ethnic base of the Movimento Popular de Libertacão de Angola.
REFERENCES: *African Encyclopedia.* 1974; Susan H. Broadhead. *Historical Dictionary of Angola.* 1992; R. H. Chilcote. *Portuguese Africa.* 1967.

MBUNGA. The Mbungas are an East African people who are part of the Ngindo* cluster of the Northeastern Bantu* language group of East Africa. Most of the Mbungas are rice farmers who raise this cash crop in the fertile, damp floodplains of the Kilombero and Rufiji rivers in Tanzania. They also

raise poultry and goats. The Mbungas trace descent through male lines. They are primarily Muslim in their religious orientation, but they generally do not observe Ramadan or many other Islamic rituals. The wearing of a white skull cap and the adoption of an Arab* name are the only religious requirements they regularly fulfill. Like other Tanzanians, the Mbungas have been dealing with the government's *ujamaa* program since the mid-1970s. The policy is designed to alter the traditional homestead settlement pattern in favor of establishing village clusters, where public education and public health campaigns can be more successful. The Mbunga population of Tanzania exceeds 30,000 people.
REFERENCE: A. R. W. Crosse-Upcott. ''Male Circumcision Among the Ngindo.'' *Journal of the Royal Anthropological Institute* 89 (1959): 169–89.

MBUNZA. The Mbunzas are a subgroup of the Herero* people.

MBUTE. *See* VUTE.

MBUTERE. *See* VUTE.

MBWELA. The Mbwelas are a subgroup of the larger Ngangela* cluster of peoples living today in Angola.

MBWELA. The Mbwelas, also known as the Lukolwes, are an ethnic group living today in Zambia. They are closely related linguistically to the Nkoyas* and the Mashashas.
REFERENCE: Sirarpi Ohannessian and Mubanga E. Kashoki. *Language in Zambia.* 1978.

MBWEN. *See* GOUIN.

MBWERA. *See* SHIRAZI.

MBWILA. The Mbwilas are a Tanzanian ethnic group whom ethnologists sometimes include in the Safwa* cluster of peoples.

MDAKA. The Mdakas are a subgroup of the Mbundus* of north-central Angola.

MDEMBO. *See* NDEMBU.

MEBAN. The Meban people are one of the subgroups of the Shilluks,* a pre-Nilotic* people of the Sudan.

MEBE. *See* DAN.

MECH'A. The Mech'a are one of the primary subgroups of the Oromo* peoples of northern Ethiopia. Most of them are Sunni Muslims of the Shafi school. They live in western Shoa Province and northern Kafa Province and work as sedentary farmers.

MÉDÉ. *See* GULA.

MEDI. *See* KURI.

MEDIA. The Media, with a population of perhaps 2,000 people, are one of the smallest of the Buduma* subgroups. They are cattle raisers and fishermen.

MEDOGO. The Medogos are one of the Lisi* peoples of Chad. They number approximately 10,000 people, all of whom are Muslims. They share judicial institutions and intermarry regularly with the Bulala* people. They are located mainly between Ati and Oum Hadjer in the Batha Prefecture.
REFERENCES: Thomas Collelo et al. *Chad: A Country Study.* 1988; Samuel Decalo. *Historical Dictionary of Chad.* 1987.

ME'EN. The Me'en are an ethnic group living today in Ethiopia. They speak a Nilo-Saharan language and make their living as pastoralists. The Me'en population is approximately 45,000 people.
REFERENCES: M. L. Bender, J. D. Bowen, R. L. Cooper, and C. A. Ferguson, eds. *Language in Ethiopia.* 1976; Harold D. Nelson et al. *Ethiopia: A Country Study.* 1980.

MEGELI. *See* MIGILI.

MEGONG. *See* EGGAN.

MEHAFALY. The Mehafaly (Mahafali) people are one of Madagascar's ethnic groups. With a population today of approximately 150,000 people, they are concentrated west of the Antandroy* people, between the Menarandra and Onilahy rivers. Their ethnic roots reach back to the Sakalavas.* The traditional Mehafaly economy revolved around raising goats and cattle and moving the animals seasonally for forage. More recently, the Mehafaly people have been drawn into the larger commercial economy.
REFERENCE: Maureen Covell. *Madagascar: Politics, Economics and Society.* 1987; Harold D. Nelson et al. *Area Handbook for the Malagasy Republic.* 1973.

MEHWEN. The Mehwens are a subgroup of the Bassa* people of Liberia. Most Mehwens live in Grand Bassa County.

MEIDAB. *See* MEIDOB.

MEIDOB. The Meidobs are a group of approximately 50,000 people who live in the Meidob Hills in Darfur Province of western Sudan. There is also a concentration of Meidobs in the city of Malha. The Meidobs call themselves the Tiddi. They speak a language that is classified as part of the Nilo-Saharan family. They trace their origins to the Nubian* groups of the Nile River in Egypt, and many contemporary Meidobs are familiar with Nubian kinship groups. Historically, the Meidobs have made their living raising livestock, particularly sheep, goats, and camels, and collecting salt, all of which they trade across the Libyan caravan routes. They also raise sorghum and vegetables for local consumption. The Meidobs are a fiercely independent people whose relationship with outsiders has often been hostile. The Meidobs are divided into three primary subgroups: the Urrti, the Shalkota (also known as Kargeddi), and the Torti.

The Meidob conversion to Islam began in the seventeenth century but was not complete until the nineteenth century. When Darfur became part of the Anglo-Egyptian Sudan in 1916, the British* recognized the Shalkota *malik* (chief) as the local political administrator. That political authority did not end until 1971 when the Sudanese government formally abolished all forms of "native administration." Today, Meidob men are devout Muslims, but Meidob women have retained and still practice a number of pre-Islamic rituals, including fertility rites and divination. During the 1980s, the Meidobs were hurt by the severe drought affecting the region, which led to the migration of increasingly large numbers of Meidob young men to Libyan cities in search of work.
REFERENCES: E. A. Hales. "Meidob Kinship, Marriage and Residence." Ph.D. Dissertation. Cambridge University. 1979; J. M. Hales. "The Pastoral System of the Meidob." Ph.D. Dissertation. Cambridge University. 1978; Robin Thelwall, "Meidob." In Richard V. Weekes, ed. *Muslim Peoples.* 1984.

MEJAT. The Mejats are a small ethnic group who traditionally lived along the northern coast of Western Sahara. They first emerged as a self-conscious ethnic group in the sixteenth century. The Mejats support themselves as fishermen. They are subdivided into the El-Gronas, the El-Beyeds, the Ahel Mohammed Ben Brahims,* and the Ahel Ali Ben Salems.
REFERENCE: Tony Hodges. *Historical Dictionary of Western Sahara.* 1982.

MEKIBO. *See* MEKYIBO.

MEKYIBO. The Mekyibo, who have also been known historically as the Mekibo, Ehotile, Eotile, Eoutilé, Vétéré, Ewutre, and Byetri, are part of the Lagoon cluster of peoples in the southern Ivory Coast. Their current population totals approximately 5,000 people, most of whom live along the Aby Lagoon in the subprefecture of Adiaké. They claim to be the true indigenous people of the region.
REFERENCE: Robert J. Mundt. *Historical Dictionary of Côte d'Ivoire.* 1995.

MENABE. The Menabes (Antaivas, Tankays) are a subgroup of the Tanala* peoples of Madagascar.

MENASIR. The Menasirs, also known as the Lemanisirs, are a small group of fishermen who live along the Atlantic Coast of Western Sahara, between Saguia el-Hamra and Dakhla. They are subdivided into two groups: the Oulad Mohammed Aidis and the Oulad Ali Sergs.
REFERENCE: Tony Hodges. *Historical Dictionary of Western Sahara.* 1982.

MENDÉ. The Mendé (Mendi, Kossa) are a patrilineal ethnic group living in Sierra Leone and Liberia in West Africa; the vast majority are in Sierra Leone. They are the largest ethnic group in the country, comprising nearly a third of the Sierra Leone population and totaling approximately 1.4 million people. They are divided into more than sixty separate chiefdoms and are concentrated in the central forests and coastal bush country of southern Sierra Leone. Another 10,000 or so Mendé live across the border in the Guma Mende chiefdom of Liberia. They speak a Manding* language. Ethnologists identify three major Mendé subgroups. The Kpa-Mende live to the west in the coastal bush, while the Sewa Mende are in the central forests. The Ko-Mende also live in the forests but generally to the north of the Sewa.

The traditional Mendé religion revolved around the supreme creator—Ngewo. It was an animistic faith. The Mendé believed that Ngewo could be approached through the spirits of their ancestors or spirits representing their various religious societies. Belief in the power of witches was central to Mendé indigenous religion. In the nineteenth century, Muslim traders—Sunni Muslims of the Maliki rite—introduced Islam to the Mendé, but the new religion took hold only very slowly until the early twentieth century, when conversion to the Muslim faith was seen as an act of defiance against the British* colonial administration. Today, approximately one-third of the Mendé are Muslims. The remainder are Christians, animists, or some syncretic mix of the original tribal religion, Christianity, and Islam.

Today, approximately 80 percent of Mendé are small farmers who raise wet or dry rice, cassava, palm kernels, coffee, cocoa, and ginger. The rice and cassava are staples, while the others are cash crops. Since the early 1970s, an increasing number of Mendé young men have migrated to Freetown, Port Loko, Makeni, Bo, Pujehun, and Sulima in search of work. The move to the cities has created a labor shortage on the rural farms.
REFERENCES: W. A. Hart. "Sculpture of the Njayei Society among the Mende." *African Arts* 26 (July 1993): 46–54; Barry L. Isaac and Shelby R. Conrad. "Child Fosterage among the Mende of Upper Bambara Chiefdom, Sierra Leone: Rural-Urban and Occupational Comparisons." *Ethnology* 21 (July 1982): 243–58; Vernon R. Darjahn. "Mende." In Richard V. Weekes, ed. *Muslim Peoples.* 1984; W. T. Harris and H. L. Sawyer. *The Springs of Mende Belief and Conduct.* 1968.

MENDI. *See* MENDÉ.

MENI-FERE. The Meni-Feres are a subgroup of the Saho* people of Ethiopia. Their current population exceeds 20,000 people.

MENING. The Menings are one of the more than thirty ethnic groups of Uganda. They speak an Eastern Nilotic* language and live in northern Uganda. Their economy revolves around transhumant pastoralism, with the men raising cattle and the women trying to raise sorghum and millet. Their entire life— economy, religion, and culture—revolves around cattle. Because of severe droughts in northeastern Africa during the 1980s and early 1990s, the Menings have faced dire economic circumstances.
REFERENCE: Peter Ladefoged, Ruth Glick, and Clive Criper. *Languages in Uganda.* 1972.

MENKA. The Menkas are a relatively small ethnic group living today in the forests of the Manyu Prefecture of Southwest Province in Cameroon. They can be found north of the headwaters of the Cross River, northeast of Mamfe Town. Their most immediate ethnic neighbors are the Kenyangs,* Ngwes,* Mundanis,* Denyas,* and Ejaghams.* Most Menkas are subsistence farmers.
REFERENCE: Samson Negbo Abangma. *Modes in Denya Discourse.* 1987.

MENSA. The Mensas are one of the principal ethnic groups of the Hamasen District in the central region of Eritrea in Ethiopia. They speak the Tegrigna language and played a central role in the Eritrean secessionist movement and Ethiopian civil war in the 1970s. Although the region itself is officially Christian, most Mensas are Muslims.
REFERENCE: Chris Prouty and Eugene Rosenfeld. *Historical Dictionary of Ethiopia and Eritrea.* 1994.

MERINA. The Merinas (Antimerinas, Hovas, Imerinas, Ovahs) are the largest ethnic group in Madagascar. Their current population is approaching three million people. Like other Madagascarene peoples, the Merinas have Indonesian, African, Indian, and Arab* origins, and their language—Malagasy—is Malayo-Polynesian in its roots. The Merinas live in the northern reaches of the Central Highlands of the island. Merina society is divided between the Fotsy, who are descendants of free Merinas, and the Mainty, who are descendants of slaves. Today, the Merinas are a well-educated people who are overrepresented in the country's elite groups. They tend to be socially conservative and clannish.
REFERENCES: Maurice Bloch. "Marriage Amongst Equals: An Analysis of the Marriage Ceremony of the Merina of Madagascar." *Man* 13 (March 1978): 21–33; Maureen Covell. *Madagascar: Politics, Economics, and Society.* 1987.

MERU. The Meru are a Tanzanian ethnic group who live in the Serengeti Plain of the Arusha Region and across the border in Kenya. They once called themselves the Ngaa and speak a Central Bantu* language. They originated on the coast of the Indian Ocean in East Africa in the early eighteenth century and began a migration that brought them to their present locations. The migration was along the Tana River, northwest toward Mount Kenya. The Meru are farmers who produce coffee, wheat, maize, and potatoes; they also raise cattle and are known for their skill as beekeepers. The total Meru population today exceeds 700,000 people, who are divided into the following subgroups: Igembe, Igoji, Imenti, Mintini, Tigania, Muthambi, Mwimbi, and Chuka.
REFERENCES: Laura Kurtz. *Historical Dictionary of Tanzania.* 1978; Bethwell A. Ogot. *Historical Dictionary of Kenya.* 1981.

MESENGO. The Mesengos are an ethnic group living today in Ethiopia. They speak a Nilo-Saharan language and make their living as pastoralists. The Mesengo population is approximately 35,000 people.
REFERENCES: M. L. Bender, J. D. Bowen, R. L. Cooper, and C. A. Ferguson, eds. *Language in Ethiopia.* 1976; Harold D. Nelson et al. *Ethiopia: A Country Study.* 1980.

MESIRIYA. *See* BAGGARA.

MESMEDJÉ. The Mesmedjé are an ethnic group in Chad. Virtually all of the 40,000 or so Mesmedjé are Muslims. They are part of the larger Nilotic* cluster of Chadian peoples. Most Mesjedjé make their living as small farmers, laborers, and semi-nomadic and nomadic pastoralists.
REFERENCES: Pierre Hugot. *Le Tchad.* 1965; J. C. Lebeuf. *Afrique Centrale.* 1972; Donald G. Morrison et al. *Black Africa: A Comparative Handbook.* 1989.

MESSELLIMIYA. *See* GEZIRA.

MESTICO. The term "Mestico" is used in the areas of formerly Portuguese* Africa to refer to those individuals of mixed racial descent—usually the offspring of Portuguese traders, administrators, and soldiers who married African women. Their total population in Angola and Mozambique exceeds 600,000, most of whom live in major urban areas and play significant roles in national economic and political life.
REFERENCE: Susan H. Broadhead. *Historical Dictionary of Angola.* 1992.

META. The Metas are a subgroup of the Bamiléké* peoples of Cameroon. They are concentrated in the northwest corner of the country, near the Atlantic Coast. The Meta economy revolves around the agricultural production of maize, millet, vegetables, and coffee.
REFERENCE: Claude Tardits. *Le royaume Bamoum.* 1980.

MÉTIS. The term "Métis" (Metisse) is used in areas of formerly French West Africa to refer to those individuals of mixed racial descent—usually the offspring of French traders, administrators, and soldiers who married African women.
REFERENCE: James S. Olson, ed. *Historical Dictionary of European Imperialism.* 1991.

METISSE. *See* MÉTIS.

METOKO. The Metokos (Mitokos) are a Bantu*-speaking people who live today on both sides of the Lualaba River, particularly on its Lilo tributary, in east-central Zaire. The Metokos have traditionally been a riverine people whose livelihood came from fishing, trading, and river-bank farming. Most Metokos still pursue a traditional lifestyle economically, although more and more are seeking work in cities and towns.
REFERENCES: Daniel Biebuyck. "Sculpture from the Eastern Zaire Forest Region." *African Arts* 9 (January 1976): 8–15; Irving Kaplan et al. *Zaire: A Country Study.* 1978.

METUME. The Metumes are an ethnic group living today southwest of Mount Kenya in Kenya in East Africa. They are closely related to the Kikuyu* and Meru* peoples. Most of them are subsistence farmers.
REFERENCE: W. H. Whiteley. *Language in Kenya.* 1974.

MFANG. *See* FANG.

MFENGU. The Mfengus are a South African ethnic group sometimes identified as "Fingoes." They speak a Xhosa* language, live in Transkei and Ciskei, and have a contemporary population of more than one million people. During the Zulu* wars under Shaka of the 1820s, the Mfengus, along with a number of other small groups, were driven south from Natal and had to settle among the Xhosa, where they were treated as second-class people. When new wars erupted in the 1830s, the Mfengus joined the Europeans in fighting the Xhosas; in return, they were rewarded with Xhosa land. Although some Mfengus retained their traditional lifestyle of raising cattle and some grains, many acculturated to European values, becoming literate converting to Christianity, and starting their own business. Mfengu success was so great that it precipitated the debates in South Africa that led to the apartheid policy. There are also influential Mfengus in Zimbabwe—descendants of Mfengus who were moved there by Cecil Rhodes in the late nineteenth century.
REFERENCES: *African Encyclopedia.* 1974; R. Kent Rasmussen. *Historical Dictionary of Zimbabwe.* 1979.

MFUNU. The Mfunus are an ethnic group located on both sides of the Zaire River in southwestern Zaire and in southeastern Congo. The Mfunus are a riverine people who have traditionally supported themselves by planting small gardens on the river banks, fishing, and trading up and down the Zaire River. REFERENCE: Irving Kaplan et al. *Zaire: A Country Study*. 1978.

MFUTE. *See* BAFUT.

MHARI. *See* MARI.

MHLANGA. The Mhlangas are one of the major clans of the Bemdzabuko* division of the Swazi* people of Swaziland.

MIANGO. *See* IRIGWE.

MIDIAS. *See* KURI.

MIDOGO. The Midogos are one of the subgroups of the Lisi* people of Chad. They are a Nilotic* people who today make their living as nomadic and semi-nomadic pastoralists, although many are also farming today.

MIGILI. The Migilis (Megilis) are an ethnic group living today in Plateau State, Nigeria, primarily in the Obi, Assaikio, Lafia, and Doma districts of the Lafia Division. Like the Jukuns* and Alagoas,* with whom they have had a long association, the Migilis have a system of sacred kingships and hereditary political offices. They are also related to the Idomas* and Gomeis.* Since their conquest by the Alagoas, they have been largely subject to them. Most Migilis are subsistence farmers, raising guinea corn, maize, and millet. They are especially concentrated in the Lafia and Awe districts.
REFERENCES: Ade Adefuye. "The Alago Kingdoms: A Political History." In Elizabeth Isichei, ed. *Studies in the History of Plateau State, Nigeria*. 1982; *Language Survey of Nigeria*. 1976.

MIJIKENDA. The Mijikendas are a cluster of Northeast Bantu*-speaking peoples who today live on the coastal strip of Kenya along the Indian Ocean, from north of the Galana River to the Tanzanian border. Included in the cluster are the Digos,* who actually live across the border in Tanzania, and the Giriyamas,* Duramas,* Rabais,* Ribes,* Kambes,* Kaumas,* Chonyis,* and Jibanas.* The Mijikendas are farmers who raise rice, maize, cassava, and coconuts. They also supply palm oil for the palm wine industry. They are nominally Sunni Muslims of the Shafi school, and their social system is based on patrilineal descent. Generally, the surrounding Swahili*-speaking people of Kenya and Tanzania look down upon the Mijikendas as an inferior group. East African demographers estimate that today the Mijikenda population exceeds 950,000 people.
REFERENCES: P. B. Bostock. *The Peoples of Kenya*. 1967; Jean Lucas Brown. "Miji

Kenda Grave Sculptures.'' *African Arts* 13 (May 1980): 36–39; Bethwell A. Ogot. *Historical Dictionary of Kenya.* 1981; Justin Willis. *Mombasa, the Swahili, and the Making of the Mijikenda.* 1993.

MIKIFORE. The Mikifores live in West Africa, particularly in Sierra Leone, Liberia, and Guinea. Their population in the early 1990s was estimated at 230,000 people, approximately one-third of whom are Muslims. They are a branch of the Mandinkas* and trace their origins back to the thirteenth-century Mali Empire; they first arrived in Guinea and Sierra Leone around 1600. Most Mikifores are small farmers who raise millet, rice, peanuts, and a variety of other crops.
REFERENCES: Cyril P. Foray. *Historical Dictionary of Sierra Leone.* 1977; Donald R. Wright. ''Manding-Speaking Peoples.'' In Richard V. Weekes, ed. *Muslim Peoples.* 1984.

MILERI. The Mileris, also known to outsiders as the Jebels, are one of the Tama*-speaking peoples of Sudan and Chad. They live on the Sudan side of the border. Their population today is approximately 9,000 people, most of whom are settled pastoralists, raising cattle, camels, and goats, as well as performing small-scale subsistence agriculture. The main Mileri settlement is Jebel Mun. They consider themselves descendants of the Missiriyya.
REFERENCE: Paul Doornbos. ''Tama-Speaking Peoples.'' In Richard V. Weekes, ed. *Muslim Peoples.* 1984.

MILTOU. The Miltous are a relatively small ethnic group living today in the Moyen-Chari Prefecture of Chad. Their language is part of the larger Chadian cluster of languages, and it represents a transition between Sara* and Massa.* Most Miltous are herdsmen and small farmer, raising sorghum, millet, maize, and cotton.
REFERENCE: Thomas Collelo et al. *Chad: A Country Study.* 1988.

MIMA. The Mimas are an ethnic group of approximately 30,000 people, located in Darfur and Kordofan provinces in Sudan. They live primarily in such urban, market centers as Woda'a, Fafa, and Magrur, or as pastoral nomads and settled farmers in rural areas. The Mimas in the cities work as merchants, craftsmen, teachers, and government civil servants. Ethnolinguists believe that they originated in the Nile Valley of Egypt, where Arabic became their language and Islam their religion. Then they migrated to the west beginning in the seventeenth century. By the early eighteenth century, the Mimas were subjects of the Darfur Sultanate. Divided into thirty smaller political subdivisions headed by territorial chiefs, they had their own king who answered to Darfur authority. By the twentieth century, the Mimas were becoming increasingly integrated into the larger political, educational, and economic life of Sudan, gradually losing much of their distinctive ethnic identity.

REFERENCE: Paul Doornbos. "Mima-Mimi." In Richard V. Weekes, ed. *Muslim Peoples.* 1984.

MIMI. The Mimis are an ethnic group of approximately 35,000 people living in Wadai Province of Chad. They are closely related to the Mimas* of Sudan. They are scattered through more than sixty villages north of the city of Biltine. The largest urban concentration of Mimis is in Agan. Rural Mimis are either pastoral nomads or sedentary farmers, raising cereals, beans, sesame, and several other crops. Ethnolinguists believe that they originated in the Nile Valley of Egypt, where Arabic became their language and Islam their religion. They then migrated to the west beginning in the seventeenth century. Only the Amdangs, a Mimi subgroup of about 8,000 people living near Biltine, have retained the ancestral language. During the late nineteenth and twentieth centuries, French* colonial authorities began to integrate some Mimis into the larger polity and economy. During the 1970s, 1980s, and early 1990s, the social and political life of the Mimis has been badly disrupted by the continuing civil wars that have devastated Chad.
REFERENCES: Paul Doornbos. "Mima-Mimi." In Richard V. Weekes, ed. *Muslim Peoples.* 1984; J. Lukas and O. Volckers. "G. Nachtigal's Aufseichnungen uber die Sprache der Mimi in Wadai." *Zeitschrift fur Eingebohrenen-sprachen* 29 (1938): 145–54.

MINA. The Mina (Popo) are one of the major ethnic groups in Togo and Benin. Most of them are subsistence farmers who raise maize, millet, manioc, and plantains. They are concentrated in the southern region of Togo and Benin, along the coast from Lomé to Ouidah, Benin. Most of them live in and around Anécho and Porto Seguro. Ethnologists believe the Mina originated in Ghana and migrated to Anécho in the seventeenth century. The term "Mina" is actually a collective word referring to two peoples—the Ga* and the Ané.* Their current population exceeds 150,000 people, and they constitute an important element in the political, commercial, and administrative elite of Togo and Benin.
REFERENCES: Samuel Decalo. *Historical Dictionary of Benin.* 1987; Donald G. Morrison et al. *Black Africa: A Comparative Handbook.* 1989.

MINDA. *See* BANDAWA-MINDA.

MINDASSA. The Mindassas are a Gabonese ethnic group living near the junction of the Leconi and the M'Passa rivers, north of Franceville, in Haut-Ogooué Province. Most of them are small farmers and are considered to be part of the Bakota,* or Kota, cluster of peoples.
REFERENCE: David E. Gardinier. *Historical Dictionary of Gabon.* 1994.

MINDOUMOU. *See* NDOUMOU.

MINI. The Minis are a small Nigerian ethnic group. They live today in the Brass Division of Rivers State.
REFERENCE: *Language Survey of Nigeria.* 1976.

MINIANKA. The Miniankas are an ethnic group of the Ivory Coast and southeastern Mali who have largely been subsumed by the Senufos.* In fact, today they are the northernmost extension of the Senufos. Their traditional homeland was near the Bani River in northern Ivory Coast, southern Mali, and southern Burkino-Faso. They were overwhelmed culturally by the northern migration of the Senufos, and, by the end of the nineteenth century, the Miniankas were part of the Kingdom of Kenedougou, a Senufo state. The arrival of the French* empire dissolved the kingdom. Today, the Miniankas are primarily small farmers living among the Senufos; their population probably exceeds 250,000 people. The Miniankas living near Koutiala in Mali are commercial farmers who raise cotton as a cash crop. Most Miniankas have resisted converson to Islam, preferring their own indigenous faith.
REFERENCES: Bohumil Holas. *Les Senufo (y compris les Minianka).* 1966; Philippe Jespers. ''L'arc et le sang des chiens.'' *Systèmes de pensée en Afrique noire* 6 (1983): 65–102.

MINTINI. The Mintinis are a Bantu*-speaking people who are a subgroup of the Meru* cluster of peoples in Kenya and Tanzania.

MINUNGO. *See* MUNUNGO.

MIRIFAB. The Mirifabs are the product of ethnogenesis between the Arab* and the Nubian* peoples of Sudan. Their population today numbers more than one million people, most of whom are small farmers and workers living in north-central Sudan. Virtually all of them are Muslims.
REFERENCE: Donald G. Morrison et al. *Black Africa: A Comparative Handbook.* 1989.

MIRRIAM. The Mirriams are a relatively small ethnic group living in Plateau State in Nigeria. They are linguistically related to the Dimmuks,* Bwals,* and Kwallas.* Their own traditions claim that an ancient ancestor sprang from Korfar Rock, and that rock remains the focus of Mirriam religion. In recent centuries, the Mirriams left the Kofyar highlands and settled in the lowlands south of Pankshin, where they farmed the land and still do today.
REFERENCE: John Ola Agi. ''The Goemai and their Neighbors: An Historical Analysis.'' In Elizabeth Isichei, ed. *Studies in the History of Plateau State, Nigeria.* 1982.

MITOKO. *See* METOKO.

MITSHOGO. *See* MITSOGO.

MITSOGO. The Mitsogos, also known as the Mitshogo or Tshogo, speak an Okandé* language and live in south-central Gabon, primarily in N'Gounié Province. They originally lived in the Ivindo River area but migrated southwest into the mountains between the Offoué and N'Gounié rivers to escape slave raiding by the Bakèlès.* French* explorers first reached the Mitsogos in 1857. At the time, the Mitsogo population was approximately 5,000 people. The Mitsogos were widely respected for their skills in iron and cloth manufacture, but they suffered at the hands of Bakèlè slave traders all through the nineteenth century. In 1899, with the establishment of a French military outpost and a Roman Catholic mission in the region, the Mitsogos came under permanent European control. They rebelled against the French in 1904 because of the oppressive labor quotas demanded by French concessionary companies. In 1937–1938, Mitsogo territory was overrun by Europeans and Africans because of the discovery of gold. Today, most Mitsogos are small farmers.
REFERENCES: David E. Gardinier. *Historical Dictionary of Gabon.* 1994; Roger Sillans. "Motombi. Mythes et Énigmes initiatiques des Mitsoghos du Gabon Central." Ph.D. dissertation. University of Paris. 1967.

MIUTINI. The Miutinis are part of the Central Bantu* cluster of peoples living today in south-central Kenya. Their population today is approximately 60,000 people, most of whom are small farmers and laborers. They are closely related to the Merus.*
REFERENCE: Donald G. Morrison et al. *Black Africa: A Comparative Handbook.* 1989.

MIWO. The Miwos live today in far northwestern Ghana, far northern Ivory Coast, and across the border in Burkina-Faso. Most of them make their living by raising livestock and through subsistence farming. Ethnologists consider them a subgroup of the Lobi* people.

MIYA. The Miyas, also known as Muyas, are a Chadic people living today in the Ganjuwa District of the Bauchi Division of Bauchi State in Nigeria. Their current population exceeds 12,000 people.
REFERENCE: *Language Survey of Nigeria.* 1976.

MMANAANA KGATLA. The Mmanaana Kgatlas are one of the five major subgroups of the Kgatla* people of Botswana. They live exclusively in Botswana. The Mmanaana Kgatlas had split away from the Kgafela Kgatla* before 1800 and lived in the Transvaal until 1820, when the Ngwaketses* conquered them. They became independent again in the 1840s, only to fall under the control of the Boers, after which they settled among the Kwenas.* From the 1940s to the early 1990s, Kgosi Letlole has governed them as chief.
REFERENCE: Fred Morton, A. Murray, and J. Ramsay. *Historical Dictionary of Botswana.* 1989.

MMANI. *See* MNAMI.

MMOFO. *See* DÉGHA.

MNAMI. The Mnamis (Mmani) are a small Senegambian* ethnic group living in Guinea, Gambia, Senegal, and Guinea-Bissau. Ethnologists classify them as part of the West Atlantic Cluster of ethnic groups. A substantial number of Mnamis are Muslims. They are primarily rice farmers. Ethnologists believe the Mnamis are of Baga* origin, but today they are being absorbed rapidly by the Sosos.* The vast majority of Mnamis speak Soso as their first language.
REFERENCES: Richard Lobban and Joshua Forrest. *Historical Dictionary of the Republic of Guinea-Bissau.* 1988; Thomas O'Toole. *Historical Dictionary of Guinea.* 1987.

MNCINA. The Mncinas are one of the clans of the Emakhandzambili* peoples, who themselves are one of the three major subgroups of the Swazi* people of Swaziland.

MNISI. The Mnisis are one of the clans of the Emakhandzambili* peoples, who themselves are one of the three major subgroups of the Swazi* people of Swaziland.

MO. The Mo people of Ghana are part of the larger Grusi* cluster of peoples. They are concentrated on the western border between the Northern Region and the Brong-Ahafo Region. They are descendants of Sasalas* who migrated from the northern part of the Northern Region and settled on the Black Volta River in the Bamboi Region and near Wa. Most Mos are farmers. Their contemporary population exceeds 20,000 people.
REFERENCE: Daniel M. McFarland. *Historical Dictionary of Ghana.* 1995.

MOAB. *See* BIMOBA.

MOARE. *See* BIMOBA.

MOBA. *See* BIMOBA.

MOBER. *See* MOBEUR.

MOBEUR. The Mobeurs (Mobers, Mavars) are an ethnic group of approximately 50,000 people living along the Komadougou River in eastern Niger and across the border in northeastern Nigeria, especially in the Mobber District of the Borno Division of Borno State. They represent a mix of the ancient So* people and the more contemporary Kanembus.* Tuareg* warriors drove them out of the Ouri area in the mid-eighteenth century, and the Mobeurs then

settled in Bosso. French* explorers considered the Mobeurs to be especially aggressive toward and suspicious of outsiders. Today, most Mobeurs are small farmers. They speak a Chadic language.
REFERENCES: Samuel Decalo. *Historical Dictionary of Niger.* 1989; *Language Survey of Nigeria.* 1976.

MOBOKO. The Mobokos are a subgroup of the Bakweri* peoples of Cameroon. They live in villages on and near the slopes of Mt. Cameroon in South West Province. They arrived in the region as part of a Bantu* migration that began in the early eighteenth century. Because of their location near the coast, the Mobokos were among the first Cameroonians to come into contact with Europeans; they lost much of their land to German* plantation owners in the late nineteenth and early twentieth centuries. In recent years, such groups as the Bakweri Union and the Bakweri Land Claim Committee have tried to recover Moboko property. Today, most Mobokos support themselves by working on the palm oil plantations, oil rigs and refineries at Cape Limbo, as well as by fishing and rice farming.
REFERENCE: Mark W. DeLancey and H. M. Mokeba. *Historical Dictionary of the Republic of Cameroon.* 1990.

MOCHA. The Mochas, who call themselves the Shekatchos, are part of the larger cluster of Omotic* peoples in Ethiopia. They live near the Kefichos,* to whom they are linguistically related, in far southwestern Ethiopia. Most Mochas are hoe cultivators who raise ensete or various other grain products. They also practice animal husbandry. They have retained many elements of their indigenous religions.
REFERENCE: Harold D. Nelson et al. *Ethiopia: A Country Study.* 1980.

MOFOU. *See* MOFU.

MOFU. The Mofus are a non-Fulbe,* non-Muslim ethnic group of northern Cameroon. The Mofus have long been isolated in the hills of northern Diamaré Department, although, in recent years, growing numbers have migrated to the lowland plains, where they have become increasingly commercialized. They arrived there fleeing Fulbe slave traders in the lowlands. The Mofus are farmers who raise crops in terraced, hillside fields. They are a subgroup of the Kirdi* peoples. The Mofu population today exceeds 85,000 people.
REFERENCE: Harold D. Nelson et al. *Area Handbook for the United Republic of Cameroon.* 1988.

MOGOGODO. *See* YAAKU.

MOGOUM. The Mogoum are one of the Hadjeray* peoples of the mountainous regions of Guéra Prefecture in Chad. They are descendants of refugees who were driven into the mountains. They speak a Chadic language and practice the *margai* cult of place and site spirits. In spite of many cultural similarities with such other groups as the Kingas,* Junkuns,* Bidios,* Dangaleats,* Sokoros,* Barains,* and Sabas,* the Mogoums rarely intermarry with them and maintain a powerful sense of identity.

REFERENCE: Thomas Collelo et al. *Chad: A Country Study.* 1988.

MOKAR. *See* GA'ANDA.

MOLÉ. *See* MOSSI.

MOLÉ-DAGBANE PEOPLES. The term ''Molé-Dagbane Peoples'' (also known as Gur or Voltaic) refers to a large linguistic group of more than nine million people who live primarily in northern Ghana, as well as in Burkina-Faso, northern Togo, and northern Ivory Coast. Historically, the Molé-Dagbane peoples have been known for their origins in the Upper Volta Basin, their skill as peasant farmers and traders, and their tendency to establish long histories as contiguous independent states. They are an extraordinary complex of dozens of subgroups identified by distinct languages, social structures, and religions, although perhaps a third of all Molé-Dagbane people are Muslims. Included in the Molé-Dagbane linguistic group are the Mossis,* Grusis,* Dogambas,* Dogons,* Basaris,* Mamprusis,* Dagaris,* Talensis,* and many others.

REFERENCES: Gregory A. Finnegan. ''Molé-Dagbane Peoples.'' In Richard V. Weekes, ed. *Muslim Peoples.* 1984; Jack Goody. *The Ethnography of the Northern Territories of the Gold Coast West of the White Volta.* 1954.

MOMA. The Momas are a relatively small ethnic group living today in the Kasai Orientale region of central Zaire. Their homeland is a heavily forested region where they support themselves by raising cassava, bananas, and kola nuts.

REFERENCE: Irving Kaplan et al. *Zaire: A Country Study.* 1978.

MONA. The Mona people (Mwanu, Mwa, Ganmu) are an ethnic group living in the Mankono Department in west-central Ivory Coast. They are closely related to the Gagus* and Guros. They are of Manding* origin and arrived in the forest several centuries ago, where they lived by farming plantains, manioc, yams, and taro. In more recent years, they have made the transition to commercial forms of farming, raising coffee, cocoa, and cotton for cash, as well as rice for their staple.

REFERENCE: Robert J. Mundt. *Historical Dictionary of Côte d'Ivoire.* 1995.

MONDJOMBO. The Mondjombos are an ethnic group living today downstream on the Ubangi River from Bangi in the Central African Republic and in northern Congo. They are a riverine people who traditionally made their

living by fishing, hunting, and planting on the river banks. After the arrival of the French,* the Mondjombos' skills as boatsmen on the Ubangi allowed them to become traders and middlemen with the inland tribes. Today, Mondjombos play key roles in the military, civil service, and police of the Central African Republic. They are considered a subgroup of the Sanga* peoples.
REFERENCE: Pierre Kalck. *Central African Republic.* 1993.

MONGO. The Mongos, or Mongo-Nkundos, are a cluster of peoples living south of the Middle Congo River in Zaire. They are concentrated in the forests of the Congo Basin and the southern uplands, bordered by the Lulonga River in the north, the Sankuru River in the south, the meeting of the Zaire and Momboyo rivers to the west, and the confluence of the Lualaba and Lukuga rivers to the east. They include such groups as the Mongos and Nkundos proper, as well as such smaller groups as the Kasai Lubas,* Tetelas,* Mboles,* Lias,* Sengeles,* Iyembis,* and Ntombas.* Their language is the lingua franca of northwestern Zaire. Since the nineteenth century, considerable mixing has occurred between the Mongo peoples and the Pygmies,* since the Pygmoid peoples live in close association with the Mongos. They practice shifting forms of agriculture to produce cassava, bananas, kola nuts, and other food crops. Farm work is done primarily by women, while men spend their time hunting and fishing. More than 2.5 million people speak one of the Mongo languages, which all belong to the larger Bantu* group.
REFERENCES: *African Encyclopedia.* 1974; F. Scott Bobb. *Historical Dictionary of Zaire.* 1988.

MONGO-NKUNDO. *See* MONGO.

MONTOL. The Montol (Teel, Baltap) people of Plateau State in Nigeria live in close relationship to Tal* and Piapung* peoples, from whom they originated. They practice subsistence horticulture, raising ginger, millet, guinea corn, beans, and citrus products. They live in social systems characterized by patrilineal descent and patrifocal residence. In recent years, they have begun migrating to towns and cities looking for work. Most Montols, however, can still be found in the Shendam District of the Shendam Division of Plateau State.
REFERENCE: Elizabeth Isichei, ed. *Studies in the History of Plateau State, Nigeria.* 1982.

MOOR. The Moors (Maures), a people of mixed Arab*-Berber* descent, are a large, Sunni Muslim ethnic group of North Africa. Since they are a migrating pastoral people, who move to find new pastures for their sheep, goats, cattle, and camels, it has been difficult to secure reliable population figures for them. Although most Moors still live as pastoralists in their movable tents of animal skins and grass matting, many now live and work in towns and cities. A few Moors also raise dates, vegetables, and wheat at oases. They have been known historically for their proclivity to raid neighbors for animals and slaves. Their population today is approaching five million people, with 1.3 million in Mauritania, 2.5 million in Morocco, 300,000 in Mali, 40,000 in Senegal, and 40,000 in Gambia. Generally, the term ''Moor'' refers to any individual, regardless of race, speaking a Hassaniya dialect. Their traditional life was a nomadic one. Today, Moorish society is divided into four major elements, based on race, lineage, and occupation. The black Moors, known as *sudan,* occupy the lower stratum of Moorish society and often live as slaves, even though the institution of slavery has been outlawed throughout North Africa. Those Moors with a heavy black African background living in towns and cities constitute a desperately poor urban proletariat. Most Moors are faithful to the Maliki school of Sunni Islam.

REFERENCES: Robert E. Handloff et al. *Mauritania: A Country Study.* 1990; Pascal Imperato. *Historical Dictionary of Mali.* 1977; Urusula Wolff. ''Mauritania's Nomadic Society Preserves Its Lifestyle.'' *Africa Report* 17 (1972): 11–16.

MOORE. *See* MOSSI.

MORÉ. *See* MOLÉ-DAGBANE PEOPLES and MOSSI.

MOROA. The Moroas are an ethnic group living in the grassy savannas and volcanic hills of the southern region of the state of Kaduna in Nigeria. Between 1810 and 1833, the Moroas fell under Fulbe* influence when the Emir of Jema'a conquered them for plunder and slaves; from 1847 to 1854, the Emir of Zaria did the same. After the imposition of British* authority in the Moroa area, the slave raids and plunder-taking gradually declined. The Moroas practice subsistence horticulture, raising ginger, millet, guinea corn, beans, and citrus products.

REFERENCE: Elizabeth Isichei, ed. *Studies in the History of Plateau State, Nigeria.* 1982.

MORONOU. The Moronous are a subgroup of the Anyis* of Ivory Coast. They are overwhelmingly Christian in their religious persuasions.

MORU. The Morus are a relatively small ethnic group living today in the central Al Istiwai region of southern Sudan. Their homeland is west of the While Nile River. The Moru language is extremely close to the language of the Madi* people of the eastern Al Istiwai region. Both groups share other cultural features, leading ethnologists to conclude that their origins are the same and their separation relatively recent. Most Morus are small farmers. They are closely related to the Madis, Bongos,* and Bakas.*

REFERENCE: Helen C. Metz et al. *Sudan: A Country Study.* 1992.

MOSHI. *See* MOSSI.

MOSSI. The Mossi (Molé, Moshi) today are a large ethnic group occupying the Volta River basin, south of the great curve in the Niger River, in West Africa. Their population exceeds 5.5 million people. The Mossi dominate the region between the Red Volta and the White Volta rivers in Burkina-Faso. They are the largest ethnic group in the country, constituting half of the population. Another 600,000 Mossi live in Ivory Coast, Ghana, Togo, and Benin, where they work on cocoa plantations or in other occupations. They call their language Molé (Moré, Moore), which is part of the Molé-Dagbane* cluster of the Niger-Congo group of the Voltaic language family. Historically, the Mossi people lived in scattered small farms where they raised millet and yams. Ethnologists argue that the Mossi originated in Nigeria and expanded north beginning in the thirteenth century. By the early sixteenth century, several politically unified Mossi states had emerged in what is today Burkina-Faso. Nearly two million Mossi are Sunni Muslims loyal to the Maliki school. The rest are Roman Catholics and animists whose worship revolves around ancestors. Like most other Voltaic societies, the Mossi tend to live in small, walled-in compounds composed of several extended families, each compound approximately 100 yards from another similar compound. In recent years, these extended families have been breaking up into nuclear families as the primary social unit. The vast majority of Mossi are subsistence hoe farmers, raising millet as the staple. Included among the Mossi are the Birifors,* Gurmas,* Grusis,* Konkombas,* Kusasis,* Nankanas,* Ouagadougous,* Talensis,* Tenkodogos,* Walas,* Yatengas,* and Zandamos.*

The Mossi kingdom was first established in the fifteenth century by migrating cavalry from the Dogamba* and the Mamprusi* kingdoms. By that time, the Songhai* empire had introduced Islam to the Mossi. Despite repeated attempts, however, Songhai never conquered them. It was Manding* traders in the late seventeenth century who began converting large numbers of Mossi to Islam. After the French* conquest of the Mossi in 1896, conversions to Islam accelerated, because many Mossi perceived Islam as a nationalistic alternative to the Roman Catholicism of the French empire. Today, Islam is gaining ground among the Mossi in Burkino-Faso.

REFERENCES: Herbert Butler. "The Absorption of Strangers and Cultural Change Among the Mossi." *Proceedings of the Central States Anthropological Society* (1977): 17–22; Gregory Finnegan. "Population Movement, Labor Migration, and Social Structure in a Mossi Village." Ph.D. dissertation. Brandeis University. 1976; Elliott P. Skinner. "Christianity and Islam Among the Mossi." *American Anthropologist* 60 (1958): 1102–19.

MOTSA. The Motsas are one of the clans of the Emakhandzambili* peoples, who themselves are one of the three major subgroups of the Swazi* people of Swaziland.

MOUBI. The Moubis are an ethnic group located primarily east of Abou Telfan in the Oum Hadjer District of Chad. Ethnologists include them in the larger cluster of Hadjeray* peoples. Moubis speak a Daju* dialect. They are farmers who raise millet, sorghum, peanuts, sesame, beans, and cotton; some Moubis have recently begun to raise cattle as well. They are Muslims whose religion has retained many elements of their pre-Islamic faith. In recent years, the Moubis have been considered politically unstable, resisting entreaties from the central government and often rebelling openly. Their population today is approximately 30,000 people.

REFERENCES: Thomas Collelo et al. *Chad: A Country Study.* 1988; Samuel Decalo. *Historical Dictionary of Chad.* 1987.

MOULOUI. The Moulouis are a small ethnic group located in the Mayo-Kebbi Prefecture of Chad, primarily in the districts of Katoa and Mousgou. In recent years, a substantial number of Moulouis have migrated to Ndjamena, where they work as laborers. They are a poor people economically, because their region is heavily inundated during the rainy season, making agriculture very difficult.

REFERENCE: Samuel Decalo. *Historical Dictionary of Chad.* 1987.

MOUNDANG. *See* MUNDANG.

MOUPOUI. *See* MUSGU.

MOURDIA. The Mourdias are tiny Chadian ethnic group who today speak Dazaga* and are rapidly assimilating into Dazaga culture. Most Mourdias are small farmers who live in the northern Ennedi region.

REFERENCE: Samuel Decalo. *Historical Dictionary of Chad.* 1987.

MOUROUM. The Mouroums are a subgroup of the Sara* people of Chad. Their contemporary population is approaching 70,000 people, most of whom live in the Dob and Lai regions. Before the French* colonial era, the Mouroums often lived in mountains and caves to avoid slave raids by the Fulbes* and Barmas.* Although the Mouroums are known for their skill as cotton farmers, especially in working poor soil, many of them in recent years have moved to towns and cities, joined the Catholic church, and become active in the Chadian government and military.

REFERENCE: Samuel Decalo. *Historical Dictionary of Chad.* 1987.

MOURRO. The Mourros are one of the major subgroups of the Tama*-speaking people of Chad. Tama is a Waddian language. Most of the Mourros live in settled villages where they have learned to rotate crops, a practice that allows them to farm the arid Sahel region. Most Mourros live in Biltine Prefecture in southeastern Chad.

REFERENCE: Thomas Collelo et al. *Chad: A Country Study.* 1988.

MOUSGOUM. *See* MUSGU.

MOUSSEY. The Mousseys (Musey) are an ethnic group closely related to the Massa* people of Chad. The Massa and Moussey languages are almost identical. Most Mousseys live in the Bongor region of Mayo-Kebbi Prefecture, where they are skilled cotton farmers. With a contemporary population of more than 130,000 people, the Mousseys supply more than 10 percent of Chad's cotton crop each year. The Mousseys are also recognized locally for their skill as horsemen. They are excellent commercial cotton farmers and encourage their children to get educations and seek success in modern Chadian society.
REFERENCES: Thomas Collelo et al. *Chad: A Country Study.* 1988; Samuel Decalo. *Historical Dictionary of Chad.* 1987.

MOWEH. The Moweh people are a subgroup of the Bassa* people of Liberia. Most Mowehs live in River Cess Territory of Liberia.

MOYO. The Moyo language is a dialect of Madi,* a Sudanic language spoken today in Uganda.

MPAMA. The Mpamas are an ethnic group living today in far western Zaire and east-central Congo on the Zaire River. Ethnologists classify them as part of the Mongo* cluster of peoples because of their similarities to the Lias,* Ntombas,* and Sengeles.* They are a riverine people who have traditionally supported themselves by fishing, farming the river banks, and trading up and down the Zaire River.
REFERENCE: Irving Kaplan et al. *Zaire: A Country Study.* 1978.

MPANGWE. *See* FANG.

MPASU. The Mpasu people live today in Kasai Occidental Province of Zaire, especially near the town of Luiza. They are surrounded by the Lundas* and Chokwes* to the southwest, the Pandes* to the northwest, and the Luluas* to the north. In terms of their political structures, they are a highly decentralized people. Most Mpasus are small farmers.
REFERENCE: Elisabeth L. Cameron. "Sala Mpasu Masks." *African Arts* 22 (November 1988): 34–43.

MPONDO. The Mpondos are an ethnic group of nearly 1.75 million people living primarily in northern Transkei in South Africa. They speak a Xhosa* language. The Mpondos are divided into the Eastern and Western Mpondos, each of which has a chief who still possesses great authority. Mpondo life during the nineteenth century was characterized by on-going wars with the Zulus* and Thembus.* In 1894, they were finally brought under the control of the British* colonial government in Cape Town. Today, most Mpondos still live in village

settings, where they raise cattle, maize, millet, pumpkins, and tea. Large numbers of Mpondo men also work in the mines of the Transvaal and the sugar plantations of Natal.
REFERENCE: *African Encyclopedia.* 1974.

MPONGWE. The Mpongwe people, who speak a Myènè* language, have inhabited the shores of the Estuary of Gabon since the sixteenth century. They arrived there to take advantage of the trading opportunities provided by the presence of Europeans. The Mpongwe migration to the coast continued in the seventeenth and eighteenth centuries. They supported themselves by hunting, fishing, and farming, but they increasingly became the key middlemen between Europeans and such interior groups as the Bakèlès* and the Sékés.* By the 1830s, they were supplying slaves, dyewood, ivory, redwood, ebony, and beeswax to Europeans, in return for textiles, firearms, gunpowder, alcohol, and metal tools. The Mpongwes had no centralized authority because of their powerful clan subdivisions. The French* were able to exploit those divisions, establishing control over Mpongwe areas in the early 1840s. Roman Catholic missions exposed Mpongwe children to European values and taught them the skills to work for French companies and in the French colonial administration. Although their population was devastated by smallpox epidemics in the nineteenth century, the Mpongwes became highly influential, owning large amounts of property in Libreville, dominating the teacher corps, and controlling much of the business establishment. Today, although the Mpongwe population does not exceed 5,000 people, they are extremely influential in Gabonese life.
REFERENCES: Henry H. Boucher. ''The Mpongwe of the Gabon Estuary: A History to 1860.'' Ph.D. dissertation. University of Wisconsin. 1977; David E. Gardinier. *Historical Dictionary of Gabon.* 1994.

MPUTU. The Mputus are one of the Luba* peoples of Zaire. They are part of the Luba-Kasai subcluster of the Lubas.

MSIMANGO. The Msimangos are one of the clans of the Emakhandzambili* peoples, who themselves are one of the three major subgroups of the Swazi* people of Swaziland.

MTSETFWA. The Mtsetfwas are one of the major clans of the Emafikamuva* people, who themselves are one of the three major subgroups of the Swazi* people of Swaziland.

MUBAKO. *See* MUMBAKE.

MUBI. The Mubi are one of the many ethnic groups in Chad. Virtually all of the 40,000 or so Mubi are Muslims. They are part of the larger Nilotic*

cluster of Sudanese peoples. Most Mubi make their living as small farmers, laborers, and semi-nomadic and nomadic pastoralists.
REFERENCES: Pierre Hugot. *Le Tchad.* 1965; J. C. Lebeuf. *Afrique Centrale.* 1972; Donald G. Morrison et al. *Black Africa: A Comparative Handbook.* 1989.

MUBI. *See* GUDE.

MUCATU. The Mucatus are a major subgroup of the Shona* peoples of Zimbabwe and Mozambique.

MUEMBA. The Muembas are an ethnic group living today in central Zambia. They are part of the larger cluster of Bemba* peoples.

MUERA. The Muera people are a subgroup of the Makonde* people of Mozambique. The Mueras live on the Rondo Plateau. During the nineteenth and early twentieth centuries, the Mueras suffered from Arab* and Nguni* slave raids. Today, the Mueras support themselves as farmers, fishermen, and hunters. Most of them are Muslims.

MUGANGA. The Mugangas are a subgroup of the Taita* peoples of East Africa, particularly Kenya. They speak a Bantu* language.

MUIKA. The Muikas are part of the Bongue cluster of the Ndowe* peoples of Equatorial Guinea.

MUKULU. The Mukulus are part of the larger cluster of Aushi* peoples in Zambia. The Mukulu population today is approximately 9,000 people.

MULLUMTCHILLOUM. *See* KURI.

MUMBAKE. The Mumbake people, also known as the Mubakos and Nyongnepas, are a Nigerian ethnic group concentrated in the Zing district of Gongola State. They can also be found across the border in western Cameroon. They speak an Adamawa language.
REFERENCE: *Language Survey of Nigeria.* 1976.

MUMUYE. The Mumuyes are one of the Bantu*-speaking peoples of Nigeria. They are classified as part of the Plateau cluster of peoples who occupy central Nigeria and can be found in the Lau, Mumuye, Kwajji, Jalingo, and Zing districts of the Muri Division of Gongola State. Most Mumuyes practice subsistence horticulture, raising ginger, millet, guinea corn, beans, and citrus products. They live in social systems characterized by patrilineal descent and patrifocal residence. In recent years, they have begun migrating to towns and cities looking for work. The Mumuye population today exceeds 400,000 people.

REFERENCES: *Language Survey of Nigeria.* 1976; Donald G. Morrison et al. *Black Africa: A Comparative Handbook.* 1989.

MUNDANG. The Mundangs (Moundang) are a non-Fulbe* ethnic group of northern Cameroon, southwestern Chad, and southeastern Nigeria, a subgroup of the Kirdis.* Closely related to the Sara* people, they live primarily in the Mayo-Kebbi Prefecture, especially in the Léré region. They originated in Cameroon and migrated into Chad. Today, only a minority of the approximately 110,000 remain in Cameroon. Their religious preferences are mixed—animist, Roman Catholic, and Muslim. Most Mundangs are small farmers who grow millet on subsistence farms. Some Mundangs raise cotton as a cash crop. They speak an Adamawa language and are closely related linguistically to the Mbuns.* The chief of the Mundang resides in Léré. The Mundang economy revolves around the commercial production of millet and corn; their cattle herds are maintained by Fulbes. They have also adopted Fulbe dress and Fulbe forms of political organization over the years.

REFERENCES: Alfred Adler. "Les Jumeaux sont rois (chez les Moundang, Tchad)." *L'Homme* 13 (1973): 167–92; Thomas Collelo et al. *Chad: A Country Study.* 1988; Samuel Decalo. *Historical Dictionary of Chad.* 1987; Harold D. Nelson, et al. *Area Handbook for the United Republic of Cameroon.* 1974.

MUNDANI. The Mundanis are a relatively small ethnic group living today in the forests of the Manyu Prefecture of Southwest Province in Cameroon. They can be found on the north bank of the headwaters of the Cross River, east of Mamfe Town. Their most immediate ethnic neighbors are the Kenyangs,* Ngwois,* Menkas,* Denyas,* and Ejaghams.* Most Mundanis are subsistence farmers.

REFERENCE: Samson Negbo Abangma. *Modes in Denya Discourse.* 1987.

MUNDAT. The Mundats are considered by many ethnologists to be a subgroup of the Ron* people of Nigeria. They can be found in the Ron District of the Pankshin Division of Plateau State.

MUNDO. *See* MUNDU.

MUNDU. The Mundus (Mundo) are an ethnic group living in southern Sudan, northwestern Uganda, and northeastern Zaire. Their most immediate neighbors are the Logos,* Alurs,* and Kakwas.* The Mundus language is part of the Central Sudanic cluster of languages. Many Mundus also live in the city of Arua on the Uganda-Zaire border. They are of Nilotic* origins. Their economy revolves around agriculture because of the excellent soil in the region. The Mundus are also known for their skill in animal husbandry.

REFERENCES: F. Scott Bobb. *Historical Dictionary of Zaire.* 1988; Irving Kaplan et al. *Zaire: A Country Study.* 1978.

MUNGA. The Mungas are an Adamawa-speaking people who are concentrated today in the Wurkum District of the Muri Division of Gongola State in Nigeria. REFERENCE: *Language Survey of Nigeria.* 1976.

MUNSHI. *See* TIV.

MUNUNGO. The Munungos (Minungos) are a subgroup of the Mbundu* people of Angola. Some ethnolinguists consider the Munungo language to be transitional between Chokwe* and Mbundu.

MUNYO YAYA. The Munyo Yayas are a subgroup of the Pokomo* people of Kenya.

MUPUN. *See* MWAHAVUL.

MURLE. The Murle are a relatively small ethnic group of perhaps 35,000 people living in the Pibor District in Upper Nile Province of southeastern Sudan. They speak an eastern Sudanic language. Some can also be found across the border in Ethiopia as well as in northern Kenya. They are especially concentrated in the Lotilla Valley, which is part of the large Upper Nile plain. During the 1970s and 1980s, the Murle were frequently in conflict with neighboring groups because of economic pressures on the southern Sudan environment. The Murle can be subdivided into the Boma Murles,* Beirs,* and Didingas.* REFERENCES: B. A. Lewis. *The Murle: Red Chiefs and Black Commoners.* 1972; Helen C. Metz et al. *Sudan: A Country Study.* 1992.

MURSI. The Mursis are an ethnic group of Ethiopia. They call themselves the Mun people and live in the Lower Omo Valley of southeastern Ethiopia, about sixty miles north of Addis Ababa. They make their living herding cattle and raising sorghum and maize. Their traditional religious life still revolves around their animals. The Mursi population exceeds 10,000 people. REFERENCE: David Turton. ''There's No Such Beast: Cattle and Colour Naming Among the Mursi.'' *Man* 15 (June 1980): 30–38.

MUSEY. *See* MOUSSEY.

MUSGU. The Musgus (Mousgoum, Musgums) live today on the plains of northern Cameroon. They can also be found in southwestern Chad and eastern Nigeria. In Chad, they are called the Moupoui and are concentrated in the Bongor region. Their current population exceeds 80,000 people. Most of them are farmers, raising groundnuts and cotton for commercial sale. In recent years, periodic droughts in the Cameroonian plains have badly damaged the Musgu economy. They are considered a subgroup of the Kirdi* peoples. Their name comes from the village of Mousgoum. They are sandwiched between the Kotoko* people, who are Muslims, to the north, and the Massa* people, who are animists, to the south. The Musgus are more closely related to the Massas, although they speak a different language. Most Musgus have converted to Islam, but pre-Islamic beliefs and rituals remain very powerful. They have recently adopted the flowing dress of Muslims and Fulbe*-type houses.

REFERENCES: Samuel Decalo. *Historical Dictionary of Chad.* 1987; Harold D. Nelson et al. *Area Handbook for the United Republic of Cameroon.* 1974.

MUSGUM. *See* MUSGU.

MUSHIKONGO. The Mushikongos are a major subgroup of the Kongo* people of Zaire and Angola.

MUTARARA. The Mutararas are a major subgroup of the Maravi* people of Mozambique.

MUTHAMBI. The Muthambis are a Bantu*-speaking people who are a subgroup of the Meru* cluster of peoples in Kenya and Tanzania.

MUWERA. The Muweras are a small ethnic group whose contemporary population numbers approximately 50,000 people. Although, in recent years, many Muweras have made the transition to commercial farming and urban labor, most Muweras continue to live as subsistence farmers and livestock raisers. They live in the lower Zambezi River Valley of Mozambique.

REFERENCE: Mario Azevedo. *Historical Dictionary of Mozambique.* 1991.

MUYA. *See* MIYA.

MVAÉ. The Mvaés are part of the larger Fang*-Pahouin* cluster of Bantu*-speaking peoples of Cameroon, Gabon, and Equatorial Guinea. The Mvaé population today exceeds 200,000 people, most of whom are Roman Catholics. They are primarily farmers, raising cocoa, rice, coffee, groundnuts, cassava, and a variety of other vegetable crops. They are actually a subgroup of the Fang proper.

REFERENCE: Mark DeLancey and H. M. Mokeba. *Historical Dictionary of the Republic of Cameroon.* 1990.

MVANIP. *See* MAGU.

MVITA. The Mvitas are a Swahili*-speaking people who today live in the coastal regions of Kenya.

MVUBA. The Mvubas are an ethnic group in Zaire whom ethnographers believe to have originated in Sudan. They are concentrated in the Haut-Zaire Region, north of the Uelé River. Historically, the Mvubas were highly decentralized politically and often under the domination of the Mamvus* and Mangbetus.* The Mvubas were unique among the peoples of the region because their political structure lacked chiefs.

REFERENCES: F. Scott Bobb. *Historical Dictionary of Zaire.* 1988; Irving Kaplan et al. *Zaire: A Country Study.* 1978.

MWA. *See* MONA.

MWAHAVUL. The Mwahavuls, also known as Suras and Mupuns, live in Plateau State, Nigeria, and are closely related to the Chips,* Dokos, Chokfiems, and Kofyars.* They can be found particularly in the Ron, Gindiri, North Sura, and South Sura districts of the Pankshin Division. Like other savanna peoples in the region, they are subsistence farmers, raising millet, maize, guinea corn, beans, and livestock. Their village political systems are decentralized.

REFERENCE: John Ola Agi. "The Goemai and Their Neighbors: An Historical Analysis." In Elizabeth Isichei, ed. *Studies in the History of Plateau State, Nigeria.* 1982.

MWAMBA. The Mwambas are a Tanzanian ethnic group whom some ethnologists classify with the Nyakyusa* peoples.

MWAN. *See* BIMOBA.

MWANDA. The Mwandas are a subgroup of the Taita* peoples of East Africa, particularly Kenya. They speak a Bantu* language.

MWANI. The Mwani people are part of the larger cluster of Interlacustrine Bantu* peoples of northwestern Tanzania. Many ethnologists include them today as part of the Haya* cluster of peoples.

MWANU. *See* MONA.

MWANYA. The Mwanyas (Mwenyis) are a major subgroup of the Shona* peoples of Zimbabwe and Mozambique. They can also be found along the Luanginga River in far western Zambia.

MWENYI. *See* MWANYA.

MWERA. *See* MWERE.

MWERE. The Mweres (Mweras) are a large ethnic group of approximately 300,000 people who live primarily in Tanzania, with smaller groups in Malawi and Mozambique. They make their living as hoe agriculturalists, raising millet and sorghum as their staples. In recent decades, substantial numbers of

Mweres have migrated to such cities as Lilongwe, Tete, Morogoro, and Dar es Salaam to work as wage laborers. Approximately 80 percent of the Mweres are nominal Sunni Muslims. The rest are nominal Christians or faithful to the indigenous Mwere religion. Many ethnologists consider them a subgroup of the Yao.*

MWILA. The Mwilas are part of the larger cluster of Nyaneka*-Humbe peoples of southwestern Angola.

MWIMBI. The Mwimbis are a Bantu*-speaking people who are a subgroup of the Meru* cluster of peoples in Kenya and Tanzania.

MWONA. The Mwonas are a small group of agricultural people living about five miles from Bambam on the Gombe-Cham-Numan Road in northeastern Nigeria. Until the completion of the road in the 1960s, they were a very isolated people. Only recently have they become more integrated into the wider commercial economy.
REFERENCE: Jonathan Slye. "Mwona Figurines." *African Arts* 10 (July 1977): 22–23.

MYÈNÈ. The term "Myènè" (Omyènè) refers to a group of Bantu* languages spoken by the Mpongwe,* Orungu,* Galoa,* Adyumba,* Nkomi,* and Enenga* peoples of Gabon. Their total population in Gabon numbers only about 30,000 people.
REFERENCE: David E. Gardinier. *Historical Dictionary of Gabon.* 1994.

MYET. *See* TAPSHIN.

MYSSIRIE. The Myssirie are a subgroup of the Djoheinas,* themselves a large Arab* subgroup in Chad.

MZABITE. The Mzabites are one of the major Berber* peoples of Algeria. They maintain a strong sense of identity, quite separate from that of the surrounding Arabs,* as well as from other Berbers. They first arrived in their homeland—five cities located approximately 330 miles south of Algiers—in the eleventh century. Unlike most Berbers, they are loyal to the Hanafi school of Islam, not the Maliki school. They are a highly urbanized people living in the cities of Ghardaya, Beni Isguen, Melika, Bou Noura, and El-Ateuf.

N

NABDAM. *See* NAMNAM.

NABÉ. *See* KULANGO.

NABTAB. *See* BENI AMER.

NACHÉRÉ. The Nachérés are an ethnic group who live in Chad. They speak a Chadian language and are concentrated in Tandjilé Prefecture. Their language represents a transition between Massa* and Sara.* Most Nachérés are small farmers, raising millet, maize, and cotton.
REFERENCE: Thomas Collelo et al. *Chad: A Country Study.* 1988.

NAFANA. The Nafanas are an ethnic group whom anthropologists classify as part of the larger cluster of Senufo* peoples of West Africa. The Nafanas are concentrated along the border of northern Ivory Coast, southern Mali, and south-western Burkina-Faso. Most of them are small farmers, raising corn, rice, yams, peanuts, sesame, and sweet potatoes.
REFERENCE: Daniel M. McFarland. *Historical Dictionary of Upper Volta.* 1978.

NAFUNFIA. *See* SHAGAWU.

NAGO. *See* NAGOT.

NAGOT. The Nagot, also known as the Nago, are a Yoruba* people of Benin. Most of the 50,000 to 60,000 Nagot people are concentrated in Ketou, Savé, north of Abomey, and in Porto Novo. In Porto Novo, they have heavily mixed with the Gouns,* another Yoruba people. They are a well-educated, upwardly mobile, political influential people.
REFERENCE: Samuel Decalo. *Historical Dictionary of Benin.* 1987.

NAGWA. The Nagwas are a subgroup of the Grusi* people of Ghana. In particular, the Nagwas live along the border of Burkina-Faso and in the Upper Region of Ghana.

NAKANYARE. *See* CHAMBA.

NAKARE. *See* JIDDA-ABU.

NAKOMSÉ. The Nakomsé are a core group of the Mossi* people of Burkina-Faso. They consider themselves the direct descendants of the original Mossi conquerors of the region.

NALOU. *See* NALU.

NALU. The Nalus (Nalou) are a small Senegambian* ethnic group living in Guinea, Gambia, Senegal, and Guinea-Bissau. Their population in Guinea-Bissau today exceeds 160,000 people. They are known as Bagas* in Gambia and Guinea. In Guinea, the Nalus live on the lower Rio Nuñez and Kogan rivers and on the Tristão Islands. Approximately half of the Nalus are Muslims. They are primarily rice farmers. In recent years, large numbers of Nalus have been assimilated into surrounding Soso* populations. They are widely known for their blacksmithing skills.
REFERENCES: Richard Lobban and Joshua Forrest. *Historical Dictionary of the Republic of Guinea-Bissau.* 1988; Thomas O'Toole. *Historical Dictionary of Guinea.* 1987.

NAMA. The term "Nama" is used in Botswana to refer to a Khoisan people, sometimes pejoratively called "Hottentots,"* who fled to what is today Botswana during the anticolonial rebellion in German South West Africa in the early 1900s. Simon Kooper led them to Botswana. German* troops pursued them there to the bitter protests of British* colonial authorities. A diplomatic settlement ended the controversy, with the Namas given permission to live in the Kgalagadi Reserve. Namas still live in the region today. Approximately 50,000 Namas can also be found today in Namibia.
REFERENCES: Fred Morton, A. Murray, and J. Ramsay. *Historical Dictionary of Botswana.* 1989; Stanley Schoeman and Elna Schoeman. *Namibia.* 1984.

NAMBALI. The Nambalis are one of the cluster of Ewe* people who live in the southern Volta Region of Ghana and across the border in southwestern Togo.

NAMCHI. The Namchis are a subdivision of the Gbaya*-Mbun* cluster of peoples in the western reaches of the Central African Republic and in eastern Cameroon. Perhaps 20 percent of them are Muslims. The others practice Christianity or a variety of tribal animist faiths. The conversion of the Namchis to Islam began early in the 1800s when Fulbe* and Hausa* groups established trading relationships with them. Christian missionaries first reached them in the 1920s. Traditional beliefs in ancestor worship and witchcraft still exist, but they are losing ground. Namchi society is organized around patrilineal clans. People live in nuclear or extended family compounds consisting of mud-walled houses protected by a fence or wall. They practice slash-and-burn agriculture and concentrate on producing maize and cassava, which they both consume themselves and market for cash. They have also learned how to raise cattle for their Fulbe neighbors.

REFERENCES: Philip Burnham. "Gbaya." In Richard V. Weekes, ed. *Muslim Peoples.* 1984; Philip Burnham. *Opportunity and Constraint in a Savanna Society.* 1980; Philip Burnham. "Regroupement and Mobile Societies: Two Cameroon Cases." *Journal of African History* 16 (1975): 577–94.

NAMNAM. The Namnams (Nabdams) are one of the Molé-Dagbane* peoples of Ghana. They are concentrated in the upper East Region, with their primary settlement at Nangodi. The Namnams are closely associated with the Talensis* and the Kusasis,* their neighbors. They speak a language known as Nabte. The Namnams can also be found across the border in Burkina-Faso. The number of Namnam people in Ghana today is approximately 35,000.

REFERENCE: Daniel M. McFarland. *Historical Dictionary of Ghana.* 1995.

NAMU. The Namus are a small ethnic group living today in Plateau State in Nigeria. They are closely related to the Dimmuks* and Bwals.* All three groups claim descent from a man known as Dimmuk. They possess a long list of kings and a well-developed oral history. Political authority tends to be highly decentralized among the various Namu villages. Most Namus are subsistence farmers.

REFERENCE: John Ola Agi. "The Goemai and Their Neighbors: An Historical Analysis." In Elizabeth Isichei, ed. *Studies in the History of Plateau State, Nigeria.* 1982.

NAMWANGA. The Namwangas (Inamwanga) are a group of approximately 80,000 people who live today in the extreme northeastern corner of Zambia. They speak a Mambwe* language. Their origins, along with their neighbors the Lungus,* Ilas,* and Mambwes, are in East Africa. They are a pastoral people also known for their skill as ironworkers. The Namwangas were among the first to sign treaties with the British,* primarily to protect themselves from the Bembas.* The Jehovah's Witnesses made thousands of converts among the Namwangas in the early twentieth century.

REFERENCE: John J. Grotpeter. *Historical Dictionary of Zambia.* 1979.

NANA. *See* KRU.

NANDE. *See* YIRA.

NANDI. The Nandis live in the western highlands of Kenya. They are a sub-group of the Kalenjin* cluster of peoples. Their population today exceeds 425,000 people, most of whom live in the highlands around Kapsabet in Rift Valley Province. Cattle were central to the traditional Nandi economy, but, in recent years, they have started raising maize and tobacco on large commercial farms, as well as moving to towns and cities for work and business opportunities. The Nandis enjoyed a reputation as fierce, skilled warriors who regularly raided the neighboring Masais,* Luos,* and Gusiis* for cattle. The arrival of British* military force in the region in 1905 ended those raids. They call their language Kalenjin, which is also spoken by the neighboring Kipsigi* people.
REFERENCE: *African Encyclopedia.* 1974.

NANDU-TARI. The Nandu-Tari people are a Nigerian ethnic group. They are one of the Eastern Plateau peoples in the Benue-Congo language family. Most of them can be found today in the Jema'a District of the Jema'a Division of Kaduna State.
REFERENCE: *Language Survey of Nigeria.* 1976.

NANÈRÈGÈ. *See* NANERGE.

NANERGE. The Nanerge (Nanergue, Nanèrègè) are an ethnic group whom anthropologists classify as part of the larger cluster of Senufo* peoples of West Africa. The Nanerge are concentrated in the border area between Mali and south-western Burkina-Faso, northwest of Bobo Dioulasso near the Ngorolaka River. They are closely related to the Miniankas.* Most of them are small farmers, raising corn, rice, yams, peanuts, sesame, and sweet potatoes.
REFERENCE: Daniel M. McFarland. *Historical Dictionary of Upper Volta.* 1978.

NANERGUE. *See* NANERGE.

NANKANA. The Nankana people are an ethnic group living today in south-central Burkina-Faso and across the border in Ghana and Togo. They are closely related to the Grusis* and make their living primarily raising sorghum and mil-let.
REFERENCE: Daniel M. McFarland. *Historical Dictionary of Upper Volta.* 1978.

NANKANSE. *See* GRUSI.

NANKANSI. *See* GRUSI.

NANKWILI. The Nankwilis are a Tanzanian ethnic group and are often included by ethnologists in the larger Nyamwezi* cluster of peoples. *See* NYAMWEZI.

NANOUMBA. *See* NUNUMA.

NANUM. *See* NUNUMA.

NANUMBA. *See* NUNUMA.

NANUNE. *See* NUNUMA.

NAO. The Nao people are one of Ethiopia's many tiny ethnic groups. They live in the southern reaches of the country where they make their living as subsistence farmers. The Naos speak an Omotic* language and have a current population of approximately 8,000 people.
REFERENCES: M. L. Bender, J. D. Bowen, R. L. Cooper, and C. A. Ferguson, eds. *Language in Ethiopia.* 1976; Harold D. Nelson et al. *Ethiopia: A Country Study.* 1980.

NAR. The Nar people are a small ethnic group in Chad. Ethnologists consider them a part of the Sara* cluster of peoples, and they are most closely related to the Madjingayé* people. Most Nars live in the Koumra region, on both banks of the Mandoul River. The Nars are known among neighboring ethnic groups for their skill as musicians and their highly democratic, individualistic culture. The current Nar population exceeds 40,000 people.
REFERENCE: Samuel Decalo. *Historical Dictionary of Chad.* 1987.

NARA. The Naras are one of the Nilo-Saharan-speaking peoples of northwestern Ethiopia. They tend to be a semi-nomadic people whose economy depends on livestock, particularly cattle. Large numbers of Naras are also hoe cultivators, raising a variety of grain crops. The Nara population is approximately 35,000 people.
REFERENCES: M. L. Bender, J. D. Bowen, R. L. Cooper, and C. A. Ferguson, eds. *Language in Ethiopia.* 1976; Harold D. Nelson et al. *Ethiopia: A Country Study.* 1980.

NARAGUTA. The Naragutas are a small ethnic group of several thousand people living today in the Gwong District of the Jos Division of Plateau State in Nigeria. Historically, they have also been known as the Igutas and Anagutas. They live in a series of villages where they have made the transition in recent decades to small farming. Hunting, however, has long been of religious and ritual significance to them. It tends to be a communal activity, complete with hunting dogs, horses, and brush fires to flush out game animals. Like other peoples in the region, they raise goats, sheep, and chickens, and they also practice subsistence forms of agriculture, raising millet, yams, cassava, maize, beans, and several other products.

REFERENCES: Samuel Akbapot. "Random Music of Birom." *African Arts* 8 (Winter 1975): 46–47; Harold Good. *The Peoples of the Northern Region of Nigeria.* 1963; Elizabeth Isichei, ed. *Studies in the History of Plateau State, Nigeria.* 1982; *Language Survey of Nigeria.* 1976; Jean-Claude Muller. "Intertribal Hunting Among the Rukuba." *Ethnology* 21 (1982): 203–14.

NATA. The Natas, who are closely related to the Issenyes,* are part of the Interlacustrine Bantu* cluster of peoples in Tanzania. They live in northwestern Tanzania, primarily along the southwestern shore of Lake Victoria. They raise cattle and farm, using the manure to keep their soil productive.
REFERENCES: Donald G. Morrison et al. *Black Africa: A Comparative Handbook.* 1989; Laura Kurtz. *Historical Dictionary of Tanzania.* 1978.

NATIMBA. The Natimbas are a subgroup of the Somba* people of Benin and Togo. Their contemporary population is approximately 50,000 people, most of whom are farmers, raising maize, millet, plantains, and cassava.
REFERENCE: Donald G. Morrison et al. *Black Africa: A Comparative Handbook.* 1989.

NAUDEBA. The Naudeba are one of the Sudanic peoples who live in northern Togo. They are animist in their religious loyalties and make their living herding cattle or camels, as well as in subsistence agriculture.
REFERENCE: Donald G. Morrison et al. *Black Africa: A Comparative Handbook.* 1989.

NAWURI. The Nawuris are a subgroup of the Kwa* peoples of Ghana.

NCHUMBULUNG. *See* NTWUMURU.

NCHUMURU. *See* NTWUMURU.

NDA DIA. *See* DADIYA.

NDAGHAN. *See* NGOSHE NDHANG.

NDAKA. The Ndakas are a Bantu*-speaking people who live today in north-eastern Zaire. Some of them can also be found in western Uganda. The most immediate neighbors of the Ndakas in Zaire are the Mbos,* Baleses,* Budus,* and Mangbetus.* Like the others, the Ndakas work small cassava and banana farms in the heavily forested region.
REFERENCE: Irving Kaplan et al. *Zaire: A Country Study.* 1978.

NDALI. The Ndalis are an ethnic group living today in Tanzania. They are part of the Rungwa* cluster of peoples and are closely associated with the Lambyas.* Their population today is approximately 100,000 people.

NDAM. The Ndams are a relatively small ethnic group living today in the Moyen-Chari Prefecture in Chad. Their language is part of the larger Chadian cluster of languages, and it represents a transition between Sara* and Massa.* Most Ndams are herdsmen and small farmers, raising sorghum, millet, maize, and cotton.
REFERENCE: Thomas Collelo et al. *Chad: A Country Study.* 1988.

NDAMBA. The Ndambas are an East African people who are part of the Ngindo* cluster of the Northeastern Bantu* language group of East Africa. Most of the Ndambas are rice farmers, who raise the cash crop in the fertile, damp floodplains of the Kilombero and Rufiji rivers in Tanzania. They also raise poultry and goats. The Ndambas trace descent through male lines. They are primarily Muslim in their religious orientation, but they generally do not observe Ramadan or many other Islamic rituals. The wearing of a white skull cap and the adoption of an Arab* name are the only religious requirements they regularly fulfill. Like other Tanzanians, the Ndambas have been dealing with the government's *ujamaa* program since the mid-1970s. The policy is designed to alter the traditional homestead settlement pattern in favor of establishing village clusters where public education and public health campaigns can be more successful. Some ethnologists include the Pogoros* among the Ndambas. Their population today in Tanzania is approximately 50,000 people.
REFERENCE: A.R.W. Crosse-Upcott. "Male Circumcision Among the Ngindo." *Journal of the Royal Anthropological Institute* 89 (1959): 169–89.

NDARA. *See* MANDARA.

NDAU. The Ndaus (Buzi, Vandau) are one of the major subgroups in the Shona* cluster of peoples in Zimbabwe and Mozambique. They claim to be descendants of the Rodzi people who were generally incorporated into Ndau military regiments. Most of them are farmers, raising cattle, millet, maize, pumpkins, and yams. The Ndaus are subdivided into the following major clans: Shanga (Machangana), Gova,* Danda, Watombodji, and Zezuru.* The Ndaus live primarily in southeastern Zimbabwe and in Mozambique, from west of the Sabi River to the Indian Ocean. Because of the occupation of their territory by the Gazas in the nineteenth century, there are many elements of Gaza culture in Ndau culture. The Ndau population of Zimbabwe exceeds 400,000 people.
REFERENCE: R. Kent Rasmussen. *Historical Dictionary of Zimbabwe.* 1994.

NDEBELE. The Ndebeles, also called the Amandebeles and Matabeles, live today primarily in Zimbabwe, especially in the southwestern districts of the country and around Bulawayo. There are smaller clusters of Ndebeles in South Africa and Botswana as well. The Ndebeles emerged as a distinct people in the 1820s and 1830s when their leader, Chief Mzilikazi, led them north out of Zululand to escape the authority of Shaka. Along the way, large numbers of

Sothos* and Tswanas* joined them. Together, they conquered a number of Shona* peoples and settled in the colony of Rhodesia. The traditional Ndebele social structure has reflected that migration process. The highest class consists of the *ebezanzi,* or the descendants of the original Zululand Ndebeles. The middle class is composed of the *abenhla,* the descendants of the Tswanas and Sothos who joined them along the way. The lower class, or *amaholi,* are descendants of the conquered Shonas.

After the death of Mzilikazi in 1868, Ndebeles granted territorial concessions to Cecil Rhodes and the British* South African Company to launch European settlement and mining projects. Futile anti-British wars erupted in 1893 and again in 1896–1897. Today, Ndebeles can be found working in the towns, cities, mines, and plantations of Zimbabwe and South Africa, as well as in rural villages where they herd cattle and raise millet and maize. They are grouped as one of the Nguni* peoples because they speak a Nguni language, (part of the Bantu* cluster). The Ndebele population today is well in excess of one million people.
REFERENCES: *African Encyclopedia.* 1974; R. Kent Rasmussen. *Historical Dictionary of Zimbabwe.* 1979.

NDEM. *See* NNAM.

NDEMBO. *See* NDEMBU.

NDEMBU. The Ndembus (Ndembos, Mdembus, Dembos) are an ethnic group living in the western Shaba Region of Zaire and in the wooded hill country northeast of Luanda in Angola. They can also be found near the Lundas* and Luvales* in northwestern Zambia. Although they speak a Mbundu* language, they have been heavily influenced by Kongo* culture as well. Many ethnologists consider them to be a subgroup of the Kongos. The Ndembu social structure is matrilineal. Because their homeland has been known for its forested hilltops and escarpments, the Ndembus have been able to maintain very independent attitudes. They had a long history of resistance to Portuguese* authority in Angola, violently rebelling from 1907 to 1909 and from 1917 to 1919. During the wars of liberation against Portugal in the 1960s, the Ndembu homeland became a stronghold for the Movimento Popular de Libertacão de Angola (MPLA). Ndembu country is a productive coffee region. In Zaire, the Ndembus are closely related to the Lundas, culturally and linguistically. In recent years, however, they have adopted anti-Lunda political attitudes, often aligning themselves with the Chokwes* in Zairean politics. Most Ndembos are small farmers.
REFERENCES: F. Scott Bobb. *Historical Dictionary of Zaire.* 1988; Susan H. Broadhead. *Historical Dictionary of Angola.* 1992; John J. Grotpeter. *Historical Dictionary of Zambia.* 1979; V. W. Turner. *Revelation and Divination in Ndembu Ritual.* 1975.

NDENDEULE. The Ndendeules are an ethnic group of approximately 70,000

people who today live in Tanzania. They speak a Bantu* language and are primarily subsistence farmers.
REFERENCE: Edgar C. Polomé and C. P. Hill, eds. *Language in Tanzania.* 1980.

NDENGELEKO. *See* NDENGEREKO.

NDENGEREKO. The Ndengerekos (Ndengeleko) are an East African people who are part of the Ngindo* cluster of the Northeastern Bantu* language group of East Africa. Most Ndengerekos are rice farmers, who raise the cash crop in the fertile, damp floodplains of the Kilombero and Rufiji rivers in Tanzania. Their population there exceeds 90,000 people. They also raise poultry and goats. Ndengerekos trace descent through male lines. They are primarily Muslim in their religious orientation, but they generally do not observe Ramadan or many other Islamic rituals. The wearing of a white skull cap and the adoption of an Arab* name are the only religious requirements they regularly fulfill. Like other Tanzanians, the Ndengerekos have been dealing with the government's *ujamaa* program since the mid-1970s. The policy is designed to alter the traditional homestead settlement pattern in favor of establishing village clusters where public education and public health campaigns can be more successful.
REFERENCE: A.R.W. Crosse-Upcott. "Male Circumcision Among the Ngindo." *Journal of the Royal Anthropological Institute* 89 (1959): 169–89.

NDENGSE. The Ndengses are a Bantu*-speaking people who live in the forests of the Kasai Orientale region of central Zaire. Most of them are small farmers who raise cassava, bananas, and kola nuts. In recent years, the Ndengses have been increasingly affected by Zaire's commercial economy, with the result that more and more Ndengses are growing cash crops or leaving the farms for work in towns and cities.
REFERENCE: Irving Kaplan et al. *Zaire: A Country Study.* 1978.

NDE-NSELE-NTA. The Nde-Nsele-Nta people are an ethnic group native to Nigeria. They speak an Ekoid Bantu* language and live in the Ikom and Obubra divisions of Cross River State.
REFERENCE: *Language Survey of Nigeria.* 1976.

NDENYE. The Ndenyes are a subgroup of the Anyis* of Ivory Coast. Most of the Ndenyes are Christians.

NDEREBO. *See* DOROBO.

N'DI. The N'dis are a subgroup of the Banda* peoples of the Central African Republic. Their population is approximately 175,000 people.

NDIA. The Ndias are an ethnic group living today southwest of Mount

Kenya in Kenya in East Africa. They are closely related to the Kikuyu* and Meru* peoples. Most of them are subsistence farmers.
REFERENCE: W. H. Whiteley. *Language in Kenya.* 1974.

NDIKPO. The Ndikpos are a subgroup of the Ibibio* peoples of Nigeria.

NDJEMBE. *See* NDEMBU.

NDOE. The Ndoes (Aneps) are one of the Ekoid Bantu* peoples of Cross River State in Nigeria. They are concentrated particularly in the Ikom Division. Most of the more than 15,000 Ndoes are small farmers.
REFERENCE: *Language Survey of Nigeria.* 1976.

NDOGO. The Ndogos are an ethnic group in southern Sudan who speak a language similar to that of the Azandés.* The Ndogos live in the region surrounding the city of Wau. Most of them are small farmers who also raise some cattle. The Ndogos are closely related to the Bviris.*
REFERENCE: Helen C. Metz, et al. *Sudan: A Country Study.* 1992.

NDOKKI. The Ndokkis are one of the many subgroups of the Igbo* people, an ethnic group of nearly fifteen million people living today in southern and southeastern Nigeria.

NDONDE. The Ndondes are a Tanzanian ethnic group whom some ethnologists classify in the Yao* cluster of peoples. They have a population today of approximately 25,000 people.

NDONGA. The Ndongas are a subgroup of the Ambo* people of Namibia.

NDONGO. The Ndongos are a subgroup of the Mbundus* and live in Western Mbundu state in Angola. By the mid-sixteenth century, the great Ndongo Kingdom ruled the region, but Portuguese* expansion, as well as the expansion of the Atlantic slave trade, destroyed the kingdom in the seventeenth century. Only the eastern Ndongos retained any real independence, maintaining a distinct political profile until the late nineteenth century.

NDOP. The Ndops are today considered a subgroup of the Tikar* peoples of the Bamenda highlands of North West Province in Cameroon. They are classified as part of the Middle-Cameroon Bantu* group of peoples. The Ndops originated farther to the north and were pushed into their present location by Fulbe* expansion. It is a savanna environment with patches of woodland and gallery forest along water courses. The Ndops are farmers and fishermen. Their

villages stretch along roads and tracks. Their traditional huts are rectangular and have a palmfrond roofing. Today, cement houses and corrugated sheet roofs are common, especially in villages near the tarmacked main roads.
REFERENCE: Mark W. Delancey and H. M. Mokeba. *Historical Dictionary of the Republic of Cameroon*. 1990.

NDORAWA. The Ndorawas are one of the Bantu*-speaking peoples of Nigeria. They are classified as part of the Plateau cluster of peoples who occupy central Nigeria. Most Ndorawas practice subsistence horticulture, raising ginger, millet, guinea corn, beans, and citrus products. They live in social systems characterized by patrilineal descent and patrifocal residence. In recent years, they have begun migrating to towns and cities looking for work.
REFERENCE: Donald G. Morrison et al. *Black Africa: A Comparative Handbook*. 1989.

NDORO. The Ndoros are an ethnic group living today in western Cameroon and in the Ndoro and Gashaka districts of the Mambilla Division of Gongola State, Nigeria. They speak a non-Bantu* language that is classified with the Mambila*-Vute* group of the Benue-Congo family.
REFERENCE: *Language Survey of Nigeria*. 1976.

NDOROBO. *See* DOROBO.

NDOUMOU. The Ndoumou, also known as the Mindoumou, speak a Mbete* language and live along the M'Passa River around Franceville in Gabon. Most of them are small farmers. The Ndoumou population today is approximately 10,000 people.
REFERENCE: David E. Gardinier. *Historical Dictionary of Gabon*. 1994.

NDOWE. The Ndowes are a large cluster of peoples living in Equatorial Guinea, primarily along the Río Muni coastal plain. They are often called *Los Playeros* (Beach People). The term ''Ndowe'' is used to refer to the speakers of the Kombe language. There are two divisions among the Ndowes. The Boumbas include the Banga* (Benga) people and the Bapuku* people. The Bongues* are composed of the Kombe, Bomoudi, Asangon, Muiko, Bujeba,* Balenki, and Baseke* peoples. The Ndowe cluster also includes, according to some anthropologists, the Bayeles,* a pygmy group. Ethnologists estimate that the Ndowes arrived in what is today eastern Equatorial Guinea in the fourteenth century. Before then, they had lived along the Ubangi River to the east. Fang* expansion eventually drove them to their present locations along the Atlantic Coast in the nineteenth century. Most Ndowes are farmers, raising cassava, malanga (taro), corn, plantains, and bananas. They have enjoyed close contacts with European merchants and missionaries since the nineteenth century. During the dictatorship of Macías Nguema in the 1970s, they suffered severe repression.

REFERENCES: Randall Fegley. *Equatorial Guinea.* 1991; Max Liniger-Goumaz. *Historical Dictionary of Equatorial Guinea.* 1988.

NDRE. The Ndres are a subgroup of the Banda* people. They live in the Bangui Region of the Central African Republic.

NDUKA. The Ndukas are one of the Sudanic peoples living today in Chad. They tend to be concentrated in southern Chad, where they make their living raising livestock and working small farms. The Nduka population today exceeds 75,000 people.
REFERENCE: Donald G. Morrison et al. *Black Africa: A Comparative Handbook.* 1989.

NDULU. The Ndulus are a subgroup of the Ovimbundu* peoples of Angola.

NDUNDULA. The Ndundulas are part of the larger cluster of Luyana* peoples of Zambia. The Luyanas are part of the Lozi* group.

NDUT. The Ndut are a subgroup of the Cangin, themselves a subdivision of the Serer* peoples of Senegal.

NDWANDWE. The Ndwandwes are one of the Bembo*-Nguni* peoples of Swaziland. They are closely related to the royal Swazi* clans, but, in the six-teenth century, they split away from the people who would eventually evolve into the Swazis. The Ndwandwes moved south of the Pongola River in what is today Swaziland and settled between the Pongola and the Umfolozi rivers. The great leader Zwide made them a powerful group in early nineteenth-century Swaziland. About that time, the Shangana* people of Mozambique broke away from the Ndwandwes and became a separate people.
REFERENCE: John J. Grotpeter. *Historical Dictionary of Swaziland.* 1975.

NDYEGEM. The Ndyegems are settled farmers living in the Mbuur region of Senegal. They are a subgroup of the Serer.*

NEEGBAN. The Neegbans are one of the Bassa* clans living in the River Cess Territory of Liberia.

NEEKREEN. The Neekreens are a subgroup of the Bassa* people of Liberia. Most of them live in Grand Bassa County.

NEEKRUM. The Neekrums are a subgroup of the Bassa* people of Liberia. Most of them live in Grand Bassa County.

NEEPU. The Neepus are a subgroup of the Bassa* people of Liberia. Most of them live in Grand Bassa County.

NEHYO. *See* NEYO.

NEILLIAM. The Neilliams are a subgroup of the Boua* people, who live along the middle Chari River in the Moyen-Chari Prefecture of Chad. Neilliams can also be found in central Guére Prefecture. The Neilliams arrived in the Chari Valley long before the Saras* did. Over the centuries, they were victimized by Boua slave traders, although the Neilliams themselves often enslaved the Tounians.* Most Neilliams today are small farmers, raising millet, sorghum, and cotton. Their population today is fewer than 5,000 people.
REFERENCE: Thomas Collelo et al. *Chad: A Country Study.* 1988.

NEMADI. The Nemadis are one of the Moor* subgroups living today in Mauritania.

NEMBA. The Nemba are a subgroup of the Ijaw* people of Nigeria. They are concentrated in the Brass Local Government Area of Rivers State and are closely related to the Akassas.*

NEW CESS. The New Cess are a subgroup of the Bassa* people of Liberia. Most of them live in Grand Bassa County.

NEYO. The Neyos are one of the Kru* cluster of peoples of the Ivory Coast. They live in two dozen villages near Sassandra. At the time of the arrival of Europeans in West Africa, the Neyos were the inhabitants of that region, but, with a population today of only about 6,000, they are a tiny minority. They speak a language closely related to that of the Bétés* and Godies,* but they are closer today to the Bakwés* because of geographical proximity and marital alliances. From the seventeenth through the nineteenth centuries, the Neyos served as commercial intermediaries between Europeans, who wanted slaves, rubber, and ivory, and inland African groups, who wanted copper utensils, cloth, marine salt, alcohol, and weapons.
REFERENCE: Robert J. Mundt. *Historical Dictionary of Côte d'Ivoire.* 1995.

NFACHARA. *See* CHARA.

NFUA. *See* BOKYI.

NGA. The Ngas are one of the Bantu*-speaking peoples of Nigeria. They are classified as part of the Plateau cluster of peoples who occupy central Nigeria. Most Ngas live in Plateau State. They are bordered to the north by the Yergan* peoples and to the east by the Kanams.* Most Ngas practice subsistence horticulture, raising ginger, millet, guinea corn, beans, and citrus products. They live in social systems characterized by patrilineal descent and patrifocal residence. In recent years, they have begun migrating to towns and cities looking for work.

REFERENCE: Elizabeth Isichei, ed. *Studies in the History of Plateau State, Nigeria.* 1982.

NGADJI. *See* KURI.

NGALA. The Ngalas are a highly influential ethnic group in northwestern Zaire. Most Ngalas live between the Zaire and the Ubangi rivers. They can also be found in Angola. The Ngala language is the lingua franca of the region and one of the four national languages of Zaire. It appears to be primarily a Bantu* language, with many adopted words from various Sudanic languages as well. The Ngalas were once a relatively small group in terms of population, but linguistic factors gave them great influence. The Ngala language became the commercial language of the lower Zaire River region, the lingua franca of the military in Zaire, and the language spoken most commonly in Leopoldville during the colonial era. During his long tenure as president of Zaire, Joseph Mobutu used the Ngala language to speak to the people of Zaire.

REFERENCE: F. Scott Bobb. *Historical Dictionary of Zaire.* 1988.

NGALANGI. The Ngalangis are a subgroup of the Ovimbundu* peoples of Angola.

NGALTUKU. *See* KANEMBU.

NGAMA. The Ngama people are a subgroup of the Sara* cluster of peoples of Chad. They are most closely related to the Madjingayes,* another Sara group. The Ngamas have a population of nearly 50,000 people, and they are among the most economically developed people in Chad. They can be found especially in the Maro, Modélé, and Nadili cantons where they work in a variety of occupations, including as businessmen, commercial farmers, civil servants, and professionals.

REFERENCE: Samuel Decalo. *Historical Dictionary of Chad.* 1987.

NGAMBAYE. The Ngambayes are one of the major subgroups of the Sara* people of Chad. They live in a large area in Logone Orientale, Logone Occidentele, and Mayo-Kebbi prefectures. Their population today exceeds 450,000 people, and many of them live in fishing villages on the Logone and Chari rivers. Ngambayes can also be found in the Garoua region of Cameroon as well as in Nigeria and the Central African Republic. The Ngambayes themselves are divided into such primary subgroups as the Makoula, Mang, Mbaoua, Kilang, Dogo, and Mbeur. From the seventeenth to the nineteenth centuries, the Ngam-

bayes suffered from Fulbe* and Baguirmi slave raids. They did not come into extensive contact with Europeans until the early 1900s, but they adapted quickly to the educational opportunities available. The Ngambayes played a central role in the formation of the Parti Progressiste Tchadien (PPT) after World War II. The Ngambayes constitute about 40 percent of the Sara people.
REFERENCE: Samuel Decalo. *Historical Dictionary of Chad.* 1987.

NGAMO. The Ngamos, also known over the years as the Gamos, are a Nigerian people. They speak a Chadic language and make their living raising livestock and working subsistence farms. Most Ngamos today live in the Fika District of the Fika Division of Borno State as well as in Bauchi State, especially in the Nafada District of the Gombe Division and the Darazo District of the Bauchi Division.
REFERENCE: *Language Survey of Nigeria.* 1976.

NGAN. *See* BENG.

NGANDJERA. The Ngandjeras are a subgroup of the Ambos* of Namibia.

NGANDU. The Ngandus are a relatively small group of Bantu*-speaking people who live in the forests of the Kasai Orientale region of north-central Zaire. Most of them are small farmers who raise cassava, bananas, and kola nuts. In recent years, the Ngandus have been increasingly affected by Zaire's commercial economy, with the result that more and more of them are growing cash crops or leaving the farms for work in towns and cities.
REFERENCE: Irving Kaplan et al. *Zaire: A Country Study.* 1978.

NGANGAN. The Ngangans are one of the subgroups of the Bimoba* cluster of peoples in Togo, West Africa.

NGANGELA. The term ''Ngangela'' (Nganguela, Ngangwela) is a pejorative reference used by the Ovimbundus,* and many others in Angola, to refer to a cluster of peoples living on the upper Kwanza and Kubango rivers. The Ngangelas are a series of highly decentralized ethnic groups. Their total population today exceeds 700,000 people. During the late nineteenth century, the Chokwes* expanded south and penetrated Ngangela territory, splitting the Ngangelas into two regions. The people in the western section refer to themselves as Ngangelas, but those in the eastern region eschew the name, preferring the names of their own individual subgroups, such as the Lwenas (Luenas), Luvales,* Mbundas,* and Luchazis* (Lutchazes). Also included in the Ngangela cluster of Angolan peoples are the Nyembas, Luimbes, Mbwelas,* Nyembes,* Mbanes, Nkanga-las,* Ngonyelos,* Avicos,* Ngongeiros,* Yahumas, Gengistas, Nkoyas,* and Camochis. Most of the western Ngangelas raise cattle, while fishing is important to the economies of the eastern groups. Modern Angolan politics has also split

the Ngangelas. Many western Ngangelas have allied themselves with the Ovimbundus in the União Nacional Para la Independência Total de Angola (UNITA), while many easterners associate with the Mbundu*-dominated Movimento Popular de Libertacão de Angola (MAPA). During the political instability of the 1980s, thousands of Ngangelas fled Angola and received political asylum in Zaire.
REFERENCES: Susan H. Broadhead. *Historical Dictionary of Angola.* 1992; Thomas Collelo et al. *Angola: A Country Study.* 1989.

NGANGUELA. *See* NGANGELA.

NGANGWELA. *See* NGANGELA.

NGAO. The Ngaos are a subgroup of the Banda* people of the Central African Republic. The French* conducted nearly genocidal wars of conquest against the Ngaos between 1897 and 1901. Their current population exceeds 175,000 people.

NGARE. The Ngares are a Swahili*-speaking people who today live in Kenya.

NGBAGA. The Ngbagas, closely related to the Mbakas* of Zaire, are located on both sides of the Ubangi River in northwestern Zaire, southeastern Congo, and southern Central African Republic where the frontiers of those three countries converge. The Ngbagas are a riverine people who have traditionally supported themselves by planting small gardens on the river banks, fishing, and trading up and down the Ubangi River.
REFERENCE: Irving Kaplan et al. *Zaire: A Country Study.* 1978.

NGBAKA. *See* MBAKA.

NGBANDI. Most anthropolosists classify the Ngbandi people as cultural relatives of the Ngala* people of Zaire. They have Sudanic origins and live in northwestern Zaire. They can be found particularly east of the town of Busingu, between the Zaire River and the Ubangi River. They tend to be widely dispersed in the region. They can also be found in north-central Zaire at the border of the Central African Republic. Traditionally, the Ngbandis have made their living as fishermen. The most famous Ngbandi in Zairean history is Joseph Mobutu, longtime president of the country. The Ngbandis can also be found in the Central African Republic, living in the vast forests upstream from Bangi. The Banziris,* Bourakas, Sangas,* Yakomas,* Dendis,* and Bangous* are all considered part of the Ngbandi group. Most Ngbandis are small farmers.

REFERENCES: F. Scott Bobb. *Historical Dictionary of Zaire.* 1988; Pierre Kalck. *Central African Republic.* 1993.

NGBO. The Ngbos are one of the many subgroups of the Igbo* people, an ethnic group of nearly fifteen million people living today in southern and southeastern Nigeria.

NGCOMPHALALA. The Ngcomphalalas are one of the clans of the Emakhandzambili,* who themselves are one of the three major subgroups of the Swazi* people of Swaziland.

NGEN. *See* BENG.

NGENE. *See* BENG.

NGE-NGE. The Nge-Nges are a ethnic group living today in Zaire and the Congo. They are located on both sides of the Zaire River in southwestern Zaire and in southeastern Congo. The Nge-Nges are a riverine people who have traditionally supported themselves by planting small gardens on the river banks, fishing, and trading up and down the Zaire River.
REFERENCE: Irving Kaplan et al. *Zaire: A Country Study.* 1978.

NGENGE. The Ngenges, who are closely related to the Gbagyis,* are a Nigerian ethnic group of approximately 110,000 people, of whom 10 percent are Muslims.
REFERENCE: *Language Survey of Nigeria.* 1976.

NGENGELE. The Ngengeles are a relatively small ethnic group living today in the Kasai Orientale region of central Zaire. Most of them live west of the Lualaba River. Their homeland is a heavily forested region where they support themselves by raising cassava, bananas, and kola nuts.
REFERENCE: Irving Kaplan et al. *Zaire: A Country Study.* 1978.

NGERE. *See* KPELLE.

NGGWAHYI. The Nggwahyis, also known as the Ngwaxis and Ngwohis, are one of Nigeria's many ethnic groups. They speak a Chadic language and make their living raising cattle and working subsistence farms. Most Nggwahyis live in the Askiva District of the Biu Division of Borno State.
REFERENCE: *Language Survey of Nigeria.* 1976.

NGIGIM. *See* KANEMBU.

NGII. The Ngii people are an ethnic group living today in northeastern

Zaire. More precisely, they are concentrated in the Irumu Zone, just south of the Lendu*-speaking peoples in the Djugu Zone in the Haut-Zaire Region. The Ngii speak a Sudanic language and are a subgroup of the Lendu peoples.

REFERENCE: Constance Lojenga. "The Secret Behind Vowelless Syllables in Lendu." *Journal of African Languages and Linguistics* 11 (October 1989): 115–26.

NGINDO. The term "Ngindo" refers to a cluster of Northeastern Bantu* people of East Africa. Included in the Ngindo cluster are the Pogoros,* Ndambas,* Mbungas,* Ndengerekos,* Matumbis,* and Rufijis.* They trace social descent along male lines. They live on the floodplains of the Kilombero and Rufiji rivers. Most Ngindos are rice farmers and also raise small stock animals. Most of them are Muslim, but their devotions are marginal in terms of identity and commitment.

REFERENCE: A.R.W. Crosse-Upcott. "Male Circumcision Among the Ngindo." *Journal of the Royal Anthropological Institute* 89 (1959): 169–89.

NGINDU. The Ngindus (Ngindo) are a Tanzanian ethnic group whom some ethnologists classify in the Yao* cluster of peoples. Their population today is approximately 175,000 people.

NGIRIL. The Ngirils are a subgroup of the Mbochi* people of eastern Gabon, central Congo, and western Zaire. Their contemporary population exceeds 30,000 people. Although they are increasingly turning to commercial agriculture, the Ngiril economy has traditionally revolved around trading and fishing, at which they are highly adept. Their social structure is based on a patrilineal clan structure.

REFERENCES: Gordon C. McDonald et al. *Area Handbook for the People's Republic of the Congo (Congo Brazzaville).* 1971; Donald G. Morrison et al. *Black Africa: A Comparative Handbook.* 1989.

NGIZM. The Ngizms are part of the larger cluster of Kanuri* peoples of Bornu State in northeastern Nigeria. Ngizm historians claim that they originated in a place called Birnin-Bedr, southwest of Mecca, in the time of the Prophet Mohammed. Their economy is a complex one, revolving around commerce, home manufacturing, personal services, and agriculture. Farmers raise guinea corn, millet, groundnuts, cattle, sheep, and goats. The Ngizms fish in Lake Chad, and, in recent years, they have begun to produce cotton as a cash crop. They are Sunni Muslims.

REFERENCES: Ronald Cohen. *The Kanuri of Bornu.* 1967; Donald G. Morrison et al. *Black Africa: A Comparative Handbook.* 1989; C. L Temple, ed. *Notes on the Tribes, Provinces, Emirates and States of the Northern Provinces of Nigeria.* 1967.

NGOK. The Ngoks are a subgroup of the Dinka* people of Sudan. The major Ngok subgroups are the Abyor, Mannyuar, Anyiel, Acueng, Alei, Acak, Bongo, Diil, and Marenga.

NGOLOGA. The Ngologas are a subgroup of the Kgalagadi* people of Botswana.

NGOMBE. The Ngombes are a Zairean people. Most Ngombes live along the Zaire River, north of the settlements of Mbandaka and Basankusu, where they traditionally pursued a riverine lifestyle—fishing, farming on the river banks, and trading goods up and down the Zaire River in northwestern Zaire.
REFERENCE: Irving Kaplan et al. *Zaire: A Country Study.* 1978.

NGONDE. The Ngonde people live in the Northern Region of Malawi, especially in the Karonga and Chitipa districts, and across the border in Zambia and Tanzania. Most of them are concentrated between the Songwe and the North Rukuru rivers. They speak the same language as the Nyakyusas,* who live on the other side of the river in Tanzania. That region has been a commercial and geographic crossroads in East Africa for centuries. Ngonde oral tradition has them arriving there from points to the east; they then seized control and mixed with the hunter-gatherers already living there. Ngonde society was unique in that they lived in what are called age-villages. When boys reached the age of ten or eleven, they left their parents' homes and built a village for themselves. They then lived as bachelors until they began to marry in their late twenties. The Ngonde economy revolved around cattle herding. German* missionaries brought Christianity to the Ngondes in 1891, but the conversion process took place over a long period of time. In recent years, Ngonde life has changed rather dramatically. An increasing number of Ngondes are switching to farming or wage labor as the commercial economy of Malawi has enveloped them; their political system, focused on traditional chieftains, has been subsumed by the larger political culture and administrative structure. Their current population in all three countries is approximately 750,000 people.
REFERENCES: Colin Black. *The Lands and Peoples of Rhodesia and Nyasaland.* 1964; Cynthia A. Crosby. *Historical Dictionary of Malawi.* 1980; Harold D. Nelson et al. *Area Handbook for Malawi.* 1975; Monica Wilson. *For Men and Elders: Change in the Relations of Generations of Men and Women among the Nyakyusa-Ngonde People, 1875–1971.* 1977.

NGONGEIRO. The Ngongeiros are a subgroup of the larger Ngangela* cluster of peoples living today in Angola.

NGONGO. The Ngongos are a Bantu*-speaking people who live today in south-central Zaire. They are closely related to the Bakubas (Kubas*) Leeles,* Sakatas,* and Njembes.*
REFERENCE: Donald G. Morrison et al. *Black Africa: A Comparative Handbook.* 1989.

NGONI. The Ngoni (Anguni, Angoni, Mangoni, Wangoni) people live in central Malawi, especially in Mzimba District, and from the south shore of Lake Malawi down to the border between the Central and Southern regions, as well as across the border in Mozambique and Tanzania. Another 180,000 Ngoni live in southeastern Zambia, where they speak a Nyanja* dialect. The Portuguese* called them the "Vatua." The Ngoni people have recent roots in South Africa, primarily in Natal, as indicated by their language and patrilineal descent systems. They speak a Zulu* tongue that also uses the "click" sound, indicating their connections with Khoikhois* and Xhosas.* In the 1830s, they migrated into central Africa from the south, fleeing from ethnic rivalries and disputes over land and cattle. The Ngoni conquered the peoples they encountered and established imperial control over them. Their domination of those other groups did not end until the arrival of British* administration in the region in the 1890s. The Ngoni population is approximately one million people today. Most of them make their living raising livestock, especially cattle, and producing maize on small farms. They can be divided into such subgroups as the Mbelwe Ngoni, Gomani Ngoni, and Chiwere Ngoni.

REFERENCES: Y. M. Chibambo. *My Ngoni of Nyasaland.* 1942; W. Elmslie. *Among the Wild Ngoni.* 1899; John J. Grotpeter. *Historical Dictionary of Zambia.* 1979; Margaret Read. *Growing Up Among the Ngoni of Nyasaland.* 1959.

NGONYELO. The Ngonyelos are a subgroup of the larger Ngangela* cluster of peoples living today in Angola.

NGOSHE NDHANG. The Ngoshe Ndhang people are a relatively small ethnic group of approximately 12,000 people who live today in the Madagali District of the Mubi Division of Gongola State in Nigeria, as well as in the Central Gwoza District of Borno State there. They speak a Chadic language that is part of the Mandara* group. Over the years, they have also been identified as the Ngweshes, Ndaghans, and Ngoshe Samas.

REFERENCE: *Language Survey of Nigeria.* 1976.

NGOSHE SAMA. *See* NGOSHE NDHANG.

NGOUNDI. The Ngoundis are a Bantu*-speaking people living in the dense forests of the southwestern reaches of the Central African Republic. The Ngoundis are primarily farmers, who live in a close, symbiotic relationship with the Aka* pygmies, whom they call the Babinga, in the region.

REFERENCE: Pierre Kalck. *Central African Republic.* 1993.

NGOVE. *See* NGOWÉ.

NGOWÉ. The Ngowé people, who have also been known historically as the Ngove, are an ethnic group living on the shores of the Fernan Vaz Lagoon in Ogooué-Maritime Province in Gabon. They are closely related to the Eshiras* and were probably once an Eshira group. Because of their coastal location, the Ngowés took advantage of the presence of Europeans in the fifteenth and six-teenth centuries to establish themselves as middlemen traders with interior groups. Europeans referred to the Ngowé region as the Kingdom of Gobby. In recent years, the Ngowés have begun assimilating with their Fang,* Nkomi,* and Orungu* neighbors. Most of the surviving Ngowés are small farmers or workers in the timber industry. Their current population is approximately 20,000 people.
REFERENCE: David E. Gardinier. *Historical Dictionary of Gabon.* 1994.

NGUERZE. *See* KPELLE.

NGUIN. *See* BENG.

NGULU. *See* NGURU.

NGUMBO. The Ngumbos are part of the larger cluster of Aushi* peoples in Zambia. Their contemporary population exceeds 60,000 people, most of whom are subsistence farmers.

NGUNI. The term ''Nguni'' refers to a group of Bantu* languages spoken in southeastern Africa, primarily in the coastal belt from Zululand to Ciskei in South Africa. The Ngunis migrated south from north of the Limpopo River in the fifteenth century, along with the Sotho* peoples. The Ngunis generally stayed east of the Drakensberg mountains, near the coast, while the Sothos remained west of the mountains. Included in the Nguni group are the Xhosas,* Swazis,* and Ndebeles.* Most Nguni peoples raise cattle and maize as their staple products. Their languages include clicks, a feature that links them to the Khoikhois.* They can be divided into the Cape Nguni, a Xhosa-speaking people, and the Natal Nguni.
REFERENCES: *African Encyclopedia.* 1974; John J. Grotpeter. *Historical Dictionary of Swaziland.* 1975; Christopher Saunders. *Historical Dictionary of South Africa.* 1983.

NGURU. The Nguru are one of the individual groups in the Zaramo* cluster of the Northeast Bantu*-speaking people of East Africa. They live in the moun-tainous highlands of coastal Tanzania where most of them work as hoe farmers, producing maize, beans, vegetables, bananas, sorghum, and cassava; they also raise sheep, goats, and poultry. During the nineteenth century, the Nguru were for the most part left alone because of their geographic isolation; the lowland Zaramo peoples were more vulnerable. Most Nguru today live in small, plastered houses with thatched roofs, although a few still reside in traditional round houses thatched all the way to the ground. Although a majority of Nguru were once Muslims, various Christian groups have established missions in the Tanzanian highlands. Today less than half of the Nguru are still Muslim. Even those are considered to be only marginally loyal, confining their religious observances to fasting at Ramadan, taking on Arab* names, and wearing the white skull cap. Their population in Tanzania exceeds 150,000 people. Since the mid-1970s, the Nguru have been dramatically affected by the Tanzanian government's *ujamaa* policy, which is designed to gather rural people out of their scattered homestead settlements into more concentrated villages where public education and public health campaigns can be more effective. Rates of malaria and schistosomiasis are relatively high among the Nguru, and only improved public health programs can alleviate the crisis. The Nguru people have also been affected in recent years by the East African drought of the late 1980s and early 1990s and by the threat of the human immunodeficiency virus (HIV) and the disease of AIDS, although their geographic isolation in the highlands has provided some protection.

REFERENCES: Laura Kurtz. *Historical Dictionary of Tanzania.* 1978; L. W. Swantz. *Ritual and Symbol in Transitional Zaramo Society.* 1970.

NGURU. *See* LOMWE.

NGURUIMI. The Nguruimis people live in northwestern Tanzania, primarily along the southwestern shore of Lake Victoria. They raise cattle and farm, using the manure to keep their soil productive. They have a population today of approximately 30,000 people.

REFERENCE: Laura Kurtz. *Historical Dictionary of Tanzania.* 1978.

NGWA. The Ngwas are one of the many subgroups of the Igbo* people, an ethnic group of nearly fifteen million people living today in southern and southeastern Nigeria.

NGWAKETSE. The Ngwaketses are one of the primary subdivisions of the Tswana* people of Botswana and South Africa. They became independent of the Kwenas* early in the 1800s, under the leadership of Makaba. At the time, the Ngwaketses made their living as cattle raiders. To escape Boer control in the 1880s, they accepted British* protection. Within a few years, however, under Bathoen I, they resisted British control as well. During the 1890s, most Ngwaketses became Christians. During the twentieth century, Bathoen II helped the Ngwaketses maintain their sense of group identity.

REFERENCE: Fred Morton, A. Murray, and J. Ramsay. *Historical Dictionary of Botswana.* 1989.

NGWANO. *See* WAN.

NGWATO. The Ngwatos are one of the primary subdivisions of the Tswana* people of Botswana and South Africa. They originated with the Kwena* people and split off from them. Under the leadership of Sekgoma I, they came to dominate central and northeastern Botswana in the mid-nineteenth century. Their power increased under Khama III in the later decades of the century. During the twentieth century, after the imposition of British* imperial authority, the Ngwatos increasingly became migrant laborers in the southern African trade and extraction industries.
REFERENCE: Fred Morton, A. Murray, and J. Ramsay. *Historical Dictionary of Botswana.* 1989.

NGWAXI. *See* NGGWAHYI.

NGWE. *See* NGWOI.

NGWELA. *See* KULANGO.

NGWENA. The Ngwenas are one of the major clans of the Bemdzabuko* division of the Swazi* people of Swaziland.

NGWESHE. *See* NGOSHE NDHANG.

NGWOHI. *See* NGGWAHYI.

NGWOI. The Ngwois—also known as Ngwes, Ungwes, Ingwes, and Nkwois—are one of the Western Plateau peoples of Nigeria. Their population numbers approximately 5,000 people, most of whom live in the Tegina and Kwangoma districts of the Minna Division in Niger State. The Ngwois also live in the forests of the Manyu Prefecture of Southwest Province in Cameroon. They can be found just east of the headwaters of the Cross River, east of Mamfe Town. Their most immediate ethnic neighbors are the Kenyangs,* Mundanis,* Menkas,* Denyas,* and Ejaghams.* Most Ngwois are subsistence farmers.
REFERENCES: Samson Negbo Abangma. *Modes in Denya Discourse.* 1987; *Language Survey of Nigeria.* 1976.

NHLENGETFWA. The Nhlengetfwas are one of the clans of the Emafika-muva* people, who themselves are one of the three major subgroups of the Swazi* people of Swaziland.

NHOHWE. *See* NHOWE.

NHOWE. The Nhowes (Nhohwes, Vanhowes, Wanoes) are a subgroup of the Zezuru* people, who are part of the Shona* cluster in Zimbabwe. Most Nhowes live in the Mrewa District.

NIABIUSSA. *See* NYAKYUSA.

NIABOUA. The Niaboua are a small ethnic group of the Ivory Coast. They live in the subprefecture of Zoukougbeu. They speak a Kru* language closely related to Guéré.* Before the arrival of the French,* most Niaboua were hunters and gatherers, but, under French tutelage, they made the transition to cocoa and coffee farming. In recent years, there has been a substantial migration of Julas* to Niaboua territory, and many Niaboua have migrated to Abidjan.
REFERENCES: Jean-Noel Loucou. *Histoire de la Côte d'Ivoire.* Volume I: *La formation des peuples.* 1984; Robert J. Mundt. *Historical Dictionary of Côte d'Ivoire.* 1995.

NIAMNIAM. *See* NYAMNYAM.

NIANJA. *See* NYANJA.

NIASSA. *See* NYANJA.

NIBULU. *See* NUNUMA.

NIÉDÉBOUA. The Niédéboua are one of the Kru* clusters of people in Ivory Coast. The Niédéboua are concentrated in the subprefecture of Vavoua. They were traditionally subsistence farmers, raising a variety of crops, but, under French* influence in the twentieth century, a substantial number of Niédéboua made the transition to commercial farming, particularly coffee and cocoa.
REFERENCE: Robert J. Mundt. *Historical Dictionary of Côte d'Ivoire.* 1995.

NIELLIM. The Niellims are a subgroup of the Sara* people of Chad. Most Niellims live in southern Chad, along the Chari River until it reaches the Salamat River. During the nineteenth century, the Niellims were a small sultanate that suffered badly from attacks at the hands of the Barmas.* Today, the Niellims are in an advanced state of assimilation with the Barmas.
REFERENCE: Samuel Decalo. *Historical Dictionary of Chad.* 1987.

NIENDÉ. The Niendés are a subgroup of the Somba* people of Benin and Togo. Their contemporary population is approximately 50,000 people, most of whom are farmers, raising maize, millet, plantains, and cassava.

NIÉNIGÉ. The Niénigés (Niéniégue, Niniga, Nienigue) are one of the Habé* peoples of Burkina-Faso. They are concentrated between Satiri, Ouarkoyé, and Boromo at the bend of the Black Volta River. They are primarily farmers, raising millet, sorghum, cotton, and peanuts.
REFERENCE: Daniel M. McFarland. *Historical Dictionary of Upper Volta.* 1978.

NIKIM. The Nikims are an ethnic group living today in Kwara State in

Nigeria. They trace their origins to the confluence of the Niger and Benue rivers in what used to be Northern Nigeria.

REFERENCES: Donald G. Morrison et al. *Black Africa: A Comparative Handbook.* 1989; A. Oyewole. *Historical Dictionary of Nigeria.* 1987.

NIKKI. The Nikkis are part of the larger group of Bariba* people. They number approximately 550,000 people and live primarily in the Department of Borghou in Benin, although some can also be found in Kwara State in Nigeria. Although some Nikkis have moved to cities in Nigeria and Benin in recent years and have taken jobs as civil servants, small businessmen, and craftsmen, most Nikkis are farmers who raise yams, sorghum, millet, and corn for their own consumption, as well as rice, peanuts, cotton, and beans as cash crops. Nikkis usually live in concentrated villages; within those villages, they dwell in walled compounds that house several families related on a paternal line. They may also have small farmhouses a few miles out in the countryside near their land and herds. Approximately one-third of the Nikkis are Muslims, and they have recently become somewhat more devout in their commitment. The rest for the most part remain loyal to indigenous beliefs, which include devotion to ancestors, shamanistic healers, and a belief in a variety of animistic forces. The Nikkis have historically been a dominant group wherever they have lived. Neighboring Fulbe* people have generally served the Nikkis by raising their cattle herds for them, while the Hausas* are usually merchants and traders supplying the Nikki with goods and services. Both the Fulbes and the Hausas acknowledge Nikki political leadership where they live in close proximity to each other.

REFERENCES: Jacques Maquet. *Civilizations of Black Africa.* 1972; Harold D. Nelson et al. *Area Handbook for Nigeria.* 1972; Carolyn F. Sargent. "Born to Die: Witchcraft and Infanticide in Bariba Culture." *Ethnology* 27 (1988): 79–95.

NILOTE. The term "Nilote" is used to refer to groups of people living near the Bahr al Jabal River and its tributaries in Sudan. Their languages are part of the Nilotic* sub-branch of the Eastern Sudan group of Nilo-Saharan languages. Historically, cattle have been central to the Nilotic economy and culture. Nilotes constitute 60 percent of the population of southern Sudan today. Included in the Nilotic cluster are such groups as the Dinkas,* Nuers,* and Shilluks.*

REFERENCE: Helen C. Metz et al. *Sudan: A Country Study.* 1992.

NILOTIC. The Nilotic peoples of Africa speak a language that is part of the eastern group of Sudanic languages. Most of them raise cattle, sheep, and goats.

REFERENCE: Carolyn Fluehr-Lobban, Richard A. Lobban, Jr., and John Obert Voll. *Historical Dictionary of Sudan.* 1992.

NILYAMBA. The Nilyambas are a relatively large ethnic group in contemporary Tanzania. They speak a Bantu* language and have a population of approximately 275,000 people. Most of them are subsistence farmers.
REFERENCE: Edgar C. Polomé and C. P. Hill. *Language in Tanzania.* 1980.

NIMBARI. *See* NYAMNYAM.

NINGO. The Ningos are one of the subgroups of the Adangbe* peoples of the Accra Plain and coastal inselbergs of southeastern Ghana. Most of them make their living as small farmers.

NINISI. The word ''Ninisi'' (Tinguimbissi) is a collective term used to describe the autochthonous peoples of Burkina-Faso in West Africa. It literally means ''children of the earth'' and refers to the Lilses,* Fulses,* Kibsis,* Kipirsis,* and Kurumbas.* Most of them are small farmers today, raising millet and sorghum. They live in the central part of the country. They were probably the original inhabitants of the region until the Mossis* invaded in the sixteenth century and became dominant.
REFERENCE: Daniel M. McFarland. *Historical Dictionary of Upper Volta.* 1978.

NINZAM. The Ninzams (Gbhus) are a relatively small Nigerian ethnic group. They speak a Bantu* language and live on the southwestern edge of the Jos Plateau in Plateau State, primarily in the Wamba District of the Akwanga Division. They can also be found in the Jema'a District of the Jema'a Division of Kaduna State. Their most immediate ethnic neighbors are the Nunkus,* Chessus,* Turkwans,* Kantanas,* and Arums.* Most Ninzams are subsistence farmers who raise millet, guinea corn, maize, and a variety of other products.
REFERENCES: Elizabeth Isichei, ed. *Studies in the History of Plateau State, Nigeria.* 1982; *Language Survey of Nigeria.* 1976.

NINZO. The Ninzos are part of a larger Hausa*-Fulbe* cluster of peoples living today in northwestern Nigeria. Some of them can also be found across the border in Niger and in northern Benin. A strong Muslim component dominates their religion, and most of them are small farmers and cattle herders.
REFERENCE: Donald G. Morrison et al. *Black Africa: A Comparative Handbook.* 1989.

NIONIOSSE. The Nioniosse are one of the autochthonous peoples of Upper Volta.
REFERENCE: Donald G. Morrison et al. *Black Africa: A Comparative Handbook.* 1989.

NITEN. *See* GANAWURI.

NIUMINKO. The Niuminkos, also known as Nyoominkoos, are considered a subgroup of the Serer* because they speak a Serer dialect. Most Niuminkos also

speak Mandinka* and Wolof* as well. They are concentrated in the coastal areas
of Gambia. Most Niuminkos make their living as fishermen and merchants.
REFERENCE: David P. Gamble. *The Gambia.* 1988.

NJABETA. The Njabeta are one of the cluster of Middle-Cameroon Bantu*
peoples who live in central Cameroon. Most of them make their living as small
farmers and fishermen, although, in recent years, increasing numbers of Njabeta
men have found work on commercial farms and in the oil fields. The recent
emphasis on commercial crops for export—coffee, cocoa, timber, palm oil, and
bananas for foreign exchange—has actually tended to impoverish most Njabeta
farmers and has contributed to a decline in their standard of living.
REFERENCE: Mark DeLancey and H. M. Mokeba. *Historical Dictionary of the Republic
of Cameroon.* 1990.

NJAI. *See* NZANGI.

NJANJA. The Njanjas (Vanjanjas) are a branch of the Zezuru* peoples, who
themselves are part of the Shona* cluster of peoples in Zimbabwe. They are
concentrated in the Charter District.

NJANYI. *See* NZANGI.

NJEI. *See* NZANGI.

NJEMBE. The Njembes are one of the cluster of Kuba* peoples of south-central
Zaire. In rural areas, most Njembes are farmers, raising maize, millet, and cassava. In towns and cities, large numbers of Njembes work in a variety of
occupations.

NJEMP. The Njemps, who are also known as the Tiamus, speak a Maa language and live in the region south and east of Lake Baringo in Kenya and in
the hill region reaching from east of Lake Baringo to the Laikipia escarpment.
They are descended from either the Samburu* people or the Laikipiak Masai.*
During the nineteenth century, the Njemps made their living supplying caravans
between Uganda and Zaire. They are known as skilled fishermen who also raise
cattle, sheep, and goats. They are rapidly adopting irrigated agriculture. The
Njemp population in Kenya today exceeds 10,000 people.
REFERENCE: Peter D. Little. ''Woman as Ol Payian (Elder): The Status of Widows
Among the Il Chamus (Njemps) of Kenya.'' *Ethnos* 52 (1987): 81–102.

NJUKU. *See* JUKUN.

NKALU. The Nkalus are one of the many subgroups of the Igbo* people, an ethnic group of nearly fifteen million people living today in southern and southeastern Nigeria.

NKAMBULE. The Nkambules are one of the clans of the Emafikamuva* people, who themselves are one of the three major subgroups of the Swazi* people of Swaziland.

NKANGALA. The Nkangalas are a subgroup of the larger Ngangela* cluster of peoples living today in Angola.

NKANU. The Nkanus are one of the many subgroups of the Igbo* people of southern and southeastern Nigeria.

NKEM-NKUM. The Nkem-Nkums are one of Nigeria's many ethnic groups. They speak an Ekoid Bantu* language in the Benue-Congo family and live primarily in the Ogoja Division of Cross River State. The Nkem-Nkum population today exceeds 70,000 people.
REFERENCE: *Language Survey of Nigeria.* 1976.

NKIM. The Nkims are an ethnic group living today in Kwara State in Nigeria. They trace their origins to the confluence of the Niger and Benue rivers in what used to be Northern Nigeria. They have long been a farming people, but, in recent decades, because Kwara State has been integrated into a larger commercial economy, large numbers of Nkims have begun working for wages and experiencing occupational diversity.
REFERENCES: Donald G. Morrison et al. *Black Africa: A Comparative Handbook.* 1989; A. Oyewole. *Historical Dictionary of Nigeria.* 1987.

NKOKOLLE. *See* NKUKOLI.

NKOLE. *See* NYANKORE.

NKOLONKATI-EUNDA. The Nkolonkati-Eundas are a subgroup of the Ambos* of Namibia.

NKOMI. The Nkomi people of Gabon have a contemporary population of several thousand people, and they speak a Myènè* language. When the Portuguese* first arrived in Gabon in the fifteenth century, the Nkomis were living on the shores of the Fernan Vaz Lagoon, making their living as small farmers, fishermen, and traders. By the early 1600s, with the Dutch firmly established in the region, the Nkomis were trading ivory, fabrics, and slaves for iron goods. By the 1800s, the Nkomis had added rubber to the list of goods that they secured from the interior for European consumption; it had become the most important product of that trade by the late 1800s. Many Nkomis were educated at Christian

mission schools in the early 1900s. Today the Nkomis are a visible group in the Fernan Vaz Lagoon region.
REFERENCE: David E. Gardinier. *Historical Dictionary of Gabon.* 1994.

NKONYA. The Nkonyas are a subgroup of the Guan* peoples of Ghana. They are concentrated in the Volta Region of southeastern Ghana, with some located across the border in Togo. The Nkonya population in Ghana today exceeds 25,000 people.

NKONYANE. The Nkonyanes are one of the major clans of the Bemdzabuko* division of the Swazi* people of Swaziland.

NKORAMFO. *See* KULANGO.

NKORO. The Nkoros are one of the many ethnic groups living in Rivers State, Nigeria. They are concentrated particularly in the Bonny Local Government Area. Ethnolinguists classify them as part of the larger cluster of Ijaw* peoples. The Nkoros are primarily subsistence farmers.
REFERENCE: E. J. Alagoa and Tekena N. Tamuno. *Land and People of Nigeria: Rivers State.* 1989.

NKOYA. The Nkoyas (Mankoyas) are descendants of the Mbwelas,* who were early Congolese immigrants to western-central Zambia. Today, the Nkoya population is approximately 45,000 people, most of whom live east of the Lozis* and west of the Ilas* and Kaondes.* They speak a Lozi language and have long been a subject people to the Lozis.
REFERENCE: John J. Grotpeter. *Historical Dictionary of Zambia.* 1979.

NKOYE. The Nkoyes are an ethnic group in Zaire. They are part of the Mawika* cluster of peoples.

NKU. The Nku people of Zaire are concentrated near the confluence of the Kwango and the Kasai rivers in southwestern Zaire. Some Nkus can also be found across the border in the southeastern Congo. Many of them live in and around the city of Bundundu. As a riverine people, the Nkus traditionally made their livings fishing, planting crops on the river banks, and trading goods in the region. Many of them still live that way.
REFERENCE: Irving Kaplan et al. *Zaire: A Country Study.* 1978.

NKUKOLI. The Nkukolis—known widely as the Nkokolles, Lokukolis, and Ekuris—are one of the Cross River peoples of the Benue-Congo language family in Nigeria. They live primarily at the juncture of the Ikom, Obubra, and Akamkpa divisions in Cross River State. They can also be found in western

Cameroon. They are closely related to the Efiks* and Ibibios.* Most of them are farmers, raising yams and palm oil.
REFERENCE: *Language Survey of Nigeria.* 1976.

NKUTSHU. The Nkutshus are a Bantu*-speaking group of people who live today primarily in the Kasai Orientale region of Zaire. Their most immediate neighbors are the Ndengses,* Yelas,* and Oolis.* The region is heavily forested, and most Nkutshus make their living there as small farmers, raising cassava, bananas, and kola nuts.
REFERENCE: Irving Kaplan et al. *Zaire: A Country Study.* 1978.

NKWOI. *See* NGWOI.

NLADJA-WRON. *See* ALLADIAN.

NNAM. The Nnams (Ndems) are an Ekoid Bantu* people of Cross River State in Nigeria. They are especially concentrated in the Ikom and Ogoja divisions. The Nnam population today exceeds 5,000 people.
REFERENCE: *Language Survey of Nigeria.* 1976.

NNERIGWE. *See* IRIGWE.

NNGA. *See* ANGA.

NOALE. *See* MBEMBE.

NOARMA. The Noarmas are a subgroup of the Daza* people of Chad. Most Noarmas live in the Borkou Subprefecture where they are nomadic pastoralists raising goats, sheep, camels, and sometimes horses.
REFERENCE: Thomas Collelo et al. *Chad: A Country Study.* 1988.

NOLE. The Nole are a subgroup of the Afran Qalla,* themselves a subgroup of the Oromo* of Ethiopia. They are primarily Muslims who live around the city of Harar and work as sedentary farmers.

NON. The Non are a subgroup of the Cangin,* themselves a subdivision of the Serer* peoples of Senegal.

NONO. The Nono are considered a Fringe Manding* group who trace their tribal origins back to the Mali Empire of the thirteenth century. There are approximately 23,000 Nonos living today in Mali. Virtually all of them are Muslims.
REFERENCE: Donald R. Wright. ''Manding-Speaking Peoples.'' In Richard V. Weekes, ed. *Muslim Peoples.* 1984.

NOUNOUMA. *See* NUNUMA.

NOUROUMA. *See* NUNUMA.

NSENGA. The Nsengas (Senga), whose contemporary population is around 290,000 people, live in the Eastern Province of Zambia and across the border in Mozambique. In Mozambique, they are especially concentrated in Tete Province, in the Tete highlands north of the Zambezi River. Although they spent centuries as part of the Chewa* kingdom, they are closely related, culturally and linguistically, to the Bembas.* Ethnologists believe that they originated in the Congo centuries ago. During the nineteenth century, the Nsengas were actively engaged in the ivory trade with Europeans. The Nsenga economy revolves around a form of agriculture in which they plant maize and millet in mounds of soil. In regions where tsetse fly infestation is minimal, they also raise cattle. Commercial agriculture started developing among the Nsengas in the 1970s.
REFERENCES: *African Encyclopedia.* 1974; John J. Grotpeter. *Historical Dictionary of Zambia.* 1979.

NSIT. The Nsits are a subgroup of the Ibibio* peoples of Nigeria.

NSO. The Nsos are today considered a subgroup of the Tikar* peoples of the Bamenda highlands of North West Province in Cameroon. They are classified as part of the Middle-Cameroon Bantu* group of peoples. The Nsos originated farther to the north and were pushed into their present location by Fulbe* expansion. Theirs is a savanna environment with patches of woodland and gallery forest along water courses. The Nsos are farmers and fishermen. Their villages stretch along roads and tracks. Their traditional huts are rectangular and have a palmfrond roofing, but today cement houses and corrugated sheet roofs are common, especially in villages near the tarmacked main roads.
REFERENCE: Mark W. Delancey and H. M. Mokeba. *Historical Dictionary of the Republic of Cameroon.* 1990.

NSUTA. The Nsutas are one of the primary subgroups of the Asante* people of Ghana.

NTANDU. The Ntandus are a subgroup of the Kongos.*

NTEMA. The Ntemas are a subgroup of the Mbundu* peoples of Angola.

NTHALI. The Nthalis are part of the Tumbuka* cluster of peoples living today in northern Malawi, primarily between Lake Nyasa and the Zambian border, south of the Tanzanian border. Some Nthalis can also be found in

Zambia and Tanzania. The Nthali population today exceeds 50,000 people. Their economy still revolves around the production of maize, sorghum, and millet.
REFERENCES: *African Encyclopedia.* 1974; John J. Grotpeter. *Historical Dictionary of Zambia.* 1979; Donald G. Morrison et al. *Black Africa: A Comparative Handbook.* 1989.

NTOMBA. The Ntomba (Ntombe) people live south of the Middle Zaire River, along the Maringa River, in Zaire. They are fishermen and farmers, raising cassava, bananas, and kola nuts. The Ntombas speak a Mongo* language, which is part of the larger Bantu* linguistic family.
REFERENCE: Irving Kaplan et al. *Zaire: A Country Study.* 1978.

NTOMBE. *See* NTOMBA.

NTOUMOU. *See* NTUMU.

NTRUBER. *See* NTRUBU.

NTRUBU. The Ntrubus, also known as the Ntrubers, are one of the cluster of Volta-Togo peoples who live in the Volta Region of Ghana. They are concentrated east of Krakye. The Ntrubu population today is approximately 8,000 people.
REFERENCE: Daniel M. McFarland. *Historical Dictionary of Ghana.* 1985.

NTUM. *See* NTUMU.

NTUMU. The Ntumus (Ntoumou, Ntums) are part of the larger Fang*-Pahouin* cluster of Bantu*-speaking peoples of Cameroon, Gabon, and Equatorial Guinea. The Ntumu population today exceeds 200,000 people, most of whom are Roman Catholics. They are primarily farmers, raising cocoa, rice, coffee, groundnuts, cassava, and a variety of other vegetable crops. They are actually a subgroup of the Fang proper.
REFERENCES: Mark DeLancey and H. M. Mokeba. *Historical Dictionary of the Republic of Cameroon.* 1990; Harold D. Nelson et al. *Area Handbook for the United Republic of Cameroon.* 1974.

NTWUMURU. The Ntwumurus, also known as the Nchumuru and Nchumbulung, are one of the clusters of Guan* peoples of Ghana. They are closely related culturally to the Krakyes.* They live around Lake Volta and make their living as farmers and fishermen. The Ntwumuru population in Ghana today is approximately 30,000 people.

NUADHU. *See* CHOMO-KARIM.

NUBA. The descriptive term "Nuba" or "Nubans" (not to be confused with the Nubians* of the Upper Nile Valley) is a generic reference to the approximately 1.2 million people of non-Arab* extraction who live in as many as 100 settlements of the Nuba Mountains on the Kordofan Province of Sudan. They do not constitute an ethnic group because more than 100 mutually unintelligible languages are spoken by Nubas. Those languages are divided into perhaps ten distinct linguistic groups. Most of the Nubas also speak Arabic because the process of Arabization has been affecting them for centuries, in spite of the geographic isolation of the region. During the past thousand years, the region has served as a place of refuge for groups fleeing natural and human disasters. The Nubas supported themselves with rainfall agriculture, raising sorghum as the staple, tobacco for personal consumption, and small amounts of cotton and peanuts. For centuries, the dry, rocky valleys and ravines of the Nuba Mountains have also served as a source of slaves for Arab raiders coming into the area from the north.

The conversion of Nubas to Islam was a phenomenon of the nineteenth century, when Arab traders initiated significant, sustained contact with the Nubas. Most Nubas living in the western, northern, and eastern mountains have become Muslims, while those to the south are more like to have remained loyal to their pre-Islamic animist faiths. British* colonial missionaries in the Anglo-Egyptian Sudan converted some of the southern Nubas to Christianity. British colonial policy, as enunciated in what were known as the Closed District Ordinances of the 1920s, sought to prevent the spread of Islam by confining Muslim clerics to certain regional areas and not permitting travel, as well as by outlawing the use of Arabic names, Arabic dress, and the Arabic language in the schools. After Sudan became independent in 1956, Islam spread and Christianity declined. Political authority in the Nuba region is highly decentralized, although, in recent years, Nuban nationalism has found expression in such groups as the General Union of Nubas, led by Phillip Abbas Gaboush.

REFERENCES: James C. Faris. ''Nuba.'' In Richard V. Weekes, ed. *Muslim Peoples.* 1984; Carolyn Fluehr-Lobban, Richard A. Lobban, Jr., and John Obert Voll. *Historical Dictionary of Sudan.* 1992; R. C. Stevenson. ''The Nuba Peoples of Kordofan Province: An Ethnographic Survey.'' M. S. thesis. University of Khartoum. 1965.

NUBAN. *See* NUBA.

NUBIAN. The Nubians (not to be confused with the Nubas* or Nubans of the Nuba Mountains of Kordofan Province of Sudan) are a people whose traditional homeland was between Aswan, Egypt, and the Dongola region of northern Sudan. Their current population in Egypt and Sudan exceeds 800,000 people. About 10,000 Nubians can also be found in Uganda. The Nubian language is part of the Sudanic branch of the Nilo-Saharan linguistic family. Historically, the Nubian homeland was at the crossroads between Egypt to the north and the African tribal kingdoms to the south. Byzantine missionaries converted the Nubians to Christianity in the sixth century. Egypt conquered Nubia in the seventh century, maintaining them as a tributary kingdom. Nubia also became a source of slaves for Arab* slave traders. In the sixteenth century, the process of converting Nubians to Islam began. By the seventeenth century, that process was complete, and, as a result, the slave raids into Nubia largely came to an end. Today, the Marghaniyya branch of Islam is especially influential among Nubians, and they are working at increasing Nubian devotions and wiping out the last vestiges of pre-Islamic Christianity and indigenous traditions.

The Nubians are divided into a number of subgroups. From the fourteenth to the sixteenth centuries, when Islamic missionaries arrived in Nubia, some peoples fled to more remote locations in Darfur and Kordofan, where they evolved into distinct Nubian groups on their own. Included among these refugee peoples are the Anags, Birkeds,* Dillings,* Kadarus, Meidobs,* and Nyamas. Unlike other Nubians, they speak Kordofian languages, which are not related to Sudanic languages. The Barbras are another Nubian subgroup. They are divided into a number of subgroups themselves. The Kenuz Nubians lived in the region from the first to the second cataracts on the Nile River. The Sukkot and Maha Nubians live between the second and third cataracts, as did the Halfawi Nubians. Some Nubians can also be found in southern Egypt.

Beginning with the construction of the dam on the Nile at Aswan in 1897, and the increases in its height in 1912 and 1927, Nubian lands were flooded, forcing a relocation of many Nubians. They received financial compensation for the loss of their lands, and large numbers of Nubians moved to Egyptian cities to live and work. The construction of the High Dam at Aswan from 1962 to 1965 brought about the relocation of another 100,000 Nubians, who settled in New Nubia, a government community twenty miles north of Aswan and in Wadi Halfa near Khartoum. The urbanization and relocation of so many Nubians has led to the emergence of a sense of Nubian ethnicity in the past thirty years, primarily because the older village and regional sub-identities are no longer relevant. The Kenuz* Nubians were relocated to Egypt, especially in the Kom Ombo region. The Sukkots, Mahas,* and Halfawis were relocated to towns in the eastern Sudan. Today, the Nubian population exceeds one million people, with half of them dispersed throughout major Egyptian cities and the other half in New Nubia, Wadi Halfa, or rural villages. Use of the Nubian language is declining rapidly as Arabic becomes the primary means of communication among Nubians.

REFERENCES: William Y. Adams. *Nubia, Corridor to Africa.* 1984; Hussein M. Fahim. *Dams, People and Development: The Aswan High Dam Case.* 1981; Robert A. Fernea. *Nubians in Egypt: Peaceful People.* 1973; Elizabeth Fernea and Robert A. Fernea. *Nubian Ethnographies.* 1991; Carolyn Fluehr-Lobban, Richard A. Lobban, Jr., and John Obert Voll. *Historical Dictionary of Sudan.* 1992.

NUER. The Nuer live in the Upper Nile River Valley of Sudan and across the border in far southwestern Ethiopia. Their homeland is flat land watered by the White Nile and the Blue Nile rivers. Their northern boundary is about 200 miles

south of Khartoum, and their southern border is the northeastern shore of Lake
Victoria. As with the neighboring Dinkas,* their economy and culture revolve
around cattle production. They are closely associated with the Atuots,* whom
many consider to be one of their subgroups. Including the Atuots, who have
adopted the Nuer language, there are several identifiable Nuer subgroups. They
include the Garjok, Garjak, and Jekiang* of the Nasser District; the Lau of the
Abwong District; the Gaweir of the Fanjak District; and the Laks and Thiangs
of Zeraf Island in the Fanjak District; and the Western Nuer in the Yivrol
District. They speak a Nilotic* language. Until the outbreak of the Sudanese
civil war in 1983, the Western Leek Nuer of southern Sudan were being incorporated into the national political economy of Sudan more effectively, and less
traumatically, than many Nuer communities east of the White Nile. The creation
of government courts, the collection of tribute, and the establishment of roads,
markets, schools, missions, and medical facilities all came more gradually to the
Western Leek Nuer than to the Eastern Jikany Nuer who were devastated by
the civil war from 1955 to 1972. The most important post-World War II Sudanese politician was Buth Diu.

REFERENCES: Carolyn Fluehr-Lobban, Richard A. Lobban, Jr., and John Obert Voll.
Historical Dictionary of Sudan. 1992; Ray Huffman. *Nuer Customs & Folklore.* 1970;
Sharon Hutchinson. ''Rising Divorce Among the Nuer, 1936–1983.'' *Man* 25 (1990):
393–411.

NUKHI. The Nukhi dialect is spoken by San* peoples in southwestern Botswana. The Nukhi people, who are primarily farmers and cattle-raisers, are
closely related to neighboring Xam, Xo, and Xegwi people.

NUMANA-NUNKU-GWANTU. The Numana-Nunku-Gwantus, also known as
Sangas,* are one of the Eastern Plateau peoples of Nigeria. They can be found
today living in the Wamba District of the Akwanga Division of Plateau State,
as well as in the Jema'a District of the Jema'a Division of Kaduna State.

REFERENCE: *Language Survey of Nigeria.* 1976.

NUNG NDEM. The Nung Ndems are a subgroup of the Ibibio* peoples of
Nigeria.

NUNGU. *See* NUNKU.

NUNGUDA. *See* LONGUDA.

NUNGURA. *See* LONGUDA.

NUNGURABA. *See* LONGUDA.

NUNKU. The Nunkus (Nungus, Rindres, Rendres, Rindiris, Lindiris, and Wambas) are a relatively small Nigerian ethnic group. They speak a Bantu* language and live on the southwestern edge of the Jos Plateau in Plateau State, especially in the Wamba District of the Akwanga Division. Their most immediate ethnic neighbors are the Ayus,* Ninzams,* Madas,* and Kagoros.* Most Nunkus are subsistence farmers who raise millet, guinea corn, maize, and a variety of other products.

REFERENCES: Elizabeth Isichei, ed. *Studies in the History of Plateau State, Nigeria.* 1982; *Language Survey of Nigeria.* 1976.

NUNUMA. The Nunumas (Nounouma, Nouna, Nourouma, Nanoumba, Nibulu), also known historically as Nanums and Nanunes, are a Molé*-Dagbane people who live in the Northern Region of Ghana. Their homeland is bounded by the Daka River to the west and the Oti River to the east. Their primary settlement in Burkina-Faso is in the town of Tchériba, which is on the road between Dédougou and Koudougou. Other Nunumas can be found in the areas of Boromo and Léo. The Nunumas are small farmers. Today their population exceeds 50,000 people.

REFERENCES: Daniel M. McFarland. *Historical Dictionary of Upper Volta.* 1978; Daniel M. McFarland. *Historical Dictionary of Ghana.* 1995.

NUPE. The Nupes are a riverine ethnic group living along the Niger and Kaduna rivers in west-central Nigeria, particularly in the vicinity of the towns of Bida, Mokwa, and Jebba. Most of the 550,000 Nupes live in Niger State, with the remainder in Kwara State on the south bank of the Niger River. Those in rural areas raise rice, guinea corn, millet, and yams. The Nupe language is related to Yoruba* and Igbo* and is part of the Benue-Kwa language. Traditionally, the Nupes were a politically powerful people who fished and traded goods along the Niger River. In 1810, an itinerant Fulbe* preacher, Mallam Dendo, brought Islam to the Nupe. He became politically influential and helped to bring about the Fulbe conquest of the Nupes. By the late nineteenth century, the Nupe economy had made a transition in which fishing and local trade gave way in significance to grain production and long-range commercial trading. The Fulbe brought the Sunni Muslim faith, Maliki school, to the Nupe elites, but conversion was much more limited among the Nupe masses, who viewed Islam as a foreign religion. Christianity was more successful in rural villages. British* missionaries brought Protestantism in the 1860s, as did agents of the Royal Niger Company in the 1890s. Today, perhaps one-third of the Nupes are Muslims, but only half of those actually practice the religion. Many rural Nupes still worship their traditional deity—Soko—whom some identify as Allah. Urban Nupes are far more likely to be more devout Muslims. Polygyny is still commonly practiced. The Nupes are divided into a number of subgroups, including the Bataus, Benis, Kyedyes, Eghagis, Ebes, and Benus.

REFERENCES: R. M. Blench. "Nupe." In Richard V. Weekes, ed. *Muslim Peoples.* 1984; A. Oyewole. *Historical Dictionary of Nigeria.* 1987.

NWENSHI. The Nwenshis are a Bantu*-speaking people who live today in the Katanga region of southeastern Zaire. Some Nwenshis can also be found across the border in Zambia, with some scattered members in southwestern Tanzania. Most Nwenshis make their living as small farmers.
REFERENCE: Irving Kaplan et al. *Zaire: A Country Study.* 1978.

NYAGOMBE. The Nyagombes are a small ethnic group whose contemporary population numbers approximately 50,000 people. In recent years, many Nyagombes have made the transition to commercial farming and urban labor, but most continue to live as subsistence farmers and livestock raisers. They live in the lower Zambezi River Valley of Mozambique.
REFERENCE: Mario Azevedo. *Historical Dictionary of Mozambique.* 1991.

NYAGTWA. The Nyagtwas are an ethnic group living today in Tanzania. They speak a Swahili* dialect and are included in the Zaramo* cluster of peoples.

NYAI. The term "Nyai" (Banyai, Manyai, Vanyai) is a reference to so many Shona* subgroups in Zimbabwe that it has become practically synonymous with Shona.
REFERENCE: R. Kent Rasmussen. *Historical Dictionary of Zimbabwe.* 1994.

NYAKUSA. *See* NYAKYUSA.

NYAKWAI. The Nyakwai people live in the Central Karamoja District of northeastern Uganda. They are especially concentrated just south of Jie County in the Nyakway Hills. The Nyakwais speak a language that ethnolinguists classify as part of the Lwo group of dialects. For centuries, they have been pastoralists, living a semi-nomadic lifestyle—the men herding their cattle seasonally in search of pasture and the women remaining in permanent villages raising maize and millet. Even though their economy is a mixed one, Nyakwai religion and culture revolve around cattle. Like other pastoral peoples in East Africa in the 1980s and early 1990s, the Nyakwais have suffered because of the persistent droughts there.
REFERENCE: John Lamphear. *The Traditional History of the Jie of Uganda.* 1976.

NYAKYUSA. The Nyakyusa (Niabiussa, Sochile, Sokile) people live on the east side of the Songwe River in Tanzania. They speak the same language as the Ngonde* people, who live on the other side of the river in Malawi. That region has been a commercial and geographic crossroads for centuries in East Africa. Included in the Nyakyusa cluster of peoples are the Kukwes, Mwambas, Ngondes, Selyas, and Sukwas. The oral traditions of the Nyakyusas have them arriving there from points to the east; they then seized control and mixed with the hunter-gatherers already living there. Nyakyusa society was unusual in that

they lived in what are called age-villages. When boys reached the age of ten or eleven, they left the parental home and built a village for themselves. They then lived as bachelors until they began to marry in their late twenties. The Nyakyusa economy revolved around cattle herding. German* missionaries brought Christianity to the Nyakyusas in 1891, but the conversion process took place over a long period of time. In recent years, Nyakyusa life has changed rather dramatically. Increasing numbers of Nyakyusas are switching to farming (raising rice, bananas, coffee, and many other crops) or wage labor as the commercial economy of Tanzania has enveloped them, and their political system focused on a traditional chieftain has been subsumed by the larger political culture and administrative structure. The Nyakyusa population today is more than 450,000 people.
REFERENCE: Monica Wilson. *For Men and Elders: Change in the Relations of Generations of Men and Women among the Nyakyusa-Ngonde People, 1875–1971.* 1977.

NYALA. The Nyalas are a subgroup of the Luhya* people of Kenya and Uganda. They are a Western Bantu* people who today live north of Lake Victoria on both sides of the Kenyan-Ugandan border. They are divided into a northern group, known as the Kakelelwa, and a southern group, known as the Lake Nyala.

NYAMA. The Nyamas are a subgroup of the Nubian* people of the Sudan.

NYAMBO. The Nyambo people are part of the larger cluster of Interlacustrine Bantu* peoples of northwestern Tanzania. Many ethnologists include them today as part of the Haya* cluster of peoples.

NYAMNYAM. The Nyamnyams, also identified historically as the Niamniams, Nimbaris, and Baris, are one of Nigeria's hundreds of ethnic groups. They speak an Adamawa language and live in the Gashaka District of the Mambilla Division of Gongola State. Nyamnyams can also be found in western Cameroon.
REFERENCE: *Language Survey of Nigeria.* 1976.

NYAMPISI. The Nyampisis are a major subgroup of the Shona* people of Mozambique.

NYAMWANGA. The Nyamwangas are an ethnic group in contemporary Tanzania. Their population is approximately 75,000 people; most of them are subsistence farmers. They speak a Bantu* language.
REFERENCE: Edgar C. Polomé and C. P. Hill. *Language in Tanzania.* 1980.

NYAMWESE. *See* NYAMWEZI.

NYAMWESI. *See* NYANWEZI.

NYAMWEZI. The Nyamwezi (Banyamwezi), or ''People of the Moon,'' are a
Tanzanian group located primarily in the Kaliama, Urambo, Tubora, Igunga,
and Nzega districts, south of Lake Victoria. They can also be found in Zaire.
Many ethnologists often include the Galas, Galaganzas, Irwanas, and Nankwilis
in the Nyamwezi group of peoples. They migrated to the region sometime before
the fourteenth century. Their population exceeds five million people. The Nyamwezi speak a language they call Kinyamwezi, which is part of the larger
Bantu* group of languages. Their homeland is approximately 4,000 feet above
sea level and is characterized by undulating steppes on which they raise maize,
rice, sweet potatoes, bananas, and cattle. Tobacco cultivation has become increasingly important in recent years. Except for a few sheep and goats, however,
they do little livestock raising. They are also known for their abilities as merchants and traders. They are traditionally subdivided into three subgroups: the
Nyamwezi proper, whose population is approaching one million people, of
whom perhaps half are Muslims; the Sukumas,* who total in excess of three
million people and occupy the rolling plains and steppe country bordering Lake
Victoria; and the Sumbwas,* whose population is approximately 300,000 people. Perhaps 5 percent of the Sumbwas and Sukumas are Muslims. The Nyamwezi living in the villages around Tabora are primarily Muslims, and there
are some Christian missions in the region, but most Nyamwezi are still loyal to
a tribal faith that emphasizes ancestor worship and animism. The key figure in
Nyamwezi religion is a diviner known as *mfumu.* Historically, the Nyamwezi
have been the most expansionist people in Tanzania, primarily because of their
involvement in the slave and ivory trades in the nineteenth century. Most of
them today are located in Kwa Mtoro and near the highway to Maxorongo.

During the nineteenth century, between one and two million Nyamwezi men
worked between the coast and the interior as porters. Slave traders first brought
Islam to the Nyamwezi in the 1840s. Of those Nyamwezi who are Muslims,
most are Sunnis of the Shafi school, although there are some Shiites as well.
Most Nyamwezi Muslims are considered to be somewhat lackadaisical in their
devotions. Traditionally, the Nyamwezi lived in isolated clusters of homesteads
composed of several nuclear families. In the 1970s, however, to improve public
education and health, as well as to rationalize government administration, Tanzania established its *ujamaa* policy to force Tanzanian families to relocate from
those isolated homesteads to larger settlements. There has been considerable
resistance to the policy. In recent years, the Nyamwezi have also suffered from
soil erosion and drought in Tanzania.

REFERENCES: R. G. Abrahams. *The Nyamwezi Today: A Tanzanian People in the
1970s.* 1981; James L. Brain. ''Nyamwezi.'' In Richard V. Weekes, ed. *Muslim Peoples.*
1984; Hans Cory. *Sukuma Law and Custom.* 1970.

NYANDANG. *See* YANDANG.

NYANEKA-HUMBE. The Nyaneka-Humbes (Haneca-Nkumbi) are a cluster of approximately 425,000 people living today in far southwestern Angola. They speak a Bantu* language. Included in the Nyaneka cluster are the Mwilas, Gambos, Handas, Kipungus, Kilengis, Donguenas, Hingas, and Kwankuas. Most of them are small farmers and cattle raisers.
REFERENCE: Thomas Collelo et al. *Angola: A Country Study.* 1989.

NYANGA. The Nyangas are a subgroup of the Kivu* peoples of Zaire. They live in the highlands of east-central Zaire, near the Rwandan and Ugandan borders, where they farm and raise cattle for milk and meat. Their current population is approximately 35,000 people. Their homeland is a mountainous rain forest. They speak a Bantu* language. The Nyanga economy revolves around hunting, trapping, and food gathering, as well as banana growing.
REFERENCES: Daniel P. Biebuyck. "Nyanga Circumcision Masks and Costumes." *African Arts* 6 (Winter 1973): 20–25; Irving Kaplan et al. *Zaire: A Country Study.* 1978.

NYANGA. *See* NYANGBO.

NYANGBARA. The Nyangbaras are an ethnic group in East Africa who speak a Central Nilotic* language. They live in southern Sudan near the Uganda border. The Nyangbaras pursue a pastoral lifestyle, with the women and children living in permanent villages and the men leaving home seasonally to take the cattle to pasture. The cattle provide the Nyangbaras with milk, blood, and hides. Nyangbara women work agricultural plots and raise millet, maize, cow peas, and some tobacco. Because of the droughts that have hit the region in the 1980s and early 1990s, the Nyangbaras have faced what can be called at best a very marginal living. Their traditional religion and culture revolve around cattle.
REFERENCES: John Lamphear. *The Traditional History of the Jie of Uganda.* 1976; Donald G. Morrison et al. *Black Africa: A Comparative Handbook.* 1989.

NYANGBO. The Nyangbos (Nyanga, Nyango, Yagbum) are a small Volta-Togo group of peoples who live in the Volta Region of Ghana; there they support themselves as small farmers and livestock raisers. The Nyangbo population today is approximately 5,000 people. They are classified as a Central Togo people.
REFERENCE: Irving Kaplan et al. *Area Handbook for Ghana.* 1971.

NYANGO. *See* NYANBGO.

NYANGO. *See* IRIGWE.

NYANG'ORI. *See* TERIK.

NYANJA. The Nyanjas (Wanyanja, Anyanja, Niassa, Nianja) are a subgroup of the Chewa* people of southern Malawi, eastern Zambia, Zimbabwe, and central Mozambique. They are descended from the sixteenth-century Maravi* people. In the fifteenth century, the Nyanjas were virtually the same as the Chewas. They lived in Shaba Province in Zaire. They then began migrating to the east, and, in the eighteenth century, the Nyanjas split away from the Chewas. They speak a dialect of Chichewa, the Chewa language. The word ''Nyanja'' literally, and appropriately, means the people of the lake, since the Nyanjas are concentrated along the shores of Lake Malawi and Lake Chilwa, as well as in the Blantyre and Zomba districts. The Nyanja population today exceeds 500,000 people, most of whom are sedentary farmers who raise maize, beans, and rice. They are predominately Roman Catholics. In Zambia, they are closely associated with the government bureaucracies in Lusaka.

NYANKOLE. *See* NYANKORE.

NYANKORE. The Nyankores (Runyankore, Nyankole, Nkole) are a Bantu*-speaking people of Uganda. Like the neighboring Nyoro* and Toro* groups, their own traditions describe alien gods who, centuries ago, brought centralized government, a kingdom, and cattle to them. Ankole is the traditional homeland of the Nyankores. Today it is a district in southwestern Uganda, bordered by the Kangera River to the south, Lake Edward and Lake George to the west, the former Toro kingdom to the north, and the Buganda plateau to the east. The Nyankore population exceeds one million people, divided into two primary subgroups, each of which is further divided by elaborate, exogamous clans. More than 90 percent of the Nyankores are Irus* who live in the west. The Iru are primarily subsistence farmers, raising plantains and millet. They also produce coffee, cotton, and tea for cash. The smaller, more dominant group—the Himas*—are pastoralists who produce cattle, hides, and skins; they subsist on milk. Traditionally, the Himas were an aristocratic elite while the Iru were a subservient peasantry.

In 1901, the Nyankore kingdom of Ankole signed a political agreement with the British,* making the kingdom an autonomous territory within British East Africa. Although the British tried to eliminate the inequalities between the Himas and the Irus, much of the disparity continued. The Himas tended to convert to Protestantism and maintain their positions of political authority, while the Irus became Roman Catholics or remained loyal to the ancestral religion, which revolved around the cult of Bagyendnawa and the royal drum (still enshrined today at the Royal Enclosure in Mbarara). Approximately 2 percent of Nyankores are Muslims.

Uganda became independent from the British in 1962. In 1967, as part of its attempt to integrate the nation politically, the Ugandan government abolished the ancient kingdoms, including Ankole, incorporating it as a political district in the larger polity. During the reign of President Idi Amin, from 1971 to 1979,

Nyankore Christians were perceived as enemies of the state and were persecuted. They also organized the military force that joined with the Tanzanian army in overthrowing the Amin regime. Today, large numbers of the Nyankores still live in grass houses constructed within the cattle *kraals*. Within the last twenty years, however, substantial numbers of Nyankores have moved to towns and cities in search of work, business opportunities, and education.

REFERENCES: H. F. Morris. *A History of Ankole.* 1962; Ayre Oded. ''Nyankole.'' In Richard V. Weekes, ed. *Muslim Peoples.* 1984.

NYASA. The Nyasas are an ethnic group living today in Tanzania. They are concentrated in the far southwestern corner of the country, on the shores of Lake Malawi and across the border in Mozambique. Most Nyasas make their living farming and fishing. Included in the Nyasa group of peoples are the Matengos, Kingas,* Pangas,* and Wanjis. The entire Nyasa population today exceeds 500,000 people.

REFERENCE: Laura Kurtz. *Historical Dictionary of Tanzania.* 1978.

NYATANZA. The Nyatanzas are a major subgroup of the Shona* peoples of Mozambique.

NYATSO. *See* KPAN.

NYATURU. The Nyaturus are a Bantu*-speaking people who live today in Tanzania. Most of the more than 350,000 Nyaturus are subsistence farmers.

REFERENCE: Edgar C. Polomé and C. P. Hill. *Language in Tanzania.* 1980.

NYEMBE. The Nyembes are a subgroup of the larger Ngangela* cluster of peoples living today in Angola.

NYENGO. The Nyengos are part of the larger cluster of Luyana* peoples of Zambia. The Luyanas are part of the Lozi* group. The Nyengos can also be found across the border in eastern Angola. The Nyengo population in Zambia today exceeds 15,000 people.

NYEYU. The Nyeyus are an Eastern Nilotic* people who live today in southern Sudan near the Uganda border. They pursue a pastoral lifestyle, raising cattle for milk, blood, and hides. Nyeyu women produce millet, maize, cow peas, and some tobacco. Recent droughts in the region have devastated the Nyeyu economy.

REFERENCES: John Lamphear. *The Traditional History of the Jie of Uganda.* 1976; Donald G. Morrison et al. *Black Africa: A Comparative Handbook.* 1989.

NYIDU. *See* ICEN.

NYIHA. The Nyihas are an ethnic group who consider themselves native to the Mbozi District of the Mbeya Region of Tanzania. Their current population exceeds 125,000 people, most of whom are farmers and cattle raisers. Some Nyihas can also be found in Zambia.
REFERENCE: Laura Kurtz. *Historical Dictionary of Tanzania.* 1978.

NYIKA. The Nyikas are a group of peoples who live along the coasts of Tanzania and Kenya in East Africa. Included in the Nyika cluster, along with a variety of smaller groups, are the Giriyamas,* Digos,* Durumas,* and Rabais. The total Nyika population today is approximately 550,000 people. Although a few Nyikas still live in their traditional fortified, hilltop settlements, most are now in farming villages, where they raise sheep, goats, maize, and millet. Many Nyikas also work on sugar cane, sisal, and cotton plantations.
REFERENCE: *African Encyclopedia.* 1974.

NYIKOBE. *See* YUKUBEN.

NYIKUBEN. *See* YUKUBEN.

NYINDU. The Nyindus are an ethnic group living today in the eastern zone, primarily in what is known as the Mwenga region. The region is heavily forested. The Nyindus make their living fishing and working small cassava and yam farms.
REFERENCES: Daniel Biebuyck. ''Sculpture from the Eastern Zaire Forest Region.'' *African Arts* 9 (January 1976): 8–14; Irving Kaplan et al. *Zaire: A Country Study.* 1978.

NYISAM. *See* PASSAM.

NYOLE. The Nyoles (Lunyoles) are a Bantu*-speaking group who today are considered to be part of the Gisu* cluster of peoples. They are concentrated north of Lake Victoria on both sides of the Ugandan-Kenyan border. They make their living as farmers and fishermen.

NYOMINKA. The Nyominka are primarily fishermen living in the Saalum estuary of Senegal. They are a subgroup of the Serer.*

NYONGNEPA. *See* MUMBAKE.

NYONNIWEIN. The Nyonniweins are a subgroup of the Bassa* people of Liberia. Most Nyonniweins live in Grand Bassa County.

NYONYO. *See* KPAN.

NYONYOSE. *See* NINISI.

NYOOMINKOO. *See* NIUMINKO.

NYORE. The Nyores are a subgroup of the Luhya* people of Kenya and Uganda. They are a Western Bantu* people who live today north of Lake Victoria on both sides of the Kenyan-Ugandan border.

NYORO. The Nyoros (Runyoro, Banyoro) are part of the western Interlacustrine Bantu* cluster of western Uganda. Their own historical traditions describe a group of alien gods who brought centralized government, a kingdom, and cattle to them in ancient times. Historians can identify a Nyoro kingdom in the region about five centuries ago—the Bunyoro-Kitara empire. They lost out to Ganda* expansion in the eighteenth and nineteenth centuries. The traditional Nyoro economy revolved around the hunting of elephants, lions, leopards, and crocodiles, although they have switched to agriculture in recent years, now raising bananas, millet, cassava, sweet potatoes, cotton, tobacco, and coffee. Today, the Nyoro population exceeds 400,000 people, most of whom are Christians or Nyoro animists. Only 2 percent of the Nyoros are Muslims.
REFERENCES: *African Encyclopedia.* 1974; Rita M. Byrnes et al. *Uganda: A Country Study.* 1990.

NYUBI. The Nyubis are a subgroup of the Karanga* people, who are part of the Shona* cluster of peoples in Zimbabwe.

NYULI. The Nyulis are one of the Eastern Lacustrine peoples who live north of Lake Victoria in Uganda. Their population today exceeds 100,000 people. Most Nyulis are small farmers, raising plantains, sweet potatoes, cassava, and millet as staples and cotton and coffee for cash. In the northern reaches of the Busoga District, where the climate is much drier than in the fertile south, they raise cattle. A substantial number of them are Muslims.
REFERENCES: N. Kasozi King and Arye Oded. *Islam and the Confluence of Religions in Uganda, 1840–1966.* 1973; Y. K. Lubogo. *History of Busoga.* 1960.

NYUNGWE. The Nyungwe (Nhungwe, Nyunwe) are a small ethnic group living in Mozambique. They are part of the Lower Zambezi cluster of peoples, which includes the Senas,* Tongas,* Chikundas,* and Chuabos.* Most of them are small subsistence farmers who live along the banks of the lower Zambezi River. During the late eighteenth and nineteenth centuries, they actively participated in the slave trade, capturing and selling other Africans to Portuguese* traders. They first emerged as a distinct ethnic group at that time, when they lived on large Portuguese plantations.
REFERENCES: Mario Azevedo. *Historical Dictionary of Mozambique.* 1991; Harold D. Nelson et al. *Mozambique: A Country Study.* 1984.

NZABI. The Nzabi people, known also as the Bandjabi people, are a large ethnic group in south-central Gabon and northwestern Congo. At the present time, they are scattered across 32,000 square miles of territory in both countries. They were hunters and shifting cultivators until the arrival of Europeans changed trading networks all across West Africa. By the early nineteenth century, the Nzabis were engaged in the rubber, tobacco, groundnuts, red dye, and slave trades. During World War I, the Nzabis violently, but unsuccessfully, resisted the growing presence of French* colonial administration. In the 1930s, Christian missionaries began working successfully among the Nzabis, and today many Nzabis are Christians.

REFERENCES: David E. Gardinier. *Historical Dictionary of Gabon.* 1994; F. A. Shank. "Nzabi Kinship: A Cognitive Approach." Ph.D. dissertation. Indiana University. 1974.

NZAKARA. The Nzakaras are a subgroup of the formerly powerful Sabanga* peoples of the Central African Republic. Their population in the nineteenth century exceeded 10,000 people, and they were prominent on the Ubanguian Plateau; they had their own kingdom. Most Nzakaras today have adopted the Banda* language and are assimilating with them.

REFERENCE: Pierre Kalck. *Historical Dictionary of the Central African Republic.* 1992.

NZANGI. Over the past century, the Nzangis have also been known as the Njanyis, Njais, Njeis, Zanys, Jenges, Jengs, and Pakas. They speak a Chadic language and live today in western Cameroon as well as in the Adamawa and Mubi divisions of Gongola State. The Nzangi population in Nigeria today stands at approximately 60,000 people.

REFERENCE: *Language Survey of Nigeria.* 1976.

NZARE. *See* MBEMBE.

NZEMA. *See* NZIMA.

N'ZIMA. *See* NZIMA.

NZIMA. The Nzima—also known historically as Nzemas, N'zimas, Appolos, Assokos, Amanyas, Appolonians, and Zémas—are a subgroup of the Akans* who are also classified with the Lagoon cluster of peoples in Ivory Coast. Their population numbers in the hundreds of thousands, and most of them live in the sub-prefectures of Grand-Bassam and Adiaké in Ivory Coast and across the border in southern and central Ghana. In Ghana, they are located in the Western Region between the Tano and Aknobra rivers. During the nineteenth century, the Nzima became important traders between interior tribes and British* ships. That came to an end in 1898 when French* merchants got the French colonial administration, in Ivory Coast at least, to tax Nzima merchants heavily and thus put them out of business. Similar discriminatory taxation policies drove Nzima merchants out of the timber business. During the early years of the French empire, a substantial number of Nzimas received French educations, giving rise to a small Nzima professional class in Ivory Coast today. Most Nzima are small farmers. The leading Nzima in African history is Kwame Nkrumah.

REFERENCES: Robert E. Handloff et al. *Côte d'Ivoire: A Country Study.* 1990; Daniel M. McFarland. *Historical Dictionary of Ghana.* 1995; Robert J. Mundt. *Historical Dictionary of Côte d'Ivoire.* 1994; Timothy Wiskel. *French Colonial Rule and the Baule Peoples: Resistance and Collaboration, 1899–1911.* 1980.

O

OBAMBA. The Obamba people, who are also known as the Mbamba people, speak a Mbèdè* language and live in the northern reaches of the Franceville and Okondja prefectures in Haut-Ogooué Province in Gabon. Several centuries ago, they lived up the Sébé River in the Congo, but attacks from the Mbochi* people drove them downriver to the region of Okondja. There they drove out the Kaniguis* and took control of the region themselves. Today most Obambas are small farmers.
REFERENCE: David E. Gardinier. *Historical Dictionary of Gabon.* 1994.

OBANLIKU. The Obanlikus (Abanlikus) are an ethnic group of Cross River State in Nigeria. They live today in the Opobo and Eket divisions and have a current population of approximately 80,000 people.
REFERENCE: *Language Survey of Nigeria.* 1976.

OBE. *See* UTUGWANG.

OBGINYA. *See* OGBIA.

OBOLO. The Obolo people, also known as the Andonis, are a Nigerian ethnic group, part of the Cross River group of Benue-Congo peoples. They are concentrated in the Opobo and Eket divisions of Cross River State and have a contemporary population of approximately 90,000 people.
REFERENCE: *Language Survey of Nigeria.* 1976.

OBORA. The Obora are a subgroup of the Afran Qalla,* themselves a subgroup of the Oromo* of Ethiopia. They are primarily Muslims living around the city of Harar who work as sedentary farmers.

OBULOM. The Obuloms are a small ethnic group living today in the Okrika Division of Rivers State in Nigeria.
REFERENCE: *Language Survey of Nigeria.* 1976.

ODERIGA. *See* MBEMBE.

ODJUKRU. *See* ADJUKRU.

ODODOP. *See* KOROP.

ODOT. The Odots are a subgroup of the Ibibio* peoples of Nigeria.

ODUAL. The Oduals, also known as the Sakas,* are one of the Cross River peoples of Nigeria. They are concentrated in the Abua/Odual Division of Rivers State. The Odual population today is approximately 35,000 people.
REFERENCE: *Language Survey of Nigeria.* 1976.

ODUT. The Oduts are a small ethnic group of perhaps 3,000 people who live today in the Calabar Division of Cross River State in Nigeria.
REFERENCE: *Language Survey of Nigeria.* 1976.

OFFOT. The Offots are a subgroup of the Ibibio* peoples of Nigeria.

OFUNABWAN. *See* MBEMBE.

OFUTOP. *See* EFUTOP.

OGADEN. The Ogaden people are part of the Eastern Hamatic cluster of peoples who live today in far northwestern Kenya, southern Ethiopia, and Somalia. They speak a Somali* language and have a current population of approximately 60,000 people. The Ogadens are a pastoral people who also cultivate small plots of land.
REFERENCE: Donald G. Morrison et al. *Black Africa: A Comparative Handbook.* 1989.

OGBIA. The Ogbias, known also as the Obginyas, are one of the Cross River peoples of Nigeria and can be found living in the Ogbia and Brass divisions of Cross River State.
REFERENCE: *Language Survey of Nigeria.* 1976.

OGBOGOLO. The Ogbogolo people live in the Abua/Odual Division of Rivers State in Nigeria.
REFERENCE: *Language Survey of Nigeria.* 1976.

OGBOIN. The Ogboins are a subgroup of the Izon* peoples of Rivers State in Nigeria.

OGBRONUAGUM. The Ogbronuagums are also known as the Bukumas. They are a Nigerian people who live in the Kalabari Division of Rivers State.
REFERENCE: *Language Survey of Nigeria.* 1976.

OGOKO. The Ogoko language is a dialect of Madi,* a Sudanic language spoken in Uganda.

OGONI. *See* KANA.

OGORI-MAGONGO. The Ogori-Magongos are a linguistically isolated ethnic group living today in the Ogori-Magongo District of the Igbirra Division of Kwara State in Nigeria.
REFERENCE: *Language Survey of Nigeria.* 1976.

OHORI. The Ohoris are one of the main subgroups of the Yoruba* people of Nigeria. Most Ohoris can be found today living east of the Weme River in Benin and along the Benin-Nigerian border in western Ogun State in Nigeria.

OIYAKIRI. The Oiyakiris are a subgroup of the Izon* peoples of Rivers State in Nigeria.

OJOR. *See* LUBILA.

OKAK. The Okaks are a subgroup of the Fang* peoples of Cameroon, Equatorial Guinea, and Gabon. They speak a Bantu* language. Ethnologists believe they arrived in their present location after a migration from the savannas in northeastern Africa in the seventeenth and eighteenth centuries. They are farmers living in forested regions and raising cocoa, peanuts, and groundnuts for export and cassava, yams, and other food products for consumption. Large numbers of Okak men also work in the timber industry.

OKAM. *See* MBEMBE.

OKANDÉ. The Okandé cluster of peoples in Gabon includes the Okandé proper as well as the Apindjis,* Mitsogos,* Poves,* Bassimbas,* and Baveyas.* They were well-known regionally for their skills as canoeman.
REFERENCES: David E. Gardinier. *Historical Dictionary of Gabon.* 1994; Donald G. Morrison et al. *Black Africa: A Comparative Handbook.* 1989.

OKANDÉ. The Okandé people today live near Booué in central Gabon. Their traditional homeland was on both sides of the Middle Ogooué River, east of its junction with the Okano River and west of Booué. When Europeans began to penetrate the Gabonese interior, the Okandés cooperated with them, providing skilled boatmen for exploring parties. Their own flat-bottomed canoes were particularly well-suited for navigating the shallows of the Middle Ogooué. Although the Okandés did not keep slaves of their own, they regularly purchased slaves from a number of tribes and sold them to the Galoa.* Because of their canoeing mobility, they became middlemen in the commercial traffic on the Ogooué River in the late nineteenth and early twentieth centuries. Most Okandés today make their living as small farmers and traders.
REFERENCE: David E. Gardinier. *Historical Dictionary of Gabon.* 1994.

OKEBU. The Okebus are an ethnic group living in southern Sudan, northwestern Uganda, and northeastern Zaire. Their most immediate neighbors are the Lugbaras,* Alurs,* and Kakwas.* The Okebus speak a language that is part of the Central Sudanic cluster of languages. Many Okebus also live in the city of Arua on the Uganda-Zaire border. They are of Nilotic* origin. Their economy revolves around agriculture because of the excellent soil in the region. The Okebus are also known for their skills in animal husbandry.
REFERENCES: F. Scott Bobb. *Historical Dictionary of Zaire.* 1988; Irving Kaplan et al. *Zaire: A Country Study.* 1978.

OKIEK. The Okieks are Kalenjin*-speakers who live in the Rift Valley Province of Kenya. Traditionally, the Masais* have looked down upon the Okieks, because the Okieks did not own cattle and preferred a life of hunting and gathering. Today, many Okieks do own cattle, but most are small farmers and laborers.

OKII. *See* BOKYI.

OKOBA. The Okobas (Okogbas) are one of the many subgroups of the Igbo* people, an ethnic group of nearly fifteen million people living today in southern and southeastern Nigeria.

OKODIA. The Okodias are a subgroup of the Ijaw* peoples of Rivers State in Nigeria. *See* IJAW.

OKOGBA. *See* OKOBA.

OKOLLO. The Okollo language is a dialect of Madi,* a Sudanic language spoken in Uganda. *See* MADI.

OKONYONG. *See* KIONG.

OKORDIA. *See* OKODIA.

OKOYONG. *See* KIONG.

OKPAMHEVI. The Okpamhevis (Opameris) are a Nigerian people whose homeland is in the Akoko-Edo Division of Bendel State. Many ethnologists classify them as an Edo* subgroup.

OKPE. The Okpes (Okpe-Idesa-Oloma-Akuku) are a subgroup of the Edo* peoples of Nigeria.

OKRIKA. The Okrikas are one of the many ethnic groups living in Rivers State, Nigeria. They are concentrated particularly in the Okrika-Tai-Eleme Local Government Area. Ethnolinguists classify them as part of the larger cluster of Ijaw* peoples. The Okrikas are primarily subsistence farmers.
REFERENCE: E. J. Alagoa and Tekena N. Tamuno. *Land and People of Nigeria: Rivers State.* 1989.

OKU. The Okus are a subgroup of the Ibibio* peoples of Nigeria.

OLI. *See* WOURI.

OLODIAMA. The Olodiamas are a subgroup of the Izon* peoples of Rivers State in Nigeria.

OLULUMO-IKOM. The Olulumo-Ikoms are one of the Cross River peoples of Nigeria. They have a contemporary population of approximately 40,000 people, most of whom live in the Ikom Division of Cross River State.
REFERENCE: *Language Survey of Nigeria.* 1976.

OMAND. The Omand are one of the cluster of Middle-Cameroon Bantu* peoples who live in central Cameroon. Most of them make their living as small farmers and fishermen, although increasing numbers of Omand men have recently found work on commercial farms and in the oil fields. The growing emphasis on commercial crops for export—coffee, cocoa, timber, palm oil, and bananas—has actually tended to impoverish most Omand farmers and has contributed to a decline in their standard of living.
REFERENCE: Mark DeLancey and H. M. Mokeba. *Historical Dictionary of the Republic of Cameroon.* 1990.

OMBÉKÉ. *See* ORUNGU.

OMETO. The Ometo are one of the subgroups of the Sadama* people of southwestern Ethiopia. They are concentrated in the Omo River Valley, where they raise tea, barley, maize, coffee, and cotton.

OMOTIC. The Omotic peoples are a cluster of more than eighty groups of people living between the lakes of the Great Rift Valley and the Omo River in southern Ethiopia. The Omotic population today exceeds 1.5 million people, most of whom are hoe cultivators, raising ensete at higher altitudes and other grains in the lowlands. They are also known for their animal husbandry and their skill as artisans.
REFERENCE: Harold D. Nelson et al. *Ethiopia: A Country Study.* 1980.

OMYÈNÈ. *See* MYÈNÈ.

ONATSHI. The Onatshis are a subgroup of the Igbo* people of Nigeria.

ONDO. The Ondos are one of the main subgroups of the Yoruba* people of Nigeria. Most Ondos today can be found living in the Ondo State of western Nigeria.

ONIONG. The Oniongs are a subgroup of the Ibibio* peoples of Nigeria.

ONITSHA. The Onitshas are one of the many subgroups of the Igbo* people, an ethnic group of nearly fifteen million people living today in southern and southeastern Nigeria.

OOHUM. *See* YUKUBEN.

OOLI. The Oolis are a Bantu*-speaking people who live in the forests of the Kasai Orientale region of central Zaire. They can also be found on the north side of the Kasai River in southwestern Zaire. Most of them are small farmers who raise cassava, bananas, and kola nuts. In recent years, the Oolis have been increasingly affected by Zaire's commercial economy, with the result that more and more Oolis are growing cash crops or leaving the farms for work in towns and cities.
REFERENCE: Irving Kaplan et al. *Zaire: A Country Study.* 1978.

OPAMERI. *See* OKPAMHEVI.

OPOROMA. The Oporomas are a subgroup of the Izon* peoples of Rivers State in Nigeria.

OQUIE. *See* AKWAMU.

ORA. The Oras are a subgroup of the Edo* peoples of south-central Nigeria.

ORATTA. The Orattas are one of the many subgroups of the Igbo* people, an ethnic group of nearly fifteen million people living today in southern and south-eastern Nigeria.

ORING. The Orings—also known as Orris and Korings—are one of the Cross River peoples of Nigeria. They live today in the Ishielu Division of Anambra State and the Utonkon District of the Oturkpo Division of Benue State. They can also be found across the border in western Cameroon. The Oring language is of Bantu* origin. Most of the Orings are farmers, raising yams and palm oil. Large numbers of them also work in Nigerian cities. The Oring population today exceeds 400,000 people.
REFERENCES: *Language Survey of Nigeria.* 1976; Donald G. Morrison et al. *Black Africa: A Comparative Handbook.* 1989.

ORMA. The Ormas are one of the major subgroups of the Oromo* people of Ethiopia. They are among the southern cluster of the Oromos. Most of the Ormas are egalitarian pastoralists who live near the Tana River in southeastern Kenya.

ORO. *See* ORON.

OROMA. *See* OROMO.

OROMO. The Oromos, who have also been known as the Galla, are a large ethnic cluster of peoples living from northeastern Ethiopia to east-central Kenya, as well as between the borders of Sudan and Somalia. Their language is part of the Eastern Cushitic branch of the Afro-Asiatic linguistic family. They practice a form of patrilineal descent, and, although they are divided into dozens of subgroups, the differences in dialect do not prevent the various Oromo groups from understanding one another. In recent years, because of economic and political integration in Ethiopia, the different Oromo subgroups are acquiring an increasing sense of common identity. The Oromo population today exceeds thirteen million people, and they constitute the majority group in the populations of Wellega, Ilubabor, Kafa, Shoa, Arusi, Harar, Bale, Sidamo, and Wollo provinces in Ethiopia. They are also a prominent ethnic group in north-central and northeastern Kenya. Most Oromos are settled farmers or pastoralists.

Ethnologists trace Oromo origins to southern Ethiopia. Beginning in the sixteenth century, the Oromos began an ambitious expansion that took them into northern Ethiopia. At the time, they were egalitarian pastoralists. More than half of the Oromos are Sunni Muslims, primarily of the Shafi school, although some are also followers of the Hanafi law. Sufi brotherhoods play a prominent role in Oromo Muslim life. The process of converting to Islam began in the nineteenth century and continues today. The traditional indigenous Oromo religion, which revolves around a belief in a single creator and an environment animated by spirit beings, still exists. Christianity has also made inroads among the Oromos.

The Oromos are divided into subgroups based on a variety of geographic and social factors, of which regional identity is among the most important. To the north, the major Oromo subgroups are the Wollo (Wello), Yejju, and Raya (Azebo), who live in Wollo Province and southern Tigre Province. They are overwhelmingly Muslims. In Shoa Province, the primary Oromo subgroups are the Tulama and the Mech'a; there are also Mech'a* in northern Kafa Province. Most of the Mech'a are Muslims. In Wellaga and Ilubabor provinces, the Wellega constitute the primary Oromo subgroup. All of these northern Oromo subgroups are settled farmers. The southernmost Oromo subgroups are more likely to be pastoralists. They include the Boran* (also known as Borana or Borena), the Gabra (Garre) living east of Lake Turkana, and the Orma, who live near the Tana River in southeastern Kenya. The Guji,* who are primarily pastoralists, live east of Lake Abaya in southern Ethiopia. The Arssi* (Arusi) live north of the Guji in Bale Province. They too are pastoralists. Most of the Oromos in Bale Province are Muslims. The Oromo groups around Harar are Muslims and sedentary farmers. They include the Ittu, Anniya, and Afran Qalla,* themselves composed of the Obora, Nole, Babile, and Alla.

REFERENCES: J. T. Hultin. "Social Structure, Ideology and Expansion: The Case of the Oromo in Ethiopia." *Ethos* 40 (1975): 273–84; G.W.B. Huntingford. *The Galla of Ethiopia.* 1955; Asmaron Legesse. *Gada: Three Approaches to the Study of an African Society.* 1973.

ORON. The Oron (Oro) are an ethnic group living in the Oron Division of Cross River State in Nigeria. They speak a language closely related to that of the neighboring Efik* and Ibibio* peoples. Their population today exceeds 200,000 people.
REFERENCE: *Language Survey of Nigeria.* 1976.

ORRI. *See* ORING.

ORU. The Orus are one of the many subgroups of the Igbo* people, an ethnic group of nearly fifteen million people living today in southern and southeastern Nigeria.

ORUMA. The Orumas are a subgroup of the Ijaw* peoples of Rivers State in Nigeria.

ORUNGOU. *See* ORUNGU.

ORUNGU. The Orungus (Orungou) are a Myènè*-speaking people who live today near Nazareth Bay on the Atlantic coast of Ogooué-Maritime Province in Gabon. They have also been known historically as the Ombéké. The Orungus are closely related to the Eshiras,* probably as a splinter group who moved down the Ogooué River to the coast in the seventeenth century. There the Orungus settled among Mpongwe* clans and adopted the Mpongwe language as well as many Mpongwe technical skills. By 1700, the Orungus were in complete control of the mouth of the Nazareth River and in full contact with Europeans. For the first half of the eighteenth century, they traded ivory, beeswax, honey, gum copal, ebony, and dyewood to British* and Portuguese* merchants, and, by the late eighteenth century, they were heavily engaged in the slave trade. Wealth from the slave trade provided the Orungus with a great deal of political and economic power. In 1862, following British attempts to wipe out the slave trade, the Orungus signed treaties recognizing French* sovereignty. As the slave trade declined in the 1870s and 1880s, so did Orungu power. Because of missionary opposition to the slave trade, the Orungus avoided contact with missionary schools, and, unlike the neighboring Mpongwes, they did not secure the education necessary to be influential in the French colonial system. Today the Orungus are a tiny minority in their homeland.
REFERENCE: David E. Gardinier. *Historical Dictionary of Gabon.* 1994.

OSOSO. Many ethnologists consider the Ososo people of the Akoko-Edo Division of Bendel State in Nigeria to be a subgroup of the Edo.*

OSUDOKU. The Osudokus are one of the subgroups of the Adangbe* peoples of the Accra Plain and coastal inselbergs of southeastern Ghana. Most of them make their living as small farmers.

OTANK. The Otank people, known at times as the Utangas, are one of the Cross River peoples of Nigeria. They are concentrated today in the Mbaikyor District of the Katsina Ala Division of Benue State and in the Obudu Division of Cross River State. Most of the more than 20,000 Otanks are small farmers.
REFERENCE: *Language Survey of Nigeria.* 1976.

OTMAN. The Otmans are a subgroup of the Amarar,* themselves a subdivision of the Beja* peoples of the Sudan. They speak a Northern Cushitic language. The Otman population today exceeds 100,000 people, most of whom live in a 25,000-square-mile region along the Red Sea, extending from Port Sudan in the south to Mohammed Ghol in the north and reaching westward to an ethnic frontier with the Bisharin,* approximately halfway to the Nile. The Otmans are Muslims, although the pastoral Amarar are somewhat perfunctory in their religious devotions. Their indigenous, animistic traditions still have a powerful hold on the people. Rural Otmans are characterized by their large crowns of curly hair, complete with long ringlets hanging down from the head. While sedentary Otmans live in permanent, mud-walled homes, the semi-nomadic pastoral herders live in portable, rectangular goat-skin houses. Their herds consist largely of camels and sheep. In recent years, Otmans have become increasingly integrated into a cash economy, primarily because of the need to pay government taxes. Severe droughts have damaged their herds of sheep, cattle, and camels, forcing growing numbers of Otmans to settle down into permanent farming communities where government-financed irrigation systems allow them to raise cotton and other crops commercially.

REFERENCES: Andrew Paul. *A History of the Beja Tribes of the Sudan.* 1954; S. A. el-Arifi. "Pastoral Nomadism in the Sudan." *East African Geographical Review* 13 (1975): 89–103; Roushdi A. Henin. "Economic Development and Internal Migration in the Sudan." *Sudan Notes and Records* 44 (1963): 100–119.

OUAGADOUGOU. The Ouagadougous are part of the larger Mossi* cluster of ethnic groups in West Africa. They are concentrated in the center of Burkina-Faso, near the city of Ouagadougou in Centre District. Those Ouagadougous living in the city are primarily wage laborers, while those still living in rural areas are farmers, raising peanuts, millet, sorghum, and cotton. Today, the Ouagadougou population exceeds one million people.

REFERENCE: Daniel M. McFarland. *Historical Dictionary of Upper Volta.* 1978.

OUAN. *See* WAN.

OUARA. *See* WARA WARA.

OUASSOULOUNKE. *See* WASULUNKA.

OUATCHI. The Ouatchi are an ethnic group whom African anthropologists classify as part of the Ewe* cluster of peoples in Togo and Benin. Their current population is approximately 250,000 people, most of whom live near Anécho and Tabligbo in southern Togo. They arrived in the region during the early nineteenth century, escaping from drought in what is today Benin. Among the Mina* and other Ewe peoples, the Ouatchi are considered backward and parochial, and the term "Ouatchi" is often said with contempt and derision. The Ouatchi language is closely related to Anlo*-Evegbé.* It is also spoken in Atakpamé and in the Grand-Popo-Athieme areas of Benin. Most of the Ouatchi are subsistence farmers who raise maize, millet, manioc, and plantains.

REFERENCE: Samuel Decalo. *Historical Dictionary of Togo.* 1976.

OUBI. *See* UBI.

OULAD ALI. The Oulad Alis are a subgroup of the Oulad Tidrarins.* They live a nomadic lifestyle in Western Sahara and southern Morocco.

OULAD ALI SERG. The Oulad Ali Sergs are a subgroup of the Menasirs* of Western Sahara.

OULAD BA AMAR. The Oulad Ba Amars are a subgroup of the Oulad Delims* of Western Sahara. The Oulad Ba Amars are subdivided into four groups, each with a strong sense of identity: the Mesidas (who are the dominant group), the Ahel Faqir Breika, the El-Amamria, and the Souaaid.

OULAD BORHIM. The Oulad Borhims are a subgroup of the Reguibat* es-Sahel people of Western Sahara. Their population today is approximately 1,000 people, most of whom are settled in El-Ayoun.

OULAD BOU SBAA. The Oulad Bou Sbaas, also known as "Sons of the Father of the Lions," first appeared as a self-conscious group in Western Sahara in the sixteenth century. They were a nomadic people, herding camels and goats over a broad area. They established commercial relations with the Spanish* in the 1880s, and, between 1884 and 1886, they signed treaties with several Spanish explorers. They are divided into three subgroups: the Oulad el-Hadj Ben Demouiss, the Oulad Sidi Mohammed Ben Demouiss, and the Oulad Brahim. Today, they are a widely dispersed people living in southern Morocco, Western Sahara, Mauritania, and Senegal. The largest cluster of them is in El-Ayoun in Western Sahara.
REFERENCE: Tony Hodges. *Historical Dictionary of Western Sahara.* 1982.

OULAD BRAHIM. The Oulad Brahims are a subgroup of the Oulad Bou Sbaa* of Western Sahara. The major subdivisions of the Oulad Brahims are the Oulad Assouss, Oulad Baggar, Embouat, and Oulad Hameida.

OULAD CHEIKH. The Oulad Cheikhs are a subgroup of the Reguibat* es-Sahel of Western Sahara in what is today Morocco. Several subgroups constitute the Oulad Cheikhs, including the Ahel Delimi, Ahel Baba Ali, Lemouissat, Lahouareth, Lahseinat, and Ahel el-Hadj. Today, there are approximately 4,000 Oulad Cheikhs. Most of them pursue sedentary lifestyles in the towns of El-Ayoun, Dakhla, Smara, and Bir Enzaren, although Oulad Cheikh nomads can still be found east of Bir Enzaren and Aoussert.
REFERENCE: Tony Hodges. *Historical Dictionary of Western Sahara.* 1982.

OULAD DAOUD. The Oulad Daouds are a subgroup of the Reguibat* es-Sahel of Western Sahara in what is today Morocco. They are divided into the Ahel Salem, Ahel Tenakha, and Ahel Baba Ammi factions.

OULAD DELIM. Of all the people of Western Sahara, the Oulad Delims are known as the people of the purest Arab* descent, with the least African genetic heritage. They were a self-conscious ethnic group by the sixteenth century and a formidable military and political force by the eighteenth century. By the late nineteenth century, the Oulad Delims tended to side with the Spanish* rather than the French,* whom they viewed as a greater threat to their own sovereignty. After Spanish domination of Western Sahara was complete, the Oulad Delims played a conspicuous role in the Spanish colonial army. Today, the Oulad Delim population exceeds 6,000 people, most of whom live in Dakhla. They are divided into five subgroups: the Oulad Tegueddi,* the Loudeikat, the Oulad Khaliga,* the Serahenna, and the Oulad Ba Amar.*

REFERENCE: Tony Hodges. *Historical Dictionary of Western Sahara.* 1982.

OULAD EL-HADJ BEN DEMOUISS. The Oulad El-Hadj Ben Demouiss are a subgroup of the Oulad Bou Sbaa* of Western Sahara.

OULAD KHALIFA. The Oulad Khalifas are a subgroup of the Arosien* people of Western Sahara in what is today Morocco.

OULAD KHALIGA. The Oulad Khaligas are a subgroup of the Oulad Delims.* The Oulad Khaligas are subdivided into the Ahel Amar Barkas, Ahel Mohammed Ben Sieds, Chehagfas, and Laouaids.

OULAD KHELAIF. The Oulad Khelaifs are a subgroup of the Taoubalt* people of Western Sahara.

OULAD MANSOUR. The Oulad Mansours are a subgroup of the Hassaunas,* a large group of ethnic Arabs* living today in Chad.

OULAD MEHAREB. The Oulad Meharebs are a subgroup of the Hassaunas,* a large group of ethnic Arabs* living today in Chad.

OULAD MOHAMMED AIDI. The Oulad Mohammed Aidis are a subgroup of the Menasirs,* a small fishing tribe in Western Sahara.

OULAD MOUMEN. The Oulad Moumens are a small ethnic group that historically has been subject to the Ait Lahsens.*

OULAD MOUSSA. The Oulad Moussas, with a contemporary population of perhaps 9,000 people, are one of the major subgroups of the Reguibat* people of Western Sahara in what is today Morocco. Most of them live in such cities as El-Ayoun and Smara, but Oulad Moussa nomads still herd livestock in the Guelta Zemmour region. The major Oulad Moussa subgroups include the Oulad El-Qadi, Ahel Bellao, Oulad Moueya, Oulad Lahsen, and Oulad Hossein.

OULAD SIDI BOU MEHDI. The Oulad Sidi Bou Mehdis are a subgroup of the Arosien* people of Western Sahara in what is today Morocco.

OULAD SIDI MOHAMMED BEN DEMOUISS. The Oulad Sidi Mohammed Ben Demouiss, who are also known as the Demouissat, are one of the subgroups of the Oulad Bou Sbaa* people of Western Sahara. They are further subdivided into the Ahel Cheikh Mokhtars and the Ahel Khanouehs.

OULAD SOULEIMAN. The Oulad Souleimans are a subgroup of the Oulad Tidrarins* of Western Sahara.

OULAD TALEB. The Oulad Talebs are a subgroup of the Reguibat* of Western Sahara in what is today Morocco. Most of them have abandoned a nomadic lifestyle and live in El-Ayoun. Their primary subgroups include the Oulad Ben Hossein, Oulad Ba Brahim, Oulad Ba Aaissa, Oulad Ba Moussa, and Ahel Dera.

OULAD TEGUEDDI. The Oulad Tegueddis are a subgroup of the Oulad Delims* of Western Sahara. Most of the more than 1,800 Oulad Tegueddis have abandoned a nomadic lifestyle for residency in Dakhla. They are divided into the following subgroups: Oulad Brahim, Ahel Atzman, Ahel Esbweir, and Ahel Ali Oulad Soueied.

OULAD TIDRARIN. The Oulad Tidrarins are one of the main ethnic groups of Western Sahara, although they can also be found living in southern Morocco and Mauritania. They are widely known in the region for their commitment to learning and education. In the eighteenth and nineteenth centuries, they came under the domination of the Oulad Delims,* having to pay tribute taxes to them. With the arrival of the Spanish* in Western Sahara, the Oulad Tidrarins emerged from Oulad Delim domination. By the early 1970s, most Oulad Tidrarins were living a sedentary lifestyle, primarily in the towns of El-Ayoun, Dakhla, and Boujdour.
REFERENCE: Tony Hodges. *Historical Dictionary of Western Sahara.* 1982.

OUNIA. The Ounias are a subgroup of the Daza* people of Chad. Most Ounias live in the Ennedi region as nomadic pastoralists, raising goats, sheep, camels, and sometimes horses.
REFERENCE: Thomas Collelo et al. *Chad: A Country Study.* 1988.

OUOBE. *See* WOBÉ.

OUOLOF. *See* WOLOF.

OVAH. *See* MERINA.

OVAHERERO. *See* HERERO.

OVAMBO. *See* AMBO.

OVANDE. *See* EVANT.

OVIEDO. *See* EDO.

OVIMBUNDU. The Ovimbundus are one of the largest ethnic groups in Angola. Their current population exceeds 3.5 million people. Their traditional homeland is in the central highlands of the country. Historically, the Ovimbundus were subdivided into distinct, autonomous kingdoms, and, in the twentieth century, those identities have acquired ethnolinguistic characteristics. The primary Ovimbundu subgroups are the Bailundus,* Biés,* Dombes,* Gandas,* Huambos,* Hanhas (Hanyas), Chicumas, Lumbos, Sumbes, Cacondas,* Chiyakas* (Kikayas), Ngalangis, Kibulas, Ndulus, Kingolos, Kalukembes, Ekeketes, Kakondas, Kitatas, Mbuis, Kissanjes, Sambus, and Seles. The central highlands of Angola are an extremely fertile agricultural region, and, since the seventeenth century, Ovimbundu women have raised maize as a staple crop. Male economic activity has revolved around hunting, raiding, and trading.

The Ovimbundu states remained isolated from Portuguese* and Afro-Portuguese traders until the mid-seventeenth century, but they were quickly incorporated into the growing Atlantic economy, especially the slave trade. During the next several centuries, the Ovimbundus actively participated in the slave, ivory, agricultural products, and wild rubber trades. They became active middlemen between European traders and such inland groups as the Lundas,* Chokwes,* Lozis,* and Kazembes.* When new transportation systems rendered the traditional Ovimbundu caravans obsolete, the Ovimbundus made the transition to commercial maize production.

During the twentieth century, the Ovimbundus witnessed the alienation of their land as Portuguese settlers took over. Many Ovimbundus were forced into contract labor, particularly on the large coffee plantations in the north. At the same time, Protestant and Catholic missionaries made inroads among the Ovimbundus, providing educations to the most promising Ovimbundu young men. Since the 1960s, the Ovimbundus have been loyal to the União Nacional Para a Independência Total de Angola (UNITA).
REFERENCE: Susan H. Broadhead. *Historical Dictionary of Angola.* 1992.

OVIOBO. *See* EDO.

OWAN. The Owans are a subgroup of the Edo* people of Bendel State in Nigeria.

OWERRI. The Owerris are a subgroup of the Igbo* people of Nigeria.

OWO. The Owos are one of the main subgroups of the Yoruba* people of Nigeria. Most Owos today can be found in the Ondo State of western Nigeria.

OYDA. The Oydas are a small ethnic group living today in southern Ethiopia. They speak an Omotic* language and make their living as subsistence farmers. Many ethnologists classify the Oydas as part of the Welamo* cluster of peoples. Today, the Oyda population is approximately 4,000 people.
REFERENCE: M. L. Bender, J. D. Bowen, R. L. Cooper, and C. A. Ferguson, eds. *Language in Ethiopia.* 1976.

OYEK. The Oyeks are a small ethnic group living in the Evinagong region of Equatorial Guinea. Most of them are small farmers, raising cassava, malanga (taro), corn, and plantain bananas. Until his assassination in the 1970s, Felipe Nsué served as the political leader of the Oyeks.
REFERENCE: Max Liniger-Goumaz. *Historical Dictionary of Equatorial Guinea.* 1988.

OYO. The Oyos are one of the main subgroups of the Yoruba* people of Nigeria. Most Oyos today can be found in Oyo State of western Nigeria. Some can also be found in Angola.

OYUWI. The Oyuwi language is a dialect of Madi,* a Sudanic language spoken in Uganda.

P

PA'A. The Pa'a people have also been identified over the years as the Palas, Afas, Fa'awas, and Fonis. They are a Nigerian ethnic group whose homeland is in the Ganjuwa District of the Bauchi Division of Bauchi State. The Pa'a population today exceeds 23,000 people.
REFERENCE: *Language Survey of Nigeria.* 1976.

PABALA. *See* ACOLI.

PABIR. The Pabirs are one of the Plateau Chadic peoples of Nigeria. Their current population exceeds 220,000 people, of whom approximately one-quarter are Muslims. Traditionally, the Pabirs lived in walled villages of 400 to 3,000 people and had a centralized political structure. They live in central Nigeria, east of the Niger River and north of the Benue River. They are closely related linguistically to the Buras.* In the 1980s, many Bura and Pabir leaders tried to bring the two peoples together to reduce their local political differences, but the movement was stillborn.
REFERENCE: Helen C. Metz et al. *Nigeria: A Country Study.* 1991.

PACABOL. *See* ACOLI.

PACUA. *See* ACOLI.

PADHOLA. The Padholas are an East African people who live in western Uganda and northeastern Zaire. They are of Nilotic* extraction. Over the course of the last several centuries, the Padholas acquired a reputation as negotiators because of their abilities to help settle disputes among more warlike groups, like the Azandés* and Mangbetus.* The Padholas divide themselves into relatively small political groupings with chiefs as executives. The chiefs also have religious authority, since the Padholas believe that they can intercede with dead ancestors to guarantee favorable conditions for the people. Some ethnologists include them in the Luo* cluster.

PADJADINCA. The Padjadincas are a Senegambian* people who first appeared in the coastal lowlands of what is today Guinea-Bissau in the fifteenth century. They are still loyal to many of their traditional animist beliefs and rituals. Their social and political structure has been characterized by petty chiefdoms. They are closely related to the Bijagos* and make their living as rice farmers.
REFERENCE: Richard Lobban and Joshua Forrest. *Historical Dictionary of the Republic of Guinea-Bissau.* 1988.

PAHOUIN. The Pahouins (Fang,* Beti-Pahouin, Pangwe, and Pamue) are an ethnic group of approximately two million people living in Equatorial Guinea, Cameroon, and Gabon. They speak a Bantu* language. Ethnologists believe that they arrived in their present location after a migration from the savannas of northeastern Africa in the seventeenth and eighteenth centuries. Their own traditions have them originating to the northeast and migrating southwest to the coast in the nineteenth century. They are farmers living in forested regions; they raise cocoa, peanuts, and groundnuts for export and cassava, yams, and other food products for consumption. Large numbers of Pahouin men also work in the timber industry. During the nineteenth century, they were very active in the ivory trade, and they also fiercely resisted French* penetration of the region. Formal colonial rule was imposed on the eve of World War I, and, during the 1920s, French labor demands forced thousands of Pahouin men into brutal forest and plantation labor. Not enough people were left to raise foods products among the Pahouins, which led to large-scale famine. Smallpox and influenza then devastated the already weakened population. These depredations created a fierce Pahouin nationalism. Today, the Pahouins are very influential in national political life. Although many of them are Christians, the religion is mixed considerably with traditional Pahouin animism, reflected in a variety of independent African Christian churches. The Pahouins are divided into dozens of subgroups and sub-subgroups, including the Betis,* Boulous, and Fangs.
REFERENCES: *African Encyclopedia.* 1974; Christopher Chamberlain. "The Migration of the Fang into Central Gabon During the Nineteenth Century." *International Journal of African Historical Studies* 11 (1978): 429–56; David E. Gardinier. *Historical Dictionary of Gabon.* 1994.

PAI. The Pai (Dalong) people, closely related to the Tals* and Montols* of Plateau State in Nigeria, are a highland people. They are concentrated especially in the Pai District of the Pankshin Division. They are surrounded by the Tals to the west, the Yergans* to the east, the Montols to the south, and the Ngas* to the north. They practice subsistence horticulture, raising ginger, millet, guinea corn, and beans. They live in social systems characterized by patrilineal descent and patrifocal residence. In recent years, they have begun migrating to towns and cities looking for work.

REFERENCES: Elizabeth Isichei, ed. *Studies in the History of Plateau State, Nigeria.* 1982; *Language Survey of Nigeria.* 1976.

PAIEM. *See* FYAM.

PAIMOL. *See* ACOLI.

PAKA. *See* NZANGI.

PAKARA. *See* CHARA.

PALA. *See* PA'A.

PALUO. The Paluos are an ethnic group living today in Uganda. They speak a Nilotic* language and are concentrated in the north-central region of the country, north of Lake Kyoga and northeast of Lake Albert. Most Paluos are small farmers. Ethnologists include them in the Luo* cluster of peoples.

PALWOL. The Palwols are a Western Nilotic* people who today live in Uganda. Their original homeland was in southern Sudan and southwestern Ethiopia; they arrived in their present location during a long, slow migration between 1200 and 1800. Most Palwols make a living raising maize, millet, cotton, rice, sugarcane, and groundnuts.

REFERENCE: Peter Ladefoged, Ruth Glick, and Clive Criper. *Language in Uganda.* 1972.

PANA. The Pana are a small ethnic group of several thousand people who live near the Mali border in Burkina-Faso. They are concentrated in the Tougan region where they make their living raising livestock.

REFERENCE: Daniel M. McFarland. *Historical Dictionary of Upper Volta.* 1978.

PANDE. The Pandes (Pende) were once a large ethnic group living in southwestern Central African Republic, northern Congo, eastern Cameroon, and west-central Zaire. They are a Bantu*-speaking people. They should not be confused with the Pandes* of Mozambique. They entered a long period of decline beginning in the mid-nineteenth century, and, today, the only remnants of the Pandes live in several villages in the Lobaye basin and the upper Sangha basin in the Central African Republic. They are concentrated especially around Bambio. In Zaire, they can be found between the Kwilu and Kasai rivers south of Gungu. The Kweses* are a Pande subgroup.

REFERENCES: F. Scott Bobb. *Historical Dictionary of Zaire.* 1988; Pierre Kalck,

Historical Dictionary of the Central African Republic. 1992; Irving Kaplan et al. *Zaire: A Country Study.* 1978.

PANDE. The Pandes, not to be confused with the Pandes* of the Central African Republic, are a small ethnic group of several thousand people living in Mozambique. Most of them are small subsistence farmers who live along the banks of the lower Zambezi River. During the late eighteenth and nineteenth centuries, they actively participated in the slave trade, capturing and selling other Africans to Portuguese* traders.
REFERENCE: Mario Azevedo. *Historical Dictionary of Mozambique.* 1991.

PANGA. The Pangas (Pangwa) are a small ethnic group living today in Zaire. They are concentrated on the north bank of the Kasai River in southwestern Zaire, between Llebo and Bandundu. As a riverine people, the Pangas have traditionally made their living by fishing, working small gardens on the river banks, and engaging in commercial trade up and down the Kasai. Most Pangas still engage in those traditional pursuits, although the numbers moving to cities and towns looking for work is rapidly increasing. Some of them can also be found in Tanzania.
REFERENCE: Irving Kaplan et al. *Zaire: A Country Study.* 1978.

PANGU. The Pangus are one of the Bantu*-speaking peoples of Nigeria. They are classified as part of the Plateau cluster of peoples who occupy central Nigeria. Most Pangus practice subsistence horticulture, raising ginger, millet, guinea corn, beans, and citrus products. They live in social systems characterized by patrilineal descent and patrifocal residence. In recent years, they have begun migrating to towns and cities looking for work.
REFERENCE: Donald G. Morrison et al. *Black Africa: A Comparative Handbook.* 1989.

PANGWA. *See* PANGA.

PANGWE. *See* PAHOUIN.

PANYAM. The Panyams are an Adamawa-speaking people who live today in the Wurkum District of the Muri Division of Gongola State in Nigeria.
REFERENCE: *Language Survey of Nigeria.* 1976.

PAPEI. The Papeis are a Senegambian* people who first appeared in the coastal lowlands of what is today Guinea-Bissau in the fifteenth century. They are still loyal to many of their traditional animist beliefs and rituals. Their social and political structure has been characterized by petty chiefdoms. They are closely related to the Bijagos* and Padjadincas.* They make their living primarily as rice farmers.

REFERENCE: Richard Lobban and Joshua Forrest. *Historical Dictionary of the Republic of Guinea-Bissau.* 1988.

PARE. The Pare (Asu) are a Northeast Bantu*-speaking people of Tanzania who are part of the larger Shambaa* cluster of peoples. They live in the highlands and mountains of Tanzania where they raise vegetables, maize, beans, cassava, cardamom, and bananas. The Pare have a current population of approximately 240,000 people. They are a patrilineal people who are divided among Christian, Muslim, and shamanistic faiths. Since the 1970s, the Pare have been affected by the Tanzanian government's program (*ujamaa*) to eliminate the homestead settlement pattern in favor of bringing groups into villages where public education and health programs can be more effective. The government has also abolished the traditional chiefdoms and is working to integrate the Pare into the larger body politic.
REFERENCES: S. T. Feierman. *The Shambaa Kingdom.* 1962; Edgar V. Winans. *Shambala: The Constitution of a Traditional State.* 1962.

PARI. The Paris are part of the Western Nilotic* cluster of peoples living today in Sudan, particularly around Lafon Hill in the Torit District of Eastern Equatorial Province. Their population is approximately 10,000 people. They are Muslims whose economy revolves around the raising of cattle. The Paris are closely related to the Dinkas,* Nuers,* Anuaks,* and Acolis.*
REFERENCE: Torben Andersen. "The Pari Vowel System with an Internal Reconstruction of Its Historical Development." *Journal of African Languages and Linguistics* 11 (April 1989): 1–20.

PARUMO. *See* ACOLI.

PASSAM. The Passam people of Nigeria have also been identified as the Nyisams. They are an Adamawa-speaking people whose homeland is in the Batta District of the Numan Division of Gongola State.
REFERENCE: *Language Survey of Nigeria.* 1976.

PATAPORI. *See* KOTOPO.

PATE. The Pates are a Swahili*-speaking people who today live in Kenya.

PATRI. The Patris (Kpatili) are a subgroup of the formerly powerful Sabanga* peoples of the Central African Republic. Their population in the nineteenth century exceeded 10,000 people, and they were prominent on the Ubanguian Plateau. Most Patris today have adopted the Banda* language and are assimilating with them.
REFERENCE: Pierre Kalck. *Historical Dictionary of the Central African Republic.* 1992.

PAXALA. *See* SITI.

PEDAH. The Pedah, also known as the Houéda, are considered to be a subgroup of the Aizo* people of Benin. There are approximately 15,000 Pedahs, most of whom live near Lake Ahèmè and make their living as fishermen.

PEDI. Today there are more than two million Pedi (Bapedi) people living in the northern Transvaal region of South Africa and in Swaziland. They are closely related, culturally and linguistically, to the Sothos,* and, during the decades of apartheid, the South African government placed them with the Sotho people in Lebowa. The traditional Pedi life focused on a village existence, with the people raising cattle, goats, maize, and sorghum. Like other Sotho-speaking people, the Pedis practice polygamy, with some men having several wives. Ethnohistorians, as well as Pedi oral traditions, have placed them in the region of Pretoria in the seventeenth century, after which they migrated to their present location. They were a powerful military force in nineteenth-century South Africa, and they were also known as skilled, long-distance traders. In the mid-1800s, Ndebele* armies drove the Pedis into the Zoutpansberg Mountains. Subsequent wars with Swazi* armies hurt them more. In the early twentieth century, the British* finished off what little military power the Pedis had left. Today, large numbers of Pedis live on small farms in Lebowa; others work in industrial areas and send their wages home.
REFERENCES: *African Encyclopedia.* 1974; John J. Grotpeter. *Historical Dictionary of Swaziland.* 1975; Christopher Saunders. *Historical Dictionary of South Africa.* 1983.

PEI. The Pei are a subgroup of the Karimojon.* They live southeast of the Jie* in central Karamoja District of Uganda, south of Mt. Toror. The Pei are cattle pastoralists who also raise millet and maize to survive. They speak a language that is part of the Central Paranilotic cluster of languages.

PEKI. *See* KREPI.

PELE. *See* KPELLE.

PEM. *See* FYAM.

PEMBA. The Pembas live on the island of Zanzibar off the coast of northeastern Tanzania. They are a subgroup of the Shirazi* people.

PEMBE. The Pembes are a small ethnic group living in the Capoche and Mucanha regions of Mozambique. Most of them are subsistence farmers, fishermen, and livestock raisers.
REFERENCE: Mario Azevedo. *Historical Dictionary of Mozambique.* 1991.

PENDE. *See* PANDE.

PERE. The Peres are closely related to the Kivu* peoples of Zaire. They live in the highlands of east-central Zaire, near the Rwandan and Ugandan borders where they farm and raise cattle for milk and meat. They live close to the Lindi River. Some Peres can also be found across the border in southwestern Uganda. They speak a Bantu* language.
REFERENCES: Daniel P. Biebuyck. "Sculpture from the Eastern Zaire Forest Regions: Mbole, Yela, and Pere." *African Arts* 10 (October 1976): 54–61; Irving Kaplan et al. *Zaire: A Country Study.* 1978.

PEREBA. *See* WOM.

PERO. The Pero people, known also as the Piperos and Filiyas, are a Chadic-speaking ethnic group who live today in the Kaltungo District of the Gombe Division of Bauchi State.
REFERENCE: *Language Survey of Nigeria.* 1976.

PETER HARRIS. The Peter Harris people, named after a leader from the recent past, are a subgroup of the Bassa* people of Grand Bassa County, Liberia.

PEUL. *See* FULBE.

PFUNGWE. The Pfungwes are a subgroup of the Korekores,* who constitute the "Northern Shona"* cluster of peoples in Zimbabwe.

PHALENG. The Phalengs are a subgroup of the Kgalagadi* people of Botswana.

PHETLA. The Phetlas (Baphetlas, Maphetlas) are a Lesotho ethnic group who migrated to their present homeland from the Tugela Valley beyond the Drakensberg Mountains. They were soon joined in the region by the Mapolanes* and the Phuthis.* Together, the three peoples are today known as Phuthis; Moorosi, a Phuthi ruler, united them. They are concentrated today in the Quthing, Qacha's Nek, and Mohale's Hoek districts of Lesotho.
REFERENCE: Gordon Haliburton. *Historical Dictionary of Lesotho.* 1977.

PHODZO. The Phodzo are a small ethnic group of several thousand people living in Mozambique. Most of them are small subsistence farmers who live along the banks of the lower Zambezi River. During the late eighteenth and nineteenth centuries, the Phodzo actively participated in the slave trade, capturing and selling other Africans to Portuguese* traders.
REFERENCE: Mario Azevedo. *Historical Dictionary of Mozambique.* 1991.

PHOKA. The Phokas are part of the Tumbuka* cluster of peoples living today in northern Malawi, primarily between Lake Nyasa and the Zambian border, south of the Tanzanian border. Some Phokas can also be found in Zambia and Tanzania. The Phoka population today exceeds 40,000 people. They speak a language closely related to that of the Tongas.* The Phoka economy still revolves around the production of maize, sorghum, and millet.
REFERENCES: *African Encyclopedia.* 1974; John J. Grotpeter. *Historical Dictionary of Zambia.* 1979; Donald G. Morrison et al. *Black Africa: A Comparative Handbook.* 1989.

PHUTHI. The Phuthi are a subgroup, or, more exactly, a chiefdom, of the Sotho* people of Lesotho and South Africa. They are located in the Qacha's Nek, Mohale's Hoek, and Quthing districts of Lesotho, where they have become united with the Phetlas* and Mapolanes.* Their great leader, Moorosi, united the three peoples.
REFERENCE: Gordon Haliburton. *Historical Dictionary of Lesotho.* 1977.

PHUTING. The Phuting are a subgroup, or, more exactly, a chiefdom, of the Sotho people* of Lesotho and South Africa.

PIA. *See* PIYA.

PIAPUNG. The Piapungs are a small ethnic group living today in Plateau State in Nigeria. Ethnologists believe that they are descended from a mixture of Tal* and Montol* immigrants, with whom they share linguistic and cultural institutions. Today, they are largely under the cultural influence of their neighbors, the Gomeis.* Most Piapungs are subsistence farmers.
REFERENCE: John Ola Agi. "The Goemai and Their Neighbors: An Historical Analysis." In Elizabeth Isichei, ed. *Studies in the History of Plateau State, Nigeria.* 1982.

PILA PILA. The Pila Pila (Yowa, Yao) are a Voltaic people in the Bariba* cluster of northern Benin. Their current population is approximately 20,000 people, most of whom live south of Natitingou in Atakora Province. Their language is closely related to the Moré language spoken by the Mossi* people in Burkina-Faso. The Pila Pila call themselves the Yao* or Yowa. They can also be found scattered in the Eastern and Asante Regions of Ghana.
REFERENCE: Samuel Decalo. *Historical Dictionary of Benin.* 1987.

PIMBWE. The Pimbwes are an ethnic group whom some ethnologists classify with the Rungwa* people of Tanzania. Their current population is approximately 25,000 people.

PIPERO. *See* PERO.

PISALA. *See* SASALA.

PITI. The Pitis (Pittis, Abisis, Bisis) are a Plateau people living today in Nigeria, particularly in the Lere District of the Saminaka Division of Kaduna State. They dwell in a series of villages where they have made the transition in recent decades to small farming. Hunting, however, has long been of religious and ritual significance to them. The Pitis are closely related to the Chawai* and Ribam* peoples. Their current population exceeds 6,000 people.
REFERENCES: Harold D. Gunn. *The Peoples of the Plateau Area of Nigeria.* 1963; *Language Survey of Nigeria.* 1976. Jean-Claude Muller. ''Intertribal Hunting Among the Rukuba.'' *Ethnology* 21 (1982): 203–14.

PITSI. The Pitsis are a subgroup of the Lendu* people of Zaire.

PITTI. *See* PITI.

PIYA. The Piya people (Pias, Wurkums) are a Chadic-speaking people of Nigeria. They are concentrated in the Wurkum District of the Muri Division of Gongola State.
REFERENCE: *Language Survey of Nigeria.* 1976.

PLA. The Pla people are one of the subgroups of the Ewe* cluster of peoples in Togo, Benin, and Ghana in West Africa.

PLATEAU CHADIC. The Plateau Chadic are a cluster of closely related ethnic groups in Nigeria, including the Gerawas, Gwandaras, Margis,* and Pabirs.* The Plateau Chadic population exceeds 640,000 people, of whom 100,000 are Muslims.
REFERENCE: *Language Survey of Nigeria.* 1976.

PLAYERO. *See* NDOWE.

PO. *See* BAULE.

PODZO. The Podzo (Marromeu, Chipango) people live near Marromeu in Mozambique and make their livings as farmers and urban workers. They are subdivided into a number of clans, each with a strong sense of identity. The Podzo clans include the Chinde, Mbadzo, Botha, Zinjo, Sase, Chilendje, Malunga, Bande, Simboti Nyamgombe, Chifungo, and a number of others.
REFERENCE: Mario Azevedo. *Historical Dictionary of Mozambique.* 1991.

POGOLU. *See* POGORO.

POGORO. The Pogoros (Pogolus) are an East African people who are part of the Ngindo* cluster of the Northeastern Bantu* language group of East Africa. Most Pogoros are rice farmers who raise the cash crop in the fertile, damp

floodplains of the Kilombero and Rufiji rivers in the Ulanga District of Tanzania. Droughts in recent years have had a serious economic impact on the Pogoros. They also raise poultry and goats. The Pogoros trace descent through male lines. They are primarily Muslim in their religious orientation. Their current population exceeds 140,000 people.
REFERENCE: A.R.W. Crosse-Upcott. ''Male Circumcision Among the Ngindo.'' *Journal of the Royal Anthropological Institute* 89 (1959): 169–89.

POI. The Pois are a Bantu-speaking people living today in the Haut-Zaire region of northeastern Zaire. Although most Pois still making their living as farmers, raising cassava as a staple, they have become increasingly integrated into the regional commercial economy in recent decades. Large numbers of Pois have moved to the city of Kisangani in search of wage labor.
REFERENCE: Irving Kaplan et al. *Zaire: A Country Study.* 1978.

POJULU. The Pojulus, also known as Fajelus, are an Eastern Nilotic* people who live today in southern Sudan near the Uganda border. They pursue a pastoral lifestyle, raising cattle for milk, blood, and hides. Pojulu women produce millet, maize, cow peas, and some tobacco. Recent droughts in the region have devastated the Pojulu economy.
REFERENCES: John Lamphear. *The Traditional History of the Jie of Uganda.* 1976; Donald G. Morrison et al. *Black Africa: A Comparative Handbook.* 1989.

POKOMO. The Pokomos are a cluster of peoples living along the banks of the Tana River in Kenya, where they live as farmers raising plantains, sugarcane, rice, and maize. They are a mixed people, composed of subgroups with Bantu* and Oromo* roots. There are four main Pokomo subgroups, each with a separate dialect that is mutually intelligible with the others. The Lower Pokomo live from Kipini to Bubesa in the Salama region. The Upper Pokomos live between Matanama and Roka. The Welwans (also known as Malakotes) dwell between Roka and Garissa. The Munyo Yayas (Northern Pokomos or Korokoros) can be found from Garissa to Mbalambala. The Pokomo population today exceeds 60,000 people.
REFERENCE: Bethwell A. Ogot. *Historical Dictionary of Kenya.* 1981.

POKOT. The Pokots (Suk) live in the western highlands of Kenya. Pokots can also be found in Uganda. They speak a Western Nilotic* language and are a subgroup of the Kalenjin* cluster of peoples. Cattle were central to the traditional Pokot economy, but, in recent years, the Pokots have started raising maize and tobacco on large commercial farms and moving to towns and cities for work and business opportunities. The Pokots had a reputation as fierce, skilled warriors who regularly raided neighboring Masais,* Luos,* and Gusiis* for cattle. The arrival of British* military force in the region in 1905 ended those raids.

POLANE. *See* MAPOLANE.

POLCI. The Polcis are a small ethnic group occupying a territory of approximately 1,000 square miles northeast of the Jos Plateau in northwestern Nigeria. Their most immediate ethnic neighbors are the Jarawas, Hausas,* Zeems,* and Dasses.* Most Polcis are subsistence farmers who raise millet, guinea corn, maize, and beans.
REFERENCE: Elizabeth Isichei, ed. *Studies in the History of Plateau State, Nigeria.* 1982.

POMBO. The Pombos are one part of the larger Kongo* cluster of peoples living today in northwestern Angola and southeastern Zaire. Their population exceeds 50,000 people, and they speak a Bantu* language. A substantial number of Pombos can be found living today in Kinshasa, Zaire. Because of their location near the coast, the Pombos had sustained contact with the Portuguese* during the colonial period, but they still participated in the nationalistic rebellion against Portuguese rule. Most Pombos are farmers today, and their main crop is coffee.
REFERENCE: Thomas Collelo et al. *Angola: A Country Study.* 1989.

PONEK. The Ponek are one of the cluster of Middle-Cameroon Bantu* peoples who live in central Cameroon. Most of them make their living as small farmers and fishermen, although, in recent years, increasing numbers of Ponek men have found work on commercial farms and in the oil fields. Their commercial farming enterprises, however, have competed poorly, reducing the Ponek lifestyle to poverty levels.
REFERENCE: Mark DeLancey and H. M. Mokeba. *Historical Dictionary of the Republic of Cameroon.* 1990.

PONGO. The Pongos are a small Cameroonian ethnic group. Most of them make their living as small farmers, urban workers, civil servants, and businessmen. Because of their location on the Atlantic coast, the Pongos came into contact with German* and British* commercial interests early, which gave them access to greater economic and educational opportunities.
REFERENCE: Harold D. Nelson et al. *Area Handbook of the United Republic of Cameroon.* 1974.

PONGU. The Pongus, also known as the Arringeus, are a small ethnic group of approximately 14,000 people living in the Tegina District of the Minna Division of Niger State in Nigeria. Their language is classified with the Kamuku*-Bassa* group of Plateau languages in the Benue-Congo family.
REFERENCE: *Language Survey of Nigeria.* 1976.

POPO. *See* MINA.

PORE. *See* TEMNE.

POROTO. The Porotos are an ethnic group living today in Tanzania. Many ethnologists classify them as part of the Sangu* peoples within the Rufiji* cluster.

PORTUGUESE. Tens of thousands of ethnic Portuguese still reside in the cities of the former Portuguese colonies in Africa. Beginning with the fifteenth-century voyages of Prince Henry the Navigator, Portugal established a colonial foothold in Africa that did not end until the great wars of rebellion in the 1960s and 1970s. From bases in the Cape Verde Islands, São Tome, and Principe in the sixteenth century, Portugal began exploiting the Upper Guinea region of West Africa, which became the colony of Portuguese Guinea (Guinea-Bissau). Portuguese settlements at Luanda and Benguela led to the penetration of what became Portuguese West Africa (Angola). On the east coast of Africa, Portugal planted isolated settlements in what is today Mozambique and developed large landed estates in the Zambezi River Valley. That entire region became known as Portuguese East Africa. Ethnic Portuguese can still be found today in Angola, Mozambique, Guinea-Bissau, São Tome, Principe, and the Cape Verde Islands, where they are usually important in the business community.
REFERENCE: James S. Olson, ed. *Historical Dictionary of European Imperialism.* 1991.

POTOPO. *See* KOTOPO.

POTOPORE. *See* KOTOPO.

POULI. The Poulis (Foulacoundas) are a subgroup of the Fulbe* peoples of Guinea in West Africa.

POUNOU. *See* BAPOUNOU.

POVE. The Poves, also known as the Pubis, speak a Okandé* language and live in the deep forests between the Lolo River and the Offoué River in Gabon. Small clusters of the Bakèlès* live among them. They arrived in the region in the late nineteenth century, migrating in from the north and colliding with the French* who were arriving from the south. The Poves suffered under the exactions of French labor and concessionary demands, but they did not violently resist. Most Poves today are small farmers.
REFERENCE: David E. Gardinier. *Historical Dictionary of Gabon.* 1981.

PRAMPRAM. The Pramprams (Gbugblas) are one of the subgroups of the Adangbe* peoples of the Accra Plain and coastal inselbergs of southeastern Ghana. Most of them make their living as small farmers.

PUBI. *See* POVE.

PUKU-GEERI-KERI-WIPSI. The Puku-Geeri-Keri-Wipsis are a Nigerian ethnic group, one of the Plateau peoples of the Benue-Congo linguistic family. They can be found today in the Dalai and Fakai districts of the Zuru Division of Sokoto State.
REFERENCE: *Language Survey of Nigeria.* 1976.

PUNA. The Punas are a subgroup of the Mbundu* peoples of Angola.

PUTUKWAM. *See* UTUGWANG.

PYAM. *See* FYAM.

PYAPUN. The Pyapuns are a Chadic-speaking people of Nigeria. Pyapuns can be found today in the Shendam District of the Shendam Division of Plateau State.
REFERENCE: *Language Survey of Nigeria.* 1976.

PYEM. *See* FYAM.

PYGMY. The term ''Pygmy'' has been used to describe a people of short stature who today number more than 200,000 people in Central Africa. The Pygmies used to occupy a much larger territory, but they have retreated from that broad area over the last thousand years because of long-term climatic changes, which have caused the tropical forest to shrink, and the expansion of Bantu* agricultural techniques, which has likewise converted large sections of the tropical forest to savanna. In recent years, more intensive forms of swidden agriculture, lumbering, and mining have also contributed to the steady elimination of tropical forest. In the process, the Pygmies have lost territory. Pygmies speak languages that they have borrowed from their neighbors. Although some Pygmies are fishermen and potters, most still survive off the forest, migrating back and forth seasonally between the farming villages of other ethnic groups and a hunting-gathering lifestyle in the forest.

There are four major subgroups of Pygmies. The Western cluster of Pygmies, who are sometimes known as the Binga* (Babinga, Babenga, Bambenga), number approximately 35,000 people and live in the northeastern reaches of Congo, southwestern Central African Republic, southern Cameroon, parts of Gabon, and across the Ubangi River in Zaire. The cluster includes the Gelli (Bagiella, Badjelli, Baguielli), who number approximately 2,500 people and live on the Atlantic coast near Kribi in Cameroon. Another group in the Western cluster of Pygmies are the Aka* people of the Central African Republic, who number approximately 5,000 people. The Central cluster of Pygmies consists of the Twa* or Cwa people. Their population today exceeds 100,000 people. The Twa live north of Lake Leopold in Zaire. The Eastern cluster of Pygmies are known as the Mbutis (Bambuti) and number approximately 40,000 people. Their homeland is the Ituri forest of northeastern Zaire. There are three subgroups of the Mbuti: the Aka to the northwest, the Efe* to the east and north, and the Sua to the south. The Southeastern cluster—also known as the Twa, Gesera, and Zigaba—live in Rwanda and Burundi. A smaller group of them live on the Uganda-Zaire border.

REFERENCE: Luigi Luca Cavalli-Sforza. *African Pygmies*. 1986.

Q

QIMANT. The Qimants are an ethnic group living today in Ethiopia. They speak a Central Cushitic language and are closely related to the Agaw* peoples. The Qimants are concentrated north of Lake Tana, near Gonder, in western Ethiopia. The Qimant population today exceeds 20,000 people, most of whom are small farmers and cattle raisers who remain loyal to their traditional religious beliefs.
REFERENCE: Harold D. Nelson et al. *Ethiopia: A Country Study.* 1980.

QIREIJAB. The Qireijab are a tiny group of Beja* people. They speak a Northern Cushitic language and actually are a subgroup of the Ababda* of southern Egypt and northern Sudan. The Qireijab are a highly Arabized Sunni Muslim people who sustain themselves by fishing in the Red Sea.
REFERENCES: Andrew Paul. *A History of the Beja Tribes of the Sudan.* 1954; John Spencer Trimingham. *Islam in Sudan.* 1949.

QUAHOE. *See* KWAHU.

QUIN. The Quin are an ethnic group living today in Burkina-Faso.
REFERENCE: Donald G. Morrison et al. *Black Africa: A Comparative Handbook.* 1989.

QUIOCO. *See* CHOKWE.

QUISSINCA. The Quissincas speak a Manding* language and live in Guinea-Bissau. Most Quissincas are subsistence farmers, raising rice as the staple and maintaining herds of cattle and goats. Quissinca society is organized around exogamous patrilineal clans.

REFERENCE: Richard Lobban and Joshua Forrest. *Historical Dictionary of the Republic of Guinea-Bissau.* 1988.

QULAUGHLI. The Qulaughli are a Muslim ethnic group of Libya. Their current population is approximately 70,000 people.
REFERENCE: Harold D. Nelson et al. *Libya: A Country Study.* 1989.

R

RABAI. The Rabais are part of the Mijikenda* cluster of people of coastal Kenya and Tanzania. Most of them are farmers, raising maize, millet, sheep, and goats, but others are laborers on sugarcane, sisal, and cotton plantations.

RACHID. The Rachids are a subgroup of the Djoheinas,* themselves a large Arab* subgroup in Chad.

RAHANWAYN. The Rahanwayns (Rahanweins) are one of the six primary clans of the Somali* people of Somalia. They are closely related to the Digils.* Like all Somalis, they claim descent from Samaale, the mythical founder of the entire ethnic group. Also, like all other Somalis, they speak the Somali language and are Sunni Muslims. Some Rahanwayns are nomadic herders, who raise camels, sheep, and cattle, but most of them are farmers. The Rahanwayn ethnic group, however, is subdivided into thousands of sub-clans and sub-sub-clans; individual Rahanwayns feel far more loyalty to their local clan than to any larger collectivity. Most Rahanwayns are concentrated in northwestern Somalia. They live primarily between the Shebelle and the Juga rivers.

During the late 1980s and early 1990s, hundreds of thousands of Rahanwayns faced starvation because of the famine and civil war in Somalia. Political instability became endemic as centralized authority broke down in the face of severe clan and sub-clan rivalries. Somalia essentially became a no-man's-land of misery and suffering, with no single individual or group enjoying enough power to impose any order. In 1991, many Rahanwayns joined the Somali National Alliance, a group headed by General Mohammed Farrah Aidid, a member of the Hawiye* clan. Even the intervention of United Nations troops in 1992 did not permanently restore stability to the region. Like millions of other Somalis, the Rahanwayns faced catastrophe.

REFERENCES: Margaret Castagno. *Historical Dictionary of Somalia.* 1975; Helen C. Metz et al. *Somalia: A Country Study.* 1992; *New York Times,* October 4, 1992.

RAHANWEIN. *See* RAHANWAYN.

RANGI. The Rangis (Rongo) are a prominent, Bantu*-speaking people who live in Central Tanzania. Their particular Bantu language is known as Kirangi. Their population today numbers approximately 250,000 people. The majority of those living in rural areas are hoe farmers, raising sorghum, millet, maize, cattle, sheep, and goats. A few Rangis also raise peanuts and castor oil plants as cash crops. The Rangi political system revolves around small chiefdoms. Until the early 1970s, most of the Rangi lived in isolated homestead settlements in the bush country of the north or the scrub region of the south. But, in 1974, Tanzania officially launched its *ujamaa* program, gathering the Rangi (and other groups) into larger villages where education, commercial agriculture, and political control would be easier to implement. Islam first reached the Rangis in the nineteenth century when slave traders came into central Tanzania; today, more than 80 percent of Rangis identify themselves as Muslims—Sunni Muslims of the Shafi school. Strong elements of their traditional animist faith, particularly worship at rain shrines, nevertheless survive, and relatively few people conduct their daily Islamic prayers or observe Ramadan. Most ethnologists believe that the gathering of the Rangis into larger villages, towns, and cities will accelerate their conversion to Islam. Like so many other people in East Africa, the Rangis, especially those in rural areas, have suffered badly from the drought affecting the region in the early 1990s.

REFERENCES: H. A. Fosbrooke. ''A Rangi Circumcision Ceremony: Blessing of a New Grove.'' *Tanganyika Notes and Records* 50 (1958): 30–38; Ioan Myrddin Lewis, ed. *Islam in Tropical Africa.* 1966; J. Spencer Trimingham. *Islam in East Africa.* 1964.

RASHAIDA. *See* BAGGARA.

RAYA. The Rayas, also known as the Azebos, are one of the major Oromo* subgroups in northern Ethiopia. Most of them are Sunni Muslims, Shafi school, who work as sedentary farmers in Wollo Province and in southern Tigre Province.

REDI. The Redis are a Tanzanian ethnic group who are sometimes classified as part of the Kerere* group of peoples. They have a contemporary population of approximately 75,000 people.

REGEIBAT. *See* REGUIBAT.

REGI. *See* REDI.

REGUIBAT. The Reguibat (Regeibat), also known as the Erguibat, are one of the largest ethnic groups in Western Sahara. Traditionally, their nomadic range included southern Morocco, much of Western Sahara, southwestern Algeria, northern Mauritania, and northwestern Mali. They are of Sanhaja origin, although they speak an Arabic dialect. The Reguibat living on the Atlantic coast of Western Sahara are known as the Reguibat es-Sahel, while those to the east are called the Reguibat es-Charg, or Lgouacem. The Reguibat es-Charg are divided into the following subgroups: the Ahel Brahim Ou Daoud,* the Lebouihat,* the Laiaicha,* and the Foqra.* The Reguibat es-Sahel are subdivided into the Oulad Moussa, the Souaad, the Lemouedenin, the Oulad Daoud, the Oulad Borhim, the Oulad Cheikh,* the Thaalat, and the Oulad Taleb. In the nineteenth century, the Reguibat acquired the warlike reputation for which they are still known today. At that time, their camel herds had grown in size, as had their need for pasturage; a Reguibat demographic expansion simultaneously occurred, which brought them into conflict with other groups. The Reguibat were at the height of their power in the early twentieth century when the French* empire tried to bring northern Mauritania, southern Morocco, and southwestern Algeria under control. The Reguibat fought the French until their defeat in 1934. Today, the Reguibat population exceeds 100,000 people, the vast majority of whom are now sedentary in their lifestyle.
REFERENCE: Tony Hodges. *Historical Dictionary of Western Sahara.* 1982.

REHEBOTH. *See* REHOBATH BASTER.

REHOBATH BASTER. The Rehobath Basters are a unique ethnic group living today in Namibia. Their current population exceeds 25,000 people. They are the result of a process of ethnogenesis between several African ethnic groups and the German* settlers who colonized German South West Africa. Before Namibian independence, they were classified by South Africa as "Coloureds."*
REFERENCE: Reginald Green, Marja-Liisa Kiljunen, and Kimmo Kiljunen. *Namibia: The Last Colony.* 1981; Stanley Schoeman and Elna Schoeman. *Namibia.* 1984.

REMBA. *See* LEMBA.

REMO. The Remos are one of the main subgroups of the Yoruba* people of Nigeria. Most Remos can be found today in southern Ogun State and northern Lagos State of western Nigeria.

RENDILLE. The Rendille people of Kenya are Cushitic speakers with close cultural and linguistic ties to the Somalis* and Sonis. Today, they live in northern Kenya, especially between Lake Turkana and Mount Marsabit. The Rendille population is approximately 25,000 people, most of whom are nomadic pastoralists raising camels.
REFERENCE: Bethwell A. Ogot. *Historical Dictionary of Kenya.* 1981.

RENDRE. *See* NUNKU.

RESHAWA. The Reshawa—known also as the Tsureshes, Tsure Jas, Gungan-cis, Bareshes, and Gungawas—are a group of approximately 125,000 people who live on the banks and islands of the Niger River in the Yauri Division of Sokoto State in Nigeria. They make their living as farmers and fishermen. They are primarily hoe cultivators, raising millet and guinea corn in the highlands and onions along the river. They are surrounded by a number of other ethnic groups, including the Hausas,* Shangawas,* Dukkawas,* Lopawas,* and Kamberis.* Except for the Dukkawas, who marry endogamously, the Reshawas are known to intermarry polygynously with the surrounding ethnic groups. They are also known for their skill at wrestling, the hostility of all their male-female relation-ships (except that between mother and son), their cultural pragmatism, and their willingness to incorporate people from other ethnic groups. Their conversion to Islam was, and often remains, a product of their need to get along with the dominant Hausas, who are also Muslims.

Ethnologists trace Reshawa origins in the Yauri District back to the fourteenth century. Briefly, during the sixteenth century, the Reshawas established political domination of the region, but the Hausas soon came to power and have remained so ever since. The Muslim religion came to the Reshawas via traders, Hausa administrators, and traveling *mullahs.* More than two-thirds of the Reshawas are now Muslims. They speak Reshe, part of the Benue-Congo branch of the Niger-Congo linguistic family. Because of the completion of the Kainji Dam Project in 1968, many Reshawas were forced to relocate off the islands and river banks into larger settlements where government schools, jobs, and health facilities are accelerating their acculturation and assimilation.
REFERENCES: Frank A. Salamone. ''All Resettled at Kainji?'' *Intellect* (1977): 231–33; Frank A. Salamone. ''Gungawa Wrestling as an Ethnic Marker.'' *Africa und Ubersee* (1974): 193–201; Frank A. Salamone. ''Reshawa.'' In Richard V. Weekes, ed. *Muslim Peoples.* 1984.

RESHE. *See* RESHAWA.

RHARHABE. The Rharhabe people are a highly independent subgroup of the Xhosa* people of the Transkei and Ciskei in southeastern Cape Province of South Africa.

RHONGA. *See* RONGA.

RIBAM. The Ribams are a people living today in Plateau State in Nigeria. They live in a series of villages where they have made the transition in recent decades to small farming. They are closely related to the Pitis,* primarily through

proximity of settlement and intermarriage. They have close links culturally to the Chawais* as well. Hunting has long been of religious and ritual significance to them.
REFERENCE: Jean-Claude Muller. "Intertribal Hunting Among the Rukuba." *Ethnology* 21 (1982): 203–14.

RIBE. The Ribes are part of the Mijikenda* cluster of people of coastal Kenya and Tanzania. Most of them are farmers, raising maize, millet, sheep, and goats, but others are laborers on sugarcane, sisal, and cotton plantations.

RIBINA. The Ribinas are an ethnic group living today north of the Jos Plateau in Plateau State in northwestern Nigeria. They are surrounded ethnically by the Jarawas, Afusaris,* Zaris,* Zeems,* Gusus,* and Dasses.* Most Ribinas are subsistence farmers who maintain close relations with neighboring Sanga* peoples. The Ribinas can be found especially in the Jere and Buji districts of Plateau State.
REFERENCES: Harold D. Gunn. *Peoples of the Plateau Area of Northern Nigeria.* 1963; Elizabeth Isichei, ed. *Studies in the History of Plateau State, Nigeria.* 1982.

RIMI. *See* TURU.

RIMIBE. The term "Rimibe" is used in Burkina-Faso to refer to an ethnic group that serves as serfs to the dominant Fulbe* people there.

RINDIRI. *See* NUNKU.

RINDRE. *See* NUNKU.

RISHUWA. *See* KUZAMANI.

RIZEGAT. The Rizegats—also known as the Mahamids, Maharges, and Mararits—are a subgroup of the Djoheinas,* themselves a large Arab* subgroup in Chad.

RO BAMBANI. *See* AGOI.

ROBA. The Robas, known also as the Lallas, Lalas, and Gworams, are one of Nigeria's Adamawa-speaking ethnic groups. They are concentrated in Gongola State, primarily in the Ga'anda, Song, and Yungur districts of the Adamawa Division and the Shellem District of the Numan Division.
REFERENCE: *Language Survey of Nigeria.* 1976.

ROLONG. The Rolongs are one of the primary subdivisions of the Tswana* people of Botswana and South Africa. They are actually a collection of peoples scattered throughout southern, northeastern, and western Botswana, as well as in northern Cape Province and the Orange Free State in South Africa. Rolongs are subdivided into such groups as the Tshidi Rolong.

RON. The Rons are one of the Bantu*-speaking peoples of Nigeria. They are classified as part of the Plateau cluster of peoples who occupy central Nigeria. Most Rons practice subsistence horticulture, raising ginger, millet, guinea corn, beans, and citrus products. They live in social systems characterized by patrilineal descent and patrifocal residence. In recent years, they have begun migrating to towns and cities looking for work.
REFERENCE: Donald G. Morrison et al. *Black Africa: A Comparative Handbook.* 1989.

RONGA. The Rongas (Rsonga, Rhonga) are a subgroup of the Tonga* people. They are concentrated in Maputo, Marracuene, Matola, Manhica, and Sabie in Mozambique, where they live as farmers and fishermen. During the nineteenth and twentieth centuries, the Rongas were known for their nationalistic opposition to Portuguese* imperial authority. They have also maintained a strong sense of independence within the Tonga cluster.

RONGO. The Rongos are a Tanzanian ethnic group whom some ethnologists classify with the Sukuma* cluster of peoples. They have a population today of about 100,000 people.

RORKEC. The Rorkecs are a major subdivision of the Atuot* people of the southern Sudan.

ROTSE. *See* LOZI.

ROUIMIAT. The Rouimiats are a subgroup of the Ait Lahsens* of Western Sahara in what is today Morocco.

ROZI. *See* LOZI.

ROZVI. The Rozvis (Rozwis, Barozwis, Varozvis, Varozwi) are a Shona* people whose origins are quite obscure. People claiming to be Rozvis are spread through Zimbabwe, and identification as a Rozvi is considered prestigious. The original Rozvis were Shona people associated with the Changamire State in the late seventeenth and eighteenth centuries. Nguni* invasions destroyed the Changamire State in the early 1800s, bringing about a widespread dispersal of the Rozvi people.
REFERENCE: R. Kent Rasmussen. *Historical Dictionary of Zimbabwe.* 1994.

ROZWI. *See* ROZVI.

RSONGA. *See* RONGA.

RUANDA. *See* RWANDA.

RUBATAB. The Rubatabs are the product of ethnogenesis between the Arab* and the Nubian* peoples of Sudan. Their population today numbers more than one million people, most of whom are small farmers and workers living in north-central Sudan. Virtually all of them are Muslims.
REFERENCE: Donald G. Morrison et al. *Black Africa: A Comparative Handbook.* 1989.

RUFIJI. The Rufijis are an East African people who are part of the Ngindo* cluster of the Northeastern Bantu* language group of East Africa. The Rufiji population of Tanzania today is in excess of 150,000 people. Most of the Rufijis are rice farmers, who raise the cash crop in the fertile, damp floodplains of the Kilombero and Rufiji rivers in Tanzania. They also raise poultry and goats. The Rufijis trace descent through male lines. They are primarily Muslim in their religious orientation, but they generally do not observe Ramadan or many other Islamic rituals. Like other Tanzanians, the Rufijis have been dealing with the government's *ujamaa* program since the mid-1970s. This policy is designed to alter the traditional homestead settlement pattern in favor of establishing village clusters where public education and public health campaigns can be more successful. Some ethnologists include the Mawanda within the Rufiji group of peoples.
REFERENCE: A. R. W. Crosse-Upcott. "Male Circumcision Among the Ngindo." *Journal of the Royal Anthropological Institute* 89 (1959): 169–89.

RUKUBA. The Rukuba (Sales, Inchazis, Kuches, Baches) are an African people numbering approximately 15,000 people. The center of their territory is located about twenty-five miles northwest of Jos, the capital city of Plateau State in Nigeria. The Rukuba are surrounded by a number of other African groups, including the Janjis,* Amos,* Pitis,* Ribams,* Chawais,* Irigwes,* Biroms,* Afusaris,* Gurrums,* Bujis,* and Charras.* They live in twenty-four villages, with each village headed by a chief and divided into five sub-villages. Three of these sub-villages are headed by section chiefs; the fourth sub-village is used for religious rituals and headed by a section chief, while the fifth arbitrates in disputes between the various village sections. The Rukuba are divided into two exogamous moieties; most villages have members of both groups in residence. In the early 1990s, their population exceeded 120,000 people.
REFERENCES: *Language Survey of Nigeria.* 1976; Jean-Claude Muller. "Intertribal Hunting Among the Rukuba." *Ethnology* 21 (1982): 203–14.

RUMAIYA. *See* RUMAYA.

RUMAYA. The Rumayas (Rumaiyas) are an ethnic group living today in the Kauru District of the Saminaka Division of Kaduna State in Nigeria. Their contemporary population is approximately 4,000 people. They speak a Western Plateau language in the Benue-Congo family.
REFERENCE: *Language Survey of Nigeria.* 1976.

RUNGA. The Rungas are one of the Sudanic peoples living today in Chad. They tend to be concentrated in southern Chad, especially in much of the Salamat Prefecture, and across the border in the Central African Republic where they make their living raising livestock and working small farms. The primary Runga crops are millet, sorghum, peanuts, and cotton. The Runga population today exceeds 35,000 people.
REFERENCES: Thomas Collelo et al. *Chad: A Country Study.* 1988; Donald G. Morrison et al. *Black Africa: A Comparative Handbook.* 1989.

RUNGU. The Rungus are a group of peoples who live along the coast of Tanzania and Kenya in East Africa. They are closely related to the Nyikas* and Fipas.* Most Rungus now live in farming villages where they raise sheep, goats, maize, and millet. They also work on sugarcane, sisal, and cotton plantations. The Rungu population of Tanzania today exceeds 25,000 people.
REFERENCES: *African Encyclopedia.* 1974; Donald G. Morrison et al. *Black Africa: A Comparative Handbook.* 1989.

RUNGWA. The Rungwas are an ethnic group living in west-central Tanzania, east of the Fipas,* who live on the shore of Lake Tanganyika. The Rungwas are primarily in Rukwa region. Most Rungwas make their living as small farmers and cattle raisers. Some ethnologists classify the Pimbwes* as a Rungwa group. The Rungwas have a population today of approximately 15,000 people.
REFERENCE: Laura Kurtz. *Historical Dictionary of Tanzania.* 1978.

RURAMA. *See* KURAMA.

RURI. The Ruris are an ethnic group living today in Tanzania. Some ethnologists cluster them with the Jiji* peoples, who are part of the Interlacustrine Bantu* group.

RUUND. *See* LUNDA.

RWAMBA. *See* RWANDA.

RWANDA. The Rwandas (Rwamba) are one of the Bantu* highland peoples of east-central Zaire, living near Lake Kivu and the Rwandan border, as well as in southwestern Uganda and Tanzania. The Rwandas speak a Bantu language and make their living as farmers who also raise cattle for milk and meat. During the genocidal civil war in Rwanda in 1994, the Rwandas were overrun by refugees fleeing the violence.

REFERENCE: Irving Kaplan et al. *Zaire: A Country Study.* 1978.

S

SAB. According to some ethnologists, the Sabs are one of the two primary lineage groups of the Somali* people of Somalia, Kenya, Ethiopia, and Djibouti. Included in the so-called Sab cluster are the Digils* and the Rahanwayns* (Rahaweins). The latter two groups, however, consider the word "Sab" to be derogatory and resent its use to describe them. They have traditionally been looked down upon by the more dominant, warlike Samale group. Most Sabs are hunter-gatherers, subsistence farmers, and craftsmen. The so-called Sabs are of Bantu* extraction and constitute roughly 20 percent of the total Somali population.

SABA. The Sabas are an ethnic group in Chad. Virtually all of the 40,000 or so Sabas are Muslims. They are part of the larger Nilotic* cluster of Chadic peoples. Most Sabas make their living as small farmers, laborers, and semi-nomadic and nomadic pastoralists. They are one of the Hadjeray* peoples of the mountainous regions of Guéra Prefecture. They are descended from refugees who were driven into the mountains. They speak a Chadic language and practice the *margai* cult of place and site spirits. In spite of many cultural similarities with such other groups as the Kingas,* Junkuns,* Bidios,* Mogoums,* Sokoros,* Barains,* and Dangaleats,* the Sabas rarely intermarry and maintain a powerful sense of separate ethnic identity.
REFERENCES: Thomas Collelo et al. *Chad: A Country Study.* 1988; Pierre Hugot. *Le Tchad.* 1965; J. C. Lebeuf. *Afrique Centrale.* 1972; Donald G. Morrison et al. *Black Africa: A Comparative Handbook.* 1989.

SABANGA. The Sabangas were once the ethnic group that dominated the Ubangian Plateau of what is today the Central African Republic. Their own traditions place their origins in the Nile Basin before their migration to the Ubangian Plateau. They were divided into such subgroups as the Dokoas,* Patris,* and Nzakaras.* Today, only three small groups of Sabangas are still left. The surviving Sabangas have adopted Banda* as their primary language and are rapidly assimilating into the Banda group.

REFERENCE: Pierre Kalck. *Historical Dictionary of the Central African Republic.* 1992.

SABAOT. The Sabaots live in the western highlands of Kenya. They are a subgroup of the Kalenjin* cluster of peoples. They are divided into four sub-groups of their own: Kony, Pok, Sapei (Sebei), and Bungomek. Cattle were formerly central to the traditional Sabaot economy, but the Sabaots have recently started raising maize and tobacco on large commercial farms and moving to towns and cities for work and business opportunities. The Sabaots enjoyed a reputation as fierce, skilled warriors who regularly raided the neighboring Ma-sais,* Luos,* and Gusiis* for cattle. The arrival of British* military force in the region in 1905 ended those raids. The Sabaot population today exceeds 75,000 people.

SABE. The Sabes are one of the main subgroups of the Yoruba* people. Most Sabes can be found today in eastern Benin and across the border in Oyo State in Nigeria.

SADAMA. The Sadama (Sidama, Sidamo) people live in southwest Ethiopia, north of Lake Abaya. Their homeland is a trapezoidal-shaped region bounded by Lake Awasa, Lake Abaya, the upper reaches of the Loghita River, and the Billate River. They are a Cushitic-speaking people, whose ethnic ancestors were closely related to the Oromo*-speaking Gujis* and Borans.* More specifically, their language is part of the Highland Eastern Cushitic group. Group mythology holds that their ancestors migrated southward from the Dawa River region be-ginning in the sixteenth century. In that expansion, the Sadama gradually drove the pastoral Guji people to the south and east. They also divided into two groups themselves, based on the lineage of their original ancestors. The Yamarico claim to be the descendants of a man named Bushe. The Aleta, who claim to be the descendants of Maldea, live south of the Gidabo River.

The Sadama homeland is drained by the Dawa, Ganale, Gidabo, and Billate rivers and consists of a long plateau approximately sixty miles long and, at its widest, approximately thirty miles wide. In the lowlands near the lake, the Sa-dama graze animals and raise small amounts of maize and millet. On the lush plateau, where the soil is excellent, they produce large quantities of maize and ensete. In the wet highlands, they also graze cattle and raise ensete, wheat, barley, and teff. The Sadama are surrounded to the north by the Arssis,* on the west by the Wolaytas (Walamo), on the south by the Guji and Darasas,* and on the east by the Jamjams, who are also known as the Northern Guji. By the late 1980s, demographers estimated the Sadama population at approximately 1,450,000 people.

The Sadama are divided into a variety of subgroups, in addition to the Yamarico and the Aleta. Most of these subgroups are based on regional location as well as religion. For example, approximately 10 percent of Sadamas are Muslims, but the Tamboro, Garo, Alaba, and Hidiya subgroups are primarily Muslim. Other Sadama subgroups include the Gimira-Majis, Ometos, Sidamos, Kambattas, and Janjeros. The rest of the Sadama are loyal either to their indigenous tribal religion, which emphasizes a single creator deity known as Magano and ancestor worship, or to various Christian sects. In recent years, the Wando Magano movement among the Sadama has fused Muslim, Christian, and animistic beliefs into a new syncretic faith that seems to gain adherents from those Sadama most disrupted by the integration of their economy and polity into the larger Ethiopian society.

The Sadama live in villages of about twenty-five families, where they cultivate their gardens. Usually, these are located near forested areas where they can gather sufficient wood for fuel. These villages are also organized into larger neighborhood groups, which cooperatively take care of home construction, irrigation maintenance, and political issues. The Sadama are also members of powerful patriclan systems. Among the Yamaricos, the clans correspond to geographical regions, while the Aleta clans, which expanded piecemeal over the years, occupied a checkerboard pattern of political residence. Unlike the Yamaricos, Aletas will allow members of other clans and even ''strangers'' to live among them. In their relationships with one another, the Sadama have a relatively egalitarian society in which artisans are allowed to cultivate land, even though artisans are not allowed to marry into cultivator clans. The Sadama also own large numbers of slaves, most of whom are of Wolayta descent. Political power among the Sadama is exercised by regional assemblies in which elders, chosen by complex generational class systems, exercise great influence.

REFERENCES: John Hamer. ''Hierarchy, Equality, and Availability of Land Resources: An Example from Two Ethiopian Ensete Producers.'' *Ethnology* 25 (July 1986): 215–28; John Hamer and Irene Hamer. ''Impact of a Cash Economy on Complementary Gender Relations Among the Sadama of Ethiopia.'' *Anthropological Quarterly* 67 (October 1993): 187–202.

SADAMO. *See* SADAMA.

SAFEN. The Safen are a subgroup of the Cangin,* themselves a subdivision of the Serer* peoples of Senegal. See SERER.

SAFWA. The Safwa are an ethnic group of 150,000 people who live east of Mbeyain, Tanzania. Until 1900, the Safwas were essentially a foraging people who did not farm or use fire. Today, they are an impoverished agricultural people who are divided into a number of smaller chiefdoms. Some ethnologists include the Gurukas, Mbwilas, and Songwes in the Safwa cluster.

REFERENCE: Laura Kurtz. *Historical Dictionary of Tanzania.* 1978.

SAGARA. The Sagaras (Saghala) are one of the individual groups in the Zaramo* cluster of the Northeast Bantu*-speaking people of East Africa. They live in the coastal lowlands of Tanzania where most of them work as hoe farmers, producing maize, sorghum, and rice, and raising sheep, goats, and poultry. During the nineteenth century, the Sagaras were victimized by the East African slave trade. In response, they built fortified villages protected by stockades. In the twentieth century, those settlement patterns gave way to the homestead system in which rural Sagaras scattered out more widely. They live primarily in mud-and-wattle homes characterized by high, thatched, cone-shaped roofs; those thatched roofs are giving way today to tin roofs. The vast majority of the Sagaras are Muslims, although they are considered to be only marginally loyal, confining their religious observances to fasting at Ramadan, taking on Arab* names, and wearing the white skull cap. They observe a matrilineal descent system. Their population today exceeds 80,000 people. Since the introduction of sisal plantations in the Usagara region, the Sagaras have increasingly come under outside influences.

Since the mid-1970s, the Sagaras have been affected dramatically by the Tanzanian government's *ujamaa* policy, which is designed to gather rural people out of their scattered homestead settlements into more concentrated villages where public education and public health campaigns can be more effective. Rates of malaria and schistosomiasis are high among the Sagaras, and only improved public health programs can alleviate the crisis. The Sagara people have also been affected in recent years by the East African drought of the late 1980s and early 1990s and by the threat of the human immunodeficiency virus (HIV) and the disease of AIDS.

REFERENCE: L. W. Swantz. *Ritual and Symbol in Transitional Zaramo Society.* 1970.

SAGHALA. *See* SAGARA.

SAGO. *See* DIRYA.

SAHAFATRA. The Sahafatras are a subgroup of the Antaisaka* peoples of the east coast of Madagascar.

SAHARAWI. The term "Saharawi" has been used as a collective reference to all of the peoples living in the Atlantic coastal deserts of what is today Western Sahara in southern Morocco.

REFERENCE: Tony Hodges. *Historical Dictionary of Western Sahara.* 1982.

SAHO. The Saho are a cluster of Ethiopian peoples closely related to one another by speaking one of the Saho languages, which are eastern Cushitic in origin. Most of them live in the coastal regions of Tegray and Eritrea. Their population today is approximately 170,000 people, about 80 percent of whom are Muslims. The major subgroups of the Saho people are the Erobs (who are

Christians), the Asawerda, and the Mini Fere. Most of the Sahos are nomadic and semi-nomadic pastoralists.
REFERENCES: Harold D. Nelson et al. *Ethiopia: A Country Study.* 1980; Chris Prouty and Eugene Rosenfeld. *Historical Dictionary of Ethiopia and Eritrea.* 1994.

SAHWI. *See* SEFWI.

SAKA. *See* ODUAL.

SAKA. The Sakas are a Bantu*-speaking people who live in the forests of the Kasai Orientale region of central Zaire. Most of them are small farmers who raise cassava, bananas, and kola nuts. In recent years, the Sakas have been increasingly touched by Zaire's commercial economy, with the result that more and more Sakas are growing cash crops or leaving the farms for work in towns and cities.
REFERENCE: Irving Kaplan et al. *Zaire: A Country Study.* 1978.

SAKAKUYE. *See* SAKUYE.

SAKALAVA. The Sakalavas are an ethnic group living today in Madagascar. They are concentrated along the west coast of the island, from Nosy Be to Tulear. In the central part of that region, the Sakalavas have been affected by Islam through contact with immigrants from the Comoros islands. The Sakalava population today exceeds 600,000 people. They are divided, according to some ethnologists, into the following ethnic groups: Antankaranas,* Antiboinas, Antifiherenas, Antimailakas, Antimarakas, Antimenas, Antimilanjas, and Vezus. Most Sakalavas are semi-nomadic pastoralists who also practice rudimentary forms of agriculture.
REFERENCES: Maureen Covell. *Madagascar: Politics, Economics and Society.* 1987; Gillian Feeley-Harnik. "Divine Kingship and the Meaning of History Among the Sakalava of Madagascar." *Man* 13 (September 1978): 402–16.

SAKATA. The Sakata are a Bantu*-speaking people living in south-central Zaire. They are closely related to the Kubas,* Leeles,* Njembes,* and Ngongos.* Ethnologists consider the Sakatas to be a subgroup of the Kongo* peoples. Most of them are small farmers today. Nearly one million people in Zaire are aware of their Sakata identity. Most of them live in the region of southwestern Zaire where the Kasai and Kwango rivers meet.
REFERENCE: Donald G. Morrison et al. *Black Africa: A Comparative Handbook.* 1989.

SAKUYE. The Sakuyes (Sakakuyes) speak a Oromo* language and live in northeastern Kenya, particularly in the region of Dabel. Culturally, they have many affinities with the Gabres.* The Sakuyes have a pastoral economy

that revolves around goats and camels, and their population is approximately 5,000 people. They are being absorbed by neighboring Somali* peoples.
REFERENCE: Bethwell A. Ogot. *Historical Dictionary of Kenya.* 1981.

SALA. The Salas are a Tonga*-speaking people of southern Zambia. They are closely related to the Ilas,* Tongas, Lenjes,* and Totelas.* They live west of Lusaka and number approximately 14,000 people today, most of whom are small farmers.
REFERENCE: John J. Grotpeter. *Historical Dictionary of Zambia.* 1979.

SALAGA. The Salagas are an ethnic group in contemporary Ghana. They are part of the larger Guan* cluster of people and are concentrated in the eastern Gonja area of the Northern Region. The Salagas were once a powerful people who flourished economically from the slave and kola nut trades. Soon after the arrival of the British* in the area in the 1870, the Salagas began to die of epidemic infectious diseases. Today there are approximately 10,000 people who are aware of their Salaga roots.
REFERENCE: Daniel M. McFarland. *Historical Dictionary of Ghana.* 1995.

SALAMAT. The Salamats are a subgroup of the Djoheina,* themselves a large Arab* subgroup in Chad.

SALAMPASO. The Salampaso people live in Zaire, primarily around the conjunction of the Kasai River with the northern frontier of Angola. Thousands of Salampasos also live across the border in Angola. The Salampasos are small farmers and fishermen.
REFERENCE: Irving Kaplan et al. *Zaire: A Country Study.* 1978.

SALE. *See* RUKUBA.

SAMA. *See* CHAMBA.

SAMAALE. *See* SAMALE.

SAMALE. The Samales (Samaales) are one of the two primary lineage groups of the Somali* people of Somalia, Kenya, Djibouti, and Ethiopia. They are primarily nomadic pastoralists who prize their status as warriors. They are of Hamitic origin and constitute 80 percent of the Somali population.

SAMBA. *See* CHAMBA.

SAMBAA. *See* SHAMBAA.

SAMBALA. The Sambalas are a subgroup of the Tetela* people of Zaire. They

are the Tetelas who became closely associated with the Afro-Arabs* and Belgians* there. During the late nineteenth century, the Sambalas occupied the Maniema region of what is today western Kivu. Today, they are considered an elite ethnic group because of their access to education, technology, and economic progress.
REFERENCE: F. Scott Bobb. *Historical Dictionary of Zaire.* 1988.

SAMBLA. *See* SAMOGHO.

SAMBU. The Sambus are one of the traditional, autonomous kingdoms and contemporary ethnic subgroups of the Ovimbundu* people of Angola.

SAMBURU. The Samburus (Burkeneji) live in Kenya, primarily in the Samburu District, which is south and southeast of Lake Turkana. They migrated to Kenya in the company of Masai* people. The Samburus call themselves the Loikops. They practice animal husbandry, raising cattle, goats, sheep, and camels. The Samburu population today is approximately 85,000 people.
REFERENCE: Bethwell A. Ogot. *Historical Dictionary of Kenya.* 1981.

SAMBYU. The Sambyus are a subgroup of the Kavanga* people of Namibia.

SAMIA. The Samias (Lusamio, Samio) are a subgroup of the Luhya* people of Kenya and Uganda. They are a Western Bantu* people who live today north of Lake Victoria on both sides of the Kenyan-Ugandan border.

SAMIO. *See* SAMIA.

SAMO. The Samo are one of the major groups living in northwestern Burkina-Faso; some can also be found across the border in southern Mali. They are a Fringe Mandinka* group whose language is part of the Manding* cluster in the Niger-Congo family. They trace their tribal origins back to the Mali Empire of the thirteenth century. Demographers place the Samo population today at 75,000 people, of whom one-third are Muslims. Most Samos are small farmers.
REFERENCE: Donald R. Wright. "Manding-Speaking Peoples." In Richard V. Weekes, ed. *Muslim Peoples.* 1984.

SAMOGHO. The Samogho (Sambla, Samoro, Don) are one of the major ethnic groups in northwestern Burkina-Faso, between Bobo Dioulasso and Sikasso, as well as across the border in northern Ivory Coast, particularly in the subprefecture of Boundiali. Like other Voltaic peoples of West Africa, they support themselves by herding cattle and by subsistence agriculture, raising manioc, yams, and millet.
REFERENCE: Daniel M. McFarland. *Historical Dictionary of Upper Volta.* 1978.

SAMORO. *See* SAMOGHO.

SAN. The San people—who have also been called Bushmen, Twa, and Sarwa (Basarwa)—were the original inhabitants of South Africa before the arrival of Bantu*-speaking Africans and Europeans in the region. The term "Sarwa" is a Tswana* name for the San people. Culturally and linguistically, the San have much in common with Khoikhois.* Traditionally, the San have been servants to the Tswana. During the eighteenth century, Boer* and British* settlers in South Africa drove both the San and the Khoikhoi into the Kalahari Desert. Some San did not resist and mixed into the Coloured* population of South Africa. Today, there are only about 35,000 pure San left alive. They live around the Kalahari Desert in South Africa, Namibia, and Botswana. Most of them are farmers and cattle raisers, but several thousand still live their traditional hunting and foraging life.
REFERENCES: Jacqueline Solway and Richard B. Lee. "Foragers, Genuine or Spurious? Situating the Kalahari San in History." *Current Anthropology* 31 (April 1990): 109–46; David N. Suggs. "Female Status and Role Transition in the Tswana Life Cycle." *Ethnology* 26 (1987): 107–20; A. Traili. "The Perception of Clicks in !Xoo." *Journal of African Languages and Linguistics* 15 (1994): 161–74.

SANDA. The Sandas are a prominent subgroup of the Temne* people of Sierra Leone.

SANDAWE. The Sandawe live in the region of Usandawe—the Mbulu, Iramba, Singida, and Kondoa districts in the central highlands of Tanzania. Their homeland is semi-arid plateau and flat plain, ranging from 3,000 to 5,000 feet in altutide. The Sandawe population today exceeds 50,000 people. Although the Sandawe have a history of hunting and gathering, the vast majority of them today are settled farmers, with an increasing majority moving to towns and cities looking for wage labor. They predate the arrival of the Bantu* peoples in Tanzania.
REFERENCE: James L. Newman. *The Ecological Basis for Subsistence Change among the Sandawe of Tanzania.* 1970.

SANGA. The Sangas (Sangos, Sanghas, Bosangos) are a Ubangian group who live in the Ubangi River Valley of the Central African Republic. Some can also be found across the river in Zaire and Congo, as well as in the Guéra, Salamat, and Moyen-Chari prefectures of Chad. There are Sangas in southeastern Zaire as well. During the colonial era, the Sanga language was used as a trade language. They are a riverine people known for their skill as canoemen and fishermen. Before the arrival of the French* in the late nineteenth century, the Sangas were commercial traders, moving up and down the tributaries of the

Ubangi River system. Their language gradually became the lingua franca of the entire Ubangi-Shari region, including contiguous areas of Chad and Middle Congo. Today, along with French, Sanga is the official language of the Central African Republic. The Sanga population today is approximately 75,000 people. They are divided into a number of subgroups, including the Bassanga, Mbimus, Bombos, Konanbembes, Besoms, Bondongos, Bondjos, Mondjombos, Bandzas, Baboles, Kabongos, Bonguilis, and Bomitabas.
REFERENCES: Thomas Collelo et al. *Chad: A Country Study.* 1988; Pierre Kalck. *Historical Dictionary of the Central African Republic.* 1992.

SANGA. The Sanga people, not to be confused with the Sangas* of Zaire and the Central African Republic, are one of the Northern Jos peoples of Nigeria. They live in the Lame District of the Bauchi Division of Bauchi State. The Sanga population today is approximately 7,000 people.
REFERENCE: *Language Survey of Nigeria.* 1976.

SANGA. *See* NUMANA.

SANGHA. *See* SANGA.

SANGO. *See* SANGA.

SANGU. The Sangus are an ethnic group living today in Tanzania. In particular, they are concentrated in the Mbeya and Iringa regions north of Lake Malawi. Most Sangus are farmers and cattle raisers. Some ethnologists classify the Porotos* with the Sangus.
REFERENCE: Laura Kurtz. *Historical Dictionary of Tanzania.* 1978.

SANTROFOKI. The Santrofokis are a small ethnic group in Ghana. They are considered to be part of the Central Togo-Volta cluster of peoples in Ghana and Togo. Most Santrofokis support themselves as small farmers, and they are concentrated demographically in the Buem*-Krakye* area of the Volta Region of Ghana. The Santrofoki population there today exceeds 5,000 people.
REFERENCE: Daniel M. McFarland. *Historical Dictionary of Ghana.* 1995.

SANWI. The Sanwis are a subdivision of the Anyi* people of Ivory Coast. They are primarily Christians in their religious persuasion.

SANYE. The Sanyes—also known as Ariangulu, Liangulu, Langulo, Laa, Waat, Waatha, Wasi, and Asi—are a Kenyan ethnic group. Although they were originally a hunting and gathering people of the southern Taru Desert where they hunted elephants, today they are scattered from the mouth of the Tana River to Tanzania along the southern Kenyan coast.
REFERENCE: Bethwell A. Ogot. *Historical Dictionary of Kenya.* 1981.

SAPO. *See* WEE.

SAR. *See* MADJINGAYE and SARA.

SAR. *See* WARJI.

SARA. The Sara (Sar) people of Chad are a cluster of farming and fishing groups living along the Chari and the Logone rivers. Saras can also be found in the northern reaches of the Central African Republic. Over the centuries, a process of ethnogenesis has fused them together into a people whose ethnic identity is both general, as Saras, and local, based on clan loyalties. With a population exceeding one million people, they constitute one-third of the population of Chad. The major Sara subgroups are the Sara proper and the Madjin-gayés,* Djiokos,* Kumras,* Nars,* Goulayes,* Ngamas,* Dayes,* Nois, Mbuns,* Sara-Kabas,* Dindjes,* Mbayes,* Bedjonds,* Gors,* Ngambayes,* Kabas,* Mouroums,* and Dobas. The Madjingayes, Nars, Goulayes, and Nga-mas consider themselves the purest of the Sara subgroups. The Dayes, Nois, and Mbuns assimilated into Sara culture at a much later date. The Sara-Kabas, Mbaye, Bedjonds, Gors, Ngambayes, Kabas, Mouroums, and Dobas have adopted the Sara language in recent years but remain culturally quite different in other ways.

During the past several centuries, the Saras were the object of repeated slave raids by Fulbes* and especially by Arabs,* a fact that explains the current an-imosities between Saras and Arabs in Chad. That animosity also explains the regional dimension of Chadian politics in recent decades, with the Sara-dominated south aligned against the north and east, whose inhabitants tradition-ally viewed the Saras as a subservient people. Although Catholic, Protestant, and Muslim missionaries have made inroads among the Saras, most Saras remain faithful to their own animist religious traditions.
REFERENCES: Mario Azevedo. "Sara Demographic Instability as a Consequence of French Colonial Policy in Chad." Ph.D. dissertation. Duke University. 1976; Samuel Decalo. *Historical Dictionary of Chad.* 1987.

SARACOLE. *See* SONINKÉ

SARACOTE. *See* SONINKÉ.

SARA-KABA. The Sara-Kabas, not to be confused with the Saras* or the Ka-bas,* are the result of a process of assimilation between groups of the two peoples living between Salamat and Bahr Keita on the Chari River in Chad. The Sara-Kaba population today exceeds 100,000 people. They can also be found in such cities as Sarh and Ndjamena. The Sara-Kabas were badly ex-ploited by the French* during the colonial era, being forced to work on the French railroad construction gangs. During the drive for independence, most

Sara-Kabas were ardent anti-French nationalists. The major Sara-Kaba political leader was Jean Charlot Bakouré.
REFERENCE: Samuel Decalo. *Historical Dictionary of Chad.* 1987.

SARAKOLÉ. *See* SONINKÉ.

SARAKOTE. *See* SONINKÉ.

SARAOUA. The Saraouas are a relatively small ethnic group living today in the Moyen-Chari Prefecture in Chad. Their language is part of the larger Chadian cluster of languages that represents a transition between Sara* and Massa.* Most Saraouas are herdsmen and small farmers, raising sorghum, millet, maize, and cotton.
REFERENCE: Thomas Collelo et al. *Chad: A Country Study.* 1988.

SARAXOLE. *See* SONINKÉ.

SARER. *See* SERER.

SARWA. *See* SAN.

SASALA. The Sasala—also known as the Pisala, Isala, Sissala, and Sisala— are a large ethnic group in northern Ghana. Their population today exceeds 100,000 people, most of whom are settled farmers. They are concentrated in the Upper West Region of Ghana and across the border in Burkina-Faso. The Sasalas are closely related to the Kasenas* and Vagalas.* More than half of all Sasalas who live in towns and cities are Muslims, while the vast majority of rural Sasalas retain their indigenous animist faith. In the history of Ghana, Dr. Hilla Limann, president of the Third Republic, has been the most prominent Sasala.
REFERENCES: Bruce Grindal. *Growing Up in Two Worlds: Education and Transition Among the Sisala of Northern Ghana.* 1972; Eugene Mendosa. *The Politics of Divination: A Processural View of Reactions to Illness and Deviance Among the Sisala of Northern Ghana.* 1982; John W. Nunley. ''Sisala Sculpture of Northern Ghana.'' Ph.D. dissertation. University of Washington. 1971.

SASARU-ENWAN-IGWE. The Sasaru-Enwan-Igwe people are a Nigerian ethnic group. They have a current population of approximately 15,000 people and speak an Edo* language. Most of them live in the Akoko-Edo Division of Bendel State.

SATE. *See* KUMBA.

SAUTSAUTA. The Sautsautas are a subgroup of the Bara* cluster of peoples of the plains of Madagascar.

SAYA. The Sayas are an ethnic group living today on the northeastern edge of the Jos Plateau in Plateau State in northwestern Nigeria. They are surrounded ethnically by the Jarawas, Kwankas,* Zaris,* and Ngas.* Most Sayas are subsistence farmers.
REFERENCE: Elizabeth Isichei, ed. *Studies in the History of Plateau State, Nigeria.* 1982.

SEBEI. The Sebei live on the north slope of a giant extinct volcano—Mount Elgon—in Uganda. Some can also be found in the Rift Valley Province of Kenya. They belong to the Kalenjin* language group, which includes the Nandis,* Kipsigis,* and Pokots* of Kenya. They are more distantly related to the Southern Nilotic* peoples who occupy much of the arid high plains extending from the Sudan and Ethiopia to central Tanzania, among whom the best known are the Masai.* The Sebei have a pastoral economy, raising cattle, sheep, goats, and sometimes camels. They are nomadic because their animals must graze. The Sebei consume milk, blood, and wild honey.
REFERENCE: Walter Goldschmidt. *The Sebei: A Study in Adaptation.* 1986.

SEEYA. The Seeyas are a subgroup of the Bassa* people of Liberia. Most Seeyas live in Grand Bassa County, Liberia.

SEFWI. The Sefwi—also known as Sahwi, Sehwi, Encassar, and Inkassa—are a subgroup of the Anyi*-Baule* people, themselves an Akan* group, of Ghana. They were once a dominant people throughout the Western Region of Ghana, north of Aowin and Wassa, but today their influence is much smaller, confined to an area between Wiawso and Bibiani, between the Tano and Ankobra rivers. During the late seventeenth century, they fell under the control of the Denkyiras,* and, after 1717, they were dominated by the Asante.* Asante control did not end until 1887 when European authority replaced them. Today there are three primary Sefwi subgroups: the Sefwi Anwiawso, the Sefwi Bekwai, and the Wiawso. The Sefwi population today is approximately 200,000 people.
REFERENCE: Daniel M. McFarland. *Historical Dictionary of Ghana.* 1995.

SEFWI ANWIAWSO. The Sefwi Anwiawso are one of the major subgroups of the Sefwi* people of Ghana.

SEFWI BEKWAI. The Sefwi Bekwais are one of the major subgroups of the Sefwi* people of Ghana.

SEGEJU. The Segeju people came from Kenya and settled in northeastern

Tanzania. Tradition has it that a Segeju war party from Kenya was cut off by the flooding of the Umba River. The war party consisted only of men, who married local Digo* and Shiraz* women. Today, they are a patriarchal people who make their living as farmers. They speak a Swahili* language. Their current population is approximately 25,000 people.

REFERENCE: Laura Kurtz. *Historical Dictionary of Tanzania.* 1978.

SEHWI. *See* SEFWI.

SÉKÉ. The Sékés, known also as the Shékianis and Boulous, are an ethnic group living today on the northern Atlantic coast of Gabon, just south of Rio Muni, as well as across the border in Equatorial Guinea and Cameroon. Although there are only a few thousand people left who are even aware of their Séké roots, they were once a highly influential, commercial people. Their own traditions place their origins on the upper Ivindo River in Cameroon, but they were driven south and west by Bakélé* aggression. By the late fourteenth century, Sékés were living along the Rio Muni, along the Noya and upper Temboni rivers, and on the Monday Bay estuary. They were trading ivory, redwood, ebony, and gum copal with the Portuguese* by the end of the century. By the 1760s, many Sékés were heavily involved in the slave trade as middlemen between interior ethnic groups and Europeans. In the nineteenth century, Pahouin* expansion drove many Sékés east into the Gabonese interior. On December 2, 1846, Séké chiefs signed treaties recognizing French* sovereignty. Today, the few remaining Sékés work as small farmers or as laborers and craftsmen in Libreville and Lambaréné. The Sékés are divided into two subgroups: the Séké proper and the Bengas.*

REFERENCES: David E. Gardinier. *Historical Dictionary of Gabon.* 1994; Harold D. Nelson et al. *Area Handbook for the United Republic of Cameroon.* 1974.

SELALKA. The Selalkas are a subgroup of the Ahel Brahim Ou Daoud* people, who are part of the Reguibat* cluster of peoples in Western Sahara. Traditionally, the Selalkas were extremely influential in the Reguibat ech-Charg, presiding over the group's war council. Their population today is approximately 1,200 people, most of whom live in El-Ayoun. The others still pursue a nomadic lifestyle west of Tifarity near the Mauritanian border.

SELE. The Seles are one of the traditional, autonomous kingdoms and contemporary ethnic subgroups of the Ovimbundu* people of Angola.

SELEIM. *See* BAGGARA.

SELEMO. *See* ITSEKIRI.

SELYA. The Selyas are a Tanzanian ethnic group whom some ethnologists classify with the Nyakyusa* cluster of peoples.

SENA. The Sena are an ethnic group living in the far southern tip of Malawi and across the border in Mozambique. Their expansion into southern Malawi is a twentieth-century phenomenon, a migration that began after World War I. Most Senas are small farmers and laborers, but they are known also for their belief in education and their activities in business and politics. They constitute the dominant group in the Malawian city of Nsanje. The Sena population in Malawi and Mozambique today exceeds 1.5 million people.
REFERENCES: Cynthia H. Crosby. *Historical Dictionary of Malawi.* 1980; Harold D. Nelson et al. *Area Handbook for Malawi.* 1975.

SENDE. The Sende people are part of the larger cluster of Ovimbundu* peoples of Angola.

SENE. *See* SENUFO.

SENEFO. *See* SENUFO.

SENEGAMBIAN. The term ''Senegambian'' is often used to describe the non-Fulbe* and non-Mandinka* peoples of the Guinea Littoral in West Africa. They are of Niger-Congo stock and include such groups as the Balantes,* Bañuns,* Beafadas,* Bijagos,* Jolas,* Nalus,* Papeis,* Drames, Manjacos,* Serers,* and Wolofs.*
REFERENCE: Richard Lobban and Marilyn Halter. *Historical Dictionary of the Republic of Cape Verde.* 1988.

SENFI. The Senfis are one of the primary subgroups of the Asante* people of Ghana.

SENGA. The Sengas are an ethnic group living today in the Luangwa Valley of eastern Zambia. They speak a Tumbuka* language and have a population of approximately 50,000 people. They originated in the Katanga region of Zaire nearly three centuries ago. Over the years, the Sengas were frequently subject to Arab* slave raids. The Sengas use a patrilineal descent system.
REFERENCE: John J. Grotpeter. *Historical Dictionary of Zambia.* 1979.

SENGELE. The Sengeles are an ethnic group who live west of Lake Mai-Ndombe in the Bandundu Region of Zaire. Ethnologists classify them as part of the Mongo* language family, but they are quite distinct from the Mongo people, primarily because of their complex, hierarchical social structure.
REFERENCE: F. Scott Bobb. *Historical Dictionary of Zaire.* 1988.

SENOUFO. *See* SENUFO.

SENUFO. The Senufos (Senefo, Sene, Senoufo, Syénambélé, Siena, and Bamana) are a large ethnic group of more than three million people living in Ivory Coast, Mali, and Burkina-Faso. Their geographical homeland is bounded by the Bagoe River to the west, the Bani River to the north, and the Black Volta River to the east; geographers refer to the region as the Middle Volta. The Senufos can be divided into three large subdivisions. The northern Senufo, known as the Supide or the Kenedougou, number approximately 750,000 people. They originated historically in the area around Odienne and migrated northward, intermarrying with the Samoghos,* Ganas, and Miniankas.* By the end of the nineteenth century, they constituted the Kingdom of Kenedougou, led by Tieba Traore. The Supide resisted Muslim missionaries and traders, and today they are the least Islamicized of the Senufo groups. The central Senufo are a conglomeration of Samoghos, Lobis,* Turkas,* Toussians, and Bobo*-Julas* and number approximately 45,000 people. The southern Senufos, whose population exceeds two million people, allowed Jula traders to settle among them in the eighteenth century. Those traders brought Islam to the southern Senufos, of whom approximately 400,000 are Muslims today. Most Senufos are subsistence farmers.

Since World War II, however, dramatic changes have come to Senufo life. The Senufo region has become increasingly integrated into the larger economy, which has increased the importance of cash and commercialized many Senufo farmers. Commercialization has tended to disrupt the traditional communal property values, as has urbanization. The rise of the commercial economy, the migration to cities, and the efforts of political leaders in Mali, Burkina-Faso, and Ivory Coast to create national identities have all placed pressures on more narrow tribal identities and increased the power of Islam. Conversion to Islam is accelerating rapidly.

REFERENCES: Robert Goldwater. *Senufo Sculpture from West Africa.* 1964; Till Forster. "Senufo Masking and the Art of Poro." *African Arts* 26 (January 1993): 30–39; LeVell Holmes. "Senufo." In Richard V. Weekes, ed. *Muslim Peoples.* 1984; Dolores Richter. "Further Considerations of Caste in West Africa: The Senufo." *Africa* 50 (1980): 37–54.

SENYA. The Senyas are a small ethnic group in Ghana. They are classified as part of the Guan* cluster of peoples, and they live along the Ghanaian coast in the Gomoa District, primarily at Senya Beraku. The Senyas make their living as farmers and fishermen.

REFERENCE: Daniel M. McFarland. *Historical Dictionary of Ghana.* 1995.

SERACULEH. *See* SONINKÉ.

SERAHENA. The Serahenas are a subgroup of the Oulad Delim* people of Western Sahara in what is today Morocco.

SERAHULI. *See* SONINKÉ.

SERAKHULLE. *See* SONINKÉ.

SERE. The Seres are part of the larger cluster of Azandé* peoples in Sudan.

SERER. The Serer (Serère, Sarer, Kegueme) are an ethnic group of more than one million people. The vast majority of them live in compact villages south and west of Dakar, Senegal. They are, with 19 percent of the total population, the second-largest ethnic group in Senegal. There are several Serer villages in Gambia, and they can also be found in Guinea-Bissau. Their language—closely related to Wolof,* Fulbe,* and Temne*—is part of the West Atlantic subgroup of the Niger-Congo family. They practice an intensive form of agriculture that revolves around the production of millet and peanuts in a three-year cycle (one year lying fallow) with cattle providing the fertilizer. The Serer are divided into two primary subgroups. The smaller of the subgroups, known as the Cangin,* number approximately 15,000 people and are themselves divided into the Safen, Ndut, and Non peoples. They are concentrated just outside the urban triangle of Dakar, Thies, and Rufisque. All of the Cangin groups are being rapidly assimilated by the surrounding Wolofs. The Serer proper exceed one million people, and they are subdivided into a number of smaller groups. The Ndyegem are concentrated in the Mbuur region; the Nyominka are fishermen on the Saalum estuary; and the Gelowar* are responsible for the traditional kingdoms in Siin and Saalum.

During the nineteenth century, the Serer violently resisted the expansion of Islam, which was brought to them by the Wolof. In 1861, the Serer found themselves the object of a Muslim *jihad* led by Ma Ba Jaxoo, a Manding* cleric. This warfare continued until the French* conquest of Senegal in 1887. But the Islamic pressures, combined with French imperialism and the spread of a cash economy, disrupted traditional Serer society. Islamic conversion rates accelerated, and, by World War I, approximately 40 percent of the Serer were Muslims. Rapid urbanization, better educational systems, and improved transportation infrastructures all strengthened Islam in Senegal. By the early 1990s, approximately 85 percent of all Serer were Muslims.

REFERENCES: Martin A. Klein. *Islam and Imperialism in Senegal.* 1968; Martin A. Klein. ''Serer.'' In Richard V. Weekes, ed. *Muslim Peoples.* 1984; W. J. Pichl. *The Cangin Group: A Language Group in Northern Senegal.* 1966.

SERÈRE. *See* SERER.

SEWA-MENDE. The Sewa-Mende are one of the three major subgroups of the Mendé.* They live in the forests of south-central Sierra Leone.

SEWEIN. The Seweins are a subgroup of the Bassa* people of Liberia. Most Seweins live in Grand Bassa County, Liberia.

SHA. The Sha people are one of Nigeria's many ethnic groups. Many ethnologists consider them to be a subgroup of the Ron* people. They live in the Monguna District of the Pankshin Division of Plateau State.
REFERENCE: *Language Survey of Nigeria.* 1976.

SHABALALA. The Shabalalas are one of the clans of the Emakhandzambili,* who themselves are one of the three major subgroups of the Swazi* people of Swaziland.

SHABANGU. The Shabangus are one of the clans of the Emakhandzambili,* who themselves are one of the three major subgroups of the Swazi* people of Swaziland.

SHAGA. The Shagas are a subgroup of the Kgalagadi* people of Botswana.

SHAGAU. *See* SHAGAWU.

SHAGAWU. The Shagawu people, also identified as the Nafunfias and Malenis, are a Chadic-speaking people of Nigeria. They live today in the Monguna District of the Pankshin Division of Plateau State.
REFERENCE: *Language Survey of Nigeria.* 1976.

SHAI. The Shais (Siade) are one of the subgroups of the Adangbe* peoples of the Accra Plain and coastal inselbergs of southeastern Ghana. Most of them make their living as small farmers. They are closely related to the Adas* and Krobous.* The Shai population today is approximately 45,000 people.

SHAIAB. The Shaiab are a small, surviving subgroup of the larger group of Beja* peoples in Sudan. They were originally not part of the Beja group, but, in the nineteenth and twentieth centuries, they gradually fell within a Beja cultural orbit. They are Sunni Muslims in their religious orientation.

SHAINI. *See* SHANI.

SHAKÉ. The Shakés are a Bakota*-speaking people who today live along the upper Ogooué River upriver from Booué, along the road from Booué to Lalara, and north of Lastourville in Gabon. They are closely related to the neigh-

boring Dambomo people. The Shamai, who are sometimes considered a Shaké subgroup, live north of Okondja in Haut-Ogooué Province. Oral traditions among the Shaké, Dambomo, and Shamai recite their departure from the upper Ivindo River region in Gabon and Cameroon because of Poupou's War. By the early nineteenth century, they had divided into three peoples and were living near Mt. Ngouadi in the Okondja District. Late in the 1800s, they drove the Chiwas* out of the Ogooué River Valley east of Booué. The Shakés, Dambomos, and Shamais are known for their iron and copper works. They established close economic relations with the French* in the early twentieth century and became fully integrated into the commercial economy.
REFERENCES: David E. Gardinier. *Historical Dictionary of Gabon.* 1994.

SHALKOTA. The Shalkotas are a subgroup of the Meidobs* of Sudan.

SHALL-ZWALL. The Shall-Zwalls are one of the many ethnic groups living in the Lere District of the Bauchi Division of Bauchi State in Nigeria. They speak an Eastern Plateau language of the Benue-Congo family.
REFERENCE: *Language Survey of Nigeria.* 1976.

SHAMAI. *See* SHAKÉ.

SHAMBAA. The term "Shambaa" (Shambala, Sambaa) refers to a cluster of Northeastern Bantu*-speaking people of Tanzania. The cluster includes the Shambala, Pare,* and Bondei* subgroups. Two-thirds of the people in the Shambaa cluster are Muslims, although they are considered to be only marginally loyal, confining their religious observances to fasting at Ramadan, taking on Arab* names, and wearing the white skullcaps. They observe a patrilineal descent system. They live in the coastal lowlands of Tanzania where most of them work as hoe farmers, producing maize, sorghum, and rice, and raising sheep, goats, and poultry. During the nineteenth century, the Shambaas were victimized by the East African slave trade; in response, they built fortified villages protected by stockades. In the twentieth century, those settlement patterns gave way to the homestead system in which rural Shambaas scattered out more widely. They live in mud-and-wattle homes characterized by high, thatched, cone-shaped roofs; those thatched roofs are now giving way to tin roofs. Their population today is approximately 400,000 people.
REFERENCES: S. T. Feierman. *The Shambaa Kingdom.* 1962; L. W. Swantz. *Ritual and Symbol in Transitional Zaramo Society.* 1970; Edgar V. Winans. *Shambala: The Constitution of a Traditional State.* 1962.

SHAMBALA. *See* SHAMBAA.

SHAMBAYE. *See* SHAKÉ.

SHANGA. *See* SHANGAWA.

SHANGAAN. The Shangaan peoples, also known as the Shanganas or Changane, are an ethnic group living today primarily in Mozambique. They are concentrated in the far southern tip of the country, with some of them across the
border in Swaziland and South Africa. The Shangaans are part of the larger
Tonga* cluster of peoples. Most of them today are subsistence farmers.
REFERENCE: Harold D. Nelson et al. *Mozambique: A Country Study.* 1984.

SHANGAMA. The Shangamas are an ethnic group in southern Ethiopia. Most
of them are small farmers who also raise livestock.
REFERENCE: M. L. Bender, J. D. Bowen, R. L. Cooper, and C. A. Ferguson, eds.
Language in Ethiopia. 1976.

SHANGANA. The Shanganas are a subgroup of the Tonga* people. Historically, they intermarried with the Nguni* during the Nguni invasions of Mozambique. Most Shanganas live in Bilene, Magude, Sabie, Chibuto, and Guija
in Mozambique.

SHANGAWA. The Shangawas (Shangas, Shongas, Kyengas, Kengas, and
Tyengas) are an ethnic group of approximately 40,000 people living on the
banks and islands of the Niger River near the city of Shanga in northwestern
Nigeria. They are surrounded by Hausas,* who tend to control political and
economic life. Shangawas constitute 85 percent of the population in the Shanga
District, part of the Yauri Division in Sokoto State. They speak Kengawa,* a
language in the Niger-Benue division of the Niger-Congo linguistic family. At
one time, the Shangawas were a subgroup of the Kengawas. Both the Kengawas
and Shangawas claim descent from the legendary Kisra, who opposed Islam
until the Prophet Mohammed defeated him in battle. The Kengawas and Shangawas were part of the Songhai* Empire by the thirteenth century and remained
so until the Moroccan invasions of the sixteenth century. During those invasions,
the Shangawas relocated to Yauri, and, during the slave raids of the nineteenth
century, they found refuge on the islands of the Niger River. The Shangawas
make their living as farmers, raising vegetables on the river banks and millet
and guinea corn in the highlands; they also fish and are known for their commercial skills. Nearly half of all Shangawas are Sunni Muslims of the Maliki
school. Traditional Shangawa religion, which revolves around the sacrifice of
black animals—oxen, goats, or chickens—is tied to the Kisra legend. Traditional
Shangawas believe that such major spirits as Gadakassa, Berkassa, and Gwar-
aswa control the key events in people's lives.
REFERENCES: Jonathan Jeness. *Fishermen of the Kainji Basin.* 1970; Frank Salamone.
Gods and Goods in Africa. 1974; Frank Salamone. "Shangawa." In Richard V. Weekes,
ed. *Muslim Peoples.* 1984.

SHANGWA. The Shangwas (Vashangwe, Shankwe, Bashangwe) are a sub-group of the Korekores,* who constitute the ''Northern Shona''* cluster of peoples in Zimbabwe. They live in the Bumi River area southeast of central Lake Kariba.

SHANI. The Shanis (Shenis, Shainis, Asennizes) live today in the Lere District of the Saminaka Division of Kaduna State in Nigeria. Their population there is fewer than 1,000 people.
REFERENCE: *Language Survey of Nigeria.* 1976.

SHANJO. The Shanjo peoples are located today in far southwestern Zambia and across the border in northern Namibia and southeastern Angola. They are a subgroup of the Tongas.*

SHANKWE. *See* SHANGWA.

SHASHI. The Shashis are a Tanzanian ethnic group whom some ethnologists classify with the Sukuma* cluster of peoples. Their population today exceeds 50,000 people.

SHAVASHA. The Shavashas are a subgroup of the Zezuru* peoples, who are part of the Shona* cluster in Zimbabwe.

SHAYQIYA. The Shayqiya (Shaiqiya) are a major Arab* group in the Sudan. Some ethnologists believe that they are closely related to the Jaaliyins.* Most Shayqiyas live in the Nile River Valley south of Dongola. Many of them herd camels for a living. There is also a group of Shayqiyas who have mixed with Nubians.*
REFERENCE: Carolyn Fluehr-Lobban, Richard A. Lobban, Jr., and John Obert Voll. *Historical Dictionary of Sudan.* 1992.

SHEBELLE. The Shebelles are a small ethnic group living in Somalia. They make their living as farmers and nomadic hunters and are concentrated in the Shebelle River area. The Shebelles speak a Bantu* language and were already living in the region before the Somali* migrations.
REFERENCE: Margaret Castagno. *Historical Dictionary of Somalia.* 1975.

SHEDE. *See* GUDE.

SHÉKIANI. *See* SÉKÉ.

SHEKIRI. *See* ITSEKIRI.

SHEKO. The Shekos are an ethnic group of approximately 28,000 people who

live today in southern Ethiopia. They speak an Omotic* language and make their living as small farmers.
REFERENCE: M. L. Bender, J. D. Bowen, R. L. Cooper, and C. A. Ferguson, eds. *Language in Ethiopia.* 1976.

SHENI. *See* SHANI.

SHERBRO. The Sherbros are an ethnic group of approximately 140,000 people living in Sierra Leone. About 40 percent of the Sherbros are Muslims. They are very closely related to the Bulloms,* another Sierra Leone ethnic group. Portuguese* explorers first described the Bulloms in 1507. By the seventeenth century, the Temne* people had expanded to the coast, cutting the Bulloms into two geographical groups. The northern Bulloms retained the name Bullom but began to assimilate into the surrounding Temne and Soso* groups. The southern Bulloms came to be known as the Sherbros. Today, the Sherbros are located on the Atlantic coast, between the Sierra Leone Peninsula and the Bum River estuary, primarily in the Bonhe and Moyamba districts. The Sherbro chiefdoms extend from twenty to thirty miles into the interior. In recent decades, the Sherbros have been increasingly absorbed by the Mendés.* Their economy revolves around fishing and the production of rice, cassava, and palm oil. The Krim* are considered to be a subgroup of the Sherbros.
REFERENCES: Cyril P. Foray. *Historical Dictionary of Sierra Leone.* 1977; Irving Kaplan et al. *Area Handbook of Sierra Leone.* 1976.

SHI. The Shis are a Zairean people. They live in the highlands of the Kivu Region, between Lake Tanganyika and Lake Kivu. They speak a Bantu* language. A large concentration of the Shis can be found near Bukavu. Ethnologists consider them to be part of the Kivu* cluster of peoples. In the highlands, where they live more than 4,000 feet above sea level, the Shi people farm and raise cattle for milk and meat. During the last thirty years, the Shis have often engaged in violent struggles for power with the Kusu* people, who live to the west.
REFERENCES: F. Scott Bobb. *Historical Dictionary of Zaire.* 1988; Irving Kaplan et al. *Zaire: A Country Study.* 1978.

SHIDLE. The Shidles are a small ethnic group living in Somalia. They make their living as farmers and nomadic hunters and are concentrated in the Shebelle River area, where they maintain close political alliances with the Mobilen clan of the Hawiye.* The Shidles speak a Bantu* language and were already living in the region before the Somali* migrations.
REFERENCE: Margaret Castagno. *Historical Dictionary of Somalia.* 1975.

SHIKONGO. The Shikongos (Bashikongo) are part of the larger Kongo* cluster of peoples living today in northwestern Angola and southeastern Zaire.

Their population exceeds 50,000 people, and they speak a Bantu* language. Because of their location near the coast, the Shikongos had the most sustained contact with the Portuguese* during the colonial period, but they still participated in the nationalistic rebellion against Portuguese rule. Most Shikongos are farmers today.
REFERENCE: Thomas Collelo et al. *Angola: A Country Study.* 1989.

SHILA. The Shilas speak a Bemba* language and live in the Luapulu River Valley and along the shores of Lake Mweru in Zambia. They make their living as fishermen. The contemporary Shila population is approximately 30,000 people.
REFERENCE: John J. Grotpeter. *Historical Dictionary of Zambia.* 1979.

SHILHA. The Shilhas are a subgroup of the Shluh* people, themselves a subgroup of the Berbers* in Morocco.

SHILLUK. The Shilluks are considered to be a pre-Nilotic* people in the Sudan. They call themselves the Collo. Before the Nilotic migration, the Shilluks had settled between the White and Blue Nile rivers, primarily on the west bank of the Bahr-al-Jabal, just north of the point at which it becomes the White Nile. Included in the large Shilluk cluster, according to many ethnologists, are the Anuaks,* Bareas,* Bertis,* Gules,* Hamajs,* Ingessanas,* and Mebans.* They speak a Semitic language and maintain matrilineal elements in their social structures. The Shilluks are sedentary farmers. They have a highly centralized political and religious structure. The Shilluks are divided into the following subgroups: the Anuaks who live on the Sobat River; the Jurs,* who live southwest of the Bahr-al-Jabal River; the Acolis,* who are northeast of Lake Albert; and the Jaluos in Uganda and Kenya.
REFERENCES: A. Arens. ''The Divine Kingship of the Shilluk: A Contemporary Reevaluation.'' *Ethnos* 44 (1979): 167–81; Carolyn Fluehr-Lobban, Richard A. Lobban, Jr., and John Obert Voll. *Historical Dictionary of Sudan.* 1992.

SHIMBA. The Shimbas, or Simbas, are a small ethnic group living today in the heavy forests of the lower Offoué River and the upper Ikoyi River in N'Gounié Province of Gabon. They speak an Okandé* language. Most Shimbas are small farmers.
REFERENCE: David E. Gardinier. *Historical Dictionary of Gabon.* 1994.

SHINASHA. The Shinashas are a tiny ethnic group living today in southern Ethiopia. Their language is part of the larger Omotic* group of languages, and they make their living as small farmers. The number of people who identify themselves as Shinashas today is approximately 5,000.
REFERENCE: M. L. Bender, J. D. Bowen, R. L. Cooper, and C. A. Ferguson, eds. *Language in Ethiopia.* 1976.

SHINJE. The Shinjes are part of the larger Mbundu* cluster of peoples of Angola.

SHIP. *See* CHIP.

SHIRA. *See* ESHIRA.

SHIRAZI. The Shirazis (Mbwera) are a Swahili*-speaking people of Tanzania. Their current population exceeds 280,000 people, all of whom are Muslims. They occupy the islands off the northeastern coast of the country. The Shirazis descend from Persian traders who arrived in the region in the thirteenth century and mixed with Africans and Arabs.* There are three Shirazi subgroups—the Hadimu,* Tumbatu, and Pemba. Most Shirazis are peasant farmers and traders.
REFERENCE: Laura Kurtz. *Historical Dictionary of Tanzania.* 1978.

SHISA. The Shisas are a subgroup of the Luhya* people of Kenya and Uganda. They are a Western Bantu* people who live today north of Lake Victoria on both sides of the Kenyan-Ugandan border.

SHLUH. The Shluhs are one of the larger Berber* groups in Morocco today. Because of their location in the western High Atlas and Sous regions, they are the southernmost of the Berber peoples in Morocco. They speak the Tashilhait language, which has three dialects: Shilha, Susi, and Drawa. Most Shluhs are farmers, although they own herds that are maintained by hired shepherds.

SHOMOH. *See* CHOMO-KARIM.

SHOMONG. *See* CHOMO-KARIM.

SHONA. The Shonas (Karanga, Vashona, Mashona, Chona) are a composite ethnic group and include several groups clustered together on the basis of cultural and linguistic associations. Historically, the Shona groups were attacked by the Ndebeles* in the 1830s and 1840s, which resulted in the loss of their lands and cattle herds. They found themselves paying tribute to the Ndebeles. In 1896–1897, the Shonas joined the Ndebeles in a bloody and ultimately unsuccessful war against the British* colonial administration. Their traditional economy is based on cattle and the agricultural production of millet, maize, pumpkins, and yams.

Their population today exceeds five million people in Zimbabwe, Botswana, and Mozambique; Shonas can also be found in Zambia. Until recently, when more centralized economic and political institutions began to affect Shona life, they did not identify themselves as Shonas. Instead, they identified themselves

as members of various subgroups. It is increasingly common today, however, for them to see themselves as generically Shona, with a subgroup identification as well. The Shona ethnic cluster includes 75 percent of the ethnic black Africans in the country of Zimbabwe. All of the Shona groups are patrilineal, with property and political authority resting in males who head extended family systems. The major Shona subgroups include the Kalangas,* Karangas,* Korekores,* Zezurus,* Abarues,* Ndaus,* Tembos,* Nyatanzas, Bandas,* Marungas, Mwanyas, Nyampisis, Chirumbas,* Makates, Mucatus, Chirwares,* Chilendjes, Manyicas (Manhica*), Mavondes, Choas,* and Atewes.*
REFERENCES: Dominique Meekers. ''The Noble Roora: The Marriage Practices of the Shona of Zimbabwe.'' *Ethnology* 32 (Winter 1993): 35–54; R. Kent Rasmussen. *Historical Dictionary of Zimbabwe.* 1990.

SHONGA. *See* SHANGAWA.

SHONGWE. The Shongwes are one of the clans of the Emakhandzambili,* who themselves are one of the three major subgroups of the Swazi* people of Swaziland.

SHOPE. The Shope (Chope, Chopi-Bitonga, Chopi) people are a group of more than 600,000 people who live in the Muchopes, Inharrime, Zavala, and Homoine regions of southern Mozambique. They are considered to be among the earliest inhabitants of the region. They identify their original ancestors as Nkumbe and Vilanculu Mrori. There are two major Shope subgroups, the Valenges and the Bitongas. Most Shopes are subsistence farmers. As an ethnic group, the Shopes first emerged in the eighteenth century from a mixture of a number of other peoples.
REFERENCES: Mario Azevedo. *Historical Dictionary of Mozambique.* 1991; Harold D. Nelson et al. *Mozambique: A Country Study.* 1984.

SHUBI. *See* SUBI.

SHUKRIYA. The Shukriyas are a subgroup of the Juhayna* Arabs* of the Sudan. They are a camel-herding people who live in the Blue Nile and Kassala regions.

SIA. The Sia (Sya) are considered a Fringe Mandinka* group who trace their tribal origins back to the Mali Empire of the thirteenth century. Today they live as pastoral nomads in Mali and Burkina-Faso. West African demographers estimate the Sia population today at approximately 150,000 people. Nearly two-thirds of them are Muslims. In the region around Bobo Dioulasso in Burkina-Faso, the Sia are mixing with the Bobos.* Most Sia raise cattle, millet, corn, and sorghum for a living.

REFERENCE: Donald R. Wright. "Manding-Speaking Peoples." In Richard V. Weekes, ed. *Muslim Peoples.* 1984.

SIADE. *See* SHAI.

SIDAMO. The Sidamo are one of the subgroups of the Sadama* people of southwestern Ethiopia.

SIENA. *See* SENUFO.

SIFUNDZA. The Sifundzas are one of the clans of the Emakhandzambili,* who themselves are one of the three major subgroups of the Swazi* people of Swaziland.

SIGINDA. The Siginda, with a population of perhaps 2,000 people, are one of the smallest of the Buduma* subgroups. They fish and raise cattle.

SIHANAKA. The Sihanakas (Antisihanakas) are an ethnic group of approximately 200,000 people living today primarily in Tamatave Province of Madagascar. Most of them are rice farmers, cattle herders, and fishermen. Although they live in close proximity with the Merinas,* they refuse to intermarry with them.
REFERENCES: Maureen Covell. *Madagascar: Politics, Economics, and Society.* 1987; Harold D. Nelson et al. *Area Handbook for the Malagasy Republic.* 1973.

SIHLONGONYANE. The Sihlongonyanes are one of the major clans of the Bemdzabuko* division of the Swazi* people of Swaziland.

SIMAA. The Simaas are part of the larger cluster of Luyana* peoples of Zambia. The Luyanas are part of the Lozi* group. The Simaa population today exceeds 17,000 people.

SIMBA. *See* SHIMBA.

SIMBOTI. The Simbotis are a small ethnic group whose contemporary population numbers approximately 50,000 people. In recent years, many Simbotis have made the transition to commercial farming and urban labor, but most Simbotis continue to live as subsistence farmers and livestock raisers. They live in the lower Zambezi River Valley of Mozambique.
REFERENCE: Mario Azevedo. *Historical Dictionary of Mozambique.* 1991.

SIMELANE. The Simelanes are one of the major clans of the Bemdzabuko* division of the Swazi* people of Swaziland.

SIMILSI. The term "Similsi" is used in Togo to refer to urbanized Fulbe* settlers.

SINYAR. The Sinyar are a Muslim people living in Chad and Sudan at the confluence of three seasonal rivers—the Wadi Azum, Wadi Kaja, and Wadi Salih. They call themselves the Shamya, a name taken from their assumed common ancestor. The Sinyar population exceeds 30,000 people; they live in forty villages, half in Chad and half in Sudan. The main Sinyar settlement is at Foro Boranga. Sinyar oral tradition traces their origins to Arabs* in Egypt, but they maintain kinship and coresidence with the Berti.* Non-Sinyars in the area reject this notion of Sinyar origins, claiming that the Sinyars are descendants of non-Muslim slaves. For centuries, the Sinyars have been organized into semi-independent, tribute-paying sultanates. They were subject to the Keira Sultanate of Dar Fur until 1863 and then to the Daju Sultanate of Dar Sila. The Sinyar homeland was overrun by a Turko-Egyptian army in 1879, and, in 1881, the slave trader Babikr Zibeir made inroads there. Sultan Abu Risha of Dar Sila invaded in 1882, and Mahdist troops arrived several years later. With the border settlement of 1924 between the French* and the British,* the international frontier between Chad and the Anglo-Egyptian Sudan split the Sinyars between two political administrations.

In recent years, the Sinyars have faced environmental and political challenges. Much of the Sinyar region is infested with the tsetse fly, and several decades of drought have forced population movements northward. Increasing human populations have brought about deforestation and severe declines in local wildlife populations. In addition, the severe civil wars in Chad in the late 1970s and 1980s forced large numbers of Sinyar refugees to seek tranquility across the border in Sudan. Most Sinyars today are farmers, raising grains or herding cattle.
REFERENCE: Paul Doornbos. "Sinyar." In Richard V. Weekes, ed. *Muslim Peoples.* 1984.

SIRI. The Siris are a Chadic-speaking people of Nigeria. They are primarily farmers and herders living in the Ganjuwa and Ningi districts of the Bauchi Division of Bauchi State. The Siri population is approximately 5,000 people.
REFERENCE: *Language Survey of Nigeria.* 1976.

SISALA. *See* SASALA.

SISSALA. *See* SASALA.

SISYA. The Sisyas are part of the Tumbuka* cluster of peoples living today in northern Malawi, primarily between Lake Nyasa and the Zambian border, south of Tanzania. Some Sisyas can also be found in Zambia and Tanzania. The Sisya population today exceeds 40,000 people. They speak a language closely related to that of the Tongas.* The Sisya economy still revolves around the production of maize, sorghum, and millet.

REFERENCES: *African Encyclopedia.* 1974; John J. Grotpeter. *Historical Dictionary of Zambia.* 1979; Donald G. Morrison et al. *Black Africa: A Comparative Handbook.* 1989.

SITI. The Sitis (Kira, Sitigo, Paxala, Konosarala) are a Voltaic people living in the subprefecture of Bouna in Ivory Coast. In terms of their population, which today is estimated at perhaps 20,000 people, they are a small group. Like most Voltaic peoples, the Sitis support themselves by herding cattle and by raising millet and cassava in subsistence gardens.

REFERENCE: Robert J. Mundt. *Historical Dictionary of Côte d'Ivoire.* 1995.

SITIGO. *See* SITI.

SIU. The Sius are a Swahili*-speaking people who today live in Kenya.

SKRUBU. *See* SURUBU.

SO. The So are a relatively small ethnic group living in Zaire. Most of them are concentrated on the east bank of the Lualaba River, downriver from the city of Bumba. As a riverine people, they have traditionally supported themselves by fishing, planting gardens on river banks, and trading. Today, more and more Sos are seeking wage labor in the towns and cities of north-central Zaire.

REFERENCE: Irving Kaplan et al. *Zaire: A Country Study.* 1978.

SOBO. *See* ISOKO.

SOCHILE. *See* NYAKYUSA.

SOGA. The Soga (Basoga, Lusoga) people of southeastern Uganda have a population that today exceeds one million people. They are one of the larger ethnic groups in the country, constituting approximately 8 percent of the population. Their language, which they call Lusoga, is part of the Interlacustrine group of the Bantu* language family. They live primarily in the Busoga District in eastern Uganda, between Lake Kyoga to the north, the Nile River to the west, Lake Victoria to the south, and the Mpologoma River to the east. Most Soga are small farmers, raising plantains, sweet potatoes, cassava, and millet as staples, plus cotton and coffee for cash. In the northern reaches of the Busoga District, where the climate is much drier than in the fertile south, they raise cattle. The main city in Busoga is Jinja.

Approximately 175,000 Soga are Muslims. In the nineteenth century, Swahili* and Arab* traders introduced Islam to the Soga, but a more powerful influence came at the end of the nineteenth century when the British* colonial administration stationed Sudanese troops in the Busoga District. The soldiers

were Muslims. Religious wars in Buganda also sent Muslim refugees into Busoga at the end of the nineteenth century. Most of the Soga Muslims are Sunnis
of the Shafi rite. Another 45 percent of the Soga are Christians, primarily Protestants converted by British missionaries. The rest of the Soga remain loyal to
their traditional religion, which worships the great creator, Mukama, maintains
an ancestor cult, and believes in powerful tree and rock spirits.

REFERENCES: L. A. Fallers. *Bantu Bureaucracy: A Century of Political Evolution
Among the Basoga of Uganda.* 1965; N. Kasozi King and Arye Oded. *Islam and the
Confluence of Religions in Uganda, 1840–1966.* 1973; Y. K. Lubogo. *History of Busoga.*
1960; Arye Oded. "Soga." In Richard V. Weekes, ed. *Muslim Peoples.* 1984.

SOHANTI. The Sohanti are a subgroup of the Songhai* peoples of West Africa.
They possess a unique ethnic identity based on their occupational role as magicians and ritual diviners for the indigenous Songhai faith. Today the Sohanti
can be found in Mali, Burkina-Faso, Niger, and Benin.

SOKILE. *See* NYAKYUSA.

SOKORO. The Sokoros are one of the Hadjeray* peoples of the mountainous
regions of Guéra Prefecture in Chad. They descend from refugees who were
driven into the mountains. They speak a Chadian language and practice the
margai cult of place and site spirits. In spite of many cultural similarities with
such other groups as the Kingas,* Junkuns,* Bidios,* Mogoums,* Barains,* and
Sabas,* the Sokoros rarely intermarry and maintain a powerful sense of identity.

REFERENCE: Thomas Collelo et al. *Chad: A Country Study.* 1988.

SOKWIA. *See* GISU.

SOLI. The Solis are a Tonga*-speaking people who live today near Lusaka in
south-central Zambia. Their population is approximately 50,000 people. They
maintain a matrilineal descent system. Most Solis are small farmers.

REFERENCE: John J. Grotpeter. *Historical Dictionary of Zambia.* 1979.

SOLONGO. The Solongos (Basolongo, Basorongo) are one of the major subgroups of the Kongo* people of Zaire and Angola. They are concentrated on
the dry coastal plain of northwestern Angola and southwestern Zaire, and they
make their living as fishermen in the Atlantic. The Solongo population today
exceeds 100,000 people.

REFERENCE: Thomas Collelo et al. *Angola: A Country Study.* 1989.

SOMAL. *See* SOMALI.

SOMALI. The Somalis (Somal) are one of Africa's largest, homogeneous ethnic groups. They occupy the Horn of Africa, speak a single language, worship as Sunni Muslims of the Shafi school, and claim a common heritage. Their population today exceeds eight million people, of whom nearly five million live in the Republic of Somalia. There are also approximately 2.7 million Somalis in Ethiopia, 650,000 in Kenya, 260,000 in Djibouti, and another 150,000 working in South Yemen and Saudi Arabia. Traditionally, the Somali economy revolved around nomadic animal husbandry, and, today, nearly two-thirds of all Somalis are still engaged in the production of camels, sheep, and goats. The Somali language is part of the Eastern Cushitic branch of the Afro-Asiatic family. Although increasingly large numbers of Somalis live in such cities as Mogadishu, most of them remain in the countryside.

Historically, the Somalis have divided themselves into two broad lineages. The Samale* comprise the more dominant of the lineages, priding themselves on their traditional status as warriors and nomadic pastoralists. Within these broad lineage systems, tribal confederations characterize Somali society. The Dirs,* Darods,* Hawiyes,* and Issaqs* are all part of the Samale lineage. The Dirs, who live primarily in southern Somalia and in the northwest, between Harar and the coast, consider themselves to be the original Somali group. The Issa* people of Djibouti are a subgroup of the Dir. The Darods (Daarood), Hawiyes, and Issaqs are either pastoralists in the Ogaden and in northeastern Kenya or traders on the Somali coast. The Digils* and Rahanwayns* are Somali peoples living between the Shebelle and Juba rivers in the southeast. Unlike the Samales, who are primarily nomadic, the Digils and Rahanwayns are primarily settled farmers. All of the Somali tribal confederations are further divided into clan and sub-clan affiliations, creating a social structure with highly centrifugal identities.

By the late nineteenth century, Somalis had been colonized into five distinct political entities. Great Britain established the protectorate of British* Somaliland in 1885 along the northern Somali coast, and France established French* Somaliland, which later became known as the French Territory of the Afars and Issas. In 1887, Menelik II of Ethiopia expanded into the Ogaden. Italy established Italian* Somaliland in southern Somalia in 1889, and, in 1910, Great Britain created the Northern Frontier District in Kenya. Somali nationalists then began a struggle for ethnic unification. In 1960, British Somaliland and Italian Somaliland united to become the independent Republic of Somalia. Further attempts at national unification failed. When Kenya became independent in 1963, its Somalis became Kenyan citizens. Somalia fought a bitter, costly civil war with Ethiopia over the Ogaden in 1978, from which Ethiopia emerged victorious. In 1977, the former French Somaliland became independent Djibouti. During the 1980s and early 1990s, savage clan and tribal rivalries devastated the Somali people, as did continuing border wars with Ethiopia over the Ogaden. Widespread starvation led the United Nations and the United States to intervene in Somali in 1992.

REFERENCES: David Lattin. *Politics, Language and Thought: The Somali Experience.* 1977; Ioan M. Lewis. *A Modern History of Somalia.* 1980; Abdi A. Sheik-Abdi. "Somalis." In Richard V. Weekes, ed. *Muslim Peoples.* 1984.

SOMBA. The Sombas, also known as the Tamberma, are an ethnic group of approximately 350,000 people. They are concentrated in the Atakora Mountains in northwestern Benin and across the border in Togo, especially in the Sansanné-Mango region; Sombas can be found in Ghana as well. They have also been described as the "castle people" because of their unique two-story homes. They are a highly individualistic people. Most Sombas are subsistence farmers, raising maize, millet, manioc, and plantains in a marginal economic environment. Ethnologists today classify them as part of the Ewe* cluster of peoples; their language is broadly classified with the Molé-Dagbane* group. In recent years, the most prominent Somba leaders in Benin have been Maurice Kouandété and Matthieu Kerekou. The Sombas are divided into a number of subgroups, which include the Berbas, Natimbas,* Niendés, Woabas, Sorubas,* and Dyes.*

REFERENCES: Suzanne Preston Blier. "Architecture of the Tamberma (Togo)." Ph.D. dissertation. Columbia University. 1981; Samuel Decalo. *Historical Dictionary of Togo.* 1976.

SOMONO. The Somono people of Mali are closely related to the Bambaras,* perhaps a Bambara caste. They speak a language that is considered to be Fringe Bambara—part of the larger Manding* cluster of languages in the Niger-Congo family. Most Somonos are fishermen, making their living off the Niger River in Mali. They trace their tribal origins to the Mali Empire of the thirteenth century. Their population today is approximately 15,000 people.

REFERENCES: Pascal Imperato. *Historical Dictionary of Mali.* 1977; Donald R. Wright. "Manding-Speaking Peoples." In Richard V. Weekes, ed. *Muslim Peoples.* 1984.

SOMRAI. The Somrais are a relatively small ethnic group living today in the Moyen-Chari Prefecture in Chad. Their language is part of the larger Chadian cluster of languages, and it represents a transition between Sara* and Massa.* Most Somrais are herdsmen and small farmers, raising sorghum, millet, maize, and cotton.

REFERENCE: Thomas Collelo et al. *Chad: A Country Study.* 1988.

SONGHAI. The term "Songhai" (Songhay, Sonhray, Songhoi, and Sonhrai) is used as a general reference to describe millions of people in West Africa who are part of a large cultural group deriving from the fifteenth- and sixteenth-century Kingdom of Songhai. The Songhai culture region extends from Timbuktu in Mali down the Niger River to Goa, Niamey, and Gaya. The Soninkés* controlled the region in the tenth and eleventh centuries, as did the Mandings* in the thirteenth and fourteenth centuries. In the power vacuum created

by the decline of the Mandings, the Songhai established a new empire. Eventually, the Songhai Empire stretched from Agadez and Kano in the east to Oualata in the west, and from Taghaza in the north to Djenne in the south. At its peak, the Songhai Empire included dozens of distinct ethnic clusters. The empire disintegrated in the sixteenth century, and the older ethnic identities reasserted themselves. Today, there a number of ethnic groups aware of their connections to the Songhai Empire, including the Songhai proper, Kados, Gabibis,* Sorkos,* Fonos,* Gows, Dendis,* Sohantis,* Maygas, Kourteys,* and Zermas.*
REFERENCES: H. M. Miner. *The Primitive Cry of Timbuctoo.* 1965; Leo F. Van Hoey. "Songhay." In Richard V. Weekes, ed. *Muslim Peoples.* 1984.

SONGHAI. The Songhai people of West Africa are part of the larger Songhai* culture group. One large grouping of Songhais exists around the great bend of the Niger River in Mali, stretching from Lake Debo along the river. More than 450,000 Songhais live in the vicinities of Goundam, Timbukto, Bandiagara, Gao, Issa Ber, Mopti, Segou, and Bamako. There is another concentration of approximately 600,000 Songhais in Tillaberi, Ayourou, and Tera in the western provinces of Niger. There are approximately 10,000 Songhais in and around Dori in Burkina-Faso, perhaps 50,000 in and around Parakou and Kandi in Benin, 12,000 along the Sokoto River in Nigeria, and 9,000 in Agadez in Niger. Several thousand also live in northern Ghana. The Songhais are divided into a number of regional subgroups. The Kado Songhais live in Tera, Ayourou, and Goroul in far western Niger. The Gabibi,* who are also known as the Gabibi Arbi, live north of Gao in Mali. The Sorko* are fishermen living on both sides of the Niger River in Mali. The lake districts south of Timbukto are inhabited by the Fono* Songhais. The Gow Songhais live in the Mali grasslands near Anzourou and the Hombori hills. Lining the Niger River banks between Niamey and Say in western Niger are the Kourtey.* The Sohanti* are a group of traveling magicians who are aware of their Songhai roots. The Zerma,* also known as Djerma and Zaberma, who live in and around Zermaganda and Zaberma in Niger. The Zerma population is about 500,000 people. The total Songhai population in Mali, Burkina-Faso, Niger, Benin, and Nigeria exceeds two million people.

The Songhais are primarily Sunni Muslims of the Maliki school. They tend to be very devout, and the intensity of their Islamic devotions increases with a rise in socioeconomic status. Loyalty to Islam became a badge of national identity during the years of the French* empire in Mali and Niger. The Songhais retain, however, many elements of their traditional religious beliefs, including rich animistic traditions and the magical powers of the Sohantis. In the cities and towns, there are large numbers of Songhai craftsmen, clerks, and professionals, but more than 95 percent of Songhais still live in the vast open spaces of the region. The Songhais were traditionally a nomadic people, herding cattle and sheep over the range of the Sahel in northeastern Burkina-Faso and Mali. They also farm, raising millet and vegetables. Because of the severe drought that has struck the Sahel in the 1980s and 1990s, large numbers of Songhais have lost their herds and faced poverty and starvation. Many have therefore relocated to towns and cities in order to find cash labor.

REFERENCES: Peter Stiller. "Sound in Songhay Cultural Experience." *American Ethnology* 11 (August 1984): 559–70; Leo F. Van Hoey. "Songhay." In Richard V. Weekes, ed. *Muslim Peoples.* 1984.

SONGHAY. *See* SONGHAI.

SONGHOI. *See* SONGHAI.

SONGO. The Songos are a subgroup of the Mbundu* people of north-central Angola.

SONGO. The Songos are a Tanzanian ethnic group whom some ethnologists classify in the Yao* cluster of peoples.

SONGOLA. The Songolas are an ethnic group living today in eastern Zaire, primarily in what is recognized as the Kindu zone. It is a heavily forested region, and the Songolas make their living fishing and working small farms, where they raise cassava, yams, and a variety of other crops.

REFERENCES: Daniel Biebuyck. "Sculpture from the Eastern Zaire Forest Region." *African Arts* 9 (January 1976): 8–14; Irving Kaplan et al. *Zaire: A Country Study.* 1978.

SONGWE. The Songwes are a Tanzanian ethnic group whom ethnologists sometimes include in the Safwa* cluster of peoples.

SONGYE. The Songyes are a subcluster of the Luba* peoples of Zaire. Included in the Songye cluster are the Bangu-Bangus.* They are concentrated near Kabinda in the southern Oriental Region, especially between the Lubufu and Lomami rivers. The Songye population today consists of more than 1.5 million people.

SONHRAI. *See* SONGHAI.

SONHRAY. *See* SONGHAI.

SONINKÉ. The Soninké—also known as the Sarakolé, Saraxole, Serahuli, Serakhulle—are an ethnic group of more than 2.6 million people in West Africa. The majority of the Soninké live in Mali, Burkina-Faso, and Ivory Coast, although they can also be found in Guinea-Bissau, Senegal, Gambia, Guinea, and Mauritania. Their own oral traditions trace Soninké beginnings to the Berbers* of North Africa. They were converted to Islam by violent Almoravid missionaries in the eleventh century, and today the Soninké are known for their

own zeal and for the training and education of their clerics. For the most part, the Soninké have abandoned their own language (called Azer) and speak the language of the most dominant group in whatever region they reside. The only Soninké who still speak Azer are those living in the purely Soninké communities of Nioro, Nara, and Guidimakha in Mauritania and Bakel in Senegal. In West Africa, they are known variously as the Ahl-Massin, Aswanik, Azor, Diakhanke, Dyankanke, Ligbe, Ouadane, Ouakore, Tubakai, Wangarbe, Wangarawa, and Wankore. Today, most Soninké are small farmers, although they are widely known in the region for their skill as traders, especially in diamond marketing. Large numbers of the Soninké work as migrant laborers in France today.
REFERENCES: David P. Gamble. *The Gambia.* 1988; Alfred G. Gerteiny. "Soninké." In Richard V. Weekes, ed. *Muslim Peoples.* 1984.

SONIWEIN. The Soniweins are a subgroup of the Bassa* people of Liberia. Most Soniweins live in Grand Bassa County, Liberia.

SONJO. The Sonjos live among the Masai* people of Tanzania. They speak a Nilo-Hamitic language. They are known for their skill as farmers, particularly for the elaborate irrigation systems they have developed. They have a population today of approximately 10,000 people.
REFERENCE: Laura Kurtz. *Historical Dictionary of Tanzania.* 1978.

SOOSOO. *See* SOSO.

SORKO. The Sorkos are a subgroup of the Songhai* peoples of West Africa. They live in fishing hamlets on the banks of the Niger River in Mali as well as in Niger. They are subdivided into two subgroups of their own—the Faran and the Fono.*

SORUBA. The Sorubas are a subgroup of the Somba* people of Benin and Togo. Their contemporary population is approximately 50,000 people, most of whom are farmers, raising maize, millet, plantains, and cassava.

SOSO. The Soso (Soosoo, Sosso, Soussou, Susu) are a Manding*-speaking people of West Africa whose language is actually part of the Mande-fu cluster of Manding languages (which in turn are part of the larger Niger-Congo family of languages). The Soso are closely related to the Yalunka.* At one time, they were one people living in the Fouta Djallon region. Today there are approximately 1.3 million Soso people. About 90 percent of them live in the Republic of Guinea, where they are extremely influential. The rest dwell in northwestern Sierra Leone and Guinea-Bissau. The Soso live primarily in the marshy coastal plain in farming villages. They originated in the western Sudan part of the Mali Empire; when the empire disintegrated, they migrated west to the region known today as Fouta Djallon. Over the next century, they continued their westward trek to the coastal region. They converted to Islam in the seventeenth century. Today, the Soso are overwhelmingly Sunni Muslims of the Maliki school, although their religion retains a number of pre-Islamic indigenous survivals. For example, many Soso, even while being Muslims, still perform ritual ceremonies to propitiate the *bari*—benign and malevolent spirits who inhabit the forests. Most Sosos are subsistence farmers, but they are also known for their skill as blacksmiths and traders. Soso farmers typically raise rice as their staple, as well as peanuts, millet, cassava, ginger, and bananas. The Sosos of Sierra Leone are skilled fishermen. Soso culture is known regionally for its ability to absorb smaller, neighboring cultures. Their language is the lingua franca of southern Guinea.

REFERENCES: Cyril P. Foray. *Historical Dictionary of Sierra Leone.* 1977; Thomas O'Toole. *Historical Dictionary of Guinea.* 1987; James S. Thayer. "Nature, Culture, and the Supernatural Among the Susu." *American Ethnology* 10 (February 1983): 117–32.

SOSSO. The Sossos are one of the major subgroups of the Kongo* people of Zaire and Angola.

SOTHO. The Sothos (Basuto) are one of the largest ethnic groups in southern Africa. Sotho is a Bantu* language spoken by more than seven million people today. Most of the Sothos live in Lesotho, formerly Basutoland. Sotho is a written language with a rich literary tradition. The best-known Sotho writers are Thomas Mafolo, who wrote *Shaka,* and A. M. Sekese. The Sothos are subdivided into several large groups, based in political loyalties to a chiefdom. The major Sotho chiefdoms are the Fokengs, Kwenas,* Phutis,* Phutings, Taungs, Tlokwas,* and Pedis.* Ethnologists estimate that the Sotho people have been living in southern Africa for more than a thousand years. Their ethnic identity first coalesced in the 1820s under the leadership of Moshoeshoe when he led his people during the attacks of Shaka and the Zulus.* The Sothos are divided into three great regional groupings. The Southern Sothos reside mostly in Lesotho. The Western Sotho are also called the Tswana,* of whom many live in Botswana. The Northern Sotho consist largely of the Pedi people, most of whom live in the Transvaal near Swaziland. In South Africa, the Sothos are divided administratively between the North Sotho, who live in the "independent homeland" of Lebowa and the South Sotho. Christianity is widespread among the Sothos. Most Sothos are still farmers, raising maize, sorghum, cattle, and goats. During the last thirty years, increasing numbers of Sotho farmers have made the transition to commercial agriculture, and large numbers of Sotho men have left home to work in the mines, plantations, towns, and cities of South Africa and Lesotho.

REFERENCES: *African Encyclopedia.* 1974; John J. Grotpeter. *Historical Dictionary of Swaziland.* 1975; Gordon Haliburton. *Historical Dictionary of Lesotho.* 1977.

SOUDIÉ. The Soudié people are the descendants of Hausas* who settled among

the Zerma* in the Dosso of Niger. Those who adopted the Zerma language and culture became known as the Soudié, while those who retained their original Hausa language became known as the Kurfey.*
REFERENCE: Samuel Decalo. *Historical Dictionary of Niger.* 1989.

SOUSSOU. *See* SOSO.

SOWE. The Sowes are a Tanzanian ethnic group many ethnologists classify with the larger Bena* cluster of peoples.

SPANIARD. Several thousand ethnic Spaniards* can be found in Africa today, primarily in the former Spanish colonies. In 1778, Portugal ceded to Spain what became known as Spanish Equatorial Guinea. To counter British* naval activity on the coast of Africa, Spain established a trading post on the Rio de Oro Bay; that post evolved into the colony of Spanish Sahara. Spanish Sahara, Spanish Equatorial Guinea, and the two small zones of Morocco known as Spanish Morocco, along with Ceuta, Melilla, and Ifni, constituted the Spanish empire in Africa. Spain lost these colonies during the revolutionary nationalism of the 1950s, 1960s, and 1970s, except for Ceuta and Melilla. Both sections of Spanish Morocco were ceded to Morocco in 1956 and 1958; Ifni went to Morocco in 1959; and Spanish Sahara was divided up between Mauritania and Morocco in 1976.
REFERENCE: James S. Olson. *Historical Dictionary of European Imperialism.* 1991.

SRIGBÉ. *See* BAKWÉ.

SRUBU. *See* SURUBU.

SUA. The Sua are a subgroup of the Mbutis, themselves a major subgroup of the Pygmies.* The Sua live in the southern reaches of the Ituri forest of Zaire.

SUBA. The Subas people live in northwestern Tanzania, primarily along the southwestern shore of Lake Victoria. They raise cattle and farm, using the manure to keep their soil productive. During the past century, they have been known widely for their skill as ironworkers.
REFERENCES: Laura Kurtz. *Historical Dictionary of Tanzania.* 1978; Donald G. Morrison et al. *Black Africa: A Comparative Handbook.* 1989.

SUBI. The Subis (Shubi) are an ethnic group living in far northwestern Tanzania, just west of the southwestern tip of Lake Victoria. Before the civil war in Rwanda in 1994, some Subis could also be found in Rwanda; virtually all of them have fled to Tanzania or Burundi to escape the violence. Most Subis

are small farmers. Some ethologists include the Hangazas with the Subis. They have a population today in excess of 130,000 people.
REFERENCE: Laura Kurtz. *Historical Dictionary of Tanzania.* 1978.

SUBIA. *See* SUBIYA.

SUBIYA. The Subiyas (Subia) are an ethnic group living today in Botswana in southern Africa. They can also be found in the Caprivi Strip of Namibia and in southwestern Zambia. Most Subiyas speak a Lozi* language, although some speak Tonga* as their first language. They make their living raising livestock and farming.
REFERENCES: John J. Grotpeter. *Historical Dictionary of Zambia.* 1979; John A. Wiseman. *Botswana.* 1992.

SUBO. *See* SUBI.

SUGUR. *See* SUKUR.

SUK. *See* POKOT.

SUKKOT. The Sukkots are a subgroup of the Nubian* people of Sudan.

SUKU. The Sukus are a subgroup of the Yaka* people of Zaire. Most Sukus live in southwestern Zaire, between the Inzia and Kwilu rivers north of Feshi.
REFERENCE: Arthur P. Bourgeois. ''Suku Drinking Cups.'' *African Arts* 12 (November 1978): 76–77.

SUKUMA. The Sukuma are a Bantu*-speaking people who are closely related to the Nyamwezi* and who live in northern and western Tanzania. Their population in 1967 totaled approximately 1,523,000; estimates place that number at more than three million people today. Sukuma land covers more than 52,000 square kilometers and consists of rolling hills and homogeneous savanna.

Traditionally, the Sukuma were subsistence farmers who lived on a particular plot of land for several years and then moved on when the soil became exhausted. For the most part, they lived in village groups and raised such food crops as sorghum, millet, and maize. They practiced an animist religion that revolved around ancestor worship. When Germany exerted its imperial power over the region in the 1890s, the residential pattern changed; the village concentrations were actively dispersed as a matter of state policy in favor of scattered homesteads. In terms of political loyalties, there was no real sense of Sukuma nationalism. Individuals were more likely to express their loyalty to chiefdom states. Chiefdoms were subdivided into sub-chiefdoms, and each sub-chiefdom was divided into villages governed by headmen.

The traditional pattern of Sukuma life changed dramatically after World War I. Germany lost control over the region, and Great Britain became the new colonial power. Increasing numbers of Protestant missionaries made superficial progress in converting the Sukuma, but the traditional tribal beliefs still prevailed. After World War II, economic changes brought more drastic alterations in Sukuma life. During the late 1940s and 1950s, the plow replaced the hoe, and Sukuma farmers began raising such cash crops as cotton and tobacco. With the introduction of tractors in the 1960s and 1970s, more and more Sukuma became commercial farmers, raising cotton, tobacco, millet, sorghum, and maize for sale in national markets. Competition for land increased, and British* colonial officials, with the blessing of the masses, implemented a series of measures to encourage democratic landholding patterns. Some ethnologists include the Rongos* and the Shashis* in the Sukuma cluster.

REFERENCES: H. H. Cory. *Sukuma Law and Custom.* 1953; Parker Shipton. "Lineage and Locality as Antithetical Principles in East African Systems of Land Tenure." *Ethnology* 23 (1984): 117–32; R. E. S. Tanner. "Land Tenure in Northern Sukumaland, Tanganyika." *East African Agricultural Journal* 2 (1955): 120–29; R. E. S. Tanner. "Sukuma Ancestor Worship and Its Relation to Social Structure." *Tanganyika Notes and Records* 50 (1958): 52–62.

SUKUR. The Sukurs—also identified frequently as the Sugurs, Adikummus, and Gemasakuns—are one of Nigeria's many ethnic groups. They speak a Chadic language and live primarily in the Madagali District of the Mubi Division of Gongola State. Their current population is approximately 20,000 people.

REFERENCE: *Language Survey of Nigeria.* 1976.

SUKWA. The Sukwas are a Tanzanian ethnic group whom some ethnologists classify with the Nyakyusa* cluster of peoples.

SUMBE. The Sumbes are one of the subgroups of the Ovimbundu* peoples of Angola.

SUMBWA. The Sumbwas, like the Sukuma,* are closely related to the Nyamwezi* of Tanzania. In fact, they are a subgroup of the Nyamwezi. Their population today is approximately 250,000 people, most of whom are hoe farmers. The Sumbwas are concentrated south of Lake Victoria in western Tanzania.

SUNDI. The Sundis (Basundi), sometimes known as the Kongo-Sundi, are the largest subgroup of the Kongo* peoples of Congo, Zaire, and Angola. Their contemporary population exceeds 200,000 people.

SUNGOR. *See* ASUNGOR.

SUPIDE. *See* SENUFO.

SURA. *See* MWAHAVUL.

SURMA. The Surma of Ethiopia are a semi-nomadic people who are part of the larger Surma linguistic group. They raise crops and cattle. Surma women are known for the cultural tradition of adorning themselves with large lip plates, which they consider a measure of their beauty and worth. Generally, the Surma people have been isolated by the 7,000-foot mountains and desolate lowlands near the Ethiopian border with Sudan in southwestern Ethiopia. The vast majority of the Surma live west of the Omo River, in the presence of other livestock raisers and subsistence farmers. Their diet consists largely of corn, millet, and sorghum, along with milk and blood from their animals. Between November and February each year, the Surma engage in brutal stick fighting with one another (each stick is a six-foot staff tipped with a carved phallus). Known as the *donga,* the stick-fighting rituals are used as a means of settling disputes and releasing emotional tension.

The Surma live in the Maji and Bero-Shasha provinces in the Kafa region of Ethiopia. Their location is geographically remote. Because rainfall is so limited, the Surma have never been able to rely totally on farming. Instead, they are agro-pastoralists who supplement their diet through hunting and gathering. Those Surma who farm tend to raise maize, cabbage, beans, sweet potatoes, and peppers. Before the era of the Italian* colonization of Ethiopia, the Surma were frequently the objects of slave raiding by other groups on the Ethiopian plateau, but that practice declined after the Italian occupation and World War II. The Surma's closest neighbors are the Dizis, Anauks,* and Nyangatoms. The main towns in the general region are Tum and Maji, but they are occupied over-whelmingly by the Dizi, not the Surma.

Before the 1970s, Surma cattle herds were extensive, with pastures ranging deep into Sudan, but, in the 1970s, a series of ecological and human conflicts devastated the tribe. Epidemics of anthrax and trypanosomiasis wiped out large numbers of cattle, as did severe droughts. Ethnic conflict over grazing land erupted between the Surma and the Nyangatoms. Conditions became so bad that, in the 1980s, the Surma started migrating north into the Upper Kibish Valley. During the late 1980s and early 1990s, the Surma continued their north-ern migration, moving as far as the southern tributaries of the Akobo-Dima River. More than 1,000 Surma now live near the eastern edge of the Boma Plateau in Sudan. By the early 1990s, severe ethnic battles between the Surma, the Dizis, and the Nyangatoms had helped destroy Surma political culture; in the process, public security became precarious at best. The Surma are known to attack non-Surma travelers in their area, a fact that has been aggravated by the extraordinarily strong Surma sense of identity.

REFERENCES: John Abbink. "Settling the Surma: Notes on an Ethiopian Relocation Experiment." *Human Organization* 51 (Summer 1992): 175–89; Carol Beckwith and Angela Fisher. "The Eloquent Surma of Ethiopia." *National Geographic* 179 (February 1991): 77–99.

SURU. *See* TAPSHIN.

SURUBU. The Surubus (Srubus, Skrubus, Zurubus, Fitis) are one of the Western Plateau peoples of Nigeria. They have a contemporary population of approximately 9,000 people and live in the Kauru District of the Saminaka Division of Kaduna State.
REFERENCE: *Language Survey of Nigeria.* 1976.

SUSI. The Susis are a subgroup of the Shilha* people, who themselves are one of the Berber* peoples of Morocco.

SUSU. *See* SOSO.

SUTU. *See* SOTHO.

SWAHILI. The Swahili are a people whose ethnogenesis is a relatively recent phenomenon, and ethnologists have had difficulty describing them. Today, their population is approaching three million people, most of whom live on the islands of Lamu, Mombasa, Pemba, Zanzibar, and Mafia and in the East African littoral, which reaches from the Somali-Kenya frontier in the north to Mozambique's central coast. They are devout Muslims, known for their emphasis on education, family unity, and commercial skills. The Swahili are concentrated particularly in the coastal cities of Lamu Town, Malindi, Mombasa, Vanga, Dar es Salaam, and Zanzibar Town.

Their name comes from the Arabic word "sawahi," meaning "coast," so they are thus the "People of the Coast." The name was coined by the Omani Arabs* who ruled the East African coast in the eighteenth and early nineteenth centuries. The Swahili had complex origins. Several thousand years ago, the East African coast was occupied by hunter-gatherer groups who eventually mixed with Cushitic groups who herded livestock in the region. The contemporary Orma people are close relatives of those Cushitic herders. Around the first or second century A.D., Bantu*-speaking peoples from the region of northern Congo arrived on the East African coast and mixed with their predecessors there. To these groups must be added a series of Indonesian, Persian, Hindi, Arab, and Portuguese* traders who settled on the coast. The Swahili language is of Bantu origin, although it is loaded with loan words from the mercantile languages of the Indian Ocean, especially Arabic, Hindi, and Portuguese. They are a Muslim people.

For several thousand years, the Swahili have occupied the East African coast, serving as middlemen between the African interior and the Indian Ocean trade routes, trading spices, slaves, ivory, gold, and grains. In the process, they have become a skilled commercial people. The so-called "Swahili coast" extends from the Bajun coast of present-day Somalia in the north to the northern coast of Mozambique in the south. Most lower-class Swahili are farmers, raising rice, sorghum, millet, maize, and cassava.

REFERENCES: John Middleton. *The World of the Swahili: An African Mercantile Civilization.* 1992; Michael Sims. "Swahili." In Richard V. Weekes, ed. *Muslim Peoples.* 1984.

SWAKA. The Swakas are a relatively small ethnic group living today in eastern Zambia. They are an offshoot of the Lala* peoples. Most Swakas are small farmers. Their contemporary population exceeds 50,000 people.

REFERENCE: John J. Grotpeter. *Historical Dictionary of Zambia.* 1979.

SWAZI. There are more than two million Swazi people today, most of whom live in Swaziland and neighboring areas of South Africa. They speak the Swazi language, known as siSwati, which is part of the Bantu* language family. The traditional Swazi economy revolved around the production of cattle, but, in recent years, most Swazis have made the transition to agriculture, raising maize, millet, groundnuts, and rice. Today, large numbers of Swazi men work in the timber, sugar, and mineral industries of South Africa. The ruling Swazi clan, known as the Dlamini, occupied the eastern region of Southern Africa before the nineteenth century, but the Zulu* wars early in the 1800s drove them into the mountains of what is today Swaziland. The various ethnic groups already in the mountains then joined the Swazis under the leadership of Chief Mswati. Later in the century, European settlers forcibly entered Swazi land for agricultural and mining purposes. After the Boer War from 1899 to 1902, the British* colonial government assumed control of Swaziland. Swaziland became independent in 1968.

Today, there are three major subgroups of the Swazis, each of which is divided into a series of clans. The Bemdzabukos* (Bomdzabukos) are one of those subgroups. They consider themselves to be "pure Swazi." The Bemdzabukos are subdivided themselves into the following clans: Mhlanga, Madonsela, Mavuso, Fakude, Hlophe, Mabuza, Simelane, Matsebula, Twala, Ngwenya, Sihlongonyane, Nkonyane, and Manana. The Emafikamuvas* are the second subgroup of the Swazi people. They are known as the "latecomers," since they arrived in Swaziland after the first Swazis had already settled there. At the time, the Emafikamuvas were fleeing Zulu expansion. They were incorporated into Swazi ethnic culture, but they are still not considered to be real Swazis by many other Swazis. The Emafikamuvas are composed of the following major clans: Nkambules, Manyatsis, Nhlengetfwas, Mtsettfwas, Hlatshwako, Tselas, Masukus, Dladlas, Vilakatis, and Masilelas. The third major subgroup of the Swazi people is the Emakhandzambilis.* They are of Ngoni* or Sotho* origins and were living in the area when it was invaded by Sobhuza I and his followers in the early nineteenth century. Over time, they were absorbed by the Swazi peoples, although, even today, they are still not considered to be "true Swazis," like the Bemdzabukos. The Emakhandzambilis are also subdivided into many clans, including the Gama, Magagula, Maziya, Kubonye, Mnisi, Maphosa, Gwebu, Shabanga, Tabetse, Sifundza, Malindza, Bhembe, Shabalala, Mncina, Makhubu, Mashinini, Msimango, Motsa, Mahlangu, Zwane, Shongwe, Thabede, and Ngcomphalala.

REFERENCES: *African Encyclopedia.* 1974; John J. Grotpeter. *Historical Dictionary of Swaziland.* 1975; E. T. Sherwood. *Swazi Personality and the Assimilation of Western Culture.* 1961.

SYA. *See* SIA.

SYÉNAMBÉLÉ. *See* SENUFO.

T

TA'AISHA. *See* BAGGARA.

TABETSE. The Tabetses are one of the clans of the Emakhandzambili,* who themselves are one of the three major subgroups of the Swazi people of Swaziland.

TABWA. The Tabwas are a relatively small ethnic group living today in southeastern Zaire, northwestern Zambia, and southwestern Tanzania. Most of the Tabwas, however, are located between Lake Mweru and Lake Tanganyika in Zaire. They live in a highland region that permits them to farm as well as to raise cattle for meat and milk. The Tabwas speak a Bemba* language and maintain a matrilineal descent system. The Tabwa population in Zambia exceeds 25,000 people.
REFERENCES: John J. Grotpeter. *Historical Dictionary of Zambia.* 1979; Irving Kaplan et al. *Zaire: A Country Study.* 1978; Allen F. Roberts. '' 'Comets Importing Change of Times and States': Ephemerae and Process Among the Tabwe of Zaire.'' *American Ethnology* 9 (November 1982): 712–29.

TACHONI. The Tachonis are a subgroup of the Luhya* people of Kenya and Uganda. They speak a Bantu language and live today north of Lake Victoria on both sides of the Kenyan-Ugandan border.

TAFI. The Tafis are one of the groups classified in the Volta-Togo cluster of peoples in eastern Ghana and western Togo. They live in the Volta Region, where their closest neighbors are the Avatimes* and the Nyangbos.* Most Tafis are small farmers. There are approximately 5,000 Tafi people living in Ghana today.
REFERENCE: Daniel M. McFarland. *Historical Dictionary of Ghana.* 1995.

TAGOUANA. *See* TAGUANA.

TAGUANA. The Taguanas are a Voltaic people living in northeastern Ivory Coast and far southwestern Burkina-Faso. They are closely related to the nearby Lobi* and Kulango* people and have a population today of approximately 50,000. Most Taguanas work small farms and raise cattle.
REFERENCE: Donald G. Morrison et al. *Black Africa: A Comparative Handbook.* 1989.

TAHAMBA. The Tahambas are one of the clans of the Bandi* Chiefdom of Lofa County in Liberia.

TAISAKA. *See* ANTAISAKA.

TAITA. The term "Taita" refers to a cluster of Northeastern Bantu*-speaking people of East Africa. The Taita live in a hill-country region about fifty miles inland from the Indian Ocean coast in Kenya, primarily in the Taita Hills of the Coast Province. They speak a Bantu language and live primarily on Dabida Hill, Sagalla Hill, and Kasigau Hill. They have close relationships with the neighboring Masais.* The Taita are farmers who raise rice, beans, bananas, tobacco, maize, and cassava. Production of cattle, sheep, and goats is also part of their economy. They maintain a patrilineal descent system. Most of them are Sunni Muslims of the Shafi school, but their devotions are marginal in terms of identity and commitment. Except for the observance of Ramadan and the taking of Arabic names, they are not strongly committed to the practices of Islam. The Taita population today exceeds 150,000 people. They are divided into a number of subgroups, including the Dabidas, Mbololos, Werughas, Mbales, Chawias, Buras, Mwandas, Kasigaus, Saghala, Dambis, Muganges, Teris, Kishambas, and Gimbas.
REFERENCES: Patrick Fleuret. "The Social Organization of Water Control in the Taita Hills, Kenya." *American Ethnology* 12 (February 1985): 103–18; A. H. J. Prins. *The Coastal Tribes of the North-Eastern Bantu: Pokomo, Nyika, and Taita.* 1952.

TAKARIR. *See* TUKULOR.

TAKRURI. *See* TUKULOR.

TAL. The Tal people, sometimes called the Amtuls and Kwabzaks, are closely related to the Pais* and Montols* of Plateau State in Nigeria. The Tals are concentrated in the Tal District of the Pankshin Division. They practice subsistence horticulture, raising ginger, millet, guinea corn, and beans. They live in social systems characterized by patrilineal descent and patrifocal residence. In recent years, they have begun migrating to towns and cities looking for work. The Tal language is Chadic in origins.

REFERENCES: Elizabeth Isichei, ed. *Studies in the History of Plateau State, Nigeria.* 1982; *Language Survey of Nigeria.* 1976.

TALA. The Talas are a Chadic-speaking people of Nigeria. They live primarily in the Zungur District of the Bauchi Division of Bauchi State.
REFERENCE: *Language Survey of Nigeria.* 1976.

TALAOTA. *See* TALAOTE.

TALAOTE. The Talaotes (Talaota, Talowta, Batalowta, Batalotes) are an ethnic group of Kalanga* origins, some of whom migrated centuries ago from Zimbabwe to Botswana. By the mid-nineteenth century, the Talaotes had been brought into the Ngwato State. Talaotes today live in the Central District of Botswana. The Talaotes in Zimbabwe are concentrated west of the Matopo Hills in the southwestern part of the country.
REFERENCES: Fred Morton, A. Murray, and J. Ramsay. *Historical Dictionary of Botswana.* 1989; R. Kent Rasmussen. *Historical Dictionary of Zimbabwe.* 1994.

TALE. *See* TALENSI.

TALEN. *See* TALENSI.

TALENE. *See* TALENSI.

TALENSI. The Talensi—also called Tale, Talen, Talene, or Tallensi—speak one of the Molé-Dagbane* languages and live in the northeast corner of Ghana in the Upper East Region. Most of them are settled farmers whose population is approaching 300,000 people. Until 1957, they lived under the administration of what was known as the Northern Territories in the British* Gold Coast colony. They can also be found across the border in Burkina-Faso. The Talensi economy revolves around the production of sorghum and millet.
REFERENCES: Meyer Fortes. *The Dynamics of Clanship Among the Tallensi.* 1945. Meyer Fortes. *Time and Social Structure.* 1970.

TALLENSI. *See* TALENSI.

TALODI. The Talodis are one of the Nuba* peoples of Sudan.

TALOWTA. *See* TALAOTE.

TAMA. The term "Tama" refers to a group of languages and ethnic groups living near the border between Chad and Sudan. The Tama language is part of the Nilo-Saharan linguistic family. There are approximately 300,000 Tama-speaking people, and they are divided into seven ethnic groups: the Tamas* proper, Gimrs,* Mararis* (Abu Sharibs* or Abu Charibs), Asungors* (Sungors), Maraits, Mourros,* Kibets,* Dagels,* Erengas,* and Mileris.* During the nineteenth century, the Tama peoples fell under the domination of the Turko-Egyptian Sudan; Turkish authority was replaced by French* or British* colonial power in the late nineteenth and early twentieth centuries. Today, the Tama peoples are citizens of independent Chad and independent Sudan. Most of them live in compounds made up of cylindrical houses constructed of reed mat walls and thatched roofs. The Tamas are subsistence farmers, raising some livestock as well as sorghum, maize, peanuts, sesame, watermelons, onions, and chili peppers.

REFERENCES: Thomas Collelo et al. *Chad: A Country Study.* 1988; Paul Doornbos. ''Tama-Speaking Peoples.'' In Richard V. Weekes, ed. *Muslim Peoples.* 1984.

TAMA. The Tama proper are a subgroup of the Tama,* a cluster of several ethnic groups inhabiting the border area between Sudan and Chad (between 21° and 23° east longitude and 13° and 15° north latitude). The Tama live in the mountains of eastern Chad, near the Sudanese border. They are surrounded by the Mimis* and Zaghawas* to the north, the Mararis* and Maraits to the west, the Asungors* (Sungor) and Masalits* to the south, and the Gimrs* to the east. The Tama intermarry with all of these groups except the Masalits. The Tama are closely related to the Daju* peoples. There are approximately 65,000 members of the Tama ethnic group. Most Tama are sedentary farmers, raising millet, sesame, peanuts, onions, chili peppers, and various vegetables; they maintain small stocks of camels, cattle, goats, and sheep as well.

Historically, they were part of the Sultanate of Tama, which still exists. Before independence came in 1960, the sultanate was under French* colonial rule. After independence, a civil war erupted in Chad in which Muslim rebels attacked the sultanates, including the sultanate of Tama, accusing them of collaborating with the non-Muslim peoples from southern Chad who controlled the central government. Most of the other sultanates have disappeared, but the Tama sultanate has survived. Although the Tama today have converted to Islam, they also remain loyal to many elements of their traditional religion, which was known for its xenophobia and animistic rituals.

REFERENCE: Paul Doornbos. ''Tama-Speaking Peoples.'' In Richard V. Weekes, ed. *Muslim Peoples.* 1984.

TAMBA. The Tambas (Tembis) are a Chadic-speaking people of central Nigeria. Many ethnolinguists classify them as a Ron* subgroup. They live primarily in the South Sura District of the Pankshin Division.

REFERENCE: *Language Survey of Nigeria.* 1976.

TAMBERMA. *See* SOMBA.

TAMBO. The Tambos are a small ethnic group living today on the upper Lu-

angwa River in extreme northeastern Zambia. Their population is approximately 15,000 people, most of whom speak a Mambwe* language. They are a patrilineal, cattle-raising people. They can also be found across the border in Tanzania.
REFERENCE: John J. Grotpeter. *Historical Dictionary of Zambia.* 1979.

TAMBORO. The Tamboro are a Muslim subgroup of the Sadama* people of southwestern Ethiopia.

TAMPOLENSE. The Tampolense people of Ghana are part of the Grusi* cluster of peoples. They are concentrated in the Northern Region, north of the Gonjas* and south of the Mamprusis.* They are closely related to the Sasalas* and the Vagalas.*
REFERENCE: Daniel M. McFarland. *Historical Dictionary of Ghana.* 1995.

TAMPOLENSI. *See* TAMPOLENSE.

TANALA. The Tanalas are an ethnic group in Madagascar. Their population today is approximately 400,000 people, most of whom live in the southern third of the eastern mountain chain of the island. They are divided into two subgroups: the Menabes and the Ikongos. Traditionally, the Tanalas have supported themselves as hunters, food gatherers, and wood collectors. They practiced a primitive form of slash-and-burn agriculture that damaged the soil. In recent decades, many Tanalas have made the transition to commercial agriculture, growing rice and coffee while using more environmentally sensitive techniques.
REFERENCES: Maureen Covell. *Madagascar: Politics, Economics and Society.* 1987; Harold D. Nelson et al. *Area Handbook for the Malagasy Republic.* 1973.

TANALANA. The Tanalanas, not to be confused with the Tanalas* of eastern Madagascar, are a small ethnic group of western Madagascar who live in close proximity, economically and geographically, with the Vezus, a subgroup of the Sakalavas.* The Tanalanas are primarily farmers who trade their products for fish from the Vezus.

TANDA. *See* TENDA.

TANDA. The Tandas are a ethnic group living today on both sides of the Ubangi River in northwestern Zaire and in northeastern Congo. The Tandas are a riverine people who have traditionally supported themselves by planting small gardens on the river banks, fishing, and trading up and down the Zaire and Ubangi rivers.
REFERENCE: Irving Kaplan et al. *Zaire: A Country Study.* 1978.

TANDE. The Tandes are a subgroup of the Korekores,* who constitute the "Northern Shona"* cluster of peoples in Zimbabwe.

TANDRUY. *See* ANTANDROY.

TANEKA. The Taneka, also known as the Tongba, are a small ethnic group of Voltaic background who live in the villages of Taneka Koko, Taneka Beri, and Pabégu in Benin. Their current population is approximately 25,000 people.
REFERENCE: Samuel Decalo. *Historical Dictionary of Benin.* 1987.

TANGALE. The Tangale people—also identified over the years as Tangles and Biliris—are a Nigerian ethnic group. They speak a Chadic language and can be found today in the Tangale and Kaltungo districts of the Gombe Division of Bauchi State.
REFERENCE: *Language Survey of Nigeria.* 1976.

TANGLE. *See* TANGALE.

TANKAY. *See* MENABE.

TANOSY. *See* ANTANOSY.

TANUSI. *See* ANTANOSY.

TAOUBALT. The Taoubalts are a small ethnic group living in Western Sahara, in what is today Morocco. They are known as *chorfas*—highly religious people who consider themselves direct descendants of the Prophet Mohammed. They are divided into two subgroups: the Oulad Sidi Djemma and the Oulad Khelaif. The Taoubalts are closely associated with the Izarguiens.* They live today between Oued Noun and the Saguia el-Hamra.
REFERENCE: Tony Hodges. *Historical Dictionary of Western Sahara.* 1982.

TAPSHIN. The Tapshin people, whom neighbors also call the Surus and Myets, are one of the Plateau peoples of Nigeria. They live in the Kaduna District of the Pankshin Division of Plateau State.
REFERENCE: *Language Survey of Nigeria.* 1976.

TAQALI. The Taqali (Taqili, Taqwe, and Teqale) are one of the non-Arabic Nuba* peoples of Kordofan Province of Sudan. Their population today exceeds 180,000 people, and they live in two clusters, as highlanders and as people of the plains. Most highlanders are subsistence farmers who use iron-tipped dibble sticks and hoes to raise sorghum, cotton, and peanuts through rainfall agricultural techniques in the granite inselbergs of the northeastern Nuba Mountains.

The Taqali who live on the plains surround the town of Abbasiya. Those in Abbasiya function in a diverse economy, while the plains farmers are often involved in large-scale commercial agriculture. The Taqali are virtually all Muslim in their religious loyalties. During the eighteenth and nineteenth centuries, the Taqali enjoyed the status of statehood, with their kingdom reaching as far south as the Tira Hills. During the years of the Anglo-Egyptian Sudan, from 1898 to 1956, the Taqali ruling families were incorporated into the local colonial administration. It was not until the Sudanese revolution of 1969 that the Taqali elites lost their relative political independence. Most Taqilis speak Arabic as a second language.
REFERENCE: Janet Ewald. "Taqalis." In Richard V. Weekes, ed. *Muslim Peoples.* 1984.

TAQILI. *See* TAQALI.

TAQWE. *See* TAQILI and NUBA.

TARA. *See* BOBO.

TARAKIRI. The Tarakiris are a subgroup of the Izon* peoples of Rivers State in Nigeria.

TARAWA. The Tarawa are an ethnic group in Mozambique. They are particularly concentrated in the Chicoa, Cachomba, Mague, and Changara regions of Tete Province. Although many Tarawas support themselves as small farmers, the ethnic group as a whole is widely known for its skill in weaving and textiles. The Tarawas consider themselves descendants of Mwenemutapa, their founding chief.
REFERENCE: Mario Azevedo. *Historical Dictionary of Mozambique.* 1991.

TARIYA. *See* CHARA.

TAROK. The Taroks (Appas, Yergams, Yergums) are a Nigerian people. Their language is part of the Benue group of the Benue-Congo family. Most Taroks live today in the Plain Yergam, Hill Yergam, and Wase districts of the Langtang Division of Plateau State.
REFERENCE: *Language Survey of Nigeria.* 1976.

TATSI. The Tatsis are a subgroup of the Lendu* peoples of Zaire.

TAUNG. The Taung are a subgroup (more exactly, a chiefdom) of the Sotho* people of Lesotho and South Africa.

TAVARA. The Tavaras are a subgroup of the Korekores,* who constitute the "Northern Shona"* cluster of peoples in Zimbabwe.

TAVETA. The Tavetas are a small ethnic group of approximately 12,000 people who live in the Taita/Taveta District of the Coast Province of Kenya. They raise cattle, sheep, and goats, and they farm as well, producing tobacco, maize, and cassava. They are classified as one of the Coastal Bantu* peoples of East Africa. They can also be found across the border in Tanzania.
REFERENCE: Bethwell A. Ogot. *Historical Dictionary of Kenya.* 1981.

TAWANA. The Tawanas (Batawanas) were part of the Ngwatos,* a Tswana* subgroup, until the late eighteenth century. After a dispute with the Ngwatos, they migrated to the Kgwebe Hills in what is today Ngamiland, Botswana. There they came to dominate the Yeis,* Mbukushus,* Kgalagadis,* and San* peoples. During the 1890s, the Tawanas came under British* control. By the 1920s, the Tawanas were the most successful cattle raisers in Bechuanaland. The tsetse fly infestation reduced those herds in the 1930s, and, in the era since World War II, large numbers of Tawanas have become laborers in the mining and commercial economy.
REFERENCES: Fred Morton, A. Murray, and J. Ramsay. *Historical Dictionary of Botswana.* 1989; R. Kent Rasmussen. *Historical Dictionary of Zimbabwe.* 1994.

TAWARA. The Tawara (Tavara) are a small ethnic group of several thousand people living in Mozambique, primarily between northern Darwin District and the Zambezi River, as well as in Zimbabwe. Most of the Tawara are small subsistence farmers who live along the banks of the lower Zambezi River. During the late eighteenth and nineteenth centuries, they actively participated in the slave trade, capturing and selling other Africans to Portuguese* traders. The Tawara population today exceeds 300,000 people.
REFERENCES: Mario Azevedo. *Historical Dictionary of Mozambique.* 1991; R. Kent Rasmussen. *Historical Dictionary of Zimbabwe.* 1994.

TBOU. *See* TEBU.

TCHADE. *See* GUDE.

TCHAMAN. *See* ABRON.

TCHAMBA. *See* BASARI.

TCHAMBA. *See* CHAMBA.

TCHARIGIRIA. *See* KURI.

TCHRIMBO. *See* EBRIÉ.

TCHUKULIA. *See* KURI.

TÉBOU. *See* TEBU.

TEBU. The Tebu—who are also called the Tébou, Tibbu, Tubu, Tbou, Toub-bou, and Toubou—inhabit the Tibesti region of the central Sahara in the northern reaches of Chad. They can also be found in the Sahel and Saharan regions of Niger and Sudan, with a small cluster of perhaps 2,500 people in southern Libya. Their total population is approximately 230,000 people. Although these people have a generic sense of ethnicity, they are divided by language. Included in the subcategory of Tebu peoples who speak one of the Saharan branches of the Nilo-Saharan linguistic family are the Kanembu* in the area of Lake Chad, the Daza* and Aza* in the Sahel of Niger and Chad, the Teda* in central Tibesti and Libya, the Ennedi,* the Bideyat (Beri*) in Sudan, and the Zaghawa* of Sudan. The Kreda* and Bulgeda are also Tebu subgroups. All of these groups have similar systems of social organization, based on patrilineal clans, and similar material cultures. They are all Muslims, converted during the early years of the Arab* conquest. Most Tebu groups practice oasis agriculture and/or nomadic pastoralism. The Tebu proper are subdivided into two groups of people. One of those groups speaks the Dazaga* language and is further subdivided into the Daza, Aza, Dowaza, and Wajunga. The other group is the Teda, who call their language Tedaga.
REFERENCES: R. R. Akester. "Tibesti—Land of the Tebou." *Geographical Magazine* 31 (1958): 12–26; Catherine Baroin. *Anarchie et Cohésion Chez les Toubou.* 1985; Catherine Baroin. "The Position of Tubu Women in Pastoral Production." *Ethnos* 5 (1987): 138–55.

TEDA. The Tedas, whose population numbers approximately 22,000 people, are one of the Tebu* (Toubou) groups of the Tibesti region of northwestern Chad; about 3,000 more Tedas live across the border in southern Libya, and smaller groups of Tedas are scattered through Niger and Chad. Most Tedas live in isolated regions of the Tibesti Mountains, where they herd goats and camels and farm the oases. Thanks to the volcanic mountains of the region, the Tibesti region enjoys more rainfall than the lowland deserts; the Tedas live in villages in the mountain valleys. Date-palm groves abound, and the Tedas support themselves by harvesting the dates and raising small amounts of food. The Tedas in Niger live in the Djado region, between Agadem and Soutellan, where they are known as the Braouia. They herd goats and camels on a semi-nomadic basis; there is not enough water for cattle. The Tedas call their language Tedaga. They are known for their taciturn hostility toward their Arab* and Taureg* neighbors. The Teda themselves subdivided into patrilineal clans, including the Tomaghera, Tarsoa, Tameurtioua, Tozoba, Gouboda, Factoa, Kosseda, Dirsina, Bardoa, Odobaya, Terintere, Keressa, Tchioda, Mogode, Aozouya, Taizera, Gounda, Fortena, Mada, Tegua, and Kamadja.

Virtually all Tedas are Muslims, their conversion dating back to the Arab conquest. During the 1970s and early 1980s, the Tedas suffered badly from the civil war in Chad. The Tibesti region became a refuge for the Muslim guerrilla forces fighting the central government, and Chadian forces regularly launched military campaigns there. Severe drought has also damaged the Teda economy, forcing men to leave the region in search of work; the women and children remain behind to watch the herds.

REFERENCES: Monique Brandily. "Songs to Birds Among the Teda of Chad." *Journal of Ethnomusicology* 26 (September 1982): 371–81; Kim Kramer. "Teda." In Richard V. Weekes, ed. *Muslim Peoples.* 1984; Helen Metz. *Libya: A Country Study.* 1987.

TEDAGA. *See* TEDA.

TEEL. *See* MONTOL.

TEGALI. The Tegalis are one of the Nuba* peoples of Sudan.

TEGRE. *See* TIGRE.

TÉGUESSIÉ. *See* LOBI.

TEIS-UM-DANAB. The Teis-um-Danabs are one of the Nuba* peoples of Sudan.

TEKARIR. *See* TUKULOR.

TÉKÉ. The Tékés, also known as Batekes, live in the grassy savanna plateaus east of Franceville in Haut-Ogooué Province in eastern Gabon and across the border in Congo. They can also be found living on both sides of the Zaire River between Kinshasa and the confluence of the Kasai and Zaire rivers. In the Congo Republic, they are known as the Téké and are very closely related to the Tyo. The Tékés are also closely related to the Mbambas, Ndoumous,* and Kaniguis.* Ethnologists believe that the Tékés originated to the northwest and began their migration to their contemporary homeland in the fifteenth century. They planted palm trees after arriving in the region and made their living trading palm oil and raphia fabrics. They also engaged in the slave trade during the eighteenth and nineteenth centuries. Their population today exceeds 150,000 people. Although most Tékés are settled farmers today, raising manioc and bananas, they still enjoy hunting antelopes, gazelles, and other animals.

REFERENCES: F. Scott Bobb. *Historical Dictionary of Zaire.* 1988; Claude Cabrol and Raoul Lehuard. *La civilisation des peuples batéké,* 1976; David E. Gardinier. *Historical Dictionary of Gabon.* 1995.

TEKNA. The Tekna people today live primarily in southern Morocco, although they can also be found in Mauritania, Algeria, Western Sahara, and Mali. They are partly sedentary and partly nomadic. Historically, the Tekna peoples were never really united. They are divided into two coalitions—the Ait Atmans* and the Ait Jmels.* The largest Tekna group is the Izarguiens.*
REFERENCE: Tony Hodges. *Historical Dictionary of Western Sahara.* 1982.

TEM. *See* KOTOKOLI.

TEMBA. *See* KOTOKOLI.

TEMBE. *See* TEMBO.

TEMBI. *See* TAMBA.

TEMBO. The Tembos are a major subgroup of the Shona* people of Mozambique. They are of Nguni* origin and speak a Bantu* language. Most Tembos live south of Delagoa Bay.

TEME. The Temes are one of the Chadic-speaking peoples of Nigeria. They are closely related to the Teras.* They live in the Mayo Belwa District of the Adamawa Division of Gongola State.
REFERENCE: *Language Survey of Nigeria.* 1976.

TEMEIN. The Temeins are one of the Nuba* peoples of Sudan.

TEMNE. The Temne, also known as Timne and Timmanee, are one of the largest ethnic groups in Sierra Leone, constituting, with approximately 1.5 million people, about a third of the country's population. They also can be found in Guinea. They dwell in the northern region of the coastal bush and in the adjacent rain forest. Ethnolinguists classify the Temne language as part of the Mel group of the Congo-Kordofanian family. Their own oral traditions place their beginnings in the Futa Jalon region of Guinea, but they migrated southwest to the Freetown peninsula before the arrival of the Portuguese* in the late fifteenth century. Today, the city of Freetown remains essentially a Temne environment. Muslim traders brought Islam to the Temne in the seventeenth century, and today approximately 475,000 of the Temne are Muslims; the others are Roman Catholic, Protestant, or Poro. The Poro religion is strong among the southern Temne, where Islam is weakest. Poro values emphasize traditional Temne religion and culture, and there is considerable animosity between Muslim Temne and Poro Temne. The Temne are also divided into such subgroups as the Sandas, Yonis, Kholifas, and Kunikes.

Between 80 and 90 percent of the Temne are farmers whose staple is rice. They produce both upland dry rice and wet, swamp rice. They also produce cassava and millet. For cash crops, the Temnes raise and sell peanuts, oil palm products, tobacco, ginger, and kola. Other Temnes work in mines, mills, factories, and a variety of urban occupations. Their social structure is based on patrilineal clans, and polygyny is common.

During the years of British* colonial power, the Temne were grouped into forty-four chiefdoms, and those chiefdoms were designated as administrative districts. Taken together, they constituted the Northern Province of Sierra Leone. Sierra Leone achieved independence in 1961, and, since then, the Temne have played an active role in national politics, particularly in the Sierra Leone People's party and the All Peoples Conference.

REFERENCES: Vernon R. Dorjahn. "Temne Household Size and Composition: Rural Changes over Time and Rural-Urban Differences." *Ethnology* 16 (1977): 105–27; Vernon R. Dorjahn. "Temne." In Richard V. Weekes, ed. *Muslim Peoples.* 1984; K. C. Wylie. *The Political Kingdoms of the Temne.* 1977.

TEN. *See* GANAWURI.

TENDA. The Tenda, also known as Tanda, are a cluster of related ethnic groups in eastern Senegal, Guinea, and Guinea-Bissau, including the Basaris,* Koñagis* (Coniagui), Badyarans* (Bajaranke, Badyaranke), Bediks,* Boenis, and Mayos. The Koñagis, Basaris, and Badyaran are concentrated around Youkoukoun in the northern part of middle Guinea. The Koñagis and Basaris actually straddle the border between Senegal and Guinea. The Boenis are probably Basaris who converted to Islam. During the years of the slave trade, the Tenda peoples fled to the isolated hills of southeastern Senegal and across the border in Guinea and Guinea-Bissau. Their population today is approximately 30,000 people.

REFERENCES: Andrew F. Clark and Lucie Colvin Phillips. *Historical Dictionary of Senegal.* 1994; Harold D. Nelson et al. *Area Handbook of Guinea.* 1975; Thomas O'Toole. *Historical Dictionary of Guinea.* 1987.

TENDE. *See* KURIA.

TENGABISSI. "Tengabissi" (Tinguimbissi) is a term referring to most of the people living east of the Red Volta in Burkina-Faso. Many consider the term synonymous with Ninisi.*

TENGKEDOGO. *See* TENKODOGO.

TENKODOGO. The Tenkodogos (Tengkedogos) are one of the Molé-Dagbane* groups living today in southeastern Burkina-Faso and across the border in northern Togo and northern Benin. They are concentrated around the town of Tenkodogo in the East Department of Burkina-Faso. Although the agricultural production of sorghum and millet is important to the Tenkodogo, they are also known for their skill at raising cattle and goats. The Tenkodogo population today exceeds one million people.

REFERENCE: Daniel M. McFarland. *Historical Dictionary of Upper Volta.* 1978.

TEPETH. The Tepeths are part of the Karimojon* cluster of peoples who live today in eastern and northeastern Uganda, as well as in Kenya. Most Tepeths are farmers, raising millet, sorghum, sweet potatoes, groundnuts, cassava, and cotton. Many Tepeth men supplement their diets with protein from fishing in the swamps and lakes of the area.

TEQALE. *See* TAQALI and NUBA.

TERA. The Teras are part of the larger cluster of Kanuri* peoples of Bornu State in northeastern Nigeria. Their economy is a complex one, revolving around commerce, home manufacturing, personal services, and agriculture. The farmers raise guinea corn, millet, groundnuts, cattle, sheep, and goats. They also fish in Lake Chad. In recent years, they have begun to produce cotton as a cash crop. They are Sunni Muslims. Some ethnologists classify the Tera as an offshoot of the Bolewa* people, although they claim themselves to have originated near the city of Mecca on the Arabian peninsula.

REFERENCES: Ronald Cohen. *The Kanuri of Bornu.* 1967; Donald G. Morrison et al. *Black Africa: A Comparative Handbook.* 1989; C. L. Temple, ed. *Notes on the Tribes, Provinces, Emirates and States of the Northern Provinces of Nigeria.* 1967.

TEREA. *See* CHARA.

TERIA. *See* CHARA.

TERIK. The Teriks, also known as Nyang'oris, live in the western highlands of Kenya. They are a subgroup of the Kalenjin* cluster of peoples. Cattle were central to the traditional Terik economy, but, in recent years, the Teriks have started raising maize and tobacco on large commercial farms and moving to towns and cities for work and business opportunities. The Teriks enjoyed a reputation as fierce, skilled warriors who regularly raided neighboring Masais,* Luos,* and Gusiis* for cattle. The arrival of British* military force in the region in 1905 ended those raids.

TERRI. *See* CHARA.

TESO. The Teso people, whose current population probably exceeds one million, are an ethnic group living east of Lake Kyoga in eastern Uganda and across the border in western Kenya. They speak a Nilotic* language and are known for the paintings of men and animals that adorn their houses. Ethnologists believe the Teso originated in the Great River Valley, north of their present lo-

cation; the Teso themselves claim to be descendants of the Karimojon.* The traditional Teso economy was based on cattle herding, but the rinderpest infestations of the nineteenth century destroyed most of their herds, forcing the Teso to make the transition to agriculture. Today, most Teso are farmers, raising millet, sorghum, sweet potatoes, groundnuts, cassava, and cotton. Many Tesos supplement their diets with protein from fishing in the swamps and lakes of the area. They are considered part of the Karimojon cluster of peoples.
REFERENCE: *African Encyclopedia.* 1974.

TETELA. The Tetela people live between Lusambo and the Upper Zaire River in Sankuru and Maniema in the Kasai Oriental and Kivu regions of Zaire. They are fishermen and farmers who raise cassava, bananas, and kola nuts. The Tetelas speak a Mongo* language, which is part of the larger Bantu* linguistic family. The Tetelas are closely related to the Kusus* and did not really separate from them until the late 1800s when Afro-Arabs and Belgian* colonial authorities arrived in the region. They had extensive contacts with the Afro-Arabs, and in the process many of them adopted Islam. The most famous Tetela in Zairean history was Patrice Lumumba.
REFERENCE: F. Scott Bobb. *Historical Dictionary of Zaire.* 1988.

TÉUESSUÉ. The Téuessués live in far northwestern Ghana, far northeastern Ivory Coast, and in Burkina-Faso, where they make their living as farmers and livestock raisers. Most African ethnologists consider them a subgroup of the Lobi* people.

TEUSO. The Teuso people today live in small towns and cities in Uganda. Until the 1960s, they lived in the Kidepo National Park in Uganda, but they were relocated at that time. Their Karimojon* neighbors despised the Teusos, who survived by subsistence farming, hunting, and cattle raiding. Displaced from the land, they moved to towns and work today as day laborers.
REFERENCE: Rita M. Byrnes et al. *Uganda: A Country Study.* 1990.

TEWE. The Tewe are a small ethnic group of several thousand people living in Mozambique. Most of them are small subsistence farmers who live along the banks of the lower Zambezi River. During the late eighteenth and nineteenth centuries, they actively participated in the slave trade, capturing and selling other Africans to Portuguese* traders.
REFERENCE: Mario Azevedo. *Historical Dictionary of Mozambique.* 1991.

TGHUADE. *See* DGHWEDE.

THAALAT. The Thaalats are a subgroup of the Reguibat* people of Western Sahara in what is today Morocco. They are subdivided themselves into the Ahel Dekhil, the Ahel Meiara, and the Ahel Rachid. Their population today exceeds 1,000 people, of whom perhaps a third live in El-Ayoun. The rest are nomads.

THABEDE. The Thabedes are one of the clans of the Emakhandzambili,* who themselves are one of the three major subgroups of the Swazi* people of Swaziland.

THARAKA. The Tharakas are part of the Central Bantu* cluster of peoples living in Kenya. The Tharaka population today exceeds 75,000 people. Most of them are farmers living in south-central Kenya near Nairobi. They are closely related to the Meru* peoples.
REFERENCE: Donald G. Morrison et al. *Black Africa: A Comparative Handbook.* 1989.

THEMBU. The Thembu are a Xhosa*-speaking group of people living in the Transkei and Ciskei regions of South Africa. Ethnohistorians estimate that the Thembu have been living in these regions for at least one thousand years. When the Thembu turned on the whites in 1846–1847, they were defeated militarily and assigned to live in Gcalekaland. Those Thembus who willingly cooperated became known as ''Emigrant Thembu,'' while those who tried to stay away from whites became known as ''True Thembu.'' Although the traditional Thembu economy was based on mixed agriculture (the production of cattle, goats, maize, shorghum, and pumpkins), the contemporary Thembu raise these products commercially or work as laborers in the mines, cities, factories, and plantations of South Africa. Today, the leader of the African National Congress, Nelson Mandela, is a Thembu.
REFERENCE: *African Encyclopedia.* 1974.

THEPU. The term ''Thepu'' (Bathepu) is sometimes used to refer to the peoples of Nguni* origin living in Lesotho. Included in this cluster are the Fengos, Pondos, Thembu,* and Vundles.*
REFERENCE: Gordon Haliburton. *Historical Dictionary of Lesotho.* 1977.

THIANG. The Thiangs are a major subdivision of the Nuer* people of southern Sudan. They are concentrated on Zeraf Island in the Fanjak District.

THONGA. *See* TONGA.

TIAN. *See* BOBO.

TIAPI. The Tiapis (Tyapis) are a small ethnic group living today in Guinea. They speak a language very close to that of the Landomas,* and, though many ethnologists consider them to be a Landoma subgroup, they have a distinct sense of identity as Tiapis. They are concentrated in the Gaoual Administrative

District of Guinea and call themselves Cocoli. They have their origins in the Fouta Djallon region. Most Tiapis are rice farmers.
REFERENCE: Harold D. Nelson et al. *Area Handbook for Guinea.* 1975.

TIBBU. *See* TEBU.

TIDDI. *See* MEIDOB.

TIEFO. The Tiefos (Tyéfo) are an ethnic group whom anthropologists classify as part of the larger cluster of Senufo* peoples of West Africa. The Tiefos are concentrated along the border of northern Ivory Coast, southern Mali, and south-western Burkina-Faso, primarily south of Bobo-Dioulasso. Their major settle-ment of Noumoudara was destroyed by Samory in 1897, when most Tiefos were killed. They never recovered ethnically. Most of them are now small farmers, raising corn, rice, yams, peanuts, sesame, and sweet potatoes.
REFERENCE: Daniel M. McFarland. *Historical Dictionary of Upper Volta.* 1978.

TIENGA. The Tiengas are considered a Fringe Manding* group who trace their tribal origins back to the Mali Empire of the thirteenth century. Today they are pastoralists and subsistence farmers who live in Burkina-Faso. The Tienga pop-ulation exceeds 40,000, of whom 25,000 are Muslims. They can also be found in northern Benin.
REFERENCE: Donald R. Wright. "Manding-Speaking Peoples." In Richard V. Weekes, ed. *Muslim Peoples.* 1984.

TIGANIA. The Tiganias are a Bantu*-speaking people who are a subgroup of the Meru* cluster of peoples in Kenya and Tanzania.

TIGONG. *See* MBEMBE.

TIGRAY. *See* TIGRE.

TIGRE. The Tigre (Tegre, Tigray) are nomadic pastoralists who live in northern and western Eritrea and Tigre provinces in Ethiopia. Their population numbers several million. Most of them are Muslims. They speak a Semitic language. As a people, they are closely related to the Tigrinya.* The Tigres raise cattle, cam-els, goats, and sheep. The first Tigre converts to Islam were living on islands in the Red Sea in the seventh century when Muslim missionaries reached them, but it was not until the nineteenth century that widespread conversions on the mainland took place. Approximately half of the Tigres are part of the Beni Amer* people, to whom they are serfs and workers. During the 1970s and 1980s, the Tigres suffered because of government policies. The Marxist government of Ethiopia was not sympathetic to the lifestyle of nomadic peoples and worked at forcing them into a sedentary life. The government also persecuted Muslims. In addition, the war associated with Ethiopia's attempt to incorporate Eritrea into the economic and political life of the country disrupted Tigre life. Tens of thousands of Tigres took refuge in Sudan.

There are a number of other groups who speak Tigre but are of different ethnic origins. Historically, the Tigres were the Muslim vassals of the Bet Asgede people, but, in the nineteenth century, the Bet Asgedes adopted the language and religion of their serfs, becoming Tigre-speaking Muslims. The Bet Asgedes are subdivided into three ethnic groups of their own: the Hababs, Ad Tekles,* and Ad Temaryams.*

REFERENCES: Dan F. Bauer. *Household and Society in Ethiopia: An Economic and Social Analysis of Tigray.* 1977; Thomas R. DeGregori. "Tigre." In Richard V. Weekes, ed. *Muslim Peoples.* 1984.

TIGRINYA. The Tigrinyas are a Semitic-speaking people who live in the northern and western sections of Eritrea and Tigre provinces of Ethiopia. They are closely related linguistically to the Tigres,* but the Tigrinyas are overwhelmingly Christians, while the Tigres are Muslims. The Tigrinyas are sedentary farmers who raise smaller amounts of livestock than the nomadic Tigre. War and drought have disrupted Tigrinya life in recent years. Today, the Tigrinya population in Ethiopia exceeds four million people.

REFERENCES: Dan F. Bauer. *Household and Society in Ethiopia: An Economic and Social Analysis of Tigray.* 1977; Thomas R. DeGregori. "Tigre." In Richard V. Weekes, ed. *Muslim Peoples.* 1984.

TIGUN. *See* MBEMBE.

TIJANJI. *See* JANJI.

TIKAR. The Tikar are one of the many ethnic groups of Cameroon. They live in the Bamenda highlands of North West Province, primarily in the Upper Mbam Valley, where most of them labor as farmers, raising a variety of cereals, coffee, groundnuts, tea, and tobacco. They are part of the Bamiléké* cluster. Along with smaller groups closely related to the Tikars, their current population exceeds 600,000 people. They are divided into many independent chiefdoms, with dialect differences so great that even groups within a few miles of each other have difficulty understanding one another's languages. Ethnologists believe the Tikars came to their present location from areas to the northeast. They live in highly centralized, densely populated settlements. They are known regionally for their skill in metal work, pottery, sculpture, and handicrafts. The Tikars are subdivided into the Kom,* Ndop,* Nso,* Wum,* and Bafut* peoples, whose cultures are identical but who are divided by loyalties to their own subchiefdoms. Most of the Tikar groups are patrilineal societies.

REFERENCES: Mark W. DeLancey and H. M. Mokeba. *Historical Dictionary of the Republic of Cameroon.* 1990; Marietta B. Joseph. "Dance Masks of the Tikar." *African*

Arts 7 (Spring 1974): 46–52; Harold D. Nelson et al. *Area Handbook for the United Republic of Cameroon.* 1974.

TIKURIMI. *See* KURAMA.

TIKUU. *See* BAJUNI.

TIMAP. *See* AMO.

TIMBARA. The Timbaras are a subgroup of the Sadama* people of Shewa Province in southwestern Ethiopia. They speak an eastern Cushitic language and are Muslims. Most Timbaras make their living raising ensete. Some ethnologists also place them with the Kembattas.*

TIMBO. The Timbos are one of the Bassa* clans living in the River Cess Territory of Liberia.

TIMENE. The Timenes are a small Senegambian* ethnic group located south of Gabu in Guinea-Bissau. During the Mandinka* expansion that began in the fifteenth century, they became isolated from other Senegambian groups. Most Timenes make their living as small farmers.
REFERENCE: Richard Lobban and Joshua Forrest. *Historical Dictionary of the Republic of Guinea-Bissau.* 1988.

TIMMANEE. *See* TEMNE.

TIMN. *See* KOTOKOLI.

TIMNE. *See* TEMNE.

TIMONJY. The Timonjys are a subgroup of the Bara* cluster of peoples of the plains of Madagascar.

TINDIGA. *See* HADZA.

TINGA. The Tingas are one of the Bantu*-speaking peoples of Nigeria. They are classified as part of the Plateau cluster of peoples who occupy central Nigeria. Most Tingas practice subsistence horticulture, raising ginger, millet, guinea corn, beans, and citrus products. They live in social systems characterized by patrilineal descent and patrifocal residence. In recent years, they have begun migrating to towns and cities looking for work.
REFERENCE: Donald G. Morrison et al. *Black Africa: A Comparative Handbook.* 1989.

TINGUIMBISSI. *See* TENGABISSI.

TIO. The Tio people live along the southern stretches of the Zaire River in southern Congo and southwestern Zaire. As early as the fifteenth century, the Tio Kingdom was established there along the river. They were a riverine people who dominated trade in the region because of their geographical access up and down the Zaire. They speak a Bantu* language.
REFERENCE: Irving Kaplan et al. *Zaire: A Country Study.* 1978.

TIRIKI. The Tirikis are a subgroup of the Luhya* people of Kenya and Uganda. They are a Western Bantu* people who live today north of Lake Victoria on both sides of the Kenyan-Ugandan border.

TIRMA. The Tirmas are a small ethnic group living in Ethiopia. They speak a Nilo-Saharan language and make their living as pastoralists. The Tirma population is approximately 10,000 people.
REFERENCE: M. L. Bender, J. D. Bowen, R. L. Cooper, and C. A. Ferguson, *Language in Ethiopia.* 1976.

TISKENA. The Tiskenas are a small ethnic group living today in Ethiopia. The Tiskenas speak a Nilo-Saharan language and live in close proximity to Majang* and Omotic* peoples. The Tiskenas are primarily plow agriculturalists who also raise cattle. Most of them live in far southwestern Ethiopia.
REFERENCE: Harold D. Nelson et al. *Ethiopia: A Country Study.* 1980.

TITA. The Titas are a linguistically isolated Nigerian people who live today in the Jalingo District of the Muri Division of Gongola State.
REFERENCE: *Language Survey of Nigeria.* 1976.

TITU. The Titus are a small ethnic group living today in Zaire. They are concentrated on the north bank of the Kasai River in southwestern Zaire, between Llebo and Bandundu. As a riverine people, the Titus have traditionally made their living by fishing, working small gardens on the river banks, and engaging in commercial trade up and down the Kasai. Most Titus still engage in those traditional pursuits, although the numbers moving to cities and towns looking for work are rapidly increasing.
REFERENCE: Irving Kaplan et al. *Zaire: A Country Study.* 1978.

TIV. There are more than 2.5 million Tiv people living in the middle Benue valley of Benue State of Nigeria. They can also be found in the Lafia Division of Plateau State and in the Wukari Division of Gongola State. They remain loyal to their traditional descent systems, based on ancestors who lived several generations ago, and trace those lineages through the male line. Each *tar*—the smallest descent group—controls property, and Tiv men are allowed to farm the land. In the southern part of their territory, the Tiv raise yams; in the north, they produce millet. Their main cash crop is soy beans. Because of their warrior tradition, the Tiv make fine soldiers, and substantial numbers of them have joined the Nigerian army.

REFERENCES: R. C. Abraham. *The Tiv People.* 1933; *African Encyclopedia.* 1974; A. Oyewelo. *Historical Dictionary of Nigeria.* 1987; Michel Vernon. "Segmentation Among the Tiv: A Reappraisal." *American Ethnology* 10 (May 1983): 290–301.

TJIMBA. The Tjimbas are a subgroup of the Kaokabanders, themselves a subgroup of the Herero* people of Namibia and Angola.

TLOKOA. *See* TLOKWA.

TLOKWA. The Tlokwa (Batlokwa, Batlokoa, Tlokoa) are a subgroup, or, more exactly, a chiefdom, of the Tswana* people of Lesotho, Botswana, and South Africa. Before the 1820s, they lived northwest of the Sotho* clans in the Caledon Valley, near what is today Harrismith. They acted as middlemen between the Ngunis* and interior ethnic groups. During repeated warfare in the 1830s, they fled their homeland and began the move to their present location. Most Tlokwas today are farmers and livestock raisers.

REFERENCE: Gordon Haliburton. *Historical Dictionary of Lesotho.* 1977.

TOF. *See* KULERE.

TOFINU. The Tofinus are a subgroup of the Goun* peoples of Benin, who themselves are part of the larger Fon* or Ewe* cluster of peoples. Some Tofinus can also be found in Togo and Ghana.

TOGBO. The Togbos are a subgroup of the Banda* people of the Central African Republic. Their current population exceeds 175,000 people.

TOGHWEDE. *See* DGHWEDE.

TOJIMA. *See* KURI.

TOKA. The Tokas are a small ethnic group living today in extreme southern Zambia, north of Victoria Falls and east along the Zambezi River. Their population is approximately 22,000 people. The Tokas speak a Tonga* language and maintain a highly decentralized political system. Most Tokas are small farmers and cattle raisers.

REFERENCE: John J. Grotpeter. *Historical Dictionary of Zambia.* 1979.

TOKOLOR. *See* TUKULOR.

TOLBA. The Tolbas are one of the Moor* subgroups living today in Mauritania.

TOLU. The Tolus are one of the two main subgroups of the Gimira* people of Ethiopia.

TOMA. *See* LOMA.

TOMBO. The Tombos are a subgroup of the Habé* peoples of Burkina-Faso. Included in this cluster of people are the Dogons,* Kados,* and Toros.* They originally inhabited the Katenga region but were displaced by Mossi* expansion toward the Mali border. Most of them make their living as small farmers, raising peanuts, millet, and sorghum.
REFERENCE: Daniel M. McFarland. *Historical Dictionary of Upper Volta.* 1978.

TON. *See* ANYI.

TON. *See* BAULE.

TONCOULEUR. *See* TUKULOR.

TONGA. The Tonga, not to be confused with the much larger Tonga* group of people in Zambia, Malawi, Mozambique, and Zimbabwe, are a small ethnic group living in Mungari and Mandie near Vila Catandica and Tete in Mozambique. They can also be found in northern Malawi. These Tongas are closely related to the Tumbukas,* who are their neighbors to the north and west. After decades of domination at the hands of the Ngonis,* the Tongas rebelled in the 1880s and allied themselves with Scottish missionaries. Most Tongas today work in South Africa, Mozambique, and Zimbabwe. Those living in Malawi are small farmers.
REFERENCES: Mario Azevedo. *Historical Dictionary of Mozambique.* 1991; Harold D. Nelson et al. *Area Handbook for Malawi.* 1975.

TONGA. The Tonga (Batonga) people are one of the main ethnic groups of southern Zambia. A substantial number of Tongas also live in Zimbabwe and in the southern reaches of the Northern Region of Malawi, along the shore of Lake Malawi. Some can also be found in Swaziland and in Mozambique, especially to the south in Gaza Province. They are an offshoot of the Zulu* people, having migrated from South Africa and displaced the Chopes and Bitongas. The Rongas,* Shanganas,* and Tswas* are subgroups of the Tongas. They have traditionally lacked a central authority, and, during the nineteenth century, they were devastated by armies of the Lozis* and Ndebeles.* Most of their cattle herds were stolen or destroyed, and large numbers of Tonga men ended up in slavery. The Tonga social system is patrilineal. They speak a Bantu* language that is closely related to the languages of the Ila,* Lenje,* Totela,* and Sala* peoples of Zambia and to the Tumbuka* of Malawi. Today, the Tongas make their living as fishermen on Lake Malawi, small farmers, and migrant laborers.

The contemporary Tonga population consists of several million people. Other groups, like the Lenjes, Solis,* Ilas, Tokas,* Leyas, Salas, and Gowas, speak a Tonga language. The Tongas in Zambia are classified in two large clusters: the Plateau Tongas and the Gwembe Tongas.

REFERENCES: *African Encyclopedia.* 1974; John J. Grotpeter. *Historical Dictionary of Zambia.* 1979; Jaap Van Velsen. *The Politics of Kinship: A Study of Social Manipulation Among the Lakeside Tonga of Nyasaland.* 1964.

TONGBA. *See* TANEKA.

TONGBO. *See* MAMBILA.

TONGWE. The Tongwe people are an ethnic group living in west-central Tanzania, in the Kigora and Tabora regions of the central highlands. Most Tongwes raise cattle and farm. Their population today is approximately 15,000 people.

REFERENCE: Laura Kurtz. *Historical Dictionary of Tanzania.* 1978.

TOPOSA. Like the Turkanas,* the Toposas are an ethnic group in East Africa who speak a Central Nilotic* language. They live in southern Sudan near the Uganda border. The Toposas pursue a pastoral lifestyle, with the women and children living in permanent villages and the men leaving home seasonally to take the cattle to pastures. The cattle provide the Toposas with milk, blood, and hides. Toposa women work agricultural plots and raise millet, maize, cow peas, and some tobacco. Because of the droughts that have hit the region in the 1980s and early 1990s, the Toposas have faced what can be called at best a very marginal living. Their traditional religion and culture revolve around cattle.

REFERENCES: John Lamphear. *The Traditional History of the Jie of Uganda.* 1976.

TORO. The Toros (Rutoro, Rutooro) are part of the western Interlacustrine Bantu* of western Uganda, which includes the Nyankores* and Nyoros.* Their own historical traditions describe a group of alien gods who brought centralized government, a kingdom, and cattle to them in ancient times. Historians can identify a Nyoro kingdom in the region about five centuries ago—the Bunyoro-Kitara empire. Toro became a separate kingdom around 1830. They lost out to Buganda expansion, however, later in the nineteenth century. The traditional Toro economy revolved around the hunting of elephants, lions, leopards, and crocodiles, but they have switched to agriculture in recent years, raising bananas, rice, millet, cassava, sweet potatoes, cotton, tobacco, and coffee. Most Toros today can be found living on Uganda's western border, south of Lake Albert. Today, the Toro population exceeds 450,000 people, most of whom are Christians or Toro animists. Only 2 percent of the Toros are Muslims.

REFERENCES: *African Encyclopedia.* 1974; Rita M. Byrnes et al. *Uganda: A Country Study.* 1990.

TORODO. *See* TUKULOR.

TOROM. The Toroms are an ethnic group in Chad. Most of the 50,000 or so Toroms are Muslims. They are part of the larger Nilotic* cluster of Chadian peoples. Most Toroms make their living as small farmers, laborers, and semi-nomadic and nomadic pastoralists.
REFERENCES: Pierre Hugot. *Le Tchad.* 1965; J. C. Lebeuf. *Afrique Centrale.* 1972; Donald G. Morrison et al. *Black Africa: A Comparative Handbook.* 1989.

TORTI. The Torti are a subgroup of the Meidobs* of Sudan.

TOTELA. The Totelas are a Bantu*-speaking people of southern Zambia. They are closely related to the Ilas,* Tongas,* Lenjes,* and Salas.* Their population today exceeds 30,000 people. They frequently intermarry with Lozis.*
REFERENCE: John J. Grotpeter. *Historical Dictionary of Zambia.* 1979.

TOUBACAYE. *See* JAHANKA.

TOUBBOU. *See* TEBU.

TOUBOU. *See* TEBU.

TOUCOULEUR. *See* TUKULOR.

TOUMAK. The Toumaks are a relatively small ethnic group living today in the Moyen-Chari Prefecture in Chad. Their language is part of the larger Chadian cluster of languages, and it represents a transition between Sara* and Massa.* Most Toumaks are herdsmen and small farmers, raising sorghum, millet, maize, and cotton.
REFERENCE: Thomas Collelo et al. *Chad: A Country Study.* 1988.

TOUNA. The Tounas, like the Tounbé live in far northwestern Ghana, far northeastern Ivory Coast, and in Burkina-Faso, where they make their living as farmers and livestock raisers. Most African ethnologists consider them a subgroup of the Lobi* people.

TOUNBÉ. The Tounbés, like the Touna, live in far northwestern Ghana, far northeastern Ivory Coast, and in Burkina-Faso. Most African ethnologists consider them a subgroup of the Lobi* people.

TOUNDJOUR. The Toundjours are a Chadian ethnic group. Most of the 60,000 or so Toundjours are Muslims. They are part of the larger Nilotic* cluster of

Chadian peoples. Most Toundjours make their living as small farmers, laborers, and semi-nomadic and nomadic pastoralists.

REFERENCES: Pierre Hugot. *Le Tchad.* 1965; J. C. Lebeuf. *Afrique Centrale.* 1972; Donald G. Morrison et al. *Black Africa: A Comparative Handbook.* 1989.

TOUNIA. The Tounians are a subgroup of the Boua* people, who live along the middle Chari River in the Moyen-Chari Prefecture of Chad. Tounians can also be found in central Guére Prefecture. The Tounians arrived in the Chari Valley long before the Sara* did. Over the centuries, they were victimized by Neilliam* slave traders, who drove them into a close relationship with neighboring Kabas,* a Sara people. Most Tounians today are small farmers, raising millet, sorghum, and cotton. Their population today is fewer than 5,000 people.

REFERENCE: Thomas Collelo et al. *Chad: A Country Study.* 1988.

TOUPOURI. *See* TUPUR.

TOURA. The Toura (Tura, Wenmebo) are today considered a peripheral Manding* ethnic group living in Biankouma Department in Ivory Coast. Beginning in the sixteenth century, expanding Mandinkas* pushed the Touras into the region, where they intermarried with the Dan.* Today, the Touras are highly assimilated with the Dan.

TOUREG. *See* TUAREG.

TOURKA. *See* TURKA.

TOUSIA. *See* TUSYAN.

TOUSSIAN. *See* TUSYAN.

TOUWÉ. *See* BAKWÉ.

TRAUDE. *See* DGHWEDE.

TSAGO. *See* DIRYA.

TSAMAY. The Tsamay people are a small ethnic group living today in Ethiopia. They speak a Cushitic language and make their living as small farmers. The Tsamay population is approximately 7,000 people.

REFERENCE: M. L. Bender, J. D. Bowen, R. L. Cooper, and C. A. Ferguson, eds. *Language in Ethiopia.* 1976.

TSAMBA. *See* CHAMBA.

TSANGUI. *See* BATSANGUI.

TSAW. The Tsaws are a subgroup of the Tonga* people.

TSCHOKOSSI. *See* CHOKOSSI.

TSCHOKWE. *See* CHOKWE.

TSELA. The Tselas are one of the clans of the Emafikamuva* people, who themselves are one of the three major subgroups of the Swazi* people of Swaziland.

TSEMAI. The Tsemais are an ethnic group in southern Ethiopia.

TSENGA. The Tsengas, who are concentrated in the Tete District in Mozambique, are a major subgroup of the Maravi* people.

TSHOGO. *See* MITSOGO.

TSHU-KWE. The Tshu-Kwe are a subgroup of the San* people in Botswana. They are divided into a number of subgroups themselves, based on closely related dialects of the same language. These groups include the Kuas, southern Kua, Ganas, Gwis, and Khute. The Tshu-Kwe peoples are scattered through central Botswana where they farm and raise cattle.
REFERENCE: Fred Morton, A. Murray, and J. Ramsay. *Historical Dictionary of Botswana.* 1989.

TSIEN. *See* BETE.

TSIMIHETY. The Tsimihety people, whose contemporary population exceeds 700,000 people, are an ethnic group living today in Madagascar. They claim to be descendants of the Sihanakas* who fled into the high valleys of the eastern coast of the island for isolation and protection. They are known today for their hard work and ambition. The Tsimihety are concentrated in Diégo-Suarez and Majunga provinces. They are divided into about forty subgroups based on kinship ties. Although they have readily intermarried into other groups as they have expanded in Madagascar, they retain a strong sense of Tsimihety identity. Rice is the staple crop of the Tsimihety, but herding cattle possesses enormous economic and cultural significance for them as well.
REFERENCES: Maureen Covell. *Madagascar: Politics, Economics and Society.* 1987; Harold D. Nelson et al. *Area Handbook for the Malagasy Republic.* 1973.

TSONGA. The Tsongas are an ethnic group living in southern Mozambique and northern Transvaal in South Africa. Their population is approaching three million people, of whom more than one million are in South Africa. They have been in the region since before the sixteenth century. Traditionally, the Tsongas have worked as farmers, raising maize, sorghum, and millet, as well as working as long-distance traders and middlemen between the East African coast and the interior of Zimbabwe and South Africa. In the early nineteenth century, the Tsongas came under the domination of Chief Shoshangane of the Ndandwe people. As a result, the Tsongas came under a Zulu* cultural influence, adopting cattle as a central aspect of their economy and the Zulu language. Today, Tsongas still farm and raise cattle, although an increasing number of Tsonga young men are working at mining and industrial sites in South Africa.

REFERENCES: *African Encyclopedia.* 1974; Thomas F. Johnston. "A Tsonga Initiation." *African Arts* 7 (Summer 1974): 60–62; Christopher Saunders. *Historical Dictionary of South Africa.* 1983.

TSONGA. *See* TONGA.

TSOTSE. The Tsotses are a subgroup of the Luhya* people of Kenya and Uganda. They are a Western Bantu* people who live today north of Lake Victoria on both sides of the Kenyan-Ugandan border.

TSUA. *See* TSWA.

TSURE JA. *See* RESHAWA.

TSURESHE. *See* RESHAWA.

TSWA. The Tswa people of Mozambique are considered to be a subgroup of the Tonga* people today. Most Tswas live between the Limpopo and the Save rivers, as well as in Mossurize and Sofala.

TSWANA. The Tswana, who are often referred to as the Western Sotho,* are a large ethnic group living in Botswana, Namibia, and across the border in South Africa. Their current population exceeds three million people. The largest Tswana settlements are near water sources on the edge of the Kalahari Desert. Ethnologists believe that, about one thousand years ago, the ancestors of the Tswana had large settlements in southwestern Transvaal. Europeans meeting the Tswanas for the first time in the early nineteenth century were surprised at Tswana social life, since the Tswana maintained large settlements of up to 20,000 people. Christian missionaries started working in those settlements in the 1820s, and the Tswana readily adapted to Christian life. The primary Tswana subdivisions are the Ngwatos,* Ngwaketses,* Birwas,* Hurutshes,* Kaas,* Kgafelas,* Kgatlas,* Khurutshes,* Bolongs, Letes,* Mmanaana Kgatlas,* Talaotes,* Tawanas,* and Kwenas.* There are high rates of labor migration among the Tswana of Botswana.

REFERENCES: I. Schapera. *A Handbook of Tswana Law and Custom.* 1959; I. Schapera. *Married Life in an African Tribe.* 1966; David N. Suggs. "Female Status and Role Transition in the Tswana Life Cycle." *Ethnology* 26 (1987): 107–20; D. N. Suggs. "Climacteric among the 'New' Women of Mochudi, Botswana." Ph.D. dissertation. University of Florida, Gainesville. 1986.

TUAREG. The Tuaregs (Touregs, Twaregs) are an ethnic group living in the western and southwestern Sahara Desert. They are a migrating pastoral people who move to find new pasture for their sheep, goats, and camels, and it has therefore been difficult to secure reliable population figures for them. Recent estimates, however, place the Tuareg population of Mali, Niger, Burkina-Faso, Libya, and southern Algeria at more than 850,000 people. A few Tuaregs raise dates, vegetables, and wheat at oases. Although most Tuaregs still live as pastoralists in their movable tents of animal skins and grass matting, many now live and work in towns and cities. They have also been known historically for their proclivity for raiding neighbors for animals and slaves. They speak Tamachek, a Berber* language. The Tuareg were traditionally a nomadic people herding cattle and sheep over the dry range of the Sahel. Because of the severe drought that has struck the Sahel in the 1980s and 1990s, large numbers of Tuaregs have lost their herds and face poverty and starvation. Many have relocated to towns and cities in order to find cash labor.

Tuareg society is divided into several castes and clans. At the top of the social order are the white Tuaregs, a nobility who dominate hundreds of thousands of black Tuaregs, many of whom are slaves known as Ikelans or Bellas.* The Tuareg nobility is divided into its own castes. At the top are the Imajeren, whose name translates as "The Proud and Free." Just below them are the Imrad, a free people but subordinate to the Imajaren. The Ineslemen* are a religious fraternity functioning as a caste. At the bottom of the social structure are the massive numbers of Tuareg slaves—the Bella or Ikelan. They are not nomadic, like their masters, but remain sedentary to care for the livestock, gardens, and palm groves.

REFERENCES: *African Encyclopedia.* 1974; Sonia Bleeker. *The Tuareg: Nomads and Warriors of the Sahara,* 1964; Andrew Bourgeot. "The Twareg Women of Ahaggar and the Creation of Value." *Etnos* 52 (1987): 103–18; Samuel Decalo. *Historical Dictionary of Niger.* 1989; Jeremy Keenan. *The Tuareg: People of Ahaggar.* 1978.

TUBACAYE. *See* JAHANKA.

TUBU. *See* TEBU.

TUER. *See* BERI.

TUGEN. The Tugens are a subgroup of the Kalenjin* peoples of the Rift Valley Province of Kenya. With a population of about 200,000 people, they are the third-largest of the Kalenjin groups. The Tugens live east of the Kerio River and in the hills above the Kerio River Valley.

TUGUN. *See* MBEMBE.

TUKI. The Tukis are an agricultural people living today in Cameroon. They speak a Bantu* language that is part of the Benue branch of the Niger-Congo family. The Tuki population today exceeds 26,000 people, most of whom are in the central region of the country.
REFERENCE: Edmond Biloa. ''Pronouns in Tuki.'' *Studies in African Linguistics* 2 (August 1990): 21–33.

TUKRI. *See* TUKULOR.

TUKULOR. The Tukulors (Toucouleurs, Tokolors, Takruris, Tekarirs, Torodos, Toncouleurs, and Tukris) are a West African ethnic groups whose population in the early 1990s exceeded 750,000 people, the vast majority of whom are Muslims. They are also known as the Takarirs and Futankobes. The Tukulors are descendants of a mixture of Fulbes,* Moors,* and Soninkés.* They speak Fulbe as their primary tongue, but they are not nomadic. The Tukulors are a sedentary people living primarily in Senegal on both sides of the Dagana River, to a point halfway between Matam and Bakel. Tukulors can also be found in the region of Kayes, Nioro-du-Sahel, Segu, eastern Massina, and Dinginray. Thousands of Tukulors are also in Guinea. In spite of their conversion to Islam, the traditional Tukulor religion remains very powerful, in a syncretic mix with Muslim beliefs. Tukulor animism revolves around a belief in witches and ghost spirits. Nevertheless, they proudly claim to be the first black Africans converted to Islam. The Tukulors are known regionally for their skill in manufacturing amulets and potions capable of warding off danger.
REFERENCES: Lucy Behrman. *Muslim Brotherhood and Politics in Senegal.* 1970; Jean-Paul Bourdier. ''The Rural Mosques of Futa Toro.'' *African Arts* 26 (July 1993): 32–45; Alfred G. Gerteiny. ''Tukulor.'' In Richard V. Weekes, ed. *Muslim Peoples.* 1984.

TUKUN. *See* MBEMBE.

TULA. The Tulas (Tures) are an Adamawa-speaking people of the Kaltungo District of the Gombe Division of Bauchi State in Nigeria.
REFERENCE: *Language Survey of Nigeria.* 1976.

TULAI. The Tulais are a subgroup of the Gezawa* people of northern Nigeria.

TULAMA. The Tulamas (Tulema) are one of the major subgroups of the Oromo* peoples of Ethiopia. Most of them are concentrated in Shoa Province, in and around Addis Ababa; they work primarily as sedentary farmers.

TULEMA. *See* TULAMA.

TUMAGRI. *See* KANEMBU.

TUMBATU. The Tumbatus are one of the subgroups of the Shirazi* people of the island of Zanzibar in Tanzania.

TUMBUKA. The Tumbuka (Tumbukwa, Matumboka, Batumbuka) peoples have lived for centuries on the Nyika Plateau of northern Malawi and north-eastern Zambia, between the Dwangwa and North Rukuru rivers. They constituted a loosely organized confederation under Chikulamayembe in the eighteenth century, but Nguni* raids destroyed it. Their current social structure is dominated by powerful, decentralized clans. Linguistically, they are related to the Tongas.* Today, the Tumbukas are mixing with the Angoni people, who recently arrived in the region. The Tumbuka economy still revolves around the production of maize, sorghum, and millet. The Tumbuka population today exceeds 200,000 people.
REFERENCES: *African Encyclopedia.* 1974; John J. Grotpeter. *Historical Dictionary of Zambia.* 1979.

TUMBUKWA. *See* TUMBUKA.

TUMBWE. The Tumbwes are a Bantu*-speaking ethnic group living today in southeastern Zaire. They live in and around the city of Kalemie on the western shore of Lake Tanganyika. Traditionally, the Tumbwes made their living by farming small plots near the lake and by fishing. In recent years, more and more Tumbwes have been seeking wage labor in towns and cities.
REFERENCE: Irving Kaplan et al. *Zaire: A Country Study.* 1978.

TUMTUM. The Tumtums are one of the Nuba* peoples of Sudan.

TUNGBO. The Tunbgos are a subgroup of the Izon* peoples of Rivers State in Nigeria.

TUNJUR. In the sixteenth century, there was a powerful Tunjur kingdom in Sudan, but its power was eclipsed by the rise of the Fur* empire in the seventeenth century. A smaller Tunjur kingdom existed at the same time in the Wadai region of what is today Chad. In Darfur Province of Chad, there are ruined palaces and citadels that attest to Tunjur power in the past. Approximately 10,000 people in Chad and Sudan identify themselves as Tunjur today. They live primarily in Darfur Province in Chad and across the border in Sudan. The Chadian Tunjur live near the Batha River in Wadai Province, in Dar Ziyud, and in the Abu Telfan hills. They no longer speak the Tunjur language, for it is has been replaced by Fur, Arabic, or Beri* as their primary tongue. They live in settled villages of reed-walled, concial-roofed houses built on hilltops or elevated ridges. They are farmers, raising a variety of crops, including millet, beans, sorghum, and haricot beans, but they are best known for their skill at cultivating date palms. The Tunjur are devout Sunni Muslims of the Maliki school.

REFERENCES: G. T. Nachtigel. *Sahara and Sudan.* vol. 4: *Wadai and Darfur.* 1971; Joseph Tubiana. "Tunjur." In Richard V. Weekes, ed. *Muslim Peoples.* 1984.

TUPUR. The Tupurs (Tupuri, Toupouri) are a non-Fulbe,* non-Muslim ethnic group of northern Cameroon, southwestern Chad, and southeastern Nigeria, a subgroup of the Kirdis.* Most of those in Chad are concentrated near the town of Fianga in Mayo-Kebbi Prefecture. They arrived there fleeing Fulbe slave traders in the lowlands. The Tupurs live by fishing and raising cattle, as well as by farming millet and sorghum in terraced, hillside fields. They also raise cattle. Their current population exceeds 160,000 people, of whom 100,000 live in Cameroon.

REFERENCE: Harold D. Nelson et al. *Area Handbook for the United Republic of Cameroon.* 1974.

TUPURI. *See* TUPUR.

TURA. *See* TOURA.

TURE. *See* TULA.

TURKA. The Turkas (Tourka, Turuka) are an ethnic group whom anthropologists classify as part of the larger cluster of Senufo* peoples of West Africa. The Turkas are concentrated along the border of northern Ivory Coast, southern Mali, and southwestern Burkina-Faso. Most of them are small farmers, raising corn, rice, yams, peanuts, sesame, and sweet potatoes. The Turka population today exceeds 150,000 people.

REFERENCE: Daniel M. McFarland. *Historical Dictionary of Upper Volta.* 1978.

TURKANA. The Turkana are an ethnic group living in far northeastern Uganda, on the escarpment there, and across the border in Kenya. They can also be found in Ethiopia. They speak a language that ethnologists classify as Central Paranilotic. The bulk of the Turkanas live in Kenya. The economy of the Turkanas is a mixed one. Men spend most of their time herding cattle, which provides milk, blood, and hides for the Turkana lifestyle. Turkana women spend much of their time trying to raise crops in what can be an inhospitable environment. They focus their farming on raising millet, maize, cow peas, and tobacco. The Turkana living near Lake Rudolf rely on fish for their protein. The Turkana population today exceeds 350,000 people.

REFERENCES: Alan Donovan. "Turkana Functional Art." *African Arts* 21 (May 1988): 44–47; John Lamphear. *The Traditional History of the Jie of Uganda.* 1976.

TURKWAM. *See* TURKWAN.

TURKWAN. The Turkwans (Turkwams) are a relatively small Nigerian ethnic group. They speak a Bantu* language and live on the southwestern edge of the Jos Plateau in Plateau State, primarily in the Mama District of the Akwanga Division. Their most immediate ethnic neighbors are the Rindres (Nunkus*), Chessus,* Arums,* Kantanas, and Ninzams.* Most Turkwans are subsistence farmers who raise millet, guinea corn, maize, and a variety of other products.
REFERENCE: Elizabeth Isichei, ed. *Studies in the History of Plateau State, Nigeria.* 1982.

TURU. The Turu (Rimi) are a prominent, Bantu*-speaking people who live in Central Tanzania. Their particular Bantu language is known as Kinyaturu. Their population today probably exceeds 500,000 people. The majority of the Turu living in rural areas are hoe farmers, raising sorghum, millet, maize, cattle, sheep, and goats. A few of the Turu also raise peanuts and castor oil plants as cash crops. The political system of the Turu revolves around independent councils of elders in each village or general settlement area. Until the early 1970s, most Turus lived in isolated homestead settlements in the bush country of the north or the scrub region of the south. Islam first reached the Turu in the nineteenth century when slave traders came into central Tanzania, and today more than half of the Turu identify themselves as Sunni Muslims of the Shafi school. Strong elements of their traditional animist faith, particularly worship at rain shrines, survive, however, and relatively few people conduct their daily Islamic prayers or observe Ramadan. The Turu also maintain a profound belief in werelions (*mbojo*) and that the frequent lion attacks on Turu men, women, and children can be blamed on these. Most ethnologists believe that the gathering of the Turu into larger villages, towns, and cities will accelerate their conversion to Islam.
REFERENCES: M. T. Jellicoe. "The Turu Resistance Movement." *Tanganyika Notes and Records* 7 (1969): 1–12; Ioan M. Lewis. *Islam in Tropical Africa.* 1966; H. K. Schneider. "The Lion Men of Singida: A Reappraisal." *Tanganyika Notes and Records* 58–59 (1962): 123–27.

TURUKA. *See* TURKA.

TURUMAWA. *See* ETULO.

TUSSI. *See* TUTSI.

TUSYAN. The Tusyans (Tousias, Toussians) are a subgroup of the Lobi* people of Burkina-Faso in West Africa. Most Tusyans live east of Banfora in the southwestern corner of the country. They are primarily farmers, raising corn, rice, yams, peanuts, sesame, and sweet potatoes. The Tusyans are closely related

to the Vigyes. The Tusyan population in Burkina-Faso today exceeds 150,000 people.
REFERENCE: Daniel M. McFarland. *Historical Dictionary of Upper Volta.* 1978.

TUTSI. The Tutsi—also known as the Tussi, Batutsi, Watutsi, and Watusi—were historically the dominant ethnic group in what is today Rwanda. They are a tall people who traditionally made their living as cattle herders. The Tutsi speak Kinyarwanda, a Bantu* language. Tutsis constitute 15 percent of the population of Burundi. The Tutsis are divided into two large subgroups—the Abanyaruguru and the Himas*—each of which is divided into approximately thirty identifiable family lineages. In terms of religious loyalties, they are about equally divided between Roman Catholicism and traditional beliefs. The Tutsis conquered other groups in the region beginning in the fifteenth century. The final conquest of the Hutus* and Twas* was completed by King Kigeri Rwabugiri in the late nineteenth century. Throughout much of the twentieth century, the Tutsis controlled the Hutus, even though the Hutus outnumbered them by twenty to one.

But, in 1956, the Hutus rebelled against what they believed to be intolerable Tutsi oppression, demanding equal rights and political control of the country. The rebellion turned violent in 1959, forcing more than 200,000 Tutsis to flee Rwanda. Belgian* colonial officials supported the Hutu majority, and, when independence came to Rwanda in 1962, the Hutus were thoroughly in control. In Burundi, the Tutsis remained in control. In 1965, a Hutu rebellion in Burundi failed, and, in the process, thousands of Hutus, especially intellectuals, were slaughtered. The failed rebellion left Burundi under complete Tutsi control. In the early 1970s, another Tutsi-Hutu civil conflict erupted in Burundi. In the fighting, more than 200,000 people were killed and another 100,000 fled. The Hutu-Tutsi rivalry festered during the 1970s and 1980s, periodically erupting into violence, but, during the early 1990s, the power struggle began to devastate Burundi. The violence forced more than 700,000 people—Hutus and Tutsis—to flee Burundi for Rwanda, Tanzania, and Zaire. In 1994, more than 500,000 Tutsis and Hutus died in the Rwanda civil war.
REFERENCES: *African Encyclopedia.* 1974; Warren Weinstein. *Historical Dictionary of Burundi.* 1976.

TWA. The term ''Twa'' has sometimes been used to refer to the San* people of South Africa.

TWA. The Central cluster of Pygmies* consists of the Twa or Cwa people. Their population today exceeds 100,000 people. The Twa live north of Lake Leopold in Zaire and in Rwanda. They live in dense forests and make their living by hunting and gathering. Over the years, they associated closely with the Tutsis in Rwanda. Those Twa who live near the Tutsis* and Hutus* in Rwanda work as potters and artisans. The civil war in Rwanda in 1994 imposed severe hardships on the Twas, many of whom fled to remote jungle areas for safety.

TWALA. The Twalas are one of the major clans of the Bemdzabuko* division of the Swazi* people of Swaziland.

TWAREG. *See* TUAREG.

TWI. The term ''Twi'' is used to refer to the Akan* language, spoken by more than six million people in Ghana. Fang,* Asante,* and Akuapem* are all Twi languages.

TWI-FANTE. *See* ASANTE.

TWIFO. *See* TWIFU.

TWIFU. The Twifus (Twifo) are an ethnic group in the Pra Valley of Ghana. They once constituted one of the prominent Akan* states, dominating the trade routes between the Asante* and the Fantes.* Today, the remnants of the Twifu state and the Twifu peoples are north of Elmina.
REFERENCE: Daniel M. McFarland. *Historical Dictionary of Ghana.* 1995.

TYAPI. *See* TIAPI.

TYÉFO. *See* TIEFO.

TYENGA. *See* SHANGAWA.

TYENGAWA. *See* SHANGAWA.

TYOKOSSI. *See* CHOKOSSI.

TYOPI. *See* LANDOMA.

U

UBAGHARA. The Ubaghara people are one of the many Cross River ethnic groups in Nigeria. Most of them are small farmers living in the Akamkpa Division of Cross River State.
REFERENCE: *Language Survey of Nigeria.* 1976.

UBANG. The Ubangs are one of the Cross River peoples in Nigeria. They can be found today living in the Obudu Division of Cross River State.
REFERENCE: *Language Survey of Nigeria.* 1976.

UBANGUIAN. The term ''Ubanguian'' has been used to describe several riverine peoples of the Central African Republic. Ethnologists place the origins of the Banziris,* Bourakas,* Sangas,* and Yakomas* in the Sudan before their migration to the Ubangi River Valley, which began in the sixteenth century. These groups live primarily along the Ubangi River between the Bangi bend and the confluence of the Ouellé and Mbomou rivers.
REFERENCE: Pierre Kalck. *Historical Dictionary of the Central African Republic.* 1992.

UBANI. The Ubanis are one of the many subgroups of the Igbo* people, an ethnic group of nearly fifteen million people living today in southern and southeastern Nigeria.

UBI. The Ubis (Oubi) are an ethnic groups who are part of the Kru* cluster of peoples in Ivory Coast. They are concentrated in the town of Tai along the Cavally River in the subprefecture of Tai in southwestern Ivory Coast. There are also Ubis living across the border in Liberia. Because of similar cultural characteristics, some ethnologists view the Ubis as a subgroup of the Bakwés.* The traditional Ubi lifestyle revolved around subsistence agriculture, but, in recent years, many Ubis have made the transition to commercial farming.
REFERENCE: Robert J. Mundt. *Historical Dictionary of Côte d'Ivoire.* 1995.

UBIUM. The Ubiums are a subgroup of the Ibibio* peoples of Nigeria.

UDOK. *See* UDUK.

UDUK. The Uduks (Udoks) are an ethnic group living today in eastern Sudan. Ethnologists believe that the Uduks have lived there in what is now Al Awsat State since antiquity. Most of them dwell near the mountainous border with Ethiopia, where they work as small farmers. They speak a language that is part of the Koman division of Nilo-Saharan. Over the years, the Uduks have been victimized by Arab* slave traders and by frequent clashes with Ethiopian ethnic groups.
REFERENCE: Helen C. Metz et al. *Sudan: A Country Study.* 1992.

UGEP. *See* LOKE.

UHAMI-IYAYU. The Uhami-Iyayu people are one of the Edo* peoples of the Owo Division of Ondo State in Nigeria.

UHROBO. *See* URHOBO.

UKAAN. The Ukaan people, also known over the years as the Ikans, Anyarans, and Augas, are a Nigerian ethnic group. Although their language is classified with the Niger-Congo family, it appears to be isolated within that group. The Ukaans live in the Akoko Division of Ondo State and the Akoko-Edo Division of Bendel State.
REFERENCE: *Language Survey of Nigeria.* 1976.

UKELE. *See* KUKELE.

UKELLE. *See* ORING.

UKI. *See* BOKYI.

UKPE-BAYOBIRI. The Ukpe-Bayobiris are one of the Cross River peoples of Nigeria. They live in the Obudu and Ikom divisions of Cross River State.
REFERENCE: *Language Survey of Nigeria.* 1976.

UKPET. *See* AKPET-EHOM.

UKPILA. *See* UPILA.

UKPUM. The Ukpums are a subgroup of the Ibibio* peoples of Nigeria.

UKUE-EHUEN. The Ukue-Ehuens, also known as Ekpennis, are one of the Edo* peoples of Nigeria. They can be found in the Ukpe and Ekpenni districts of the Akoko Division in Ondo State.

ULA. *See* URA.

ULEME. *See* UNEME.

ULUKWUMI. The Ulukwumis are one of the Yoruba* peoples of the Aniocha Division in Bendel State, Nigeria.

UM ALI. The Um Ali are a subgroup of the Bisharin,* themselves a subgroup of the Beja* peoples of Sudan. Like other Beja people, the Um Ali speak a Northern Cushitic language. The Bisharin homeland extends from between Mohammed Gol to the Egyptian border along the coast of the Red Sea, then west to the Nile River Valley, and south along the Atbara River Plain. The Um Ali live in the steppes and deserts of the Atbai subregion, where they work primarily as camel raisers and herders.
REFERENCES: Paul Andrew. *A History of the Beja Tribes of the Sudan.* 1954; P. E. H. Hair. ''A Layman's Guide to the Languages of the Sudan Republic.'' *Sudan Notes and Records* 46 (1966): 65–78.

UM NAGI. The Um Nagi are a subgroup of the Bisharins,* themselves a subgroup of the Beja* peoples of Sudan. Like other Beja people, the Um Nagi speak a Northern Cushitic language. The Bisharin homeland extends from between Mohammed Gol to the Egyptian border along the coast of the Red Sea, then west to the Nile River Valley, and south along the Atbara River Plain. Two of the Um Nagi clans live close to the Um Ali* and raise cattle. The other Um Nagi clans are camel, sheep, and cattle herders and farmers who live in the more arable regions south of Sidon.
REFERENCES: Paul Andrew. *A History of the Beja Tribes of the Sudan.* 1954; P. E. H. Hair. ''A Layman's Guide to the Languages of the Sudan Republic.'' *Sudan Notes and Records* 46 (1966): 65–78.

UMON. The Umons (Amons) are a Nigerian people. They live in twenty-five agricultural villages in the Biase District of the Akamkpa Division of Cross River State. Their language is part of the Cross River cluster of the Benue-Congo family.
REFERENCE: *Language Survey of Nigeria.* 1976.

UNAY. *See* BERI.

UNEME. The Unemes (Ulemes, Ilemes, Inemes) are one of the Edo* peoples of Nigeria. Their population is approximately 25,000 people, most of whom live in the Etsako, Ishan, and Akoko-Edo divisions of Bendel State.
REFERENCE: *Language Survey of Nigeria.* 1976.

UNGA. The Ungas are a small ethnic group in Zambia. They are an offshoot of the Bemba* people and live in the vicinity of Lake Bangwedu, primarily in the swamps where they work as fishermen. Because of their isolation in the swamps, the Ungas managed until quite recently to maintain their independence from both Europeans and other Africans. Their population today is approximately 25,000 people.
REFERENCE: John J. Grotpeter. *Historical Dictionary of Zambia.* 1979.

UNGU. *See* LUNGU.

UPILA. The Upilas (Okpellas, Ukpilas) are a subgroup of the Edo* peoples of south-central Nigeria. They are concentrated approximately seventy-five miles north of Benin City and about thirty miles west of the Niger River. Today, they number about 25,000 people who live in nine villages.
REFERENCE: Jean M. Borgatti. "Okpella Masking Traditions." *African Arts* 9 (July 1976): 24–33.

URA. The Uras (Ulas) are a small ethnic group of approximately 4,000 people living today in the Kwongoma District of the Minna Division of Niger State in Nigeria. They are closely related to Kamukus* and Bassas.*
REFERENCE: *Language Survey of Nigeria.* 1976.

URHOBO. The Urhobo (Uhrobo, Biotu, and the pejorative Sobo) people live in Bendel State in Nigeria, primarily in the Western and Eastern Urhobo divisions. They are closely related to the neighboring Edo* people. Both groups make their living raising yams, cassava, and oil palm products, as well as by fishing. In recent years, the Urhobos have increasingly mixed with the Edo, Ijaw,* and Itsekiri* peoples of the region, but they still maintain a distinct sense of separate ethnic identity. Their population today exceeds 600,000 people. The primary Urhobo settlements in Nigeria can be found in Sapele, Ughelli, and Effurin.
REFERENCES: *African Encyclopedia.* 1974; Perkins Foss. "Urhobo Statuary for Spirits and Ancestors." *African Arts* 9 (July 1976): 12–23; A. Oyewelo. *Historical Dictionary of Nigeria.* 1987.

URRTI. The Urrti are a subgroup of the Meidobs* of Sudan.

URSAWA. The Ursawas, with a population of perhaps 2,000 people, are one of the smallest of the Buduma* subgroups. They are cattle raisers and fishermen.

URUAN. The Uruans are a subgroup of the Ibibio* peoples of Nigeria.

USHI. The Ushis are part of the larger cluster of Aushi* peoples in Zambia.

UTANGA. *See* OTANK.

UTOR. *See* ETULO.

UTSE. *See* ICHEVE.

UTSER. *See* ICHEVE.

UTSEU. *See* ICHEVE.

UTUGWANG. The Utugwangs, also known as Putukwams, Mbe Afals, and Obes, are one of the Cross River peoples of Nigeria. Their language is part of the Bendi group of the Cross River cluster in the Benue-Congo family. They live in the Obudu and Ogoja divisions of Cross River State.
REFERENCE: *Language Survey of Nigeria.* 1976.

UTUTU. The Ututus are one of the many subgroups of the Igbo* people, an ethnic group of nearly fifteen million people living today in southern and south-eastern Nigeria.

UWET. *See* BAKPINKA.

UZEKWE. The Uzekwes (Ezekwes) are one of the Cross River peoples of Nigeria. They live in the Ogoja Division of Cross River State.
REFERENCE: *Language Survey of Nigeria.* 1976.

V

VA. *See* JULA.

VADUMA. *See* DUMA.

VAGALA. The Vagalas, also known as the Vigalas and Vageles, are a Grusi* group of people in Ghana. They are concentrated in the Gonja area northeast of Bole in the Northern Region. They can also be found across the border in Burkina-Faso where they live among the Mamprusi. The Vagalas are closely related to the Kasenas.* Their contemporary population is approximately 8,000 people.
REFERENCE: Daniel M. McFarland. *Historical Dictionary of Ghana.* 1995.

VAGELE. *See* VAGALA.

VAHERA. *See* HERA.

VAI. The Vai people, also known as Vey, Vei, and Mande-tan, are an ethnic group in West Africa. They are closely related to the Kono* and trace their origins to the Manding* peoples of Mali, but they migrated southwest into the rain forest near the Mano River in what are today Liberia and Sierra Leone. The Vai have been living there for approximately five hundred years. Because they have maintained contacts with the savanna Mandinka* to their north, the Vai still have a savanna culture, even though they live in the forests. There are roughly 70,000 Vais in Liberia, 65,000 in Guinea, and 20,000 in Sierra Leone. In recent years, those Vais living in Sierra Leone have been rapidly assimilating into the larger Mendé culture. They are swidden agriculturalists who raise rice as their staple. They also carry on trading relationships between the coastal shipping economy and groups in the interior. Traditional Vai religion, which still survives among a minority of the Vai people, worshipped a supreme being named Konga, but, late in the eighteenth century, Muslim traders reached them. The conversion process accelerated under the impact of Muslim Fulbe* traders in the nineteenth century. In 1928 and 1930, when Sierra Leone and Liberia abolished slavery among the Vai, conversion to Islam became a mass phenomenon, and most Vai today are Sunni Muslims. The Vai have their own written script, which is still used, especially in Liberia. A small subgroup of the Vai— the Gallina—maintains a distinct identity and lives in the Yakemo Kpukumu Krim Chiefdom region.

REFERENCES: Svend E. Holsoe. "Vai." In Richard V. Weekes, ed. *Muslim Peoples.* 1984; S. J. Johnson. *Traditional History, Customary Laws, Mores, Folkways and Legends of the Vai Tribe.* 1954; Lester P. Monts. "Dance in the Vai Sande Society." *African Arts* 17 (August 1984): 53–59.

VAKALANGA. *See* KALANGA.

VALEMBA. *See* LEMBA.

VALENGE. The Valenges are one of the two major subgroups of the Shope* people of Mozambique.

VALUNDE. *See* LUNDA.

VAMARI. *See* MARI.

VANDAU. *See* NDAU.

VANHOWE. *See* NHOWE.

VANJANJA. *See* NJANJA.

VANNEROKI. *See* BOKYI.

VANYAI. *See* NYAI.

VARAMA. The Varama people of southwestern Gabon live along the Rembo Ndogo River in N'Gounié Province. They are closely related linguistically to the Eshira.* Most Varamas are small farmers today.

REFERENCE: David E. Gardinier. *Historical Dictionary of Gabon.* 1994.

VARMBO. The Varmbos are a subgroup of the Bassa* people of Liberia. Most Varmbos live in Grand Bassa County, Liberia.

VAROZWI. *See* ROZVI.

VASHANGWE. *See* SHANGWA.

VASHONA. *See* SHONA.

VATUA. *See* NGONI.

VEI. *See* VAI.

VEIAO. *See* YAO.

VEMBA. The Vembas are a Tanzanian ethnic group that many ethnologists classify with the larger Bena* cluster of peoples.

VENDA. The Venda (Bavenda) people, whose current population exceeds 550,000 people, have lived in recent years as a "national unit" in South Africa. Their homeland is located in northeastern Transvaal; there are also Vendas living across the border in Zimbabwe. The Vendas were intricately involved with the Rozvi* Kingdom, and their Bantu* language is closely related to that of the Karangas.* Some ethnolinguists classify their language as transitional between Sotho* and Shona.* The Venda kingdom was united and strongly resisted British* imperialism until the end of the nineteenth century. Most Vendas still support themselves by raising cattle, sorghum, and maize. They maintain close spiritual ties to their traditional animist faith. Men and women still belong to the traditional age-group associations, and Venda chiefs still exercise considerable authority.
REFERENCES: *African Encyclopedia.* 1974; R. Kent Rasmussen. *Historical Dictionary of Zimbabwe.* 1994.

VERE. *See* DURU-VERRE.

VERRE. *See* DURU-VERRE.

VESO. *See* VEZU.

VÉTÉRÉ. *See* MEKYIBO.

VEY. *See* VAI.

VEZU. The Vezus (Vesos) are a subgroup of the Sakalava* peoples of the plains of Madagascar. They make their living as fishermen and trade their fish for agricultural products to the Tanalanas,* a nearby group.

VIDRI. The Vidri are a subgroup of the Banda* people of the Central African Republic. Located primarily in the Yalinga and Bria regions, the Vidri have a

reputation as a particularly fierce people who have bitterly resisted both African and European conquerers. Baram-Bakié, the leader of the anti-French* insurrection of 1909 in the Central African Republic, was a Vidri.
REFERENCE: Pierre Kalck. *Historical Dictionary of the Central African Republic.* 1992.

VIDUNDA. The Vidunda are one of the individual groups in the Zaramo* cluster of the Northeast Bantu*-speaking people of East Africa. They live in the mountainous highlands of coastal Tanzania, where most of them work as hoe farmers, producing maize, beans, vegetables, cardamom, bananas, sorghum, and cassava, as well as raising sheep, goats, and poultry. During the nineteenth century, the Vidunda were, for the most part, left alone because of their geographic isolation. The lowland Zaramo peoples were more vulnerable. Most Vidunda today live in small, plastered houses with thatched roofs, although a few still reside in traditional round houses that are thatched all the way to the ground. Although a majority of the Vidunda were once Muslims, various Christian groups have established missions in the Tanzanian highlands; less than half of the Vidundas are still Muslim today. Even those are considered to be only marginally loyal, confining their religious observances to fasting at Ramadan, taking on Arab* names, and wearing the white skull cap. The Vidundas maintain a matrilineal social structure. In Tanzania today, there are more than 30,000 Vidundas.
REFERENCE: L. W. Swantz. *Ritual and Symbol in Transitional Zaramo Society.* 1970.

VIGALA. *See* VAGALA.

VIGNE. *See* VIGYE.

VIGYE. The Vigyes (Vignes) are a subgroup of the Lobi* people of Burkina-Faso in West Africa. Most Vigyes live east of Banfora in the southwestern corner of the country. They are primarily farmers, raising corn, rice, yams, peanuts, sesame, and sweet potatoes. The Vigyes are closely related to the Tusyans.*
REFERENCE: Daniel M. McFarland. *Historical Dictionary of Upper Volta.* 1978.

VILAKATI. The Vilakatis are one of the clans of the Emafikamuva* people, who themselves are one of the three major subgroups of the Swazi* people of Swaziland.

VILI. The Vili are a subgroup of the Kongo* people of Gabon, Congo, Zaire, and Angola. They are concentrated in southwestern Gabon and across the border in Congo. The Vili language is part of the Kongo language family, itself part of the West Central Bantu* group. Vili oral traditions claim affinity with the Kongos, Tékés,* Tyos, and Woyos, who were all once part of the inland Nguunu Kingdom. They began scattering in the eleventh century, moving to the

lower Congo River. The groups that evolved into the Vili people moved to the Loango coast in the late thirteenth and early fourteenth centuries. When the Portuguese* arrived in the 1480s, the Vilis were found along the Atlantic coast of southern Gabon and northern Congo. Their traditional lifestyle revolved around fishing, hunting, and small-scale farming; for trading purposes, the Vilis manufactured salt and palm cloth. During the seventeenth century, they participated in the ivory trade, and they broadened out into the slave trade in the eighteenth century. Late in the nineteenth century, when French* control was established over the Vilis, they became porters and agents for French firms doing business in West Africa. Small but influential Vili populations developed in Libreville and Port-Gentil. Jean-Félix Tchicaya, a Vili, was an influential Gabonese politician in the late colonial and early independence period.
REFERENCES: David E. Gardinier. *Historical Dictionary of Gabon.* 1994; Phyllis M. Martin. *The External Trade of the Loango Coast, 1576–1870: The Effects of Changing Commercial Relations on the Vili Kingdom of Loango.* 1972.

VINDA. The Vindas are a subgroup of the Bara* cluster of peoples of the plains of Madagascar.

VINZA. The Vinzas are an ethnic group living east of Lake Tanganyika in west-central Tanzania. They are especially concentrated around the town of Vinza. Until the twentieth century, they traded salt that they produced from brine springs in the area. Today, most Vinzas are small farmers. Many ethnologists include them in the Ha* group of peoples. The Vinza population today is approximately 8,000 people.
REFERENCE: Laura Kurtz. *Historical Dictionary of Tanzania.* 1978.

VIYE. *See* BIE.

VOLTAIC. *See* MOLÉ-DAGBANE PEOPLES.

VOUMBOU. *See* VOUNGOU.

VOUNGOU. The Voungou (Voumbou) people of southwestern Gabon are closely linked linguistically to the Eshira* people. They originally lived on the upper N'Gounié River, before aggressive Bapounou* warriors pushed them into the thick forests in the mountains west of the Moukabala River. The Voungous still live there, on both sides of the border between Ogooué-Maritime and N'Gounié provinces. During the eighteenth century, the Voungous actively supplied slaves to Portuguese* and British* traders, and, in the nineteenth and twentieth centuries, they became active in the rubber traffic. Today, most Voungous are small farmers and laborers.
REFERENCE: David E. Gardinier. *Historical Dictionary of Gabon.* 1994.

VUELA. *See* HWELA.

VUMBA. The Vumbas are a Swahili*-speaking people who today live in Kenya.

VUNDLE. The Vundles (AmaVundles) are a Nguni*-speaking people who were probably once a Sotho* clan before mixing with the Thembu* in the seventeenth century. They are concentrated today in the Mjanyane Valley of the Quthing District of Lesotho. They arrived in Lesotho after the Xhosa* defeat in the War of the Axe. Most of the Vundle are farmers and cattle raisers today.
REFERENCE: Gordon Halibuton. *Historical Dictionary of Lesotho.* 1977.

VUNGARA. The Vungaras are one of the two major subgroups of the Azandé* people of Zaire. They speak an Adamawa-Eastern language and live in Haut-Zaire.

VUTE. The Vutes (Mbute, Bute, Mbutere) are a tiny ethnic group in contemporary Cameroon. They are a subdivision of the Gbaya*-Mbun* cluster of peoples in the western reaches of the Central African Republic and in eastern Cameroon. Some can also be found in Nigeria. Their population today is around 35,000 people, a third of whom are Muslims. The others practice Christianity or a variety of tribal animist faiths. The conversion of the Vutes to Islam began early in the 1800s when Fulbe* and Hausa* groups established trading relationships with them. Christian missionaries first reached them in the 1920s. Traditional beliefs in ancestor worship and witchcraft still exist, but they are losing ground. Vute society is organized around patrilineal clans. People live in nuclear or extended family compounds consisting of mud-walled houses protected by a fence or wall. The Vutes practice slash-and-burn agriculture and concentrate on producing maize and cassava, which they both consume themselves and market for cash. They have also learned to raise cattle for their Fulbe neighbors.
REFERENCES: Philip Burnham. *Opportunity and Constraint in a Savanna Society.* 1980; Philip Burnham. "Regroupement and Mobile Societies: Two Cameroon Cases." *Journal of African History* 16 (1975): 577–94; Rhonda Thwing and John Watters. "Focus in Vute." *Journal of African Languages and Linguistics.* 9 (October 1987): 95–122.

W

WA'A. *See* DGHWEDE.

WAAT. *See* SANYE.

WAATHA. *See* SANYE.

WA BAMBANI. *See* AGOI.

WA-BONI. The Wa-Bonis are a group of hunters, fishermen, and foragers who live in the southern coastal area of Somalia, particularly near major towns in the Gado Region. Historically, the Wa-Bonis supplied hides from rhinos, giraffes, and antelopes to the Somalis,* who would then manufacture sandals and shields from them. They also sold the ivory to Somalis for export.
REFERENCE: Margaret Castagno. *Historical Dictionary of Somalia.* 1975.

WADAI. *See* MABA.

WADJIRIMA. *See* KURI.

WAGANDA. *See* GANDA.

WAGGA. *See* WAJA.

WA-GOSHA. The Wa-Goshas are a small ethnic group living in Somalia. They make their living mostly as farmers and nomadic hunters, and they are concentrated in the Juba River area. They speak a Bantu* language and were already living in the region before the Somali* migrations.
REFERENCE: Margaret Castagno. *Historical Dictionary of Somalia.* 1975.

WAHYAO. *See* YAO.

WAJA. The Wajas (Waggas) are part of a larger Hausa*-Fulbe* cluster of peoples living today in northwestern Nigeria, primarily in the Waja District of the Gombe Division of Bauchi State. Some of them can also be found across the border in Niger and in northern Benin. Their religion has a strong Muslim component. Most Wajas are small farmers and cattle herders.
REFERENCE: *Language Survey of Nigeria.* 1976.

WAJUNGA. The Wajunga are a subgroup of the Dazaga,* themselves a subgroup of the Tebu* of the Sahel and Sahara regions of Chad, Niger, and Sudan. In particular, the Wajunga live near two lakes east of the Tibesti Mountains in northwestern Chad. They no longer speak Wajunga, having adopted Dazaga as their primary language, and they intermarry freely with the Teda* and Daza* peoples. During the Chadian civil war of the 1970s and 1980s, the Wajunga found themselves opposed to the Teda and engaged in guerrilla warfare against them. The civil war has badly disrupted social and economic life among the Wajunga. They are a settled people today.

WAKA. The Waka are an Adamawa-speaking people of Nigeria. They can be found in the Lau District of the Muri Division of Gongola State.
REFERENCE: *Language Survey of Nigeria.* 1976.

WAKANDE. *See* MBEMBE.

WAKHUTU. *See* HUTU.

WALA. The Walas—Walba, Walo, Oule, Wilé—are one of the Molé-Dagbane* peoples of northern Ghana and Togo. Their population today exceeds 120,000 people, of whom more than 90 percent are Muslims. Their own traditions, confirmed by ethnological research, have them coming from Mamprusi in the seventeenth century and establishing control over the Dagari* and Lobi* peoples. They settled in the area around Wa in the upper West Region. In 1894, after severe attacks from the Gonjas,* the Walas signed a treaty for protection with the British.* They signed a similar treaty with the French* in 1895.
REFERENCES: Mona Fikry. ''Wa: A Case Study of Social Values and Social Tensions as Reflected in the Oral Traditions of the Wala of Northern Ghana.'' Ph.D. dissertation. Indiana University. 1969; Daniel M. McFarland. *Historical Dictionary of Ghana.* 1995.

WALAGA. *See* WELLEGA.

WALAMO. *See* WELAMO.

WALBA. *See* WALA.

WALLA. The Wallas are one of the major subgroups of the Oromo* people of Ethiopia.

WALO. *See* WALA.

WAMBA. *See* NUNKU.

WAMBO. *See* HUAMBO.

WAMIA. *See* ITESO.

WAN. The Wan (Ouan, Ngwano) are a patrilineal ethnic group of approximately 16,000 people living in the subprefectures of Kounahiri, Beoumi, and Mankono in central Ivory Coast. Although they are a southern Manding* group, French* colonial authorities classified them with the neighboring Baules* and Guros (Kweni*). They were traditionally a sedentary, hoe-farming people who raised a variety of crops, but, in the last several decades, many Wans have switched to coffee and cotton cultivation to earn cash and function in the commercial economy.
REFERENCE: Philip L. Ravenhill. ''The Social Organization of the Wan: A Patrilineal People of the Ivory Coast.'' Ph.D. dissertation. New School for Social Research. 1975.

WANDA. *See* WANDYA.

WANDALA. *See* MANDARA.

WANDYA. The Wandyas (Wandas) are an ethnic group living today in Tanzania and Zambia. They are part of the Rukwa cluster of peoples and closely associated with the Lambyas.* They have a population today of approximately 20,000 people.

WANÉ. *See* KRU.

WANGA. The Wangas are a subgroup of the Luhya* people of Kenya and Uganda. They are a Western Bantu* people who today live north of Lake Victoria on both sides of the Kenyan-Ugandan border.

WANGARA. *See* JULA.

WANGONI. *See* NGONI.

WANIRAMBA. *See* IRAMBA.

WANJI. The Wanjis are a Tanzanian ethnic group who are included in the Nyasa* cluster of peoples. Their population today is approximately 50,000 people.

WANOE. *See* NHOWE.

WANWUMA. The Wanwumas are one of the clans of the Bandi* Chiefdom of Lofa County in Liberia.

WANYANJA. *See* NYANJA.

WARA WARA. The Wara Waras (Ouara) are an ethnic group whom anthropologists classify as part of the larger cluster of Senufo* peoples of West Africa. The Wara Waras are a small group living in five villages in the hills of southwestern Burkina-Faso. Most of them are small farmers, raising corn, rice, yams, peanuts, sesame, and sweet potatoes. The call themselves the Saamas.
REFERENCE: Daniel M. McFarland. *Historical Dictionary of Upper Volta.* 1978.

WA-RIBI. The Wa-Ribis are a small ethnic group who live today between Bardera and Lugh in Somalia. Ethnographers identify them as some of the pre-Cushitic inhabitants of the region. They are a hunting people.
REFERENCE: Margaret Castagno. *Historical Dictionary of Somalia.* 1975.

WARJI. The Warjis (Sars) are a Chadic-speaking people who live in the Warji and Ganjuwa districts of the Bauchi Division of Bauchi State in Nigeria. They have a population today of approximately 55,000 people.
REFERENCE: *Language Survey of Nigeria.* 1976.

WARRI. *See* ITSEKIRI.

WARSHA. *See* WASSA.

WASA. *See* WASSA.

WASAW. *See* WASSA.

WASI. *See* SANYE.

WASSA. The Wassa people—also known as Warshas, Wasas, Wassaws, and Wasaws—are a major Akan* group in Ghana. They are concentrated in the Western Region and across the border in Ivory Coast. The Wassas are surrounded ethnically by the Nzima* and Ahanta* to the south, the Aowins* and Sefwis* to the west and north, and the Denkyiras* and Fantes* to the east. There are two subdivisions of the Wassas: the Amanfis and the Fiasos. Through-

out the seventeenth, eighteenth, and nineteenth centuries, the Wassas were at war with the Asantes,* a rivalry the British* exploited deftly to their advantage. Most Wassas today are small farmers and industrial workers. Their current population exceeds 200,000 people.
REFERENCE: Daniel M. McFarland. *Historical Dictionary of Ghana.* 1985.

WASSALUNKE. *See* WASULUNKA.

WASSAW. *See* WASSA.

WASULUNKA. The Wasulunka (Wassalunke, Ouassoulounke) are a Manding*-speaking people whose language is actually considered part of the Fringe Manding cluster of Manding languages. Most Wasulunkas are settled rice and peanut farmers living in Wasulu, a region south of the Niger River in southwestern Mali, near the Mali-Guinea frontier, primarily in the *cercles* of Yanfolila and Bougouni. There are also some Wasulunkas living across the border in northern Guinea, east of Kankan, and in Ivory Coast. The Wasulunkas are Muslims who were originally Fulbe* people and were conquered by Samory Touré.
REFERENCES: Carleton T. Hodge, ed. *Papers on the Manding.* 1971; Pascal Imperato. *Historical Dictionary of Mali.* 1977; Thomas O'Toole. *Historical Dictionary of Guinea.* 1987.

WASWAHILI. *See* SWAHILI.

WATUSI. *See* TUTSI.

WATUTSI. *See* TUTSI.

WATYI. *See* OUATCHI.

WAYAO. *See* YAO.

WAYTO. The Wayto live in the region of Lake Tana in north-central Ethiopia. Lake Tana is a large but shallow freshwater lake, and the Waytos live on its shores, its offshore islands, and in the plains area extending out from it. The Wayto population is approximately 2,000 people, with most of them in scattered villages along the lake and others dispersed among the Amhara* peoples in the plains. Wayto homes are of wattle-and-daub construction or are reed-walled cylinders with thatched conical roofs. They are in a state of assimilation with the Amhara. Until the late eighteenth century, the Waytos were a hunting-fishing-gathering culture, loyal to their own language and their ancestral religion. Both the economy and the religion revolved around the hippopotamus, an animal that was abundant in the lake. The Waytos lost the use of their language in the nineteenth century, adopting Amhara, and they converted to Islam as well. Within the last forty years, the Waytos have made the transition from a foraging economic lifestyle to a settled, mixed economy based on subsistence farming, fishing, and craftsmanship. By 1940, to secure cash from sales of hippo ivory, the Wayto had all but destroyed the hippopotamus herds, necessitating the economic transition. Today, large numbers of Waytos also labor on the large farms of non-Wayto groups.

REFERENCE: Frederick C. Gamst. "Wayto." In Richard V. Weekes, ed. *Muslim Peoples.* 1984.

WE. *See* WEE.

WÉ. *See* GUÉRÉ.

WÉ. *See* WOBÉ.

WEE. The Wee, also known as the Krahn, are an ethnic group of approximately 40,000 people in Liberia and Ivory Coast. They are closely affiliated with the Sapo people of the same region. In Liberia, they are concentrated in Nimba, Grand Gedeh, and Sinoe countries. They are divided into several chiefdoms and the following clans: Kpiarplay, Biai, Krazohn-Plo, Gbo, Gbaboh, Nizohni, Gbohbo-Niabo, Tchien Menyon-Kana, Tchien Menzon-Gbohbo, Gbilibo, Blio-Gbalu, Gbagbo, Jibehgbo, Juarzon, Karbardae, Seekon, and Wedjah. Most of the Wee people are subsistence farmers.

REFERENCES: D. Elwood Dunn and Svend H. Holsoe. *Historical Dictionary of Liberia.* 1985; Harold D. Nelson et al. *Liberia: A Country Study.* 1984.

WEELA. *See* HWELA.

WEGAM. *See* KUGAMA.

WEGELE. *See* GENGLE.

WEIN. The Weins are a subgroup of the Bassa* people of Liberia. Most Weins live in Grand Bassa County, Liberia.

WELAMO. The Welamos (Wolayta) are an ethnic group living between the Belati and Omo rivers in Ethiopia. They are part of the Omotic* cluster of peoples. Their own legends claim that Christianity came to them in the thirteenth century from St. Tekle Haymanot. The Welamos were conquered by the forces of Menelik II after a fierce resistance in 1894. Also known as the Walamo, they are a pastoral people living in far southwestern Ethiopia. In addition to raising cattle, they also produce millet and maize. Their population today exceeds 550,000 people.

REFERENCES: Harold D. Nelson et al. *Ethiopia: A Country Study.* 1980; Chris Prouty and Eugene Rosenfeld. *Historical Dictionary of Ethiopia and Eritrea.* 1994.

WELLEGA. The Wellegas (Walaga) are a major subgroup of the Oromo* peoples of Ethiopia. Most of them live in Wellega and Ilubabor provinces and work as mixed agriculturalists.

WELWAN. The Welwans (Malakotes) are a subgroup of the Pokomo* people of Kenya.

WEMBA. *See* BEMBA.

WEN-GBA-KON. The Wen-Gba-Kons are a subgroup of the Bassa* people of Liberia. Most Wen-Gba-Kons live in Grand Bassa County, Liberia.

WENMEBO. *See* TOURA.

WENSOHN. The Wensohns are a subgroup of the Bassa* people of Liberia. Most Wensohns live in Grand Bassa County, Liberia.

WENYA. The Wenyas are part of the Tumbuka* cluster of peoples living today in northern Malawi, primarily between Lake Nyasa and the Zambian border, south of the Tanzanian border. Some Wenyas can also be found in Zambia and Tanzania. The Wenya population today exceeds 40,000 people. They speak a language closely related to that of the Tongas.* The Wenya economy still revolves around the production of maize, sorghum, and millet.
REFERENCES: *African Encyclopedia.* 1974; John J. Grotpeter. *Historical Dictionary of Zambia.* 1979; Donald G. Morrison et al. *Black Africa: A Comparative Handbook.* 1989.

WERE. *See* DURU-VERRE.

WERIZE. The Werizes are a subgroup of the Gawwada* people of Ethiopia.

WERUGHA. The Werughas are a subgroup of the Taita* peoples of East Africa, particularly Kenya. They speak a Bantu* language.

WESTERN NUER. The Western Nuers are a major subdivision of the Nuer* people of Southern Sudan. They are concentrated in the Yivrol District.

WESTERN SOTHO. *See* TSWANA.

WETAWIT. The Wetawits are a small group of people living today in Ethiopia. They speak a Nilo-Saharan language and make their living as pastoralists. The Wetawit population exceeds 35,000 people today.

REFERENCE: M. L. Bender, J. D. Bowen, R. L. Cooper, and C. A. Ferguson, eds. *Language in Ethiopia.* 1976.

WIAWSO. The Wiawso are one of the major subgroups of the Sefwi* people of Ghana.

WIDEKUM. The Widekums are a subgroup of the Bamiléké* peoples of Cameroon. They are concentrated in the northwest corner of the country near the Atlantic Coast. They probably originated in the Congo Basin and migrated to their present location. The Widekum economy revolves around the production of maize, millet, vegetables, and coffee. There are probably 230,000 people in Cameroon who identify themselves as Widekum or Widekum-related peoples. They can also be found in eastern Nigeria.
REFERENCES: Harold D. Nelson et al. *Area Handbook for the United Republic of Cameroon.* 1974; Claude Tardits. *Le royaume Bamoum.* 1980.

WIILI. The Wiili are a Dagari* group.

WILÉ. *See* WALA.

WIMTIM. The Wimtims (Vimtims, Yimtims) are a subgroup of the Gude* people of Nigeria. They can be found in the Mubi District of the Mubi Division of Gongola State. The Wimtims speak a Chadic language.
REFERENCE: *Language Survey of Nigeria.* 1976.

WINAMWANGE. The Winamwanges are part of the larger cluster of Mambwe* peoples in Zambia.

WIWA. The Wiwas are part of the larger cluster of Mambwe* peoples in Zambia.

WIYAP. *See* JIRU-KIR.

WOABA. The Woabas are a subgroup of the Somba* people of Benin and Togo. Their contemporary population is approximately 50,000 people, most of whom are farmers, who raise maize, millet, plantains, and cassava.

WOBÉ. The Wobés (Ouobe, Wé) are a Kru*-speaking people living near the town of Man and in the subprefectures of Kouibly, Fakobly, Logoualé, and Bangolo in western Ivory Coast and in Liberia. Because of close similarities with the Guérés,* as well as their own sense of unity with them, ethnologists consider the Wobés and the Guérés to have been the same people until a recent split. Their population today in Ivory Coast and Liberia is approaching 200,000 people.

REFERENCES: Robert E. Handloff et al. *Côte d'Ivoire: A Country Study.* 1990; Robert J. Mundt. *Historical Dictionary of Côte d'Ivoire.* 1987; John Singler. "On the Underlying Representation of Contour Tones in Wobé." *Studies in African Linguistics* 15 (1984): 59–75.

WODAABE. *See* BORORO.

WOGO. The Wogos are a relatively small ethnic group living today in Mali, Nigeria, and Niger. They represent a mixture of Sarakolé (Soninké) and Sorko* culture. They spread out of Mali, down the Niger River, and reached present-day Niger and Nigeria early in the 1800s. Already Islamicized, they settled among and then did battle with the Kurtey* people in the region. Most Wogos are fine farmers, many of whom earn extra cash by working seasonally in Ghana. They are a homogeneous people who maintain close ties across international boundaries. Wogos speak a Songhai* language.
REFERENCE: Samuel Decalo. *Historical Dictionary of Niger.* 1989.

WOKUMBE. The Wokumbe are one of the so-called "grasslands" peoples of northwestern Cameroon. Most of them are farmers, raising a variety of cereal crops and vegetables, along with cocoa and coffee in some locations. They are well-known regionally for their skill at sculpture, pottery, and metalworking.
REFERENCE: Mark W. DeLancey and H. M. Mokeba. *Historical Dictionary of the Republic of Cameroon.* 1990.

WOLAYTA. *See* WELAMO.

WOLLO. The Wollos are a major subgroup of the Oromo* peoples of Ethiopia. Most of them are Muslims who live in Wollo Province and work as mixed agriculturalists.

WOLLOF. *See* WOLOF.

WOLOF. The Wolof (Wollof, Jolof, Ouolof) people dominate the Senegambia region of West Africa. Approximately 2.5 million Wolofs live in the area from the Senegal River in the north to the Gambia River in the south. They are closely related to the neighboring Serers,* Pepels, and Jolas.* The Wolofs were in the region by the fifteenth century when Portuguese* traders first reached them, and today the Wolofs constitute more than 36 percent of the total population in Senegal and 15 percent in Gambia. There are also some Wolofs in Mauritania and in the Casamance region of Senegal. The Wolof conversion to Islam began in the eleventh century, and today the vast majority of Wolofs are Muslims. The few Wolofs who are Christians live mostly in the coastal cities of Dakar, Goree, and Banjul. A few pre-Islamic religious traditions persist among older, rural Wolof women. The Wolof language, which is a lingua franca in the region and which is developing into a written form, is part of the West Atlantic group of the Niger-Congo linguistic family.

With the arrival of the Portuguese, a Wolof migration toward the coastal region began. By the mid-nineteenth century, when peanuts became an important cash crop, tens of thousands of Wolofs migrated into southwestern Senegal, where the land was best suited for peanut cultivation. Demands for new peanut land have triggered a relatively recent expansion to the south and east. Most recently, urbanization has accelerated as Wolofs have headed for Dakar and other cities in search of wage labor. In rural areas, the Wolofs still live in small, walled-off compounds of several hundred people. Each compound has a central square, a mosque, a cemetery, and homes constructed of reed or millet-stalk walls, with roofs thatched with palm leaves. Mud-walled homes with corrugated sheet roofs are recent additions. Rural Wolofs are farmers who raise millet, sorghum, and maize as staples and peanuts for cash. They also own cattle, which they contract out to Fulbe* herders. In such cities as Dakar, St. Louis, Kaolack, and Banjul, the Wolofs are the dominant group; there they work as merchants, traders, clerks, civil servants, skilled craftsmen, professionals, and artists.

REFERENCES: David P. Gamble. "Wolof." In Richard V. Weekes, ed. *Muslim Peoples.* 1984; David P. Gamble. *The Wolof of Senegambia.* 1967; L. B. Venema. *The Wolof of Saloum.* 1978.

WOM. The Woms (Perebas) are a Nigerian ethnic group. They are closely associated with the Duru-Verres* and live in the Verre District of the Adamawa Division of Gongola State, as well as across the border in Cameroon.

REFERENCE: *Language Survey of Nigeria.* 1976.

WOUMBOU. The Woumbous, also identified as the Bavumbus, are a small ethnic group living in several villages west of Franceville on the upper Ogooué River in Gabon. Historically, they have intermarried frequently with various Pygmy* groups, with whom they have lived in close proximity. Most Woumbous are small farmers who also hunt and fish to supplement their diets.

REFERENCE: David E. Gardinier. *Historical Dictionary of Gabon.* 1994.

WOURI. The Wouris (Olis) are an ethnic group of approximately 60,000 people living along the Atlantic coast of Cameroon, Gabon, and Equatorial Guinea. Approximately four centuries ago, they migrated to their present location from Zaire. They were among the first Cameroonian people to meet and interact with Europeans, and they became active middlemen in the Atlantic slave trade during the seventeenth and eighteenth centuries. During the century of French* administration, the Wouris became one of the most thoroughly educated and acculturated groups in Cameroon.

REFERENCES: *African Encyclopedia.* 1974; Mark DeLancey and H. M. Mokeba. *Historical Dictionary of the Republic of Cameroon.* 1990.

WOVEA. The Woveas are a subgroup of the Bakweri* peoples of Cameroon. They live in villages on the slopes surrounding Mt. Cameroon in South West Province. They arrived in the region as part of a Bantu* migration beginning in the early eighteenth century. Because of their location near the coast, the Woveas were among the first Cameroonians to come into contact with Europeans. They lost much of their land to German* plantation owners in the late nineteenth and early twentieth centuries. In recent years, such groups as the Bakweri Union and the Bakweri Land Claim Committee have tried to recover Wovea property. Today, most Woveas support themselves by working on the palm oil plantations, oil rigs, and refineries at Cape Limbo, as well as by fishing and rice farming.
REFERENCE: Mark W. DeLancey and H. M. Mokeba. *Historical Dictionary of the Republic of Cameroon.* 1990.

WOYO. The Woyos are one of the major subgroups of the Kongo* people of Zaire and Angola.

WULUKOHA. The Wulukohas are one of the clans of the Bandi* Chiefdom of Lofa County in Liberia.

WUM. The Wums are a subgroup of the Tikar* peoples of the Bamenda highlands of North West Province in Cameroon. Unlike most Tikar peoples, who have patrilineal descent systems, the Wums are matrilineal. They are classified as part of the Middle-Cameroon Bantu* group of peoples. The Wums originated farther to the north and were pushed into their present location by Fulbe* expansion. Theirs is a savanna environment with patches of woodland and gallery forest along water courses. The Wums are farmers and fishermen, whose villages stretch along roads and tracks. Traditional huts are rectangular and have a palm-frond roofing, but today cement houses and corrugated sheet roofs are common, especially in villages near the tarmacked main roads.
REFERENCE: Mark W. DeLancey and H. M. Mokeba. *Historical Dictionary of the Republic of Cameroon.* 1990.

WUNGU. The Wungus are a Bantu*-speaking people of Tanzania. Their population today is approximately 30,000 people.
REFERENCE: Edgar C. Polomé and C. P. Hill. *Language in Tanzania.* 1980.

WURKUM. *See* KULUNG.

WUTE. *See* BAFUT.

X

XAM. The Xam dialect is spoken by San* peoples in southwestern Botswana. The Xam people, who are primarily farmers and cattle raisers, are closely related to neighboring Xo,* Nukhi,* and Xegwi* people.

XAMTANGA. The Xamtanga are an ethnic group living today in Ethiopia. They speak a Central Cushitic language and are closely related to the Agaw* peoples. The Xamtangas are concentrated east of Lake Tana and the city of Gonder, in north-central Ethiopia. The Xamtanga population today exceeds 3,000 people, most of whom are small farmers and cattle raisers. Most are members of the Ethiopian Orthodox Church, a Christian organization.
REFERENCES: M. L. Bender, J. D. Bowen, R. L. Cooper, and C. A. Ferguson, eds. *Language in Ethiopia.* 1976; Harold D. Nelson et al. *Ethiopia: A Country Study.* 1980.

XEGWI. The Xegwi dialect is spoken by San* peoples in southwestern Botswana. The Xegwi people, who are primarily farmers and cattle raisers, are closely related to neighboring Xam,* Nukhi,* and Xo* people.

XESIBE. The Xesibe are a Xhosa*-speaking people who today live in the northeastern corner of the Transkei in South Africa.
REFERENCE: M. C. O'Connell. "Spirit Possession and Role Stress Among the Xesibe of Eastern Transkei." *Ethnology* 21 (January 1982): 21–38.

XHOSA. The Xhosa people, whose contemporary population exceeds 600,000 people, live in the Transkei and Ciskei of southeastern Cape Province in South Africa. They are divided into several independent subgroups, including the Xesibe, Gcaleka, and Rharhabe. The Xhosa language, along with Ndebele,* Swazi, and Zulu,* is part of the Nguni* group of Bantu* languages. Other groups in South Africa, such as the Thembu* and Mfengu,* speak Xhosa as well. The

Xhosa have been in the Transkei and Ciskei for hundreds of years. Conflict with Boer settlers in South Africa started in the late eighteenth century, when the Boers started moving east from the Cape of Good Hope. Those wars lasted for more than a century. In the mid-nineteenth century (1856–1857, to be exact), the Xhosa prophetess Nongquase promised the destruction of all Europeans and the restoration of all cattle herds if the Xhosa would only destroy all of their cattle and food supplies. Most Xhosa obeyed, and the next decades were noted for poverty, starvation, and suffering. Today, most Xhosas are farmers, raising maize, sorghum, and pumpkins. Xhosa chiefs still maintain considerable local authority, and there are tens of thousands of Xhosa working as businessmen, professionals, and craftsmen in South Africa. The most prominent Xhosa writers are Sinxo and John Bokwe.

REFERENCES: *African Encyclopedia.* 1974; B. A. Pauw. *Christianity and Xhosa Tradition.* 1975; Christopher Saunders. *Historical Dictionary of South Africa.* 1983.

XHU. *See* KUNG.

XO. The Xo dialect is spoken by San* peoples in southwestern Botswana. The Xo people, who are primarily farmers and cattle raisers, are closely related to neighboring Xam,* Nukhi,* and Xegwi* people.

XU-ANGOLA. *See* MALIGO.

Y

YAAKU. The Yaakus (Mogogodos) are a small ethnic group in Kenya. They live near Doldol, approximately thirty miles from Mt. Kenya. Their homeland is in the Mukoodo Forest. The Yaakus speak an eastern Cushitic language. Since 1930, they have been engaged in the transition from a hunting-gathering economy to a pastoral lifestyle revolving around the production of goats and cattle. They are rapidly adopting Masai* culture.
REFERENCE: Bethwell A. Ogot. *Historical Dictionary of Kenya.* 1981.

YACOUBA. *See* DAN.

YAGALA. The Yagalas live today in far northwestern Ghana, far northeastern Ivory Coast, and across the border in Burkina-Faso. Most of them make a living from raising livestock and subsistence farming. Ethnologists consider them a subgroup of the Lobi* people.

YAGBA. The Yagbas are one of the main subgroups of the Yoruba* people of Nigeria. Most Yagbas can be found today living in Kwara State in western Nigeria.

YAGBUM. *See* NYANGBO.

YAGHWATADAXA. *See* GUDUF.

YAGOUT. The Yagout are a nomadic group of the Tekna* peoples of Western Sahara in what is today Morocco. The Yagout population currently exceeds 1,000 people. Their traditional homeland was in northern Western Sahara, particularly south of the Zini Mountains and in the western Ouarkizz Mountains. Today, large numbers of Yagouts live in El-Ayoun.
REFERENCE: Tony Hodges. *Historical Dictionary of Western Sahara.* 1982.

YAHUMA. The Yahumas are a subgroup of the larger Ngangela* cluster of peoples living today in Angola.

YAJU. *See* YEJJU.

YAKA. The Yakas are a Bantu*-speaking people whose original homeland was between the Kwango and Wamba rivers in southwestern Zaire and northern Angola. They are considered by many ethnologists to be a subgroup of the Kongos.* Known widely for their powerful sense of independence, the Yakas first tried to avoid and then resisted the arrival of Belgian* colonial administration. Since Zairean independence, the Yakas have frequently clashed with the Kongos and resisted the authority of the central government. Their population today exceeds one million people. The Sukus* are a subgroup of the Yakas.
REFERENCES: Kenneth Lee Adelman. ''The Art of the Yaka.'' *African Arts* 9 (October 1975): 41–43; F. Scott Bobb. *Historical Dictionary of Zaire.* 1988; Susan H. Broadhead. *Historical Dictionary of Angola.* 1992.

YAKI. The Yakis are an ethnic group living today in southern Cross River State in Nigeria, as well as across the border in western Cameroon. They are closely related to the Efiks* and Ibibios.* The Yaki language is of Bantu* origins. Most of the Yakis are farmers, raising yams and palm oil. Large numbers of them also work in Nigerian cities. The Yaki population today exceeds 350,000 people.
REFERENCE: Donald G. Morrison et al. *Black Africa: A Comparative Handbook.* 1989.

YAKO. *See* LOKE.

YAKOMA. The Yakomas are part of what some ethnologists call the Ubanguian* people of the Central African Republic. Some can also be found across the river in Zaire. Most of them have lived historically near the confluence of the Kotto and Ubangi rivers. They fiercely resisted the inroads of King Leopold and the Belgians* in the region and eventually sided with the French* against the Belgians. The Yakomas are a riverine people. There are approximately 80,000 Yakoma people today.
REFERENCE: Pierre Kalck. *Historical Dictionary of the Central African Republic.* 1992.

YAKORO. *See* BEKWARRA.

YAKPA. The Yakpas are a subgroup of the Banda* people of the Central African Republic. The French* conducted nearly genocidal wars of conquest against the Yakpas between 1897 and 1901. Their current population exceeds 175,000 people.

YAKUDI. *See* KURI.

YAKURR. *See* LOKE.

YALA. The Yalas (Iyalas) are a subgroup of the Idoma* people of Nigeria. They have a population today of approximately 100,000 people, most of whom live in the Ogoja, Ikom, and Obubra divisions of Cross River State.

YALNA. The Yalnas are an ethnic group in Chad. Many of the 50,000 or so Yalnas are Muslims. They are part of the larger Nilotic* cluster of Chadian peoples. Most Yalnas make their living as small farmers, laborers, and semi-nomadic and nomadic pastoralists.
REFERENCES: Pierre Hugot. *Le Tchad.* 1965; J. C. Lebeuf. *Afrique Centrale.* 1972; Donald G. Morrison et al. *Black Africa: A Comparative Handbook.* 1989.

YALUNKA. The Yalunka—who have also been known historically as the Di-alonke, Djalonke, Dyalonké, Jalonké, Jallonké, Jalonca, and Jalunka—are an ethnic group of approximately 100,000 people living in northeastern Sierra Le-one and across the border in Guinea. They can also be found in Guinea-Bissau. They consider themselves to be the original inhabitants of the Futa Jalon plateau of West Africa. They speak a Manding* language that is closely related to Soso.* Most Yalunkas are subsistence farmers, raising rice as the staple and maintaining herds of cattle and goats. Yalunka society is organized around ex-ogamous patrilineal clans. Since the 1950s, increasing numbers of the Yalunka have left the rural areas for the diamond fields of Sierra Leone or for such cities as Freetown where they work for wages. Large numbers of Fulbes* and Man-dinkas* have moved into the Yalunka region in recent decades, creating a mul-ticultural social environment.

Until the late nineteenth century, the Yalunka were violently anti-Islam. But, in 1884, the Mandinka empire of Samory Touré conquered the Yalunka and forcible conversions began. British* and French* troops expelled the Mandinkas in 1892 and divided up the area, the British taking Sierra Leone and the French taking Guinea. Christian missionaries affiliated with the Church Missionary So-ciety tried but failed to convert the Yalunka; instead, the Yalunka turned to Islam in increasing numbers. Today, more than 95 percent of the Yalunka are Sunni Muslims.
REFERENCES: Leland Donald. "Yalunka." In Richard V. Weekes, ed. *Muslim Peoples.* 1984; M. C. Fyle. *The Solima Yalunka Kingdom: Precolonial Politics, Economics and Society.* 1979.

YAMARICO. The Yamarico are one of the major subgroups of the Sadama* people of southwestern Ethiopia.

YAMBESSA. The Yambessa are one of the cluster of Middle-Cameroon Bantu*
peoples who live in central Cameroon. They are part of the Bamiléké* cluster.
Most of them make their living as small farmers and fishermen, although, in
recent years, increasing numbers of Yambessa men have found work on commercial farms and in the oil fields. The increasing emphasis on commercial crops
for export—coffee, cocoa, timber, palm oil, and bananas—has actually tended
to impoverish most Yambessa farmers and has contributed to a decline in their
standard of living.
REFERENCE: Mark W. DeLancey and H. M. Mokeba. *Historical Dictionary of the
Republic of Cameroon.* 1990.

YAMMA. The Yamma are a subgroup of the Gbagyi* people of Nigeria. Demographers estimate the Yamma population at 110,000 people, of whom half
are Muslims.

YANBASA. *See* YAMBESSA.

YANDANG. The Yandangs—also known over the years as the Yendams, Hen-
dangs, Yundums, and Nyandangs—are an Adamawa-speaking people of Nigeria. They have a population today of approximately 35,000 people, most of
whom live in Gongola State, especially in the Jalingo and Lau districts of the
Muri Division and the Jereng and Kwajji districts of the Adamawa Division.
REFERENCE: *Language Survey of Nigeria.* 1976.

YANS. *See* YANZI.

YANZI. The Yanzis (Yans) are a Bantu*-speaking people whom many ethnologists consider to be a subgroup of the Kongos.* Known widely for their powerful sense of independence, the Yanzis first tried to avoid and then resisted the
arrival of Belgian* colonial administration. Since Zairean independence, the
Yanzis have frequently clashed with the Kongos and resisted the authority of
the central government. Their population today exceeds one million people.
Many of them live south of the Kasai River and east of the Kwango River, in
the triangle where those two rivers meet in southwestern Zaire.
REFERENCES: F. Scott Bobb. *Historical Dictionary of Zaire.* 1988; Susan H. Broadhead. *Historical Dictionary of Angola.* 1992.

YAO. The Yao—also known historically as the Wayao, Wahyao, Veiao,
Achawa, and Adjao (Ajaua)—are an ethnic group of approximately one million
people living in Malawi, Mozambique, and Tanzania. They are closely related
to the Chewas* and Lomwes.* They are not to be confused with the Pila Pila*
people of Benin who call themselves Yao. Some ethnologists include the
Mweres,* Kiturikas, Makuas, Makondes,* Matambwes, Mawias, Ngindos,*
Ndondes, Machingas, and Songos in the Yao cluster. Yao traditions trace their

origins to the region between the Lujenda and Rovuma rivers near Lake Malawi. Very closely related to the Yao are another seven million Mwere, Makua, and Makonde people, who live primarily in Tanzania. Some ethnologists classify all eight million of these people as Yao. Until the colonial conquest of the nineteenth century, the Yao were known widely as traders who exchanged ivory, slaves, beeswax, tobacco, guns, gunpowder, beads, and cloth between Arab* and Swahili* traders on the East African coast and interior ethnic groups. They lived in autonomous villages where they raised millet and sorghum. With the arrival of the German* and British* colonial administrations in the nineteenth and twentieth centuries, the slave and ivory trade disappeared, forcing large numbers of Yao men to seek wage labor in the cities. Today, at any given time of the year, as many as one of every three Yao men will be working far from his own village. Today, approximately 75 percent of the Yao proper are Sunni Muslims of the Shafi school, as are more than a third of the Mweres, Makuas, and Makondes. They are not known to be particularly devout, however, and many elements of their indigenous religious beliefs have mixed with Islam and Christianity to create syncretic religions. Since 1974, when Tanzania began the forced relocation of its citizens into larger demographic clusters for purposes of education and public health, the Yao have found themselves crowded together in large settlements, which they do not particularly enjoy.

REFERENCES: Y. B. Abdallah. *The Yaos.* 1919; Edward A. Alpers. *Ivory and Slaves.* 1975; James L. Brain. "Yao." In Richard V. Weekes, ed. *Muslim Peoples.* 1984; J. Clyde Mitchell. *The Yao Village.* 1956.

YAO. *See* PILA PILA.

YARSÉ. The Yarsé are an ethnic group living today among the Mossi* in Burkina-Faso. Late in the 1600s, Manding* traders brought Islam to the Mossis and settled among them. In 1780, the king of the Mossi extended formal permission to these people to settle throughout his kingdom. Over the years, they adopted the Mossi language as their primary tongue, acculturated to Mossi institutions, and often married other Mossis. But the Yarsé did not convert to Roman Catholicism or the indigenous Mossi religion; most of them remained faithful to Islam. Today, the Yarsé continue their mercantile pursuits, although a substantial number of them have settled down to become subsistence millet farmers. Current population estimates for the Yarsé are approximately 190,000 people, of whom 90 percent are Muslims.

REFERENCES: Peter B. Hammond. *Yatenga: Technology in the Culture of a West African Kindgom.* 1971; Michael Izard. "The Yarsé and Pre-Colonial Trade in Yatenga." In C. Meillassoux, ed. *The Development of Indigenous Trade and Markets in West Africa.* 1971.

YASGUA. *See* YESKWA.

YASHI. The Yashis are one of Nigeria's many ethnic groups. They live in the Mana District of the Akwanga Division of Plateau State.
REFERENCE: *Language Survey of Nigeria.* 1976.

YATENGA. The Yatengas are a Molé-Dagbane* people living in northwestern Burkina-Faso and across the border in Mali. In the sixteenth century, Yadega founded the Yatenga Kingdom as part of the larger Mossi* Empire. It became a French* protectorate in 1895. The major Yatenga towns are Gourcy and Ouahigouya. Yatenga farmers raise peanuts, millet, and sorghum, and Yatenga herders raise cattle. The Yatenga population today exceeds 800,000 people.
REFERENCE: Peter B. Hammond. *Yatenga: Technology in the Culture of a West African Kindgom.* 1971.

YAWIYASU. The Yawiyasus are one of the clans of the Bandi* Chiefdom of Lofa County in Liberia.

YAWOTATAXA. *See* GUDUF.

YEDINA. *See* BUDUMA.

YEI. The Yei (Bayei) people live today in Ngamiland, on the western edges of the Okavango swamps in Botswana. They migrated there from southern Zambia in the early eighteenth century. Unlike their Tawana* neighbors, who built centralized political states, the Yeis did not live in villages, preferring scattered homesteads. Eventually, the Yeis became dominated by the Tawanas. During the past two centuries, the Yeis have moved away from their traditional fishing and hunting economy toward agriculture and stock-raising. After World War II, Yei separatism, from both British* and Tawana control, emerged in the Yei community. Botswanan independence and local political reforms giving them more political autonomy had satisfied most of the Yei grievances by the 1970s.
REFERENCES: Frank L. Lambrecht and Dora J. Lambrecht. "Leather and Beads in N'gamiland." *African Arts* 10 (January 1977): 34–35; Fred Morton, A. Murray, and J. Ramsay. *Historical Dictionary of Botswana.* 1989.

YEJJU. The Yejjus (Yaju) are one of the major Oromo* subgroups in northern Ethiopia. Most of them are Sunni Muslims of the Shafi school, who work as sedentary farmers in Wollo Province and southern Tigre Province.

YEKE. The Yekes are a Bantu*-speaking people who live in the southern Shaba region of Zaire, especially between Kolwezi and Kazanga near the border with Zambia. Some Yekes also live across the border in Zambia. In the 1800s, Nyamwezi* traders established their own kingdom in the region, and the Yekes are descended from them. The Yeke Kingdom began to disintegrate in

the late 1800s. In the late 1950s, the Yekes joined with the Lundas* in forming the CONAKAT political party and demanding independence.
REFERENCE: F. Scott Bobb. *Historical Dictionary of Zaire.* 1988.

YEKHEE. The Yekhees—Iyekhees, Afemmais, and Etsakos—are one of the Edo* peoples of Nigeria. They have a population of approximately 290,000 people. They live in the Etsako and Isham divisions of Bendel State.

YELA. The Yelas are a Bantu*-speaking people who live in the forests of the Kasai Orientale region of eastern Zaire. Most of them are small farmers who raise cassava, bananas, and kola nuts. In recent years, the Yelas have been increasingly touched by Zaire's commercial economy, with the result that more and more Yelas are growing cash crops or leaving their farms for work in towns and cities. Most Yelas can be found near the Tshuapa River.
REFERENCES: Daniel P. Biebuyck. "Sculpture from the Eastern Zaire Forest Regions: Mbole, Yela, and Pere." *African Arts* 10 (October 1976): 54–61; Irving Kaplan et al. *Zaire: A Country Study.* 1978.

YENDAM. *See* YANDANG.

YENDI. The Yendi are one of the Molé-Dagbane* peoples of northern Ghana.
REFERENCE: Paul Andre Ladouceur. "The Yendi Chieftancy Dispute and Ghanian Politics." *Canadian Journal of African Studies* 6 (1972): 97–115.

YERGAN. The Yergans (Yergams, Yergums, Yerguns) are one of the Bantu*-speaking peoples of Nigeria. They are classified as part of the Plateau cluster of peoples who occupy central Nigeria. Most Yergans live in the Langtang Government Council Area in Plateau State. They are bordered to the south and southwest by the Gerkawa,* Gomei,* and Montol* peoples, to the east by the Hausas,* and to the north and northwest by the Kanams* and Ngans (Bengs*). Most Yergans practice subsistence horticulture, raising ginger, millet, guinea corn, beans and citrus products. They live in social systems characterized by patrilineal descent and patrifocal residence. In recent years, they have begun migrating to towns and cities looking for work.
REFERENCE: Stephan Banfa. "Towards a Yergam History: Some Explorations." In Elizabeth Isichei, ed. *Studies in the History of Plateau State, Nigeria.* 1982.

YERIMA. *See* KURI.

YESKWA. The Yeskwas (Yasguas) are one of the Eastern Plateau peoples of Nigeria. They live in the Jema'a District of the Jema'a Division of Kaduna State and the Gitate and Kokona districts of the Nasarawa Division of Plateau State.
REFERENCE: *Language Survey of Nigeria.* 1976.

YIDDA. *See* MADA.

YIGHA. *See* LEYIGHA.

YIMTIM. *See* WIMTIM.

YIRA. The Yiras (Nandes) are a subgroup of the Kivu* peoples of Zaire. They live in the highlands of east-central Zaire, near the Rwandan and Ugandan borders where they farm and raise cattle for milk and meat. They speak a Bantu* language.
REFERENCE: Irving Kaplan et al. *Zaire: A Country Study.* 1978.

YIWOM. The Yiwoms (Gerkas, Gurkas) are a Chadic-speaking people of Nigeria. They live in the Shendam Division of Plateau State.
REFERENCE: *Language Survey of Nigeria.* 1976.

YOKOBOUÉ. The Yokoboué are a subgroup of the Dida* people of Ivory Coast.

YOMBE. The Yombe are a subgroup of the Kongo* people of Congo, Zaire, Zambia, and Angola. They are concentrated in the Yombe mountain area of Congo, especially in and around Ncesse, Chimpeze, Kakamocka, and Mvouti. The contemporary Yombe population in Congo exceeds 30,000 people. There are also 10,000 Yombes in Zambia. Most of them are farmers, raising maize, beans, and millet. Some ethnologists classify them in the Tumbuka* cluster.
REFERENCE: G. C. Bond. "Kinship and Conflict in a Yombe Village." *Africa* 52 (October 1972): 116–30.

YONI. The Yonis are a prominent subgroup of the Temne* people of Sierra Leone.

YORDA. *See* KPAN.

YORUBA. The Yoruba are a large ethnic group numbering more than twenty million people in Sierra Leone, Ghana, Benin, Togo, Niger, and Nigeria. The largest group—more than eighteen million people—live in southwestern Nigeria. The Yoruba constitute the entire populations of the states of Ogun, Ondo, and Oyo in Nigeria, as well as the majority of the population in Lagos State. In Kwara State, they are the majority group in the Ilorin region. Because of differences in dialect and regional identity, the Yoruba can be divided into such subgroups as the Ogun Yoruba, Ondo Yoruba, Oyo Yoruba, Ilorin Yoruba, Ekiti Yoruba, Ife Yoruba, Ijebu Yoruba, Ijesa Yoruba, Holli, Dassa, Ketu, Manigri, Itsha, Chabe, Egba, and Anago. The Yoruba language is part of the Kwa* group of the Niger-Congo linguistic family.

All of the Yoruba groups consider themselves originally a Sudanic people who conquered the indigenous groups of the forested regions of Nigeria; ethnolinguists and anthropologists agree. They all accept Ile-Ife as the original city of the Yoruba. The original Yoruba religion consisted of hundreds of *orishas,* or gods, of whom Ifa was the greatest. Fulbe* and Hausa* traders brought Islam to the Yoruba savannas in the north, and Christian missionaries—many of them freed American slaves returning to their Yoruba homeland—introduced Christianity in the southern regions. Today, approximately 45 percent of the Yoruba are Muslims, 45 percent Christians, and 10 percent still loyal to Ifa, but even Islam and Christianity among the Yoruba possess strong elements of the traditional animistic faith.

The Yoruba today can be seen in all walks of life in West Africa. In rural areas, they still live in their walled, windowless compounds of approximately 1,000 people and work as farmers. In the cities, they function in every occupation, from day laborers to professionals, civil servants, and businessmen and businesswomen. The Yoruba dominate the University of Lagos, the University of Ibadan, and the University of Ife. Their culture is among the most cohesive and resilient in the world.

REFERENCES: J. S. Eades. *The Yoruba Today.* 1980; G. J. Ojo. *Yoruba Culture: A Geographical Analysis.* 1966; Robert Wren. ''Yoruba.'' In Richard V. Weekes, ed. *Muslim Peoples.* 1984.

YOWA. *See* PILA PILA.

YUKUBEN. The Yukubens—known also as Nyikubens, Nyikobes, Ayikibens, Boritsus, Balaabes, and Oohums—are a Nigerian ethnic group living in the Ayikiben District of the Wukari Division of Gongola State.

REFERENCE: *Language Survey of Nigeria.* 1976.

YUKUTARE. *See* BITARE.

YUNDUM. *See* YANDANG.

YUNGUR. The Yungurs (Ebenas, Ebinas, Benas, Binnas) are an Adamawa-speaking people of Nigeria. They live in the Shellen District of the Numan Division and the Song and Yungur districts in the Adamawa Division of Gongola State. They have a population of 95,000 people.

REFERENCE: *Language Survey of Nigeria.* 1976.

Z

ZABARIMA. *See* ZERMA.

ZABARMA. *See* ZERMA.

ZABAYDIYA. The Zabaydiyas are one of the major Arabic*-speaking groups living today in Sudan.

ZABERMA. *See* ZERMA.

ZABERMAWA. *See* ZERMA.

ZAGHAWA. The Zaghawas are a subgroup of the Beri* peoples of Chad and Sudan. Their population exceeds 300,000 people, virtually all of whom are Muslims. The Zaghawas are scattered around Sudan and southwestern Ethiopia. A remnant of the Garamantes people, they are closely related to the Bertis* and Bideyats. They live in small, sedentary villages of no more than 100 people each and make their living raising millet, sorghum, peanuts, okra, sesame, watermelons, cucumbers, and pumpkins. Some Zaghawas raise cattle, goats, sheep, and sometimes donkeys, camels, and horses. Because of changing economic patterns in recent years, more and more Zaghawa young men travel seasonally to Libya in search of wage labor. The Zaghawas are Sunni Muslims, but their devotions are lukewarm, at least when compared to many other Muslim groups. They also practice *karama*—the sacrifice of a bull, goat, or lamb to ward off evil or to bring rain and a good harvest. Political power among the Zaghawas was once exercised by *omdas,* or chiefs, but, in recent decades, the Sudanese government has imposed a series of village, division, and regional councils. The *omdas,* however, are still recognized as important judicial officials.
REFERENCES: Carolyn Fluehr-Lobban, Richard A. Lobban, Jr., and John Obert Voll.

Historical Dictionary of Sudan. 1992; L. T. Holy. *Neighbours and Kinsmen: A Study of the Berti Peoples of Darfur.* 1974.

ZAGHMANA. *See* DGHWEDE.

ZAHR-FLAHN. The Zahr-Flahns are one of the Bassa* clans living in the River Cess Territory of Liberia.

ZALAMO. *See* ZARAMO.

ZAMFARA. The Zamfaras are a subgroup of the Hausa* peoples of Nigeria.

ZANAKI. The Zanakis are an ethnic group of approximately 70,000 people who live east of Lake Victoria in northern Tanzania. They are subdivided into two groups, the Birus and the Baturis.* Under German* control from the 1890s to World War I, the Zanakis were divided into twelve separate chiefdoms. The British* tried to unite them into a single group after World War II, but centrifugal social forces kept the Zanakis divided into a number of separate chiefdoms. Most Zanakis today are farmers, cattle raisers, or city workers. Julius Nyerere is the most famous representative of the Zanaki people.
REFERENCE: Laura Kurtz. *Historical Dictionary of Tanzania.* 1978.

ZANDAMO. The Zandamo Kingdom was founded by Rawa in the sixteenth century as part of the larger Mossi* empire. Located between the Red Volta River and the White Volta River, the kingdom was later absorbed by the Ya-tengas* in what is today Burkina-Faso and Mali. Most Zandamos make their living raising peanuts, sorghum, millet, and cattle.
REFERENCE: Daniel M. McFarland. *Historical Dictionary of Upper Volta.* 1978.

ZANDE. *See* AZANDÉ.

ZANGAL. The Zangals are a Chadic-speaking people of Nigeria. They live in the Zungur District of the Bauchi Division of Bauchi State.
REFERENCE: *Language Survey of Nigeria.* 1976.

ZANY. *See* NZANGI.

ZAOSE. The Zaoses are a small ethnic group of several thousand who live in Burkina-Faso. They tend to be concentrated southeast of the town of Koupéla in the southeastern part of the country. Most Zaoses make their living raising cattle and/or producing sorghum and millet on small farms.
REFERENCE: Daniel M. McFarland. *Historical Dictionary of Upper Volta.* 1978.

ZARAMO. The Zaramo (Zalamo) are a cluster of Northeast Bantu*-speaking people who live along the East African coast in Tanzania. Included in the Zaramo cluster are the Zaramo proper as well as the Kutus,* Kweres,* Zigalus,* Kamis,* Sagaras,* Lugurus,* Ngulus, Kagurus,* and Vidundas.* Although distinct, the Nyagtwas are included with the Zaramos by many ethnologists. Except for the Zaramo proper and the Kutus, the Zaramo cluster traces descent matrilineally. Most Zaramo peoples are Muslims. They make their living as hoe agriculturalists, producing maize, sorghum, and rice as well as raising sheep, goats, and poultry. Generally, the Zaramo do not raise cattle. During the last two decades, increasing numbers of the Zaramo peoples have made their way to the cities in search of work. Many of them have also suffered from the drought that struck East Africa in the late 1980s and early 1990s. Most Zaramos tend to live inland from the coast, behind Dar es Salaam, the capital of Tanzania. The Zaramo population today exceeds 375,000 people.
REFERENCE: L. W. Swantz. *Ritual and Symbol in Transitional Zaramo Society.* 1970.

ZARAMO. The term "Zaramo," which refers to a cluster of Northeast Bantu*-speaking peoples in East Africa, also refers to one of the individual groups in that cluster—the Zaramo proper. They live in the coastal lowlands of Tanzania where most of them work as hoe farmers, producing maize, sorghum, and rice, as well as raising sheep, goats, and poultry. During the nineteenth century, the Zaramo were victimized by the East African slave trade. In response, they built fortified villages protected by stockades. In the twentieth century, those settlement patterns gave way to the homestead system in which rural Zaramos scattered out more widely. They live in mud-and-wattle homes characterized by high, thatched, cone-shaped roofs, but thatch is now giving way to tin. The vast majority of the Zaramo are Muslims, although they are considered to be only marginally loyal, confining their religious observances to fasting at Ramadan, taking on Arab* names, and wearing the white skull cap.

Since the mid-1970s, the Zaramo have been dramatically affected by the Tanzanian government's *ujamaa* policy, which is designed to gather rural people out of their scattered homestead settlements into more concentrated villages, where public education and public health campaigns can be more effective. Rates of malaria and schistosomiasis are high among the Zaramo, and only improved public health programs can alleviate the crisis. The Zaramo people have also been affected in recent years by the East African drought of the late 1980s and early 1990s and by the threat of the human immunodeficiency virus (HIV) and the disease of AIDS.
REFERENCE: L. W. Swantz. *Ritual and Symbol in Transitional Zaramo Society.* 1970.

ZARANDAWA. *See* GEZAWA.

ZARI. The Zaris are a relatively small Nigerian ethnic group. They speak a Bantu* language and live on the northeastern edge of the Jos Plateau

in Plateau State. Their most immediate ethnic neighbors are the Sayas,* Jarawas, Dasses,* Zeems,* and Afusaris.* Most Zaris are subsistence farmers who raise millet, guinea corn, maize, and a variety of other products.
REFERENCE: Elizabeth Isichei, ed. *Studies in the History of Plateau State, Nigeria.* 1982.

ZARMA. *See* ZERMA.

ZAYZE. The Zayzes (Zayze-Zergula) people are an ethnic group living today in Ethiopia. The Zayzes are part of the Omotic* cluster of peoples in southern Ethiopia. They plant ensete and other grains and practice animal husbandry for a living. Like most other Omotic peoples in the region, the Zayzes have remained loyal to their indigenous religious traditions. Their population today exceeds 15,000 people.
REFERENCE: Harold D. Nelson et al. *Ethiopia: A Country Study.* 1980.

ZAZZAGAWA. The Zazzagawas are a subgroup of the Hausa* peoples of Nigeria.

ZEEM. The Zeems are an ethnic group living today north of the Jos Plateau in Plateau State in northwestern Nigeria. They are surrounded ethnically by the Jarawas, Afusaris,* Zaris,* and Dasses.* Most Zeems are subsistence farmers.
REFERENCE: Elizabeth Isichei, ed. *Studies in the History of Plateau State, Nigeria.* 1982.

ZEEWEIN. The Zeeweins are a subgroup of the Bassa* people of Liberia. Most Zeeweins live in Grand Bassa County, Liberia.

ZELA. The Zelas are a small ethnic group living in the foothills of the Mitumba Mountains in southeastern Zaire. The Zelas speak a Bantu* language and make their living as farmers.
REFERENCE: Irving Kaplan et al. *Zaire: A Country Study.* 1978.

ZÉMA. *See* NZIMA.

ZENAGA. The Zenagas are one of the Moor* subgroups living today in Mauritania.

ZERGULA. The Zergulas are an ethnic group living today in Ethiopia. They are part of the Omotic* cluster of peoples in southern Ethiopia. Zergulas raise ensete and other grains and practice animal husbandry for a living. Like most other Omotic peoples in the region, the Zergulas have remained loyal to

their indigenous religious traditions. Their population today exceeds 12,000 people.
REFERENCE: Harold D. Nelson et al. *Ethiopia: A Country Study.* 1980.

ZERMA. The Zerma (Zabarma, Zaberma, Zabarima, Zabermawa, Zarma, Djerma, Dyarma, Dyerma) are an ethnic group residing near Djibo, Airbinda, and Dori in Burkina-Faso. There are also large concentrations of Zerma in Niger, where they live in and around Zermaganda on both sides of the Niger River, and in Zaberma, which is a wadi region near Dosso. Smaller groups can be found in northwestern Nigeria, northern Benin, northern Ghana, and Ivory Coast. The Zerma are divided into a number of subgroups based on a powerful sense of kinship. Included in these kinship groups are the Kalles, Golles, Kados, Kourteys,* and Loqas. Most of the more than 1.2 million Zerma live in 2,000 villages where they are subsistence farmers. The Zerma possess small cattle herds, which they contract out to Fulbe* herders. The Zerma are also the majority group in the population of Niamey, the capital city of Niger. They are a subgroup of the Songhai* peoples of West Africa. During the nineteenth century, the Zerma were highly expansionist, but the arrival of the French* colonial administration in West Africa confined them to their present area. They are Muslims of the Maliki school.

During the colonial period, the French first encountered the Zerma in 1898. The Zermas and the French established a close working relationship, and the Zerma became widely known among other indigenous peoples for their pro-French attitudes. An aggressive and aristocratic people, the Zerma assisted the French in crushing local rebellions against imperial authority. They enjoy a reputation today as a particularly hardworking and honest people.
REFERENCE: Allan Joseph Atreicher. "On Being Zarma: Scarcity and Stress in the Nigerien Sahel." Ph.D. dissertation. Northwestern University. 1980.

ZEZURU. The Zezuru (Vazezuru) are one of the major subgroups in the Shona* cluster of peoples in Zimbabwe and Mozambique. They constitute about one-quarter of the Shona-speaking people in Zimbabwe. The Zezurus are sometimes known as the Central Shona. Most of them are farmers, raising cattle, millet, maize, pumpkins, and yams. In Zimbabwe, they are concentrated between Sinoia in the east, Wedza in the west, Bikita in the southeast, and Que Que in the southwest. They surround the Salisbury region. The major Zezuru subgroups are the Shavashas, Heras,* Govas,* Njanjas,* and Mbires.
REFERENCE: R. Kent Rasmussen. *Historical Dictionary of Zimbabwe.* 1994.

ZHIRU. *See* JIRU-KIR.

ZHU. *See* KUNG.

ZIBA. The Ziba people are part of the larger cluster of Interlacustrine Bantu* peoples of northwestern Tanzania. Many ethnologists include them today as part of the Haya* cluster of peoples.

ZIGABA. *See* TWA and PYGMY.

ZIGALU. The Zigalu (Zigula) are one of the individual groups in the Zaramo* cluster of the Northeast Bantu*-speaking people of East Africa. They live in the coastal lowlands of Tanzania where most of them work as hoe farmers, producing maize, sorghum, and rice, as well as raising sheep, goats, and poultry. During the nineteenth century, the Zigalu were victimized by the East African slave trade. In response, they built fortified villages protected by stockades. In the twentieth century, those settlement patterns gave way to the homestead system in which rural Zigalu scattered out more widely. They live in mud-and-wattle homes characterized by high, thatched, cone-shaped roofs, but thatch is now giving way to tin. The vast majority of the Zigalu are Muslims.
REFERENCE: L. W. Swantz. *Ritual and Symbol in Transitional Zaramo Society.* 1970.

ZIGUA. The Ziguas are an ethnic group living in the western Tanga and northern Coast regions of Tanzania. A warlike people, the Ziguas resisted first German* and then British* attempts to incorporate them into a modern commercial economy. They are largely cotton farmers today, and their population exceeds 275,000 people. They are closely related culturally to the Ngulus, Shambalas, and Bondeis.*
REFERENCE: Allison Herrick et al. *Area Handbook for Tanzania.* 1968.

ZIGULA. *See* ZIGALU.

ZILI. The Zilis are a small group of Nguni*-speaking people who first entered the Caledon Valley of contemporary Lesotho around 1600. They evolved into the Phetlas.*

ZILMAMU. The Zilmamus are one of Ethiopia's many small ethnic groups. They speak a Nilo-Saharan language and work as pastoralists. The Zilmamu population today stands at approximately 3,000 people.
REFERENCE: M. L. Bender, J. D. Bowen, R. L. Cooper, and C. A. Ferguson, eds. *Language in Ethiopia.* 1976.

ZIMBA. The Zimbas are a major subgroup of the Maravi* people of Mozambique and Zaire.

ZINZA. The Zinza people live in northwestern Tanzania, primarily along the southwestern shore of Lake Victoria. They raise cattle and farm, using the ma-

nure to keep their soil productive. During the past century, the Zinzas have become famous for their skill as ironworkers. They have a population today of about 100,000 people.
REFERENCE: Laura Kurtz. *Historical Dictionary of Tanzania.* 1978.

ZODUAN. The Zoduans are a clan with the chiefdom of Mambahn, a subgroup of the Bassa* people of Liberia. Most Zoduans live in the Marshall Territory of Liberia.

ZOMBO. The Zombos are a subgroup of the Kongo* people of Zaire and Angola. They are Kongo people from the old Kongo Kingdom. Zombos flourished as traders and merchants from the seventeenth to the twentieth centuries. The Zombos in Zaire maintain close ties to the Zombos in Angola. In Kinshasa during the 1950s, they formed mutual aid societies that eventually evolved into nationalistic and pan-Zombo political organizations. They established ALIAZO (Alliance des Ressortissants de Zombo) in Angola in 1959, which became known as the Partido Democratico de Angola (PDA). Today, the Zombos still maintain a distinct sense of ethnic identity.
REFERENCE: Susan H. Broadhead. *Historical Dictionary of Angola.* 1992.

ZUL. The Zuls are a subgroup of the Gezawa* people of northern Nigeria.

ZULU. The Zulus today number more than five million people. Most of them live in KwaZulu, the "homeland" for them in South Africa, and in Natal Province in South Africa. The Zulu language, which carries a rich literary tradition, is part of the Bantu* language group; among the most prominent Zulu writers are the poet B. W. Vilikazi and N. L. S. Nyembezi. The Zulu probably migrated to South Africa from the Great African Lakes region in the fifteenth century, but they did not become a major political force until the nineteenth century, when King Shaka fashioned a highly organized and disciplined army of 40,000 soldiers. They conquered the neighboring tribes, and, by the 1820s, they controlled most of Natal. During much of the rest of the decade, the Zulus were at war with the British.* It was not until 1883 that Cetshwayo, the Zulu king, came to terms with the British administration and accepted their dominion. There were other revolts, but the British quickly crushed them. Today, most Zulu now live in KwaZulu, where they raise cattle, sheep, goats, millet, maize, peas, and beans.
REFERENCES: *African Encyclopedia.* 1974; Christopher Saunders. *Historical Dictionary of South Africa.* 1983; B. G. M. Sundkler. *Zulu Zion.* 1976.

ZUMPER. *See* KUTED.

ZURUBU. *See* SURUBU.

ZWANE. The Zwanes are one of the clans of the Emakhandzambili,* who themselves are one of the three major subgroups of the Swazi* people of Swaziland.

APPENDIX A

Chronology of African History

BCE (Before Christian Era)

3–1.5 million   *Australopithecus africanus* and *Homo habilis* emerge in East Africa.

750 000   Homo erectus spreads out over Africa and Asia.

50 000   Homo sapiens settle the Nile Valley.

3100–2700   Lower Egypt and Upper Egypt unify and the Old Kingdom civilization emerges.

2000   Nilotic and Bantu-speaking peoples begin to occupy the Great Lakes region of East Africa.

1200   Phoenician civilization reaches present-day Algeria.

1000   Hutu farmers settle in present-day Rwanda.
Southern Kushites migrate into present-day Tanzania and meet up with the San people living there.

950   Kushite Kingdom begins to appear in Sudan.

814   Carthage is founded.

800   Berger kingdoms first emerge in North Africa.

529   Persians enter the Nile Valley.

332   Alexander the Great conquers Egypt.

218   Hannibal of Carthage crosses the Alps and invades Italy.

48   Romans enter the Nile Valley.

43   Romanization and Christianization of the Maghrib region begins.

30   Roman occupation of Egypt begins.

CE (Christian Era)

500   Bantu-speaking peoples spread out from present-day Zaire toward the Indian Ocean.

600   The Ghana Empire begins to develop.

640	Arab-Muslim conquest of Egypt and northern Sudan begins.
642	Roman occupation of Egypt ends.
647	Arab and Islamic invasion of the Maghrib begins.
700	Ancestors of today's Somali clans arrive at the Horn of Africa.
711	North African Moors begin the occupation of the Iberian Peninsula.
800	Berbers introduce Islam to the Sahel region.
900	Savanna peoples reach the West African coastal region.
1000	The Ghana Empire reaches its peak. Tuaregs found a settlement at Timbuktu. Bantu-speaking peoples begin to spread throughout the Congo Basin. Nilotic pastoralists expand into southern Sudan.
1076	The Almoravids conquer Ghana.
1135	Almoravid rule in Ghana collapses.
1200	Guan people expand out of the upper Volta River region into present-day Ghana. Islamic missionaries begin winning many converts in coastal West Africa.
1240	Soundiata Keita conquers the Ghana Empire and starts the Mali Empire.
1249	The final reconquest of Christian Portugal occurs.
1290	Islam begins spreading throughout coastal East Africa.
1298	The Abron Kingdom is founded in Ghana.
1300	Jolof Empire is founded in West Africa.
1329	The Mossi attack and ransack Timbuktu.
1400	The Mali Empire begins its decline and is replaced by the rise of the Songhai Empire. The Kongo Kingdom is founded.
1441	The Portuguese take the first slaves from the West African coast.
1446	Portuguese explorers reach Guinea-Bissau.
1469	The Portuguese navigators Lope Gonsalvez and Fernão do Poo begin their explorations of what later became Equatorial Guinea. The Songhai Empire becomes dominant on the Niger River.
1472	The Portuguese explorer Fernando Gomes reaches the Wouri River in Cameroon and the estuary of the Como River in Gabon.
1482	Diego Cam, a Portuguese mariner, reaches the mouth of the Congo River.
1483	The Portuguese arrive in Kongo.
1488	Portuguese ships round the Cape of Good Hope.
1493	Askia Mohammed becomes the emperor of Songhai.
1494	The Treaty of Tordesillas recognizes the Portuguese claim to West Africa.
1497	Vasco da Gama begins his epic voyage from Portugal to India.

1500	Tutsis begin arriving in present-day Burundi.
1504	The Funj Sultanate begins in Sudan.
1509	In the Treaty of Cintra between Spain and Portugal, Spain surrenders its claim to the Saharan coast of West Africa, except for Santa Cruz de Mar Puqueña.
1510	Leo Africanus visits the Western Sudan.
	Portugal establishes a captaincy in the Cape Verde islands.
1517	The Ottoman rule of Egypt begins.
1531	Muslim armies occupy the Christian highlands of Ethiopia.
1541	Portuguese seafarers reach Ethiopia.
1544	The first Portuguese trading center is established at Quelimane in Mozambique.
1546	The Mali Empire collapses.
1550	The Mande people begin the conquest of Gonja in Ghana.
	The Jolof Empire collapses.
1551	The Ottoman rule of Libya begins.
1562	Sir John Hawkins reaches the coast of Sierra Leone and purchases slaves.
1565	The Portuguese build a base in Accra, Ghana.
1576	The Portuguese establish a colony at Luanda in present-day Angola.
1591	Defeated by a Moroccan invasion, the Songhai Empire falls.
1592	The Portuguese capture Mombasa, Kenya.
1600	The Kingdom of Bouna is established.
1616	The Portuguese explorer Gaspar Boccaro travels through the Maravi Empire on the south coast of West Africa.
1618	The Company of Adventurers of London Trading to Africa is formed.
1638	The Dutch establish a settlement on Mauritius.
1652	Jan van Riebeeck founds Cape Town, and the Dutch occupation of the Cape of Good Hope begins.
1659	The first European-Khoikhoi war erupts in southern Africa.
1662	The Company of Royal Adventurers is formed in England to trade in Africa (it is replaced by the Royal African Company in 1672).
1668	The Gambia Adventurers Company is formed.
1672	The French Senegal Company is formed.
1673	The Second European-Khoikhoi war erupts in southern Africa.
1696	The French Royal Senegal Company is formed.
1700	The Masai expansion into present-day Tanzania begins.
1711	The Asante conquests begin in Ghana.
1714	The French Senegal Company establishes a trading post on the Guinea coast.
1740	Portugal establishes control over Fernando Po.

1742	The Asante defeat Akyem forces and become the dominant people in present-day coastal Ghana.
1750	The Company of Merchants Trading in Africa is formed.
	Azande peoples begin their expansion into Sudan.
1765	Mauritius becomes a French colony.
1769	The Oromo people begin to emerge as the dominant group in Ethiopia.
1772	France establishes a trading post on Gambia Island.
	The Scottish explorer James Bruce visits the central Sudan.
1788	The African Association is founded in Great Britain.
1790	The Sierra Leone Company is formed.
1795	Mungo Park begins his first exploratory expedition to West Africa.
	The British occupy the Cape of Good Hope for the first time.
1798	The French under Napoleon conquer Egypt.
1800	Afro-Arab trade begins to flourish in Zaire.
1802	Denmark becomes the first nation to outlaw the African slave trade.
1803	The Muslim holy wars begin in Northern Nigeria.
1805	Mungo Park begins his second exploratory expedition to West Africa.
1807	Great Britain and the United States outlaw the African slave trade.
1808	Sierra Leone becomes a British crown colony.
1814	In the Treaty of Paris, France cedes Mauritius to Great Britain.
1816	The American Colonization Society is established in the United States.
1817	The British and Asante negotiate a peace treaty in Ghana.
1820	The Ottomans conquer the Funj Sultanate in Sudan.
1821	The first black colonists settle the Cape Mesurado colony in Liberia with the backing of the American Colonization Society.
	The wars of the Mfecane begin in southern Africa.
1833	Portugal abolishes the *prazo* landed estates in Mozambique.
1834	Slavery is abolished throughout the British Empire.
	The Cape-Xhosa War begins.
1836	Slavery is formally abolished throughout the Portuguese Empire.
	The Great Trek of the Boers begins in southern Africa.
1837	The Fang peoples begin their large-scale migration to the region of Cameroon-Guinea.
	The exportation of groundnuts from West Africa begins on a commercial scale.
	The Voortrekkers enter Natal.
1838	The French establish a post at Asinie in Ivory Coast.
1840	Commercial production of palm oil begins in coastal West Africa.
	Ngoni expansion north into present-day Tanzania begins.
1842	France makes a formal claim to Asinie and Grand Bassam in Ivory Coast.

1843	Great Britain takes control of English trading posts in Gold Coast.
	Gambia is created as a separate British colony.
	Great Britain annexes Natal.
1846	The Swazi people first encounter the Boer settlers.
1847	Liberia declares its independence from the American Colonization Society.
	Great Britain annexes what becomes known as British Kaffraria in South Africa.
1849	France founds Libreville (Gabon) as a settlement for Vili people freed from slave traders.
1850	Great Britain issues formal charters to the Gold Coast settlements.
	Several independent Tutsi states emerge in present-day Burundi and Rwanda.
1852	The Anglo-Duala Treaty ends the slave trade in Cameroon.
	The South African Republic is established in the Transvaal.
1854	David Livingstone reaches Lake Dilolo in present-day Zaire.
	Al Hajj Umar begins his holy war in Guinea.
	The Orange River State is founded in southern Africa.
1856	A Zulu civil war begins in southern Africa, as does the Xhosa cattle-killing movement.
	Construction of the Suez Canal begins.
1857	Heinrich Barth, the German explorer, arrives in Timbuktu.
1858	David Livingstone makes the first of four visits to Malawi.
	Richard Burton and John Speke reach Lake Tanganyika.
1860	Samuel Baker reaches Lake Albert.
1861	King Dosumu cedes Lagos, Nigeria, to the British.
1862	Arthur Verdier establishes his *Compagnie de Kong*.
1867	Diamonds are discovered at Kimberley in South Africa.
1868	Great Britain annexes Basutoland.
1869	Heinrich Nachtigel begins his exploration of Libya, Chad, Sudan, and Niger.
	Construction of the Suez Canal is completed.
1871	Henry Stanley and David Livingstone visit Lake Tanganyika.
1872	The Ndembu of Angola rebel against the Portuguese.
1874	Great Britain establishes the Gold Coast Colony.
1877	The London Missionary Society begins missionary work in Central Africa.
	Great Britain annexes Transvaal.
1878	Internal slavery is abolished in Angola and Mozambique.
1879	The Boers found a colony in southern Angola.
	The British-Zulu War and the British-Pedi War begin in southern Africa.

1880   A British Royal Commission establishes the boundary between Swaziland and the Transvaal.

The Gun War begins in South Africa.

The first Anglo-Boer War begins.

1881   The French launch the first of many attacks on Samory Touré.

The Mahdist conquest of Sudan begins.

Colonel Ahmad Urabi launches the nationalist movement in Egypt.

1882   An Anglo-French Condominium establishes the boundary between Sierra Leone and Guinea.

The British occupation of Egypt begins.

1884   Chief Mlapa III of Togo signs a protectorate treaty with Germany, as do the Duala chiefs of Cameroon.

The Congress of Berlin defines a process for the European colonization of Africa. Mahdist forces defeat the British at Khartoum.

1885   The Berlin Act of 1885 is signed, designating Burundi and Rwanda as German spheres of influence.

A Franco-German treaty establishes the border between the Cameroons.

A Yoni Temne rebellion begins in Sierra Leone.

A Franco-Portuguese convention establishes the boundary between Portuguese Guinea and French Guinea.

Great Britain proclaims the Bechuanaland Protectorate.

1886   French Congo and Gabon are established as an autonomous colony.

The Anglo-German Agreement divides East Africa between the two powers and places Kenya in the British sphere; the two powers also agree to the boundary between Gold Coast and Togoland.

1887   The Swahili War begins.

Louis Binger begins his explorations between the Atlantic Ocean and the Niger River.

A Franco-Belgian convention gives France control of the north bank of the Ubangi River in the present-day Central African Republic.

Britain proclaims the Niger River delta region as the Oil Rivers Protectorate.

1888   The British East Africa Company acquires leases to the southern coast of present-day Somalia from Zanzibar.

Lobengula, the Ndebele king, signs the Rudd Concession.

1889   A British-French treaty establishes the boundary between Senegal and Gambia.

France establishes a protectorate over Ivory Coast.

The Battle of Toshki ends Mahdist expansion into Egypt.

The Fante National Political Society, a nationalist group, is formed in Ghana.

The French and British agree to the boundary between Gold Coast and Ivory Coast.

1890   The Heligoland Agreement between Germany and Great Britain delineates the boundary between Togo and Gold Coast.

1891	A British protectorate is established over Malawi.
	An Anglo-Portuguese Treaty determines the southern border of Malawi, in which Portugal formally abandons its claim to a band of land reaching all the way across Africa.
1892	The territory of French Sudan is created with its capital at Kayes, Mali.
	The First Pass Laws are issued in Rhodesia.
1893	Guinea and Ivory Coast are proclaimed French colonies.
	The Société du Haut-Ogooué receives large concessions in Gabon and Congo.
	The Oil Rivers Protectorate becomes the Niger Coast Protectorate.
1894	A Franco-German Convention establishes the border between French Congo and German Cameroons.
	Dahomey becomes a French colony.
	Afro-Arab traders are driven from Zaire, ending the slave trade there.
1895	The colony of French West Africa is proclaimed with its capital in Saint Louis, Senegal.
	Construction begins on the Sierra Leone Railroad.
	The South African Republic assumes control of Swaziland.
	Britain declares a protectorate over Kenya.
	The Adansi in Gold Coast sign a treaty of protection with Britain.
1896	The British claim a protectorate over the Asante in Gold Coast.
	The Jameson Raid occurs in the Transvaal.
	The conquest of Mahdist forces by Anglo-Egyptian forces begins in Sudan.
1897	A Franco-German treaty fixes the northern border of Togo. Germany surrenders its claim to the Gourma region of present-day Burkina-Faso.
1898	The Hut Tax Rebellion begins in Sierra Leone.
	Mahdist forces are defeated in the Battle of Omdurman.
1899	The Bubi insurrection in Spanish Guinea begins.
	The second Anglo-Boer War begins.
	A Franco-British Convention gives Bahr-el-Ghazal to the Anglo-Egyptian Sudan and places Wadai in the French zone of authority.
	The Fashoda incident between Great Britain and France occurs.
	Rwanda becomes part of German East Africa.
1900	A Franco-Spanish convention establishes the border between Gabon and Spanish Guinea.
	The Asante launch a war against the British in Gold Coast.
	France establishes a military protectorate in Chad.
1901	France ends domestic slavery in West Africa.
1902	Germany abolishes slavery in Cameroon.
	The Mbailundu rebellion begins in Angola.
	The second Anglo-Boer War ends.
	Great Britain assumes administrative control of Swaziland.

1903	France creates the colony of Ubangui-Shari.
	The Fulbe Empire comes under British control.
	The British occupy the Sokoto Caliphate in Northern Nigeria.
1904	The Lunda rebellion begins in Angola.
1905	The Maji-Maji Rebellion begins in British East Africa.
1906	The Colony of Lagos is merged with the protectorate of Southern Nigeria to form the Colony and Protectorate of Southern Nigeria.
	The Bambatha Rebellion begins in southern Africa.
1907	Malawi becomes known as the Nyasaland Protectorate.
1910	Protocols are signed delineating the border between German East Africa, the Belgian Congo, and British East Africa.
	French Congo and its dependent territories become known as French Equatorial Africa.
	The Union of South Africa is formed.
1911	Italy invades Libya.
1913	Severe famine sweeps through Chad and Sudan.
	Albert Schweitzer begins his medical mission in French Gabon.
1914	World War I begins, and British and French forces invade Togo.
	Muslims in present-day Burkina-Faso declare a *jihad* against France.
1915	The Chilembwe Uprising occurs in Malawi.
	Coffee production begins in Ivory Coast.
	French troops crush the Bambara Rebellion in Mali, while the Teda revolt against the French in Chad.
	Great Britain passes the Crown Lands Ordinance.
1916	Belgian forces capture Rwanda from German control.
	France detaches Chad from Ubangui-Chari.
	Tauregs rebel against France in present-day Burkina-Faso.
1917	The Ndembu rise up in rebellion against the Portuguese.
1918	World War I ends.
1919	In the Treaty of Versailles, Germany surrenders its African colonies; Togo is divided between France and Great Britain under mandates from the League of Nations.
	Belgium receives a League of Nations mandate over Rwanda-Burundi.
1920	The Congress of British West Africa is formed.
1922	The colony of Niger is established.
	The nationalistic White Flag League rebels against the British in Sudan.
1924	The White Flag League nationalist rebellion occurs in Sudan.
1925	Great Britain cedes Jubaland to Italy.
1927	Domestic slavery is abolished in Sierra Leone.
1928	The Gbaya War erupts in French Equatorial Africa, and the Awandjis of Gabon rebel against French administration.
1929	Italy unites Tripolitania, Cyrenaica, and the Fezzan into one colony known as Libya.

1933	Ivory Coast and a large section of present-day Burkina-Faso are merged into a single colony.
1934	France completes the military pacification of the Moroccan-Mauritanian-Algerian border region.
1935	The Italo-Ethiopian War begins.
1936	The Anglo-Egyptian Treaty is signed, limiting British occupation of Egypt.
1939	World War II begins in Europe.
1941	The Portuguese crush the Herero rebellion in Angola.
1942	The Allied invasion of North Africa begins.
1944	The Brazzaville Conference on Africa convenes. The Ibo Federal Union is formed in Nigeria.
1945	The Mossis begin demanding that Upper Volta be recreated. The Pan-African Congress convenes in London.
1946	Ivory Coast becomes a colony in the French Union. France outlaws all involuntary labor in its colonies. Spanish West Africa, including Ifni and Western Sahara, is created.
1947	Ivory Coast and present-day Burkina-Faso are redivided into separate colonial entities. The United Gold Coast Convention begins in Ghana. Nationalist rebellion erupts in Madagascar.
1948	The Nationalist Party comes to power in South Africa and begins to implement apartheid.
1949	Kwame Nkrumah forms the Convention People's Party in Gold Coast.
1950	Great Britain declares the Mau Mau society in Kenya to be illegal. The Action Group Party is formed in Nigeria. Apartheid laws are passed in South Africa.
1951	Libya gains its independence. The Sierra Leone People's Party is formed.
1952	The Mau Mau rebellion begins in Kenya. The African National Congress launches its Defiance Campaign against apartheid.
1953	The Federation of Nyasaland and Rhodesia is established.
1954	The Asante form the National Liberation Movement in Ghana. The Northern People's Party is formed in Gold Coast. The Southern Liberal Party is formed in Sudan. The Tanganyikan African National Union is founded.
1955	The Union des Populations du Cameroun (UPC) launches a rebellion against France.
1956	*Loi cadre* reforms are passed in France. In a democratic plebiscite, the people of British Togoland vote to merge with Gold Coast.

Kwame Nkrumah calls for the independence of Ghana.

Sudan proclaims its independence.

Egypt nationalizes the Suez Canal and precipitates the Suez Crisis.

The Popular Movement for the Liberation of Angola is founded.

1957   The Gold Coast Colony, united with former British Togoland, becomes
                the independent nation of Ghana.

Several Hutu intellectuals issue the Bahutu Manifesto in Rwanda, pro-
testing the social, economic, and political power of the Tutsis.

1958   French West Africa is dissolved.

French Sudan becomes the Republic of Sudan.

The Republic of Chad is proclaimed.

The Republic of Benin is proclaimed.

Ubangui-Chari proclaims itself the Central African Republic.

Spanish West Africa is dissolved, and Western Sahara becomes a Spanish province.

Guinea becomes an independent republic.

1959   Patrice Lumumba calls for independence for the Belgian Congo.

The Mali Federation, with Senegal and Sudan as members, is established.

A Hutu rebellion against Tutsi power begins in Rwanda.

French West Africa is dissolved. Niger, Ivory Coast, and Upper Volta
are created.

The People's Progressive Party is founded in The Gambia.

1960   British Prime Minister Harold Macmillan delivers his "Winds of
                Change" speech.

The Mali Federation dissolves.

Togo declares its independence.

Ivory Coast declares its independence, and Felix Houphouet-Boigny begins his long reign as president.

The Republic of Mali is proclaimed.

ameroon declares its independence.

Gabon becomes an independent republic.

Benin declares its formal independence.

The Central African Republic and Senegal declare their independence.

Upper Volta becomes independent.

Belgian Congo (Zaire) becomes independent.

British Somaliland becomes independent.

Niger declares independence.

Congo (Brazzaville) declares its independence.

The Ghanian Republic is proclaimed with Kwame Nkrumah as president.

The Somali Republic is proclaimed.

Nigeria becomes independent.

Katanga Province secedes from Belgian Congo (Zaire).

1961   Plebiscites in British Cameroon result in Northern Cameroons joining
                Nigeria and Southern Cameroons joining the Republic of Cameroon.

Sierra Leone becomes independent.

Widespread anti-Portuguese violence begins in Angola with the Luanda Rebellion.

Tanganyika becomes independent.

Zimbabwe African People's Union is founded.

1962   Rwandwa-Burundi declares its independence.

FRELIMO is founded at Dar es Salaam, Tanganyika.

Uganda becomes independent.

Eritrean guerrilla war against Ethiopia begins.

1963   The Federation of Nyasaland and Rhodesia is dissolved.

The Organization of African Unity is formed.

The Katanga secession movement in present-day Zaire ends.

Kenya becomes independent.

Nigeria becomes a republic.

Tutsi-Hutu violence erupts in Rwanda and Burundi; Rwanda and Burundi begin to separate administratively.

Zanzibar becomes independent.

The Zimbabwe African National Union is founded.

1964   Malawi declares its independence from Great Britain.

Jonas Savimbi becomes president of UNITA in Angola.

Tanganyika and Zanzibar unite to become Tanzania.

Hutus massacre Tutsis in Rwanda.

FRELIMO begins its armed struggle against the Portuguese in Mozambique.

1965   The Failed Hutu rebellion in Burundi leads to thousands of Hutu deaths.

Gambia achieves independence from Great Britain.

Rhodesia unilaterally declares its independence from Great Britain.

1966   Malawi is declared a republic, and H. Kamazu Banda becomes president.

Mauritius gains its independence from Great Britain.

The last British troops leave Swaziland.

Botswana gains its independence.

Lesotho declares its independence.

1967   The Nigerian civil war begins when Biafra attempts to secede.

Julius Nyerere anounces his *ujamaa* socialism program for Tanzania.

1968   Equatorial Guinea declares its independence.

Swaziland becomes independent.

Armed rebellion by Zimbabwean nationalists begins in Rhodesia.

1970   The Nigerian civil war ends.

1971   The former Belgian Congo becomes Zaire.

1972   Severe drought begins in the Sahel.

Bloody Hutu uprising in Burundi is crushed.

1973   Hutu attacks on Tutsis in Rwanda escalate; Tutsi refugees flee to Burundi.

The Tutsi-Hutu civil war in Burundi results in the deaths of hundreds of thousands of Hutus.

The Polisario Front is established in Western Sahara.

The Yom Kippur War erupts.

1974   A Marxist-Leninist state is proclaimed in Benin.

Guinea-Bissau becomes independent.

Libya and Tunisia form the Arab Islamic Republic.

1975   The Transcameroon Railroad is completed.

Mozambique declares its independence from Portugal.

Cape Verde becomes independent.

Angola declares its independence from Portugal.

1977   Djibouti becomes independent.

Somali forces invade the Ogaden but are defeated by Ethiopian troops.

The United Nations imposes an arms embargo on South Africa.

1978   The Camp David accords are signed between Israel and Egypt.

War erupts between Uganda and Tanzania.

1979   The Lancaster House Agreement ends the Zimbabwe liberation war.

The Israeli-Egyptian Peace Treaty is signed.

1980   A coup d'état in Liberia ends the century-long rule of the America-Liberian elite.

Libya invades Chad.

1981   Libya withdraws from Chad.

South Africa attacks SWAPO guerrilla bases in Angola.

1982   Nigeria expels 120,000 Cameroonians living within its border.

The Chad-Sudan border conflict is resolved.

1983   The Economic Community of the States of Central Africa is formed.

Civil war between the Arabic north and the African south of Sudan intensifies.

South Africa attacks African National Congress bases in Mozambique.

1984   France and Libya reach an agreement on the withdrawal of troops from Chad.

Upper Volta is renamed Burkina-Faso.

Drought and famine hit Ethiopia.

1986   News of the threat of AIDS in Africa becomes headlines throughout the world.

Widespread famine hits southern Sudan.

The United States conducts air strikes against Libya.

South Africa attacks guerrilla bases in Botswana, Zambia, and Zimbabwe.

1988   Hutu-Tutsi violence breaks out in Burundi.

Libya formally ends its state of war with Chad.

1989   Civil war begins in Liberia.

1990   The ban on the African National Congress is lifted in South Africa.

Namibia becomes independent.

1991	Bitter civil war erupts in Liberia.
	The Tigray People's Liberation Front occupies Addis Ababa in Ethiopia.
1992	The U.S. and U.N. forces enter Somalia to end the civil war.
1993	Eritrea declares its independence from Ethiopia.
1994	A bloody civil war in Rwanda between Hutus and Tutsis takes hundreds of thousands of lives.
	The African National Congress wins the first free elections in South Africa, beginning the end of apartheid.
1995	Violence between Hutus and Tutsis erupts in Burundi.

APPENDIX B

Selected Bibliography

Abun-Nasr, J. *The Tijaniyya: A Sufi Order in the Modern World.* 1967.

Adams, W. Y. *Nubia: Corridor to Africa.* 1976.

Adamson, J. *The Peoples of Kenya.* 1967.

African Encyclopedia. 1974.

Ajayi, J.F.A., and M. Crowder. *History of West Africa.* 1975.

Akintola, J. G. Wise. *H. C. Bankole-Bright and Politics in Colonial Sierra-Leone, 1919–1958.* 1990.

Allman, J. M. *The Quills of the Porcupine: Asante Nationalism in an Emergent Ghana.* 1993.

Ambler, C. H. *Kenyan Communities in the Age of Imperialism: The Central Region in the Late Nineteenth Century.* 1988.

Austen, R. A. *Northwest Tanzania Under German and British Rule: Colonial Policy and Tribal Politics, 1889–1939.* 1968.

Azevedo, M. *Historical Dictionary of Mozambique.* 1991.

Barth, F. *Ethnic Groups and Boundaries.* 1969.

Bascom, W. R., and M. J. Herskovitz, eds. *Continuity and Change in African Cultures.* 1959.

Baxter, P. T. W. "Absence Makes the Heart Grow Fonder: Some Suggestions Why Witchcraft Accusations are Rare Among East African Pastoralists." In M. Gluckman, ed., *The Allocation of Responsibility.* 1972.

———, and U. Almagor, eds. *Age, Generation and Time.* 1978.

Baxter, P. T. W., and B. Sansom. *Race and Social Difference.* 1972.

Beck, A. *Medicine, Tradition, and Development in Kenya and Tanzania, 1920–1970.* 1981.

Behrman, L. *Muslim Brotherhoods and Politics in Senegal.* 1970.

Beidelman, T. O. "Beer Drinking and Cattle Theft in Ukagaru: Intertribal Relations in a Tanganyika Chiefdom." *American Anthropologist* 63 (1978): 534–49.

Bell, L. V. *Mental and Social Disorder in Sub-Saharan Africa: The Case of Sierra Leone, 1787–1990.* 1991.

Bender, M. L., J. D. Bowen, R. L. Cooper, and C. A. Ferguson, eds. *Language in Ethiopia.* 1976.

Benjamin, C. R. *Myth, Ritual, and Kingship in Buganda.* 1991.

Bennett, N. R. *Arab Versus European: Diplomacy and War in Nineteenth-Century East-Central Africa.* 1986.

Berat, L. *Walvis Bay: Decolonization and International Law.* 1990.

Berkman, J. A. *The Healing Imagination of Olive Schreiner: Beyond South African Colonialism.* 1989.

Berridge, G. R. *South Africa, the Colonial Powers and "African Defence": The Rise and Fall of the White Entente, 1948–60.* 1992.

Berry, S. *Cocoa, Custom, and Socio-Economic Change in Southwestern Nigeria.* 1975.

———. *No Condition Is Permanent: The Social Dynamics of Agrarian Change in Sub-Saharan Africa.* 1993.

Bezuneh, T., and A. Feleke. "Production and Utilization of the Genus Ensete in Ethiopia." *Economic Botany* 20 (1970): 66–70.

Binns, M., and T. Binns. *Sierra Leone.* 1992.

Black, C. *The Lands and Peoples of Rhodesia and Nyasaland.* 1961.

Black, R. *Angola.* 1991.

Boahen, A. A. *General History of Africa.* Vol. 7: *Africa Under Colonial Domination, 1880–1935.* 1985.

Bobb, F. S. *Historical Dictionary of Zaire.* 1988.

Bohannan, P. *Africa and Africans.* 1964.

———. *Markets in Africa.* 1962.

Bonner, P. *Kings, Commoners, and Concessionaires: The Evolution and Dissolution of the Nineteenth-Century Swazi State.* 1982.

Bozzoli, B. *The Political Nature of a Ruling Class: Capital and Ideology in South Africa, 1890–1933.* 1981.

———. *Women of Phokeng: Consciousness, Life Strategy, and Migrancy in South Africa, 1900–1983.* 1991.

Brantley, C. *The Giriama and Colonial Resistance in Kenya, 1800–1920.* 1981.

Bravemann, R. A. *Islam and Tribal Art in West Africa.* 1974.

Briggs, L. C. *Tribes of the Sahara.* 1960.

Broadhead, S. H. *Historical Dictionary of Angola.* 1992.

Bryan, M. A. *The Bantu Languages of Africa.* 1959.

Bulliet, R. *The Camel and the Wheel.* 1975.

Burton, J. W. "Nilotic Studies: Some Past Problems and Prospects." *Anthropos* 83 (1988): 453–68.

Byrnes, R. M., et al. *Uganda: A Country Study.* 1992.

Caldwell, J., et al., eds. *Population Growth and Socio-Economic Change in West Africa.* 1975.

Castagno, M. *Historical Dictionary of Somalia.* 1975.

Chanock, M. *Law, Custom, and Social Order: The Colonial Experience in Malawi and Zambia.* 1985.

Citino, R. *Germany and the Union of South Africa in the Nazi Period.* 1991.

Clark, A. F., and L. C. Phillips. *Historical Dictionary of Senegal.* 1994.

Clough, M. S. *Fighting Two Sides: Kenyan Chiefs and Politicians, 1918–1940.* 1990.

Cobley, A. G. *Class and Consciousness: The Black Petty Bourgeoisie in South Africa, 1924–1950.* 1990.

Collelo, T., et al. *Angola: A Country Study.* 1991.

———. *Chad: A Country Study.* 1990.

Collins, R. O. *Shadows in the Grass: Britain in the Southern Sudan, 1918–1956.* 1983.

———, and F. M. Deng, eds. *The British in the Sudan, 1898–1956: The Sweetness and the Sorrow.* 1984.

Colson, E., and M. Gluckman. *Seven Tribes of British Central Africa.* 1951.

Colson, E., and T. Scudder. *For Prayer and Profit: The Changing Role of Beer in Gwembe District, 1950–1983.* 1988.

Comaroff, J. *Body of Power, Spirit of Resistance: The Culture and History of a South African People.* 1985.

Cooper, F. *From Slaves to Squatters: Plantation Labor and Agriculture in Zanzibar and Coastal Kenya, 1890–1925.* 1980.

———. *On the African Waterfront: Urban Disorder and the Transformation of Work in Colonial Mombasa.* 1987.

Craig, C. C. *White Supremacy and Black Resistance in Pre-Industrial South Africa: The Making of the Colonial Order in the Eastern Cape, 1770–1865.* 1992.

Crosby, C. *Historical Dictionary of Malawi.* 1980.

Crowder, M. *The Flogging of Phineas McIntosh: A Tale of Colonial Folly and Injustice, Bechuanaland, 1911.* 1988.

———, ed. *The Cambridge History of Africa.* Vol. 8: *From c. 1940 to c. 1975.* 1984.

Crush, J. *The Struggle for Swazi Labour, 1890–1920.* 1987.

Daakubu, M. E. *The Languages of Ghana.* 1988.

Dakeyne, R. B. "The Pattern of Settlement in Central Nyanza, Kenya." *Australian Geographer* 8 (1962): 183–91.

Daly, M. W. *Imperial Sudan: The Anglo-Egyptian Condominium, 1934–1956.* 1991.

Daniels, M. *Burundi.* 1992.

Decalo, S. *Historical Dictionary of Benin.* 1994.

———. *Historical Dictionary of Chad.* 1987.

———. *Historical Dictionary of Niger.* 1989.

———. *Historical Dictionary of Togo.* 1976.

DeLancey, M. W. *Somalia.* 1988.

———, and H. M. Mokeba. *Historical Dictionary of the Republic of Cameroon.* 1990.

Demeny, P. T. *The Demography of the Sudan.* 1968.

Deng, F. M. "Property and Value Inter-play Among the Nilotes of the Southern Sudan." *Iowa Law Review* 51 (1966): 541–60.

Dorjahn, V. R., ed. *Essays on the Economic Anthropology of Liberia and Sierra Leone.* 1979.

Dusgate, R. H. *The Conquest of Northern Nigeria.* 1985.

Edgarton, R. B. *Like Lions They Fought: The Zulu War and the Last Black Empire in South Africa.* 1988.

———. *Mau Mau: An African Crucible.* 1989.

Eldridge, E. A. *A South African Kingdom: The Pursuit of Security in Nineteenth-Century Lesotho.* 1993.

Fadiman, J. A. *When We Began There Were Witchmen: An Oral History from Mount Kenya.* 1993.

Fage, J. D. *A History of West Africa.* 1969.

Farer, T. J. *War Clouds on the Horn of Africa.* 1979.

Fegley, R. *Equatorial Guinea.* 1991.

Fernandez, J. W. *Bwiti: An Ethnography of the Religious Imagination in Africa.* 1982.

Fetter, B. *Colonial Rule and Regional Imbalance in Central Africa.* 1983.

Finucane, J. R. *Rural Development and Bureaucracy in Tanzania: The Case of Mwanza Region.* 1974.

Fisher, H. *Ahmadiyah: A Study in Contemporary Islam on the West African Coast.* 1974.

Floyd, B. *Eastern Nigeria.* 1969.

Fluehr-Lobban, C., R. A. Lobban, Jr., and J. O. Voll. *Historical Dictionary of Sudan.* 1992.

Foray, C. P. *Historical Dictionary of Sierra Leone.* 1977.

Forde, D. *African Worlds: Studies in the Cosmological Ideas and Social Values of African Peoples.* 1954.

Fortes, M. *Marriage in Tribal Societies.* 1962.

————, and G. Dieterlen. *African Systems of Thought.* 1965.

Furlong, P. J. *Between Crown and Swastika: The Impact of the Radical Right on the Afrikaner Nationalist Movement in the Fascist Era.* 1991.

Gailey, H. A. *Historical Dictionary of The Gambia.* 1988.

Galli, R. *Guinea-Bissau.* 1990.

Gamble, D. P. *The Gambia.* 1988.

Gardinier, D. E. *Gabon.* 1992.

————. *Historical Dictionary of Gabon.* 1994.

Giblin, J. L. *The Politics of Environmental Control in Northeastern Tanzania, 1840–1940.* 1992.

Gifford, P. *Christianity and Politics in Doe's Africa.* 1993.

————, and L. R. Williams, eds. *Decolonization and African Independence: The Transfers of Power, 1960–1980.* 1988.

Godwin, P., and I. Hancock. *"Rhodesians Never Die": The Impact of War and Political Change on White Rhodesia, c. 1970–1980.* 1993.

Gomez, M. A. *Pragmatism in the Age of Jihad: The Precolonial State of Bundu.* 1992.

Good, H. *The Peoples of the Northern Region of Nigeria.* 1969.

Goody, J. "A Note on the Penetration of Islam into the West of the Northern Territories of the Gold Coast." *Transactions of Gold Coast and Togoland Historical Society* 1 (1953): 45–46.

————. *Contexts of Kinship.* 1972.

————. *Technology, Tradition and State in Africa.* 1971.

————, ed. *Kinship.* 1971.

Greenberg, J. H. *The Languages of Africa.* 1970.

Grotpeter, J. J. *Historical Dictionary of Swaziland.* 1975.

————. *Historical Dictionary of Zambia.* 1979.

Gunn, H. D. *Peoples of the Plateau Area of Northern Nigeria.* 1953.

Hafkin, N. J., and E. G. Bay. *Women in Africa.* 1976.

Haliburton, G. *Historical Dictionary of Lesotho.* 1977.

Handloff, R. E., et al. *Côte d'Ivoire: A Country Study.* 1990.

————. *Mauritania: A Country Study.* 1990.

Handwerker, P. "Productivity, Marketing Efficiency, and Price-Support Programs: Alternative Paths to Rural Development in Liberia." *Human Organization* 40 (1981): 27–39.

Hansen, H. B. *Mission, Church, and State in a Colonial Setting: Uganda, 1890–1925.* 1984.

Harris, J. F. *Repatriates and Refugees in a Colonial Society: The Case of Kenya.* 1987.

Hasan, Y. F. *The Arabs and the Sudan.* 1967.

Heath, D. "Spatial Politics and Verbal Performance in Urban Senegal." *Ethnology* 29 (1990): 209–24.

Hecht, R. M. "Cocoa and the Dynamics of Socio-Economic Change in Southern Ivory Coast." Ph.D. Dissertation. Cambridge University. 1981.

———. "The Transformation of Lineage Production in Southern Ivory Coast, 1920–1980." *Ethnology* 23 (1984): 261–78.

Herbert, E. W. *Iron, Gender, and Power: Rituals of Transformation in African Societies.* 1993.

Hertzon, R. *Ethiopian Semitic: Studies in Classification.* 1972.

Hill, P. *Migrant Cocoa Farmers of Southern Ghana.* 1963.

Hodges, T. *Historical Dictionary of Western Sahara.* 1982.

Hunwick, J. O. "The Influence of Arabic in West Africa." *Transactions of the Historical Society of Ghana* 7 (1964): 24–41.

———. *Islam in Africa: Friend or Foe?* 1976.

Hyden, G. *Political Development in Rural Tanzania: Tanu Yajenge Nchi.* 1969.

Imperato, P. J. *Historical Dictionary of Mali.* 1986.

Isichei, E., ed. *Studies in the History of Plateau State, Nigeria.* 1982.

Jeater, D. *Marriage, Perversion, and Power: The Construction of Moral Discourse in Southern Rhodesia, 1894–1930.* 1993.

Johnson, D. L. *The Nature of Nomadism.* 1969.

Johnston, G. *Of God and Maxim Guns: Presbyterians in Nigeria, 1846–1966.* 1988.

Jules-Rosette, B. "Faith Healers and Folk Healers: The Symbolism and Practice of Indigenous Therapy in Urban Africa." *Religion* 11 (1981): 127–49.

July, R. *A History of the African People.* 1970.

Kaba, L. *The Wahhabiyya: Islamic Reform and Politics in French West Africa.* 1974.

Kadzombe, E. D., W. D. Michie, and M. R. Naidoo. *Lands and Peoples of Central Africa.* 1973.

Kalck, P. *Central African Republic.* 1993.

———. *Historical Dictionary of the Central African Republic.* 1992.

Kamoche, J. G. *Imperial Trusteeship and Political Evolution in Kenya, 1923–1963: A Study of the Official Views and the Road to Decolonization.* 1981.

Kanogo, T. *Squatters and the Roots of Mau Mau, 1905–63.* 1987.

Kaplan, I., et al. *Area Handbook for Ghana.* 1971.

———. *Tanzania: A Country Study.* 1978.

———. *Zaire: A Country Study.* 1978.

———. *Zambia: A Country Study.* 1979.

Karp, I. "Beer Drinking and Social Experience in an African Society." In I. Karp and C. S. Bird, eds., *Explorations in African Systems of Thought.* 1980.

Keppel-Jones, A. *Rhodes and Rhodesia: The White Conquest of Zimbabwe, 1884–1902.* 1983.

Kimambo, I. N. *Penetration and Protest in Tanzania: The Impact of the World Economy on the Pare, 1860–1960.* 1991.

Kindy, H. M. *Life and Politics in Mombasa.* 1972.

King, N. K., and A. Oded. *Islam and the Confluence of Religions in Uganda, 1840–1966.* 1973.

Kitching, G. *Class and Economic Change in Kenya: The Making of an African Petite Bourgeoisie, 1905–1970.* 1980.

Klein, M. A. *Islam and Imperialism in Senegal.* 1968.

Kuper, A. *Wives for Cattle: Wealth and Marriage in Southern Africa.* 1982.

Kurtz, L. S. *Historical Dictionary of Tanzania.* 1978.

Labouret, H. *Africa Before the White Man.* 1962.

Ladefoged, P., R. Glick, and C. Criper. *Language in Uganda.* 1972.

Ladouceur, P. A. *Chiefs and Politicians: The Politics of Regionalism in Northern Ghana.* 1979.

Larsson, B. *Conversion to Greater Freedom? Women, Church and Social Change in North-Western Tanzania under Colonial Rule.* 1991.

Laughlin, C. D., and E. R. Laughlin. *Age Generations and Political Process in South Africa.* 1974.

Leatherdale, C. *Britain and South Africa, 1925–1939: The Imperial Oasis.* 1983.

Le Cordeur, B. A. *The Politics of Eastern Cape Separatism, 1820–1854.* 1981.

Leinhardt, R. G. ''Nilotic Kings and Their Mother's Kin.'' *Africa* 25 (1955): 29–41.

Levine, V. T., and R. P. Nye. *Historical Dictionary of Cameroon.* 1990.

Levtzion, N. *Muslims and Chiefs in West Africa: A Study of Islam in the Middle Volta Basin in the Pre-Colonial Period.* 1968.

Lewis, D. L. *The Race to Fashoda: European Colonialism and African Resistance in the Scramble for Africa.* 1987.

Lewis, G. *Between the Wire and the Wall: A History of South African ''Coloured'' Politics.* 1987.

Lewis, I. M., ed. *Islam in Tropical Africa.* 1966.

Liniger-Goumaz, M. *Historical Dictionary of Equatorial Guinea.* 1988.

Lipsky, G. *Ethiopia: Its Peoples, Its Society, Its Culture.* 1962.

Lipton, M. *Capitalism and Apartheid: South Africa, 1910–84.* 1985.

Lobban, R., and J. Forrest. *Historical Dictionary of the Republic of Guinea-Bissau.* 1988.

Lobban, R., and M. Halter. *Historical Dictionary of the Republic of Cape Verde.* 1988.

Lyons, M. *The Colonial Disease: A Social History of Sleeping Sickness in Northern Zaire, 1900–1940.* 1992.

McCarthy, M. *Social Change and the Growth of British Power in the Gold Coast: The Fante States, 1807–1874.* 1983.

McDonald, G. C., et al. *Area Handbook for Burundi.* 1969.

———. *Area Handbook for the People's Republic of the Congo (Congo Brazzaville).* 1971.

McFarland, D. M. *Historical Dictionary of Ghana.* 1995.

———. *Historical Dictionary of Upper Volta.* 1978.

Mandala, E. A. *Work and Control in a Peasant Economy: A History of the Lower Tchiri Valley in Malawi, 1859–1960.* 1990.

Maquet, J. *Civilizations of Black Africa.* 1972.

Markaris, J. *National and Class Conflict in the Horn of Africa.* 1987.

Martin, E. B. *The History of Malindi: A Geographical Analysis of an East African Coastal Town from the Portuguese Period to the Present.* 1973.

Maughn-Brown, D. *Land, Freedom, and Fiction: History and Ideology in Kenya.* 1985.

Maxon, R. M. *Struggle for Kenya: The Loss and Reassertion of Imperial Initiative, 1912–1923.* 1993.

Meek, C. K. *The Northern Tribes of Nigeria.* 1969.

Meillassoux, C., ed. *The Development of Indigenous Trade and Markets in West Africa*. 1971.

Mendelsohn, J. *God, Allah and Juju: Religion in Africa Today*. 1962.

Metz, H. C., et al. *Egypt: A Country Study*. 1991.

———. *Libya: A Country Study*. 1989.

———. *Nigeria: A Country Study*. 1991.

———. *Somalia: A Country Study*. 1992.

———. *Sudan: A Country Study*. 1992.

Middleton, J. *The World of the Swahili: An African Mercantile Civilization*. 1992.

———, and I. Campbell. *Zanzibar: Its Society and Politics*. 1965.

Mier, S., and R. Roberts, eds. *The End of Slavery in Africa*. 1988.

Mollison, S. *Kenya's Coast*. 1971.

Moore, H. I., and V. Vaughn. *Cutting Down Trees: Gender, Nutrition, and Agricultural Change in the Northern Province of Zambia, 1890–1990*. 1994.

Moore, S. F. *Social Facts and Fabrication: "Customary" Law on Kilimanjaro, 1880–1908*. 1986.

Morrison, D. G., et al. *Black Africa: A Comparative Handbook*. 1989.

Morton, F. *Children of Ham: Freed Slaves and Fugitive Slaves on the Kenya Coast, 1873 to 1907*. 1990.

———, A. Murray, and J. Ramsay. *Historical Dictionary of Botswana*. 1989.

Mundt, R. J. *Historical Dictionary of Côte d'Ivoire*. 1995.

Munson, H. *Religion and Power in Morocco*. 1993.

Murdock, G. P. *Africa: Its Peoples and Their Culture History*. 1959.

Myers, R. A. *Ghana*. 1986.

———. *Nigeria*. 1989.

Nachtigel, G. *Sahara and Sudan*. Vol. 4: *Wadai and Darfur*. 1971.

Nasson, B. *Abraham Esau's War: A Black South African War in the Cape, 1899–1902*. 1991.

Nelson, H. D., et al. *Area Handbook for Guinea*. 1975.

———. *Area Handbook for Malawi*. 1975.

———. *Area Handbook for Nigeria*. 1972.

———. *Area Handbook for Senegal*. 1974.

———. *Area Handbook for the Malagasy Republic*. 1973.

———. *Area Handbook for the United Republic of Cameroon*. 1974.

———. *Ethiopia: A Country Study*. 1980.

———. *Kenya: A Country Study*. 1983.

———. *Liberia: A Country Study*. 1984.

———. *Morocco: A Country Study*. 1985.

———. *Mozambique: A Country Study*. 1984.

———. *Zimbabwe: A Country Study*. 1982.

Newbury, C. *The Diamond Ring: Business, Politics, and Precious Stones in South Africa, 1867–1947*. 1989.

Newbury, D. *Kings and Clans: Ijwi Island and the Lake Kivu Rift, 1780–1840*. 1991.

Nicolls, C. S. *The Swahili Coast*. 1971.

Nyrop, R. F., et al. *Rwanda: A Country Study*. 1989.

Obudho, R. A., and S. El-Shaikh, eds. *Urban Systems in Africa*. 1979.

Oded, A. *Islam in Uganda*. 1974.

Odendaal, A. *Black Protest Politics in South Africa to 1912.* 1984.

Ogot, B. A. *Historical Dictionary of Kenya.* 1981.

Ohannessian, S., and M. E. Kashoki. *Language in Zambia.* 1978.

Oliver, R., and G. N. Sanderson, eds. *The Cambridge History of Africa.* Vol. 6: *From 1870–1905.* 1985.

O'Toole, T. *Historical Dictionary of Guinea.* 1995.

Ottenberg, S. *African Religious Groups and Beliefs: Papers in Honor of William R. Bascom.* 1982.

———, and P. Ottenberg. *Cultures and Societies of Africa.* 1960.

Packard, R. M. *White Plague, Black Labor: Tuberculosis and the Political Economy of Health and Disease in South Africa.* 1989.

Pankhurst, R. *Economic History of Ethiopia.* 1968.

Parkin, D. J. *Palms, Wine, and Witnesses: Public Spirit and Private Gain in an African Farming Community.* 1972.

Pearce, R. D. *The Turning Point in Africa: British Colonial Policy, 1938–48.* 1982.

Phillips, A. *The Enigma of Colonialism: British Policy in West Africa.* 1989.

Pichl, W. J. *The Cangin Group: A Language Group in Northern Senegal.* 1966.

Polomé, E. C., and C. P. Hill. *Language in Tanzania.* 1980.

Prins, G. *The Hidden Hippopotamus: Reappraisal in African History; The Early Colonial Experience in Western Zambia.* 1980.

Prouty, C., and E. Rosenfeld. *Historical Dictionary of Ethiopia and Eritrea.* 1994.

Radcliffe-Brown, A. R., and D. Forde. *African Systems of Kinship and Marriage.* 1950.

Rahim, M. A. *Imperialism and Nationalism in the Sudan: A Study in Constitutional and Political Development, 1899–1956.* 1986.

Rasmussen, R. K. *Historical Dictionary of Zimbabwe.* 1994.

Rathbone, R. *Murder and Politics in Colonial Ghana.* 1993.

Robbins, M. C. "Problem-Drinking and the Integration of Alcohol in Rural Buganda." *Medical Anthropology* 1 (1977): 1–24.

Ross, R. *Beyond the Pale: Essays on the History of Colonial South Africa.* 1993.

St. John, R. B. *Historical Dictionary of Libya.* 1991.

Salamone, F. A. *Gods and Goods in Africa.* 1974.

Salim, A. L. *Swahili-Speaking Peoples of Kenya's Coast.* 1973.

Samarin, W. J. *The Black Man's Burden: African Colonial Labor on the Congo and Ubangi Rivers, 1880–1900.* 1989.

Sargent, C. "Obstetrical Choice among Urban Women in Benin." *Social Science and Medicine* 20 (1984): 287–92.

Saul, M. "Beer, Sorghum and Women: Production for the Market in Rural Upper Volta." *Africa* 51 (1981): 746–64.

Schildkrout, E. "The Fostering of Children in Urban Ghana: Problems of Ethnographic Analysis in a Multi-Cultural Context." *Urban Anthropology* 2 (1973): 48–73.

———. *People of the Zongo: The Transformation of Ethnic Identities in Ghana.* 1978.

Schoeman, S., and E. Schoeman. *Namibia.* 1984.

Schraeder, P. J. *Djibouti.* 1991.

Schreuder, D. M. *The Scramble for Southern Africa, 1877–1895.* 1980.

Schultz, E. A., ed. *Image and Reality in African Interethnic Relations: The Fulbe and Their Neighbors.* 1980.

Seitel, P. *See So That We May See: Performances and Interpretations of Traditional Tales from Tanzania.* 1980.

Seligman, C. G., and B. Z. Seligman. *Pagan Tribes of the Nilotic Sudan.* 1950.

Shack, W. "Some Aspects of Ecology and Social Structure in the Ensete Complex in South-West Ethiopia." *Journal of the Royal Anthropological Institute* 93 (1963): 72–79.

Shaw, C. S. *Cape Verde.* 1988.

Shillington, K. *The Colonisation of the Southern Tswana, 1870–1900.* 1985.

Simmons, A. S. *Modern Mauritius: The Politics of Decolonization.* 1982.

Simmons, F. J. *Northwest Ethiopia: Peoples and Economy.* 1960.

Sinclair, J. "Educational Assistance, Kinship, and the Social Structure in Sierra Leone." *Africana Research Bulletin* 2 (1972): 30–62.

Skinner, E. P. *African Urban Life: The Transformation of Ouagadougou.* 1974.

Smith, D. R. *The Influence of the Fabian Colonial Bureau on the Independence Movement in Tanganyika.* 1985.

Spencer, J. *The Kenyan African Union.* 1985.

Spencer, P. *Nomads in Alliance.* 1973.

Switzer, L. *Power and Resistance in an African Society: The Ciskei Xhosa and the Making of South Africa.* 1993.

Temperley, H. *White Dreams, Black Africa: The Antislavery Expedition to the River Niger, 1841–1842.* 1991.

Tew, M. *The People of the Lake Nyasa Region.* 1950.

Thompson, L. *African Societies in Southern Africa.* 1969.

Thompson, V., and R. Adloff. *Djibouti and the Horn of Africa.* 1968.

———. *Historical Dictionary of the People's Republic of the Congo.* 1984.

Throup, D. *Economic and Social Origins of Mau Mau, 1945–1953.* 1988.

Trimingham, J. S. *The Influence of Islam Upon Africa.* 1969.

———. *Islam in East Africa.* 1964.

———. *Islam in Ethiopia.* 1965.

———. *Islam in West Africa.* 1959.

Ullendorf, E. *The Ethiopians.* 1973.

Vansina, J., R. Mauny, and L. V. Thomas, eds. *The Historian in Tropical Africa.* 1964.

Watson, J. *Asian and African Systems of Slavery.* 1980.

Watson, R. L. *The Slave Question: Liberty and Property in South Africa.* 1990.

Weinstein, W. *Historical Dictionary of Burundi.* 1976.

Were, G. S., and D. A. Wilson. *East Africa Through a Thousand Years: A History of the Years A.D. 1000 to the Present Day.* 1968.

Wheatcroft, G. *The Randlords.* 1985.

White, J. *Central Administration in Nigeria, 1914–1948: The Problem of Polarity.* 1981.

White, L. *The Comforts of Home: Prostitution in Colonial Nairobi.* 1990.

Whiteley, W. H. *Language in Kenya.* 1974.

Williams, T., ed. *Socialization and Communication in Primary Groups.* 1975.

Wilson, M. *The Peoples of the Nyasa-Tanganyika Corridor.* 1958.

Wolcott, H. F. *The African Beer Gardens of Bulawayo: Integrated Drinking in a Segregated Society.* 1974.

Worger, W. H. *South Africa's City of Diamonds: Mine Workers and Monopoly Capitalism in Kimberley, 1867–1895.* 1987.

Zein, A. H. M. *The Sacred Meadows: A Structural Analysis of Religious Symbolism in an East African Town.* 1974.

Index

Boldface page numbers indicate location of main entries.

About the Author

JAMES S. OLSON is Distinguished Professor of History at Sam Houston State University, where he has taught since 1972. He is the author of more than 20 books on U.S. and world history.

ISBN 0-313-27918-7

90000>

EAN

9 780313 279188

HARDCOVER BAR CODE